Developing Management Skills

Developing Management Skills

Fourth Edition

David A. Whetten
Brigham Young University

Kim S. Cameron
Brigham Young University

▲▲ **ADDISON-WESLEY**

An imprint of Addison Wesley Longman, Inc.

Reading, Massachusetts • Menlo Park, California • New York • Harlow, England
Don Mills, Ontario • Sydney • Mexico City • Madrid • Amsterdam

Acquisitions Editor: Michael Roche
Editorial Assistant: Ruth Berry
Production Supervisor: Louis C. Bruno, Jr.
Project Coordination: Electronic Publishing Services Inc., NYC
Text Designer and Illustrations: Electronic Publishing Services Inc., NYC
Cover Designer: Linda Wade
Cover Coordinator: Regina Hagen
Compositor: Electronic Publishing Services Inc., NYC
Marketing Manager: Jodi Fazio
Marketing Coordinator: Joyce Cosentino

For permission to use copyrighted material, grateful acknowledgment is made to the copyright holders in source notes throughout the text, which are hereby made part of this copyright page.

Library of Congress Cataloging-in-Publication Data

Whetten, David A. (David Allred), 1946—
    Developing management skills / David A. Whetten, Kim S. Cameron
  – 4th ed.
      p.   cm.
Includes bibliographical references and index.
ISBN 0-321-01308-5 (pbk.)
    1. Management—Study and teaching. 2. Management—Problems, exercises, etc.
I. Cameron, Kim S. II. Title.
HD30.4.W46   1998
658.4'0071'173—dc21
                                                                             97-39234
                                                                              CIP

Copyright © 1998 by Addison-Wesley Educational Publishers Inc.

ISBN 0-321-01308-5
  45678910—RNV—0100999

Reprinted with corrections, November 1998

Contents

Preface

Preparing to Meet the Challenges of the New Millenium

As you prepare for your managerial careers in the new millenium, the environment that you will face will undoubtedly be very different from the one managers faced a decade ago, or the one facing you as you read this preface. The impact that globalization is having on businesses, both small and large, is challenging the problem-solving skills of managers. The increased diversity in the workplace at home and abroad requires refined communication skills. While the business pressures that lead to a wave of reengineering, six-sigma quality efforts, downsizing, and speed-to-market have caused a radical transformation in the way business appears to function, the personal, interpersonal, and group skills of all workers remain as important as ever.

Today's business students are learning the latest tools for analyzing their specialized fields of study. Accounting and operations management majors learn how computing power has given them the ability to analyze financial information that provides new insights into operational and financial performance. Finance majors learn to appreciate the latest trading techniques in derivative markets. Human resource majors are learning how to assess programs and strategize how a planned global expansion will affect an organization's human resource needs. Marketing majors learn how scanner data can be analyzed so that they can better understand customer needs and preferences. These techniques, and the frenetic pace of work, have created a dynamic, constantly changing work environment that challenges individuals to continually adapt and learn new methods of accomplishing objectives.

The business landscape painted by the changing workplace does not absolve managers of the need to acquire, practice, and utilize a set of managerial skills that allow them to work effectively. Questions like "How do I get my people to accept this idea?," "How do I explain the need to change to my 'old-timers' without creating a defensive reaction?," "How do I help the 'survivors' of a downsizing manage with their sense of loss, grief, and guilt?," and "How do I use existing organizational rewards to reinforce the need for change?" are just some of the questions that managers need to address on a daily basis.

A wave of downsizing and reengineering has created flatter workplaces with less formal hierarchies. Companies that have adopted fluid, project-based team approaches to organizing their work forces have found that the requisite personal, interpersonal, and group skills are still vital as the mantle of leadership is passed from one team member to another.

Will Rogers's dictum that "Common sense ain't necessarily common practice" underscores the problem with most content-based discussions of management. It is one thing to catalogue the "best practices" associated with world-class quality, efficiency, or customer satisfactions. It is far more challenging to prepare the members of an organization to accept the need for change, to help them understand the new approach, to obtain their commitment to implement the proposal, to manage the transition period effectively, and to institutionalize the new approach by "hard wiring" it into the organization's communication, evaluation, and reward systems. As one experienced manager noted, "Good ideas are not in scarce supply. What is rare is the ability to translate a good idea into accepted practice."

The goal of this book is to provide current and prospective managers with the personal, interpersonal, and group skills necessary to reduce the gap between good ideas and accepted practice. Managers can hire content knowledge, but they cannot hire stand-ins to represent them in critical staff meetings, conversations with angry customers, scheduling discussions with their secretaries, counseling sessions with troubled employees, or performance evaluations. Skillful performance in these settings has been documented by literally dozens of studies (see the Introduction that immediately follows this Preface) as the essential and indispensable foundation of effective management practice.

Background of this Book

We have been convinced for a decade or so that management skills must be a crucial part of the business school and corporate training curricula. Not only does a recent study of business school education (Porter and McKibbin, 1988) corroborate that view, but our experience with business school students and managers in executive education seminars has continually reaffirmed our commitment to the skill development approach.

Originally, the motivation for writing *Developing Management Skills* grew out of our frustration with teaching management courses following conventional methods. When we used texts based on the traditional "principles of management" framework, we felt uncomfortable with their lack of theoretical and research grounding. Because principles of management have been generally derived from recollections and interpretations of practicing managers, empirical research and theory regarding their validity in modern organizations is limited.

When we used an organization and management theory approach, students complained that the practical relevance of the material was difficult to discern. Not enough "hows" were included to be useful to students who aspired to be practicing managers.

When we used a traditional "organizational behavior" approach, colleagues teaching the elective organizational behavior courses reported that students complained about redundancy. It became increasingly difficult to differentiate among topics covered by organizational behavior and management books.

When we emphasized the "experiential learning" approach, centered around simulations, case discussions, and games, students complained they weren't gaining enough substantive knowledge about how to be effective managers. Few students brought enough practical experience, theoretical knowledge, or self-analytic skills to those exercises to get much benefit from them. As a result, the exercises were entertaining but not very useful.

After years of experimentation, we determined that while each approach had its place in a management program and each could contribute to a student's education, none, taken alone, could help students develop into competent managers.

In our search for alternatives, we asked recent graduates and senior executives to evaluate the organizational behavior and management curricula in terms of their experiences as managers. In general, they criticized behavioral science courses for not teaching them job-relevant skills.

They were acutely award of the challenges posed by "people problems" in their work, and they felt that their education had not prepared them for that component of their job.

Based on this feedback, we began formulating the teaching methodology, and we examined the way such skills as education, social work, engineering, medicine, and law are taught in other professional schools. We also drew heavily on recent innovations in training programs for practicing managers that emphasize behavior modification through role modeling. To identify the relevant management skills, we surveyed over 400 managers in public and private organizations and combed the professional literature for statements by management experts identifying the characteristics of effective managers. As our teaching model began to evolve, it became apparent that a supporting textbook would need to be developed. Further, it would necessarily have to be a hybrid, containing diverse teaching methods and material that would give equal emphasis to concept acquisition and skill practice.

Early in this project it was clear that our text would be at variance with prevailing views regarding what behavioral science courses should offer management students. Typically, these courses either present an array of general principles and concepts derived from research in industrial/organizational psychology, sociology, OB, industrial administration, and so on, or they rely heavily on group exercises, games, or cases to illustrate certain management activities. They either describe management practice and provide students with theories for analyzing common problems encountered by managers, or they eschew theory and research in favor of activity and involvement. Through our experience we became convinced that the strengths of each approach, used in combination, were needed for students to develop (not just know about) management skills. Therefore, the hallmark of this text is a balanced integration of theory and practice, understanding and application.

We have found that using theories of behavior as a means to the end of developing behavioral skills not only increases students' interest in and acceptance of the conceptual material in our field, but it also significantly increases their ability to apply the concepts they have learned. Overall, the preparation of students to become productive members of organizations is markedly improved by participation in a management skills course. In fact, the research cited in the Introduction makes it clear that personal and interpersonal skill competence contributes more to the long-term success of managers than does their proficiency in analytic and quantitative skills.

Organization of the Material

The purpose of this book is to help practicing managers and management students develop the skills necessary to cultivate and implement good ideas in organizations. Based on years of research and personal observation of effective managers, we have identified nine fundamental management skills, organized into three categories. Each chapter in this book addresses one of these skills.

▶ *Personal*
Developing Self-Awareness
Managing Stress
Solving Problems Creatively

▶ *Interpersonal*
Communicating Supportively
Gaining Power and Influence
Motivating Others
Managing Conflict

▶ *Group Skills*
Empowering and Delegating
Building Effective Teams

In addition to these core skills, we have included sections on two skills involving applied communications: "Making Written and Oral Presentations," "Conducting Interviews," and "Conducting Meetings."

The shift from learning management principles or programs to learning management skills requires an associated shift in learning objectives. The goal of purely cognitive or content-oriented learning is *understanding*. In contrast, the goal of skill development is *application*. In other words, the goal of "changing my mind" is replaced with the goal "changing my behavior." This qualitative change in learning objectives requires an entirely new system of learning. The learning model used to organize the skill development process in each chapter parallels the four requirements for personal and organizational change.

Requirements for Change	Skill Development Steps
Accept the need to change	Skill Assessment
Understand what to change	Skill Learning
	Skill Analysis
Commit to and practice/pilot change	Skill Practice
Apply change	Skill Application

New to this Edition

Our primary objectives in preparing this edition were (1) to expand the range of skills covered, (2) to make the book more user-friendly for independent learners outside the traditional classroom, (3) to improve the quality of the accompanying instructor's manual, and (4) to make available new supplemental teaching materials. We are confident that adopters familiar with previous editions will recognize improvements in these areas.

Supplements

To augment the improvements in the text, the supplements have been revised, expanded, and improved as well. The available supplements include:

Instructor's Manual   Greatly expanded and revised for this edition by Pat Seybolt of the University of Utah. The manual features:

▶ A revamped design with more of "point form" style and a larger font size that allows earlier course planning and lectures.

▶ A section on how to organize a skill-building course, including tips on how to use teaching assistants effectively for large courses.

▶ An extensive overview of course philosophy, including comparisons with traditional pedagogical approaches.

▶ Sample course outlines and general guidelines for teaching the course in small or very large sections.

▶ Suggestions for conducting role plays and managing class discussion.

- Extensive teaching hints and discussion questions for each chapter.

- Supplemental high-involvement classroom exercises for introducing each chapter.

- Several "campus life" problems for helping undergraduates see opportunities for immediate application of the course material.

- Norm data for "Skill Assessment" surveys so students can compare their scores with a sample of 500 other students.

- Transparency masters for many of the tables and figures, plus behavioral guidelines, to facilitate classroom discussion. All of the selected images are also contained in electronic format that will allow users to project the images through the use of a PC and a projection pad.

- A resource guide for identifying all available teaching materials for specific learning objectives in each chapter.

- Descriptions of the brief scenes from popular movies that can be used to introduce each topic. Discussion questions for linking the video clip to the chapter material area also included.

- A list of films that can be used in conjunction with each chapter.

Test Bank   Greatly expanded and revised for this edition by Forrest F. Aven of the University of Houston—Downtown. The manual features approximately 60 multiple choice and 20 short answer questions for each chapter and includes page references from the text. The test bank is available in both a printed form and in Test Gen EQ format.

Test Gen Eq (Windows)   This computerized test generator lets instructors construct tests by choosing questions from item banks that were prepared specifically for the textbook and course. The test construction process involves the use of a simple form that is filled in on the computer screen, where the test questions can be edited, saved, and printed. In addition, instructors can add questions to any test or item bank, or even create their own item banks of test questions and graphics.

Videos   The video package that accompanies *Developing Management Skills* includes interviews with experienced executives discussing the cases in the book, a series of three cases developed specifically for the text that illustrate three firms interacting with each other, and a video that parallels the opening "In-Basket" exercise that is designed to introduce the course (SSS Software).

Two New Supplements   We recognize that many of today's students are taking continuing education courses for continuous improvement and enhancing their career opportunities. These students may not have the access to the resources that the traditional students have. To meet the need of this growing constituency, we offer two new supplements with the fourth edition of *Developing Management Skills*:

- *Web Site*   A dynamic web site that includes chapter links to related sites and interactive assessment tests has been developed to supplement this book. The web site was developed by Forrest F. Aven and James E. Weber and programmed by Erping Zhu, all of the University of Houston. Visit the web site at http://hepg.awl.com/whetten/dms4/.

- *Self-Directed Learning Manual*   Prepared by Sue Campbell Clark of the University of Idaho, this manual allows the student to tailor what they learn to their own need, and be more productive in the learning process.

Program Features

▶ Tests and item banks can include five types of questions: multiple-choice, true-false, matching, short answer (any kind, including fill-in and completion), and essay.

▶ A supplementary page attached to each item's bank questions can contain its topic, objective, skill, difficulty, and other user-added information.

▶ Test questions can be chosen in a variety of ways, including manual selection, random selection, choice while viewing, and choice while searching.

▶ Questions chosen for a test can be viewed and edited without affecting the original versions of the questions in the item bank.

▶ Test size is limited only by the memory capacity of the computer and the length of questions chosen.

▶ Test questions can be printed in the exact order specified or grouped and sorted automatically by the program.

▶ Test questions can be imported to or exported from the program and the computer's own word-processing software.

▶ Printer files can be created or modified to take advantage of the capabilities of the printer.

Acknowledgements

In addition to the informal feedback that we have received from colleagues at conferences, and electronically via the OBTC network, we would especially like to thank the following people who have formally reviewed material and provided valuable feedback:

Forrest F. Aven, *University of Houston*

Lloyd Baird, *Boston University*

John D. Bigelow, *University of Idaho*

David Cherrington, *Brigham Young University*

Andrew J. DuBrin, *Rochester Institute of Technology*

Barbara A. Gorski, *St. Thomas University*

Stanley Harris, *Auburn University*

Richard E. Hunt, *Rockhurst College*

Daniel F. Jennings, *Baylor University*

Avis L. Johnson, *The University of Akron*

Jay T. Knippen, *University of South Florida*

Roy J. Lewicki, *The Ohio State University*

Michael Lombardo, *Center for Creative Leadership*

Charles C. Manz, *Arizona State University*

Ralph F. Mullin, *Central Missouri State University*

Jon L. Pierce, *University of Minnesota-Duluth*

Lyman Porter, *University of California-Irvine*

Lyle F. Schoenfeldt, *Appalachian State University*

Jacob P. Siegel, *University of Toronto*

Noel M. Tichy, *University of Michigan*

Wanda V. Trenner, *Ferris State University*

Kenneth M. York, *Oakland University*

We would also like to thank the contributions of our collaborators for producing adapted versions of *Developing Management Skills* for the European and Australian markets.

We are grateful for the assistance of many dedicated associates in putting together the fourth edition. We would especially like to thank Nancy Keesham and Don Clement, both of the Fuqua School of Business at Duke University for her work on the communication chapter and the supplement on making oral and written presentations; Gretchen Spreitzer of the University of Southern California for her work on the chapter on gaining power and influence; Richard M. Steers of the University of Oregon for his work on the motivation chapter; and Pat Seybolt and Troy Nielsen of the University of Utah for their work on the managing conflict.

We gratefully acknowledge Cathy German of Miami University for her assistance in revising the Skill Learning portion of the chapter on communication. Special thanks are also due to Susan Schor, Joseph Seltzer, and James Smither for writing the SSS Software In-Basket Exercise.

We would like to thank Mike Roche, Elizabeth MacDonnell, Ruth Berry, Lou Bruno, Jodi Fazio, Gina Hagen, Karen Stevenson and Mike Hodges of Addison Wesley and Anthony Calcara of Electronic Publishing Services Inc. for their help in making this book a reality.

We also express appreciation to our families for their patience and support, which is reflected in their willingness to share their time with this competing "labor of love" and to forgive our own gaps between common sense and common practice.

David A. Whetten

Kim S. Cameron

Introduction

The Critical Role of Management Skills in America's Future

For the first time in history, a book on management became this country's best-seller approximately one decade ago. It was succeeded by a litany of popular books discussing management principles and organizational success stories that continue to sell hundreds of thousands of copies a year. One management guru's book has been on the best-seller list for almost five straight years. Business services and organizational consulting have become the second most rapidly growing area in the U.S. service sector, lagging behind only health care services. Why has management become a hot topic in America? Why has so much attention been turned to the management of organizations?

Our intent in this book is not to try to duplicate the popular appeal of the best-selling books nor to utilize the common formula of recounting anecdotal incidents of successful organizations and well-known managers. Rather, *Developing Management Skills* is designed specifically to help guide individuals in improving their own personal management competencies. It is more of a practicum and a guide to effective managerial behavior than a discussion of what someone else has done to successfully manage an organization.

We begin by discussing the current conditions in American business. This helps illuminate the reason that competent management is such a critical concern right now. Then we discuss the extent to which effective management education and training are being provided by business schools and other executive training programs. The characteristics and qualities of successful managers derived from several investigations are summarized, and a model is presented that describes how these characteristics and qualities can best be developed. The chapter concludes with a brief description of the organization of the rest of the book.

Current Conditions in Business

Just a few years ago, businesses in the United States were largely alone among the major industrialized countries in facing lost competitiveness, perceptions of poor quality, and eroding consumer confidence. Now, most European and Asian firms are experiencing the same environmental conditions and the same difficult challenges. No one is feeling smug anymore. We begin this introduction, therefore, by using U.S. business as an example. This is not because the management skills in this book are exclusively American, but because focusing on the United States can serve as a case study to illustrate the critical role management skills play in the health of almost any country's economy. Most businesses and managers worldwide will likely face similar challenges in the coming decade.

In approximately one decade, America's position as the undisputed world economic leader was transformed into that of the world's largest debtor nation. In just five years at the beginning of the 1980s, the United States went from a trade balance surplus to the largest trade deficit in the history of the world. Until recently, most of that debt resulted from trade deficits in manufactured goods, but the same trend has come to characterize services as well. The service sector, which accounts for 71 percent of America's GNP and 75 percent of its jobs, experienced a trade deficit for the first time in early 1988, which has continued to the present.

The decline of U.S. business in a global environment in the 1980s was dramatic and rapid. Few countries have ever experienced as extensive and as rapid an economic decline as did the United States during the 1980s. In most years starting in the mid-1980s, for example, two-thirds of the net investment in the United States for housing, capital equipment, R&D, and plant construction was funded by foreign capital. The biggest export was IOUs. In every previous decade, Americans consumed slightly less than 90 percent of what they produced, but since the beginning of the 1980s they consumed 235 percent of production growth. Only 30 percent of this growth in consumption was accounted for by increases in productivity. The other 70 percent was funded by cutbacks in domestic investment and foreign debt. Over the course of the 1980s the U.S. investment rate was second lowest in the industrialized world, while the growth in output per worker was the absolute lowest. It took Britain 75 years to slide from the world's economic leader to second-class status by having productivity growth rates one-half a percentage point below competitor nations, but the U.S. rate is three times lower than that, and the slide proceeded much more rapidly (see Peterson, 1987).

The number of business failures per 10,000 concerns was at record levels in the 1980s, eclipsing the levels recorded during the Great Depression of 1929–1932. Beginning in 1986, failure rates more than doubled those during the Depression. Failure rates in the service sector, especially, were at record levels. Bank failures continue to set all-time records, and the list of "problem banks" was at record levels.

During the 1980s, the United States experienced a 25-percent decline in patent applications (innovations), and almost half of the U.S. patents awarded in 1994 were to foreigners. A variety of explanations and rationales were proposed for this slide in U.S. organizational performance, such as tax codes, restrictive trade barriers, and government regulations. However, most observers now agree that at least part of the blame, and maybe even the lion's share of the blame, rests with America's managers. Thurow (1984), for example, represented this point of view by asserting that there has been a serious flaw in U.S. management:

> America is not experiencing a benevolent second industrial revolution, but a long-run economic decline that will affect its ability to competitively produce goods and services for world markets. If American industry fails, the managers are ultimately

accountable. While we cannot fire all of America's managers any more than we can fire the American labor force, there is clearly something wrong with management. That something is going to have to be corrected if America is to compete in world markets.

Roy H. Pollock, former executive vice president at RCA, characterized America's condition this way: "With the exception of the Civil War, it's doubtful that America has ever faced such an awesome trauma. Recovering from this situation won't be painless. But the alternative is to accept continuing economic decline and the end to America's greatness."

As a response to these changes, American and world businesses have adapted and changed. Reengineering and the move to "cut management fat" have resulted in fewer managerial positions and increased the importance of effective management skills. New processes have increased the necessity of cross-functional teams to work together, and the recent proliferation of corporate alliances has challenged managers to apply their skills to projects where different organizational cultures and differing agendas present new challenges for managers.

The Role of Management

These trials, of course, are not over for American businesses, and they are just beginning or are in full bloom in most other industrial nations. Managers throughout the world will continue to be required to make wrenching adjustments. However, discouragement, fear, or resignation are neither appropriate nor predestined. There are reasons to be hopeful. One is that there are no secrets regarding how to manage an effective firm or to turn around ineffective performance. There is no magic to effective competitiveness. Two scientific studies illustrate this point.

The first study was an investigation of the factors that best accounted for financial success over a five-year span in 40 major manufacturing firms (Hanson, 1986). The question was, "What explains the financial success of the firms that are highly effective?" The five most powerful predictors were identified and assessed. They included market share (assuming that the higher the market share of a firm, the higher its profitability), firm capital intensity (assuming that the more a firm is automated and up-to-date in technology and equipment, the more profitable it is), size of the firm in assets (assuming that economies of scale and efficiency can be used in large firms to increase profitability), industry average return on sales (assuming that firms would reflect the performance of a highly profitable industry), and the ability of managers to effectively manage their people (assuming that an emphasis on good people management helps produce profitability in firms). The results of statistical analyses revealed that one factor—the ability of managers to manage their people effectively—was three times more powerful than all other factors combined in accounting for firm financial success over a five-year period. Good management was more important than all other factors in predicting profitability.

A second study was conducted by the U.S. Office of the Controller of the Currency. It studied the reasons for the failures of national banks in the United States during the decade of the 1980s. The total number of national banks that failed during that period was 162. Two major factors were found to account for the record number of bank failures during that eight-year period: distressed economic conditions and poor management. However, the relative impact of those two factors was somewhat surprising. A total of 89 percent of the failed banks were judged to have had poor management. Only 35 percent of the failures had experienced depressed economic conditions in the region in which they operated, and in only 7 percent of the cases was a depressed economic condition the sole cause of bank failure. The government research team concluded the following.

We found oversight and management deficiencies to be the primary factors that resulted in bank failure. In fact, poor policies, planning, and management were significant causes of failure in 89 percent of the banks surveyed. The quality of a bank's board and management depends on the experience, capability, judgment, and integrity of its directors and senior officers. Banks that had directors and managers with significant shortcomings made up a large portion of the banks that we surveyed.

These studies indicate that good management fosters financial success, while bad management fosters financial distress. Loss of firm competitiveness and financial decline are more products of shoddy management in U.S. firms than of macroeconomic factors or offshore price advantages.

This argument for the importance of good management for organization success is also supported by practical examples in two separate industries. Two different organizations have undergone a change in top management, and the results produced by the introduction of a new management approach were dramatic.

The first example comes from the General Motors automobile assembly plant in Fremont, California. The plant was built in the 1950s and, at the beginning of the 1980s, was assembling the Chevrolet Nova model. The plant had a history of labor and productivity problems, however, and by the end of 1982 the performance statistics were dismal. Absenteeism was running at 20 percent. The number of formal grievances filed by employees totaled almost 5,000 (an average of more than 20 grievances per day for every workday of the year), and over 2,000 grievances were still unresolved at year's end. An average of three to four wildcat strikes per year had occurred during the previous few years, and both the productivity quantity and quality of production by the 5,000 employees were the worst in the corporation. Costs of Fremont's Chevy Nova were about 30 percent above the Asian competitor's cars. In light of these data, corporate headquarters issued an order to close the plant and lay off the workers at the end of 1982.

In 1985, General Motors signed a joint operating agreement with one of its major competitors, Toyota. Much had been written about the Japanese method of managing, so General Motors asked Toyota to reopen and manage the Fremont plant. Most of the former U.S. auto workers were rehired, and the Japanese agreed to manage the plant. The primary difference between 1982 and 1985 was that a new management team was put in place; the workforce was essentially the same. At the end of 1986, in just one year's time, the performance data looked like this:

Absenteeism:	2 percent
Grievances:	2 outstanding
Strikes:	None
Employees:	2,500 (producing 20 percent more cars)
Productivity:	Highest in the corporation
Quality:	Highest in the corporation
Costs:	Equal to those of the competition
Product:	Geo Prism—rated AAA's best car in its price range in 1994

The remarkable thing about this turnaround is that it did not take five or 10 years to produce major improvements in productivity, cohesion, and commitment. It occurred in just over a year simply by changing the way workers were managed.

The second example involves a television manufacturing plant near Chicago. It was sold by its American owner to a Japanese company. Half of the white collar employees were let go, but the rest of the American workforce remained. In addition, the top management group was brought in from Japan. Essentially, the plant continued to produce the same product with the same workforce. The only difference was a new top management team. The difference between performance statistics under American management and Japanese management was dramatic. Under U.S. management, defects averaged 150 per 100 TV sets. Under Japanese management, the average was 4. Product rejects averaged 60 per 100 TVs under U.S. management and only 3.8 under Japanese management. Warranty costs were $17 million per year with U.S. managers and $3 million with Japanese managers. In addition, productivity per day doubled under the new management team from 1,000 sets per day to 2,000 sets per day.

These illustrations point out, as Thurow and others assert, that management is a key factor in both firm success and firm failure. When excellent management is present, dramatic and rapid improvements can be effected. In surveys of CEOs, executives, and business owners, they consistently say that the factor most responsible for business failure is "bad management" and the best way to overcome business failures is to "provide better management." Of much less importance are factors such as interest rates, foreign competition, taxes, inflation, and government regulation. To the question, "What are the factors that are most important in overcoming business failure?," two answers outnumber all other responses: "Provide better managers," and "Train and educate current managers."

By using Japanese comparisons in the examples above, we do not intend to imply that a uniquely Japanese management system exists at all or is superior to an American system. We also emphasize that we are not advocating that what are normally labeled Japanese methods be adopted wholesale in American firms. In fact, what are commonly labeled "Japanese management methods"—quality circles, continuous improvement philosophy, employee empowerment, just-in-time inventories, integrated manufacturing systems, process design, teamwork—all were initially invented and practiced in the United States, primarily in the 1910s and 1920s. This explains why, in our own interviews with Japanese managers, many have explained their success by saying, "We just practice what you preach." Good management, we emphasize, is not the prerogative of any single nationality or culture. Equally dramatic examples of firm and industry turnaround and excellence are prevalent in firms throughout the world, such as Xerox, Motorola, American Express, Philips, ICI, Sony, and S.A.S. Airlines. Changing the way managers behave in organizations can bring about quick and dramatic improvements. Preachments about how to do that have been around for a long time. Neither the Japanese nor any other culture has discovered many new principles that were not being advocated 50 years ago. The difference lies in the practice.

It is clear from the research and from these examples that the role of management in America's future is critical. What is less obvious, however, is what specifically constitutes "good management." Questions such as what attributes and what behaviors are displayed by effective managers and how an individual can learn to be a good manager are still left unaddressed. Identifying attributes of effective management and teaching management to individuals has been the role accepted by business schools and by management education programs. Unfortunately, this role may not have been performed as effectively as it could have been.

For the past decade, management education has been assailed as a culprit in contributing to economic decline. This criticism was often aimed at business schools and other management education programs. Over 200 articles have appeared in the last decade in a wide array of academic and popular publications with such titles as "Managing Our Way to Economic Decline," "Overhauling America's Business Management," "The Failure of Business Education," "The Crisis in Business Education," "Are Business Schools Doing Their Job?," "Business Schools and Their Critics," and "What Good are B-Schools?" The criticisms are pointed. For example, Donald E. Peterson (1990) asserted: "The business schools . . . are doing more harm than good. I no longer flippantly say, as I used to, 'close their doors,' because now I'm beginning to believe that maybe this idea has serious merit." Wrapp (1982, p. 35) added: "Business schools have done more to ensure the success of the Japanese and West German invasion of America than any one thing I can think of." Samuelson (1990) stated: "For three decades we've run an experiment on the social utility of business schools. They've flunked. If they were improving the quality of U.S. management, the results ought to be obvious by now. They aren't."

Even the American Assembly of Collegiate Schools of Business (AACSB) (1985), the accreditation agency for America's business schools, admitted:

> In recent years, as the U.S. seems to have lost its edge in worldwide industrial competitiveness, nearly every sector of society has criticized U.S. corporate management. Critics say that the U.S. manager is short-term oriented, naively quantitative, averse to risk, self-centered, deficient in ethics and loyalty, impatient for promotion, overpriced, and unconcerned with real productivity. Not all managers fit such descriptions by any means. But enough apparently do to prompt the question, how did they become that way? What kind of managers are the business schools and other management development programs producing?

Pfeffer (1981) argued that the main problem in business schools and management education is the type of training imparted:

> Management education or performance in management schools does not predict subsequent career success for managers. But why not? It is because of the type of training imparted. Management schools impart both the ideology and skills of analysis. . . . Optimization techniques for the core of current courses. . . . Students emerge from such a program believing that there is an optimal answer or set of answers discoverable through quantitative analysis.

Mintzberg (1987) expressed a similar point of view:

> Ideal management education should reorient its priorities. My ideal management training would emphasize skill training, experiential education, if you like. Perhaps forty percent of the effort should be devoted to it. . . . A great deal is known about inculcating such skills. But not in the business schools.

Scientific data support the assertions of these and other authors that, in the absence of skill training, performance in school is not predictive of subsequent career success. Cohen (1984) summarized the results of 108 studies of the relationship between performance in college courses (as measured by grade-point average) and subsequent life success. Life success was measured in these studies by a variety of factors, including job performance, income, promotions, personal satisfaction, eminence, and graduate degrees. The mean correlation between performance in school and performance in life in these 108 studies was 0.18, and in no case did the correlation exceed 0.20. These low correlations suggest that school performance and successful performance in subsequent life activities are related only marginally.

What is the explanation for these dismal results? Why should students strive hard to excel in formal education programs? Do grades matter at all? Should students and executives invest in formal education and training to try to improve their managerial competencies, or can good management be learned on the job? Should anyone go into debt to attend a business school?

Obviously, we believe that formal education and management training can positively affect managerial performance. We also believe that there must be a concerted effort to help develop such management talent in order to foster turnaround and excellence in most firms. Those beliefs, however, are not based on blind optimism. Scientific evidence exists that such training can make a difference both to an individual and to the bottom-line performance of a firm. We summarize two studies below that provide support for this contention. First, however, we must address the question, "What constitutes effective management?" Then we can discuss how formal education can help one improve management competence and the extent to which improvement will affect the performance of an organization.

Effective Management

In an effort to identify what constitutes effective management, we conducted an investigation in which we identified individuals who were rated as highly effective managers in their own organizations. We contacted organizations in the fields of business, health care, education, and state government and asked senior officers to name the most effective managers in their organizations. We then interviewed these people to determine what attributes they associated with managerial effectiveness. We also reviewed studies done by other researchers that attempted to identify the characteristics of effective managers.

In our own study, 402 highly effective managers were identified by their peers and superiors in this sample of organizations. We interviewed these individuals and tried to discover what made them such successful managers. Among the questions were:

- How have you become so successful in this organization?

- Who fails and who succeeds in this organization and why?

- If you had to train someone to take your place, what knowledge and what skills would you make certain that person possessed?

- If you could design an ideal course or training program to teach you to be a better manager, what would it contain?

- Think of other effective managers you know. What skills do they demonstrate that explain their success?

Our analysis of the interviews produced about 60 characteristics of effective managers. The 10 identified most often are listed in Table 1. Notice that these 10 characteristics are all behavioral skills. They are not personality attributes or styles, nor are they generalizations such as "luck" or "timing." They also are not very surprising. The characteristics of effective managers are not a secret.

---

1. Verbal communication (including listening)
2. Managing time and stress
3. Managing individual decisions
4. Recognizing, defining, and solving problems
5. Motivating and influencing others
6. Delegating
7. Setting goals and articulating a vision
8. Self-awareness
9. Team building
10. Managing conflict

Table 1   The Most Frequently Cited Skills of Effective Managers

The attributes derived from our study are similar to those resulting from several other surveys published in the management literature. Table 2, for example, lists the results of several studies using a variety of kinds of respondents. Not surprisingly, the two lists are highly similar. Regardless of whether respondents are CEOs or first-line supervisors, whether they work in the public sector or the private sector, their skills are generally well marked and agreed upon by observers. It is not hard to identify and describe the skills of effective managers.

Three notable characteristics are typical of most of these skills. First, the skills are behavioral. They are not personality attributes or stylistic tendencies. They consist of an identifiable set of actions that individuals perform and that lead to certain outcomes. An important implication, therefore, is that individuals can learn to perform these actions and can improve their current level of performance. Whereas people with different styles and personalities may apply the skills differently, there are, nevertheless, a core set of observable attributes of effective skill performance that are common across a range of individual differences.

A second characteristic is that these skills seem, in several cases, to be contradictory or paradoxical. For example, they are neither all soft and humanistic in orientation nor all hard-driving and directive. They are oriented neither toward teamwork and interpersonal relations exclusively nor toward individualism and entrepreneurship exclusively. A variety of skills are present.

To illustrate, Cameron and Tschirhart (1988) assessed the skill performance of over 500 mid-level and upper-middle managers in about 150 organizations. They used the 25 most frequently mentioned management skills taken from those in Tables 1 and 2 as well as from research by Ghiselli (1963), Livingston (1971), Miner (1973), Katz (1974), Mintzberg (1975), Flanders (1981), and Boyatzis (1982). Through statistical analyses, Cameron and Tschirhart discovered that the skills could be sorted into four main groups. One group of skills focused on participative and human relations skills (for example, supportive communication and teambuilding), while another group focused on just the opposite, that is, competitiveness and control (for example, assertiveness, power, and influence skills). A third group focused on innovativeness and entrepreneurship (such as creative problem solving), while a fourth group emphasized quite the opposite type of skills, namely, maintaining order and rationality (for example, managing time and rational decision making).

One conclusion from that study was that effective managers are required to demonstrate paradoxical skills. That is, the most effective managers are both participative and hard-driving, both nurturing and competitive. They were able to be flexible and creative while also being controlled, stable, and rational. The second characteristic associated with effective management, then, is the mastery of diverse and seemingly contradictory skills.

Third, these critical skills were interrelated and overlapping. No effective manager performed one skill or one set of skills independent of others. For example, in order to effectively motivate others, skills such as supportive communication, influence, and delegation were also required. Effective managers, therefore, develop a constellation of skills that overlap and support one another and that allow flexibility in managing diverse situations.

Improving Management Skills

Successful management, of course, is more than just following a cookbook list of sequential behaviors. Developing highly competent management skills is much more complicated than developing skills such as those associated with a trade (for example, welding) or a sport (for example, shooting baskets). Management skills are (1) linked to a more complex knowledge base than other types of skills and (2) inherently connected to interaction with other (frequently unpredictable) individuals. A standardized approach to welding or shooting baskets may be feasible, but no standardized approach to managing human beings is possible.

STUDY • RESPONDENTS • FOCUS	RESULTS	
• Prentice (1984) • 230 executives in manufacturing, retail, and service firms • Critical skills for managing organizations	Listening Communication Leadership Problem solving Time management	Interpersonal relations Formal presentations Stress management Adaptability to change
• Margerison and Kakabadse (1984) • 721 chief executive officers in U.S. corporations • Most important things you've learned in order to be a chief executive	(1) Communication Managing people Delegation Patience Respect Control Understanding people Evaluating personnel Tolerance Team spirit	(2) Strategic planning Decision making Self-discipline Analytic abilities Hard work Flexibility Financial management Time management Knowledge of the business Clear thinking
• Margerison and Kakabadse (1984) • 721 chief executive officers in U.S. corporations • Key management skills to develop in others to help them become senior executives	Human relations Communication Planning and goal setting People management and leadership Teamwork	Decision making Financial management Entrepreneurial skills Delegating Broad experience
• Cameron (1984) • 50 consultants, professors, management development experts, and public administrators • Critical management skills needed by state government managers	Managing conflict Motivating others Managing stress and time Decision making Delegation	Goal setting Problem solving Design jobs Gaining and using power Career planning
• Hunsicker (1978) • 1,854 Air Force officers • Skills that most contribute to successful management	Communication Human relations General management ability Technical competence	Leadership Knowledge and experience
• Luthans, Rosenkrantz, and Hennessey (1985) • 52 managers in 3 organizations • Participant observation of skills demonstrated by most effective versus least effective managers	Managing conflict Building power and influence Communicating with outsiders	Decision making Communicating with insiders Developing subordinates Processing paperwork Planning and goal setting
• Benson (1983) • A survey of 25 studies in business journals • A summary of the skills needed by students entering the professions	Listening Written communication Oral communication Motivating/persuading	Interpersonal skills Informational interviewing Group problem solving

Table 2   Identifying Critical Management Skills: A Sample of Studies

STUDY • RESPONDENTS • FOCUS	RESULTS	

• Curtis, Winsor, and Stephens (1989)
• 428 members of the American Society of Personnel Administrators in the United States
• (1) Skills needed to obtain employment,
   (2) skills important for successful job performance
   (3) skills needed to move up in the organization
	(1)
	Verbal communication
	Listening
	Enthusiasm
	Written communication
	Technical competence
	Appearance
		(2)
		Interpersonal skills
		Verbal communication
		Written communication
		Persistence/determination
		Enthusiasm
		Technical competence

	(3)
	Ability to work well with
	   others one-on-one
	Ability to gather information
	   and make a decision
	Ability to work well in groups
	Ability to listen and
	   give counsel
	Ability to give
	   effective feedback
	Ability to write
	   effective reports
	Knowledge of the job
		Ability to present a
		   good image for
		   the firm
		Ability to use computers
		Knowledge of
		   management theory
		Knowledge of finance
		Knowledge of marketing
		Knowledge of accounting
		Ability to use
		   business machines

Table 2   *(continued)*

On the other hand, what all skills do have in common is the potential for improvement through practice. Any approach to developing management skills, therefore, must involve a heavy dose of practical application. At the same time, practice without the necessary conceptual knowledge is sterile and ignores the need for flexibility and adaptation to different situations. Therefore, developing skill competency is inherently tied to both conceptual learning and behavioral practice.

The method we have found to be most successful in helping individuals develop management skills is based on social learning theory (Bandura, 1977; Davis & Luthans, 1980). This approach marries rigorous conceptual knowledge with opportunities to practice and apply observable behaviors. Variations on this general approach have been used widely in on-the-job supervisory training programs (Goldstein & Sorcher, 1974) as well as in allied professional education classrooms such as teacher development and social work (Rose, Crayner, & Edleson, 1977; Singleton, Spurgeon, & Stammers, 1980).

This learning model, as originally formulated, consisted of four steps: (1) the presentation of behavioral principles or action guidelines, generally using traditional instruction methods; (2) demonstration of the principles by means of cases, films, scripts, or incidents; (3) opportunities to practice the principles through role plays or exercises; and (4) feedback on performance from peers, instructors, or experts.

Our own experience in teaching complex management skills has convinced us that three important modifications are necessary in order for this model to be most effective. First, the behavioral principles must be grounded in social science theory and in reliable research results. Commonsense generalizations and panacea-like prescriptions appear regularly in the popular management literature. To ensure the validity of the behavioral guidelines being prescribed, the learning approach must include scientifically based knowledge about the effects of the management principles being presented.

Second, individuals must be aware of their current level of skill competency and be motivated to improve upon that level in order to benefit from the model. Most people receive very little feedback about their current level of skill competency. Most organizations provide some kind of annual or semiannual evaluation (for example, course grades in school or performance appraisal interviews in firms), but these evaluations are almost always infrequent and narrow in scope, and they fail to assess performance in most critical skill areas. To help a person understand what skills to improve and why, therefore, an assessment activity must be part of the model.

In addition, most people find change rather uncomfortable and therefore avoid taking the risk to develop new behavior patterns. An assessment activity in the learning model helps encourage these people to change by illuminating their strengths and weaknesses. People then know where weaknesses lie and what things need to be improved. Assessment activities generally take the form of self-evaluation instruments, case studies, or problems that help highlight personal strengths and weaknesses in a particular skill area.

Third, an application component is needed in the learning model. Most management skill training takes place in a classroom setting where feedback is immediate and it is relatively safe to try out new behaviors and make mistakes. Therefore, transferring learning to an actual job setting is often problematic. Application exercises help to apply classroom learning to examples from the real world of management. Application exercises often take the form of an outside-of-class intervention, a consulting assignment, or a problem-centered intervention, which the student then analyzes to determine its degree of success or failure.

In summary, evidence suggests that a five-step learning model is most effective for helping individuals develop management skills (see Cameron & Whetten, 1984; Whetten & Cameron, 1983). Table 3 outlines such a model. Step 1 involves the assessment of current levels of skill competency and knowledge of the behavioral principles. Step 2 consists of the presentation of validated, scientifically based principles and guidelines for effective skill performance. Step 3 is an analysis step in which models or cases are made available in order to analyze behavioral principles in real organizational settings. This step also helps demonstrate how the behavioral guidelines can be

COMPONENTS	CONTENTS	OBJECTIVES
1. Skill assessment	Survey instruments Role plays	Assess current level of skill competence and knowledge; create readiness to change.
2. Skill learning	Written text Behavioral guidelines	Teach correct principles and present a rationale for behavioral guidelines.
3. Skill analysis	Cases	Provide examples of appropriate and inappropriate skill performance. Analyze behavioral principles and reasons they work.
4. Skill practice	Exercises Simulations Role plays	Practice behavioral guidelines. Adapt principles to personal style. Receive feedback and assistance.
5. Skill application	Assignments (behavioral and written)	Transfer classroom learning to real-life situations. Foster ongoing personal development.

Table 3   A Model for Developing Management Skills

adapted to different personal styles and circumstances. Step 4 consists of practice exercises in which experimentation can occur and immediate feedback can be received in a relatively safe environment. Step 5, finally, is the application of the skill to a real-life setting outside the classroom with follow-up analysis of the relative success of that application.

Research on the effectiveness of training programs using this general learning model has shown that it produces results superior to those based on the traditional lecture-discussion approach (Moses & Ritchie, 1976; Burnaska, 1976; Smith, 1976; Latham & Saari, 1979; Porras & Anderson, 1981). In addition, evidence suggests that management skill training can have significant impact on the bottom-line performance of a firm. The U.S. Postal Service completed a study a few years ago in which 49 of the largest 100 post offices in America were evaluated. An important question in the study was, "How can we make post offices more effective?" Productivity and service quality were both monitored over a period of five years. The two major factors that had impact on these effectiveness measures were (1) degree of mechanization (automation), and (2) investment in training. Two kinds of training were provided: maintenance training (training in operating and maintaining the equipment) and management training (training in developing management skills). The overall conclusion of the study was: "Performance levels in these organizations vary systematically and predictably as training levels vary. The training-performance relationship is positive and statistically significant." More specifically, the study found that (1) providing management training was more important than providing maintenance training in accounting for improved productivity and service in the post offices, and (2) both kinds of training were more important than having automated or up-to-date equipment in the post office (mechanization). Low-tech offices outperformed high-tech offices when managers were provided with management skill training. In short, its five-year study convinced the U.S. Postal Service that helping employees to develop management skills was the best way to improve organizational effectiveness.

Management skill training, then, is a critical developmental activity for both potential and practicing managers. We have provided evidence that many organizations are in danger of losing their global competitiveness as well as their credibility here at home. Moreover, evidence suggests that it is, to a significant extent, the managers who are at fault. We suggest that one important way to improve management and organizational performance is to train more managers in critical management skills. Mintzberg (1975, p. 60) made this point two decades ago:

> Management schools will begin the serious training of managers when skill training takes its place next to cognitive learning. Cognitive learning is detached and informational, like reading a book or listening to a lecture. No doubt much important cognitive material must be assimilated by the manager-to-be. But cognitive learning no more makes a manager than it does a swimmer. The latter will drown the first time he jumps into the water if his coach never takes him out of the lecture hall, gets him wet, and gives him feedback on his performance. Our management schools need to identify the skills managers use, select students who show potential in these skills, put the students into situations where these skills can be practiced, and then give them systematic feedback on their performance.

Porter and McKibbin (1988), after completing a study of management education in American business schools sponsored by the American Assembly of Collegiate Schools of Business, concluded:

> The challenge of how to develop stronger people skills needs to be faced by both business schools in the education of their degree program students and by corporations and firms in their management development activities.

Donald E. Peterson (1990), retired chairman and CEO at Ford Motor Company, agreed: "The element that is still not as well-instilled as I might wish is the importance of people skills in being a successful manager. Most schools still stress individual performance."

These perspectives match those of our own students and colleagues in business organizations who, based on their own personal experience and observations, have reached the same conclusions. For example, a vice president of a major computer manufacturer observed:

> Many management school graduates have a hard time adjusting to organizational reality. They are long on analytic skills and short on implementation skills. The best solution in the world is worthless unless you can get others to support it. We call this malady paralysis by analysis.

A partner in a Big Six accounting firm similarly observed:

> The higher up the organization you go, the less relevant technical knowledge becomes. It is important for your first couple of promotions, but after that, people skills are what count.

A recent graduate from a Big Ten management school also reported:

> I can't believe it. I went for my second interview with a company last week, and I spent the first half-day participating in simulation exercises with ten other job candidates. They videotaped me playing the role of a salesman handling an irate customer, a new director of personnel putting down a revolt by the "old guard," and a plant manager trying to convince people of the need to install a radically new production process. Boy, was I unprepared for that!

The message behind these personal observations is clear—from all perspectives, competence in personal, interpersonal, and group skills is a critical prerequisite for success in management. Strong analytical and quantitative skills are important, but they are not sufficient. Successful managers must be able to work effectively with people. Unfortunately, interpersonal and management skills have not always been a high priority for business school students and aspiring executives. In a survey of 110 Fortune 500 CEOs, 87 percent were satisfied with the level of competence and analytic skills of business school graduates, 68 percent were satisfied with conceptual skills of graduates, but only 43 percent of the CEOs were satisfied with graduates' management skills, and only 28 percent were satisfied with their interpersonal skills!

To assist you in improving your own management skills, this book emphasizes practicing management skills, rather than just reading about them. We have organized the book with this specific approach in mind.

Leadership and Management

Before outlining for you the organization of this book, it is important to discuss briefly the place of leadership in this volume. Some writers differentiate between the concepts of "leadership" and "management." They have wondered why we concentrate on "management" skills instead of "leadership" skills in this book. We have also been asked by professors, business executives, and students why we have not either changed the title of the book to include "leadership," or at least included one chapter on leadership in this volume. These queries and suggestions have motivated us to be clear at the outset of this volume about what we mean by "management" and why we believe it encompasses "leadership" as typically defined.

Traditionally, **leadership** is used to describe what individuals do under conditions of change. When organizations are dynamic and undergoing transformation, people at the top are supposed to exhibit leadership. **Management,** on the other hand, has traditionally been used to describe what executives do under conditions of stability. Thus, management has been linked with the status quo. In addition, leadership has sometimes been defined as "doing the right things," whereas management has been defined as "doing things right." Leaders have been said to focus on setting the direction, articulating a vision, and creating something new. Managers have been said to focus on monitoring, directing, and refining current performance. Leadership has been equated with dynamism, vibrancy, and charisma; management with hierarchy, equilibrium, and control.

Although such distinctions between leadership and management may have been appropriate in previous decades, that is no longer the case. Managers cannot be successful without being good leaders, and leaders cannot be successful without being good managers. No longer do organizations and individuals have the luxury of holding on to the status quo: worrying about doing things right but failing to do the right things; keeping the system stable instead of leading change and improvement; monitoring current performance instead of formulating a vision of the future; concentrating on equilibrium and control instead of vibrancy and charisma. Effective management and leadership are inseparable. The skills required to do one are also required of the other. No organization in a post-industrial, hyper-turbulent environment will survive without executives capable of providing both management and leadership. Some reasons for this assertion are illustrated in Figure 1. By staying the same, we get worse. Because our circumstances are constantly changing and expectations for performance are continually escalating, the traditional definition of management is outmoded and irrelevant today. Effective managers and leaders do exactly the same things.

This book, therefore, focuses on management skills because not only is it more parsimonious to write "management skills" instead of "management and leadership skills," but, more importantly, effective management subsumes effective leadership. As pointed out earlier in studies of organizational and managerial success (see Table 2), leadership is one of the attributes of effective managers. Effective managers must have leadership abilities. Therefore, each skill contained in this book is as essential for an effective leader as it is for an effective manager. Leadership and management, from our perspective, are indistinguishable.

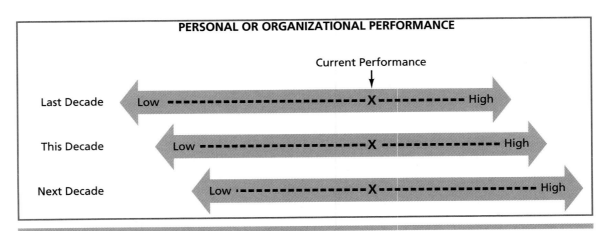

Figure 1   The Necessity of Developing Leadership and Management Skills

Organization of the Book

This book focuses on management skills that research has identified as critically important. Part I contains three chapters on personal skills: Developing Self-Awareness, Managing Stress, and Solving Problems Creatively. Each chapter contains a cluster of related skills, and each skill area overlaps with other skill areas. No skill stands alone. The specific skill content in each chapter is listed in Figure 2.

Part II focuses on interpersonal skills: Communicating Supportively, Gaining Power and Influence, Motivating Employees, and Managing Conflict. These skill areas also overlap; managers must rely on parts of many skill areas in order to perform any one skill effectively.

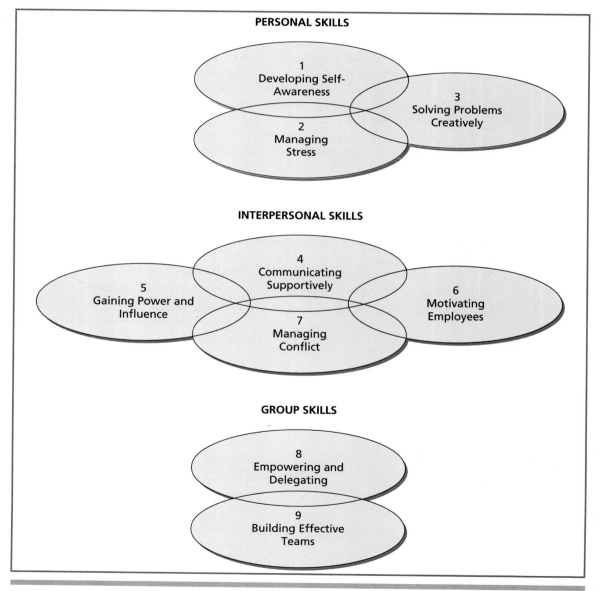

Figure 2 A Model of Critical Management Skills

Part III includes two chapters on group skills: Empowering and Delegating, and Building Effective Teams. These two chapters overlap substantially with one another as well as with the skill areas in Parts I and II. Thus, as one progresses from personal to interpersonal to group skills, the core competencies developed in the previous area help support successful performance of the new skill area.

In addition to the nine core management skill chapters in Parts I, II, and III, Part IV contains three supplements: Making Oral and Written Presentations, Conducting Interviews, and Conducting Meetings. These supplements cover specialized communication skills that are especially relevant for students who have had little managerial experience or skill training. Also these supplements foster the skill development needed to implement assignments typically included in a management skill-building course. Writing reports, giving class presentations, interviewing managers, and conducting group meetings are all prerequisites for building skills in the core management skill areas, so we have provided material on these three topics that students will find helpful.

The reengineering trend of the 1990s has left businesses with leaner and flatter organizational structures. These pared-down organizations, and a newfound emphasis on cross-functional teams, have changed the environment that managers work in, but they have not diminished the importance of the skills presented and illustrated in this book. The reader should be aware that Figure 2 is a useful way of grouping individual skills, but many of the skills are also applicable to group as well as interpersonal situations.

Appendix I contains scoring keys and forms for use with assignments in the chapters; Appendix II is a glossary of key terms in the text; and Appendix III lists references for excerpted material in the book.

Each chapter is organized on the basis of the learning model summarized in Table 3. The chapter begins with Skill Assessment instruments. Their purpose is to help you focus attention on areas of personal competence as well as areas needing improvement in both knowledge and performance.

An explanation of the key behavioral guidelines, as well as a rationale for why these guidelines work, is found in the Skill Learning section. This section explains the core behavioral principles associated with each skill. We present a model of each skill, along with evidence from research that the principles identified are effective in practice. Our objective is to provide a sound rationale for the action guidelines summarized at the end of the section.

COMPONENTS	CONTENTS	OBJECTIVES
1. Skill assessment	Survey instruments Role plays	Assess current level of skill competence and knowledge; create readiness to change.
2. Skill learning	Written text Behavioral guidelines	Teach correct principles and present a rationale for behavioral guidelines.
3. Skill analysis	Cases	Provide examples of appropriate and inappropriate skill performance. Analyze behavioral principles and reasons they work.
4. Skill practice	Exercises Simulations Role plays	Practice behavioral guidelines. Adapt principles to personal style. Receive feedback and assistance.
5. Skill application	Assignments (behavioral and written)	Transfer classroom learning to real-life situations. Foster ongoing personal development.

Table 3 A Model for Developing Management Skills

In the Skill Analysis section, you will find brief case histories that illustrate both effective and ineffective applications of the behavioral principles. The purpose of this section is to bridge the gap between intellectual understanding and behavioral application. Critiquing a manager's performance in a real-life case enhances your understanding of the skill learning material. Each case provides a model of effective or ineffective performance and helps identify ways that the skill can be adapted to your personal style.

The Skill Practice section provides exercises, problems, and role-play assignments. The goal of this section is to provide opportunities to practice the behavioral guidelines in simulated managerial situations and to receive feedback from peers and instructors. Practicing these managerial skills in a classroom setting is not only safer and less costly than in a real-life management job, but others' observation and feedback can be more precise and more timely as well.

The last section of each chapter is Skill Application. It contains a form for helping you generate your own improvement agenda, as well as assignments and ideas for applying the skill in an out-of-class situation. The purpose of these assignments is to help you transfer behavioral guidelines into everyday practice. You may be directed to teach the skill to someone else, consult with another manager to help resolve a relevant problem, or apply the skill in an organization or family.

Practice and Application

The philosophy of this book is that improvement in management skills is primarily the learner's responsibility. If the application of the principles covered in this book is not conscientiously applied outside the classroom, little or no progress can be achieved. Our intention, therefore, is to have the course carry over into the life activities of learners.

Effectiveness in management is no different from effectiveness in most other human enterprises. It requires the same kinds of skills to live a productive and successful life as it does to manage people effectively. That is why, even though some users of this book may not presently be managers of other employees—and indeed may never become managers—they should neither dismiss these skills as irrelevant nor wait until they become managers before attempting to practice them.

Psychological research has confirmed that when people are forced to perform under stress, they rely on what is called a "dominant response pattern" (Staw, Sandelands, & Dutton, 1981). That is, they rely on the behavior patterns that are most deeply ingrained in their response repertoire. For example, if a person who has been accustomed to responding to conflict combatively, but who has recently begun practicing a more supportive response pattern, is faced with an intense, emotional confrontation, that person may begin by reacting supportively. But as pressure mounts, he or she is likely to revert to the more practiced, combative style.

Thus it is important that learners not make the mistake of thinking they can delay applying skill training until they become managers. When problems and conflicts occur then, it is too late for learners to change their behavior to handle issues effectively. Learners, therefore, should practice and apply the skills discussed in this book to part-time jobs, friendships, student organizations, families, church groups, and so forth. Employees, of course, will want to use the guidelines provided here with their coworkers, managers, subordinates, and customers. With conscientious practice, following the behavioral guidelines will become second nature.

A second reason that nonmanagers should not delay the application of management skills is that individuals learn faster and remember better that which they experience both intellectually and emotionally. That is, people learn best that which affects them, and they feel affected by something if they see an immediate effect on their lives. For example, individuals can more quickly acquire a working knowledge of a foreign language and retain it longer if they spend a summer living in a country where the language is spoken than if they merely take a language course in their own country.

Simply stated, application is a crucial component of the skill improvement process, but it generally takes extra effort and ingenuity to make application exercises effective and worthwhile. We encourage you to put that extra effort into improving your management skills.

Developing Management Skills is not intended just for individuals who plan to enter managerial positions or who currently manage organizations. It is meant to help people in general better manage many aspects of their lives and relationships. In fact, John Holt (1964, p. 165) succinctly summarized our intention by equating management skill to intelligence:

> When we talk about intelligence, we do not mean the ability to get a good score on a certain kind of test or even the ability to do well in school; these are at best only indicators of something larger, deeper and far more important. By intelligence we mean a style of life, a way of behaving in various situations. The true test of intelligence is not how much we know how to do, but how we behave when we don't know what to do.

Fostering the development of such intelligence is the goal of *Developing Management Skills*.

Supplementary Material

Diagnostic Survey and Exercises

Personal Assessment of Management Skills

Step 1: To get an overall profile of your level of skill competence, respond to the following statements using the rating scale below. Please rate your behavior as it is, not as you would like it to be. If you have not engaged in a specific activity, answer according to how you think you would behave based on your experience in similar activities. Be realistic; this instrument is designed to help you tailor your learning to your specific needs. After you have completed the survey, the scoring key in Appendix I will help you generate an overall profile of your management skill strengths and weaknesses.

Step 2: Get copies of the Associates' version of this instrument from your instructor. An alternate version has been provided in the *Instructor's Manual* that uses "he" or "she" instead of "I" in the questions. Give copies to at least three other people who know you well or who have observed you in a managerial situation. They should complete the instrument by rating your behavior. Bring the completed surveys back to class and compare your own ratings to your associates' ratings, your associates' ratings to the ratings received by others in the class, and the ratings you received to those of a national norm group.

Subsections of this instrument appear in each chapter throughout the book.

Rating Scale

1	Strongly disagree	4	Slightly agree
2	Disagree	5	Agree
3	Slightly disagree	6	Strongly agree

In regard to my level of self-knowledge:

_____ 1. I seek information about my strengths and weaknesses from others as a basis for self-improvement.

_____ 2. In order to improve, I am willing to be self-disclosing to others (that is, to share my beliefs and feelings).

_____ 3. I am very much aware of my preferred style in gathering information and making decisions.

_____ 4. I have a good sense of how I cope with situations that are ambiguous and uncertain.

_____ 5. I have a well-developed set of personal standards and principles that guide my behavior.

When faced with stressful or time-pressured situations:

_____ 6. I use effective time-management methods such as keeping track of my time, making to-do lists, and prioritizing tasks.

_____ 7. I frequently affirm my priorities so that less important things don't drive out more important things.

_____ 8. I maintain a program of regular exercise for fitness.

_____ 9. I maintain an open, trusting relationship with someone with whom I can share my frustrations.

_____ 10. I know and practice several temporary relaxation techniques such as deep breathing and muscle relaxation.

_____ 11. I strive to redefine problems as opportunities for improvement.

When I approach a typical, routine problem:

_____ 12. I state clearly and explicitly what the problem is. I avoid trying to solve it until I have defined it.

_____ 13. I always generate more than one alternative solution to the problem, instead of identifying only one obvious solution.

_____ 14. I keep steps in the problem-solving process distinct; that is, I define the problem before proposing alternative solutions, and I generate alternatives before selecting a single solution.

When faced with a complex or difficult problem that does not have an easy solution:

_____ 15. I try out several definitions of the problem. I don't limit myself to just one way to define it.

_____ 16. I try to unfreeze my thinking by asking lots of questions about the nature of the problem before considering ways to solve it.

_____ 17. I try to think about the problem from both the left (logical) side of my brain and the right (intuitive) side of my brain.

_____ 18. I do not evaluate the merits of an alternative solution to the problem before I have generated a list of alternatives. That is, I avoid deciding on a solution until I have developed many possible solutions.

_____ 19. I have some specific techniques that I use to help develop creative and innovative solutions to problems.

When trying to foster more creativity and innovation among those with whom I work:

_____   20. I make sure there are divergent points of view represented in every problem-solving group.

_____   21. I try to acquire information from customers regarding their preferences and expectations.

_____   22. I provide recognition not only to those who are idea champions but also to those who support others' ideas and who provide resources to implement them.

_____   23. I encourage informed rule-breaking in pursuit of creative solutions.

In situations where I have to provide negative feedback or offer corrective advice:

_____   24. I help others recognize and define their own problems when I counsel them.

_____   25. I understand clearly when it is appropriate to offer advice and direction to others and when it is not.

_____   26. I always give feedback that is focused on problems and solutions, not on personal characteristics.

_____   27. My feedback is always specific and to the point, rather than general or vague.

_____   28. I am descriptive in giving negative feedback to others. That is, I objectively describe events, their consequences, and my feelings about them.

_____   29. I take responsibility for my statements and point of view by using, for example, "I have decided" instead of "They have decided."

_____   30. I convey flexibility and openness to conflicting opinions when presenting my point of view, even when I feel strongly about it.

_____   31. I don't talk down to those who have less power or less information than I.

_____   32. I don't dominate conversations with others.

In a situation where it is important to obtain more power:

_____   33. I always put forth more effort and take more initiative than expected in my work.

_____   34. I am continually upgrading my skills and knowledge.

_____   35. I strongly support organizational ceremonial events and activities.

_____   36. I form a broad network of relationships with people throughout the organization at all levels.

_____   37. In my work I consistently strive to generate new ideas, initiate new activities, and minimize routine tasks.

_____   38. I consistently send personal notes to others when they accomplish something significant or when I pass along important information to them.

_____   39. I refuse to bargain with individuals who use high-pressure negotiation tactics.

_____   40. I always avoid using threats or demands to impose my will on others.

When another person needs to be motivated:

_____   41. I always determine if the person has the necessary resources and support to succeed in a task.

_____   42. I use a variety of rewards to reinforce exceptional performances.

_____ 43. I design task assignments to make them interesting and challenging.

_____ 44. I make sure the person gets timely feedback from those affected by task performance.

_____ 45. I always help the person establish performance goals that are challenging, specific, and time bound.

_____ 46. Only as a last resort do I attempt to reassign or release a poorly performing individual.

_____ 47. I consistently discipline when effort is below expectations and capabilities.

_____ 48. I make sure that people feel fairly and equitably treated.

_____ 49. I provide immediate compliments and other forms of recognition for meaningful accomplishments.

When I see someone doing something that needs correcting:

_____ 50. I avoid making personal accusations and attributing self-serving motives to the other person.

_____ 51. I encourage two-way interaction by inviting the respondent to express his or her perspective and to ask questions.

_____ 52. I make a specific request, detailing a more acceptable option.

When someone complains about something I've done:

_____ 53. I show genuine concern and interest, even when I disagree.

_____ 54. I seek additional information by asking questions that provide specific and descriptive information.

_____ 55. I ask the other person to suggest more acceptable behaviors.

When two people are in conflict and I am the mediator:

_____ 56. I do not take sides but remain neutral.

_____ 57. I help the parties generate multiple alternatives.

_____ 58. I help the parties find areas on which they agree.

In situations where I have an opportunity to empower others:

_____ 59. I help people feel competent in their work by recognizing and celebrating their small successes.

_____ 60. I provide regular feedback and needed support.

_____ 61. I try to provide all the information that people need to accomplish their tasks.

_____ 62. I exhibit caring and personal concern for each person with whom I have dealings.

When delegating work to others:

_____ 63. I specify clearly the results I desire.

_____ 64. I specify clearly the level of initiative I want others to take (for example, wait for directions, do part of the task and then report, do the whole task and then report, and so forth).

_____ 65. I allow participation by those accepting assignments regarding when and how work will be done.

_____ 66. I avoid upward delegation by asking people to recommend solutions, rather than merely asking for advice or answers, when a problem is encountered.

_____ 67. I follow up and maintain accountability for delegated tasks on a regular basis.

When I am attempting to build and lead an effective team:

_____ 68. I help team members establish a foundation of trust among one another and between themselves and me.

_____ 69. I help members learn to play roles that assist the team in accomplishing its tasks as well as building strong interpersonal relationships.

_____ 70. I encourage a win/win philosophy in the team—that is, when one member wins, every member wins.

_____ 71. I encourage the team to achieve dramatic breakthrough innovations as well as small continuous improvements.

_____ 72. I manage difficult team members effectively, through supportive communication, collaborative conflict management, and empowerment.

What Does It Take to Be an Effective Manager?

The purpose of this exercise is to help you get an in-depth picture of the role of a manager and the skills required to perform that job successfully.

Your assignment is to interview at least three managers who are employed full-time. You should use the questions below in your interviews, but you are not restricted to them. The purpose of these interviews is to give you a chance to learn about critical managerial skills from those who have to use them.

Please treat the interviews as confidential. The names of the individuals do not matter—only their opinions, perceptions, and behaviors. Assure the managers that no one will be able to identify them from their responses.

Keep notes on your interviews. These notes should be as detailed as possible so you can reconstruct the interviews for class. Be sure to keep a record of each person's job title and a brief description of his or her organization.

1. Please describe a typical day at work.

2. What are the most critical problems you face as a manager?

3. What are the most critical skills needed to be a successful manager in your line of work?

4. What are the major reasons managers fail in positions like yours?

5. What are the outstanding skills or abilities of other effective managers you have known?

6. If you had to train someone to replace you in your current job, what key abilities would you focus on?

7. On a scale of 1 (very rarely) to 5 (constantly), can you rate the extent to which you use the following skills or behaviors during your workday?

_____ Managing personal stress	_____ Managing time
_____ Facilitating group decision making	_____ Making private decisions
_____ Recognizing or defining problems	_____ Using verbal communication skills
_____ Appraising others' performance	_____ Motivating others
_____ Managing conflict	_____ Achieving self-awareness
_____ Gaining and using power	_____ Orchestrating change
_____ Delegating	_____ Setting goals
_____ Listening	_____ Disciplining others
_____ Interviewing	_____ Empathizing
_____ Team building	_____ Solving problems
_____ Conducting meetings	_____ Negotiating

SSS Software In-Basket Exercise

NOTE: The SSS Software exercise is used with permission. Copyright © 1995 by Susan Schor, Joseph Seltzer, and James Smither. All rights reserved.

One way to assess your own strengths and weaknesses in management skills is to engage in an actual managerial work experience. The following exercise gives you a realistic glimpse of the tasks faced regularly by practicing managers. Complete the exercise, and then compare your own decisions and actions with those of classmates.

SSS Software designs and develops customized software for businesses. It also integrates this software with the customer's existing systems and provides system maintenance. SSS Software has customers in the following industries: airlines, automotive, finance/banking, health/hospital, consumer products, electronics, and government. The company has also begun to generate important international clients. These include the European Airbus consortium and a consortium of banks and financial firms based in Kenya.

SSS Software has grown rapidly since its inception eight years ago. Its revenue, net income, and earnings per share have all been above the industry average for the past several years. However, competition in this technologically sophisticated field has grown very rapidly. Recently, it has become more difficult to compete for major contracts. Moreover, although SSS Software's revenue and net income continue to grow, the rate of growth declined during the last fiscal year.

SSS Software's 250 employees are divided into several operating divisions with employees at four levels: Nonmanagement, Technical/Professional, Managerial, and Executive. Nonmanagement employees take care of the clerical and facilities support functions. The Technical/Professional staff perform the core technical work for the firm. Most Managerial employees are group managers who supervise a team of Technical/Professional employees working on a project for a particular customer. Staff who work in specialized areas such as finance, accounting, human resources, nursing, and law are also considered Managerial employees. The Executive level includes the 12 highest-ranking employees at SSS Software. An organization chart in Figure 3 illustrates SSS Software's structure. There is also an Employee Classification Report that lists the number of employees at each level of the organization.

In this exercise, you will play the role of Chris Perillo, Vice President of Operations for Health and Financial Services. You learned last Wednesday, October 13, that your predecessor, Michael Grant, had resigned and gone to Universal Business Solutions, Inc. You were offered his former job, and you accepted it. Previously, you were the Group Manager for a team of 15 software developers assigned to work on the Airbus consortium project in the Airline Services Division. You spent all of Thursday, Friday, and most of the weekend finishing up parts of the project, briefing your successor, and preparing for an interim report you will deliver in Paris on October 21.

It is now 7 A.M. Monday morning and you are in your new office. You have arrived at work early so you can spend the next two hours reviewing material in your in-basket (including some memos and messages to Michael Grant), as well as your voice mail and E-mail. Your daily planning book indicates that you have no appointments today or tomorrow but will have to catch a plane for Paris early Wednesday morning. You have a full schedule for the remainder of the week and all of next week.

Assignment

During the next two hours, review all the material in your in-basket, as well as your voice mail and E-mail. Take only two hours. Using the response form below as a model, indicate how you want to respond to each item (that is, via letter/memo, E-mail, phone/voice mail, or personal meeting). If you decide not to respond to an item, check "no response" on the response form. All your responses must be written on the response forms. Write your precise, detailed response (do not merely jot down a few notes). For example, you might draft a memo or write out a message that you will deliver via phone/voice mail. You may also decide to meet with an individual (or individuals) during the limited time available on your calendar today or tomorrow. If so, prepare an agenda for a personal meeting and list your goals for the meeting. As you read through the items, you may occasionally observe some information that you think is relevant and want to remember (or attend to in the future) but that you decide not to include in any of your responses to employees. Write down such information on a sheet of paper titled "note to self."

Sample Response Form

RELATES TO:

Memo #_____   E-mail # _____   Voice mail # _____

RESPONSE FORM:

_____ Letter/Memo_____ Meet with person (when, where)

_____ E-mail   _____ Note to self

_____ Phone call/Voice mail   _____ No response

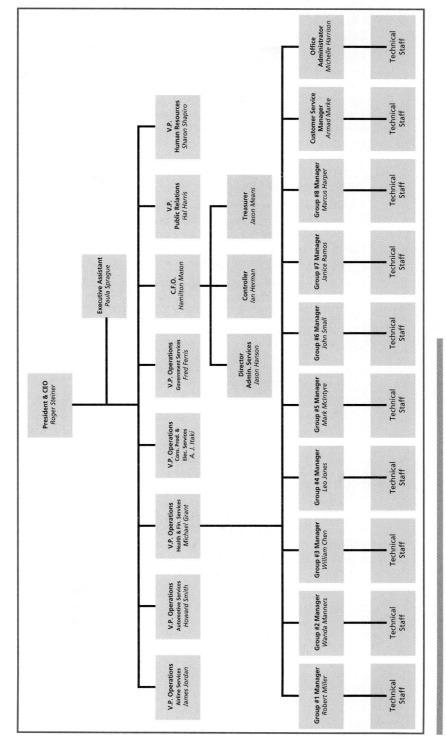

Figure 3 Partial Organization Chart of Health and Financial Services Division

ITEM 1
Memo

TO: All Employees
FROM: Roger Steiner, Chief Executive Officer
DATE: October 15

I am pleased to announce that Chris Perillo has been appointed as Vice President of Operations for Health and Financial Services. Chris will immediately assume responsibility for all operations previously managed by Michael Grant. Chris will have end-to-end responsibility for the design, development, integration, and maintenance of custom software for the health and finance/banking industries. This responsibility includes all technical, financial, and staffing issues. Chris will also manage our program of software support and integration for the recently announced merger of three large health maintenance organizations (HMOs). Chris will be responsible for our recently announced project with a consortium of banks and financial firms operating in Kenya. This project represents an exciting opportunity for us, and Chris's background seems ideally suited to the task.

Chris comes to this position with an undergraduate degree in Computer Science from the California Institute of Technology and an M.B.A. from the University of Virginia. Chris began as a member of our technical/professional staff six years ago and has most recently served for three years as a Group Manager supporting domestic and international projects for our airlines industry group, including our recent work for the European Airbus consortium.

I am sure you all join me in offering congratulations to Chris for this promotion.

ITEM 2
Memo

TO: All Managers
FROM: Hal Harris, Vice President, Community and Public Relations
DATE: October 15

For your information, the following article appeared on the front page of the business section of Thursday's *Los Angeles Times*.

> In a move that may create problems for SSS Software, Michael Grant and Janice Ramos have left SSS Software and moved to Universal Business Solutions Inc. Industry analysts see the move as another victory for Universal Business Solutions Inc. in their battle with SSS Software for share of the growing software development and integration business. Both Grant and Ramos had been with SSS Software for over 7 years. Grant was most recently Vice President of Operations for all SSS Software's work in two industries: health and hospitals, and finance and banking. Ramos brings to Universal Business Solutions Inc. her special expertise in the growing area of international software development and integration.
>
> Hillary Collins, an industry analyst with Merrill Lynch, said "the loss of key staff to a competitor can often create serious problems for a firm such as SSS Software. Grant and Ramos have an insider's understanding of SSS Software's strategic and technical limitations. It will be interesting to see if they can exploit this knowledge to the advantage of Universal Business Solutions Inc."

ITEM 3
Memo

TO: Chris Perillo
FROM: Paula Sprague, Executive Assistant to Roger Steiner
DATE: October 15

Chris, I know that in your former position as a Group Manager in the Airline Services Division, you probably have met most of the group managers in the Health and Financial Services Division, but I thought you might like some more personal information about them. These people will be your direct reports on the management team.

Group #1: Bob Miller, 55-year-old white male, married (Anna) with two children and three grandchildren. Active in local Republican politics. Well regarded as a "hands-off" manager heading a high-performing team. Plays golf regularly with Mark McIntyre, John Small, and a couple of V.P.s from other divisions.

Group #2: Wanda Manners, 38-year-old white female, single with one school-age child. A fitness "nut," has run in several marathons. Some experience in Germany and Japan. Considered a hard-driving manager with a constant focus on the task at hand. Will be the first person to show up every morning.

Group #3: William Chen, 31-year-old male of Chinese descent, married (Harriet), two young children from his first marriage. Enjoys tennis and is quite good at it. A rising star in the company, he is highly respected by his peers as a "man of action" and a good friend.

Group #4: Leo Jones, 36-year-old white male, married (Janet) with an infant daughter. Recently returned from paternity leave. Has travelled extensively on projects, since he speaks three languages. Has liked hockey ever since the time he spent in Montreal. Considered a strong manager who gets the most out of his people.

Group #5: Mark McIntyre, 45-year-old white male, married (Mary Theresa) to an executive in the banking industry. No children. A lot of experience in Germany and Eastern Europe. Has been writing a mystery novel. Has always been a good "team player," but several members of his technical staff are not well respected and he hasn't addressed the problem.

Group #6: John Small, 38-year-old white male, recently divorced. Three children living with his wife. A gregarious individual who likes sports. He spent a lot of time in Mexico and Central America before he came to SSS Software. Recently has been doing mostly contract work with the federal government. An average manager, has had some trouble keeping his people on schedule.

Group #7: This position vacant since Janice Ramos left. Roger thinks we ought to fill this position quickly. Get in touch with me if you want information on any in-house candidates for any position.

Group #8: Marcus Harper, 42-year-old black male, married (Tamara) with two teenage children. Recently won an award in a local photography contest. Considered a strong manager who gets along with peers and works long hours.

Customer Services: Armad Marke, 38-year-old Armenian male, divorced. A basketball fan. Originally from Armenia. Previously a Group Manager. Worked hard to establish the Technical Services Phone Line, but now has pretty much left it alone.

Office Administrator: Michelle Harrison, 41-year-old white female, single. Grew up on a ranch and still rides horses whenever she can. A strict administrator.

There are a number of good folks here, but they don't function well as a management team. I think Michael played favorites, especially with Janice and Leo. There are a few cliques in this group and I'm not sure how effectively Michael dealt with them. I expect you will find it a challenge to build a cohesive team.

ITEM 4

Memo

TO: Chris Perillo
FROM: Wanda Manners, Group 2 Manager
DATE: October 15

CONFIDENTIAL AND RESTRICTED

Although I know you are new to your job, I feel it is important that I let you know about some information I just obtained concerning the development work we recently completed for First National Investment. Our project involved the development of asset management software for managing their international funds. This was a very complex project due to the volatile exchange rates and the forecasting tools we needed to develop.

As part of this project, we had to integrate the software and reports with all their existing systems and reporting mechanisms. To do this, we were given access to all of their existing software (much of which was developed by Universal Business Solutions Inc.). Of course, we signed an agreement acknowledging that the software to which we were given access was proprietary and that our access was solely for the purpose of our system integration work associated with the project.

Unfortunately, I have learned that some parts of the software we developed actually "borrow" heavily from complex application programs developed for First National Investment by Universal Business Solutions Inc. It seems obvious to me that one or more of the software developers from Group 5 (that is, Mark McIntyre's group) inappropriately "borrowed" algorithms developed by Universal Business Solutions Inc. I am sure that doing so saved us significant development time on some aspects of the project. It seems very unlikely that First National Investment or Universal Business Solutions Inc. will ever become aware of this issue.

Finally, First National Investment is successfully using the software we developed and is thrilled with the work we did. We brought the project in on time and under budget. You probably know that they have invited us to bid on several other substantial projects.

I'm sorry to bring this delicate matter to your attention, but I thought you should know about it.

ITEM 5A

Memo

TO: Chris Perillo
FROM: Paula Sprague, Executive Assistant to Roger Steiner
DATE: October 15
RE: Letter from C.A.R.E. Services (copies attached)

Roger asked me to work on this C.A.R.E. project and obviously wants some fast action. A lot of the staff are already booked solid for the next couple of weeks. I knew that Elise Soto and Chu Hung Woo have the expertise to do this system and when I checked with them, they were relatively free. I had them pencil in the next two weeks and wanted to let you know. Hopefully, it will take a "hot potato" out of your hands.

ITEM 5B

Copy of Fax

C.A.R.E.
Child and Adolescent Rehabilitative and Educational Services
A United Way Member Agency
200 Main Street
Los Angeles, California 90230

DATE: October 11

Roger Steiner, CEO
SSS Software
13 Miller Way
Los Angeles, California 90224

Dear Roger,

This letter is a follow-up to our conversation after last night's board meeting. I appreciated your comments during the board meeting about the need for sophisticated computer systems in non-profit organizations and I especially appreciate your generous offer of assistance to have SSS Software provide assistance to deal with the immediate problem with our accounting system. Since the board voted to fire the computer consultant, I am very worried about getting our reports done in time to meet the state funding cycle.

Thanks again for your offer of help during this crisis.

Sincerely yours,

Janice Polocizwic

Janice Polocizwic
Executive Director

ITEM 5C

Copy of Letter

SSS SOFTWARE
13 Miller Way
Los Angeles, CA 90224

DATE: October 12

Janice Polocizwic
Executive Director, C.A.R.E. Services
200 Main Street
Los Angeles, California 90230

Dear Janice,

I received your fax of October 11. I have asked Paula Sprague, my executive assistant, to line up people to work on your accounting system as soon as possible. You can expect to hear from her shortly.

Sincerely,

Roger Steiner

Roger Steiner

cc: Paula Sprague, Executive Assistant

ITEM 6

Memo

TO: Michael Grant
FROM: Harry Withers, Group 6 Technical Staff
DATE: October 12

PERSONAL AND CONFIDENTIAL

Our team is having difficulty meeting the submission deadline of November 5 for the Halstrom project. Kim, Fred, Peter, Kyoto, Susan, Mala, and I have been working on the project for several weeks, but we are experiencing some problems and may need additional time. I hesitate to write this letter, but the main problem is that our group manager, John Small, is involved in a relationship with Mala. Mala gets John's support for her ideas and brings them to the team as required components of the project. Needless to say, this has posed some problems for the group. Mala's background is especially valuable for this project, but Kim and Fred, who have both worked very hard on the project, do not want to work with her. In addition, one member of the team has been unavailable recently because of child-care needs. Commitment to the project and team morale have plummeted. However, we'll do our best to get the project finished as soon as possible. Mala will be on vacation the next two weeks, so I'm expecting that some of us can complete it in her absence.

ITEM 7

Voice Mail

Hello, Michael. This is Jim Bishop of United Hospitals. I wanted to talk with you about the quality assurance project that you are working on for us. When Jose Martinez first started talking with us, I was impressed with his friendliness and expertise. But recently, he doesn't seem to be getting much accomplished and has seemed distant and on-edge in conversations. Today, I asked him about the schedule and he seemed very defensive and not entirely in control of his emotions. I am quite concerned about our project. Please give me a call.

ITEM 8
Voice Mail

Hi, Michael. This is Armand. I wanted to talk with you about some issues with the Technical Services Phone Line. I've recently received some complaint letters from Phone Line customers whose complaints have included long delays while waiting for a technician to answer the phone, technicians who are not knowledgeable enough to solve problems, and, on occasion, rude service. Needless to say, I'm quite concerned about these complaints.

I believe that the overall quality of the Phone Line staff is very good, but we continue to be understaffed, even with the recent hires. The new technicians look strong, but are working on the help-line before being fully trained. Antolina, our best tech, often brings her child to work, which is adding to the craziness around here.

I think you should know that we're feeling a lot of stress here. I'll talk with you soon.

ITEM 9
Voice Mail

Hi, Chris, it's Pat. Congratulations on your promotion. They definitely picked the right person. It's great news—for me, too. You've been a terrific mentor so far, so I'm expecting to learn a lot from you in your new position. How about lunch next week?

ITEM 10
Voice Mail

Chris, this is Bob Miller. Just thought you'd like to know that John's joke during our planning meeting has disturbed a few of the women in my group. Frankly, I think the thing's being blown out of proportion, especially since we all know this is a good place for both men and women to work. Give me a call if you want to chat about this.

ITEM 11
Voice Mail

Hello. This is Lorraine Adams from Westside Hospital. I read in today's Los Angeles Times that you will be taking over from Michael Grant. We haven't met yet, but your division has recently finished two large million-dollar projects for Westside. Michael Grant and I had some discussion about a small conversion of a piece of existing software to be compatible with the new systems. The original vendor had said that they would do the work, but they have been stalling, and I need to move quickly. Can you see if Harris Wilson, Chu Hung Woo, and Elise Soto are available to do this work as soon as possible? They were on the original project and work well with our people.

Um . . . (long pause) I guess I should tell you that I got a call from Michael offering to do this work. But I think I should stick with SSS Software. Give me a call.

ITEM 12
Voice Mail

Hi, Chris, this is Roosevelt Moore calling. I'm a member of your technical/professional staff. I used to report to Janice Ramos, but since she left the firm, I thought I'd bring my concerns directly to you. I'd like to arrange some time to talk with you about my experiences since returning from six weeks of paternity leave. Some of my major responsibilities have been turned over to others. I seem to be out of the loop and wonder if my career is at risk. Also, I am afraid that I won't be supported or seriously considered for the opening created by Janice's departure. Frankly, I feel like I'm being screwed for taking my leave. I'd like to talk with you this week.

ITEM 13

E-mail

TO: Michael Grant
FROM: Jose Martinez, Group 1 Technical Staff
DATE: October 12

I would like to set up a meeting with you as soon as possible. I suspect that you will get a call from Jim Bishop of United Hospitals and want to be sure that you hear my side of the story first. I have been working on a customized system design for quality assurance for them using a variation of the J-3 product we developed several years ago. They had a number of special requirements and some quirks in their accounting systems, so I have had to put in especially long hours. I've worked hard to meet their demands, but they keep changing the ground rules. I keep thinking, this is just another J-3 I'm working on, but they have been interfering with an elegant design I have developed. It seems I'm not getting anywhere on this project. Earlier today, I had a difficult discussion with their Controller. He asked for another major change. I've been fighting their deadline and think I am just stretched too thin on this project. Then Jim Bishop asked me if the system was running yet. I was worn out from dealing with the Controller, and I made a sarcastic comment to Jim Bishop. He gave me a funny look and just walked out of the room.

I would like to talk with you about this situation at your earliest convenience.

ITEM 14

E-mail

TO: Chris Perillo
FROM: John Small, Group 6 Manager
DATE: October 15

Welcome aboard, Chris. I look forward to meeting with you. I just wanted to put a bug in your ear about finding a replacement for Janice Ramos. One of my technical staff, Mala Abendano, has the ability and drive to make an excellent group manager. I have encouraged her to apply for the position. I'd be happy to talk with you further about this, at your convenience.

ITEM 15

E-mail

TO: Chris Perillo
FROM: Paula Sprague, Executive Assistant to Roger Steiner
DATE: October 15

Roger asked me to let you know about the large contract we have gotten in Kenya. It means that a team of four managers will be making a short trip to determine current needs. They will assign their technical staff the tasks of developing a system and software here over the next six months, and then the managers and possibly some team members will be spending about 10 months on site in Kenya to handle the implementation. Roger thought you might want to hold an initial meeting with some of your managers to check on their interest and willingness to take this sort of assignment. Roger would appreciate an E-mail of your thoughts about the issues to be discussed at this meeting, additional considerations about sending people to Kenya, and about how you will put together an effective team to work on this project. The October 15 memo I sent to you will provide you with some information you'll need to start making these decisions.

ITEM 16

E-mail

TO: Chris Perillo
FROM: Sharon Shapiro, V.P. of Human Resources
DATE: October 15
RE: Upcoming meeting

I want to update you on the rippling effect of John Small's sexual joke at last week's planning meeting. Quite a few women have been very upset and have met informally to talk about it. They have decided to call a meeting of all people concerned about this kind of behavior throughout the firm. I plan to attend, so I'll keep you posted.

ITEM 17

E-mail

TO: All SSS Software Managers
FROM: Sharon Shapiro, V.P. of Human Resources
DATE: October 15
RE: Promotions and External Hires

Year-to-Date (January through September) Promotions and External Hires

Level	Race					Sex		Total
	White	Black	Asian	Hispanic	Native American	M	F	
Hires into Executive Level	0 (0%)	0 (0%)	0 (0%)	0 (0%)	0 (0%)	0 (0%)	0 (0%)	0
Promotions to Executive Level	0 (0%)	0 (0%)	0 (0%)	0 (0%)	0 (0%)	0 (0%)	0 (0%)	0
Hires into Management Level	2 (67%)	1 (33%)	0 (0%)	0 (0%)	0 (0%)	2 (67%)	1 (33%)	3
Promotions to Management Level	7 (88%)	0 (0%)	1 (12%)	0 (0%)	0 (0%)	7 (88%)	1 (12%)	8
Hires into Technical/ Professional Level	10 (36%)	6 (21%)	10 (36%)	2 (7%)	0 (0%)	14 (50%)	14 (50%)	28
Promotions to Technical/ Professional Level	0 (0%)	0 (0%)	0 (0%)	0 (0%)	0 (0%)	0 (0%)	0 (0%)	0
Hires into Non-Management Level	4 (20%)	10 (50%)	2 (10%)	4 (20%)	0 (0%)	6 (30%)	14 (70%)	20
Promotions to Non-Management Level	NA	NA	NA	NA	NA	NA	NA	NA

SSS Software Employee (EEO) Classification Report as of June 30

Level	Race					Sex		Total
	White	Black	Asian	Hispanic	Native American	M	F	
Executive Level	11 (92%)	0 (0%)	1 (8%)	0 (0%)	0 (0%)	11 (92%)	1 (8%)	12
Management Level	43 (90%)	2 (4%)	2 (4%)	1 (2%)	0 (0%)	38 (79%)	10 (21%)	48
Technical/ Professional Level	58 (45%)	20 (15%)	37 (28%)	14 (11%)	1 (1%)	80 (62%)	50 (38%)	130
Non-Management Level	29 (48%)	22 (37%)	4 (7%)	4 (7%)	1 (2%)	12 (20%)	48 (80%)	60
Total	141 (56%)	44 (18%)	44 (18%)	19 (8%)	2 (1%)	141 (56%)	109 (44%)	250

Developing Self-Awareness

skill development

Skill Assessment

Diagnostic Surveys for Self-Awareness

Self-Awareness

Step 1: Before you read the material in this chapter, please respond to the following statements by writing a number from the rating scale below in the left-hand column (Preassessment). Your answers should reflect your attitudes and behavior as they are now, not as you would like them to be. Be honest. This instrument is designed to help you discover how self-aware you are so you can tailor your learning to your specific needs. When you have completed the survey, use the scoring key in Appendix I to identify the skill areas discussed in this chapter that are most important for you to master.

Step 2: After you have completed the reading and the exercises in this chapter and, ideally, as many of the Skill Application assignments at the end of this chapter as you can, cover up your first set of answers. Then respond to the same statements again, this time in the right-hand column (Postassessment). When you have completed the survey, use the scoring key in Appendix I to measure your progress. If your score remains low in specific skill areas, use the behavioral guidelines at the end of the Skill Learning section to guide further practice.

Rating Scale

1	Strongly disagree	4	Slightly agree
2	Disagree	5	Agree
3	Slightly disagree	6	Strongly agree

Assessment

Pre-   Post-

_3_   _____ 1. I seek information about my strengths and weaknesses from others as a basis for self-improvement.

_4_   _____ 2. When I receive negative feedback about myself from others, I do not get angry or defensive.

_5_   _____ 3. In order to improve, I am willing to be self-disclosing to others (that is, to share my beliefs and feelings).

_4_   _____ 4. I am very much aware of my personal style of gathering information and making decisions.

_4_   _____ 5. I am very much aware of my own interpersonal needs when it comes to forming relationships with other people.

_u_   _____ 6. I have a good sense of how I cope with situations that are ambiguous and uncertain.

_6_   _____ 7. I have a well-developed set of personal standards and principles that guide my behavior.

_5_ _____ 8. I feel very much in charge of what happens to me, good and bad.

_5_ _____ 9. I seldom, if ever, feel angry, depressed, or anxious without knowing why.

_5_ _____ 10. I am conscious of the areas in which conflict and friction most frequently arise in my interactions with others.

_5_ _____ 11. I have a close personal relationship with at least one other person with whom I can share personal information and personal feelings.

The Defining Issues Test

This instrument assesses your opinions about controversial social issues. Different people make decisions about these issues in different ways. You should answer the questions for yourself without discussing them with others. You are presented with three stories. Following each story are 12 statements or questions. Your task after reading the story is to rate each statement in terms of its importance in making a decision. After rating each statement, select the four most important statements and rank them from one to four in the spaces provided. Each statement should be ranked in terms of its relative importance in making a decision.

Some statements will raise important issues, but you should ask yourself whether the decision should rest on that issue. Some statements sound high and lofty but are largely gibberish. If you cannot make sense of a statement, or if you don't understand its meaning, mark it 5—"Of no importance."

For information about interpreting and scoring the Defining Issues Test, refer to Appendix I. Use the following rating scale for your response.

Rating Scale

1	Of great importance	This statement or question makes a crucial difference in making a decision about the problem.
2	Of much importance	This statement or question is something that would be a major factor (though not always a crucial one) in making a decision.
3	Of some importance	This statement or question involves something you care about, but it is not of great importance in reaching a decision.
4	Of little importance	This statement or question is not very important to consider in this case.
5	Of no importance	This statement or question is completely unimportant in making a decision. You would waste your time thinking about it.

The Escaped Prisoner

A man had been sentenced to prison for 10 years. After one year, however, he escaped from prison, moved to a new area of the country, and took on the name of Thompson. For eight years he worked hard, and gradually he saved enough money to buy his own business. He was fair to his customers, gave his employees top wages, and gave most of his own profits to charity. Then one day, Ms. Jones, an old neighbor, recognized him as the man who had escaped from prison eight years before and for whom the police had been looking.

Should Ms. Jones report Mr. Thompson to the police and have him sent back to prison? Write a number from the rating scale on the previous page in the blank beside each statement.

_____6_____ Should report him

_____ Can't decide

_____ Should not report him

Importance

_____5_____ 1. Hasn't Mr. Thompson been good enough for such a long time to prove he isn't a bad person?

_____5_____ 2. Every time someone escapes punishment for a crime, doesn't that just encourage more crime?

_____5_____ 3. Wouldn't we be better off without prisons and the oppression of our legal systems?

_____6_____ (4.) Has Mr. Thompson really paid his debt to society?

_____5_____ 5. Would society be failing what Mr. Thompson should fairly expect?

_____5_____ 6. What benefit would prison be apart from society, especially for a charitable man?

_____5_____ 7. How could anyone be so cruel and heartless as to send Mr. Thompson to prison?

_____3_____ (8.) Would it be fair to prisoners who have to serve out their full sentences if Mr. Thompson is let off?

_____5_____ 9. Was Ms. Jones a good friend of Mr. Thompson?

_____4_____ 10. Wouldn't it be a citizen's duty to report an escaped criminal, regardless of the circumstances?

_____2_____ (11.) How would the will of the people and the public good best be served?

_____5_____ 12. Would going to prison do any good for Mr. Thompson or protect anybody?

From the list of questions above, select the four most important:

_____4_____ Most important

_____11_____ Second most important

_____8_____ Third most important

_____10_____ Fourth most important

The Doctor's Dilemma

A woman was dying of incurable cancer and had only about six months to live. She was in terrible pain, but was so weak that a large dose of a pain killer such as morphine would probably kill her. She was delirious with pain, and in her calm periods, she would ask her doctor to give her enough morphine to kill her. She said she couldn't stand the pain and that she was going to die in a few months anyway.

What should the doctor do? (Check one.)

_____ He should give the woman an overdose that will make her die

_____ Can't decide

___6___ Should not give the overdose

Importance

___5___   1.   Is the woman's family in favor of giving her the overdose?

___3___   2.   Is the doctor obligated by the same laws as everybody else?

___5___   3.   Would people be better off without society regimenting their lives and even their deaths?

___5___   4.   Should the doctor make the woman's death from a drug overdose appear to be an accident?

___5___   5.   Does the state have the right to force continued existence on those who don't want to live?

___5___   6.   What is the value of death prior to society's perspective on personal values?

___5___   7.   Should the doctor have sympathy for the woman's suffering, or should he care more about what society might think?

___5___   8.   Is helping to end another's life ever a responsible act of cooperation?

___4___   9.   Can only God decide when a person's life should end?

___5___   10.   What values has the doctor set for himself in his own personal code of behavior?

___1___   11.   Can society afford to let anybody end his or her life whenever he or she desires?

___2___   12.   Can society allow suicide or mercy killing and still protect the lives of individuals who want to live?

From the list of questions above, select the four most important:

___11___   Most important

___12___   Second most important

___2___   Third most important

___9___   Fourth most important

The Newspaper

Fred, a senior in high school, wanted to publish a mimeographed newspaper for students so that he could express his opinions. He wanted to speak out against military build-up and some of the school's rules, such as the rule forbidding boys to wear long hair.

When Fred started his newspaper, he asked his principal for permission. The principal said it would be all right if before every publication Fred would turn in all his articles for the principal's approval. Fred agreed and turned in several articles for approval. The principal approved all of them and Fred published two issues of the paper in the next two weeks.

But the principal had not expected that Fred's newspaper would receive so much attention. Students were so excited by the paper that they began to organize protests against the hair regulation and other school rules. Angry parents objected to Fred's opinions. They phoned the principal telling him that the newspaper was unpatriotic and should not be published. As a result of the rising excitement, the principal wondered if he should order Fred to stop publishing on the grounds that the controversial newspaper articles were disrupting the operation of the school.

What should the principal do? (Check one.)

_____6_____ Should stop it

_____ Can't decide

_____ Should not stop it

Importance

_4_	1.	Is the principal more responsible to the students or to the parents?
_5_	2.	Did the principal give his word that the newspaper could be published for a long time, or did he just promise to approve the newspaper one issue at a time?
_5_	3.	Would the students start protesting even more if the principal stopped the newspaper?
_2_	4.	When the welfare of the school is threatened, does the principal have the right to give orders to students?
_5_	5.	Does the principal have the freedom of speech to say no in this case?
_5_	6.	If the principal stopped the newspaper, would he be preventing full discussion of important problems?
_5_	7.	Would the principal's stop order make Fred lose faith in him?
_5_	8.	Is Fred really loyal to his school and patriotic to his country?
_2_	9.	What effect would stopping the paper have on the students' education in critical thinking and judgment?
_1_	10.	Is Fred in any way violating the rights of others in publishing his own opinions?
_5_	11.	Should the principal be influenced by some angry parents when it is the principal who knows best what is going on in the school?
_5_	12.	Is Fred using the newspaper to stir up hatred and discontent?

From the list of questions above, select the four most important:

_10_	Most important
_9_	Second most important
_4_	Third most important
_1_	Fourth most important

Source: Rest, 1979.

The Cognitive Style Instrument

In this instrument, you should put yourself in the position of someone who must gather and evaluate information. The purpose is to investigate the ways you think about information you encounter. There are no right or wrong answers, and one alternative is just as good as another. Try to indicate the ways you do or would respond, not the ways you think you should respond.

For each scenario, there are three pairs of alternatives. For each pair, select the alternative that comes closest to the way you would respond. Answer each item. If you are not sure, make your best guess. When you have finished answering all the questions, compare the scoring key in Appendix I as a basis for comparing your score with others.

Suppose you are a scientist in NASA whose job it is to gather information about the moons of Saturn. Which of the following would you be more interested in investigating?

_b_ 1.   a. *How the moons are similar to one another*

        b. How the moons differ from one another

_a_ 2.   a. *How the whole system of moons operates*

        b. The characteristics of each moon

_a_ 3.   a. *How Saturn and its moons differ from Earth and its moon*

        b. How Saturn and its moons are similar to Earth and its moon

Suppose you are the chief executive of a company and have asked division heads to make presentations at the end of the year. Which of the following would be more appealing to you?

_b_ 4.   a. *A presentation analyzing the details of the data*

        b. A presentation focused on the overall perspective

_a_ 5.   a. *A presentation showing how the division contributed to the company as a whole*

        b. A presentation showing the unique contributions of the division

_b_ 6.   a. *Details of how the division performed*

        b. General summaries of performance data

Suppose you are visiting an Asian country, and you are writing home to tell about your trip. Which of the following would be most typical of the letter you would write?

_b_ 7.   a. *A detailed description of people and events*

        b. General impressions and feelings

_b_ 8.   a. *A focus on similarities of our culture and theirs*

        b. A focus on the uniqueness of their culture

_a_ 9.   a. *Overall, general impressions of the experience*

        b. Separate, unique impressions of parts of the experience

Suppose you are attending a concert featuring a famous symphony orchestra. Which of the following would you be most likely to do?

_b_ 10. a. *Listen for the parts of individual instruments*

b. Listen for the harmony of all the instruments together

_a_ 11. a. *Pay attention to the overall mood associated with the music*

b. Pay attention to the separate feelings associated with different parts of the music

_a_ 12. a. *Focus on the overall style of the conductor*

b. Focus on how the conductor interprets different parts of the score

Suppose you are considering taking a job with a certain organization. Which of the following would you be more likely to do in deciding whether or not to take the job?

_a_ 13. a. *Systematically collect information on the organization*

b. Rely on personal intuition or inspiration

_a_ 14. a. *Consider primarily the fit between you and the job*

b. Consider primarily the politics needed to succeed in the organization

_a_ 15. a. *Be methodical in collecting data and making a choice*

b. Mainly consider personal instincts and gut feelings

Suppose you inherit some money and decide to invest it. You learn of a new high-technology firm that has just issued stock. Which of the following is most likely to be true of your decision to purchase the firm's stock?

_b_ 16. a. *You would invest on a hunch*

b. You would invest only after a systematic investigation of the firm

_b_ 17. a. *You would be somewhat impulsive in deciding to invest*

b. You would follow a pre-set pattern in making your decision

_a_ 18. a. *You could rationally justify your decision to invest in this firm and not in another*

b. It would be difficult to rationally justify your decision to invest in this firm and not another

Suppose you are being interviewed on TV, and you are asked the following questions. Which alternative would you be most likely to select?

_a_ 19. *How are you more likely to cook?*

a. With a recipe

b. Without a recipe

_b_ 20. *How would you predict the Super Bowl winner next year?*

a. After systematically researching the personnel and records of the teams

b. On a hunch or by intuition

___b___   21.   *Which games do you prefer?*

            a. Games of chance (like Bingo)

            b. Chess, checkers, or Scrabble

Suppose you are a manager and need to hire an executive assistant. Which of the following would you be most likely to do in the process?

___a___   22.   *a. Interview each applicant using a set outline of questions*

            b. Concentrate on your personal feelings and instincts about each applicant

___a___   23.   *a. Consider primarily the personality fit between yourself and the candidates*

            b. Consider the match between the precise job requirements and the candidates' capabilities

___a___   24.   *a. Rely on factual and historical data on each candidate in making a choice*

            b. Rely on feelings and impressions in making a choice

Locus of Control Scale

This questionnaire assesses your opinions about certain issues. Each item consists of a pair of alternatives marked with *a* or *b*. Select the alternative with which you most agree. If you believe both alternatives to some extent, select the one with which you most strongly agree. If you do not believe either alternative, mark the one with which you least strongly disagree. Since this is an assessment of opinions, there are obviously no right or wrong answers. When you have finished each item, turn to the Scoring Key in Appendix I for instructions on how to tabulate the results and for comparison data.

This questionnaire is similar, but not identical, to the original locus of control scale developed by Julian Rotter. The comparison data provided in Appendix I comes from research using Rotter's scale instead of this one. However, the two instruments assess the same concept, are the same length, and their mean scores are similar.

___b___   1.   *a. Leaders are born, not made.*

          b. Leaders are made, not born.

___b___   2.   *a. People often succeed because they are in the right place at the right time.*

          b. Success is mostly dependent on hard work and ability.

___a___   3.   *a. When things go wrong in my life, it's generally because I have made mistakes.*

          b. Misfortunes occur in my life regardless of what I do.

___b___   4.   *a. Whether there is war or not depends on the actions of certain world leaders.*

          b. It is inevitable that the world will continue to experience wars.

___a___   5.   *a. Good children are mainly products of good parents.*

          b. Some children turn out bad no matter how their parents behave.

___b___   6.   *a. My future success depends mainly on circumstances I can't control.*

          b. I am the master of my fate.

_b_   7.   a. *History judges certain people to have been effective leaders mainly because circumstances made them visible and successful.*

               b. Effective leaders are those who have made decisions or taken actions that resulted in significant contributions.

_a_   8.   a. *To avoid punishing children guarantees that they will grow up irresponsible.*

               b. Spanking children is never appropriate.

_b_   9.   a. *I often feel that I have little influence over the direction my life is taking.*

               b. It is unreasonable to believe that fate or luck plays a crucial part in how my life turns out.

_b_   10.   a. *Some customers will never be satisfied no matter what you do.*

               b. You can satisfy customers by giving them what they want when they want it.

_b_   11.   a. *Anyone can get good grades in school if he or she works hard enough.*

               b. Some people are never going to excel in school no matter how hard they try.

_a_   12.   a. *Good marriages result when both partners continually work on the relationship.*

               b. Some marriages are going to fail because the partners are just incompatible.

_a_   13.   a. *I am confident that I can improve my basic management skills through learning and practice.*

               b. It is a waste of time to try to improve management skills in a classroom.

_a_   14.   a. *More management skills courses should be taught in business schools.*

               b. Less emphasis should be put on skills in business schools.

_a_   15.   a. *When I think back on the good things that happened to me, I believe they happened mainly because of something I did.*

               b. The bad things that have happened in my life have mainly resulted from circumstances outside my control.

_b_   16.   a. *Many exams I took in school were unconnected to the material I had studied, so studying hard didn't help at all.*

               b. When I prepared well for exams in school, I generally did quite well.

_b_   17.   a. *I am sometimes influenced by what my astrological chart says.*

               b. No matter how the stars are lined up, I can determine my own destiny.

_b_   18.   a. *Government is so big and bureaucratic that it is very difficult for any one person to have any impact on what happens.*

               b. Single individuals can have a real influence on politics if they will speak up and let their wishes be known.

_a_   19.   a. *People seek responsibility in work.*

               b. People try to get away with doing as little as they can.

_b_   20.   a. *The most popular people seem to have a special, inherent charisma that attracts people to them.*

               b. People become popular because of how they behave.

_____ b 21. a. *Things over which I have little control just seem to occur in my life.*

b. Most of the time I feel responsible for the outcomes I produce.

_____ a 22. a. *Managers who improve their personal competence will succeed more than those who do not improve.*

b. Management success has very little to do with the competence possessed by the individual manager.

_____ b 23. a. *Teams that win championships in most sports are usually the teams that, in the end, have the most luck.*

b. More often than not, teams that win championships are those with the most talented players and the best preparation.

_____ a 24. a. *Teamwork in business is a prerequisite to success.*

b. Individual effort is the best hope for success.

_____ b 25. a. *Some workers are just lazy and can't be motivated to work hard no matter what you do.*

b. If you are a skillful manager, you can motivate almost any worker to put forth more effort.

_____ a 26. a. *In the long run, people can improve this country's economic strength through responsible action.*

b. The economic health of this country is largely beyond the control of individuals.

_____ a 27. a. *I am persuasive when I know I'm right.*

b. I can persuade most people even when I'm not sure I'm right.

_____ a 28. a. *I tend to plan ahead and generate steps to accomplish the goals that I have set.*

b. I seldom plan ahead because things generally turn out OK anyway.

_____ b 29. a. *Some things are just meant to be.*

b. We can change anything in our lives by hard work, persistence, and ability.

Tolerance of Ambiguity Scale

Please respond to the following statements by indicating the extent to which you agree or disagree with them. Fill in the blanks with the number from the rating scale that best represents your evaluation of the item. The scoring key is in Appendix I.

Rating Scale

1	Strongly disagree	5	Slightly agree
2	Moderately disagree	6	Moderately agree
3	Slightly disagree	7	Strongly agree
4	Neither agree nor disagree		

_____ 4 1. An expert who doesn't come up with a definite answer probably doesn't know too much.

_____ 3 2. I would like to live in a foreign country for a while.

_____ 5 3. There is really no such thing as a problem that can't be solved.

_____ 3 4. People who fit their lives to a schedule probably miss most of the joy of living.

3	5. A good job is one where what is to be done and how it is to be done are always clear.
6	6. It is more fun to tackle a complicated problem than to solve a simple one.
5	7. In the long run it is possible to get more done by tackling small, simple problems rather than large and complicated ones.
6	8. Often the most interesting and stimulating people are those who don't mind being different and original.
6	9. What we are used to is always preferable to what is unfamiliar.
4	10. People who insist upon a yes or no answer just don't know how complicated things really are.
5	11. A person who leads an even, regular life in which few surprises or unexpected happenings arise really has a lot to be grateful for.
6	12. Many of our most important decisions are based upon insufficient information.
7	13. I like parties where I know most of the people more than ones where all or most of the people are complete strangers.
5	14. Teachers or supervisors who hand out vague assignments give one a chance to show initiative and originality.
5	15. The sooner we all acquire similar values and ideals the better.
4	16. A good teacher is one who makes you wonder about your way of looking at things.

Source: Budner, 1962.

Fundamental Interpersonal Relations Orientation-Behavior (FIRO-B)

For each statement below, decide which of the following answers best applies to you. Place the number of the answer at the left of the statement. When you have finished, turn to the scoring key in Appendix I.

Rating Scale

1	Usually	4	Occasionally
2	Often	5	Rarely
3	Sometimes	6	Never

4	1. I try to be with people.
2	2. I let other people decide what to do.
5	3. I join social groups.
5	4. I try to have close relationships with people.
5	5. I tend to join social organizations when I have an opportunity.
5	6. I let other people strongly influence my actions.
5	7. I try to be included in informal social activities.
5	8. I try to have close, personal relationships with people.

Skill Assessment

2	9.	I try to include other people in my plans.
5	10.	I let other people control my actions.
5	11.	I try to have people around me.
5	12.	I try to get close and personal with people.
4	13.	When people are doing things together, I tend to join them.
5	14.	I am easily led by people.
5	15.	I try to avoid being alone.
5	16.	I try to participate in group activities.

For each of the next group of statements, choose one of the following answers:

Rating Scale

1	Most people	4	A few people
2	Many people	5	One or two people
3	Some people	6	Nobody

1	17.	I try to be friendly to people.
2	18.	I let other people decide what to do.
4	19.	My personal relations with people are cool and distant.
3	20.	I let other people take charge of things.
4	21.	I try to have close relationships with people.
5	22.	I let other people strongly influence my actions.
4	23.	I try to get close and personal with people.
5	24.	I let other people control my actions.
3	25.	I act cool and distant with people.
5	26.	I am easily led by people.
4	27.	I try to have close, personal relationships with people.
4	28.	I like people to invite me to things.
4	29.	I like people to act close and personal with me.
4	30.	I try to influence strongly other people's actions.
4	31.	I like people to invite me to join in their activities.
5	32.	I like people to act close toward me.
3	33.	I try to take charge of things when I am with people.
4	34.	I like people to include me in their activities.
5	35.	I like people to act cool and distant toward me.
6	36.	I try to have other people do things the way I want them done.
4	37.	I like people to ask me to participate in their discussions.
2	38.	I like people to act friendly toward me.

Chapter One   47

_____3_____ 39.   I like people to invite me to participate in their activities.

_____5_____ 40.   I like people to act distant toward me.

For each of the next group of statements, choose one of the following answers:

Rating Scale

1	Usually		4	Occasionally
2	Often		5	Rarely
3	Sometimes		6	Never

_____5_____ 41.   I try to be the dominant person when I am with people.

_____3_____ 42.   I like people to invite me to things.

_____4_____ 43.   I like people to act close toward me.

_____4_____ 44.   I try to have other people do things I want done.

_____4_____ 45.   I like people to invite me to join their activities.

_____5_____ 46.   I like people to act cool and distant toward me.

_____3_____ 47.   I try to influence strongly other people's actions.

_____2_____ 48.   I like people to include me in their activities.

_____3_____ 49.   I like people to act close and personal with me.

_____4_____ 50.   I try to take charge of things when I'm with people.

_____4_____ 51.   I like people to invite me to participate in their activities.

_____5_____ 52.   I like people to act distant toward me.

_____3_____ 53.   I try to have other people do things the way I want them done.

_____2_____ 54.   I take charge of things when I'm with people.

Source: Schutz, 1958.

▪ Skill Learning

Key Dimensions of Self-Awareness

For more than 300 years, knowledge of the self has been considered to be at the very core of human behavior. The ancient dictum "Know thyself" has been variously attributed to Plato, Pythagoras, Thales, and Socrates. Plutarch noted that this inscription was carved on the Delphic Oracle, that mystical sanctuary where kings and generals sought advice on matters of greatest importance to them. As early as 42 B.C., Publilius Syrus proposed: "It matters not what you are thought to be, but what you are." Alfred Lord Tennyson said: "Self-reverence, self-knowledge, self-control, these three alone lead to sovereign power." Probably the most oft-quoted passage on the self is Polonius' advice in Hamlet: "To thine own self be true, and it must follow as the night the day, thou canst not then be false to any man."

This chapter on self-awareness, along with the material on time and stress management in the next chapter, allows us to construct a hierarchy of self-management skills. As Messinger reminded us, "He that would govern others must first master himself." Self-management depends first and foremost on self-awareness, but as illustrated in Figure 1, other skills are also closely linked to, and build upon, self-awareness. Setting personal priorities and goals, for example, helps individuals direct their own lives, and time and stress management helps indi-

viduals adapt to and organize their environments. This chapter centers around the core aspects of self-management and serves as the foundation for the following chapter on stress and time management. Moreover, as Figure 1 illustrates, when problems arise in personal management, the easily recognized symptoms are often time pressures or experienced stress. However, those symptoms are often linked to more fundamental problems with self-awareness and out-of-balance priorities. Enhancing these aspects of self-awareness leads to long-term strategic improvement.

Students of human behavior have long known that knowledge of oneself—self-awareness, self-insight, self-understanding—is essential to one's productive personal and interpersonal functioning and in understanding and empathizing with other people. A host of techniques and methods for achieving self-knowledge have therefore been devised. Various therapies, group methods, meditation techniques, and exercise programs have been touted as enhancing insight into the self and bringing inner peace. This chapter does not aim to summarize those procedures, nor does it espouse any one procedure in particular. Rather, we discuss here the importance of self-awareness in managerial behavior and introduce several

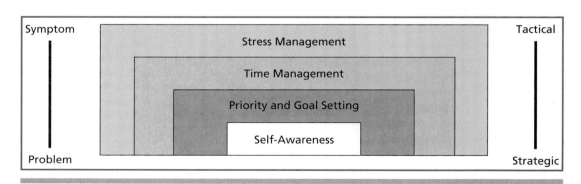

Figure 1　A Hierarchy of Personal Life-Management Skills

self-assessment instruments that research has shown to relate to managerial success. Our emphasis is on scientifically validated information linking self-awareness to the behavior of managers, and we try to avoid generalizations that have not been tested in research.

The Enigma of Self-Awareness

Erich Fromm (1939) was one of the first behavioral scientists to observe the close connection between one's self-concept and one's feelings about others: "Hatred against oneself is inseparable from hatred against others." Carl Rogers (1961) later proposed that self-awareness and self-acceptance are prerequisites for psychological health, personal growth, and the ability to know and accept others. In fact, Rogers suggested that the basic human need is for self-regard, which he found to be more powerful in his clinical cases than physiological needs. Hayakawa (1962) has asserted that the first law of life is not self-preservation, but self-image preservation. "The self-concept," he states, "is the fundamental determinant of all our behavior. Indeed, since it is an organization of our past experiences and perceptions as well as our values and goals, it determines the character of the reality we see" (p. 229). There is considerable empirical evidence that self-awareness and self-acceptance are strongly related to personal adjustment, interpersonal relationships, and life success. Brouwer (1964, p. 156) asserted:

> The function of self-examination is to lay the groundwork for insight, without which no growth can occur. Insight is the "Oh, I see now" feeling which must consciously or unconsciously precede change in behavior. Insights—real, genuine glimpses of ourselves as we really are—are reached only with difficulty and sometimes with real psychic pain. But they are the building blocks of growth. Thus, self-examination is a preparation for insight, a groundbreaking for the seeds of self-understanding which gradually bloom into changed behavior.

There is little question that the knowledge we possess about ourselves, which makes up our self-concept, is central to improving our management skills. We cannot improve ourselves or develop new capabilities unless and until we know what level of capability we currently possess. On the other hand, self-knowledge may inhibit personal improvement rather than facilitate it. The reason is that individuals frequently evade personal growth and new self-knowledge. They resist acquiring additional information in order to protect their self-esteem or self-respect. If they acquire new knowledge about themselves, there is always the possibility that it will be negative or that it will lead to feelings of inferiority, weakness, evilness, or shame. So they avoid new self-knowledge. As Maslow (1962, p. 57) notes:

> We tend to be afraid of any knowledge that would cause us to despise ourselves or to make us feel inferior, weak, worthless, evil, shameful. We protect ourselves and our ideal image of ourselves by repression and similar defenses, which are essentially techniques by which we avoid becoming conscious of unpleasantness or dangerous truths.

We avoid personal growth, then, because we fear finding out that we are not all that we would like to be. If there is a better way to be, our current state must therefore be inadequate or inferior. The realization that one is not totally adequate or knowledgeable is difficult for many people to accept. This resistance is the "denying of our best side, of our talents, of our finest impulses, of our highest potentialities, of our creativeness. In brief, this is the struggle against our own greatness" (Maslow, 1962, p. 58). Freud (1956) asserted that to be completely honest with oneself is the best effort an individual can make, because complete honesty requires a continual search for more information about the self and a desire for self-improvement.

Seeking knowledge of the self, therefore, seems to be an enigma. It is a prerequisite for and motivator of growth and improvement, but it may also inhibit growth and improvement. It may lead to stagnation because of fear of knowing more. How, then, can improvement be accomplished? How can management skills be developed if the self-knowledge necessary for the development of those skills is resisted?

The Sensitive Line

One answer relies on the concept of the **sensitive line.** This concept refers to the point at which individuals become defensive or protective when encountering information about themselves that is inconsistent with their self-concept or when encountering pressure to alter their behavior. Most people regularly experience information about themselves that doesn't quite fit or that is marginally inconsistent. For example, a friend might say, "You look tired today. Are you feeling okay?" If you are feeling fine, the information is inconsistent with your self-awareness. But because the discrepancy is relatively minor, it would not be likely to offend you or evoke a strong defensive reaction. That is, it would probably not require that you reexamine and change your self-concept. On the other hand, the more discrepant the information or the more serious its implications for your self-concept, the closer it would approach your sensitive line, and you would feel a need to defend yourself against it. For example, having a coworker judge you incompetent as a manager may cross your sensitive line if you think you have done a good job as a manager. This would be especially true if the coworker was an influential person. Your response would probably be to defend yourself against the information to protect the image you hold of yourself.

Hayakawa (1962, p. 230) stated the point differently. He asserted that the self-concept "tends to rigidify under threat," so that if an individual encounters discrepant information that is threatening, the current self-concept is reasserted with redoubled force. Haney (1979) refers to a "comfort zone" similar to a thermostat. When the situation becomes too uncomfortable, protective measures are brought into play that bring the situation back to normal. When marked discrepancies in the self-image are experienced, in other words, the validity of the information or its source is denied, or other defensive mechanisms are used to ensure that the self-concept remains stable.

In light of this defensiveness, then, how can increased self-knowledge and personal change ever occur? There are at least two answers. One is that information that is verifiable, predictable, and controllable is less likely to cross the sensitive line than information without those characteristics. That is, if an individual can test the validity of the discrepant information (for example, if some objective standard exists), if the information is not unexpected or "out-of-the-blue" (for example, if it is received at regular intervals), and if there is some control over what, when, and how much information is received (for ex-

ample, if it is requested), it is more likely to be heard and accepted. The information you receive about yourself in this chapter possesses those three characteristics. You have already completed several self-assessment instruments that have been used extensively in research. Their reliability and validity have been established. Moreover, they have been found to be associated with managerial success. Therefore, in your analysis of your scores, you can gain important insight that can prove helpful to you.

A second answer to the problem of overcoming resistance to self-examination lies in the role other people can play in helping insight to occur. It is almost impossible to increase skill in self-awareness unless we interact with and disclose ourselves to others. Unless one is willing to open up to others, to discuss aspects of the self that seem ambiguous or unknown, little growth can ever occur. Self-disclosure, therefore, is a key to improvement in self-awareness. Harris (1981) points out:

> In order to know oneself, no amount of introspection or self-examination will suffice. You can analyze yourself for weeks, or meditate for months, and you will not get an inch further—any more than you can smell your own breath or laugh when you tickle yourself.
>
> You must first be open to the other person before you catch a glimmering of yourself. Our self-reflection in a mirror does not tell us what we are like; only our reflection in other people. We are essentially social creatures, and our personality resides in association, not in isolation.

As you engage in the practice exercises in this chapter, therefore, you are encouraged to discuss your insights with someone else. A lack of self-disclosure not only inhibits self-awareness but also may affect adversely other aspects of managerial skill development. For example, several studies have shown that low self-disclosers are less healthy and more self-alienated than high self-disclosers. College students give the highest ratings for interpersonal competence to high self-disclosers. Individuals are liked best who are high self-disclosers, and excessive or insufficient self-disclosure results in less liking and acceptance by others (see, for example, Jourard, 1964; Covey, 1989). Some of the exercises in this chapter will require you to discuss your experiences with others. This is done because involving others in your acquisition of self-understanding will be a critical aspect of your personal growth.

The enigma of self-awareness can be managed, then, by exercising some control over when and what kind of information you receive about yourself, and by involving others in your pursuit of self-understanding. The social support individuals receive from others during the process of self-disclosure, besides helping to increase feedback and self-awareness, helps information contribute to greater self-awareness without crossing the sensitive line.

Important Areas of Self-Awareness

We focus on four major areas of self-awareness that have been found to be key in developing successful management: personal values, cognitive style, orientation toward change, and interpersonal orientation. These areas of self-awareness have been found to be important predictors of various aspects of effective management such as successful team membership and team leadership, life success, personal learning and development, creativity, communication competency, and effective empowerment (Schutz, 1989; Lawrence & Kleiner, 1987; Marshall, 1986; Parker & Kram, 1993; Atwater & Yammarino, 1992). **Personal values** are discussed first because they are "the core of the dynamics of behavior, and play so large a part in unifying personality" (Allport, Gordon, & Vernon, 1931, p. 2). That is, all other attitudes, orientations, and behaviors arise out of individuals' values. Two major types of values are considered: instrumental and terminal (Rokeach, 1973). We present research findings that relate personal development in these two types of values to successful managerial performance. The assessment instrument designed to assess your values development is discussed, along with information concerning the scores of other groups of people so that you can compare your scores with those of more and less successful managers. Because this discussion of values development is connected to ethical decision making, the implications of managerial ethics are also discussed.

The second area of self-awareness is **cognitive style,** which refers to the manner in which individuals gather and process information. A discussion of the critical dimensions of cognitive style is presented, based on the assessment instrument that you used to assess your own style. Empirical research linking cognitive style to managerial behavior is discussed, and your scores are compared to other successful managers in a variety of organizations.

Third, a discussion of **orientation toward change** focuses on the methods people use to cope with change in their environment. Everyone, but especially a manager, is faced with increasingly fragmented, rapidly changing, tumultuous conditions. It is important that you become aware of your orientation toward adapting to these conditions. Two important dimensions—locus of control and intolerance of ambiguity—have been measured by two assessment instruments. Research connecting these two dimensions to effective management is discussed in the sections that follow.

Finally, **interpersonal orientation,** or the tendency to interact in certain ways with other people, is explained. We provided an assessment instrument for measuring certain aspects of interpersonal orientation, and in this section we discuss its relevance to managerial behavior. By analyzing your scores, you can obtain useful insights not only into yourself but also into the quality of your relationships with others.

These four areas of self-awareness—personal values, cognitive style, orientation toward change, and interpersonal orientation—constitute the very core of the self-concept. Values define an individual's basic *standards* about what is good and bad, worthwhile and worthless, desirable and undesirable, true and false, moral and immoral. Cognitive style determines individual *thought processes* and perceptions. It determines not only what kind of information is received by an individual, but how that information is interpreted, judged, and responded to. Orientation toward change identifies the *adaptability* of individuals. It includes the extent to which individuals are tolerant of ambiguous, uncertain conditions, and the extent to which they are inclined to accept personal responsibility for their actions under changing conditions. Interpersonal orientation determines the *behavior patterns* that are most likely to emerge in interactions with others. The extent to which an individual is open or closed, assertive or retiring, controlling or dependent, affectionate or aloof depends to a large degree on interpersonal orientation. Figure 2 summarizes these four aspects of self-awareness, along with their functions in defining the self-concept.

Of course, there are many other aspects of self-awareness that could be considered in this chapter, for

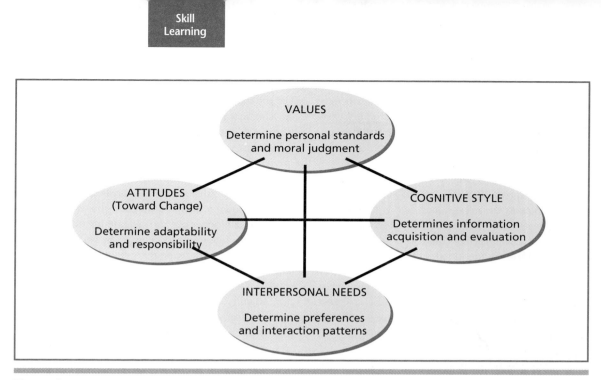

Figure 2   Four Core Aspects of the Self-Concept

example, emotions, attitudes, temperament, personality, and interests. But all these aspects of the self are related fundamentally to the four core concepts. What we value, how we feel about things, how we behave toward others, what we want to achieve, and what we are attracted to all are strongly influenced by our values, cognitive style, orientation toward change, and interpersonal orientation. These are among the most important building blocks upon which other aspects of the self emerge. On the other hand, if you want to do a more in-depth analysis of multiple aspects of self-awareness, instruments such as the Strong-Campbell Vocational Inventory, the Minnesota Multiphasic Personality Inventory, the Myers-Briggs Type Indicator, the Sanford-Binet Intelligence Test, and a host of other instruments are available in most college counseling centers or testing centers. No one, it should be emphasized, can get too much self-knowledge.

Values

Values are among the most stable and enduring characteristics of individuals. They are the foundation upon which attitudes and personal preferences are formed. They are the basis for crucial decisions, life directions, and personal tastes. Much of what we are is a product of the basic values we have developed throughout our

lives. An organization, too, has a value system, usually referred to as its organizational culture. Research has found that employees who hold values that are congruent with their organization's values are more productive and satisfied (Posner & Kouzes, 1993). Holding values that are inconsistent with company values, on the other hand, is a major source of frustration, conflict, and nonproductivity. Being aware of one's own priorities and values, therefore, is important if one expects to achieve compatibility at work and in a long-term career (Lobel, 1992).

However, as Simon (1974) and others have suggested, people sometimes lose touch with their own values, behaving in ways that are inconsistent with those values. That is, they pursue lower priorities at the expense of higher priorities, substituting goals with immediate payoffs for those with more long-term, central value. They may pursue an immediate reward or a temporary satisfaction, for example, in place of longer-term happiness and inner peace. Not being cognizant of one's own value priorities can lead to misdirected decisions and frustration in the long term.

As in many areas of self-awareness, however, many people feel that they have a clear understanding of their values. Because their values are seldom challenged, they don't think much about the extent to which they hold certain values more highly than others. On the other hand, it is precisely because they are seldom challenged that people tend to forget value priorities and behave in incongruous ways. Until people encounter a contradiction or threat to their values, they seldom assert them or seek to clarify them.

Rokeach (1973) argued that the total number of values people possess is relatively small and that all individuals possess the same values, but in different degrees. For example, everyone values peace, but some make it a higher priority than others. Two general types of values were identified by Rokeach, and independent priority ratings have been found to exist for each type (that is, the two sets of values are largely unrelated). One general type of values is labeled instrumental, or means-oriented; the other type is terminal, or ends-oriented.

Instrumental values prescribe desirable standards of conduct or methods for attaining an end. Two types of instrumental values relate to morality and competence. Violating moral values (for example, behaving wrongly) causes feelings of guilt, while violating competence values (for example, behaving incapably) brings about feelings of shame.

Terminal values prescribe desirable ends or goals for the individual. There are fewer of them, according to Rokeach, than there are instrumental values, so the sum total for all individuals in all societies can be identified. Terminal values are either personal (for example, peace of mind) or social (for example, world peace). Rokeach has found that an increase in the priority of one personal value tends to increase the priority of other personal values and decrease the priority of social values. Conversely, an increase in the priority of one social value tends to increase the priority of other social values and decrease the value of personal values. Individuals who increase their priority for "a world at peace," for example, would also increase their priority for "equality" while decreasing their priority for "pleasure" or "self-respect." People tend to differ, in other words, in the extent to which they are self- versus others-orientated in their values. Table 1 lists the 18 terminal values "judged to represent the most important values in American society" (Rokeach, 1973, p. 29).

In a national study of 1,460 American managers, Schmidt and Posner (1982) assessed which of these values were most important in the workplace. Using Rokeach's instrumental values list, they asked managers

TERMINAL VALUES	INSTRUMENTAL VALUES
A comfortable life (a prosperous life)	Ambitious (hard-working, aspiring)
An exciting life (a stimulating, active life)	Broadminded (open-minded)
A sense of accomplishment (lasting contribution)	Capable (competent, effective)
A world at peace (free of war and conflict)	Cheerful (lighthearted, joyful)
A world of beauty (beauty of nature and the arts)	Clean (neat, tidy)
Equality (brotherhood, equal opportunity for all)	Courageous (standing up for your beliefs)
Family security (taking care of loved ones)	Forgiving (willing to pardon others)
Freedom (independence, free choice)	Helpful (working for the welfare of others)
Happiness (contentedness)	Honest (sincere, truthful)
Inner harmony (freedom from inner conflict)	Imaginative (daring, creative)
Mature love (sexual and spiritual intimacy)	Independent (self-reliant, self-sufficient)
National security (protection from attack)	Intellectual (intelligent, reflective)
Pleasure (an enjoyable, leisurely life)	Logical (consistent, rational)
Salvation (saved, eternal life)	Loving (affectionate, tender)
Self-respect (self-esteem)	Obedient (dutiful, respectful)
Social recognition (respect, admiration)	Polite (courteous, well-mannered)
True friendship (close companionship)	Responsible (dependable, reliable)
Wisdom (a mature understanding of life)	Self-controlled (restrained, self-disciplined)

Table 1 Terminal and Instrumental Values
Source: Rokeach, 1973.

to identify those that were most desired in the workplace. "Responsible" and "honest" were by far the most desired values in employees (over 85 percent of the managers selected them), followed by "capable" (65 percent), "imaginative" (55 percent), and "logical" (49 percent). "Obedient," "clean," "polite," and "forgiving" were the least important, being selected by fewer than 10 percent of the managers.

Different groups of people tend to differ in the values they hold. For example, business school students and professors tend to rate "ambition," "capability," "responsibility," and "freedom" higher than people in general. They tend to place lower importance than people in general on concern and helpfulness to others, aesthetics and cultural values, and overcoming social injustice (Cavanaugh, 1980). In a study that compared highly successful, moderately successful, and unsuccessful managers, highly successful managers gave significantly higher scores to values relating to economic (for example, a comfortable life) and political values (for example, social recognition) than less successful managers (Rokeach, 1973).

Compared to the population in general, managers place substantially more value on "sense of accomplishment," "self-respect," "a comfortable life," and "independence" (Clare & Sanford, 1979). The instrumental value managers held highest for themselves, in fact, was "ambition"; their highest held terminal value was "sense of accomplishment." In other words, personal values (rather than social values) and those oriented toward achievement predominate among managers.

These value preferences may explain why business students and even managers themselves have been criticized for being too self-centered and impatient for personal achievement and promotion (see Introduction). A balance of personal values and social values, such as justice and helpfulness, may characterize a more adaptable manager in the future.

Simply esteeming certain personal and achievement-oriented values does not mean, of course, that one will be a successful manager. On the other hand, it is clear that values do affect individual behavior. For example, Kohlberg (1969), Graves (1970), and Flower, Hughes, Myers, and Myer (1975) all argue that the behavior displayed by individuals (that is, the means used to achieve their valued ends) is a product of their level of values maturity. Individuals differ in their level of values development, according to these authors, so different sets of instrumental values are held by individu-

als at different stages of development. People progress from one level of maturity to another, and as they do, their value priorities change. Individuals who have progressed to more mature levels of values development possess a qualitatively different set of instrumental values than individuals who are at less mature levels.

This theory of values or moral development has received a great deal of attention from researchers, and research findings have some important implications for self-awareness and managerial effectiveness. Therefore, we shall discuss in some detail this notion of values maturity.

Kohlberg's model is the best known and most widely researched approach to values maturity. It focuses on the kind of reasoning used to reach a decision about an issue that has value or moral connotations. The model consists of three major levels, each of which contains two stages. Table 2 summarizes the characteristics of each stage. In brief, the stages are sequential (for example, a person can't progress to stage 3 before passing through stage 2), and each stage represents a higher level of maturity. Kohlberg uses the terms *preconventional, conventional,* and *postconventional* to describe these three levels. In the following discussion, we have chosen to use different terms that capture the dominant characteristics of each stage.

The first level of maturity, the **self-centered level,** includes the first two stages of values development. Moral reasoning and instrumental values are based on personal needs or wants and on the consequences of an act. For example, something could be judged as right or good if it helped an individual obtain a reward or avoid punishment and if the consequences were not negative for someone else. Stealing $50,000 is worse than stealing $500 in the self-centered level because the consequences (that is, the losses) are more negative for someone else.

The second level, or **conformity level,** includes stages 3 and 4. Moral reasoning is based on conforming to and upholding the conventions and expectations of society. This level is sometimes referred to as the "law and order" level because the emphasis is on conformity to laws and norms. Right and wrong are judged on the basis of whether or not behaviors conform to the rules of those in authority. Respect from others based on obedience is a prized outcome. Stealing $50,000 and stealing $500 are equally wrong in this level because both violate the law. Most American adults function at this level of values maturity.

LEVEL	BASIS OF MORAL JUDGMENT	STAGE OF DEVELOPMENT
I	Moral value resides in external, quasiphysical happenings, in bad acts, or in quasiphysical needs, rather than in persons and standards.	1. *Obedience and punishment orientation.* Egocentric deference to superior power or prestige, or a trouble-avoiding set. Objective responsibility. 2. *Naively egotistic orientation.* Right action is that instrumentally satisfying the self's needs and occasionally others'. Awareness of relativism of value to each actor's needs and perspectives. Naive egalitarianism and orientation to exchange and reciprocity.
II	Moral value resides in performing good or right roles, in maintaining the conventional order and the expectancies of others.	3. *Good-person orientation.* Orientation to approval and to pleasing and helping others. Conformity to stereotypical images of majority or natural role behavior, and judgment by intentions. 4. *Orientation to "doing duty,"* showing respect for authority, and maintaining the social order for its own sake. Regard for earned expectations of others.
III	Moral value resides in conformity by the self to shared or sharable standards, rights, or duties.	5. *Contractual legalistic orientation.* Recognition of an arbitrary element or starting point in rules or expectations for the sake of agreement. Duty defined in terms of contract, general avoidance of violation of the will or rights of others, and majority will and welfare. 6. *Conscience of principle orientation.* Orientation not only to actually ordained social rules, but to principles of choice involving appeal to logical universality and consistency. Orientation to conscience as a directing agent and to mutual respect and trust.

Table 2 Classification of Moral Judgment into Levels and Stages of Development
Source: Kohlberg, 1969.

Third is the **principled level.** It includes the final two stages of maturity and represents the most mature level of moral reasoning and the most mature set of instrumental values. Right and wrong are judged on the basis of the internalized principles of the individual. That is, judgments are made on the basis of a set of principles or core values that have been developed from individual experience. In the highest stage of maturity, this set of principles is comprehensive (it covers all contingencies), consistent (it is never violated), and universal (it does not change with the situation or circumstance). Thus, stealing $50,000 and stealing $500 are still judged to be wrong, but the basis for the judgment is not the violation of laws or rules; rather, it is the violation of a set of comprehensive, consistent, universal prin-

ciples developed by the individual. Few individuals, according to Kohlberg, reach this highest level of maturity on a consistent basis.

In short, self-centered individuals view rules and laws as outside themselves, but they obey because, by doing so, they may obtain rewards or avoid punishment. Conformist individuals view rules and laws as outside themselves, but they obey because they have learned and accepted those rules and laws, and they seek the respect of others. Principled individuals examine the rules and laws and develop a set of internal principles that they believe are morally right. If there is a choice to be made between obeying a law or obeying a principle, they choose the principle. Internalized principles supersede rules and laws in principled individuals.

To understand the different levels of values maturity, consider the following story used by Kohlberg (1969):

In Europe a woman was near death from a special kind of cancer. There was one drug that the doctors thought might save her. It was a form of radium that a druggist in the same town had recently discovered. The drug was expensive to make, but the druggist was charging ten times what the drug cost to make. He paid $200 for radium and charged $2000 for a small dose of the drug. The sick woman's husband, Heinz, went to everyone he knew to borrow the money, but he could get together only about $1000, which was half of what it cost. He told the druggist that his wife was dying and begged him to sell the drug at a lower price or let him pay later. But the druggist said, "No, I discovered the drug and I'm going to make money from it." So Heinz grew desperate and began to think about breaking into the store to steal the drug for his wife.

Now answer the following questions in reaction to the story:

YES   NO

☑ ____   1. Would it be wrong for Heinz to break into the store?

☑ ____   2. Did the druggist have the right to charge that much for the product?

____ ☑   3. Did Heinz have an obligation to steal the drug for his wife?

____ ☑   4. What if Heinz and his wife did not get along? Should Heinz steal the drug for her?

____ ☑   5. Suppose Heinz's best friend were dying of cancer, rather than Heinz's wife. Should Heinz steal the drug for his friend?

____ ☑   6. Suppose the person dying was not personally close to Heinz. Should Heinz steal the drug?

____ ☑   7. Suppose Heinz read in the paper about a woman dying of cancer. Should he steal the drug for her?

____ ☑   8. Would you steal the drug to save your own life?

____ ☑   9. Suppose Heinz was caught breaking in and brought before a judge. Should he be sentenced to jail?

For individuals in the self-centered level of maturity, stealing the drug might be justified because Heinz's wife had instrumental value: she could provide companionship, help rear the children, and so on. A stranger, however, would not have the same instrumental value for Heinz, so it would be wrong to steal the drug for a stranger. Individuals in the conformity level would base their judgments on the closeness of the relationship and on law and authority. Heinz has an obligation to steal for family members, according to this reasoning, but not for nonfamily members. A governing principle is whether or not an action is against the law (or society's expectations). Principled individuals base their judgments on a set of universal, comprehensive, and consistent principles. They may answer any question yes or no, but their reasoning will be based on their own internal principles, not on externally imposed standards or expectations. (For example, they might feel an obligation to steal the drug for anyone because they value human life more than property.)

Research on Kohlberg's model of values development reveals some interesting findings that have relevance to managerial behavior. For example, moral judgment stories were administered to college students who had earlier participated in Milgram's (1963) obedience study. Under the guise of a reinforcement-learning experiment, Milgram's subjects had been directed to give increasingly intense electric shocks to a person who was observed to be in great pain. Of the respondents at the principled level (stages 5 and 6), 75 percent refused to administer the shocks (i.e., to hurt someone), while only 12.5 percent of the respondents at the conformity level refused. Higher levels of values development were associated with more humane behavior toward other people. Haan, Smith, and Block (1968) found that although both principled and self-centered individuals are inclined to join in mass social protests, the self-centered individuals are motivated by the desire to better themselves individually, while principled individuals are motivated by a sense of justice and by a desire to uphold the rights of the larger community.

It should also be noted that Kohlberg's model has been criticized by Carol Gilligan (1979, 1980, 1982, 1988) as containing a male bias. In her investigations of moral dilemmas among women, Gilligan indicated that women tend to value care, relationships, and commitment more highly than do males. The Kohlberg model, which tends to emphasize justice as the highest moral value, is more typical of males than females, she claimed. Whereas Gilligan's criticisms are somewhat controversial among researchers, they are less relevant to our discussion here because of our emphasis on the development of internalized principles for guiding behavior, whatever their basis. For our purposes in this chapter, the debate about whether justice is a male value and caring is a female value is largely beside the point.

Becoming more mature in values development requires that individuals develop a set of internalized principles by which they can govern their behavior. The development of those principles is enhanced and values maturity is increased as value-based issues are confronted, discussed, and thought about. Lickona (1976, p. 25) notes, "Simply increasing the amount of reciprocal communication that occurs among people is likely to enhance moral development."

To help you determine your own level of values maturity, an instrument developed by James Rest at the University of Minnesota's Moral Research Center was included in the Assessment section. It has been used extensively in research because it is easier to administer than Kohlberg's method for assessing maturity. According to Kohlberg (1976, p. 47), "Rest's approach does give a rough estimate of an individual's moral maturity level." Rather than placing a person on one single level of values maturity, it identifies the stage that the person relies on most. That is, it assumes that individuals use more than one level of maturity (or set of instrumental values), but that one level generally predominates. By completing this instrument, therefore, you will identify your predominant level of values maturity. To determine your maturity level, refer to the self-scoring instructions in the Appendix at the end of this chapter. An exercise in the Skill Practice section will help you develop or refine principles at the stage 5 and stage 6 level of maturity.

Ethical Decision Making and Values

In addition to its benefits for self-understanding, awareness of your own level of values maturity also has important practical implications for ethical decision making. By and large, the American public rates the honesty, integrity, and concern for moral values of American business executives as abysmal. A large majority of the public indicate that they think executives are dishonest, overly profit-oriented, and willing to step on other people to get what they want (Andrews, 1989). Although nine out of 10 companies have a written code of ethics, evidence exists to support public perceptions that these documents are not influential in assuring high moral conduct. For example, Ford Motor Company refused to alter the dangerous gas tank on the Pinto in order to save $11 per car. It cost Ford millions of dollars in lawsuits and cost many people their lives. Equity Funding tried to hide 64,000 phony insurance claims, but went bankrupt when the truth came out. Firestone denied that its 500-series tire was defective, but eventually took losses in the millions when the accident reports were publicized. A. H. Robins knew of problems with its Dalcon Shield for years before informing the public. The billion dollars set aside for lawsuits against the company was dwarfed by the actual claims, and the company filed Chapter 11. E. F. Hutton, General Dynamics, General Electric, Rockwell, Martin Marietta, Lockheed, Bank of Boston, Dow Corning, and a host of other firms have also been in the news for violating ethical principles. One cartoon that seems to summarize these goings-on shows a group of executives sitting at a conference table. The leader remarks, "Of course, honesty is one of the better policies."

Corporate behavior that exemplifies unethical decision making is not our principal concern here. More to the point is a study by the American Management Association that included 3,000 managers in the United States. It reported that most individual managers felt they were under pressure to compromise personal standards to meet company goals (Cavanaugh, 1980). As an illustration, consider the following true incident (names have been changed). How would you respond? Why?

Dale Monson, a top manufacturing manager at Satellite Telecommunications, walked into the office of Al Lake, the head of quality control.

Dale was carrying an assembled part that was to be shipped to a customer on the West Coast. Dale handed Al the part and said, "Look Al, this part is in perfect shape electronically, but the case has a gouge in it. I've seen engineering and they say that the mark doesn't affect form, fit, or function. Marketing says the customer won't mind because they are just going to bury the unit anyway. We can't rework it, and it would cost $75,000 to make new cases. We will only do 23 units, and they're already made. The parts are due to be shipped at the end of the week." Al responded, "Well, what do you want from me?" "Just sign off so we can move forward," said Dale. "Since you're the one who needs to certify acceptable quality, I thought I'd better get this straightened out now rather than waiting until the last minute before shipping."

Would you ship the part or not? Discuss this with class members. Generate a recommendation for Al.

This case exemplifies the major values conflict faced over and over again by managers. It is a conflict between maximizing the economic performance of the organization (as indicated by revenues, costs, profits, and so forth) or the social performance of the organization (as indicated by obligations to customers, employees, suppliers, and so forth). Most ethical tradeoffs are conflicts between these two desirable ends: economic versus social performance (Hosmer, 1987). Making these kinds of decisions effectively is not merely a matter of selecting between right and wrong alternatives or between good and bad choices. Most of these choices are between right and right or between one good and another. Individuals who effectively manage these kinds of ethical tradeoffs are those who have a clear sense of their own values and who have developed a principled level of moral maturity. They have articulated and clarified their own internal set of universal, comprehensive, and consistent principles upon which to base their decisions. It is seldom the case, of course, that a manager could choose economic performance goals every time or that he or she could choose social performance goals every time. Tradeoffs are inevitable.

It is not a simple matter, on the other hand, to generate a personal set of universal, comprehensive, and consistent principles that can guide decision making. According to Kohlberg's research, most adults have nei-

ther constructed, nor do they follow, a well-developed set of principles in making decisions. One reason is that they have no model or example of what such principles might be. We offer some standards against which to test your own principles for making moral or ethical choices. These standards are neither comprehensive nor absolute, nor are they independent of one another. They simply serve as reference against which to test the principles that you include in your personal values statement.

Front page test: Would I be embarrassed if my decision became a headline in the local newspaper? Would I feel comfortable describing my actions or decision to a customer or stockholder?

Golden rule test: Would I be willing to be treated in the same manner?

Dignity and liberty test: Are the dignity and liberty of others preserved by this decision? Is the basic humanity of the affected parties enhanced? Are their opportunities expanded or curtailed?

Equal treatment test: Are the rights, welfare, and betterment of minorities and lower status people given full consideration? Does this decision benefit those with privilege but without merit?

Personal gain test: Is an opportunity for personal gain clouding my judgment? Would I make the same decision if the outcome did not benefit me in any way?

Congruence test: Is this decision or action consistent with my espoused personal principles? Does it violate the spirit of any organizational policies or laws?

Procedural justice test: Can the procedures used to make this decision stand up to scrutiny by those affected?

Cost-benefit test: Does a benefit for some cause unacceptable harm to others? How critical is the benefit? Can the harmful effects be mitigated?

Good night's sleep test: Whether or not anyone else knows about my action, will it produce a good night's sleep?

In the Skill Application section of this chapter, you may want to consider these alternatives when constructing your own set of comprehensive, consistent, and universalistic principles. You also should be aware, however, that your set of personal principles will also be influenced by your orientation for acquiring and responding to the information you receive. This orientation is called cognitive style.

Cognitive Style

Cognitive style consists of a large number of factors that relate to the way individuals perceive, interpret, and respond to information. There are literally scores of dimensions used in the research literature to define cognitive style (for examples, see Eckstrom, French, & Harmon, 1979). In this chapter, however, we consider the two major dimensions of cognitive style discussed in research literature that have been shown to have particular relevance to managerial behavior: (1) the manner in which individuals gather information; and (2) the manner in which they evaluate information they receive.

The basic premise underlying cognitive style is that every individual is faced with an overwhelming amount of information, and only part of it can be given attention and acted upon at any one time. Individuals, therefore, develop strategies for assimilating and interpreting the information they receive. No strategy is in-

herently good or inherently bad, and not everyone adopts an identifiable, consistent set of strategies that become part of his or her cognitive style. However, about 80 percent of individuals do eventually develop (mostly unconsciously) a preferred set of information-processing strategies, and these make up their particular cognitive styles. The Cognitive Style instrument in the Assessment section assesses the two core dimensions of your information-processing preferences.

In order for your scores on the Cognitive Style instrument to be meaningful to you, you must understand the theory on which the model is based. It is grounded in the work of Jung (1923). Figure 3 illustrates the two cognitive dimensions. The information-gathering dimension distinguishes an intuitive strategy from a sensing strategy, and the information evaluation dimension distinguishes a thinking strategy from a feeling strategy.

Different strategies for taking in, coding, and storing information (information gathering) develop as a result of certain cognitive filters used by individuals to select the information to which they pay attention. An **intuitive strategy** takes a holistic view and emphasizes commonalities and generalizations, that is, the relationships among the various elements of data. Intuitive

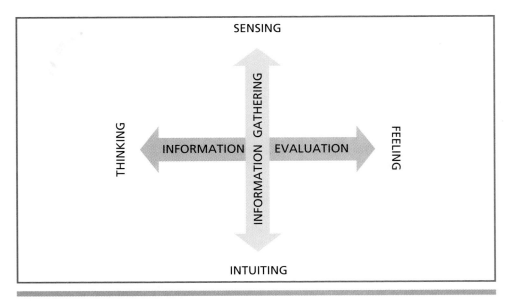

Figure 3 Model of Cognitive Style Based on Two Dimensions

thinkers often have preconceived notions about what sort of information may be relevant, and they look at the information to find what is consistent with their preconceptions. They tend to be convergent thinkers.

The **sensing strategy** focuses on detail, or on the specific attributes of each element of data, rather than on relationships among the elements. Sensing thinkers are rational and have few preconceptions about what may be relevant, so they insist on a close and thorough examination of the information. They are sensitive to the unique attributes of various parts of the information they encounter and tend to be divergent thinkers.

In simple terms, an intuitive strategy focuses on the whole whereas a sensing strategy looks at the parts of the whole. An intuitive strategy seeks commonalities and overall categories, while a sensing strategy looks for uniqueness, detail, and exceptions to general rules.

The second dimension of Jung's model refers to strategies for interpreting and judging information (information evaluation). These strategies develop from reliance on a particular problem-solving pattern. A **thinking strategy** evaluates information using a systematic plan with specific sequential steps. There is a focus on appropriate methods and logical progressions. Individuals who use a thinking style generally rely on objective data. Attempts are made to fit problems into a known model or framework. When such people defend their solutions, they emphasize the methods and procedures used to solve the problems. Vertinsky (1976) refers to these individuals as members of a "continuous culture," meaning that they operate consistently with existing patterns of thought.

A **feeling strategy,** on the other hand, approaches a problem on the basis of "gut feel," or an internal sense of how to respond. Problems are often defined and redefined, and approaches are based on trial and error rather than logical procedures. Feeling individuals have a penchant for subjective or impressionistic rather than objective data, and frequently cannot describe their own problem-solving processes. Problem solutions are often found through using analogies or seeing unusual relationships between the problem and a past experience. Vertinsky (1976) refers to these individuals as members of a "discontinuous culture."

These different strategies have important implications for managerial behavior. Each has advantages and disadvantages. For example, when faced with a large amount of data, sensing managers, because they focus on detail, experience information overload and personal stress more readily than intuitive managers do. When they encounter too much detail, or too much heterogeneity, sensing managers become overloaded because each detail receives attention.

Intuitive managers, on the other hand, focus on the relationships among elements and the whole and handle additions of detail relatively easily. However, when diversity or ambiguity is encountered in the information, when aberrations from expected relationships occur, or when preformed categories don't fit, intuitive managers are likely to have more difficulty processing the information than sensing managers are. Encountering exceptions or the absence of a clear set of relationships among elements is particularly problematic for intuitive managers. Sensing managers are likely to handle these situations more easily because of their tendency to do "fine-grained analyses" of problems.

Thinking managers are less likely to be effective when encountering problems requiring creativity and discontinuous thinking or when encountering highly ambiguous problems that have only partial information available. When no apparent system exists for solving a problem, these individuals are likely to have more difficulty than feeling managers are.

On the other hand, when one program or system will solve a variety of problems, that is, when the information suggests a straightforward, computational solution, feeling managers are less effective because of their tendency to try new approaches, to redefine problems, and to reinvent the solution over and over without following past programs. This generally leads to inefficient problem solving or even solving the wrong problem. Thinking managers have less difficulty in such situations.

Research on these cognitive dimensions has found that no matter what type of problem they face, most individuals use their preferred cognitive style to approach it. They prefer, and even seek, decision situations and problem types that are consistent with their own cognitive style (for example, individuals scoring high on thinking prefer problems with a step-by-step method of solution). In one study, for example, managers who were more thinking-oriented than feeling-oriented implemented more computer-based systems and rational procedures for decision making. Managers in another study defined identical problems differently depending on their different cognitive styles. Another study found that differences in cognitive style led to significantly different decision-making processes in managers (see Henderson & Nutt, 1980; Chenhall & Morris, 1991; Ruble & Cosier, 1990).

Students with different cognitive styles also have been found to approach learning differently, and different kinds of educational experiences hold meaning for different types of people. For example, individuals who emphasize intuitive strategies tend to do better in conceptual courses; they learn more easily through reading and through discussing general relationships. Exam questions with only one right answer may be easier for them than for those who emphasize sensing. Individuals who emphasize sensing strategies tend to do better in factual courses or courses in which attention to detail and dissimilarity is important. Critical and analytical learning activities (for example, debates) facilitate their learning, and exams emphasizing implications and applications may be easiest for these individuals.

Individuals who emphasize a thinking strategy do best in courses (such as mathematics) that take an orderly, step-by-step approach to the subject and where what is learned builds on, and follows directly from, what was learned earlier. On the other hand, feeling individuals do best in courses requiring creativity and idea generation. Learning activities in which the student must rely on a personal sense of what is appropriate (for example, sculpting) are likely to be preferred by these individuals.

Knowing one's own cognitive style can prove advantageous to managers in numerous ways, such as identifying career options, choosing appropriate business environments and managerial assignments, and selecting teams of complementary members to solve problems. It also is useful in helping students to capitalize on their academic strengths and enhance their study skills. Table 3 summarizes some personal characteristics associated with each of these major cognitive orientations.

Attitude Toward Change

In order to capitalize fully on the strengths of your own cognitive style, you also should be aware of your orientation toward change. This is important because, as the environment in which managers operate continues to become more chaotic, more temporary, more complex, and more overloaded with information, your ability to process information is at least partly constrained by your fundamental attitude about change.

Almost no one disagrees with the prediction that change will increase. Toffler (1980) stated it this way:

> A powerful tide is surging across much of the world today, creating a new, often bizarre, environment in which to work, play, marry, raise children, or retire. In this bewildering context, businessmen swim against highly erratic economic currents; politicians see their ratings bob wildly up and down; universities, hospitals, and other institutions battle desperately against inflation. Value systems splinter and crash, while lifeboats of family, church, and state are hurled madly about.

Many observers have suggested that we have now entered a "post-industrial environment," characterized by more and increasing information, more and increasing turbulence, and more and increasing complexity (Huber, 1984; Grayson & O'Dell, 1988). For example, the number of academic journals currently is increasing at the rate of 11 percent per year from a base of approximately 100,000. Laser disc technology makes possible the storage of the equivalent of a law library on a 10.5-inch disc, and visual scanners can rapidly transfer the contents of printed material to a disc. The information explosion, including instantaneous mail and voice communication, immediate document retrieval, and desktop libraries, has changed the environment of modern management dramatically. Access to more information in increasing amounts almost instantaneously leads to increased turbulence and complexity for managers. They must make decisions ever faster as both the amount and the rapidity of the information encountered increase (Cameron & Ulrich, 1986; Peters, 1987). On the other hand, the human mind is capable of processing only a certain amount of information at a time, so more and more decisions have to be made on the basis of incomplete and ambiguous information (Simon, 1973). Individuals must manage now more than ever in conditions of ambiguity and turbulence, and cognitive style is sometimes at the mercy of orientation toward change.

Being aware of your own orientation toward change, therefore, is an important prerequisite for successfully coping with it. Two dimensions of change orientation particularly relevant for managers are discussed on the following pages.

INFORMATION GATHERING

INTUITIVE TYPES	SENSING TYPES
Like solving new problems.	Dislike new problems unless there are standard ways to solve them.
Dislike doing the same thing over and over again.	Like an established routine.
Enjoy learning a new skill more than using it.	Enjoy using skills already learned more than learning new ones.
Work in bursts of energy powered by enthusiasm, with slack periods in between.	Work more steadily, with realistic idea of how long it will take.
Jump to conclusions frequently.	Must usually work all the way through to reach a conclusion.
Are patient with complicated situations.	Are impatient when the details are complicated.
Are impatient with routine details.	Are patient with routine details.
Follow inspirations, good or bad.	Rarely trust inspirations, and don't usually feel inspired.
Often tend to make errors of fact.	Seldom make errors of fact.
Dislike taking time for precision.	Tend to be good at precise work.

INFORMATION EVALUATION

FEELING TYPES	THINKING TYPES
Tend to be very aware of other people and their feelings.	Are relatively unemotional and uninterested in people's feelings.
Enjoy pleasing people, even in unimportant things.	May hurt people's feelings without knowing it.
Like harmony. Efficiency may be badly disturbed by office feuds.	Like analysis and putting things into logical order. Can get along without harmony.
Often let decision be influenced by their own or other people's personal likes and wishes.	Tend to decide impersonally, sometimes ignoring people's wishes.
Need occasional praise.	Need to be treated fairly.
Dislike telling people unpleasant things.	Are able to reprimand people or fire them when necessary.
Relate well to most people.	Tend to relate well only to other thinking types.
Tend to be sympathetic.	May seem hardhearted.

Table 3   Characteristics of Cognitive Styles

Tolerance of Ambiguity

The first important dimension is **tolerance of ambiguity,** which refers to the extent to which individuals are threatened by or have difficulty coping with situations that are ambiguous, where change occurs rapidly or unpredictably, where information is inadequate or unclear, or where complexity exists. Stimulus-rich and information-overloaded environments (for example, air traffic control towers) are examples. Regardless of their cognitive style, people vary in their aptitude for operating in such circumstances.

People differ in the extent to which they are "cognitively complex" or in the extent to which they can cope with ambiguous, incomplete, unstructured, dynamic situations. Individuals who have a high tolerance of ambiguity also tend to be more cognitively complex. They tend to pay attention to more information, interpret more cues, and possess more sense-making categories than less complex individuals do. Research has found that cognitively complex and tolerant individuals are better transmitters of information (Bieri et al., 1966), more sensitive to internal (non-superficial) characteristics of others when evaluating their performance at work (Schneier, 1979), and more behaviorally adaptive and flexible under ambiguous and overloaded conditions than less tolerant and less cognitively complex individuals (Haase, Lee, & Banks, 1979). Managers with higher tolerance-of-ambiguity scores are more likely to be entrepreneurial in their actions (Schere, 1982), to screen out less information in a complex environment (Haase et al., 1979), and to choose specialties in their occupations that possess less-structured tasks (Budner, 1962). It also should be pointed out, however, that individuals who are more tolerant of ambiguity have more difficulty focusing on a single important element of information—they are inclined to pay attention to a variety of items—and they may have somewhat less ability to concentrate without being distracted by interruptions. However, for the most part, in an information-rich environment, tolerance of ambiguity and cognitive complexity are more adaptive than the opposite characteristics.

In the Skill Assessment section of this chapter, a Tolerance of Ambiguity Scale (Budner, 1962) assesses the extent to which you have a tolerance for these kinds of complex situations. In scoring the Tolerance of Ambiguity Scale (see Appendix I) three different sub-scale scores are assessed. One is the **Novelty** score, which indicates the extent to which you are tolerant of new, unfamiliar information or situations. The second sub-scale is the **Complexity** score, which indicates the extent to which you are tolerant of multiple, distinctive, or unrelated information. The third sub-scale is the **Insolubility** score, which indicates the extent to which you are tolerant of problems that are very difficult to solve because, for example, alternative solutions are not evident, information is unavailable, or the problem's components seem unrelated to each other. In general, the more tolerant people are of novelty, complexity, and insolubility, the more likely they are to succeed as managers in information-rich, ambiguous environments. They are less overwhelmed by ambiguous circumstances.

It is important to note that cognitive complexity and tolerance for ambiguity are not related to intelligence (Smith & Leach, 1972), and your score on the Tolerance of Ambiguity Scale is not an evaluation of how smart you are. Most important, individuals can learn to tolerate more complexity and more flexibility in their information-processing abilities. The first step toward increasing tolerance is becoming aware of where you are now by completing the Skill Assessment section. Then the Skill Analysis and Skill Practice sections of this chapter, along with discussions such as the one in the chapters on problem solving and creativity, provide ways to improve your tolerance for ambiguity and your cognitive complexity.

It is also interesting to note that a positive correlation exists between tolerance of ambiguity and the second dimension of orientation toward change discussed here, internal locus of control.

Locus of Control

The second dimension of orientation toward change is **locus of control.** It is one of the most studied and written-about aspects of orientation toward change. Locus of control refers to the attitude people develop regarding the extent to which they are in control of their own destinies. When individuals receive information about the success or failure of their own actions, or when something changes in the environment, they differ in how they interpret that information. People receive reinforcements, both positive or negative, as they attempt to make changes around them. If individuals interpret the reinforcement they receive to be contingent upon their own actions, it is called an **internal locus** of control (that is, "I was the cause of the success or failure of the change"). If they interpret the reinforcement as being a product of outside forces, it is called an **external locus** of control (that is, "Something or someone else caused the success or failure"). Over time, people develop a "generalized expectancy" about the dominant sources of the reinforcements they receive. Thus, they become largely internally focused or largely externally focused with regard to the source of control they perceive in a changing environment.

Over 1,000 studies have been done using the locus of control scale. In general, the research suggests that, in American culture, internal locus of control is associated with the most successful managers (for reviews of the literature, see Hendricks, 1985; Spector, 1982). For example, the author of the scale, Julian B. Rotter (1966), summarized several studies of locus of control and reported that people with an internal locus of control are more likely to (1) be attentive to aspects of the environment that provide useful information for the future, (2) engage in actions to improve their environment, (3) place greater emphasis on striving for achievement, (4) be more inclined to develop their own skills, (5) ask more questions, and (6) remember more information than people with an external locus of control (see also Seeman, 1982).

In the management literature, individuals who have an internal locus of control are less alienated from the work environment (Mitchell, 1975; Seeman, 1982; Wolf, 1972), more satisfied with their work (Organ & Green, 1974; Pryer & Distefano, 1971), and experience less job strain and more position mobility (promotions and job changes) than do individuals with an external locus of control (Gennill & Heisler, 1972; Newton & Keenan, 1990). A study of leadership and group performance found that internals were more likely to be leaders and that groups led by internals were more effective than those led by externals (Anderson & Schneider, 1978; Blau, 1993). Internals also were found to outperform externals in stressful situations (Anderson, Hellriegel, & Slocum, 1977), to engage in more entrepreneurial activity (Durand & Shea, 1974; Cromie, Callahan, & Jansen, 1992; Bonnett & Furnharn, 1991), to be more active in managing their own careers (Hammer & Vardi, 1981), and to have higher levels of job involvement than externals (Runyon, 1973; Kren, 1992). Differences have also been found regarding how power and authority are utilized by externals and internals (see the chapter on Gaining Power and Influence). External leaders tend to use coercive power and threat, whereas internal leaders rely more on persuasion and expertise as a source of power (Goodstadt & Hjelle, 1973; Mitchell, Smyser, & Weed, 1975; Sweeney, McFarlin, & Cotton, 1991). Moreover, internals both demonstrate and are more satisfied with a participative management style than externals are (Runyon, 1973; Colarelli & Bishop, 1990). A study of locus of control among top executives found that the firms led by internals engaged in more innovation, more risky projects, more leadership in the marketplace, longer planning horizons, more scanning of

the environment, and a more highly developed technology than external-led firms did (Miller, Kets de Vries, & Toulouse, 1982). In summarizing his conclusions about locus of control, McDonald (1970) stated, "all research points to the same conclusion: In the American culture, people are handicapped by external locus of control."

On the other hand, research also has found that an internal locus of control is not a panacea for all management problems. Internal locus of control is not always a positive attribute. For example, individuals with an external locus of control have been found to be more inclined to initiate structure as leaders (to help clarify roles) and to show consideration to people (Durand & Shea, 1974). Internals are less likely to comply with leader directions and are less accurate in processing feedback about successes and failures than are externals (Cravens & Worchel, 1977). Internals also have more difficulty arriving at decisions with serious consequences for someone else (Wheeler & Davis, 1979).

It is important to note that locus of control can shift over time, particularly as a function of the position held at work (Harvey, 1971), and that external locus of control does not inhibit individuals from attaining positions of power and influence at the top of organizations (Rothenberg, 1980). Therefore, no matter what your Internal-External score, you can be a successful manager in the right setting, or you can alter your locus of control. Research has shown that people who interpret information about change as if they are in control of it, and who perceive themselves to be in charge of their own performance (and hence able to control outcomes related to that performance), are more likely to be effective managers in most circumstances in our culture.

The Locus of Control Scale in the Skill Assessment section helps you generate a score showing the extent to which you have an internal or external locus of control. The scoring key and some comparison information are located in Appendix I.

In summary, two key attitudes toward change, tolerance of ambiguity and locus of control, have been found to be associated with success in management roles. Knowing your scores on these two factors can help you capitalize on your strengths and enhance your potential for management success. While substantial research exists associating some positive managerial behaviors with internal locus of control and tolerance of ambiguity, possessing these orientations is neither an assurance of success as a manager nor a solution to the problems that managers face. By knowing your scores, however, you will be able to choose situations in which you are more likely to feel comfortable, perform effectively, and understand the point of view of those whose perspectives differ from yours. Self-understanding is a prerequisite to self-improvement and change.

Interpersonal Orientation

The fourth critical area of self-awareness is interpersonal orientation. This aspect of self-awareness differs from the first three in that it relates to behavioral tendencies and to relationships with other people, not just to one's own personal inclinations and psychological attributes. Because the manager's job has been characterized as overwhelmingly interpersonal, interpersonal orientation, or the tendency to behave in certain ways around other people, is an especially important aspect of self-awareness. Sayles (1964, p. 38) suggests that management involves virtually constant contact with people, and managers whose personalities do not dispose them toward a high amount of interpersonal activity are likely to be frustrated and dissatisfied. The quality and type of this interpersonal activity can vary widely, however. Therefore, it is important for you to know your own interpersonal tendencies and inclinations to maximize the probabilities of successful interactions.

Interpersonal orientation does not reflect the actual behavior patterns displayed in interpersonal situations. Rather, it refers to the underlying tendencies to behave in certain ways, regardless of the other person involved or the circumstance. Interpersonal orientation generally arises from certain basic needs in the individual that relate to relationships with others.

A well-known and thoroughly researched theory of interpersonal orientation was proposed by Schutz (1958). The basic assumption of his model is that people need people and that all individuals seek to establish compatible relationships with other individuals in their social interactions. As people form relationships and begin striving for compatibility in interactions, three interpersonal needs develop that must be satisfied if the individual is to function effectively and avoid unsatisfactory relationships.

The first is the **need for inclusion.** Everyone needs to maintain a relationship with other people, to be included in their activities, and to include them in one's own activities. To some extent all individuals seek to belong to a group, but at the same time they want to be

left alone. They need to ensure that others are not left out while at the same time giving them independence. There is always a tradeoff between tendencies toward extroversion and introversion. Therefore, individuals differ in the strength of their relative needs: (1) the need to include others, or expressed inclusion, and (2) the need to be included by others, or wanted inclusion.

A second interpersonal need is the **need for control.** This is the need to maintain a satisfactory balance of power and influence in relationships. All individuals need to exert control, direction, or structure over other people while also remaining independent from them. All individuals also have a need to be controlled, directed, or structured by others but at the same time to maintain freedom and discretion. Essentially, this is a tradeoff between authoritarianism and dependency. Individual differences arise, therefore, in the need to control others, or expressed control, and the need to be controlled by others, or wanted control.

A third need is the **need for affection,** or the need to form close personal relationships with others. This need is not restricted to physical affection or romantic relationships but includes needs for warmth, intimacy, and love apart from overt behaviors. All individuals need to form close, personal relationships with other people, but at the same time they want to avoid becoming overcommitted or smothered. All individuals need to have others show warmth and affection to them but also need to maintain some distance. This is a tradeoff between high affiliative needs and high independence needs. Individuals therefore vary in their needs for expressing affection toward other people and for wanting affection to be expressed toward them.

Each of the three interpersonal needs has two aspects, a desire to express the need and a desire to receive the needed behavior from others. These three needs determine an individual's interpersonal orientation. Individuals differ uniquely in their need to give or receive certain behaviors when interacting with others. Table 4 summarizes these three needs and illustrates characteristics of each.

In the Skill Assessment section, we provided the instrument Schutz developed to assess inclusion, control, and affection needs. Using the scoring sheet and instructions in Appendix I, compute your score for each interpersonal need. The discussion of interpersonal orientation in this section will be more meaningful to you if you have completed the FIRO-B survey in the Assessment section. If you have not done so, please take

	INCLUSION	CONTROL	AFFECTION
Expressed Toward Others	I join other people, and I include others.	I take charge, and I influence people.	I get close and personal with people.
Wanted from Others	I want other people to include me.	I want others to lead me or give me directions.	I want people to get close and personal with me.

Table 4 Descriptors of Fundamental Interpersonal Relations Orientation-Behavior (FIRO-B) Needs

time to complete it now. It should take you no more than 10 minutes.

There are several ways your scores on this questionnaire can be analyzed and interpreted. For example, you can compare your *expressed* total with your *wanted* total to determine the extent to which you are willing to give as much behavior as you want to get. Individuals who have high expressed scores and low wanted scores are called "controllers" by Ryan (1970) because they want to express but are unwilling to accept in return. The reverse pattern, high wanted scores and low expressed scores, is called a "passive" pattern by Ryan because these individuals want to receive but are unwilling to initiate interaction.

By comparing each need score, you can determine which is your most important interpersonal need. Your highest score may indicate the need that is least satisfied.

Another way to interpret your scores is to compare them with the national norm data in Table 5. The numbers at the top of each box (for example, 4 to 7) refer to the average range of scores. At least 50 percent of adults fall within that range. The numbers at the bottom (for example, 5.4) refer to the average scores in the cells. At least 50 percent of adults score within 1.5 of those scores. If you scored 6 in the expressed control cell, for example, you score higher than 75 percent of the people on that need; if you scored 2 in the expressed affection cell, you score lower than 75 percent.

The score in the lower-right-hand corner (the total of the expressed and wanted scores) is called the *social interaction index*. This score represents the overall interpersonal need level. The highest possible score is 54. Individuals with high scores have strong needs to interact with other people. They are likely to be gregarious, friendly, and involved with others. Low scores are more typical of shy, reserved people.

Hill (1974) found that business school students differ significantly on the social interaction index, depending on their majors. Accounting and systems analysis students in his study had means of 22.3 and 22.6, respectively (lower than average), while marketing and human resource majors had means of 31.0 and 31.9, respectively (higher than average). Finance, small business, and engineering students were in the middle.

	INCLUSION	CONTROL	AFFECTION	ROW TOTALS
Expressed Toward Others	4 to 7 5.4 *1*	2 to 5 3.9 *2*	3 to 6 4.1 *2*	9 to 18 13.4 *5*
Wanted from Others	5 to 8 6.5 *6*	3 to 6 4.6 *3*	3 to 6 4.6 *5*	11 to 20 15.9 *8*
Column Totals	9 to 15 11.9 *1*	5 to 11 8.5 *5*	6 to 12 8.9 *7*	20 to 38 29.3 *13*

Table 5 Average FIRO-B Scores and Ranges

This difference turned out to be statistically significant, which suggests that career selection may have something to do with interpersonal orientation.

Probably the greatest usefulness of the scores lies in analyzing **interpersonal compatibility**—that is, in matching one person's scores with those of another. Individuals can be interpersonally incompatible in three ways. To explain these three incompatibilities, two hypothetical scores are used in Table 6.

The first type of incompatibility is **reciprocal.** It refers to the match between one person's expressed behavior and another person's wanted behavior. For example, if one person has a high need to express control but the other person does not want to be controlled, there is a reciprocal incompatibility. The formula for computing reciprocal incompatibility is

$$| \text{Manager's } e - \text{Subordinate's } w | + | \text{Subordinate's } e - \text{Manager's } w |$$

The straight lines indicate absolute values (no minus numbers). The data in Table 6 show that in the inclusion area, for example, a reciprocal incompatibility exists between the manager and the subordinate. Using the formula above, we have

$$| 9 - 2 | + | 3 - 8 | = 12$$

Any score higher than 6 means that there is a strong possibility of incompatibility. In this case, the manager has a strong need to include others and to be included by them, but the subordinate has low needs in both aspects of inclusion. There is a potential for interpersonal conflict to arise in this area, particularly if inclu-

sion behavior (for example, teamwork) is required in the relationship.

Originator incompatibility is the second type. This refers to the match between the expressed scores of both individuals. Originator incompatibility occurs either when both people want to initiate in an area or when neither wants to initiate. The formula for computing originator incompatibility is

$$(\text{Manager's } e - \text{Manager's } w) + (\text{Subordinate's } e - \text{Subordinate's } w)$$

The parentheses in the formula indicate that minus numbers should be computed. The data from Table 6 in the control area make clear that an originator incompatibility exists. Both the manager and the subordinate want to control, but neither has a high need to be controlled. Their incompatibility score is computed as follows:

$$(9 - 4) + (8 - 2) = +11$$

Any score higher than +6 indicates high competitive originator incompatibility. A score of less than -6 indicates high apathetic originator incompatibility. Apathetic incompatibility occurs either when neither individual wants to initiate in the area or, in this case, when neither person wants to control or take charge; both want the other to do it.

The third type of incompatibility is **interchange.** This refers to the extent to which two individuals emphasize the same or different interpersonal needs. For example, interchange incompatibility exists if one person emphasizes control needs highly while the other

	MANAGER			
	INCLUSION	CONTROL	AFFECTION	
Expressed *(e)*	9	9	1	19
Wanted *(w)*	8	4	3	15
	17	13	4	34
	SUBORDINATE			
	INCLUSION	CONTROL	AFFECTION	
Expressed *(e)*	3	8	6	17
Wanted *(w)*	2	2	8	12
	5	10	14	29

Table 6 Examples of Two FIRO-B Scores

emphasizes affection needs highly. When interpersonal problems arise, one person would likely define the problem as one of control, direction, or influence, while the other person would likely define the problem as one of closeness, warmth, and affection. The difficulty would be in getting the two people to see the situation as the same problem. The formula for computing interchange incompatibility is

$$| \text{Manager's } e + \text{Manager's } w | - | \text{Subordinate's } e + \text{Subordinate's } w |$$

Again, the straight lines in the formula enclose absolute values. In the affection area in Table 6, an interchange incompatibility exists. Affection is a high need area for the subordinate but a low need area for the manager. (The reverse case exists in the inclusion area.) Computing the interchange incompatibility score gives us

$$| 1 + 3 | - | 6 + 8 | = 10$$

Scores above 6 indicate a strong possibility of incompatibility. The need of the subordinate in the affection area is likely to be ignored or rejected in the relationship.

Using these three incompatibility formulas allows us to compute a **total incompatibility** score, which combines the three types of incompatibilities in the three need areas. These are computed in Table 7 for the hypothetical manager and subordinate.

The incompatibility scores indicate that this manager and subordinate have a high probability of interpersonal difficulty in their relationship. Potential problems of not meeting one another's needs in any of the three interpersonal need categories (reciprocal incompatibility), of both wanting to control but not wanting to be controlled (originator incompatibility in

the control area), and of having different need emphases (interchange incompatibility in the inclusion and affection areas) would probably lead these two people to have a conflict-ridden relationship.

Research confirms this prediction. For example, DiMarco (1974) has found that low incompatibility scores result in more favorable attitudes of subordinates toward managers. Obradovic (1962) has found teacher attitudes are more favorable toward students when compatibility scores are high. Hutcherson (1963) has found that students achieve higher levels in classes when compatibility with the teacher is high. More often, friends are chosen from among those with compatible scores. Sapolsky (1965) and Mendelsohn and Rankin (1969) have even found that the success of therapist-patient treatment is affected by interpersonal incompatibility.

There is strong evidence that groups composed of compatible individuals are more satisfying to members and more effective than groups composed of incompatible individuals. The following are some characteristics that studies have found typical of interpersonally compatible groups (Hewett, O'Brien, & Hornik, 1974; Liddell & Slocum, 1976; Reddy & Byrnes, 1972; Shalinsky, 1969; Schutz, 1958; Smith & Haythorn, 1973):

1. More interpersonal attraction among members.

2. More positive group climate.

3. More cooperative behavior on tasks.

4. More productivity in accomplishing tasks.

5. Faster problem solving.

6. Fewer errors in solving problems.

7. Less hostility among members.

	INCLUSION	CONTROL	AFFECTION
Reciprocal incompatibility	12	11	10
Originator incompatibility	2	11	−4
Interchange incompatibility	12	3	10
Total incompatibility (Sum of absolute values)			75

Table 7 Incompatibility Scores for a Hypothetical Manager and a Subordinate

Knowing your interpersonal orientation, then, can be an important factor in your managerial success. Not only does it enhance good interpersonal relations by helping you diagnose potential areas of incompatibility, but it also helps you generate alternatives for behavior when you attempt to solve interpersonal difficulties. For example, some problems can be solved simply by increasing inclusion activities, by allowing someone else to express a little more control, or by redefining an issue as an affection problem instead of a control problem.

Summary

Corporate America increasingly has begun to discover the power of developing self-awareness among its managers. Each year, millions of executives complete instruments designed to increase self-awareness in companies such as Apple, AT&T, Citicorp, Exxon, General Electric, Honeywell, 3M, and the U.S. Army. An awareness of how individuals differ in their values priorities and values maturity, cognitive style, orientation toward change, and interpersonal orientation has helped many companies cope better with interpersonal conflicts, botched communications, breakdowns in trust, and misunderstandings. For example, after requiring his top 100 managers to undergo self-awareness training, the president of the computer reservations company of Hilton Hotels and Budget Rent-a-Car stated:

> We had some real morale problems. I realized I had a mixed bag of people reporting to me and that this training could help us better understand each other and also understand how we make decisions. We wouldn't have made it through [a recent company crisis] without self-awareness training (Moore, 1987).

Not only does self-awareness training assist individuals in their ability to understand, and thereby manage, themselves, but it also is important in helping individuals develop understanding of the differences in others. Most people will regularly encounter individuals who possess different styles, different sets of values, and different perspectives than they do. Most work forces are becoming more, not less, diverse. Self-awareness training as discussed in this chapter, therefore, can be a valuable tool in helping individuals develop empathy and understanding for the expanding diversity they will face in work and school settings. The relationship between the four critical areas of self-awareness and these management outcomes is summarized in Figure 4.

Most of the following chapters relate to skills in interpersonal or group interaction, but successful skill development in those areas will occur only if individuals

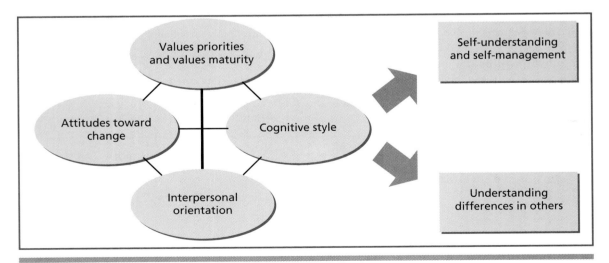

Figure 4   Core Aspects of Self-Awareness and the Managerial Implications

have a firm foundation in self-awareness. In fact, there is an interesting paradox in human behavior: *We can know others only by knowing ourselves, but we can know ourselves only by knowing others.* Our knowledge of others, and therefore our ability to manage or interact successfully with them, comes from relating what we see in them to our own experience. If we are not self-aware, we have no basis for knowing certain things about others. Self-recognition leads to recognition and understanding of others. As Harris (1981) puts it:

> Nothing is really personal that is not first interpersonal, beginning with the infant's shock of separation from the umbilical cord. What we know about ourselves comes only from the outside, and is interpreted by the kind of experiences we have had; and what we know about others comes only from analogy with our own network of feelings.

Behavioral Guidelines

Following are the behavioral guidelines relating to the improvement of self-awareness. These guidelines will be helpful to you as you engage in practice and application activities designed to improve your self-awareness.

1. Identify your sensitive line. Determine what information about yourself you are most likely to defend against.

2. Identify a comprehensive, consistent, and universal set of principles on which you will base your behavior. Identify the most important terminal and instrumental values that guide your decisions.

3. Expand your cognitive style, your tolerance of ambiguity, and your internal locus of control by increasing your exposure to new information and engaging in different kinds of activities than you are used to. Seek ways to expand and broaden yourself.

4. Compute incompatibility scores on those with whom you regularly interact and identify areas in which potential incompatibilities may arise. Apply principles of supportive communication (Chapter 4) and conflict management (Chapter 7) when disagreements do arise.

5. Engage in honest self-disclosure with someone who is close to you and accepting of you. Check out aspects of yourself that you are not sure of.

6. Keep a journal, and make time regularly to engage in self-analysis. Balance life's activities with some time for self-renewal.

Skill Analysis

Cases Involving Self-Awareness

Communist Prison Camp

To find examples of an intensive destruction of identification with family and reference groups and the destruction of social role and self-image, we turn to the experiences of civilian political prisoners interned in Chinese Communist prisons.

In such prisons the total regimen, consisting of physical privation, prolonged interrogation, total isolation from former relationships and sources of information, detailed regimentation of all daily activities, and deliberate humiliation and degradation, was geared to producing a confession of alleged crimes, the assumption of a penitent role, and the adoption of a Communist frame of reference. The prisoner was not informed what his crimes were, nor was he permitted to evade the issue by making up a false confession. Instead, what the prisoner learned he must do was reevaluate his past from the point of view of the Communists and recognize that most of his former attitudes and behavior were actually criminal from this point of view. For example, a priest who had dispensed food to needy peasants in his mission church had to "recognize" that he was actually a tool of imperialism and was using his missionary activities as cover for exploitation of the peasants. Even worse, he had used food as blackmail to accomplish his aims.

The key technique used by the Communists to produce social alienation to a degree sufficient to allow such redefinition and reevaluation to occur was to put the prisoner into a cell with four or more other prisoners who were somewhat more advanced in their "thought reform" than he. Such a cell usually had one leader who was responsible to the prison authorities, and the progress of the whole cell was made contingent upon the progress of the least "reformed" member. This condition meant in practice that four or more cell members devoted all their energies to getting their least "reformed" member to recognize "the truth" about himself and to confess. To accomplish this they typically swore at, harangued, beat, denounced, humiliated, reviled, and brutalized their victim twenty-four hours a day, sometimes for weeks or months on end. If the authorities felt that the prisoner was basically uncooperative, they manacled his hands behind his back and chained his ankles, which made him completely dependent on his cellmates for the fulfillment of his basic needs. It was this reduction to an animal-like existence in front of other humans which constituted the ultimate humiliation and led most reliably to the destruction of the prisoner's image of himself. Even in his own eyes he became something which was not worthy of the regard of his fellow man.

If, to avoid complete physical and personal destruction, the prisoner began to confess in the manner desired of him, he was usually forced to prove his sincerity by making irrevocable behavioral commitments, such as denouncing and implicating his friends and relatives in his own newly recognized crimes. Once he had done this he became further alienated from his former self, even in his own eyes, and could seek security only in a new identity and new social relationships. Aiding this process of confessing was the fact that the crimes gave the prisoner something concrete to which to attach the free-floating guilt which the accusing environment and his own humiliation usually stimulated.

. . . A good example was the plight of the sick and wounded prisoners of war who, because of their physical confinement, were unable to escape from continual conflict with their interrogator or instructor, and who therefore often ended up forming a close relationship with him. Chinese Communist instructors often encouraged prisoners to take long walks or have informal talks with them and offered as incentives cigarettes, tea, and other rewards. If the prisoner was willing to cooperate and become a "progressive," he could join with other "progressives" in an active group life.

Within the political prison, the group cell not only provided the forces toward alienation but also offered the road to a "new self." Not only were there available among the fellow prisoners individuals with whom the prisoner could identify because of their shared plight, but once he showed any tendency to seek a new identity by truly trying to reevaluate his past, he received again a whole range of rewards, of which perhaps the most important was the interpersonal information that he was again a person worthy of respect and regard.

Source: Schein, 1960.

Discussion Questions

1. To what extent is the self-concept a product of situational factors or inherited factors?

2. What is the relationship between self-knowledge and social pressure?

3. Is self-awareness constant, or do people become more and less self-aware over time?

4. What mechanisms could have been used by prisoners of war to resist the destruction of their self-concepts?

5. What could have been done to facilitate the reform of the self-concepts of prisoners? What can be done to enhance an already-positive self-concept?

Decision Dilemmas

For each of the five scenarios below, select the choice you would make if you were in the situation.

1. A young manager in a high technology firm was offered a position by the firm's chief competitor for almost double her salary. Her firm sought to prevent her from changing jobs, arguing that her knowledge of certain specialized manufacturing processes would give the competitor unfair advantage. Since she had acquired that knowledge through special training and unique opportunities in her current position, the firm argued that it was unethical for her to accept the competitor's offer. What should the young manager do?

_____ Accept the offer

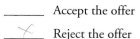 Reject the offer

2. A consumer advocate organization conducted a survey to determine whether Wendy's hamburgers were really any more "hot and juicy" than any other hamburgers. After testing a Big Mac, a Whopper, a Teen Burger, and a Wendy's Hot and Juicy, each hamburger brand received approximately the same number of votes for being the juiciest. The consumer group advocated that Wendy's not advertise its hamburgers to be the juiciest. The

company indicated that its own tests showed different results and that the image of the burger was the important thing, not the test results. Should the advertisements cease or not?

_____ Cease to advertise

___X___ Continue to advertise

3.   After several profitable years, the Bob Cummings Organic Vitamin Company was made available for sale. Bob's movie and TV appearances precluded him from keeping track of a large company, and it became apparent that, if present trends continued, the company would either have to expand substantially or lose a large share of the market. Several firms were interested in purchasing the company for the asking price, but one firm was particularly aggressive. It sponsored several parties and receptions in Bob's honor; a 35-foot yacht was made available for his use during the summer; and several gifts for family members arrived during the holidays. Bob's wife questioned the propriety of these activities. Was it appropriate for Bob to accept the gifts? Should he sell to that firm?

_____ Proper to accept

___X___ Not proper

___X___ Should not sell

_____ Should sell

4. John Waller was hired to coach football. After two seasons, he was so successful that he was named coach of the year by UPI, *Sporting News,* and ESPN. He was also very vocal about the need to clean up cheating in college athletics, especially among competitor schools in his own conference. He heard rumors about inappropriate alumni gifts to some of his own athletes, but after confronting those involved, he received assurances that the rumors weren't true. At the beginning of the next season, however, he received conclusive evidence that seven of the starters on his team, including an All-American, had received financial benefits from a wealthy booster. What should Waller do?

___X___ Kick them off the team

_____ Suspend them for several games

_____ Warn them but do nothing

5. Roger's company had been battered by competition from Asian firms. Not only were Asian products selling for less money, but their quality was substantially higher. By investing in some high technology equipment and fostering better union-management relations, Roger was relatively certain that the quality gap could be overcome. But his overhead rate was more than 40 percent above that of the competitor firms. He reasoned that the most efficient way to lower costs would be to close one of his older plants, lay off the employees, and increase production in the newer plants. He knew just which plant would be the one to close. The trouble was, the community was dependent on that plant as its major employer and had recently invested a great deal of money for highway repair and streetlight construction around the plant. Most of the work force were older people who had lived in the area most of their lives. It was improbable that they could obtain alternative employment in the same area. Should Roger close the plant or not?

_____ Close the plant

___X___ Do not close

Discussion Questions

Form a small group and discuss the following questions regarding these five scenarios:

1. Why did you make the choices you did in each case? Justify each answer.

2. What principles or basic values for decision making did you use in each case?

3. What additional information would you need in order to be certain about your choices?

4. What circumstances might arise to make you change your mind about your decision? Could there be a different answer to each case in a different circumstance?

5. What do your answers tell you about your own values, cognitive style, attitude toward change, and interpersonal orientation?

Skill Practice

Exercises for Improving Self-Awareness Through Self-Disclosure

Through the Looking Glass

In the 19th century, the concept of "looking-glass self" was developed to describe the process used by people to develop self-awareness. It means simply that other people serve as a "looking-glass" for each of us. They mirror back our actions and behaviors. In turn, we form our opinions of ourselves as a result of observing and interpreting this mirroring. The best way to form accurate self-perceptions, therefore, is to share your thoughts, attitudes, feelings, actions, and plans with others. This exercise helps you do that by asking you to analyze your own styles and inclinations and then share and discuss them with others. They may provide insights that you haven't recognized before.

Assignment

In a group of two or three, share your scores on the Skill Assessment instruments. Determine what similarities and differences exist among you. Do systematic ethnic or gender differences exist? Now read aloud the 11 statements listed below. Each person should complete each statement, but take turns going first. The purpose of your completing the statements aloud is to help you articulate aspects of your self-awareness and to receive reactions to them from others.

1. In taking the assessment instruments, I was surprised by . . .

2. Some of my dominant characteristics captured by the instruments are . . .

3. Among my greatest strengths are . . .

4. Among my greatest weaknesses are . . .

5. The time I felt most successful was . . .

6. The time I felt least competent was . . .

7. My three highest priorities in life are . . .

8. The way in which I differ most from other people is . . .

9. I get along best with people who . . .

10. The best analogy that captures how I think of myself is . . .

11. From what you've said, I have noticed about you . . .

Exercise for Identifying Aspects of Personal Culture

Family Lineage and Autobiography

Not only do our experiences and interactions affect our self-concept, but each person enters this world with certain inclinations and talents, sometimes called "temperament" by psychologists. This temperament may be developed both socially by our close family interactions and as a result of genetic factors. This exercise helps you identify and analyze the major family influences that may have had an important impact on your values, attitudes, styles, and personality. Not only is each person's physiology different, but each person's family culture varies as well. This exercise can help you highlight important aspects of your family culture.

The outcome of this exercise will be a written autobiography. In order to help you prepare such a document, the following four steps should be completed. Then use the results to construct an autobiography.

Step 1: On the chart in Figure 5, plot the points in each area of self-awareness that correspond to where you would like to have scored. The vertical axis in the figure ranges from Very Satisfied to Very Unsatisfied. Your plots will represent your level of satisfaction with the scores you received on each instrument. For example, if you are satisfied with the score on the Defining Issues Test, make a mark near the top for 1. If you are dissatisfied with your score on FIRO-B, make a mark near the bottom on 5. Connect each point so you have a "self-awareness satisfaction profile."

Step 2: On the chart in Figure 6, draw your lifeline, plotting the major activities and events of your life. The vertical axis represents the importance or significance of events in terms of their impact on who you are today and how you think. The horizontal axis represents time in years. Your line should identify times that had major impact on forming your values, styles, and orientations. Label each of these "peak" experiences on your lifeline.

Step 3: On the chart in Figure 7, complete as much of your family tree as you can. Below each name, identify the major traits you associate with the person and the major way in which the person influenced your life. Then identify the way in which your family differs from other families you know.

Step 4: Now combine all the information you have generated in steps 1 through 3 and write an autobiography, which is essentially an answer to the question, "Who am I?" Include in the autobiography your answers to the five questions on page 79. Your analysis should include more than just the answers to these questions, but be sure to include them.

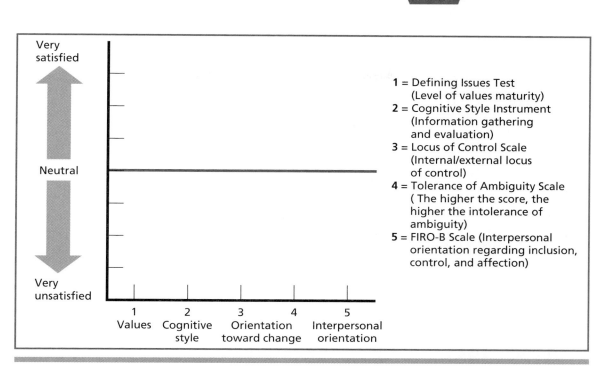

Figure 5   Satisfaction with Self-Awareness Scores

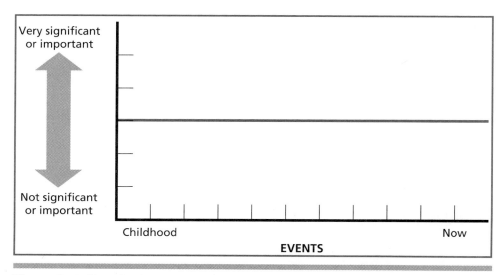

Figure 6   Lifeline of Peak Experiences

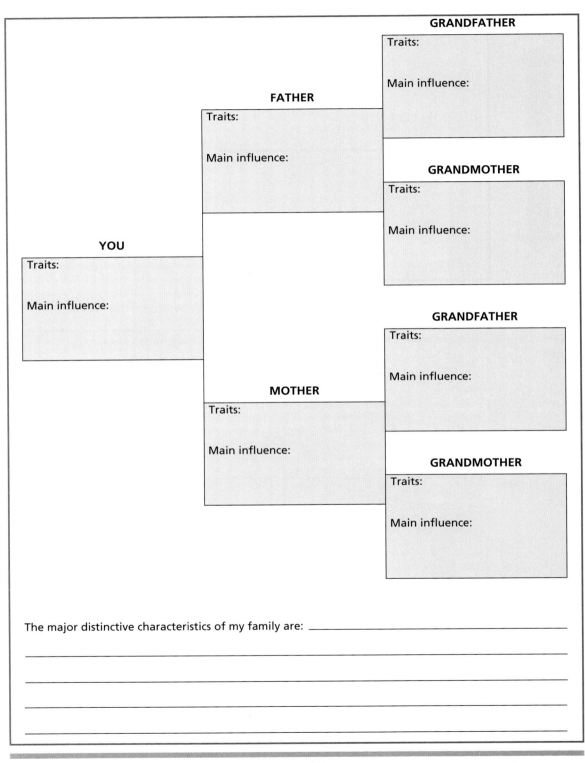

GRANDFATHER
Traits:

Main influence:

FATHER
Traits:

Main influence:

GRANDMOTHER
Traits:

Main influence:

YOU
Traits:

Main influence:

GRANDFATHER
Traits:

Main influence:

MOTHER
Traits:

Main influence:

GRANDMOTHER
Traits:

Main influence:

The major distinctive characteristics of my family are: _____

_____

_____

_____

_____

Figure 7   Family Genealogy with Important Influences Identified

Assignment

1. How would you describe your personal style?

2. What are your main strengths and weaknesses?

3. What behavioral principles lie at the center of your life?

4. What do you want to achieve in the next five years?

5. What legacy do you want to leave?

Skill Application

Activities for Developing Self-Awareness

Suggested Assignments

1. Keep a journal for at least the remainder of this course. Record significant discoveries, insights, learnings, and personal recollections, not just daily activities. Write in your journal at least twice a week. Give yourself some feedback.

2. Write down the comprehensive, consistent, and universal principles that guide your behavior under all circumstances and that you will rarely violate.

3. After completing these personal assessment instruments and discussing their implications with someone else, write a statement or an essay responding to the following four questions: (1) Who am I? (2) What are my main strengths and weaknesses? (3) What do I want to achieve in my life? (4) What legacy do I want to leave?

4. Spend an evening with a close friend or relative discussing your values, cognitive style, attitude toward change, and interpersonal orientation. You may want to have that person complete the instruments, giving his or her impressions of you, so you can compare and contrast your scores. Discuss implications for your future and for your relationship.

5. Teach someone else the value of self-awareness in managerial success and explain the relevance of values maturity, cognitive style, attitudes toward change, and interpersonal orientation. Describe the experience in your journal.

Application Plan and Evaluation

The intent of this exercise is to help you apply this cluster of skills in a real-life, out-of-class setting. Now that you have become familiar with the behavioral guidelines that form the basis of effective skill performance, you will improve most by trying out those guidelines in an everyday context. Unlike a classroom activity, in which feedback is immediate and others can assist you with their evaluations, this skill application activity is one you must accomplish and evaluate on your own. There are two parts to this activity. Part 1 helps prepare you to apply the skill. Part 2 helps you evaluate and improve on your experience. Be sure to write down answers to each item. Don't short-circuit the process by skipping steps.

Part 1. Planning

1. Write down the two or three aspects of this skill that are most important to you. These may be areas of weakness, areas you most want to improve, or areas that are most salient to a problem you face right now. Identify the specific aspects of this skill that you want to apply.

2. Now identify the setting or the situation in which you will apply this skill. Establish a plan for performance by actually writing down a description of the situation. Who else will be involved? When will you do it? Where will it be done?

   Circumstances:

   Who else?

   When?

   Where?

3. Identify the specific behaviors you will engage in to apply this skill. Operationalize your skill performance?

4. What are the indicators of successful performance? How will you know you have been effective? What will indicate you have performed competently?

Part 2. Evaluation

5. After you have completed your implementation, record the results. What happened? How successful were you? What was the effect on others?

6. How can you improve? What modifications can you make next time? What will you do differently in a similar situation in the future?

7. Looking back on your whole skill practice and application experience, what have you learned? What has been surprising? In what ways might this experience help you in the long term?

Managing Stress

skill development

Skill Assessment

Diagnostic Surveys for Managing Stress

Stress Management

Step 1: Before you read the material in this chapter, please respond to the following statements by writing a number from the rating scale below in the left-hand column (Preassessment). Your answers should reflect your attitudes and behavior as they are now, not as you would like them to be. Be honest. This instrument is designed to help you discover your level of competency in stress management so you can tailor your learning to your specific needs. When you have completed the survey, use the scoring key in Appendix I to identify the skill areas discussed in this chapter that are most important for you to master.

Step 2: After you have completed the reading and the exercises in this chapter and, ideally, as many as you can of the Skill Application assignments at the end of this chapter, cover up your first set of answers. Then respond to the same statements again, this time in the right-hand column (Postassessment). When you have completed the survey, use the scoring key in Appendix I to measure your progress. If your score remains low in specific skill areas, use the behavioral guidelines at the end of the Skill Learning section to guide further practice.

Rating Scale

1	Strongly disagree	4	Slightly agree
2	Disagree	5	Agree
3	Slightly disagree	6	Strongly agree

Assessment

Pre-   Post-   *When faced with stressful or time-pressured situations:*

_____ _____ 1. I use effective time-management methods such as keeping track of my time, making to-do lists, and prioritizing tasks.

_____ _____ 2. I maintain a program of regular exercise for fitness.

_____ _____ 3. I maintain an open, trusting relationship with someone with whom I can share my frustrations.

_____ _____ 4. I know and practice several temporary relaxation techniques such as deep breathing and muscle relaxation.

_____ _____ 5. I frequently affirm my priorities so that less important things don't drive out more important things.

_____ _____ 6. I maintain balance in my life by pursuing a variety of interests outside of work.

_____ _____ 7. I have a close relationship with someone who serves as my mentor or advisor.

_____ _____ 8. I effectively utilize others in accomplishing work assignments.

_____ _____ 9. I encourage others to generate recommended solutions, not just questions, when they come to me with problems or issues.

_____ _____ 10. I strive to redefine problems as opportunities for improvement.

Time Management

In responding to the statements below, fill in each blank with the number from the rating scale that indicates the frequency with which you do each activity. Assess your behavior as it is, not as you would like it to be. How useful this instrument will be to you depends on your ability to accurately assess your own behavior.

The first section of the instrument can be completed by anyone. The second section applies primarily to individuals currently serving in a managerial position.

Turn to Appendix I to find the scoring key and an interpretation of your scores.

Rating Scale

0	Never	3	Usually
1	Seldom	4	Always
2	Sometimes		

Section I

_____ 1. I read selectively, skimming the material until I find what is important, then highlighting it.

_____ 2. I make a list of tasks to accomplish each day.

_____ 3. I keep everything in its proper place at work.

_____ 4. I prioritize the tasks I have to do according to their importance and urgency.

_____ 5. I concentrate on only one important task at a time, but I do multiple trivial tasks at once (such as signing letters while talking on the phone).

_____ 6. I make a list of short five- or ten-minute tasks to do.

_____ 7. I divide large projects into smaller, separate stages.

_____ 8. I identify which 20 percent of my tasks will produce 80 percent of the results.

_____ 9. I do the most important tasks at my best time during the day.

_____ 10. I have some time during each day when I can work uninterrupted.

_____ 11. I don't procrastinate. I do today what needs to be done.

_____ 12. I keep track of the use of my time with devices such as a time log.

_____ 13. I set deadlines for myself.

_____ 14. I do something productive whenever I am waiting.

_____ 15. I do redundant "busy work" at one set time during the day.

_____	16.	I finish at least one thing every day.
_____	17.	I schedule some time during the day for personal time alone (for planning, meditation, prayer, exercise).
_____	18.	I allow myself to worry about things only at one particular time during the day, not all the time.
_____	19.	I have clearly defined long-term objectives toward which I am working.
_____	20.	I continually try to find little ways to use my time more efficiently.

Section II

_____	1.	I hold routine meetings at the end of the day.
_____	2.	I hold all short meetings standing up.
_____	3.	I set a time limit at the outset of each meeting.
_____	4.	I cancel scheduled meetings that are not necessary.
_____	5.	I have a written agenda for every meeting.
_____	6.	I stick to the agenda and reach closure on each item.
_____	7.	I ensure that someone is assigned to take minutes and to watch the time in every meeting.
_____	8.	I start all meetings on time.
_____	9.	I have minutes of meetings prepared promptly after the meeting and see that follow-up occurs promptly.
_____	10.	When subordinates come to me with a problem, I ask them to suggest solutions.
_____	11.	I meet visitors to my office outside the office or in the doorway.
_____	12.	I go to subordinates' offices when feasible so that I can control when I leave.
_____	13.	I leave at least one-fourth of my day free from meetings and appointments I can't control.
_____	14.	I have someone else who can answer my calls and greet visitors at least some of the time.
_____	15.	I have one place where I can work uninterrupted.
_____	16.	I do something definite with every piece of paper I handle.
_____	17.	I keep my workplace clear of all materials except those I am working on.
_____	18.	I delegate tasks.
_____	19.	I specify the amount of personal initiative I want others to take when I assign them a task.
_____	20.	I am willing that others get the credit for tasks they accomplish.

Type A Personality Inventory

Rate the extent to which each of the following statements is typical of you most of the time. Focus on your general way of behaving and feeling. There are no right or wrong answers.

When you have finished, turn to Appendix I to find the scoring key and an interpretation of your scores.

Rating Scale

    3   The statement is very typical of me.

    2   The statement is somewhat typical of me.

    1   The statement is not at all typical of me.

_____   1.   My greatest satisfaction comes from doing things better than others.

_____   2.   I tend to bring the theme of a conversation around to things I'm interested in.

_____   3.   In conversations, I frequently clench my fist, bang on the table, or pound one fist into the palm of another for emphasis.

_____   4.   I move, walk, and eat rapidly.

_____   5.   I feel as though I can accomplish more than others.

_____   6.   I feel guilty when I relax or do nothing for several hours or days.

_____   7.   It doesn't take much to get me to argue.

_____   8.   I feel impatient with the rate at which most events take place.

_____   9.   Having more than others is important to me.

_____   10.   One aspect of my life (e.g., work, family care, school) dominates all others.

_____   11.   I frequently regret not being able to control my temper.

_____   12.   I hurry the speech of others by saying "Uh huh," "Yes, yes," or by finishing their sentences for them.

_____   13.   People who avoid competition have low self-confidence.

_____   14.   To do something well, you have to concentrate on it alone and screen out all distractions.

_____   15.   I feel others' mistakes and errors cause me needless aggravation.

_____   16.   I find it intolerable to watch others perform tasks I know I can do faster.

_____   17.   Getting ahead in my job is a major personal goal.

_____   18.   I simply don't have enough time to lead a well-balanced life.

_____   19.   I take out my frustration with my own imperfections on others.

_____   20.   I frequently try to do two or more things simultaneously.

_____   21.   When I encounter a competitive person, I feel a need to challenge him or her.

_____   22.   I tend to fill up my spare time with thoughts and activities related to my work (or school or family care).

_____   23.   I am frequently upset by the unfairness of life.

_____   24.   I find it anguishing to wait in line.

Source: Friedman and Rosenman, 1974.

Social Readjustment Rating Scale

Circle any of the following you have experienced in the past year. Using the weightings at the left, total up your score.

Mean Value	Life Event	
100	1.	Death of spouse
73	2.	Divorce
65	3.	Marital separation from mate
63	4.	Detention in jail or other institution
63	5.	Death of a close family member
53	6.	Major personal injury or illness
50	7.	Marriage
47	8.	Being fired
45	9.	Marital reconciliation with mate
45	10.	Retirement from work
44	11.	Major change in the health or behavior of a family member
40	12.	Pregnancy
39	13.	Sexual difficulties
39	14.	Gaining a new family member (e.g., birth, adoption, relative moving in, etc.)
39	15.	Major business readjustment (e.g., merger, reorganization, bankruptcy, etc.)
38	16.	Major change in financial state (e.g., a lot worse off or a lot better off than usual)
37	17.	Death of a close friend
36	18.	Change to a different line of work
35	19.	Major change in the number of arguments with spouse (e.g., either a lot more or a lot less than usual regarding childbearing, personal habits, etc.)
31	20.	Taking out a mortgage or loan for a major purchase (e.g., for a home, business, etc.)
30	21.	Foreclosure on a mortgage or loan
29	22.	Major change in responsibilities at work (e.g., promotion, demotion, lateral transfer)
29	23.	Son or daughter leaving home (e.g., marriage, attending college, etc.)
29	24.	Trouble with in-laws
28	25.	Outstanding personal achievement
26	26.	Spouse beginning or ceasing work outside the home
26	27.	Beginning or ending formal schooling
25	28.	Major change in living conditions (e.g., building a new home, remodeling, deterioration of home or neighborhood)
24	29.	Revision of personal habits (dress, manners, association, etc.)
23	30.	Troubles with the boss
20	31.	Major change in working hours or conditions
20	32.	Change in residence
20	33.	Change to a new school
19	34.	Major change in usual type or amount of recreation
19	35.	Major change in outside activities (e.g., a lot more or a lot less than usual)
18	36.	Major change in social activities (e.g., clubs, dancing, movies, visiting, etc.)

17	37.	Taking out a mortgage or loan for a lesser purchase (e.g., for a car, TV, freezer, etc.)
16	38.	Major change in sleeping habits (a lot more or a lot less sleep, or change in part of day when asleep)
15	39.	Major change in number of family get-togethers (e.g., a lot more or a lot less than usual)
15	40.	Major change in eating habits (a lot more or a lot less food intake, or very different meal hours or surroundings)
13	41.	Vacation
12	42.	Christmas
11	43.	Minor violations of the law (e.g., traffic tickets, jaywalking, disturbing the peace)

Total of Circled Items:

Source: Holmes and Rahe, 1967.

Sources of Personal Stress

1. Identify the factors that produce the most stress for you right now. What is it that creates feelings of stress in your life?

   Source of Stress   **Rating**

2. Now give each of those stressors above a rating from 1 to 100 on the basis of how powerful each is in producing stress. Refer to the Social Readjustment Rating Scale for relative weightings of stressors. A rating of 100, for example, might be associated with the death of a spouse or child, while a rating of 10 might be associated with the overly slow driver in front of you.

3. Use these specific sources of stress as targets as you discuss and practice the stress management principles presented in the rest of the chapter.

Skill Learning

Improving the Management of Stress and Time

The National Institute for Occupational Safety and the American Psychological Association estimate that the growing problem of stress on the job siphons off more than $500 billion from the nation's economy. In California alone, workers' compensation claims for mental stress increased more than 700 percent during the 1980s. In a nationwide survey by Northwestern National Life (1992), 4 in 10 American workers rated their job as very or extremely stressful. Fifty percent said that job stress reduced their productivity, and 46 percent said that they experience more job stress now than they did a few years ago. Those who report high levels of stress were three times more likely than workers with low stress to suffer from frequent illnesses. Minor illnesses such as headaches, backaches, anxiety, and fatigue, as well as major illnesses such as heart attacks, ulcers, high blood pressure, and strokes are far more frequent in people who experience high levels of stress than in those who don't. Stress-related illnesses cost American industry 132 million workdays of lost production each year.

As an illustration of the debilitating effects of job-related stress, consider the following story reported by the Associated Press.

> **Baltimore (AP)** The job was getting to the ambulance attendant. He felt disturbed by the recurring tragedy, isolated by the long shifts. His marriage was in trouble. He was drinking too much.
>
> One night it all blew up.
>
> He rode in back that night. His partner drove. Their first call was for a man whose leg had been cut off by a train. His screaming and agony were horrifying, but the second call was worse. It was a child beating. As the attendant treated the youngster's bruised body and snapped bones, he thought of his own child. His fury grew.
>
> Immediately after leaving the child at the hospital, the attendants were sent out to help a heart attack victim seen lying in a street. When they arrived, however, they found not a cardiac patient but a drunk—a wino passed out. As they lifted the man into the ambulance, their frustration and anger came to a head. They decided to give the wino a ride he would remember.
>
> The ambulance vaulted over railroad tracks at high speed. The driver took the corners as fast as he could, flinging the wino from side to side in the back. To the attendants, it was a joke.
>
> Suddenly, the wino began having a real heart attack. The attendant in back leaned over the wino and started shouting. "Die, you sucker!" he yelled. "Die!"
>
> He watched as the wino shuddered. He watched as the wino died. By the time they reached the hospital, they had their stories straight. Dead on arrival, they said. Nothing they could do.
>
> The attendant, who must remain anonymous, talked about that night at a recent counseling session on "professional burnout"—a growing problem in high-stress jobs.

As this story graphically illustrates, stress can produce devastating effects. Personal consequences can range from inability to concentrate, anxiety, and depression to stomach disorders, low resistance to illness, and heart disease. For organizations, consequences range from absenteeism and job dissatisfaction to high accident and turnover rates.

The Role of Management

Amazingly, a 25-year study of employee surveys revealed that incompetent management is the largest cause of workplace stress! Three out of four surveys listed employee relationships with immediate supervisors as the worst aspect of the job (Snider, 1990). Moreover, research in psychology has found that stress not only affects workers negatively, but it also produces less visible (though equally detrimental) consequences for managers themselves. For example, when managers experience stress, they tend to:

▶ selectively perceive information and see only that which confirms their previous biases

- become very intolerant of ambiguity and demanding of right answers

- fixate on a single approach to a problem

- overestimate how fast time is passing (hence, they often feel rushed)

- adopt a short-term perspective or crisis mentality and cease to consider long-term implications

- have less ability to make fine distinctions in problems, so that complexity and nuances are missed

- consult and listen to others less

- rely on old habits to cope with current situations

- have less ability to generate creative thoughts and unique solutions to problems (Staw, Sandelands, & Dutton, 1981; Weick, 1993).

Thus, not only do the results of stress negatively affect employees in the workplace, but they also drastically impede effective management behaviors—for example, listening, making good decisions, solving problems effectively, planning, and generating new ideas. Developing the skill of managing stress, therefore, can have significant payoffs. The ability to deal appropriately with stress not only enhances individual self-development but can also have an enormous bottom-line impact on entire organizations.

Unfortunately, most of the scientific literature on stress focuses on its consequences. Too little examines how to cope effectively with stress, and even less addresses how to prevent stress. We begin our discussion by presenting a framework for understanding stress and learning how to cope with it. This model explains the major types of stressors faced by managers, the primary reactions to stress, and the reasons some people experience more negative reactions than others do. The last section presents principles for managing and adapting to stress, along with specific examples and behavioral guidelines.

Major Elements of Stress

One way to understand the dynamics of stress is to think of it as the product of a "force field" (Lewin, 1951). Kurt Lewin suggested that all individuals and organizations exist in an environment filled with reinforcing or opposing forces (i.e., stresses). These forces act to stimulate or inhibit the performance desired by the individual. As illustrated in Figure 1, a person's level of performance in an organization results from factors that may either complement or contradict one another. Certain forces drive or motivate changes in behavior, while other forces restrain or block those changes.

According to Lewin's theory, the forces affecting individuals are normally balanced in the force field. The strength of the driving forces is exactly matched by the strength of the restraining forces. (In the figure, longer arrows indicate stronger forces.) Performance changes when the forces become imbalanced. That is, if the driving forces become stronger than the restraining forces,

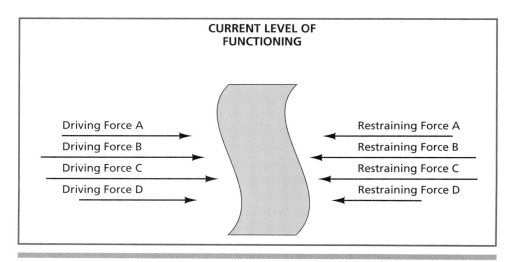

Figure 1   Model of Force Field Analysis

or more numerous or enduring, change occurs. Conversely, if restraining forces become stronger or more numerous than driving forces, change occurs in the opposite direction.

Feelings of stress are a product of certain stressors inside or outside the individual. These stressors can be thought of as driving forces in the model. That is, they exert pressure on the individual to change present levels of performance physiologically, psychologically, and interpersonally. Unrestrained, those forces can lead to pathological results (e.g., anxiety, heart disease, and mental breakdown). However, most people have developed a certain amount of resiliency or restraining forces to counter stressors and inhibit pathological results. These restraining forces include behavior patterns, psychological characteristics, and supportive social relationships. Strong restraining forces lead to low heart rates, good interpersonal relationships, emotional stability, and effective stress management. An absence of restraining forces leads to the reverse.

Of course, stress produces positive as well as negative effects. In the absence of any stress, people feel completely bored and lack any inclination to act. Even when high levels of stress are experienced, equilibrium can be restored quickly if there is sufficient resiliency. In the case of the ambulance driver, for example, multiple stressors overpowered the available restraining forces and burnout occurred. Before reaching such an extreme state, however, individuals typically progress through three stages of reactions: an *alarm* stage, a *resistance* stage, and an *exhaustion* stage.

Reactions to Stress

The **alarm** stage is characterized by acute increases in anxiety or fear if the stressor is a threat or by increases in sorrow or depression if the stressor is a loss. A feeling of shock or confusion may result if the stressor is particularly acute. Physiologically, the individual's energy resources are mobilized and heart rate, blood pressure, and alertness increase. These reactions are largely self-correcting if the stressor is of brief duration. However, if it continues, the individual enters the **resistance** stage, in which defense mechanisms predominate and the body begins to store up excess energy.

Five types of defense mechanisms are typical of most people who experience extended levels of stress. The first is *aggression,* which involves attacking the stressor directly. It may also involve attacking oneself, other people, or even objects (e.g., whacking the computer). A second is *regression,* which is the adoption of a behavior pattern or response that was successful at some earlier time (e.g., responding in childish ways). A third defense mechanism, *repression,* involves denial of the stressor, forgetting, or redefining the stressor (e.g., deciding that it isn't so scary after all). *Withdrawal* is a fourth defense mechanism, and it may take both psychological and physical forms. Individuals may engage in fantasy, inattention, or purposive forgetting, or they may actually escape from the situation itself. A fifth defense mechanism is *fixation,* which is persisting in a response regardless of its effectiveness (e.g., repeatedly and rapidly redialing a telephone number when it is busy).

If these defense mechanisms reduce a person's feeling of stress, negative effects such as high blood pressure, anxiety, or mental disorders are never experienced. The primary evidence that prolonged stress has occurred may simply be an increase in psychological defensiveness. However, when stress is so pronounced as to overwhelm defenses or so enduring as to outlast available energy for defensiveness, **exhaustion** may result, producing pathological consequences.

While each reaction stage may be experienced as temporarily uncomfortable, the exhaustion stage is the most dangerous one. When stressors overpower or outlast the resiliency capacities of individuals, or their ability to defend against them, chronic stress is experienced and negative personal and organizational consequences generally follow. Such pathological consequences may be manifest physiologically (e.g., heart disease), psychologically (e.g., severe depression), or interpersonally (e.g., dissolution of relationships). These changes result from the damage done to an individual for which there was no defense (e.g., psychotic reactions among prisoners of war), from an inability to defend continuously against a stressor (e.g., becoming exhausted), from an overreaction (e.g., an ulcer produced by excessive secretion of body chemicals), or from lack of self-awareness so that stress is completely unacknowledged.

Figure 2 identifies the major categories of stressors (driving forces) that managers experience, as well as the major attributes of resiliency (restraining forces) that inhibit the negative effects of stress. Each of these forces is discussed in some detail in this chapter, so that it will become clear how to identify stressors, how to eliminate them, how to develop more resiliency, and how to cope with stress on a temporary basis.

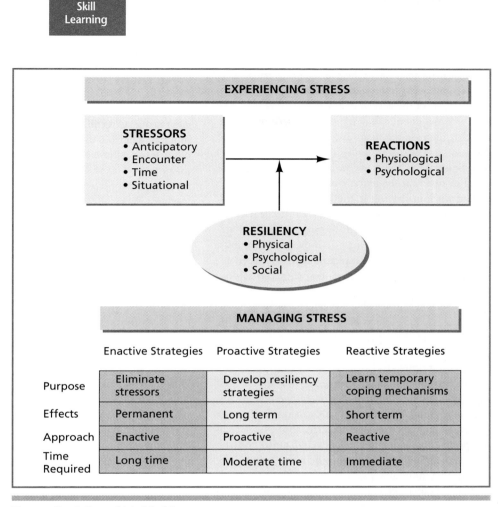

Figure 2 A General Model of Stress

Coping with Stress

Individuals vary in the extent to which stressors lead to pathologies and dysfunctions. Some people are what Eliot and Breo (1984) labeled "hot reactors," meaning they have a predisposition to experience extremely negative reactions to stress. For others, stress is experienced more favorably. Their physical condition, personality characteristics, and social support mechanisms mediate the effects of stress and produce resiliency, or the capacity to cope effectively with stress. In effect, resiliency serves as a form of inoculation against the effects of stress. It eliminates exhaustion. This helps explain why some athletes do better in "the big game," while others do worse. Some managers appear to be brilliant strategists when the stakes are high; others fold under the pressure.

In managing stress, using a particular hierarchy of approaches has been found to be most effective. First, the best way to manage stress is to eliminate or minimize stressors with **enactive strategies**. These create, or enact, a new environment for the individual that does not contain the stressors (Weick, 1979). The second most effective approach is for individuals to enhance their overall capacity to handle stress by increasing their personal resiliency. These are called **proactive strategies** and are designed to initiate action that resists the negative effects of stress. Finally, developing short-term techniques for coping with stressors is necessary when an immediate response is required. These are **reactive strategies**; they are applied as on-the-spot remedies to reduce temporarily the effects of stress.

To understand why the above hierarchy of stress management techniques is recommended, consider the following analogy. When the human body experiences a stressor, it reacts like an automobile engine when the driver steps on the accelerator pedal: It "revs up." The body releases chemicals, such as adrenaline and cortisol, that increase the heart and breathing rates, blood flow, energy level, and so on. A continual or repetitive revving up of the body's engine can have the same damaging or toxic consequences over time as racing a car's engine without driving it anywhere. Burnout occurs. Individuals are better off if they can eliminate harmful stressors and the potentially negative effects of frequent, potent stress reactions. However, because most individuals do not have complete control over their environments or their circumstances, they can seldom eliminate all harmful stressors. Their next-best alternative, therefore, is to develop a greater capacity to withstand the negative effects of stress and to mobilize the energy generated by stressors. Developing personal resiliency that helps the body return to normal levels of activity more quickly—or that directs the "revved up engine" in a productive direction—is the next best strategy to eliminating the stressors altogether. Finally, on a temporary basis, individuals can respond to the revved-up state by using constructive strategies such as temporary relaxation techniques and mind control. Such techniques are designed to help the "engine" return to idle more quickly, at least for a short time.

Unfortunately, most people reverse the order of coping strategies presented above—that is, they rely first on temporary reactive methods to cope with stress because these actions can be implemented immediately. But reactive strategies also have to be repeated whenever stressors are encountered because their effects are short-lived. Moreover, some common reactive strategies, such as drinking, taking sleeping pills, or letting off steam through anger, can become habit-forming and harmful in themselves. Without more long-term strategies, relying on repetitive reactive strategies can create a vicious circle.

It takes more effort to develop proactive resiliency strategies, but the effects are more long-lasting. However, resiliency strategies can take time to implement; hence, the payoff, while substantial, is not immediate. The best and most permanent strategies are those that eliminate stressors altogether. They require the longest time to implement, and they may involve complex arrangements. But because stress is purged, the payoff is enduring.

Managing Stress

In the following sections, each of the three major strategies for managing stress is discussed in detail. Each section first describes the elements of the model and then discusses specific techniques for effectively managing that aspect of stress. Because elimination of stress is the most important stress management tool, we cover it in the most detail.

Stressors

Table 1 lists the four main types of stressors illustrated in the story of the ambulance driver. The first, **time stressors,** generally result from having too much to do in too little time. These are the most common and most pervasive sources of stress faced by managers in corporations (Mintzberg, 1973; Carlson, 1951; Sayles, 1964). One reason for time stressors is that our culture is extremely time conscious and continues to be even more so year by year. Fifteen years ago, when asked for the time, a person might have responded, "It's about 2:30." Now the response is more likely to be, "It's 2:28," or even, "It's 15 seconds before 2:28." The emphasis on time is also evidenced by the many ways we have of talking about time. We have time, keep time, buy time, save time, mark time, spend time, sell time, waste time, kill time, pass time, give time, take time, and make time.

TIME STRESSORS
- Work overload
- Lack of control

ENCOUNTER STRESSORS
- Role conflicts
- Issue conflicts
- Action conflicts

SITUATIONAL STRESSORS
- Unfavorable working conditions
- Rapid change

ANTICIPATORY STRESSORS
- Unpleasant expectations
- Fear

Table 1 Sources of Stress

This fascination with time makes it an important source of stress. A variety of researchers, for example, have studied the relationships between role overload and chronic time pressures, on the one hand, and psychological and physiological dysfunction on the other (French & Caplan, 1972; Kahn et al., 1964). They found significant relationships between the presence of time stressors and job dissatisfaction, tension, perceived threat, heart rate, cholesterol levels, skin resistance, and other factors.

In the story of the ambulance drivers presented earlier, time stressors were evidenced by the drivers' work overload—that is, they felt compelled to accomplish a large number of tasks in a short time and were not in control of the time available. When experienced on a daily basis, time stressors can be highly detrimental. The presence of temporary time stressors may serve as motivators for getting work done, and some individuals accomplish much more when faced with an immediate deadline than when left to work at their own pace. However, a constant state of time pressure—having too much to do and not enough time to do it—is usually harmful.

Encounter stressors are those that result from interpersonal interactions. Most people have experienced the debilitating effects of a quarrel with a friend, roommate, or spouse; of trying to work with an employee or supervisor with whom there has been an interpersonal conflict; or of trying to accomplish a task in a group that is divided by lack of trust and cohesion. Each of these stressors results from some kind of conflictual interpersonal encounter. Encounter stressors are especially common for managers. They generally arise from three types of conflicts: *role conflicts,* in which roles performed by group members are incompatible; *issue conflicts,* in which disagreement exists over how to define or solve a problem; and *interaction conflicts,* in which individuals fail to get along well because of mutual antagonism (Hamner & Organ, 1978).

Our own research has revealed that encounter stressors in organizations have significant negative effects on productivity and satisfaction (Cameron, 1994; Cameron & Whetten, 1987), and encounter stressors have been found by other researchers to be at the very heart of most organizational dysfunction (Likert, 1967; Schutz, 1958; Peters, 1988). Not surprisingly, encounter stressors more frequently affect managers with responsibility for people rather than equipment. The highest levels of encounter stress exist among managers who interact frequently with other people and have responsibility for individuals in the workplace (French & Caplan, 1972). Poor relationships with others cause particularly high levels of stress. Mishra (1993) reviewed literature on interpersonal trust, for example, and reported that lack of trust among individuals not only blocks quality communication, information sharing, decision competence, and problem-solving capabilities, but also results in high levels of personal stress.

In a national survey of workers by Northwest National Life (1992), encounter stressors were cited as a major cause of burnout. Table 2 summarizes the results of that study. When workers reported not feeling free to interact socially, experienced workplace conflict, didn't talk openly to managers, felt unsupported by fellow employees, were stifled by red tape, and did not feel recognized, burnout was significantly higher than when those encounter stressors were not present. Of the 10 most significant stressors associated with burnout, 7 dealt with encounter stressors. The other 3 were situational stressors, to which we turn next.

The third category of stressors, **situational stressors,** arise from the environment in which a person lives or from an individual's circumstances. One of the most common forms of situational stress is unfavorable working conditions. For the ambulance drivers, these would include continual crises, long hours, and isolation from colleagues. In addition, wide-reaching and increasingly rapid change also creates an increase in stress. Cameron and his colleagues (1987, 1991, 1994), for example, reported that a large majority of organizations in industrialized nations have downsized or restructured in the last five years. Their research identified an almost universal increase in situational stress as a result. The following quotation from one employee is illustrative:

My husband and I both work for a huge conglomerate. We are carrying workloads that used to be handled by three or four employees. We come home exhausted after putting in 12-hour days, drag ourselves behind lawn mowers and vacuum cleaners at 9:00 at night, miss our children's soccer games and school plays, and barely see each other. Because of today's business climate, we feel totally helpless to make a move. Nobody dares quit a job these days. It's too risky. But the stress is killing us.

WORK SITE CHARACTERISTICS	PERCENTAGE OF EMPLOYEES REPORTING BURNOUT
Employees are *not* free to talk with one another.	48%
Employees are free to talk with one another.	28%
Personal conflicts on the job are *common.*	46%
Personal conflicts on the job are rare.	22%
Employees are given *too little* control.	46%
Employees are given enough control.	25%
Staffing or expense budgets are *inadequate.*	45%
Staffing or expense budgets are adequate.	21%
Management and employees *do not* talk openly.	44%
Management and employees talk openly.	20%
Management is *unsupportive* of employees.	44%
Management is supportive of employees.	20%
Sick and vacation benefits are *below average.*	44%
Sick and vacation benefits are average or better.	26%
Employee benefits have been *reduced.*	42%
Employee benefits have been maintained.	24%
Dealing with red tape is *common.*	40%
Dealing with red tape is rare.	22%
Employees are *not* recognized and rewarded.	39%
Employees are recognized and rewarded.	20%

Table 2   Causes of Burnout

Data are from NWNL's 1992 research study, "Employee Burnout: Causes and Cures." Sample size: 1,299 private-sector employees in 37 organizations. Characteristics are ranked by the highest employee burnout level

Source: "Employee Burnout: Causes and Cures." Northwestern National Life Insurance Company, Minneapolis, MN, 1992, p. 6. Copyright © 1993 by Northwestern National Life Insurance Company. All rights reserved. No part of this information may be reproduced without the prior written permission of NWNL.

One of the most well-researched links between situational stressors and negative consequences involves rapid change, particularly the effects of changes in life events (Wolff, Wolf, & Hare, 1950; Holmes & Rahe, 1970). The *Social Readjustment Rating Scale (SRRS)* was introduced in 1967 to track the number of changes individuals had experienced over the past 12 months. Since changes in some events were thought to be more stressful than others, a scaling method was used to assign weights to each life event. Numerous studies among a variety of cultures, age groups, and occupations have confirmed the relative weightings in the 1967 instrument (see Rahe, Ryman, & Ward, 1980) which generally hold true regardless of culture, age, or occupation. You completed this instrument in the Assessment section.

Statistical relationships between the amount of life-event change and physical illness and injury have been found consistently among managers (Kobasa, 1979), sports figures (Holmes & Masuda, 1974), naval personnel (Rahe, 1974), and the general population (Jenkins, 1976). For example, scores of 150 points or below result in a probability of less than 37 percent that a serious illness will occur in the next year, but the probability increases to about 50 percent with scores of 150–300. Those who score over 300 on the SRRS have an 80 percent chance of serious illness (Holmes & Rahe, 1967).

Several studies have been conducted using college and high school football players to determine if life-event change is related to injury as well as to illness (Bramwell, Masuda, Wagner, & Holmes, 1975;

Coddington & Troxell, 1980). Bramwell and colleagues found that college players with the lowest scores on the SRRS had a rate of injury (they missed three or more practices) of 35 percent. Those with medium scores had an injury rate of 44 percent, and those with high scores were injured at the amazing rate of 72 percent. Coddington and Troxell's results showed an injury rate five times as great for high scorers on the SRRS as for low scorers among high school athletes. Holmes and Holmes (1970) studied the extent to which daily health changes occurred as a result of life-event changes. Rather than focusing on major illness or injuries, they recorded minor symptoms such as headache, nausea, fever, backache, eyestrain, and so forth over 1,300 workdays. The results revealed high correlations between scores in life-event changes and the chronic presence of these symptoms.

We must caution, of course, that scoring high on the SRRS does not necessarily mean a person is going to become ill or be injured. A variety of coping skills and personal characteristics, to be discussed later, may counteract those tendencies. The point to be made here is that situational stressors are important factors to consider in learning to manage stress skillfully.

Anticipatory stressors, the fourth category, includes potentially disagreeable events that threaten to occur—unpleasant things that have not yet happened, but might happen. Stress results from the anticipation or fear of the event. In the case of the ambulance drivers, the constant threat of anticipating having to witness one more incident of human suffering or death served as an anticipatory stressor. In organizations that experience rapid change, restructuring, or downsizing, anticipatory stressors are also pervasive. People fear that they will lose their jobs, they fear that their friends will be ousted from the company, they become anxious about new reporting and interpersonal relationships that result from restructuring, and they worry that the future will be unpredictable and frightful. Brockner and his colleagues (1993) documented the negative effects of layoffs and plant closings on survivors (those who kept their jobs), and a paramount problem they identified is the presence of anticipatory stressors.

In other contexts, American hostages in Iran and Beirut were heavily stressed by threats of death or punishment by their kidnapper guards. Schein (1960) reported that dramatic behavioral and psychological changes occurred in American prisoners in the Korean War. He identified anticipatory stressors (e.g., threat of

severe punishment) as major contributors to psychological and physiological pathology among the prisoners (see the Skill Analysis section of Chapter 1, Communist Prison Camp).

Anticipatory stressors need not be highly unpleasant or severe, however, to produce stress. Schachter (1959), Milgram (1963), and others induced high levels of stress by telling individuals that they would experience a loud noise or a mild shock or that someone else might become uncomfortable because of their actions. Fear of failure or fear of embarrassment in front of peers is a common anticipatory stressor. Anxieties about retirement and losing vitality during middle age have been identified by Levinson (1978), Hall (1976), and others as common stress producers as well.

Eliminating Stressors

Because eliminating stressors is a permanent stress reduction strategy, it is by far the most desirable. Although it is impossible, and even undesirable, for individuals to eliminate all the stressors they encounter, they can effectively eliminate those that are harmful. One way is to "enact" the environment rather than merely "react" to it (Weick, 1979). That is, individuals can actively work to create more favorable environmental circumstances in which to work and live. By so doing, they can rationally and systematically eliminate stressors. Table 3 outlines several ways to eliminate each of the four types of stressors.

TYPE OF STRESSOR	ELIMINATION STRATEGY
Time	Effective time management
	Efficient time management
	Delegating
Encounter	Collaboration and clan building
	Interpersonal competence
Situational	Work redesign
Anticipatory	Goal setting
	Small wins

Table 3 Management Strategies for Eliminating Stressors

Eliminating Time Stressors Through Time Management

As pointed out earlier, time stressors often are the greatest sources of stress for managers. Research by Mintzberg (1973) and Kotter (1987) showed, for example, that managers experience frequent interruptions (over 50 percent of their activities last nine minutes or less); they seldom engage in long-range planning; and fragmentation, brevity, and variety characterize their time use. On the average, no manager works more than 20 minutes at a time without interruption, and most of a manager's time is controlled by the most bothersome, persistent, and energetic people (Carlson, 1951). Guest (1956) found that an industrial foreman engages in between 237 and 1,073 separate incidents a day with no real breaks. Effective time management can enable managers to gain control over their time and organize their fragmented, chaotic environment.

Two different sets of skills are important for effectively managing time and for eliminating time stressors. One set focuses on *efficiently* using time each day. The other set focuses on *effectively* using time over the long term. Because the effectiveness approach to time management serves as the foundation for the efficiency approach, we explain it first. Then we review the tools and techniques for achieving efficiency in time use.

Effective Time Management

As pointed out above, overload and lack of control are the greatest sources of time stress for managers. In fact, one doesn't have to be a manager to feel overloaded and out of control. Almost everyone suffers now and then from a pervasive feeling of time stress. Somehow, no matter how much time is available, it seems to get filled up and squeezed out. Probably the most commonly prescribed solutions for attacking problems of time stress are to use calendars and planners, to generate to-do lists, and to learn to say no. But although almost everyone has tried such tactics, almost everyone still claims to be under enormous time stress. This is not to say that calendars, lists, and saying no are never useful. However, they are examples of an *efficiency* approach to time management rather than an *effectiveness* approach. In eliminating time stressors, efficiency without effectiveness is fruitless.

Managing time with an effectiveness approach means that (1) individuals spend their time on important matters, not just urgent matters; (2) people are able to distinguish clearly between what they view as important versus what they view as urgent; (3) results rather than methods are the focus of time management strategies; and (4) people have a reason not to feel guilty when they must say no.

A number of time management experts have pointed out the usefulness of a "time management matrix" in which activities are categorized in terms of their relative importance and urgency (Covey, 1989; Lakein, 1989). *Important* activities are those that produce a desired result. They accomplish a valued end, or they achieve a meaningful purpose. *Urgent* activities are those that demand immediate attention. They are associated with a need expressed by someone else, or they relate to an uncomfortable problem or situation that requires a solution as soon as possible. Figure 3 outlines this matrix and provides examples of types of activities that fit in each quadrant.

Activities such as handling employee crises or customer complaints are both urgent and important (Cell 1). A ringing telephone, the arrival of the mail, or unscheduled interruptions might be examples of urgent but potentially unimportant activities (Cell 2). Important but nonurgent activities include developmental opportunities, innovating, planning, and so on (Cell 3). Unimportant and nonurgent activities are escapes and routines that people may pursue but which produce little valuable payoff: for example, small talk, daydreaming, shuffling paper, and arguing (Cell 4).

Activities in the Important/Urgent quadrant (Cell 1) usually dominate the lives of managers. They are seen as "have to" activities that demand immediate attention. Attending a meeting, responding to a call or request, interacting with a customer, or completing a report might all legitimately be defined as Important/Urgent activities. The trouble with spending all one's time on activities in this quadrant, however, is that they all require the manager to react. They are usually controlled by someone else, and they may or may not lead to a result the manager wants to achieve.

The problem is even worse in the Unimportant/Urgent quadrant (Cell 2). Demands by others that may meet their needs but that serve only as deflections or interruptions to the manager's agenda only escalate a sense of time stress. Because they may not achieve re-

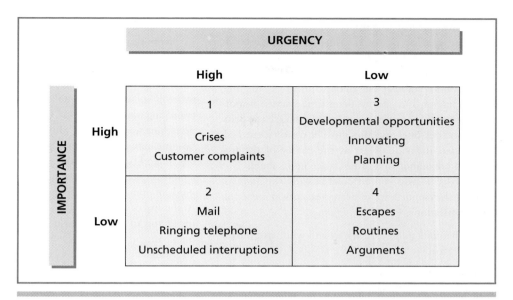

Figure 3 Types of Activities That Determine Time Use

sults that are meaningful, purposeful, and valued—that is, important—feelings of time stress will never be overcome. Experiencing overload and loss of control can be guaranteed. Managers are simply reactive.

Moreover, when these time stressors are experienced over an extended period of time, people generally try to escape into Nonimportant/Nonurgent activities (Cell 4) to relieve the stress. They escape, shut out the world, or put everything on hold. But although feelings of stress may be temporarily relieved, no long-term solutions are implemented, so time stress is never permanently reduced. That means lives are spent battling crises 95 percent of the time and escaping 5 percent of the time.

A better alternative is to focus on activities in the Important/Nonurgent quadrant (Cell 3). Activities that are Important/Nonurgent might be labeled opportunities instead of problems. They are oriented toward accomplishing high-priority results. They prevent problems from occurring or build processes that eliminate problems rather than just coping with them. Preparation, preventive maintenance, planning, building resiliency, and organizing are all "non-have-to" activities that are crucial for long-term success. Because they are not urgent, however, they often get driven out of managers' time schedules.

Important/Nonurgent activities should be the top priority on the time management agenda. By ensuring that these kinds of activities get priority, the urgent problems being encountered can be reduced. Time stressors can be eliminated.

One of the most difficult yet crucially important decisions one must make in managing time effectively is determining what is important and what is urgent. There are no rules for dividing all activities, demands, or opportunities into those neat categories. Problems don't come with an "Important/Nonurgent" tag attached. In fact, for someone, every problem or time demand may hold some degree of importance. But if managers let others determine what is and is not important, they will never effectively manage their time.

Barry Sullivan, CEO at First Chicago, for example, reorganized the way he manages his time. Instead of leaving his appointments calendar in the control of his secretary, he now decides what activities he wants to accomplish, then he allocates specific blocks of time to work on those activities. Only after he has made these determinations does he make his calendar available to his secretary to schedule other appointments.

The question still remains, however: How can people make certain that they focus on activities that are important, not just urgent? The answer is to identify clear and specific personal priorities. In Chapter 1, Developing Self-Awareness, we pointed out how important it is for people to be aware of their own core values and to establish a set of basic principles to guide their behavior. In order to determine what is important in time management, those core values, basic principles, and personal priorities must be clearly identified. Otherwise, individuals are at the mercy of the unremitting demands that others place upon them.

In order to help you articulate clearly the basis for judging the importance of activities, consider the following questions:

1. What do I stand for? What am I willing to die (or live) for?

2. What do I care passionately about?

3. What legacy would I like to leave? What do I want to be remembered for?

4. If I could persuade everyone in the world to follow a few basic principles, what would they be?

5. What do I want to have accomplished 20 years from now?

Answering these questions can help you create a personal principles statement. A personal principles statement is an articulation of the criteria you use for evaluating what is important. Other people generally help determine what is urgent. But judging importance must be done in relation to a set of personal principles and values. Table 4 presents two different types of personal principles statements. They are provided as examples of the kinds of principles statements you can write for yourself. At the end of the Developing Self-Awareness chapter, we urged you to take time to develop a statement of your own basic principles. These are the criteria upon which you judge activities to be important. Without such a statement, it is unlikely that you will be able to overcome the tyranny of urgent time demands.

Basing time management on core principles to judge the importance of activities is also the key to being able to say no without feeling guilty. When you have decided what it is that you care about passion-

FROM MAHATMA GHANDI	FROM WILLIAM ROLFE KERR
Let then our first act every morning be to make the following resolve for the day: • I shall not fear anyone on earth. • I shall fear only God. • I shall not bear ill will toward anyone. • I shall not submit to injustice from anyone. • I shall conquer untruth by truth. • And in resisting untruth I shall put up with all suffering.	Prime Personal and Professional Principles: • Succeed at home first. • Seek and merit Divine help. • Never compromise with honesty. • Remember the people involved. • Plan tomorrow today. • Develop one new proficiency a year. • Attain visibility by productivity. • Hustle while I wait. • Facilitate the success of my colleagues. • Pursue excellence in all my endeavors. • Be sincere and gentle yet decisive. • Be a creative and innovative person. • Don't fear mistakes. • Concentrate all abilities on the task at hand. • Obtain the counsel of others. • Defend those who are absent. • Listen twice as much as I speak. • Be orderly in work and person. • Maintain a positive attitude and sense of humor.

Table 4 Personal Principles Statements

ately, what it is you most want to accomplish, and what legacy you want to leave, you can more easily say no to activities that aren't congruent with those principles. Everyone is always saying no to something anyway. But usually they are saying no to Important/Nonurgent activities (Cell 3) that are most congruent with their personal missions. People who experience the most time stress are those who allow others to generate their personal principles statement for them through their time demands. Making core principles precise and public not only helps make them more powerful but also provides a basis for saying no without feeling guilty. You can opt for prevention, planning, personal development, and continuous improvement, knowing that these Important/Nonurgent activities will help eliminate and prevent the problems that create time stress. Effectiveness in time management, then, means that you accomplish what you want to accomplish with your time. How you achieve those accomplishments relates to efficiency of time use, to which we now turn.

Efficient Time Management

In addition to approaching time management from the point of view of effectiveness (i.e., aligning time use with core personal principles), it is also important to adopt the efficiency point of view (i.e., accomplishing more during a day by not wasting time). Techniques are available to help managers utilize more efficiently the time they have each day.

One way to enhance efficient time use is to be alert to your own tendencies to use time inefficiently. The list of propositions in Table 5 shows general patterns of behavior for most individuals in their use of time. In many situations, these tendencies may represent appropriate responses. In others, however, they can get in the way of efficient time management and increase time stressors unless individuals are aware of them and their possible consequences. For example, if "we do things that are planned before things that are unplanned," some important tasks may never get done unless consciously scheduled. Because many people have a tendency to "do things that are urgent before things that are important," they may find themselves saying no to important things in order to attend to urgent things, thereby perpetuating feelings of overload. If "we do the things that are easiest before the things that are difficult," our time may be taken up dealing with mundane and easy-to-resolve issues while difficult but important problems go unresolved.

Time is such a universal stressor, and time management is such an effective means for coping with it, that

---

- We do what we like to do before we do what we don't like to do.
- We do the things we know how to do faster than the things we do not know how to do.
- We do the things that are easiest before things that are difficult.
- We do things that require a little time before things that require a lot of time.
- We do things for which the resources are available.
- We do things that are scheduled (e.g., meetings) before nonscheduled things.
- We sometimes do things that are planned before things that are unplanned.
- We respond to demands from others before demands from ourselves.
- We do things that are urgent before things that are important.

- We readily respond to crises and to emergencies.
- We do interesting things before uninteresting things.
- We do things that advance our personal objectives or that are politically expedient.
- We wait until a deadline before we really get moving.
- We do things that provide the most immediate closure.
- We respond on the basis of who wants it.
- We respond on the basis of the consequences to us of doing or not doing something.
- We tackle small jobs before large jobs.
- We work on things in the order of arrival.
- We work on the basis of the squeaky-wheel principle (the squeaky wheel gets the grease).
- We work on the basis of consequences to the group.

Table 5 Typical Patterns of Time Use

we included in the Assessment section an instrument to help you diagnose your own time management competency: the Time Management Survey. The first section of that survey applies to everyone in daily life. The second section is most applicable to individuals who have managed or worked in an organization. The scoring information in Appendix I will show you how well you manage your time compared to others. The rules set forth below correspond to the item numbers in the assessment survey.

The Time Management Survey lists guidelines or techniques that have been derived from research on the management of time. Whereas one kind of time stressor is having too much time available (i.e., boredom), that is not usually the one facing managers and students. These particular rules, therefore, relate to the opposite problem, that is, having too little time available due to an overloaded schedule.

Of course, no individual can or should implement all of these time management techniques at once. The amount of time spent trying to implement all the techniques would be so overwhelming that time stressors would only increase. Therefore, it is best to incorporate a few of these techniques at a time into everyday life. Implement first those hints that will lead to the most improvement in your use of time. Saving just 10 percent more time or using an extra 30 minutes a day more wisely can produce astounding results over months and years. Effective time management, then, not only helps a person accomplish more in a typical work day but also helps eliminate feelings of stress and overload that are so detrimental to personal accomplishment and satisfaction.

What follows is a brief discussion of these 40 techniques. The first 20 are applicable to anyone in all aspects of life; the remaining relate more directly to managers and the management role.

Rule 1. Read selectively. This applies mainly to individuals who find themselves with too much material they must read such as mail, magazines, newspapers, books, brochures, instructions, and so on. Except when you read for relaxation or pleasure, most reading should be done the way you read a newspaper, that is, skim most of it, but stop to read what seems most important. Even the most important articles don't need a thorough reading because important points are generally at the beginnings of paragraphs or sections. Furthermore, if you underline or highlight what you find important, you can review it quickly when you need to.

Rule 2. Make a list of things to perform today. This is a common-sense rule that implies that you need to do some advance planning each day and not rely solely on your memory. (It also suggests that you should have only one list, not multiple lists on multiple scraps of paper.)

Rule 3. Have a place for everything and keep everything in its place. Letting things get out of place robs you of time in two ways: You need more time to find something when you need it, and you are tempted to interrupt the task you are doing to do something else. For example, if material for several projects is scattered on top of your desk, you will be continually tempted to switch from one project to another as you shift your eyes or move the papers.

Rule 4. Prioritize your tasks. Each day you should focus first on important tasks and then deal with urgent tasks. During World War II, with an overwhelming number of tasks to perform, General Dwight D. Eisenhower successfully managed his time by following rule 4 strictly. He focused his attention rigorously on important matters that only he could resolve, while leaving urgent, but less important matters to be dealt with by subordinates.

Rule 5. Do one important thing at a time but several trivial things simultaneously. You can accomplish a lot by doing more than one thing at a time when tasks are routine, trivial, or require little thought. This rule allows managers to get rid of multiple trivial tasks in less time (e.g., signing letters while talking on the phone).

Rule 6. Make a list of some 5- or 10-minute discretionary tasks. This helps use the small bits of time almost everyone has during his or her day (waiting for something to begin, between meetings or events, talking on the telephone, etc.). Beware, however, of spending all your time doing these small discretionary tasks while letting high-priority items go unattended.

Rule 7. Divide up large projects. This helps you avoid feeling overwhelmed by large, important, urgent tasks. Feeling that a task is too big to accomplish contributes to a feeling of overload and leads to procrastination.

Rule 8. Determine the critical 20 percent of your tasks. Pareto's law states that only 20 percent of the work produces 80 percent of the results. Therefore, it is important to analyze which tasks make up the most important 20 percent and spend the bulk of your time on those.

Rule 9. Save your best time for important matters. Time spent on trivial tasks should not be your "best time." Do routine work when your energy level is low, your mind is not sharp, or you aren't on top of things. Reserve your high-energy time for accomplishing the most important and urgent tasks. As Carlson (1951) pointed out, managers are often like puppets whose strings are being pulled by a crowd of unknown and unorganized people. Don't let others interrupt your best time with unwanted demands. You, not others, should control your time.

Rule 10. Reserve some time during the day when others don't have access to you. Use this time to accomplish Important/Nonurgent tasks, or spend it just thinking. This might be the time before others in the household get up, after everyone else is in bed, or at a location where no one else comes. The point is to avoid being in the line of fire all day, every day, without personal control over your time.

Rule 11. Don't procrastinate. If you do certain tasks promptly, they will require less time and effort than if you put them off. Of course, you must guard against spending all your time on trivial, immediate concerns that crowd out more important tasks. The line between procrastination and time wasting is a fine one, but if you keep in mind the rules in Table 6, you can avoid both procrastination and being overburdened by trivia.

Rule 12. Keep track of time use. This is one of the best time management strategies. It is impossible to improve your management of time or decrease time stressors unless you know how you spend your time. You should keep time logs in short enough intervals to capture the essential activities, but not so short that they create a recording burden (e.g., 30-minute periods). Parts of the Skill Practice and Skill Application sections suggest that you keep a time log for at least two weeks. One way to analyze a time log after it is has been recorded is to use the rating scales in Table 6. Eliminate those activities that consistently receive C's and D's.

Rule 13. Set deadlines. This helps improve your efficient use of time. Work always expands to fill the time available, so if you don't specify a termination time, tasks tend to continue longer than they need to.

Rule 14. Do something productive while waiting. Some estimate that up to 20 percent of an average person's time is spent in waiting. During such time, try reading, planning, preparing, rehearsing, reviewing,

---

Analyze each activity based on the following four criteria:

1. IMPORTANCE: How important is this activity?
   a. Very Important: It must be done.
   b. Important: It should be done.
   c. Not so Important: It may be useful, but it's not necessary.
   d. Unimportant: It doesn't accomplish anything.

2. URGENCY: How urgent is this activity?
   a. Very Urgent: It must be done now.
   b. Urgent: It should be done now.
   c. Not Urgent: It can be done sometime later.
   d. Time is not a relevant factor.

3. DELEGATION: Do I have to do it?
   a. I am the only one who can do this.
   b. I can delegate it to someone close to me (immediate subordinate) whom I trust implicitly.
   c. I can delegate it to someone not close to me (staff) whom I assume can be trusted.
   d. I can delegate it to anyone.

4. INVOLVEMENT: How often must others be involved?
   a. I must interact with others very frequently and consistently.
   b. I need to interact with others quite frequently.
   c. I should interact with others sometime.
   d. I don't need to involve anyone else at all.

Table 6 Criteria for Analyzing Time Commitments

---

outlining, or doing other things that help you accomplish your work.

Rule 15. Do busy work at one set time during the day. Because it is natural to let simple tasks drive out difficult tasks (see Table 5), specify a certain period of time to do busy work. Refusing to answer mail or read the newspaper until a specified time, for example, can help ensure that those activities don't supersede priority time.

Rule 16. Reach closure on at least one thing every day. Reaching the end of a day with nothing completely finished (even a 10-minute task) serves to increase a sense of overload and time stress. Finishing a task, on the other hand, produces a sense of relief and releases stress.

Rule 17. Schedule some personal time. You need some time when no interruptions will occur, when you can get off the "fast track" for awhile and be alone. This time should be used to plan, prioritize, take stock, pray, meditate, or just relax. Among other advantages, personal time also helps you maintain self-awareness.

Rule 18. Don't worry about anything continually. Allow yourself to worry only at a specified time and avoid dwelling on a worrisome issue at other times. This keeps your mind free and your energy focused on the task at hand.

Rule 19. Have long-term objectives. This helps you maintain consistency in activities and tasks. You can be efficient and organized but still accomplish nothing unless you have a clear direction in mind.

Rule 20. Be on the alert for ways to improve your management of time. Make continuous improvement in time use a part of your lifestyle.

Efficient Time Management for Managers

The second list of rules encompasses the major activities in which managers engage at work. The first nine rules deal with conducting meetings, since managers report that approximately 70 percent of their time is spent in meetings (Mintzberg, 1973; Cooper & Davidson, 1982).

Rule 1. Hold routine meetings at the end of the day. Energy and creativity levels are highest early in the day and shouldn't be wasted on trivial matters. Furthermore, an automatic deadline—quitting time—will set a time limit on the meeting.

Rule 2. Hold short meetings standing up. This guarantees that meetings will be kept short. Getting comfortable helps prolong meetings.

Rule 3. Set a time limit. This establishes an expectation of when the meeting should end and creates pressure to conform to a time boundary. Set such limits at the beginning of every meeting and appointment.

Rule 4. Cancel meetings once in a while. Meetings should be held only if they are needed. Thus, meetings that are held are more productive and more time efficient.

Rules 5, 6, and 7. Have agendas, stick to them, and keep minutes and time. These rules help people prepare for a meeting, stick to the subject, and remain work oriented. Many things will be handled outside of meetings if they have to appear on a formal agenda to be discussed. Managers can set a verbal agenda at the beginning of even impromptu meetings. Keeping a record of the meeting ensures that assignments are not forgotten, that follow-up and accountability occur, and that everyone is clear about expectations. Keeping track of the time motivates people to be efficient and non-wasteful in the meeting.

Rule 8. Start meetings on time. This helps guarantee that people will arrive on time. (Some managers set meetings for odd times, such as 10:13 A.M., to make attendees minute conscious.) People who arrive on time should be rewarded, not asked to wait for laggards.

Rule 9. Prepare minutes promptly and follow up. This practice keeps items from appearing again in a meeting without having been resolved. It also creates the expectation that most work should be done outside the meeting. Commitments and expectations made public through minutes are more likely to be fulfilled.

Rule 10. Insist that subordinates suggest solutions to problems. This rule is discussed in the Empowering and Delegating chapter. Its purpose is to eliminate the tendency toward upward delegation, that is, for subordinates to delegate difficult problems back to managers by asking for their ideas and solutions. It is more efficient for managers to choose among alternatives devised by subordinates than to generate their own.

Rule 11. Meet visitors in the doorway. This helps managers maintain control of their time by controlling the use of their office space. It is easier to keep a meeting short if you are standing in the doorway rather than sitting in your office.

Rule 12. Go to subordinates' offices. This is useful if it is practical. The advantage is that it helps managers control the length of a meeting by being free to leave. Of course, if managers spend a great deal of time traveling between subordinates' offices, the rule is not practical.

Rule 13. Don't overschedule the day. Effective managers stay in control of at least some of their time. Others' meetings and demands can undermine managers' personal control of their schedules unless they make an effort to maintain control. This doesn't mean that the day can be free of all appointments or meetings. But the manager initiates, rather than responds to, schedule requirements.

Rule 14. Have someone else answer calls. This provides managers with a buffer from interruptions for at least some part of the day.

Rule 15. Have a place to work uninterrupted. This helps guarantee that when a deadline is near, the manager can concentrate on the task at hand. Trying to get one's mind focused once more on a task or project after interruptions wastes a lot of time. "Gearing up" is wasteful if done repeatedly.

Rule 16. Do something definite with every piece of paperwork handled. This keeps managers from shuffling the same items over and over. Not infrequently, "doing something definite" with a piece of paper means throwing it away.

Rule 17. Keep the workplace clean. This minimizes distractions and reduces the time it takes to find things.

Rules 18 (delegate work), **19** (identify the amount of initiative recipients should take), **and 20** (give others credit for their success).   These rules all relate to effective delegation, a key time management technique. These last three rules are discussed in the Empowering and Delegating chapter.

Remember that these techniques for managing time are a means to an end, not the end itself. If trying to implement techniques creates more rather than less stress, they should not be applied. However, research has indicated that managers who use these kinds of techniques have better control of their time, accomplish more, have better relations with subordinates, and eliminate many of the time stressors most managers ordinarily encounter. Therefore, you will find that as you select a few of these hints to apply in your own life, the efficiency of your time use will improve and your time stress will decrease.

Most time management techniques involve single individuals changing their own work habits or behaviors by themselves. Greater effectiveness and efficiency in time use occurs because individuals decide to institute personal changes; the behavior of other people is not involved. However, effective time management must often take into account the behavior of others, because that behavior may tend to inhibit or enhance effective time use. For this reason, effective time management sometimes requires the application of other skills discussed in this book. The Empowering and Delegating chapter provides principles for efficient time management by involving other people in task accomplishment. The Motivating Employees chapter explains how to help oth-

ers be more effective and efficient in their own work. The Communicating Supportively chapter identifies ways in which interpersonal relationships can be strengthened, thus relieving stressors resulting from interpersonal conflicts. It is to these encounter stressors that we now turn.

Eliminating Encounter Stressors Through Collaboration and Interpersonal Competence

As pointed out earlier, dissatisfying relationships with others, particularly with a direct manager or supervisor, are prime causes of job stress among workers. These encounter stressors result directly from abrasive, non-fulfilling relationships. Even though work is going smoothly, when encounter stress is present, everything else seems wrong. It is difficult to maintain positive energy when you are fighting or at odds with someone, or when feelings of acceptance and amiability aren't characteristic of your important relationships at work.

Collaboration

One important factor that helps eliminate encounter stress is membership in a stable, closely knit group or community. It was discovered 25 years ago by Dr. Stewart Wolf that in the town of Roseto, Pennsylvania, residents were completely free from heart disease and other stress-related illnesses. He suspected that their protection sprang from the town's uncommon social cohesion and stability. The town's population consisted entirely of descendants of Italians who had moved there 100 years ago from Roseto, Italy. Few married outside the community, the firstborn was always named after a grandparent, conspicuous consumption and displays of superiority were avoided, and social support among community members was a way of life.

Wolf predicted that residents would begin to display the same level of stress-related illnesses as the rest of the country if the modern world intruded. It did, and they did. By the mid-1970s, residents in Roseto had Cadillacs, ranch-style homes, mixed marriages, new names, competition with one another, and a rate of coronary disease the same as any other town's (Farnham, 1991). They had ceased to be a cohesive, collaborative clan and instead had become a community of selfishness. Self-centeredness, it was discovered, was dangerous to health.

The number one psychological discovery resulting from the Vietnam and the Persian Gulf wars was the strength associated with the small, primary work group. In Vietnam, unlike Desert Storm, strong primary groups of soldiers who stayed together over time were not formed. The constant injection of new personnel into squadrons, and the constant transfer of soldiers from one location to another, made soldiers feel isolated, without loyalty, and vulnerable to stress-related illnesses. In the Persian Gulf War, by contrast, soldiers were kept in the same unit throughout the campaign, brought home together, and given lots of time to debrief together after the battle. Using a closely knit group to provide interpretation of, and social support for, behavior was found to be the most powerful deterrent to post-battle trauma. David Marlowe, chief of psychiatry at Walter Reed Army Institute of Research, indicated that "Squad members are encouraged to use travel time en route home from a war zone to talk about their battlefield experience. It helps them detoxify. That's why we brought them back in groups from Desert Storm. Epistemologically, we know it works" (Farnham, 1991).

Developing collaborative, clan-like relationships with others is a powerful deterrent to encounter stress. One way of developing this kind of relationship is by applying a concept introduced by Stephen Covey (1989) in describing habits of highly effective people. Covey used the metaphor of an emotional bank account to describe the trust or feeling of security that one person has toward another. The more "deposits" made in an emotional bank account, the stronger and more resilient the relationship becomes. Conversely, too many "withdrawals" from the account weaken relationships by destroying trust, security, and confidence. "Deposits" are made through treating people with kindness, courtesy, honesty, and consistency. The emotional bank account grows when people feel they are receiving love, respect, and caring. "Withdrawals" are made by not keeping promises, not listening, not clarifying expectations, or not allowing choice. Because disrespect and autocratic rule devalue people and destroy a sense of self-worth, relationships are ruined because the account becomes overdrawn.

The more people interact, the more deposits must be made in the emotional bank account. When you see an old friend after years of absence, you can often pick up right where you left off, because the emotional bank account has not been touched. But when you interact with someone frequently, the relationship is constantly being fed or depleted. Cues from everyday interactions are interpreted as either deposits or withdrawals. When the emotional account is well-stocked, mistakes, disappointments, and minor abrasions are easily forgiven and ignored. But when no reserve exists, those incidents may become creators of distrust and contention.

The common-sense prescription, therefore, is to base relationships with others on mutual trust, respect, honesty, and kindness. Make deposits into the emotional bank accounts of others. Collaborative, cohesive communities are, in the end, a product of the one-on-one relationships that people develop with each other. As Dag Hammarskjöld, former Secretary-General of the United Nations, stated: "It is more noble to give yourself completely to one individual than to labor diligently for the salvation of the masses." That is because building a strong, cohesive relationship with an individual is more powerful, and more difficult, than the leadership of masses. Feeling trusted, respected, and loved is, in the end, what most people desire as individuals. We want to experience those feelings personally, not just as a member of a group. Therefore, because encounter stressors are almost always the product of abrasive individual relationships, they are best eliminated by building strong emotional bank accounts with others.

Interpersonal Competence

In addition to one-on-one relationship building, a second major category of encounter stress eliminators is developing interpersonal competence. The skillful management of groups and interpersonal interactions is also an effective way to eliminate encounter stressors. For example, the ability to resolve conflict, to build and manage high-performing teams, to conduct efficient meetings, to coach and counsel employees needing support, to provide negative feedback in constructive ways, to influence others' opinions, to motivate and energize employees, and to empower individuals on the job all help eliminate the stress associated with abrasive, uncomfortable relationships. A national survey of workers found that employees who rated their manager as supportive and interpersonally competent had lower rates of burnout, lower stress levels, lower incidence of stress-related illnesses, higher productivity, more loyalty to their organizations, and more efficiency in work than employees with nonsupportive and interpersonally incompetent managers (NWNL, 1992).

A third category of factors that can eliminate encounter stressors is the development of *emotional intelligence* (Goleman, 1995). After reviewing a large number of studies, Goleman made the case that human beings have at least two kinds of intelligence, the traditional rational (IQ) intelligence, including reasoning ability, numeracy, and logic, and a newer form of intelligence called emotional intelligence (EQ). These two kinds of intelligence are independent, although a small correlation does exist between some aspects of emotional intelligence and IQ. The correlation between life success (e.g., achieving high occupational positions, satisfaction with life, family happiness) and traditional IQ intelligence is marginal. Very smart people have no greater likelihood of achieving success in life or achieving personal happiness than people with low IQ scores. On the other hand, emotional intelligence has strong relationships to success in life and to a reduced degree of encounter stress.

Emotional intelligence consists of five dimensions:

1. Knowing one's own emotions, or self-knowledge. This is the ability to recognize and understand one's own feelings from moment to moment.

2. Managing emotions, or emotional self-control. This is the ability to control and keep in check both negative emotions (such as irritability, gloom, and anxiety) and positive emotions (such as excitement or ecstasy) resulting from encounters or events.

3. Motivating oneself. This is the ability to marshal emotions in support of one's goal or desire and, contrarily, to delay immediate gratification of one's desires.

4. Recognizing emotions in others, or empathy. This is the extent to which one is in tune with the subtle social signals that others display.

5. Handling relationships, or social competence. This is the ability to manage others' emotions and to interact smoothly with others.

A large number of studies suggest that emotional intelligence can be taught and influenced positively, that is, people can achieve higher levels of emotional intelligence with careful teaching and training. This teaching follows the suggestions contained in the guidelines in the chapter on Developing Self-Awareness, the guidelines in the chapter on Communicating Supportively, and the guidelines in the chapter on Managing Conflict. In other words, eliminating encounter stress by developing emotional intelligence is closely tied to developing key management skills.

The remaining chapters in this book address these topics in detail. They provide techniques and behavioral guidelines designed to assist you in improving your interpersonal competence and emotional intelligence. After completing the book, including the practice and application exercises, you will have improved several skills related to interpersonal competence and emotional intelligence, thereby enhancing your ability to eliminate many forms of encounter stress.

Eliminating Situational Stressors Through Work Redesign

Most people would never admit that they feel less stress now than a year ago, that they have less pressure, or that they are less overloaded. Most people report feeling stress because it is the "in" thing to be stressed. "I'm busier than you are" is a common theme in social conversations. On the other hand, it is also true that a third of U.S. workers are thinking of quitting their jobs, that repeated downsizings have introduced new threats to the workplace, that highways are increasingly congested, financial pressures are escalating, crime is pervasive, and worker compensation claims for stress-related illness are ballooning. Unfortunately, in medical treatment and time lost, stress-related illnesses are almost twice as expensive as workplace injuries because of longer recovery times, the need for psychological therapy, and so on (Farnham, 1991). Situational stressors, in other words, are costly. And they are escalating.

For decades, researchers in the area of occupational health have examined the relationship between job strain and stress-related behavioral, psychological, and physiological outcomes. Studies have focused on various components of job strain, including level of task demand (e.g., the pressure to work quickly or excessively), the level of individual control (e.g., the freedom to vary the work pace), and the level of intellectual challenge (e.g., the extent to which work is interesting).

Research in this area has challenged the common myth that job strain occurs most frequently in the executive suite (Karasek et al., 1988). A federal government study of nearly 5,000 workers found that after controlling for age, sex, race, education, and health status (measured by blood pressure and serum cholesterol level), low-level workers tended to have a higher incidence of heart disease than their bosses who were in high-status, presumably success-oriented, managerial or professional occupations. This is true because certain characteristics of lower-level positions—high demand, low control, low discretion, and low interest— tend to produce higher levels of job strain.

A review of this research suggests that the single most important contributor to stress is lack of freedom (Adler, 1989). In a study of administrators, engineers, and scientists at the Goddard Space Flight Center, researchers found that individuals provided with more discretion in making decisions about assigned tasks experienced fewer time stressors (e.g., role overload), situational stressors (e.g., role ambiguity), encounter stressors (e.g., interpersonal conflict), and anticipatory stressors (e.g., job-related threats). Individuals without discretion and participation experienced significantly more stress (French & Caplan, 1972).

In response to these findings, Hackman and his colleagues (1975) proposed a model of job redesign that has proved effective in reducing stress and in increasing satisfaction and productivity. A detailed discussion of their job redesign model is provided in the chapter on Motivating Employees. Here we give their remedies for stress-producing job strain.

Combine tasks.　When individuals are able to work on a whole project and perform a variety of related tasks (e.g., programming all components of a computer software package), rather than being restricted to working on a single repetitive task or subcomponent of a larger task, they are more satisfied and committed. In such cases, they are able to use more skills and feel a pride of ownership in their job.

Form identifiable work units.　Building on the first step, individuals feel more integrated, productivity improves, and the strain associated with repetitive work is diminished when teams of individuals performing related tasks are formed. When these groups combine and coordinate their tasks, and decide internally how to complete the work, stress decreases dramatically. This formation of natural work units has received a great deal of attention in Japanese auto plants in America as workers have combined in teams to assemble an entire car from start to finish, rather than do separate tasks on an assembly line. Workers learn one another's jobs, rotate assignments, and experience a sense of completion in their work.

Establish customer relationships.　One of the most enjoyable parts of a job is seeing the consequences of one's labor. In most organizations, producers are buffered from consumers by intermediaries, such as customer relations departments and sales personnel. Eliminating those buffers allows workers to obtain firsthand information concerning customer satisfaction as well as the needs and expectations of potential customers. Stress resulting from filtered communication also is eliminated.

Increase decision-making authority.　Managers who increase the autonomy of their subordinates to make important work decisions eliminate a major source of job stress for them. Being able to influence the what, when, and how of work increases an individual's feelings of control. Cameron, Freeman, and Mishra (1990) found a significant decrease in experienced stress in firms that were downsizing when workers were given authority to make decisions about how and when they did the extra work required of them.

Open feedback channels.　A major source of stress is not knowing what is expected and how task performance is being evaluated. As managers communicate their expectations more clearly and give timely and accurate feedback, subordinates' satisfaction and performance improve. A related form of feedback in production tasks is quality control. Firms that allow the individuals who assemble a product to test its quality, instead of shipping it off to a separate quality assurance group, find that quality increases substantially and that conflicts between production and quality control personnel are eliminated.

These practices are used widely today in all types of organizations, from the Social Security Administration to General Motors. When Travelers Insurance Companies implemented a job redesign project, for example, productivity increased dramatically, absenteeism and errors fell sharply, and the amount of distractions and stresses experienced by managers decreased significantly (Hackman, Oldham, Janson, & Purdy, 1975). In brief, work redesign can effectively eliminate situational stressors associated with the work itself.

Eliminating Anticipatory Stressors Through Prioritizing, Goal Setting, and Small Wins

While redesigning work can help structure an environment where stressors are minimized, it is much more difficult to eliminate entirely the anticipatory stressors experienced by individuals. Stress associated with anticipating an event is more a product of psychological anxiety than current work circumstances. To eliminate that source of stress requires a change in thought processes, priorities, and plans. In the Developing Self-Awareness chapter, we discussed the central place of cognitive style (thought processes), values (priorities), and moral maturity (personal principles) for effective management. Earlier in this chapter, we discussed the central importance of establishing clear personal priorities, such as identifying what is to be accomplished in the long term, what cannot be compromised or sacrificed, and what lasting legacy one desires. Establishing this core value set or statement of basic personal principles helps eliminate not only time stressors but also eliminates anticipatory stress by providing clarity of direction. When traveling on an unknown road for the first time, having a road map reduces anticipatory stress. You don't have to figure out where to go or where you are by trying to diagnose the unknown landmarks along the roadside. In the same way, a personal principles statement acts as a map or guide. It makes clear where you will eventually end up. Fear of the unknown, or anticipatory stress, is thus eliminated.

Goal Setting

Similarly, establishing short-term plans also helps eliminate anticipatory stressors by focusing attention on immediate goal accomplishment instead of a fearful future. Short-term planning, however, implies more than just specifying a desired outcome. Several action steps are needed if short-term plans are to be achieved. The model in Figure 4 outlines the four-step process associated with successful short-term planning.

The first step is to identify the desired goal. Most goal-setting, performance appraisal, or management by objectives (MBO) programs specify that step, but most also stop at that point. Unfortunately, the first step alone is not likely to lead to goal achievement or stress elimination. Merely establishing a goal, while helpful, is not sufficient. Steps 2, 3, and 4 are also essential. Step 2 is to identify, as specifically as possible, the activities and behaviors that will lead toward accomplishing the goal. The more difficult the goal is to accomplish, the more rigorous, numerous, and specific should be the behaviors and activities.

A friend once approached one of us with a problem. She was a wonderfully sensitive, caring, kind single woman of about 25 who was experiencing a high degree of anticipatory stress because of her size. She weighed well over 300 pounds, but she had had great difficulty losing any weight over the last several years. She was afraid of both the health consequences and the social

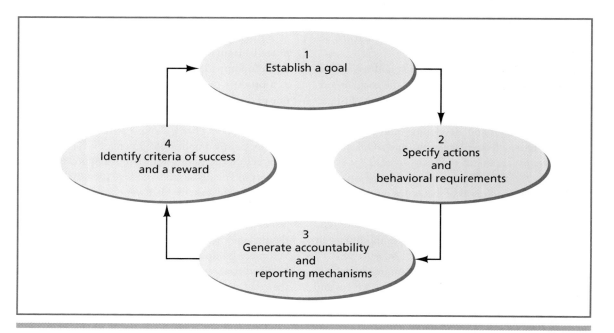

Figure 4   A Model for Short-Term Planning and Goal Setting

consequences of not being able to reduce her weight. She set a goal, or short-term plan, to lose 100 pounds in the next 10 months. Because it was to be such a difficult goal to reach, however, we helped her identify a dozen or so specific actions and guidelines that would help her reach that goal: for example, never shop alone and without a menu, never carry more than 25 cents in change (in order to avoid the temptation to buy a doughnut), exercise with friends each day at 5:30 P.M., arise each morning at 7:00 A.M. and eat a specified breakfast with a friend, forgo watching TV to reduce the temptation to snack, and go to bed by 10:30 P.M. The behaviors were rigid, but the goal was so difficult that they were necessary to ensure progress. In each case, these specific behaviors had a direct effect on the ultimate goal of losing 100 pounds.

Step 3 involves establishing accountability and reporting mechanisms. The principle at the center of this step is to make it more difficult to stay the same than to change. This is done by involving others in ensuring adherence to the plan, establishing a social support network to obtain encouragement from others, and instituting penalties for nonconformance. In addition to announcing to coworkers, friends, and a church group that she would lose the 100 pounds, our friend had her doctor register her for a hospital stay at the end of the 10-month period. If she did not achieve the goal on her own, she was to go on an intravenous feeding schedule in the hospital to lose the weight, at a cost of over $250 per day. It was clearly more uncomfortable and costly not to succeed than to accomplish the goal.

Step 4 is establishing an evaluation and reward system. What evidence will there be that the goal has been accomplished? In the case of losing weight, it's just getting on the scales. But for improving management skills, becoming a better friend, developing more patience, establishing more effective leadership, and so on, the criteria of success are not so easily identified. That is why this step is crucial. "I'll know it when I see it" isn't good enough. Specific indicators of success, or specific changes that will have been produced when the goal is achieved, must be identified. Carefully outlining these criteria serves as a motivation toward goal accomplishment by making the goal more observable and measurable.

The purpose of this short-term planning model is to eliminate anticipatory stress by establishing a focus and direction for activity. The anxiety associated with uncertainty and potentially negative events is dissipated when mental and physical energy are concentrated on purposeful activity. (By the way, the last time we saw our friend, her weight was well below 200 pounds.)

Small Wins

Another principle related to eliminating anticipatory stressors is the small-wins strategy. By "small win," we mean a tiny but definite change made in a desired direction. One begins by changing something that is relatively easy to change. Then another "easy change" is added, and so on. Although each individual success may be relatively modest when considered in isolation, the multiple small gains eventually mount up, generating a sense of momentum that creates the impression of substantial movement toward a desired goal. This momentum helps convince ourselves, as well as others, of our ability to accomplish our objective. The fear associated with anticipatory change is eliminated as we build self-confidence through small wins. We also gain the support of others as they see progress being made.

In the case of our overweight friend, one key was to begin changing what she could change, a little at a time. Tackling the loss of 100 pounds all at once would have been too overwhelming a task. But she could change the time she shopped, the time she went to bed, and the menu she ate for breakfast. Each successful change generated more and more momentum that, when combined together, led to the larger change that she desired. Her ultimate success was a product of multiple small wins.

Similarly, Weick (1993) has described Poland's peaceful transition from a communistic command-type economy to a capitalistic free-enterprise economy as a product of small wins. Not only is Poland now one of the most thriving economies in eastern Europe, but it made the change to free enterprise without a single shot being fired, a single strike being called, or a single political upheaval. One reason for this is that long before the Berlin Wall fell, small groups of volunteers in Poland began to change the way they lived. They adopted a theme that went something like this: If you value freedom, then behave freely; if you value honesty, then speak honestly; if you desire change, then change what you can. Polish citizens organized volunteer groups to help at local hospitals, assist the less fortunate, and clean up parks. They behaved in a way that was outside the control of the central government but reflected their free choice. Their changes were not on a large enough scale to attract attention and official opposition from the central government.

But their actions nevertheless reflected their determination to behave in a free, self-determining way. They controlled what they could control, namely, their own voluntary service. These voluntary service groups spread throughout Poland; thus, when the transition from communism to capitalism occurred, a large number of people in Poland had already gotten used to behaving in a way consistent with self-determination. Many of these people simply stepped into positions where independent-minded managers were needed. The transition was smooth because of the multiple small wins that had previously spread throughout the country relatively unnoticed.

In summary, the rules for instituting small wins are simple: (1) identify something that is under your control; (2) change it in a way that leads toward your desired goal; (3) find some other small thing to change, and change it; (4) keep track of the changes you are making; and (5) maintain the small gains you have made. Anticipatory stressors are eliminated because the fearful unknown is replaced by a focus on immediate successes.

Developing Resiliency

Now that we have examined various causes of stress and outlined a series of preventive measures, we turn our attention to a second major strategy for managing stress in Figure 2, the development of resiliency to handle stress that cannot be eliminated. People vary widely in their ability to cope with stress. Some individuals seem to crumble under pressure, while others appear to thrive. A major predictor of which individuals cope well with stress and which do not is the amount of resiliency that they have developed. Resiliency is associated with balancing the various aspects of one's life.

Assume that the wheel in Figure 5 represents resiliency development. Each wedge in the figure identifies an important aspect of life that must be developed in order to achieve resiliency. The most resilient individuals are those who have achieved **life balance.** For example, if the center of the figure represents the zero point of resiliency development and the outside edge of the figure represents maximum development, shading in a portion of the area in each wedge would represent the amount of development achieved in each area. (This exercise is included in the Skill Practice section.) Individuals who are best able to cope with stress would

shade in a majority of each wedge, indicating they have not only spent time developing a variety of aspects of their lives, but also that the overall pattern is relatively balanced. A lopsided pattern is as nonadaptive as are minimally shaded areas. Either pattern suggests that an individual who cannot eliminate stressors should seek to develop resiliency through life balance.

This is a counterintuitive prescription. Generally, when people are feeling stress in one area of life, such as work, they respond by devoting more time and attention to it. While this is a natural reaction, it is counterproductive for several reasons. First, the more that individuals concentrate exclusively on work, the more restricted and less creative they become. As we shall see in the discussion of creativity in Chapter 3, many breakthroughs in problem solving come from using analogies and metaphors gathered from unrelated activities. That is why several major corporations send senior managers on high adventure wilderness retreats, invite thespian troupes to perform plays before the executive committee, require volunteer community service, or encourage their managers to engage in completely unrelated activities outside of work (*Business Week,* Sept. 30, 1985, pp. 80–84).

Second, refreshed and relaxed minds think better. A bank executive commented recently during an executive development workshop that he gradually has become convinced of the merits of taking the weekend off from work. He finds that he gets twice as much accomplished on Monday as his colleagues who have been in their offices all weekend.

Third, the cost of stress-related illness decreases markedly when employees participate in well-rounded wellness programs. A study by the Association for Fitness in Business concluded that companies receive an average return of $3 to $4 on each dollar invested in health and wellness promotion. AT&T, for example, expects to save $72 million in the next 10 years as a result of investment in wellness programs for employees.

Well-developed individuals, who give time and attention to cultural, physical, spiritual, family, social, and intellectual activities in addition to work, are more productive and less stressed than those who are workaholics. In this section, therefore, we concentrate on three common areas of resiliency development for managers: physical resiliency, psychological resiliency, and social resiliency. Development in each of these areas requires initiative on the part of the individual and takes a moderate amount of time to achieve. These are not activities that can be accomplished by

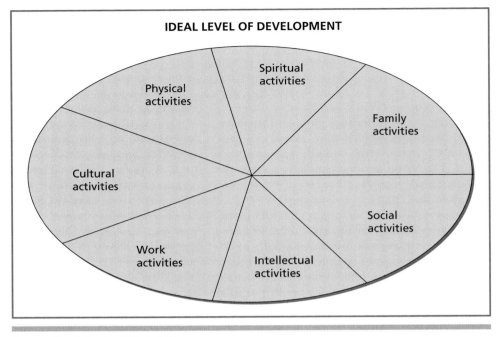

IDEAL LEVEL OF DEVELOPMENT

Spiritual activities

Physical activities

Family activities

Cultural activities

Social activities

Work activities

Intellectual activities

Figure 5   Balancing Life Activities

lunchtime or by the weekend. Rather, achieving life balance and resiliency requires ongoing initiative and continuous effort. Components of resiliency are summarized in Table 7.

Physiological Resiliency

One of the most crucial aspects of resiliency development involves one's physical condition because physical condition significantly affects the ability to cope with stress. Two aspects of physical condition combine to determine physical resiliency: cardiovascular conditioning and dietary control.

Cardiovascular Conditioning

Henry Ford is reputed to have stated, "Exercise is bunk. If you are healthy, you don't need it. If you are sick, you shouldn't take it." Fortunately, American business has not taken Ford's advice; thousands of major corporations now have in-house fitness facilities. An emphasis on physical conditioning in business has resulted

PHYSIOLOGICAL RESILIENCY	PSYCHOLOGICAL RESILIENCY	SOCIAL RESILIENCY
Cardiovascular conditioning	Balanced lifestyle	Supportive social relations
Proper diet	Hardy personality	Mentors
	High internal control	Teamwork
	Strong personal commitment	
	Love of challenge	
	Small-wins strategy	
	Deep-relaxation techniques	

Table 7   Resiliency: Moderating the Effects of Stress

partly from overwhelming evidence that individuals in good physical condition are better able to cope with stressors than those in poor physical condition. Table 8 shows the benefits of regular physical exercise.

Mesa Petroleum experienced an annual savings of $1.6 million in health care costs for its 650 employees as a result of its physical fitness program. As a result of its Live for Life program, Johnson and Johnson lowered absenteeism and slowed the rate of health care expenses, resulting in savings of $378 per employee in 1982. Exercisers at General Electric Aircraft in Cincinnati were absent from work 45 percent fewer days than nonexercisers. Prudential Life Insurance found a 46 percent reduction in major medical expenses over five years resulting from a workplace fitness program. The Scoular Grain Company opened a fitness center for its 600 employees and reaped an annual savings in health care costs of a million dollars— $1,500 per employee. The advantages of physical conditioning, both for individuals and for companies, are irrefutable.

Three primary purposes exist for a regular exercise program: maintaining optimal weight, increasing psychological well-being, and improving the cardiovascular system.

One indirect cause of stress is the sedentary lifestyle adopted by many individuals. An office worker burns up only about 1,200 calories during an eight-hour day. That is fewer calories than are contained in the typical lunch of a hamburger, french fries, and a milkshake. It is little wonder that an estimated 29 percent of the adult American population is at least 10 percent overweight (Health United States, 1988). The resulting excessive strain on both the heart and the self-image makes overweight individuals more vulnerable to stress (Wolman, 1982).

An advantage of regular physical exercise is that it also improves mental as well as physical outlook. It increases self-esteem. It gives individuals the energy to be more alert and attentive throughout the day. Episodes of depression are far less frequent. Exercise fosters the necessary energy to cope with the stresses of both unexpected events and dull routine. Physically active individuals are less prone to anxiety, have less illness, and miss fewer days of work (Griest et al., 1979). Researchers have found a chemical basis for the psychological benefit of exercise: The brain releases endorphins (similar to morphine) during periods of intense physical activity. This substance numbs pain and produces a feeling of well-being, sometimes referred to as "jogger's high," which is a euphoric, relaxed feeling reported by long-distance runners.

Another vital benefit of exercise is a strengthened cardiovascular system (Greenberg, 1987). The best results come from aerobic exercises that do not require more oxygen than a person can take in comfortably (as compared with all-out sprinting or long-distance swimming). This type of exercise includes brisk walking,

---

- Blood pressure is lowered.
- Resting heart rate is lowered; the heart is better able to distribute blood where needed under stress.
- Cardiac output is increased; the heart is better able to distribute blood where needed under stress.
- Number of red blood cells is increased; more oxygen can be carried per quart of blood.
- Elasticity of arteries is increased.
- Triglyceride level is lowered.
- Blood cholesterol level is decreased. High-density cholesterol, which is more protective of blood vessels than low-density cholesterol, is proportionately increased.
- Adrenal secretions in response to emotional stress are lowered.
- Lactic acid is more efficiently eliminated from the muscles. (This has been associated with decreased fatigue and tension.)
- Fibrin, a protein that aids in the formation of blood clots, is decreased.
- Additional routes of blood supply are built up in the heart.

Table 8 Confirmed Benefits of Regular Vigorous Exercise
Source: Goldberg, 1978.

jogging, riding a bicycle, or climbing stairs. However, the cardiovascular system is improved by exercise only when the following two conditions are met:

1. The target heart rate is sustained throughout the exercise. This rate is 60–80 percent of the heart's maximum. To figure your target rate, subtract your age in years from 220, then take 60–80 percent of that number. You should begin your exercise program at the 60-percent level and gradually increase to the 80-percent rate. To check your heart rate during your exercise, periodically monitor your heartbeat for 6 seconds and multiply by 10.

2. The exercise occurs for 20 to 30 minutes, three or four days each week. Since cardiovascular endurance decreases after 48 hours, it is important to exercise at least every other day.

Dietary Control

The adage that "You are what you eat" is sobering, especially given the fact that Americans annually consume an average of 100 pounds of refined sugar, 125 pounds of fat, 36 gallons of carbonated beverages, and 25 times more salt than the human body requires (Perl, 1980). Since diet has received a great deal of attention among Americans in the past decade or so, most people are well informed about healthy foods and eating habits, but the key principles can't be repeated too often. Important guidelines for improving your diet are summarized in the following "Ten Steps to Good Nutrition" (Davis, Eshelman, & McKay, 1980).

Eat a variety of foods. There are approximately 40–60 nutrients you need to stay healthy. Nutritionists recommend the following balanced diet for adults each day: five or six servings of fruits and vegetables; four servings of bread or cereal; two servings of milk, cheese, or yogurt; and two servings of meat, poultry, fish, eggs, beans, or peas.

Maintain optimal weight. Optimal weight is best maintained through a combination of proper diet and exercise. To lose a pound in a week, you need to burn 500 more calories a day than you consume. Although there are a number of fad diets, sound and simple practices that can help individuals avoid overeating include:

- Start each meal with a filling, low-calorie appetizer, such as a clear broth or salad.

- Curb between-meal hunger pangs with large glasses of water or fruit juices such as grapefruit and cranberry.

- A half hour before mealtime, eat a carbohydrate food such as two soda crackers or half a wheat bagel.

- Use vegetables to provide low-calorie bulk in a meal.

- Eat slowly. (It takes approximately 20 minutes after you begin eating for your brain to get the message that you are doing so.)

- Eat regularly (every three to five hours) to avoid binge eating.

- Eat smaller portions. Concentrate on your eating (rather than, for example, on watching TV) so you are aware of how much you've eaten.

- Don't eat to cope with being bored, angry, tired, or anxious. Try exercise instead.

Avoid fats. Fat is an essential nutrient, but Americans tend to eat too much of it. They get approximately 45 percent of their calories from fat, whereas a healthy diet should contain no more than about 30 percent fat. Current medical research indicates that saturated fats (those that are solid at room temperature, such as meat fat, butter, and heavy cream) tend to elevate the level of cholesterol in the blood, contributing to heart disease.

Eat more whole foods. These include raw or lightly steamed vegetables, fruits, whole grains and cereals, brown rice, beans, dried peas, nuts, and seeds. These are complex-carbohydrate foods that contain a mix of starch, fiber, sugar, vitamins, and minerals. Simple-carbohydrate foods to avoid are white flour, white rice, refined sugar, processed fruit products, and overcooked vegetables.

Avoid sugar. Americans get 25 percent of their calories from sugar in various forms, consuming an average of 160 pounds of sugar a year per adult. Sugar gives people a boost of energy and a feeling of restlessness. However, it also stimulates the pancreas to produce insulin, which counteracts the sugar in the blood. Sixty percent of the population have pancreases that overreact, creating feelings of irritability, depression, nausea, anxiety, and, potentially, diabetes.

Avoid sodium. Sodium is an important mineral, but Americans, on the average, consume approximately 10 times more than they need. Sodium is found in table salt (40 percent sodium), as well as many condiments, processed foods, soft drinks, and salty snacks. Consuming more than five grams a day is unwise, especially for individuals with high blood pressure.

Avoid alcohol. Alcohol is high in calories and low in other nutrients. It also depletes the body of Vitamin B, which is important for coping with stress.

Avoid caffeine. Caffeine is a stimulant that chemically induces the fight or flight reaction discussed earlier. In addition, it also depletes the body's supply of Vitamin B. Although many people seek a cup of coffee or a Coke when they are under stress, caffeine actually makes stress worse.

Take vitamin and mineral supplements. Although there is disagreement among nutritionists regarding the need for supplemental vitamins and minerals, it is a good idea to make sure you are getting an adequate supply during periods of high stress. Deficiencies in the B vitamins, Vitamin C, and calcium/magnesium have been linked to stress-related symptoms such as insomnia, irritability, depression, and fatigue.

Make eating a relaxing time. Take time to enjoy nutritious meals eaten in peaceful surroundings. Frequent, small meals, associated with periods of relaxation, are more beneficial than two or three large, frantic meals.

Psychological Resiliency

Another important moderator of the effects of stress is an individual's psychological resiliency. Individuals with certain psychological characteristics, sometimes referred to as "personality types," tend to handle stress better than others. We will focus especially on two examples that show best the relationship between personality and vulnerability to stress: the hardy personality and the Type A personality. First we will introduce the concept of "hardiness" and use it to discuss general psychological attributes that foster resiliency. Then we will focus on three stress-prone elements of the Type A personality and outline techniques for eliminating them.

Hardiness

In their book *The Hardy Executive,* Maddi and Kobasa (1984) described three elements that characterize a hardy, or highly stress-resistant, personality. Hardiness results from (1) feeling in control of one's life, rather than powerless to shape external events; (2) feeling committed to and involved in what one is doing, rather than alienated from one's work and other individuals; and (3) feeling challenged by new experiences rather than viewing change as a threat to security and comfort. According to these authors, hardy individuals tend to interpret stressful situations positively and optimistically, and they respond to stress constructively. As a result, their incidence of illness and emotional dysfunction under stressful conditions is considerably below the norm.

These three concepts—control, commitment, and challenge—are central to the development of a variety of management skills, and are crucial for mitigating the harmful effects of stress (Kobasa, 1982). As we discussed in the Developing Self-Awareness chapter, individuals who score high on internal locus of control feel that they are in charge of their own destinies. They take responsibility for their actions and feel they can neutralize negative external forces. They generally believe that stressors are the result of their personal choices rather than uncontrollable, capricious, or even malicious external forces. The belief that one can influence the course of events is central to developing high self-esteem. Self-esteem, in turn, engenders self-confidence and the optimistic view that bad situations can be improved and that problems can be overcome. Confidence in one's own efficacy produces low fear of failure, high expectations, willingness to take risks, and persistence under adversity (Mednick, 1982; Anderson, 1977; Ivancevich & Matteson, 1980), all of which contribute to resiliency under stress.

Commitment implies both selection and dedication. Hardy individuals not only feel that they choose what they do, but they also strongly believe in the importance of what they do. This commitment is both internal (that is, applied to one's own activities) and external (that is, applied to a larger community). The feeling of being responsible to others is an important buffer against stress (Antonovsky, 1979). Whereas self-esteem and a sense of purpose help provide a psychological support system for coping with stressful events, an individual's belief that others are counting on him or her to succeed and that he or she belongs to a larger community fosters psychological resiliency during stressful periods. Feeling part of a group, feeling cared about, and feeling trusted by others engender norms of cooperation and commitment and encourage constructive responses to stress.

Hardy people also welcome challenge. They believe that change, rather than stability, is the normal and preferred mode of life. Therefore, much of the disruption associated with a stressful life event is interpreted as an opportunity for personal growth rather than as a threat to security. This mode of thinking is consistent with the Chinese word for crisis, which has two meanings: "threat" and "opportunity." Individuals who seek challenges search for new and interesting experiences and accept stress as a necessary step toward learning. Because these individuals prefer change over stability, they tend to have high tolerance for ambiguity and high resiliency under stress (Ivancevich & Matteson, 1980; Maddi & Kobasa, 1984). The three characteristics of hardy personalities—control, commitment, and challenge—have been found to be among the most powerful mitigators of the adverse consequences of stress. By contrast, a different complex of personality attributes, the so-called Type A

Syndrome, is associated with reduced hardiness and higher levels of psychological stress.

The Type A Personality

A second important aspect of psychological resiliency relates to a personality pattern many individuals develop as they enter the competitive worlds of advanced education and of management. By far, the most well-known connection between personality and resiliency relates to a combination of attributes known as the Type A personality. For at least three decades, scientists have been aware of a link between certain personality attributes and stress-related behavioral, psychological, and physiological problems such as anxiety, deteriorating relationships, and heart disease (Friedman & Rosenman, 1959). Table 9 summarizes the primary attributes of Type A personalities that have emerged from the research.

The manner in which Friedman and Rosenman (both cardiologists) discovered the link between personality and heart disease is intriguing. Observing that their waiting room was becoming a bit shabby, they decided to have their chairs reupholstered. The decorator pointed out that only the front edges of the chairs were worn. The doctors suddenly realized that their pa-

- Signs of personal tension, such as a clenched jaw, tight muscles, tics.
- Personal commitment to having, rather than being.
- Unawareness of the broader environment.
- Ignorance of elements outside the immediate task.
- Strong need to be an expert on a subject; otherwise, lack of involvement.
- Compulsion to compete with other Type A's rather than understand and cooperate with them.
- Speech characterized by explosive accentuation, acceleration of the last few words of a sentence, impatience when interrupted.
- Chronic sense of being in a hurry.
- Polyphasic thoughts and actions, that is, a tendency to do several things simultaneously.
- Impatience with the normal pace of events. Tendency to finish others' sentences.
- Doing everything rapidly.
- Feelings of guilt when relaxing.
- Tendency to evaluate all activities in terms of measurable results.
- Belief that Type A attributes are what lead to success.
- Frequent knee-jiggling or finger-tapping.
- Determination to win every game, even when playing with those who are less skilled or experienced.

Table 9   Characteristics of the Type A Personality

tients seemed to be "on edge," literally sitting on the edges of their seats, prepared for action.

Following up their observations with intensive interviews, they noted that during interviews, many of their patients showed signs of impatience and hostility such as fidgeting, eye blinking, grimaces, rapid or explosive speech, interrupting, and filling in incomplete sentences during a pause. The opposite personality types, which they labeled Type B, appeared more relaxed, patient, and able to listen without interrupting. Over 15 percent of Friedman and Rosenman's Type A's had had heart attacks, compared to 7 percent of Type B's.

Subsequent research has found that in America about 70 percent of men and 50 percent of women exhibit Type A personality traits, such as extreme competitiveness, strong desires for achievement, haste, impatience, restlessness, hyperalertness, explosiveness of speech, tenseness of facial muscles, free-floating hostility, and so on. Rosenman suggested that anger, impatience, and competitiveness were the most debilitating factors in the Type A personality; others have proposed hostility (Greenberg, 1987); and some have blamed a feeling of urgency that keeps adrenaline constantly flowing (Kobasa, 1979). Regardless of the key ingredient, the Type A personality is certainly a high risk factor in maintaining personal well-being.

In the most extensive study of personality effects on heart disease ever conducted, an eight-year survey of 3,400 men found that Type A individuals in the 39- to 49-year age group had approximately 6.5 times the likelihood of heart disease as Type B's. Even when factors such as cigarette smoking, parental medical history, blood pressure, and cholesterol levels were factored out, the Type A personality still accounted for a two to three times greater likelihood of heart disease. This research concluded that personality is a better predictor than physiology of cardiovascular illness (Friedman & Rosenman, 1974). Ironically, subsequent research has also found that whereas Type A personalities are more prone to experience heart attacks, they are also more likely to recover from them.

Most Type A individuals believe it is their Type A personality that has led to their success. Many are unwilling to give up that orientation because hard-driving, intense, persistent action is generally admired and valued among managers. This has often been associated with the traditional male management role, but it has also been connected to the disproportionately high incidence of heart disease among men. In fact,

Goldberg (1976) and Jourard (1964) initially linked Type A personality characteristics to certain sex-linked behavior patterns.

Specifically, males or females who followed stereotypic views of appropriate male behavior were found to be more likely to experience stress-related illness. They tended to equate low self-disclosure, low emotional involvement, low display of feelings, high defensiveness, and high insensitivity to the acquisition of power and control—the presumed prerequisites for success. These were so typical of male behavior in the workplace that they became known as "the lethal aspects of the male role" (Jourard, 1964). As more women began to enter the workforce, this same pattern became less and less gender-linked. Many women also behaved as if acceptance in the workplace required "acting as masculine" as their male counterparts. As a result, the gap between stress-related illness among professional men and women has narrowed. In recent years, female stress-related illnesses (e.g., heart attacks, suicides, migraine headaches) actually have surpassed those of males in some professions. This trend is not only tragic but ironic, because corporations are spending millions of dollars each year on training workshops designed to encourage their managers to become more sensitive, understanding, and supportive. The folly of the Type A approach to management, and to life, is illustrated in the following story from the lore of Zen Buddhism.

Matajura wanted to become a great swordsman, but his father said he wasn't quick enough and could never learn. So Matajura went to the famous dueller, Banzo, and asked to become his pupil. "How long will it take me to become a master?" he asked. "Suppose I become your servant, and spend every minute with you; how long?"

"Ten years," said Banzo.

"My father is getting old. Before 10 years have passed, I will have to return home to take care of him. Suppose I work twice as hard; how long will it take me?"

"Thirty years," said Banzo.

"How is that?" asked Matajura. "First you say 10 years. Then when I offer to work twice as hard, you say it will take three times as long. Let me make myself clear: I will work unceasingly; no hardship will be too much. How long will it take?"

"Seventy years," said Banzo. "A pupil in such a hurry learns slowly."

This Type A sense of urgency, of being able to overcome any obstacle by working harder and longer, works against the ability to develop psychological hardiness. When stressors are encountered, arousal levels increase, and the tendency is to combat them by increasing arousal levels, or effort, even further. But at high arousal levels, coping responses become more primitive (Staw, Sandelands, & Dutton, 1981). Patterns of response that were learned most recently are the first ones to disappear, which means that the responses that are most finely tuned to the current stressful situation are the first ones to go. The ability to distinguish among fine-grained stimuli actually deteriorates, so the extra energy expended by individuals trying to cope becomes less and less effective. Weick (1984) pointed out that highly stressed people consequently find it difficult to learn new responses, to brainstorm, to concentrate, to resist relying on old nonadaptive behavior patterns, to perform complex responses, to delegate, and to avoid the vicious spiral of escalating arousal. Resiliency deteriorates.

The Small-Wins Strategy

An effective antidote to this Type A escalation problem is working for "small wins," discussed earlier in this chapter. When individuals work for small wins, they consciously remain sensitive to their small successes, and celebrate them, while coping with a major stressor.

A hypothetical example introduced by Kuhn and Beam (1982, pp. 249–250) illustrates the power of small wins.

Your task is to count out a thousand sheets of paper while you are subject to periodic interruptions. Each interruption causes you to lose track of the count and forces you to start over. If you count the thousand as a single sequence, then an interruption could cause you to lose count of as many as 999. If the sheets are put into stacks of 100, however, and each stack remains undisturbed by interruptions, then the worst possible count loss from interruption is 108. That number represents the recounting of nine stacks of 100 each plus 99 single sheets. Further, if sheets are first put into stacks of 10, which are then joined into stacks of 100, the worst possible loss from interruption would be 27. That number represents nine stacks of 100

plus nine stacks of 10 plus nine single sheets. Not only is far less recounting time lost by putting the paper into "subsystems" of tens and hundreds, but the chances of completing the count are vastly higher.

When individuals work for a small, concrete outcome, giving them a chance to enjoy visible success, heightened confidence, excitement, and optimism result, which motivate an attempt to accomplish another small win. By itself, a small win may seem unimportant. A series of wins at seemingly insignificant tasks, however, reveals a pattern that tends to attract allies, deter opponents, and lower resistance to further action. Once a small win has been accomplished, forces are set in motion that favor another small win. When one solution has been identified, the next solvable problem often becomes more visible. Additional resources also tend to flow toward winners, so the probability of additional successes increases.

Research clearly demonstrates that a small-wins strategy is superior to a strategy of trying to cope with stressors in large chunks. For example, successive small requests are more likely to be approved and achieve compliance than one large request (Freedman & Fraser, 1966). Positions advocated within the latitude of acceptance (i.e., that are only slightly different from current positions) modify opinions more than does advocacy of a position that exceeds those limits (i.e., large differences exist between current and proposed positions). People whose positions are close to one's own tend to be the targets of the most intensive persuasion attempts, while those whose positions are farther away are dismissed, isolated, or derogated. Cognitive therapy is most successful when the patient is persuaded to do just one thing differently that changes his or her pattern of coping up to that point. Learning tends to occur in small increments rather than in large, all-or-nothing chunks. Retention of learning is better when individuals are in an emotional state similar to the one in which they learned the original material. Over 75 percent of the changes and improvements in both individuals and organizations over time can be accounted for by minor improvements, not major alterations (Hollander, 1965). The point is that the incremental approach used in a small-wins strategy is the most basic and the one most compatible with human preferences for learning, perception, motivation, and change (Weick, 1984).

What does this have to do with hardiness and resiliency? A small-wins strategy both engenders hardiness and helps overcome the Type A personality syndrome, which is basically a large-win, winner-takes-all approach to stress. Recall that hardiness is composed of control, commitment, and challenge. The deliberate cultivation of a strategy of small wins helps produce precisely those psychological states. Small wins reinforce the perception that individuals can influence what happens to them (being in control); it helps motivate further action by building on the confidence of past successes (which creates commitment); and it produces changes of manageable size that serve as incentives to broaden, learn, and seek new opportunities or challenges. "Continuing pursuit of small wins can build increasing resistance to stress in people not originally predisposed toward hardiness" (Weick, 1984, p. 46).

Deep-Relaxation Strategies

In addition to a small-wins strategy, a second approach to building psychological resiliency is to learn and practice a deep-relaxation technique. Research demonstrates a marked decrease in Type A personality characteristics for regular users of meditation and deep-relaxation techniques. Using the automotive analogy, individuals who use deep-relaxation exercises find that when stress occurs, their "engines" don't rev up as high, and they return to idle faster (Curtis & Detert, 1981; Greenberg, 1987; Davis, Eshelman, & McKay, 1980). Deep-relaxation techniques differ from temporary, short-term relaxation techniques, which we will discuss later.

Deep-relaxation techniques include meditation, yoga, autogenic training or self-hypnosis, biofeedback, and so on. Considerable evidence exists that individuals who practice such techniques regularly are able to condition their bodies to inhibit the negative effects of stress (Cooper & Aygen, 1979; Stone & Deleo, 1976; Orme-Johnson, 1973; Beary & Benson, 1977; Benson, 1975). Most of these deep-relaxation techniques must be practiced over a period of time to develop fully, but they are not difficult to learn. Most deep-relaxation techniques require the following conditions:

1. A quiet environment in which external distractions are minimized.

2. A comfortable position so that muscular effort is minimized.

3. A mental focus. Transcendental meditation (TM) advocates recommend concentrating on one word, phrase, or object. Benson (1975) suggests the word "one." Others suggest picturing a plain vase.

The ancient Chinese used a carved jade object that resembled a mountain and sat on a desktop. The purpose of focusing on a word or object is to rid the mind of all other thoughts.

4. Controlled breathing (i.e., deliberate breathing) with pauses between breaths. Thoughts are focused on rhythmic breathing, which helps clear the mind and aids concentration.

5. A passive attitude, so that if other thoughts enter the mind, they are ignored.

6. Focused bodily changes. While meditation uses the mind to relax the body, autogenic training uses bodily sensations of heaviness and warmth to change the psychological state. Feelings of warmth and heaviness are induced in different parts of the body which, in turn, create deep relaxation (Luthe, 1962; Kamiya, 1978).

7. Repetition. Because physiological and psychological results depend on consistent practice, the best results occur when such techniques are practiced from 20 to 30 minutes each day.

The Skill Practice section contains an example of a deep-relaxation exercise.

Social Resiliency

The third factor moderating the harmful effects of stress and contributing to resiliency involves developing close social relationships. Individuals who are embedded in supportive social networks are less likely to experience stress and are better equipped to cope with its consequences (Beehr, 1976). Supportive social relations provide opportunities to share one's frustrations and disappointments, to receive suggestions and encouragement, and to experience emotional bonding. Such supportive interactions provide the empathy and bolstering required to cope with stressful events. They are formed most easily among individuals who share close emotional ties (e.g., family members) or common experiences (e.g., coworkers).

Poignant testimony to the value of social support systems during periods of high stress comes from the experiences of soldiers captured during World War II and the Korean and Vietnam wars. When it was possible for prisoners to form permanent, interacting groups, they maintained better health and morale and were able to resist their captors more effectively than when they were isolated or when groups were unstable. Indeed, the well-documented technique used by the Chinese during the Korean War for breaking down soldiers' resistance to their indoctrination efforts involved weakening group solidarity through planting seeds of mistrust and doubt about members' loyalty.

Aside from personal friendships or family relations, two types of social support systems can be formed as part of a manager's job. One is a mentor relationship; the other is a task team. Most individuals, with the possible exception of the most senior managers, can profit from a mentoring relationship. The research is clear, in fact, that career success, work satisfaction, and resiliency to stress are enhanced by a mentoring relationship (Hall, 1976; Kram, 1985). Individuals need someone else in the organization who can provide a role model, from whom they can learn, and from whom they can receive personal attention and a reinforcement of self-worth, especially under uncertain, crucial, and stressful situations.

Many organizations formally prescribe a mentoring system by assigning a senior manager to shepherd a younger manager when he or she enters the organization. With rare exceptions, when the contact is one-way, from the top down, these relationships don't work out (Kram, 1985). The junior manager must actively seek and foster the mentoring relationship as well. The junior manager can do this, not by demonstrating overdependence or overingratiation, but by expressing a desire to use the senior person as a mentor and then by making certain that the relationship does not become a one-way street. The subordinate can pass along important information and resources to the potential mentor, while both will share in working out solutions to problems. That way, the mentoring relationship becomes mutually satisfying and mutually beneficial for both parties, and resiliency to stress is enhanced because of the commitment, trust, and cooperation that begin to characterize the relationship. A mentor's guidance can both help avoid stressful situations and provide support for coping with them.

Smoothly functioning work teams also enhance social resiliency. The social value of working on a team has been well documented in research (Dyer, 1981). The more cohesive the team, the more support it provides its members. Members of highly cohesive teams communicate with one another more frequently and more positively and report higher satisfaction, lower stress, and higher commitment levels than do individ-

uals who do not feel as though they are part of a work team (Shaw, 1976).

The value of work teams has been amply demonstrated in practice as well. In the introductory chapter to this book, for example, we recounted a dramatic change that occurred in the Fremont, California, plant of General Motors when U.S. workers came under Japanese management. In just one year, marked improvements in productivity, morale, and quality occurred, due in large part to the use of effective work teams. Relationships were formed based not only on friendship but on a common commitment to solving work-related problems and to generating ideas for improvement. Teams met regularly during work hours to discuss ideas for improvement and to coordinate and resolve issues. Similar dynamics have been fostered in most of the successful companies in the United States and abroad. The "Japanese miracle" has been attributed largely to the effective use of work teams. Each company that has won the Malcolm Baldrige National Quality Award (e.g., Motorola, Westinghouse, Xerox, Millikin) fostered teamwork among employees as a crucial part of its improvement efforts. The marked improvements that occur in individual satisfaction and lowered stress levels suggest that each person should likewise help facilitate similar teamwork in his or her work setting as part of a social resiliency repertoire. To do so, individuals might consider identifying and structuring team tasks or team issues, facilitating a culture of continuous improvement among coworkers where everyone takes responsibility for generating and sharing ideas for improvement, and sharing information or resources in such a way that the team, rather than independent individuals, becomes the basic unit of action. A detailed discussion of these and other team dynamics is found in the Building Effective Teams chapter.

Temporary Stress-Reduction Techniques

Thus far, we have emphasized eliminating sources of stress and developing resiliency to stress. These are the most desirable stress-management strategies. However, even under ideal circumstances it may be impossible to eliminate all stressors, and individuals must use temporary reactive mechanisms in order to maintain equilibrium. Although increased resilience can buffer the harmful effects of stress, people must sometimes take immediate action in the short term to cope with stress. Implementing short-term strategies reduces stress temporarily so that longer-term stress-elimination, or resiliency, strategies can operate. Short-term strategies are largely reactive and must be repeated whenever stressors are encountered because, unlike other strategies, their effects are only temporary. On the other hand, they are especially useful for immediately calming feelings of anxiety or apprehension. Individuals can use them when they are asked a question they can't answer, when they become embarrassed by an unexpected event, when they are faced with a presentation or an important meeting, or almost any time they are suddenly stressed and must respond in a short period of time. Five of the best-known and easiest to learn techniques are briefly described below. The first two are physiological; the last three are psychological.

Muscle relaxation involves easing the tension in successive muscle groups. Each muscle group is tightened for five or 10 seconds and then completely relaxed. Starting with the feet and progressing to the calves, thighs, stomach, and on to the neck and face, one can relieve tension throughout the entire body. All parts of the body can be included in the exercise. One variation is to roll the head around on the neck several times, shrug the shoulders, or stretch the arms up toward the ceiling for five to 10 seconds, then release the position and relax the muscles. The result is a state of temporary relaxation that helps eliminate tension and refocus energy.

A variation of muscle relaxation involves **deep breathing.** This is done by taking several successive, slow, deep breaths, holding them for five seconds, and exhaling completely. You should focus on breathing itself, so that the mind becomes cleared for a brief time while the body relaxes. After each deep breath, muscles in the body should consciously be relaxed.

A third technique uses **imagery and fantasy** to eliminate stress temporarily by changing the focus of one's thoughts. Imagery involves visualizing an event, using "mind pictures." In addition to visualization, however, imagery also can include recollections of sounds, smells, and textures. The mind focuses on pleasant experiences from the past (e.g., a fishing trip, family vacation, visit with relatives, day at the beach) that can be recalled vividly. Fantasies, on the other hand, are not past memories but make-believe events or images. It is especially well known, for example, that children often construct imaginary friends, make-be-

lieve occurrences, or special wishes that are comforting to them when they encounter stress. Adults also use daydreams or other fantasy experiences to get them through stressful situations. The purpose of this technique is to relieve anxiety or pressure temporarily by focusing on something pleasant so that other, more productive stress-reducing strategies can be developed for the longer term.

The fourth technique is called **rehearsal.** Using this technique, people work themselves through potentially stressful situations, trying out different scenarios and alternative reactions. Appropriate reactions are rehearsed, either in a safe environment before stress occurs, or "off-line," in private, in the midst of a stressful situation. Removing oneself temporarily from a stressful circumstance and working through dialogue or reactions, as though rehearsing for a play, can help one regain control and reduce the immediacy of the stressor.

The last strategy, **reframing,** involves temporarily reducing stress by optimistically redefining a situation as manageable. Although reframing is difficult in the midst of a stressful situation, it can be facilitated by using the following cues:

"I understand this situation."

"I've solved similar problems before."

"Other people are available to help me get through this situation."

"Others have faced similar situations and made it through."

"In the long run, this really isn't so critical."

"I can learn something from this situation."

"There are several good alternatives available to me."

Each of these statements can assist an individual to reframe a situation in order to develop long-term proactive or enactive strategies.

Summary

We began this chapter by explaining stress in terms of a relatively simple model. Four kinds of stressors—time, encounter, situational, and anticipatory—cause negative physiological, psychological, and social reactions in individuals. These reactions are moderated by the resiliency that individuals have developed for coping with stress. The best way to manage stress is to eliminate it through time management, delegation, collaboration, interpersonal competence, work redesign, prioritizing, goal setting, and small wins.

The next most effective stress management strategy is improving one's resiliency. Physiological resiliency is strengthened through increased cardiovascular conditioning and improved diet. Psychological resiliency and hardiness is improved by practicing small-wins strategies and deep relaxation. Social resiliency is increased by fostering mentoring relationships and teamwork among coworkers.

When circumstances make it impossible to apply longer-term strategies for reducing stress, short-term relaxation techniques can temporarily alleviate the symptoms of stress.

Behavioral Guidelines

Following are specific behavioral guidelines for improving one's stress management skills.

1. Use effective time management practices. Make sure that you use time effectively as well as efficiently by generating your own personal mission statement. Make sure that low-priority tasks do not drive out time to work on high-priority activities. Make better use of your time by using the guidelines in the Time Management Survey in the Assessment Section.

2. Build collaborative relationships with individuals based on mutual trust, respect, honesty, and kindness. Make "deposits" into the "emotional bank accounts" of other people. Form close, stable communities among those with whom you work.

3. Consciously work to improve your interpersonal competency by learning and practicing the princi-

ples discussed in other chapters of this book (e.g., Communicating Supportively, Managing Conflict, Empowering and Delegating).

4. Redesign your work to increase its skill variety, importance, task identity (comprehensiveness), autonomy, and feedback. Make the work itself stress-reducing, rather than stress-inducing.

5. Reaffirm priorities and short-term plans that provide direction and focus to activities. Give important activities priority over urgent ones.

6. Increase your general resiliency by leading a balanced life and consciously developing yourself in physical, intellectual, cultural, social, family, and spiritual areas, as well as in your work.

7. Increase your physical resiliency by engaging in a regular program of exercise and proper eating.

8. Increase your psychological resiliency and hardiness by implementing a small-wins strategy. Identify and celebrate the small successes that you and others achieve.

9. Learn at least one deep-relaxation technique and practice it regularly.

10. Increase social resiliency by forming an open, trusting, sharing relationship with at least one other person. Facilitate a mentoring relationship with someone who can affirm your worth as a person and provide support during periods of stress.

11. Establish a teamwork relationship with those with whom you work or study by identifying shared tasks and structuring coordinated action among team members.

12. Learn at least two short-term relaxation techniques and practice them consistently.

Skill Analysis

Cases Involving Stress Management

The Turn of the Tide

Not long ago I came to one of those bleak periods that many of us encounter from time to time, a sudden drastic dip in the graph of living when everything goes stale and flat, energy wanes, enthusiasm dies. The effect on my work was frightening. Every morning I would clench my teeth and mutter: "Today life will take on some of its old meaning. You've got to break through this thing. You've got to!"

But the barren days went by, and the paralysis grew worse. The time came when I knew I had to have help.

The man I turned to was a doctor. Not a psychiatrist, just a doctor. He was older than I, and under his surface gruffness lay great wisdom and compassion. "I don't know what's wrong," I told him miserably, "but I just seem to have come to a dead end. Can you help me?"

"I don't know," he said slowly. He made a tent of his fingers and gazed at me thoughtfully for a long while. Then, abruptly, he asked, "Where were you happiest as a child?"

"As a child?" I echoed. "Why, at the beach, I suppose. We had a summer cottage there. We all loved it."

He looked out the window and watched the October leaves sifting down. "Are you capable of following instructions for a single day?"

"I think so," I said, ready to try anything.

"All right. Here's what I want you to do."

He told me to drive to the beach alone the following morning, arriving not later than nine o'clock. I could take some lunch; but I was not to read, write, listen to the radio, or talk to anyone. "In addition," he said, "I'll give you a prescription to be taken every three hours."

He then tore off four prescription blanks, wrote a few words on each, folded them, numbered them, and handed them to me. "Take these at nine, twelve, three, and six."

"Are you serious?" I asked.

He gave a short bark of laughter.

"You won't think I'm joking when you get my bill!"

The next morning, with little faith, I drove to the beach. It was lonely, all right. A northeaster was blowing; the sea looked gray and angry. I sat in the car, the whole day stretching emptily before me. Then I took out the first of the folded slips of paper. On it was written: LISTEN CAREFULLY.

I stared at the two words. "Why," I thought, "the man must be mad." He had ruled out music and newscasts and human conversation. What else was there?

I raised my head and I did listen. There were no sounds but the steady roar of the sea, the creaking cry of a gull, the drone of some aircraft high overhead. All these sounds were familiar.

I got out of the car. A gust of wind slammed the door with a sudden clap of sound. "Am I supposed to listen carefully to things like that?" I asked myself.

I climbed a dune and looked out over the deserted beach. Here the sea bellowed so loudly that all other sounds were lost. And yet, I thought suddenly, there must be sounds beneath sounds—the soft rasp of drifting sand, the tiny wind-whisperings in the dune grasses—if the listener got close enough to hear them.

On an impulse I ducked down and, feeling fairly ridiculous, thrust my head into a clump of sea-oats. Here I made a discovery: If you listen intently, there is a fractional moment in which everything seems to pause, wait. In that instant of stillness, the racing thoughts halt. For a moment, when you truly listen for something outside yourself, you have to silence the clamorous voices within. The mind rests.

I went back to the car and slid behind the wheel. LISTEN CAREFULLY. As I listened again to the deep growl of the sea, I found myself thinking about the white-fanged fury of its storms.

I thought of the lessons it had taught us as children. A certain amount of patience: you can't hurry the tides. A great deal of respect: the sea does not suffer fools gladly. An awareness of the vast and mysterious interdependence of things: wind and tide and current, calm and squall and hurricane, all combining to determine the paths of the birds above and the fish below. And the cleanness of it all, with every beach swept twice a day by the great broom of the sea.

Sitting there, I realized I was thinking of things bigger than myself—and there was relief in that.

Even so, the morning passed slowly. The habit of hurling myself at a problem was so strong that I felt lost without it. Once, when I was wistfully eyeing the car radio, a phrase from Carlyle jumped into my head: "Silence is the element in which great things fashion themselves."

By noon the wind had polished the clouds out of the sky, and the sea had merry sparkle. I unfolded the second "prescription." And again I sat there, half amused and half exasperated. Three words this time: TRY REACHING BACK.

Back to what? To the past, obviously. But why, when all my worries concerned the present or the future?

I left the car and started tramping reflectively along the dunes. The doctor had sent me to the beach because it was a place of happy memories. Maybe that was what I was supposed to reach for: the wealth of happiness that lay half-forgotten behind me.

I decided to experiment: to work on these vague impressions as a painter would, retouching the colors, strengthening the outlines. I would choose specific incidents and recapture as many details as possible. I would visualize people complete with dress and gestures. I would listen (carefully) for the exact sound of their voices, the echo of their laughter.

The tide was going out now, but there was still thunder in the surf. So I chose to go back twenty years to the last fishing trip I made with my younger brother. (He died in the Pacific during World War II and was buried in the Philippines.) I found that if I closed my eyes and really tried, I could see him with amazing vividness, even the humor and eagerness in his eyes that far-off morning.

In fact, I could see it all: the ivory scimitar of beach where we were fishing; the eastern sky smeared with sunrise; the great rollers creaming in, stately and slow. I could feel the backwash swirl warm around my knees, see the sudden arc of my brother's rod as he struck a fish, hear his exultant yell. Piece by piece I rebuilt it, clear and unchanged under the transparent varnish of time. Then it was gone.

I sat up slowly. TRY REACHING BACK. Happy people were usually assured, confident people. If, then, you deliberately reached back and touched happiness, might there not be released little flashes of power, tiny sources of strength?

This second period of the day went more quickly. As the sun began its long slant down the sky, my mind ranged eagerly through the past, reliving some episodes, uncovering others that had been completely forgotten. For example, when I was around thirteen and my brother ten, Father had promised to take us to the circus. But at lunch there was a phone call: Some urgent business required his attention downtown. We braced ourselves for disappointment. Then we heard him say, "No, I won't be down. It'll have to wait."

When he came back to the table, Mother smiled. "The circus keeps coming back, you know."

"I know," said Father. "But childhood doesn't."

Across all the years I remembered this and knew from the sudden glow of warmth that no kindness is ever wasted or ever completely lost.

By three o'clock the tide was out and the sound of the waves was only a rhythmic whisper, like a giant breathing. I stayed in my sandy nest, feeling relaxed and content—and a little complacent. The doctor's prescriptions, I thought, were easy to take.

But I was not prepared for the next one. This time the three words were not a gentle suggestion. They sounded more like a command. REEXAMINE YOUR MOTIVES.

My first reaction was purely defensive. "There's nothing wrong with my motives," I said to myself. "I want to be successful—who doesn't? I want to have a certain amount of recognition—but so does everybody. I want more security than I've got—and why not?"

"Maybe," said a small voice somewhere inside my head, "those motives aren't good enough. Maybe that's the reason the wheels have stopped going around."

I picked up a handful of sand and let it stream between my fingers. In the past, whenever my work went well, there had always been something spontaneous about it, something uncontrived, something free. Lately it had been calculated, competent—and dead. Why? Because I had been looking past the job itself to the rewards I hoped it would bring. The work had ceased to be an end in itself, it had been merely a means to make money, pay bills. The sense of giving something, of helping people, of making a contribution, had been lost in a frantic clutch at security.

In a flash of certainty, I saw that if one's motives are wrong, nothing can be right. It makes no difference whether you are a mailman, a hairdresser, an insurance salesman, a housewife—whatever. As long as you feel you are serving others, you do the job well. When you are concerned only with helping yourself, you do it less well. This is a law as inexorable as gravity.

For a long time I sat there. Far out on the bar I heard the murmur of the surf change to a hollow roar as the tide turned. Behind me the spears of light were almost horizontal. My time at the beach had almost run out, and I felt a grudging admiration for the doctor and the "prescriptions" he had so casually and cunningly devised. I saw, now, that in them was a therapeutic progression that might well be of value to anyone facing any difficulty.

LISTEN CAREFULLY: To calm a frantic mind, slow it down, shift the focus from inner problems to outer things.

TRY REACHING BACK: Since the human mind can hold but one idea at a time, you blot out present worry when you touch the happiness of the past.

REEXAMINE YOUR MOTIVES: This was the hard core of the "treatment," this challenge to reappraise, to bring one's motives into alignment with one's capabilities and conscience. But the mind must be clear and receptive to do this—hence the six hours of quiet that went before.

The western sky was a blaze of crimson as I took out the last slip of paper. Six words this time. I walked slowly out on the beach. A few yards below the high water mark I stopped and read the words again: WRITE YOUR TROUBLES ON THE SAND.

I let the paper blow away, reached down and picked up a fragment of shell. Kneeling there under the vault of the sky, I wrote several words on the sand, one above the other. Then I walked away, and I did not look back. I had written my troubles on the sand. And the tide was coming in.

Source: Arthur Gordon, 1959.

Discussion Questions

1. What is effective about these strategies for coping with stress? Why did they work? Upon what principles are they based?

2. Which of these techniques can be used on a temporary basis without going to the beach?

3. Are these prescriptions effective coping strategies or merely escapes?

4. What other prescriptions could the author take besides the four mentioned here? Generate your own list.

5. What do these prescriptions have to do with the model of stress management presented in this chapter?

The Case of the Missing Time

At approximately 7:30 A.M. on Tuesday, June 23, 1959, Chet Craig, manager of the Norris Company's Central Plant, swung his car out of the driveway of his suburban home and headed toward the plant located some six miles away, just inside the Midvale city limits. It was a beautiful day. The sun was shining brightly and a cool, fresh breeze was blowing. The trip to the plant took about 20 minutes and sometimes gave Chet an opportunity to think about plant problems without interruption.

The Norris Company owned and operated three printing plants. Norris enjoyed a nationwide commercial business, specializing in quality color work. It was a closely held company with some 350 employees, nearly half of whom were employed at the Central Plant, the largest of the three Norris production operations. The company's main offices were also located in the Central Plant building.

Chet had started with the Norris Company as an expediter in its Eastern Plant in 1948, just after he graduated from Ohio State. After three years Chet was promoted to production supervisor, and two years later he was made assistant to the manager of the Eastern Plant. Early in 1957 he was transferred to the Central Plant as assistant to the plant manager and one month later was promoted to plant manager when the former manager retired (see Figure 6).

Chet was in fine spirits as he relaxed behind the wheel. As his car picked up speed, the hum of the tires on the newly paved highway faded into the background. Various thoughts occurred to him, and he said to himself, "This is going to be the day to really get things done."

He began to run through the day's work, first one project, then another, trying to establish priorities. After a few minutes he decided that the open-end unit scheduling was probably the most important, certainly the most urgent. He frowned for a moment as he recalled that on Friday the vice president and general manager had casually asked him if he had given the project any further thought. Chet realized that he had not been giving it much thought lately. He had been meaning to get to work on this idea for over three months, but something else always seemed to crop up. "I haven't had much time to sit down and really work it out," he said to himself. "I'd better get going and hit this one today for sure." With that he began to break down the objectives, procedures, and installation steps of the project. He grinned as he reviewed the principles involved and calculated roughly the anticipated savings. "It's about time," he told himself. "This idea should have been followed up long ago." Chet remembered that he had first conceived of the open-end unit scheduling idea nearly a year and a half ago, just prior to his leaving Norris's Eastern Plant. He had spoken to his boss, Jim Quince, manager of the Eastern Plant, about it then, and both agreed that it was worth looking into. The idea was temporarily shelved when he was transferred to the Central Plant a month later.

A blast from a passing horn startled him, but his thoughts quickly returned to other plant projects he was determined to get underway. He started to think through a procedure for simpler transport of dies to and from the Eastern Plant. Visualizing the notes on his desk, he thought about the inventory analysis he needed to identify and eliminate some of the slow-moving stock items, the packing controls that needed revision, and the need to design a new special-order form. He also decided that this was the day to settle on a job printer to do the simple outside printing of office forms. There were a few other projects he couldn't recall off-

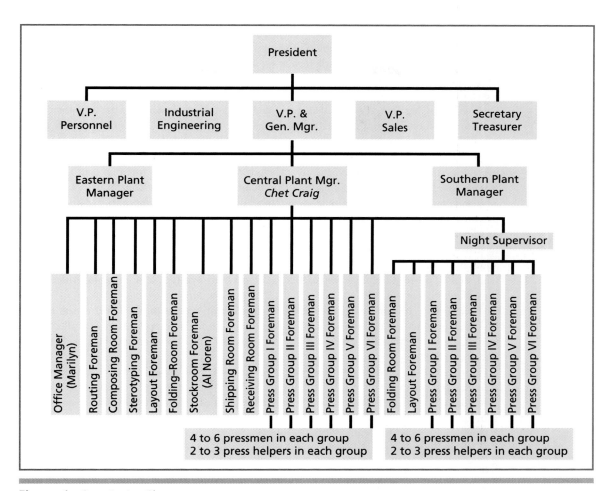

Figure 6 Organization Chart

hand, but he could tend to them after lunch, if not before. "Yes, sir," he said to himself, "this is the day to really get rolling."

Chet's thoughts were interrupted as he pulled into the company parking lot. When he entered the plant Chet knew something was wrong as he met Al Noren, the stockroom foreman, who appeared troubled. "A great morning, Al," Chet greeted him cheerfully.

"Not so good, Chet; my new man isn't in this morning," Noren growled.

"Have you heard from him?" asked Chet.

"No, I haven't," replied Al.

Chet frowned as he commented, "These stock handlers assume you take it for granted that if they're not here, they're not here, and they don't have to call in and verify it. Better ask Personnel to call him."

Al hesitated for a moment before replying, "Okay, Chet, but can you find me a man? I have two cars to unload today."

As Chet turned to leave he said, "I'll call you in half an hour, Al, and let you know."

Making a mental note of the situation, Chet headed for his office. He greeted the group of workers huddled around Marilyn, the office manager, who was discussing the day's work schedule with them. As the meeting broke up, Marilyn picked up a few samples from the clasper, showed them to Chet, and asked if they should be shipped that way or if it would be necessary to inspect them. Before he could answer, Marilyn went on to ask if he could suggest another clerical operator for the sealing machine to replace the regular operator, who was home ill. She also told him that Gene, the industrial engineer, had called and was waiting to hear from Chet.

After telling Marilyn to go ahead and ship the samples, he made a note of the need for a sealer operator for the office and then called Gene. He agreed to stop by Gene's office before lunch and started on his routine morning tour of the plant. He asked each foreman the types and volumes of orders they were running, the number of people present, how the schedules were coming along, and the orders to be run next; helped the folding-room foreman find temporary storage space for consolidating a carload shipment; discussed quality control with a pressman who had been running poor work; arranged to transfer four people temporarily to different departments, including two for Al in the stockroom; and talked to the shipping foreman about pickups and special orders to be delivered that day. As he continued through the plant, he saw to it that reserve stock was moved out of the forward stock area, talked to another pressman about his requested change of vacation schedule, had a "heart-to-heart" talk with a press helper who seemed to need frequent reassurance, and approved two type and one color-order okays for different pressmen.

Returning to his office, Chet reviewed the production reports on the larger orders against his initial productions and found that the plant was running behind schedule. He called in the folding-room foreman and together they went over the lineup of machines and made several necessary changes.

During this discussion, the composing-room foreman stopped in to cover several type changes, and the routing foreman telephoned for approval of a revised printing schedule. The stockroom foreman called twice, first to inform him that two standard, fast-moving stock items were dangerously low, later to advise him that the paper stock for the urgent Dillion job had finally arrived. Chet made the necessary subsequent calls to inform those concerned.

He then began to put delivery dates on important and difficult inquiries received from customers and salesmen. (The routine inquiries were handled by Marilyn.) While he was doing this he was interrupted twice, once by a sales correspondent calling from the West Coast to ask for a better delivery date than originally scheduled, once by the personnel vice president asking him to set a time when he could hold an initial training and induction interview with a new employee.

After dating the customer and salesmen inquiries, Chet headed for his morning conference in the executive offices. At this meeting he answered the sales vice president's questions in connection with "hot" orders, complaints, and the status of large-volume orders and potential new orders. He then met with the general manager to discuss a few ticklish policy matters and to answer "the old man's" questions on several specific production and personnel problems. Before leaving the executive offices, he stopped at the office of the secretary-treasurer to inquire about delivery of cartons, paper, and boxes and to place a new order for paper.

On the way back to his own office, Chet conferred with Gene about two current engineering projects concerning which he had called earlier. When he reached his desk, he looked at his watch. It was 10 minutes before lunch, just time enough to make a few notes of the details he needed to check in order to answer the knotty questions raised by the sales manager that morning.

After lunch Chet started again. He began by checking the previous day's production reports, did some rescheduling to get out urgent orders, placed appropriate delivery dates on new orders and inquiries received that morning, and consulted with a foreman on a personal problem. He spent some 20 minutes at the TWX going over mutual problems with the Eastern Plant.

By mid afternoon Chet had made another tour of the plant, after which he met with the personnel director to review with him a touchy personal problem raised by one of the clerical employees, the vacation schedules submitted by his foremen, and the pending job-evaluation program. Following this conference, Chet hurried back to his office to complete the special statistical report for Universal Waxing Corporation, one of Norris's best customers. As he finished the report, he discovered that it was 10 minutes after six and he was the only one left in the office. Chet was tired. He put on his coat and headed through the plant toward the parking lot; on the way he was stopped by both the night supervisor and night layout foremen for approval of type and layout changes.

With both eyes on the traffic, Chet reviewed the day he had just completed. "Busy?" he asked himself. "Too much so—but did I accomplish anything?" His mind raced over the day's activities. "Yes and no" seemed to be the answer. "There was the usual routine, the same as any other day. The plant kept going and I think it must have been a good production day. Any creative or special-project work done?" Chet grimaced as he reluctantly answered, "No."

With a feeling of guilt, he probed further. "Am I an executive? I'm paid like one, respected like one, and have a responsible assignment with the necessary authority to carry it out. Yet one of the greatest values a company derives from an executive is his creative thinking and accomplishments. What have I done about it? An executive needs some time for thinking. Today was a typical day, just like most other days, and I did little, if any, creative work. The projects that I so enthusiastically planned to work on this morning are exactly as they were yesterday. What's more, I have no guarantee that tomorrow night or the next night will bring me any closer to their completion. This is the real problem and there must be an answer."

Chet continued, "Night work? Yes, occasionally. This is understood. But I've been doing too much of this lately. I owe my wife and family some of my time. When you come down to it, they are the people for whom I'm really working. If I am forced to spend much more time away from them, I'm not meeting my own personal objectives. What about church work? Should I eliminate that? I spend a lot of time on this, but I feel I owe God some time, too. Besides, I believe I'm making a worthwhile contribution in this work. Perhaps I can squeeze a little time from my fraternal activities. But where does recreation fit in?"

Chet groped for the solution. "Maybe I'm just rationalizing because I schedule my own work poorly. But I don't think so. I've studied my work habits carefully and I think I plan intelligently and delegate authority. Do I need an assistant? Possibly, but that's a long-term project and I don't believe I could justify the additional overhead expenditure. Anyway, I doubt whether it would solve the problem."

By this time Chet had turned off the highway onto the side street leading to his home—the problem still uppermost in his mind. "I guess I really don't know the answer," he told himself as he pulled into his driveway. "This morning everything seemed so simple, but now . . ." His thoughts were interrupted as he saw his son running toward the car calling out, "Mommy, Daddy's home."

Discussion Questions

1. Which of Chet's personal characteristics inhibit his effective management of time?

2. What are his organizational problems?

3. What principles of time and stress management are violated in this case?

4. If you were hired as a consultant to Chet, what would you advise him to do?

Skill Practice

Exercises for Long-Term and Short-Run Stress Management

In this section, we provide four relatively short exercises to help you practice good stress management. We strongly urge you to complete the exercises with a partner who can give you feedback and who will monitor your progress in improving your skill. Because managing stress is a personal skill, most of your practice will be done in private. But having a partner who is aware of your commitment will help foster substantial improvement.

The Small-Wins Strategy

An ancient Chinese proverb states that long journeys are always made up of small steps. In Japan, the feeling of obligation to make small, incremental improvements in one's work is known as kaizen. In this chapter the notion of small wins was explained as a way to break apart large problems and identify small successes in coping with them. Each of these approaches represents the same basic philosophy—to recognize incremental successes—and each helps an individual build up psychological resiliency to stress.

Assignment

Answer the following questions. An example is given to help clarify each question, but your response need not relate to the example.

1. What major stressor do you currently face? What creates anxiety or discomfort for you? (For example, "I have too much to do.")

2. What are the major attributes or components of the situation? Divide the major problem into smaller parts or subproblems. (For example, "I have said 'yes' to too many things. I have deadlines approaching. I don't have all the resources I need to complete all my commitments right now.")

3. What are the subcomponents of each of those subproblems? Divide them into yet smaller parts. (For example, "I have the following deadlines approaching: a report

due, a large amount of reading to do, a family obligation, an important presentation, a need to spend some personal time with someone I care about, a committee meeting that requires preparation.")

Attribute 1:

Attribute 2:

Attribute 3:

And so on:

4. What actions can I take that will affect any of these subcomponents? (For example, "I can engage the person I care about in helping me prepare for the presentation. I can write a shorter report than I originally intended. I can carry the reading material with me wherever I go.")

5. What actions have I taken in the past that have helped me cope successfully with similar stressful circumstances? (For example, "I have found someone else to share some of my tasks. I have gotten some reading done while waiting, riding, and eating. I have prepared only key elements for the committee meeting.")

6. What small thing should I feel good about as I think about how I have coped or will cope with this major stressor? (For example, "I have accomplished a lot when the pressure has been on in the past. I have been able to use what I had time to prepare to its best advantage.")

Repeat this process each time you face major stressors. The six specific questions may not be as important to you as (1) breaking the problem down into incremental parts and then breaking those parts down again, and (2) identifying actions that can be done and that have been done in the past that have been successful in coping with components of the stressor.

Life-Balance Analysis

The prescription to maintain a balanced life seems both intuitive and counterintuitive. On the one hand, it makes sense that life should have variety and that each of us should develop multiple aspects of ourselves. Narrowness and rigidity are not highly valued by anyone. On the other hand, the demands of work, school, or family, for example, can be so overwhelming that we don't have time to do much except respond to those demands. Work could take all of one's time. So could school. So could family. The temptation for most of us, then, is to focus on only a few areas of our lives that place a great deal of pressure on us and leave the other areas undeveloped. This exercise helps you discover which areas those might be and which areas need more attention.

Assignment

Use Figure 5 to complete this exercise. In responding to the four items in the exercise, think of the amount of time you spend in each area, the amount of experience and development you have had in the past in each area, and the extent to which development in each area is important to you.

1. In Figure 5, shade in the portion of each section that represents the extent to which that aspect of your life has been well developed. How satisfied are you that each aspect is adequately cultivated?

2. Now write down at least one thing you can start doing to improve your development in the areas that need it. For example, you might do more outside reading to develop culturally, invite a foreign visitor to your home to develop socially, engage in regular prayer or meditation to develop spiritually, and so on.

3. Because the intent of this exercise is not to add more pressure and stress to your life but to increase your resiliency through life balance, identify the things you will stop doing that will make it possible to achieve better life balance.

4. To make this a practice exercise and not just a planning exercise, do something today that you have on your list for items 2 and 3 above. Write down specifically what you'll do and when. Don't let the rest of the week go by without implementing something you've written.

Deep Relaxation

To engage in deep relaxation, you need to reserve time that can be spent concentrating on relaxing. Cognitive control and physiological control are involved. By focusing your mind, you can positively affect both your mental and physical states. This exercise describes one technique that is easily learned and practiced.

The deep-relaxation technique presented below combines key elements of several well-known formulas. It is recommended that this technique be practiced for 20 minutes a day, three times a week (Robinson, 1985; Davis, Eshelman, & McKay, 1980). Reserve at least 30 minutes to engage in this exercise for the first time. Find a quiet spot with your partner, and have that person read the instructions below. When you have finished, switch roles. Since you will practice this exercise later in a different setting, you may want to make a tape recording of these instructions or do the exercise with a friend or a spouse.

Assignment

Step 1: Assume a comfortable position. You may want to lie down. Loosen any tight clothing. Close your eyes and be quiet.

Step 2: Assume a passive attitude. Focus on your body and on relaxing specific muscles. Tune out all other thoughts.

Step 3: Tense and relax each of your muscle groups for 5 to 10 seconds, in the following order:

Forehead. Wrinkle your forehead. Try to make your eyebrows touch your hairline for five seconds, then relax.

Eyes and nose. Close your eyes as tightly as you can for five seconds, then relax.

Lips, cheeks, and jaw. Draw the corners of your mouth back and grimace for five seconds, then relax.

Hands. Extend your arms in front of you. Clench your fists tightly for five seconds, then relax.

Forearms. Extend your arms out against an invisible wall and push forward for five seconds, then relax.

Upper arms. Bend your elbows and tense your biceps for five seconds, then relax.

Shoulders. Shrug your shoulders up to your ears for five seconds, then relax.

Back. Arch your back off the floor for five seconds, then relax.

Stomach. Tighten your stomach muscles by lifting your legs off the ground about two inches for five seconds, then relax.

Hips and buttocks. Tighten your hip and buttock muscles for five seconds, then relax.

Thighs. Tighten your thigh muscles by pressing your legs together as tightly as you can for five seconds, then relax.

Feet. Bend your ankles toward your body as far as you can for five seconds, then point your toes for five seconds, then relax.

Toes. Curl your toes as tightly as you can for five seconds, then relax.

Step 4: Focus on any muscles that are still tense. Repeat the exercise for that muscle group three or four times until it relaxes.

Step 5: Now focus on your breathing. Do not alter it artificially, but focus on taking long, slow breaths. Concentrate exclusively on the rhythm of your breathing until you have taken at least 45 breaths.

Step 6: Now focus on the heaviness and warmth of your body. Let all the energy in your body seep away. Let go of your normal tendency to control your body and mobilize it toward activity.

Step 7: With your body completely relaxed, relax your mind. Picture a plain object such as a glass ball, an empty white vase, the moon, or some favorite thing. Don't analyze it; don't examine it; just picture it. Concentrate fully on the object for at least three minutes without letting any other thoughts enter your mind. Begin now.

Step 8: Now open your eyes, slowly get up, and return to your hectic, stressful, anxiety-ridden, Type A environment better prepared to cope with it effectively.

Monitoring and Managing Time

Time management is the most often identified problem faced by managers and business school students. Most people feel overwhelmed at least part of the time with having too much to accomplish in too little time. It is interesting, however, that even though people may be extremely busy, if they feel that their time is discretionary—that is, it can be used in any way that they choose, such as in recreation, playing with friends or family, or by themselves—they feel less stress. Increasing discretionary time, therefore, is a key to effective time management. This exercise helps you identify and better manage your discretionary time. It takes one full week to complete. It requires that you record how you spend your time for the next seven days. Virtually every executive who is a good time manager has completed this exercise and, in fact, regularly repeats this exercise.

Assignment

Complete the following five steps, then use your partner to get feedback and ideas for improving and refining your plans.

Step 1: Beginning tomorrow, keep a time log for a whole week. Record how you spend each 30-minute block in the next seven 24-hour periods. Using the following format, record the log in your own notebook, diary, or journal.

Time	Activity	Required/Discretionary	Productive/Unproductive
1:00–1:30			
1:30–2:00			
2:00–3:00			
.			
.			
.			
23:00–23:30			
23:30–24:00			

Step 2: Beneath the heading "Required/Discretionary," write whether the time spent in each 30-minute block was required by someone or something else (R) or was discretionary (D).

Step 3: Beneath the heading "Productive/Unproductive," and beside only the discretionary time blocks, rate the extent to which you used each one productively, that is, whether or not it led to improvements of some kind. Use the following scale for your rating:

4 Used productively   2 Used somewhat unproductively

3 Used somewhat productively   1 Used unproductively

Step 4: Draw up a plan for increasing the amount of discretionary time you have during the week. Refer to the Time Management Survey in the Assessment Section for suggestions. Write down the things you will implement.

Step 5: Identify ways in which you can use your discretionary time more productively, especially any blocks of time you rated 1 or 2 in step 3. What will you do to make sure the time you control is used for more long-term benefit? What will you stop doing that impedes your effective use of time?

Skill Application

Activities For Managing Stress

Suggested Assignments

1. Do a systematic analysis of the stressors you face in your job, family, school, and social life. List the types of stressors you face, and identify strategies to eliminate or sharply reduce them. Record this analysis in your journal.

2. Find someone you know well who is experiencing a great deal of stress. Teach him or her how to manage that stress better by applying the concepts, principles, techniques, and exercises in this chapter. Describe what you taught and record the results in your journal.

3. Implement at least three of the time management techniques suggested in the Time Management Survey or elsewhere that you are not currently using but think you might find helpful. In your time log, keep track of the amount of time these techniques save you over a one-month period. Be sure to use that extra time productively.

4. With a coworker or colleague, identify ways in which your work at school, job, or home can be redesigned to reduce stress and increase productivity. Use the hints provided in the chapter to guide your redesign.

5. Write a personal principles statement. Specify precisely your core principles; those things you consider to be central to your life and your sense of self-worth; and the legacy you want to leave. Identify at least one thing that you want to accomplish in your life that you would like to be known for. Begin working on it today.

6. Establish a short-term goal or plan that you wish to accomplish this year. Make it compatible with the top priorities in your life. Specify the behavioral action steps, the

reporting and accounting mechanisms, and the criteria of success and rewards as outlined in Figure 4. Share this plan with others you know so that you have an incentive to pursue it even after you finish this class.

7. Get a physical examination, then outline and implement a regular physical fitness and diet program. Even if it is just regular walking, do some kind of physical exercise at least three times a week. Preferably, institute a regular, vigorous cardiovascular fitness program. Record your progress in your journal.

8. Pick at least one long-term deep-relaxation technique. Learn it and practice it on a regular basis. Record your progress in your journal.

9. Establish a mentoring relationship with someone with whom you work or go to school. Your mentor may be a professor, a senior manager, or someone who has been around longer than you have. Make certain that the relationship is reciprocal and that it will help you cope with the stresses you face at work or school.

Application Plan and Evaluation

The intent of this exercise is to help you apply this cluster of skills in a real-life, out-of-class setting. Now that you have become familiar with the behavioral guidelines that form the basis of effective skill performance, you will improve most by trying out those guidelines in an everyday context. Unlike a classroom activity, in which feedback is immediate and others can assist you with their evaluations, this skill application activity is one you must accomplish and evaluate on your own. There are two parts to this activity. Part 1 helps prepare you to apply the skill. Part 2 helps you evaluate and improve on your experience. Be sure to write down answers to each item. Don't short-circuit the process by skipping steps.

Part 1. Planning

1. Write down the two or three aspects of this skill that are most important to you. These may be areas of weakness, areas you most want to improve, or areas that are most salient to a problem you face right now. Identify the specific aspects of this skill that you want to apply.

2. Now identify the setting or the situation in which you will apply this skill. Establish a plan for performance by actually writing down a description of the situation. Who else will be involved? When will you do it? Where will it be done?

Circumstances:

Who else?

When?

Where?

3. Identify the specific behaviors you will engage in to apply this skill. Operationalize your skill performance.

4. What are the indicators of successful performance? How will you know you have been effective? What will indicate you have performed competently?

Part 2. Evaluation

5. After you have completed your implementation, record the results. What happened? How successful were you? What was the effect on others?

6. How can you improve? What modifications can you make next time? What will you do differently in a similar situation in the future?

7. Looking back on your whole skill practice and application experience, what have you learned? What has been surprising? In what ways might this experience help you in the long term?

Chapter

3

Solving Problems Creatively

skill development

Skill Assessment

Diagnostic Surveys for Creative Problem Solving

Problem Solving, Creativity, and Innovation

Step 1: Before you read the material in this chapter, please respond to the following statements by writing a number from the rating scale below in the left-hand column (Preassessment). Your answers should reflect your attitudes and behavior as they are now, not as you would like them to be. Be honest. This instrument is designed to help you discover your level of competency in problem solving and creativity so you can tailor your learning to your specific needs. When you have completed the survey, use the scoring key in Appendix I to identify the skill areas discussed in this chapter that are most important for you to master.

Step 2: After you have completed the reading and the exercises in this chapter and, ideally, as many as you can of the Skill Application assignments at the end of this chapter, cover up your first set of answers. Then respond to the same statements again, this time in the right-hand column (Postassessment). When you have completed the survey, use the scoring key in Appendix I to measure your progress. If your score remains low in specific skill areas, use the behavioral guidelines at the end of the Skill Learning section to guide further practice.

Rating Scale

1	Strongly disagree	4	Slightly agree
2	Disagree	5	Agree
3	Slightly disagree	6	Strongly agree

Assessment

Pre-   Post-   *When I encounter a routine problem:*

_____   _____   1. I state clearly and explicitly what the problem is. I avoid trying to solve it until I have defined it.

_____   _____   2. I always generate more than one alternative solution to the problem, instead of identifying only one obvious solution.

_____   _____   3. I keep in mind both long-term and short-term consequences as I evaluate various alternative solutions.

_____   _____   4. I gather as much information as I can about what the problem is before trying to solve it.

_____   _____   5. I keep steps in the problem-solving process distinct; that is, I define the problem before proposing alternative solutions, and I generate alternatives before selecting a single solution.

When faced with an ambiguous or difficult problem that does not have an easy solution:

_____ _____ 6. I try out several definitions of the problem. I don't limit myself to just one way to define it.

_____ _____ 7. I try to be flexible in the way I approach the problem by trying out several different alternatives rather than relying on conventional approaches.

_____ _____ 8. I try to find underlying patterns among elements in the problem so that I can uncover underlying dimensions or principles that help me understand the problem.

_____ _____ 9. I try to unfreeze my thinking by asking lots of questions about the nature of the problem before considering ways to solve it.

_____ _____ 10. I try to think about the problem from both the left (logical) side of my brain and the right (intuitive) side of my brain.

_____ _____ 11. To help me understand the problem and generate alternative solutions, I use analogies and metaphors that help me identify what else this problem is like.

_____ _____ 12. I frequently try to reverse my initial definition of the problem to consider whether or not the exact opposite is also true.

_____ _____ 13. I do not evaluate the merits of an alternative solution to the problem before I have generated a list of alternatives. That is, I avoid selecting one solution until I have developed several possible solutions.

_____ _____ 14. I often break down the problem into smaller components and analyze each one separately.

_____ _____ 15. I have some specific techniques that I use to help develop creative and innovative solutions to problems.

When trying to foster more creativity and innovation among those with whom I work:

_____ _____ 16. I help arrange opportunities for individuals to work on their ideas outside the constraints of normal procedures.

_____ _____ 17. I make sure there are divergent points of view represented in every problem-solving group.

_____ _____ 18. I sometimes make outrageous suggestions, even demands, to stimulate people to find new ways of approaching problems.

_____ _____ 19. I try to acquire information from customers regarding their preferences and expectations.

_____ _____ 20. I sometimes involve outsiders (e.g., customers or recognized experts) in problem-solving discussions.

_____ _____ 21. I provide recognition not only to those who are idea champions but also to those who support others' ideas and who provide resources to implement them.

_____ _____ 22. I encourage informed rule-breaking in pursuit of creative solutions.

How Creative Are You?© (REVISED)

How creative are you? The following test helps you determine if you have the personality traits, attitudes, values, motivations, and interests that characterize creativity. It is based on several years' study of attributes possessed by men and women in a variety of fields and occupations who think and act creatively.

For each statement, write in the appropriate letter:

A   Agree

B   Undecided or Don't Know

C   Disagree

Be as frank as possible. Try not to second-guess how a creative person might respond. Turn to Appendix I to find the answer key and an interpretation of your scores.

_____	1.	I always work with a great deal of certainty that I am following the correct procedure for solving a particular problem.
_____	2.	It would be a waste of time for me to ask questions if I had no hope of obtaining answers.
_____	3.	I concentrate harder on whatever interests me than do most people.
_____	4.	I feel that a logical step-by-step method is best for solving problems.
_____	5.	In groups I occasionally voice opinions that seem to turn some people off.
_____	6.	I spend a great deal of time thinking about what others think of me.
_____	7.	It is more important for me to do what I believe to be right than to try to win the approval of others.
_____	8.	People who seem uncertain about things lose my respect.
_____	9.	More than other people, I need to have things interesting and exciting.
_____	10.	I know how to keep my inner impulses in check.
_____	11.	I am able to stick with difficult problems over extended periods of time.
_____	12.	On occasion I get overly enthusiastic.
_____	13.	I often get my best ideas when doing nothing in particular.
_____	14.	I rely on intuitive hunches and the feeling of "rightness" or "wrongness" when moving toward the solution of a problem.
_____	15.	When problem solving, I work faster when analyzing the problem and slower when synthesizing the information I have gathered.
_____	16.	I sometimes get a kick out of breaking the rules and doing things I am not supposed to do.
_____	17.	I like hobbies that involve collecting things.
_____	18.	Daydreaming has provided the impetus for many of my more important projects.
_____	19.	I like people who are objective and rational.
_____	20.	If I had to choose from two occupations other than the one I now have, I would rather be a physician than an explorer.

_____ 21. I can get along more easily with people if they belong to about the same social and business class as myself.

_____ 22. I have a high degree of aesthetic sensitivity.

_____ 23. I am driven to achieve high status and power in life.

_____ 24. I like people who are sure of their conclusions.

_____ 25. Inspiration has nothing to do with the successful solution of problems.

_____ 26. When I am in an argument, my greatest pleasure would be for the person who disagrees with me to become a friend, even at the price of sacrificing my point of view.

_____ 27. I am much more interested in coming up with new ideas than in trying to sell them to others.

_____ 28. I would enjoy spending an entire day alone, just "chewing the mental cud."

_____ 29. I tend to avoid situations in which I might feel inferior.

_____ 30. In evaluating information, the source is more important to me than the content.

_____ 31. I resent things being uncertain and unpredictable.

_____ 32. I like people who follow the rule "business before pleasure."

_____ 33. Self-respect is much more important than the respect of others.

_____ 34. I feel that people who strive for perfection are unwise.

_____ 35. I prefer to work with others in a team effort rather than solo.

_____ 36. I like work in which I must influence others.

_____ 37. Many problems that I encounter in life cannot be resolved in terms of right or wrong solutions.

_____ 38. It is important for me to have a place for everything and everything in its place.

_____ 39. Writers who use strange and unusual words merely want to show off.

_____ 40. Below is a list of terms that describe people. Choose 10 words that best characterize you.

_____ energetic	_____ persuasive	_____ observant
_____ fashionable	_____ self-confident	_____ persevering
_____ original	_____ cautious	_____ habit-bound
_____ resourceful	_____ egotistical	_____ independent
_____ stern	_____ predictable	_____ formal
_____ informal	_____ dedicated	_____ forward-looking
_____ factual	_____ open-minded	_____ tactful
_____ inhibited	_____ enthusiastic	_____ innovative
_____ poised	_____ acquisitive	_____ practical
_____ alert	_____ curious	_____ organized
_____ unemotional	_____ clear-thinking	_____ understanding

_____ dynamic	_____ self-demanding	_____ polished
_____ courageous	_____ efficient	_____ helpful
_____ perceptive	_____ quick	_____ good-natured
_____ thorough	_____ impulsive	_____ determined
_____ realistic	_____ modest	_____ involved
_____ absent-minded	_____ flexible	_____ sociable
_____ well-liked	_____ restless	_____ retiring

Source: Raudsepp, 1981.

Innovative Attitude Scale

Indicate the extent to which each of the following statements is true of either your actual behavior or your intentions at work. That is, describe the way you are or the way you intend to be on the job. Use the scale for your responses.

Rating Scale

5	Almost always true		2	Seldom true
4	Often true		1	Almost never true
3	Not applicable			

Scoring: To score the "Innovative Attitude Scale" turn to Appendix I to find the answer key and an interpretation of your score.

_____	1.	I openly discuss with my boss how to get ahead.
_____	2.	I try new ideas and approaches to problems.
_____	3.	I take things or situations apart to find out how they work.
_____	4.	I welcome uncertainty and unusual circumstances related to my tasks.
_____	5.	I negotiate my salary openly with my supervisor.
_____	6.	I can be counted on to find a new use for existing methods or equipment.
_____	7.	Among my colleagues and coworkers, I will be the first or nearly the first to try out a new idea or method.
_____	8.	I take the opportunity to translate communications from other departments for my work group.
_____	9.	I demonstrate originality.
_____	10.	I will work on a problem that has caused others great difficulty.
_____	11.	I provide critical input toward a new solution.
_____	12.	I provide written evaluations of proposed ideas.
_____	13.	I develop contacts with experts outside my firm.
_____	14.	I use personal contacts to maneuver into choice work assignments.

_____	15.	I make time to pursue my own pet ideas or projects.
_____	16.	I set aside resources for the pursuit of a risky project.
_____	17.	I tolerate people who depart from organizational routine.
_____	18.	I speak out in staff meetings.
_____	19.	I work in teams to try to solve complex problems.
_____	20.	If my coworkers are asked, they will say I am a wit.

Source: Ettlie & O'Keefe, 1982.

■ Skill Learning

Problem Solving, Creativity, and Innovation

Problem solving is a skill that is required of every person in almost every aspect of life. Seldom does an hour go by without an individual's being faced with the need to solve some kind of problem. The manager's job is inherently a problem-solving job. If there were no problems in organizations, there would be no need for managers. Therefore, it is hard to conceive of an incompetent problem solver succeeding as a manager.

In this chapter we offer specific guidelines and techniques for improving problem-solving skills. Two kinds of problem solving—rational and creative—are addressed. Effective managers are able to solve problems both rationally and creatively, even though different skills are required for each type of problem. First we discuss rational problem solving—the kind of problem solving that managers use many times each day. Then we turn to creative problem solving, a kind of problem solving that occurs less frequently. Yet this creative problem-solving ability often separates career successes from career failures, the heroes from the goats, and the achievers from the derailed executives. It can also produce a dramatic impact on organizational effectiveness. The chapter provides guidelines for how one can become a more effective problem solver, both rational and creative, and concludes with a brief discussion of how managers can foster creative problem solving and innovation among the people with whom they work.

Steps in Rational Problem Solving

Most people, including managers, don't particularly like problems. Problems are time consuming, they create stress, and they never seem to go away. In fact, most people try to get rid of problems as soon as they can. Their natural tendency is to select the first reasonable solution that comes to mind (March & Simon, 1958). Unfortunately, that first solution is often not the best one. In typical problem solving, most people implement a marginally acceptable or merely satisfactory solution instead of the optimal or ideal solution. In fact, many observers have attributed the decline in U.S. quality and competitiveness in the 1970s and 1980s primarily to the abandonment of correct problem-solving principles. Short cuts, they argue, had a major negative effect on the American economy. Effective problem solving, on the other hand, approaches problems from a rational or logical perspective. It involves at least four steps, which are explained next.

Defining the Problem

The most widely accepted model of rational problem solving is summarized in Table 1. This method is well known and lies at the heart of the quality movement.

It is widely asserted that to improve quality as individuals and as organizations, an essential step is to learn and apply this rational method of problem solving (see, for example, Juran, 1988; Ichikawa, 1986; Greene, 1993). Many large organizations (e.g., Ford Motor, General Electric, Dana) spend hundreds of thousands of dollars to teach their managers this type of problem solving as part of their quality improvement process.

The first step is to define a problem. This involves diagnosing a situation so that the focus is on the real problem, not just its symptoms. For example, suppose you must deal with an employee who consistently fails to get work done on time. Slow work might be the problem, or it might be only a symptom of another underlying problem such as bad health, low morale, lack of training, or inadequate rewards. Defining the problem, therefore, requires a wide search for information. The more information that is acquired, the more likely it is that the problem will be defined accurately. As Charles Kettering put it, "It ain't the things you don't know that'll get you in trouble, but the things you know for sure that ain't so."

Following are some attributes of good problem definition:

1. Factual information is differentiated from opinion or speculation. Objective data are separated from perceptions and suppositions.

2. All individuals involved are tapped as information sources. Broad participation is encouraged.

3. The problem is stated explicitly. This often helps point out ambiguities in the definition.

4. The problem definition clearly identifies what standard or expectation has been violated. Problems, by their very nature, involve the violation of some standard or expectation.

STEP	CHARACTERISTICS
1. Define the problem.	• Differentiate fact from opinion. • Specify underlying causes. • Tap everyone involved for information. • State the problem explicitly. • Identify what standard is violated. • Determine whose problem it is. • Avoid stating the problem as a disguised solution.
2. Generate alternative solutions.	• Postpone evaluating alternatives. • Be sure all involved individuals generate alternatives. • Specify alternatives that are consistent with goals. • Specify both short-term and long-term alternatives. • Build on others' ideas. • Specify alternatives that solve the problem.
3. Evaluate and select an alternative.	• Evaluate relative to an optimal standard. • Evaluate systematically. • Evaluate relative to goals. • Evaluate main effects and side effects. • State the selected alternative explicitly.
4. Implement and follow up on the solution.	• Implement at the proper time and in the right sequence. • Provide opportunities for feedback. • Engender acceptance of those who are affected. • Establish an ongoing monitoring system. • Evaluate based on problem solution.

Table 1 A Model of Problem Solving

5. The problem definition must address the question "Whose problem is this?" No problems are completely independent of people.

6. The definition is not simply a disguised solution. Saying "The problem is that we need to motivate slow employees" is inappropriate because the problem is stated as a solution.

Managers often propose a solution before an adequate definition of a problem has been given. This may lead to solving the "wrong" problem. The definition step in problem solving, therefore, is extremely important.

Generating Alternatives

The second step is to generate alternative solutions. This requires postponing the selection of any one solution until several alternatives have been proposed. Maier (1970) found that the quality of solutions can be significantly enhanced by considering multiple alternatives. Judgment and evaluation, therefore, must be postponed so the first acceptable solution suggested isn't the one immediately selected. As Broadwell (1972, p. 121) noted:

> The problem with evaluating [an alternative] too early is that we may rule out some good ideas by just not getting around to thinking about them. We hit on an idea that sounds good and we go with it, thereby never even thinking of alternatives that may be better in the long run.

Many alternative solutions should be generated before any of them are evaluated. A common problem in managerial decision making is that alternatives are evaluated as they are proposed, so the first acceptable (although frequently not optimal) one is chosen.

Some attributes of good alternative generation follow:

1. The evaluation of each proposed alternative is postponed. All alternatives should be proposed before evaluation is allowed.

2. Alternatives are proposed by all individuals involved in the problem. Broad participation in alternative proposals improves solution quality and group acceptance.

3. Alternative solutions are consistent with organizational goals or policies. Subversion and criticism

are detrimental to both the organization and the alternative generation process.

4. Alternatives take into consideration both short-term and long-term consequences.

5. Alternatives build on one another. Bad ideas may become good ones if they are combined with or modified by other ideas.

6. Alternatives solve the problem that has been defined. Another problem may also be important, but it should be ignored if it does not directly affect the problem being considered.

Evaluating Alternatives

The third problem-solving step is to evaluate and select an alternative. This step involves careful weighing of the advantages and disadvantages of the proposed alternatives before making a final selection. In selecting the best alternative, skilled problem solvers make sure that alternatives are judged in terms of the extent to which they will solve the problem without causing other unanticipated problems; the extent to which all individuals involved will accept the alternative; the extent to which implementation of the alternative is likely; and the extent to which the alternative fits within organizational constraints (e.g., is consistent with policies, norms, and budget limitations). Care is taken not to short-circuit these considerations by choosing the most conspicuous alternative without considering others. As March and Simon (1958, p. 141) point out:

> Most human decision making, whether individual or organizational, is concerned with the discovery and selection of satisfactory alternatives; only in exceptional cases is it concerned with the discovery and selection of optimal alternatives. To optimize requires processes several orders of magnitude more complex than those required to satisfy. An example is the difference between searching a haystack to find the sharpest needle in it and searching the haystack to find a needle sharp enough to sew with.

Given the natural tendency to select the first satisfactory solution proposed, this step deserves particular attention in problem solving.

Some attributes of good evaluation are:

1. Alternatives are evaluated relative to an optimal, rather than a satisfactory standard.

2. Evaluation of alternatives occurs systematically so each alternative is given due consideration. Short-circuiting evaluation inhibits selection of optimal alternatives.

3. Alternatives are evaluated in terms of the goals of the organization and the individuals involved. Organizational goals should be met, but individual preferences should also be considered.

4. Alternatives are evaluated in terms of their probable effects. Both side-effects and direct effects on the problem are considered.

5. The alternative ultimately selected is stated explicitly. This can help uncover latent ambiguities.

Implementing the Solution

The final step is to implement and follow up on the solution. Implementation of any solution requires sensitivity to possible resistance from those who will be affected by it. Almost any change engenders some resistance. Therefore, the best problem solvers are careful to select a strategy that maximizes the probability that the solution will be accepted and fully implemented. This may involve ordering that the solution be implemented by others, "selling" the solution to others, or involving others in the implementation. Tannenbaum and Schmidt (1958) and Vroom and Yetton (1973) provide guidelines for managers to determine which of these implementation behaviors is most appropriate under which circumstances. Generally speaking, participation by others in the implementation of a solution will increase its acceptance and decrease resistance.

Effective implementation also requires follow-up to prevent negative side-effects and ensure solution of the problem. Follow-up not only helps ensure effective implementation but also serves a feedback function by providing information that can be used to improve future problem solving. Drucker (1974, p. 480) explained:

A feedback has to be built into the decision to provide continuous testing, against actual events, of the expectations that underlie the decision. Few decisions work out the way they are intended to. Even the best decision usually runs into snags, unexpected obstacles, and all kinds of surprises. Even the most effective decision eventually becomes obsolete. Unless there is feedback from the results of the decision, it is unlikely to produce the desired results.

Some attributes of effective implementation and follow-up are these:

1. Implementation occurs at the right time and in the proper sequence. It does not ignore constraining factors, and it does not come before steps 1, 2, and 3 in the problem-solving process.

2. The implementation process includes opportunities for feedback. How well the selected solution works needs to be communicated.

3. Implementation engenders support and acceptance by those affected by a decision. Participation is often the best way to ensure acceptance by others.

4. An ongoing monitoring system is set up for the implemented solution. Long-term as well as short-term effects should be assessed.

5. Evaluation of success is based on problem solution, not on side benefits. Although the solution may provide some positive outcomes, it is unsuccessful unless it solves the problem being considered.

Limitations of the Rational Problem-Solving Model

Most experienced problem solvers are familiar with the preceding steps in rational problem solving, which are based on empirical research results and sound rationale (Maier, 1970; Huber, 1980; Elbing, 1978; Filley, House, & Kerr, 1976). Unfortunately, managers do not always practice these steps. The demands of their jobs often pressure managers into circumventing some steps, and problem solving suffers as a result. When these four steps (defining the problem, generating alternatives, evaluating alternatives, and implementing the solution) are followed, however, effective problem solving is markedly enhanced.

On the other hand, simply learning about and practicing these four steps does not guarantee that an individual will effectively solve all types of problems. These problem-solving steps are useful mainly when the problems faced are straightforward, when alternatives are readily definable, when relevant information is available, and when a clear standard exists against which to judge the correctness of a solution. Thompson and Tuden (1959) call problems with these characteristics "computational problems," for which the main tasks are to gather information, generate alternatives, and make an informed choice. But many managerial problems are not of this type. Definitions, information, alternatives, and standards are seldom unambiguous or readily available. Hence, knowing the steps in problem solving and being able to implement them are not necessarily the same thing. For example, problems such as discovering why morale is so low, determining how to implement downsizing without antagonizing employees, developing a new process that will double productivity and eliminate all errors, or identifying ways to overcome resistance to change are common—and often very complicated—problems faced by most managers. Such problems may not always have an easily identifiable definition or set of alternative solutions available. It may not be clear how much information is needed, what the complete set of

alternatives is, or how one knows if the information being obtained is accurate. Rational problem solving may help, but something more is needed to address these problems successfully.

Table 2 summarizes some reasons why rational problem solving is not always effective in day-to-day managerial situations. Constraints exist on each of these four steps and stem from other individuals or from organizational processes that make it difficult to follow the prescribed model.

Another reason why the rational problem-solving model is not always effective for managers is that some problems are not amenable to systematic or rational analysis. Sufficient and accurate information may not be available, outcomes may not be predictable, or means-ends connections may not be evident. In order to solve such problems, a new way of thinking may be required, multiple or conflicting definitions may be needed, and unprecedented alternatives may have to be generated. In short, creative problem solving must be used.

STEP	CONSTRAINTS
1. Define the problem.	• There is seldom consensus as to the definition of the problem. • There is often uncertainty as to whose definition will be accepted. • Problems are usually defined in terms of the solutions already possessed.
2. Generate alternative solutions.	• Solution alternatives are usually evaluated one at a time as they are proposed. • Few of the possible alternatives are usually known. • The first acceptable solution is usually accepted. • Alternatives are based on what was successful in the past.
3. Evaluate and select an alternative.	• Limited information about each alternative is usually available. • Search for information occurs close to home—in easily accessible places. • The type of information available is constrained by factors such as primacy versus recency, extremity versus centrality, expected versus surprising, and correlation versus causation. • Gathering information on each alternative is costly. • Preferences of which is the best alternative are not always known. • Satisfactory solutions, not optimal ones, are usually accepted. • Solutions are often selected by oversight or default. • Solutions often are implemented before the problem is defined.
4. Implement and follow up on the solution.	• Acceptance by others of the solution is not always forthcoming. • Resistance to change is a universal phenomenon. • It is not always clear what part of the solution should be monitored or measured in follow-up. • Political and organizational processes must be managed in any implementation effort. • It may take a long time to implement a solution.

Table 2 Some Constraints on the Rational Problem-Solving Model

Impediments to Creative Problem Solving

Most people have trouble solving problems creatively. They have developed certain conceptual blocks in their problem-solving activities of which they are not even aware. These blocks inhibit them from solving certain problems effectively. The blocks are largely personal, as opposed to interpersonal or organizational, so skill development is required to overcome them.

Conceptual blocks are mental obstacles that constrain the way problems are defined and limit the number of alternative solutions thought to be relevant (Allen, 1974). Every individual has conceptual blocks, but some people have more numerous and more intense ones. These blocks are largely unrecognized or unconscious, so the only way individuals can be made aware of them is to be confronted with problems that are unsolvable because of them. Conceptual blocks result largely from the thinking processes that problem solvers use when facing problems. Everyone develops some conceptual blocks over time. In fact, we need some of them to cope with everyday life. Here's why.

At every moment, each of us is bombarded with far more information than we can possibly absorb. For example, you are probably not conscious right now of the temperature of the room, the color of your skin, the level of illumination overhead, or how your toes feel in your shoes. All of this information is available to you and is being processed by your brain, but you have tuned out some things and focused on others. Over time, you must develop the habit of mentally filtering out some of the information to which you are exposed; otherwise, information overload would drive you crazy. These filtering habits eventually become conceptual blocks. Though you are not conscious of them, they inhibit you from registering some kinds of information and, therefore, from solving certain kinds of problems.

Paradoxically, the more formal education individuals have, and the more experience they have in a job, the less able they are to solve problems in creative ways. It has been estimated that most adults over 40 display less than 2 percent of the creative problem-solving ability of a child under 5 years old. That's because formal education often prescribes "right" answers, analytic rules, or thinking boundaries. Experience in a job leads to "proper" ways of doing things, specialized knowledge, and rigid expectation of appropriate actions.

Individuals lose the ability to experiment, improvise, or take mental detours. Consider the following example:

> If you place in a bottle half a dozen bees and the same number of flies, and lay the bottle down horizontally, with its base to the window, you will find that the bees will persist, till they die of exhaustion or hunger, in their endeavor to discover an issue through the glass; while the flies, in less than two minutes, will all have sallied forth through the neck on the opposite side. . . . It is [the bees'] love of light, it is their very intelligence, that is their undoing in this experiment. They evidently imagine that the issue from every prison must be there when the light shines clearest; and they act in accordance, and persist in too logical an action. To them glass is a supernatural mystery they never have met in nature; they have had no experience of this suddenly impenetrable atmosphere; and the greater their intelligence, the more inadmissible, more incomprehensible, will the strange obstacle appear. Whereas the feather-brained flies, careless of logic as of the enigma of crystal, disregarding the call of the light, flutter wildly, hither and thither, meeting here the good fortune that often waits on the simple, who find salvation where the wiser will perish, necessarily end by discovering the friendly opening that restores their liberty to them (Sill, 1968, p. 189).

This illustration identifies a paradox inherent in learning to solve problems creatively. On the one hand, more education and experience may inhibit creative problem solving and reinforce conceptual blocks. Like the bees in the story, individuals may not find solutions because the problem requires less "educated," more "playful" approaches. On the other hand, as several researchers have found, training directed toward improving thinking significantly enhances creative problem-solving abilities and managerial effectiveness (Barron, 1963; Taylor & Barron, 1963; Torrance, 1965).

Parnes (1962), for example, found that training in thinking increased the number of good ideas produced in problem solving by 125 percent. Bower (1965) recorded numerous examples of organizations that increased profitability and efficiency through training their employees to improve their thinking skills. Many organizations such as IBM, General Electric, and AT&T now send their executives to creativity workshops in order to improve their creative-thinking abilities. Creative problem-solving experts are currently hot property on the consulting circuit, and about a million copies of books on creativity are sold each year in North America. Several well-known products have been produced as a direct result of this kind of training, for example, NASA's Velcro snaps, G.E.'s self-diagnostic dishwashers, Mead's carbonless copy paper, and Kodak's Trimprint film.

Resolving this paradox is not just a matter of more exposure to information or education. Rather, one must master the process of thinking about certain problems in a creative way. As John Gardner (1965, p. 21) stated, people must learn to use their minds, rather than merely filling them up.

> All too often we are giving our young people cut flowers when we should be teaching them to grow plants. We are stuffing their heads with the products of earlier innovation rather than teaching them to innovate. We think of the mind as a storehouse to be filled when we should be thinking of it as an instrument to be used.

In the next section, we focus on problems that require creative rather than rational solutions. These are problems for which no acceptable alternative seems to be available, all reasonable solutions seem to be blocked, or no obvious best answer is accessible. This situation may exist because conceptual blocks inhibit the implementation of rational problem solving. Our focus, therefore, must be on tools and techniques that help overcome conceptual blocks and unlock problem-solving creativity.

Two examples help illustrate the kinds of problems that require creative problem-solving skills. They also illustrate several conceptual blocks that inhibit problem solving and several techniques and tools you can use to overcome such blocks.

Percy Spencer's Magnetron

During World War II, the British developed one of the best-kept military secrets of the war, a special radar detector based on a device called the magnetron. This radar was credited with turning the tide of battle in the war between Britain and Germany and helping the British withstand Hitler's Blitzkrieg. In 1940, Raytheon was one of several U.S. firms invited to produce magnetrons for the war effort.

The workings of magnetrons were not well understood, even by sophisticated physicists. Even among the firms that made magnetrons, few understood what made them work. A magnetron was tested, in those early days, by holding a neon tube next to it. If the neon tube got bright enough, the magnetron tube passed the test. In the process of conducting the test, the hands of the scientist holding the neon tube got warm. It was this phenomenon that led to a major creative breakthrough that eventually transformed lifestyles throughout the world.

At the end of the war, the market for radar essentially dried up, and most firms stopped producing magnetrons. At Raytheon, however, a scientist named Percy Spencer had been fooling around with magnetrons, trying to think of alternative uses for the devices. He was convinced that magnetrons could be used to cook food by using the heat produced in the neon tube. But Raytheon was in the defense business. Next to its two prize products—the Hawk and Sparrow missiles—cooking devices seemed odd and out of place. Percy Spencer was convinced that Raytheon should continue to produce magnetrons, even though production costs were prohibitively high. But Raytheon had lost money on the devices, and now there was no available market for magnetrons. The consumer product Spencer had in mind did not fit within the bounds of Raytheon's business.

As it turned out, Percy Spencer's solution to Raytheon's problem produced the microwave oven and a revolution in cooking methods throughout the world. Later, we will analyze several problem-solving techniques illustrated by Spencer's creative triumph.

Spence Silver's Glue

A second example of creative problem solving began with Spence Silver's assignment to work on a temporary project team within the 3M company. The team was searching for new adhesives, so Silver obtained some material from AMD, Inc., that had potential for a new polymer-based adhesive. He described one of his experiments in this way: "In the course of this exploration, I tried an experiment with one of the monomers in which I wanted to see what would happen if I put a lot of it into the reaction mixture. Before, we had used amounts that would correspond to conventional wisdom" (Nayak & Ketteringham, 1986). The result was a substance that failed all the conventional 3M tests for adhesives. It didn't stick. It preferred its own molecules to the molecules of any other substance. It was more cohesive than adhesive. It sort of "hung around without making a commitment." It was a "now-it-works, now-it-doesn't" kind of glue.

For five years, Silver went from department to department within the company trying to find someone interested in using his newly found substance in a product. Silver had found a solution; he just couldn't find a problem to solve with it. Predictably, 3M showed little interest. The company's mission was to make adhesives that adhered ever more tightly. The ultimate adhesive was one that formed an unbreakable bond, not one that formed a temporary bond.

After four years the task force was disbanded, and team members were assigned to other projects. But Silver was still convinced that his substance was good for something. He just didn't know what. As it turned out, Silver's solution has become the prototype for innovation in American firms, and it has spawned a half-billion dollars in annual revenues for 3M—in a unique product called Post-It Notes.

These two examples are positive illustrations of how solving a problem in a unique way can lead to phenomenal business success. Creative problem solving can have remarkable effects on individuals' careers and on business success. To understand how to solve problems creatively, however, we must first consider the blocks that inhibit creativity.

Conceptual Blocks

Table 3 summarizes four types of conceptual blocks that inhibit creative problem solving. Each is discussed and illustrated below with problems or exercises. We encourage you to complete the exercises and solve the problems as you read the chapter, because doing so will help you become aware of your own conceptual blocks. Later, we shall discuss in more detail how you can overcome those blocks.

Constancy

Constancy, in the present context, means that an individual becomes wedded to one way of looking at a problem or to using one approach to define, describe, or solve it. It is easy to see why constancy is common in problem solving. Being constant, or consistent, is a highly valued attribute for most of us. We like to appear at least moderately consistent in our approach to life, and constancy is often associated with maturity, honesty, and even intelligence. We judge lack of constancy as untrustworthy, peculiar, or airheaded. Several prominent psychologists theorize, in fact, that a need for constancy is the primary motivator of human behavior (Festinger, 1957; Heider, 1946; Newcomb, 1954). Many psychological studies have shown that once individuals take a stand or employ a particular approach to a problem, they are highly likely to pursue

1. Constancy	
Vertical thinking	Defining a problem in only one way without considering alternative views.
One thinking language	Not using more than one language to define and assess the problem.
2. Commitment	
Stereotyping based on past experience	Present problems are seen only as the variations of past problems.
Ignoring commonalities	Failing to perceive commonalities among elements that initially appear to be different.
3. Compression	
Distinguishing figure from ground	Not filtering out irrelevant information or finding needed information.
Artificial constraints	Defining the boundaries of a problem too narrowly.
4. Complacency	
Noninquisitiveness	Not asking questions.
Nonthinking	A bias toward activity in place of mental work.

Table 3 Conceptual Blocks That Inhibit Creative Problem Solving

that same course without deviation in the future (see Cialdini, 1988, for multiple examples).

On the other hand, constancy can inhibit the solution of some kinds of problems. Consistency sometimes drives out creativity. Two illustrations of the constancy block are vertical thinking and using only one thinking language.

Vertical Thinking

The term **vertical thinking** was coined by Edward deBono (1968). It refers to defining a problem in a single way and then pursuing that definition without deviation until a solution is reached. No alternative definitions are considered. All information gathered and all alternatives generated are consistent with the original definition. In a search for oil, for example, vertical thinkers determine a spot for the hole and drill the hole deeper and deeper until they strike oil. Lateral thinkers, on the other hand, generate alternative ways of viewing a problem and produce multiple definitions. Instead of drilling one hole deeper and deeper, lateral thinkers drill a number of holes in different places in search of oil. The vertical-thinking conceptual block arises from not being able to view the problem from multiple perspectives—to drill several holes—or to think laterally as well as vertically in problem solving. Problem definition is restricted.

Plenty of examples exist of creative solutions that occurred because an individual refused to get stuck with a single problem definition. Alexander Graham Bell was trying to devise a hearing aid when he shifted definitions and invented the telephone. Harland Sanders was trying to sell his recipe to restaurants when he shifted definitions and developed his Kentucky Fried Chicken business. Karl Jansky was studying telephone static when he shifted definitions, discovered radio waves from the Milky Way galaxy, and developed the science of radio astronomy.

In the development of the microwave industry described earlier, Percy Spencer shifted the definition of the problem from "How can we save our military radar business at the end of the war?" to "What other applications can be made for the magnetron?" Other problem definitions followed, such as: "How can we make magnetrons cheaper?" "How can we mass-produce magnetrons?" "How can we convince someone besides the military to buy magnetrons?" "How can we enter a consumer products market?" "How can we make microwave ovens practical and safe?" And so on. Each

new problem definition led to new ways of thinking about the problem, new alternative approaches, and, eventually, to a new microwave oven industry.

Spence Silver at 3M is another example of someone who changed problem definitions. He began with "How can I get an adhesive that has a stronger bond?" but switched to "How can I find an application for an adhesive that doesn't stick firmly?" Eventually, other problem definitions followed: "How can we get this new glue to stick to one surface but not another (e.g., to notepaper but not normal paper)?" "How can we replace staples, thumbtacks, and paperclips in the workplace?" "How can we manufacture and package a product that uses nonadhesive glue?" "How can we get anyone to pay $1.00 a pad for scratch paper?" And so on.

Shifting definitions is not easy, of course, because it is not natural. It requires individuals to deflect their tendency toward constancy. Later, we will discuss some hints and tools that can help overcome the constancy block while avoiding the negative consequences of inconsistency.

A Single Thinking Language

A second manifestation of the constancy block is the use of only one thinking language. Most people think in words—that is, they think about a problem and its solution in terms of verbal language. Rational problem solving reinforces this approach. Some writers, in fact, have argued that thinking cannot even occur without words (Vygotsky, 1962). Other thought languages are available, however, such as nonverbal or symbolic languages (e.g., mathematics), sensory imagery (e.g., smelling or tactile sensation), feelings and emotions (e.g., happiness, fear, or anger), and visual imagery (e.g., mental pictures). The more languages available to problem solvers, the better and more creative will be their solutions. As Koestler (1967) puts it, "[Verbal] language can become a screen which stands between the thinker and reality. This is the reason that true creativity often starts where [verbal] language ends."

Percy Spencer at Raytheon is a prime example of a visual thinker:

> One day, while Spencer was lunching with Dr. Ivan Getting and several other Raytheon scientists, a mathematical question arose. Several men, in a familiar reflex, pulled out their slide rules, but before any could complete the equation, Spencer gave the answer. Dr. Getting was

astonished. "How did you do that?" he asked. "The root," said Spencer shortly. "I learned cube roots and squares by using blocks as a boy. Since then, all I have to do is visualize them placed together." (Scott, 1974, p. 287).

The microwave oven depended on Spencer's command of multiple thinking languages. Furthermore, the new oven would never have gotten off the ground without a critical incident that illustrates the power of visual thinking. By 1965, Raytheon was just about to give up on any consumer application of the magnetron when a meeting was held with George Foerstner, president of the recently acquired Amana Refrigeration Company. In the meeting, costs, applications, manufacturing obstacles, and so on were discussed. Foerstner galvanized the entire microwave oven effort with the following statement, as reported by a Raytheon vice president.

George says, "It's no problem. It's about the same size as an air conditioner. It weighs about the same. It should sell for the same. So we'll price it at $499." Now you think that's silly, but you stop and think about it. Here's a man who really didn't understand the technologies. But there is about the same amount of copper involved, the same amount of steel as an air conditioner. And these are basic raw materials. It didn't make a lot of difference how you fit them together to make them work. They're both boxes; they're both made out of sheet metal; and they both require some sort of trim. (Nayak & Ketteringham, 1986, p. 181).

In several short sentences, Foerstner had taken one of the most complicated military secrets of World War II and translated it into something no more complex than a room air conditioner. He had painted a picture of an application that no one else had been able to capture by describing a magnetron visually, as a familiar object, not as a set of calculations, formulas, or blueprints.

A similar occurrence in the Post-It Note chronology also led to a breakthrough. Spence Silver had been trying for years to get someone in 3M to adopt his unsticky glue. Art Fry, another scientist with 3M, had heard Silver's presentations before. One day while singing in North Presbyterian Church in St. Paul, Minnesota, Fry was fumbling around with the slips of paper that marked the various hymns in his book. Suddenly, a visual image popped into his mind.

I thought, "Gee, if I had a little adhesive on these bookmarks, that would be just the ticket." So I decided to check into that idea the next week at work. What I had in mind was Silver's adhesive. . . . I knew I had a much bigger discovery than that. I also now realized that the primary application for Silver's adhesive was not to put it on a fixed surface like bulletin boards. That was a secondary application. The primary application concerned paper to paper. I realized that immediately." (Nayak & Ketteringham, 1986, pp. 63–64).

Years of verbal descriptions had not led to any applications for Silver's glue. Tactile thinking (handling the glue) also had not produced many ideas. However, thinking about the product in visual terms, as applied to what Fry initially called "a better bookmark," led to the breakthrough that was needed.

This emphasis on using alternative thinking languages, especially visual thinking, is now becoming the new frontier in scientific research. With the advent of supercomputers, scientists are more and more working with pictures and simulated images rather than with numerical data. "Scientists who are using the new computer graphics say that by viewing images instead of numbers, a fundamental change in the way researchers think and work is occurring. People have a lot easier time getting an intuition from pictures than they do from numbers and tables or formulas. In most physics experiments, the answer used to be a number or a string of numbers. In the last few years the answer has increasingly become a picture" (Markoff, 1988, p. D3).

To illustrate the differences among thinking languages, consider the following two simple problems:

1. Below is the Roman numeral 9. By adding only a single line, turn it into a 6.

IX

2. Figure 1 shows seven matchsticks. By moving only one matchstick, make the figure into a true equality (i.e., the value on one side equals the value on the other side). Before looking up the answers in Appendix I, try defining the problems differently, and try using different thinking languages. How many answers can you find?

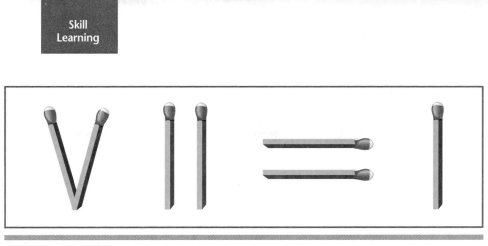

Figure 1 The Matchstick Configuration

Commitment

Commitment can also serve as a conceptual block to creative problem solving. Once individuals become committed to a particular point of view, definition, or solution, it is likely that they will follow through on that commitment. Freedman and Fraser (1966), for example, found that only 17 percent of a sample of Californians agreed to have a large, poorly lettered DRIVE CAREFULLY sign placed on their front lawn. However, in another study, another group of Californians were asked to sign a petition favoring "keeping California beautiful." Two weeks later, a full 76 percent of them were then willing to put up the DRIVE CAREFULLY sign. By signing a petition, they had become committed to the idea that they were responsible citizens. The large, unsightly sign became the visible evidence of their commitment.

A host of other studies have demonstrated the same phenomenon: that commitment can sometimes lead to dysfunctional or foolish decisions, rigidly defended. Two forms of commitment that produce conceptual blocks are *stereotyping based on past experiences* and *ignoring commonalities.*

Stereotyping Based on Past Experiences

March and Simon (1958) point out that a major obstacle to innovative problem solving is that individuals tend to define present problems in terms of problems they have faced in the past. Current problems are usually seen as variations on some past situation, so the alternatives proposed to solve the current problem are ones that have proven successful in the past. Both problem definitions and proposed solutions are therefore restricted by past experience. This restriction is referred to as **perceptual**

stereotyping (Allen, 1974). That is, certain preconceptions formed on the basis of past experience determine how an individual defines a situation.

When individuals receive an initial cue regarding the definition of a problem, all subsequent problems are frequently framed in terms of the initial cue. Of course, this is not all bad, because perceptual stereotyping helps organize problems on the basis of a limited amount of data, and the need to consciously analyze every problem encountered is eliminated. On the other hand, perceptual stereotyping prevents individuals from viewing a problem in novel ways.

The creation of microwave ovens and of Post-It Notes provide examples of overcoming stereotyping based on past experiences. Scott (1974) described the first meeting of John D. Cockcroft, technical leader of the British radar system that invented magnetrons, and Percy Spencer of Raytheon.

> Cockcroft liked Spencer at once. He showed him the magnetron, and the American regarded it thoughtfully. He asked questions—very intelligent ones—about how it was produced, and the Britisher answered at length. Later Spencer wrote, "The technique of making these tubes, as described to us, was awkward and impractical." *Awkward and impractical!* Nobody else dared draw such a judgment about a product of undoubted scientific brilliance, produced and displayed by the leaders of British science.

> Despite his admiration for Cockcroft and the magnificent magnetron, Spencer refused to abandon his curious and inquisitive stance. Rather than adopting the position of other scientists and assuming that since the

British invented it and were using it, they surely knew how to produce a magnetron, Spencer broke out of the stereotypes and pushed for improvements.

Similarly, Spence Silver at 3M described his invention in terms of breaking stereotypes based on past experience.

> The key to the Post-It adhesive was doing the experiment. If I had sat down and factored it out beforehand, and thought about it, I wouldn't have done the experiment. If I had really seriously cracked the books and gone through the literature, I would have stopped. The literature was full of examples that said you can't do this (Nayak & Ketteringham, 1986, p. 57).

This is not to say that one should avoid learning from past experience or that failing to learn the mistakes of history does not doom us to repeat them. Rather, it is to say that commitment to a course of action based on past experience can sometimes inhibit viewing problems in new ways, and can even prevent us from solving some problems at all. Consider the following problem as an example.

There are four volumes of Shakespeare on the shelf (see Figure 2). The pages of each volume are exactly two inches thick. The covers are each one-sixth of an inch thick. A bookworm started eating at page 1 of Volume 1 and ate straight through to the last page of Volume IV. What distance did the worm cover? (See Appendix I for the answer.) Solving this problem is relatively simple, but it requires that you overcome a stereotyping block to get the correct answer.

Ignoring Commonalities

A second manifestation of the commitment block is failure to identify similarities among seemingly disparate pieces of data. This is among the most commonly identified blocks to creativity. It means that a person becomes committed to a particular point of view, to the fact that elements are different, and, consequently, becomes unable to make connections, identify themes, or perceive commonalities.

The ability to find one definition or solution for two seemingly dissimilar problems is a characteristic of creative individuals (Dellas & Gaier, 1970; Steiner, 1978). The inability to do this can overload a problem solver by requiring that every problem encountered be solved individually. The discovery of penicillin by Sir Alexander Fleming resulted from his seeing a common theme among seemingly unrelated events. Fleming was working with some cultures of staphylococci that had accidentally become contaminated. The contamination, a growth of fungi, and isolated clusters of dead staphylococci led Fleming to see a relationship no one else had ever seen previously and thus to discover a wonder drug

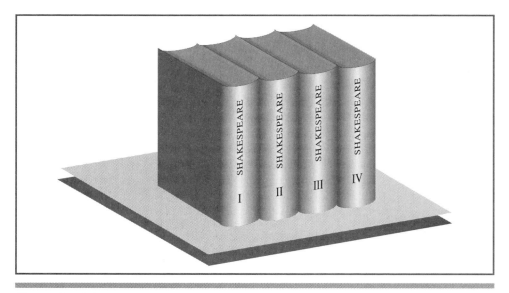

Figure 2 Shakespeare Riddle.
Source: Raudsepp & Hough, 1977.

(Beveridge, 1960). The famous chemist Friedrich Kekule saw a relationship between his dream of a snake swallowing its own tail and the chemical structure of organic compounds. This creative insight led him to the discovery that organic compounds such as benzene have closed rings rather than open structures (Koestler, 1967).

For Percy Spencer at Raytheon, seeing a connection between the heat of a neon tube and the heat required to cook food was the creative connection that led to his breakthrough in the microwave industry. One of Spencer's colleagues recalled: "In the process of testing a bulb [with a magnetron], your hands got hot. I don't know when Percy really came up with the thought of microwave ovens, but he knew at that time—and that was 1942. He [remarked] frequently that this would be a good device for cooking food." Another colleague described Spencer this way: "The way Percy Spencer's mind worked is an interesting thing. He had a mind that allowed him to hold an extraordinary array of associations on phenomena and relate them to one another" (Nayak & Ketteringham, 1986, pp. 184, 205). Similarly, the connection Art Fry made between a glue that wouldn't stick tightly and marking hymns in a choir book was the final breakthrough that led to the development of the revolutionary Post-It Note business.

To test your own ability to see commonalities, answer the following three questions: (1) What are some common terms that apply to both water and finance? (2) What is humorous about the following story? "Descartes, the philosopher, walked into a university class. Recognizing him, the instructor asked if he would like to lecture. Descartes replied, 'I think not,' and promptly disappeared." (3) What does the single piece of wood look like that will pass through each hole in the block in Figure 3 but that will perfectly fill each hole as it passes through? (Answers are in Appendix I.)

Compression

Conceptual blocks also occur as a result of compression of ideas. Looking too narrowly at a problem, screening out too much relevant data, and making assumptions that inhibit problem solution are common examples. Two especially cogent examples of compression are *artificially constraining problems* and *not distinguishing figure from ground.*

Artificial Constraints

Sometimes people place boundaries around problems, or constrain their approach to them, in such a way that the problems become impossible to solve. Such constraints arise from hidden assumptions people make about problems they encounter. People assume that some problem definitions or alternative solutions are off-limits, so they ignore them. For an illustration of this conceptual block, look at Figure 4. Without lifting your pencil from the paper, draw four straight lines that pass through all nine dots. Complete the task before reading further.

By thinking of the figure as more constrained than it actually is, the problem becomes impossible to solve. Try to break out of your own limiting assumptions on the problem. (One four-line answer is presented in Appendix I.) Now that you have been cued, can you do the same task with only three lines? Work on this problem for a minute. If you are successful, try to do

Figure 3   A Block Problem
Source: McKim, 1972.

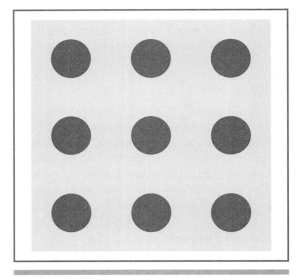

Figure 4 The Nine-Dot Problem

the task with only one line. Can you determine how to put a single straight line through all nine dots without lifting your pencil from the paper? Both the three-line solution and some one-line solutions are in the Appendix.

Artificially constraining problems means that the problem definition and the possible alternatives are limited more than the problem requires. Creative problem solving requires that individuals become adept at recognizing their hidden assumptions and expanding the alternatives they consider.

Separating Figure from Ground

Another illustration of the compression block is the reverse of artificial constraints. It is the inability to constrain problems sufficiently so that they can be solved. Problems almost never come clearly specified, so problem solvers must determine what the real problem is. They must filter out inaccurate, misleading, or irrelevant information in order to define the problem correctly and generate appropriate alternative solutions. The inability to separate the important from the unimportant, and to compress problems appropriately, serves as a conceptual block because it exaggerates the complexity of a problem and inhibits a simple definition.

How well do you filter out irrelevant information? Consider Figure 5. For each pair, find the pattern on the left that is embedded in the more complex pattern

on the right. On the complex pattern, outline the embedded pattern. Now try to find at least two figures in each pattern. (See Appendix I for a solution.)

This compression block—separating figure from ground and artificially constraining problems—played an important role in the microwave oven and Post-It Note breakthroughs. George Foerstner's contribution to the development and manufacture of the microwave oven was to compress the problem, that is, to separate out all the irrelevant complexity that constrained others. Whereas the magnetron was a device so complicated that few people understood it, Foerstner focused on its basic raw materials, its size, and its functionality. By comparing it to an air conditioner, he eliminated much of the complexity and mystery, and, as described by two analysts, "He had seen what all the researchers had failed to see, and they knew he was right" (Nayak & Ketteringham, 1986, p. 181).

On the other hand, Spence Silver had to *add* complexity, to *overcome* compression, in order to find an application for his product. Because the glue had failed every traditional 3M test for adhesives, it was categorized as a useless configuration of chemicals. The potential for the product was artificially constrained by traditional assumptions about adhesives—more stickiness, stronger bonding is best—until Art Fry visualized some unconventional applications—a better bookmark, a bulletin board, scratch paper, and, paradoxically, a replacement for 3M's main product, tape.

Complacency

Some conceptual blocks occur not because of poor thinking habits or inappropriate assumptions but because of fear, ignorance, insecurity, or just plain mental laziness. Two especially prevalent examples of the complacency block are a *lack of questioning* and a *bias against thinking*.

Noninquisitiveness

Sometimes the inability to solve problems results from an unwillingness to ask questions, obtain information, or search for data. Individuals may think they will appear naive or ignorant if they question something or attempt to redefine a problem. Asking questions puts them at risk of exposing their ignorance. It also may be threatening to others because it implies that what they accept may not be correct. This may create resistance, conflict, or even ridicule by others.

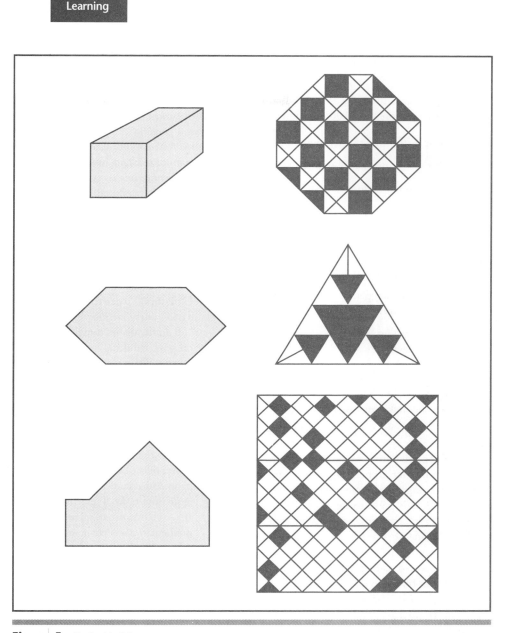

Figure 5 Embedded Pattern

Creative problem solving is inherently risky, therefore, because it potentially involves interpersonal conflict. It is risky also because it is fraught with mistakes. As Linus Pauling, the Nobel laureate, said, "If you want to have a good idea, have a lot of them, because most of them will be bad ones." Years of nonsupportive socialization, however, block the adventuresome and inquisitive stance in most people. Most of us are not rewarded for bad ideas. To illustrate, answer the following questions for yourself:

1. When would it be easier to learn a new language, when you were 5 years old or now? Why?

2. How many times in the last month have you tried something for which the probability of success was less than 50 percent?

3. When was the last time you asked three "why" questions in a row?

David Feldman authored a 1988 book in which he asks and answers more than 100 questions such as:

Why are people immune to their own body odor?

Why are there 21 guns in a 21-gun salute?

What happens to the tread that wears off tires?

Why doesn't sugar spoil or get moldy?

Why doesn't a two-by-four measure two inches by four inches?

Why doesn't postage-stamp glue have flavoring?

Why is a telephone keypad arranged differently from that of a calculator?

Why do hot dogs come 10 in a package while buns come 8 in a package?

How do military cadets find their caps after throwing them in the air at football games and graduation?

Why is Jack the nickname for John?

How do they print "M&M" on M&M candies?

Most of us are a little too complacent to even ask such questions, let alone find out the answers. We often stop being inquisitive as we get older because we learn that it is good to be intelligent, and being intelligent is interpreted as already knowing the answers, instead of asking good questions. Consequently, we learn less well at 35 than at 5, take fewer risks, avoid asking why, and function in the world without trying to understand it. Creative problem solvers, on the other hand, are frequently engaged in inquisitive and experimental behavior. Spence Silver at 3M described his attitude about the complacency block this way:

> People like myself get excited about looking for new properties in materials. I find that very satisfying, to perturb the structure slightly and just see what happens. I have a hard time talking people into doing that—people who are more highly trained. It's been my experience that people are reluctant just to try, to experiment—just to see what will happen (Nayak & Ketteringham, 1986, p. 58).

Bias Against Thinking

A second manifestation of the complacency block is in an inclination to avoid doing mental work. This block, like most of the others, is partly a cultural bias as well as a personal one. For example, assume that you passed by your subordinate's office one day and noticed him leaning back in his chair, staring out the window. A half-hour later, as you passed by again, he had his feet up on the desk, still staring out the window. And 20 minutes later, you noticed that his demeanor hadn't changed much. What would be your conclusion? Most of us would assume that the fellow was not doing any work. We would assume that unless we saw action, he wasn't being productive.

When was the last time you heard someone say, "I'm sorry. I can't go to the ball game (or concert, dance, party, or movie) because I have to think"? Or, "I'll do the dishes tonight. I know you need to catch up on your thinking"? That these statements sound humorous illustrates the bias most people develop toward action rather than thought, or against putting their feet up, rocking back in their chair, looking off into space, and engaging in solitary mental activity. This does not mean daydreaming or fantasizing, but *thinking*.

There is a particular conceptual block in our culture against the kind of thinking that uses the right hemisphere of the brain. **Left-hemisphere thinking,** for most people, is concerned with logical, analytical, linear, or sequential tasks. Thinking using the left hemisphere is apt to be organized, planned, and precise. Language and mathematics are left-hemisphere activities. **Right-hemisphere thinking,** on the other hand, is concerned with intuition, synthesis, playfulness, and qualitative judgment. It tends to be more spontaneous, imaginative, and emotional than left-hemisphere thinking. The emphasis in most formal education is toward left-hemisphere thought development. Problem solving on the basis of reason, logic, and utility is generally rewarded, while problem solving based on sentiment, intuition, or pleasure is frequently considered tenuous and inferior.

A number of researchers have found that the most creative problem solvers are **ambidextrous** in their thinking. That is, they use both left- and right-hemisphere thinking and easily switch from one to the other (Bruner, 1966; Hermann, 1981; Martindale, 1975). Creative ideas arise most frequently in the right hemisphere but must be processed and interpreted by the left, so creative problem solvers use both hemispheres equally well.

Try the exercise in Table 4, the idea for which came from von Oech (1986). It illustrates this ambidextrous principle. There are two lists of words. Take a minute to memorize the first list. Then, on a piece of paper, write down as many words as you can remember. Now take a minute and memorize the words in the second list. Repeat the process of writing down as many words as you can remember.

Most people remember more words from the second list than from the first. This is because the second list contains words that relate to visual perceptions. They connect with right-brain activity as well as left-brain activity. People can draw mental pictures or fantasize about them. The same is true for creative ideas. The more both sides of the brain are used, the more creative the ideas.

Review of Conceptual Blocks

So far, we have suggested that certain conceptual blocks prevent individuals from solving problems creatively. These blocks, summarized in Table 3, narrow the scope of problem definition, limit the consideration of alternative solutions, and constrain the selection of an optimal solution. Unfortunately, many of these conceptual blocks are unconscious, and it is only by being confronted with problems that are unsolvable because of conceptual blocks that individuals

become aware that they exist. We have attempted to make you aware of your own conceptual blocks by asking you to solve problems that require you to overcome these mental barriers. These conceptual blocks are not all bad, of course; not all problems can be addressed by creative problem solving. But research has shown that individuals who have developed creative problem-solving skills are far more effective with complex problems that require a search for alternative solutions than others who are conceptually blocked (Dauw, 1976; Basadur, 1979; Guilford, 1962; Steiner, 1978).

In the next section, we provide some techniques and tools that help overcome these blocks and improve creative problem-solving skills.

Conceptual Blockbusting

Conceptual blocks cannot be overcome all at once because most blocks are a product of years of habit-forming thought processes. Overcoming them requires practice in thinking in different ways over a long period of time. You will not become a skilled creative problem solver just by reading this chapter. On the other hand, by becoming aware of your conceptual blocks and practicing the following techniques, you can enhance your creative problem-solving skills.

Stages in Creative Thought

A first step in overcoming conceptual blocks is recognizing that creative problem solving is a skill that can be developed. Being a creative problem solver is not an inherent ability that some people naturally have and others do not have. As Dauw (1976, p. 19) has noted,

> Research results [show] . . . that nurturing creativity is not a question of increasing one's ability to score high on an IQ test, but a matter of improving one's mental attitudes and habits and cultivating creative skills that have lain dormant since childhood.

Researchers generally agree that creative problem solving involves four stages: preparation, incubation, illumination, and verification. (See Haefele, 1962, for

LIST 1	LIST 2
decline	sunset
very	perfume
ambiguous	brick
resources	monkey
term	castle
conceptual	guitar
about	pencil
appendix	computer
determine	umbrella
forget	radar
quantity	blister
survey	chessboard

Table 4   Exercise to Test Ambidextrous Thinking

literature reviews of the stages of creative problem solving.) The **preparation** stage includes gathering data, defining the problem, generating alternatives, and consciously examining all available information. The primary difference between skillful creative problem solving and rational problem solving is in how this first step is approached. Creative problem solvers are more flexible and fluent in data gathering, problem definition, alternative generation, and examination of options. In fact, it is in this stage that training in creative problem solving can significantly improve effectiveness (Allen, 1974; Basadur, 1979; McKim, 1972) because the other three steps are not amenable to conscious mental work. The following discussion, therefore, is limited primarily to improving functioning in this first stage. The **incubation** stage involves mostly unconscious mental activity in which the mind combines unrelated thoughts in pursuit of a solution. Conscious effort is not involved. **Illumination,** the third stage, occurs when an insight is recognized and a creative solution is articulated. **Verification** is the final stage, which involves evaluating the creative solution relative to some standard of acceptability.

In the preparation stage, two types of techniques are available for improving creative problem-solving abilities. One technique helps individuals think about and define problems more creatively; the other helps individuals gather information and generate more alternative solutions to problems.

One major difference between effective, creative problem solvers and other people is that creative problem solvers are less constrained. They allow themselves to be more flexible in the definitions they impose on problems and the number of solutions they identify. They develop a large repertoire of approaches to problem solving. In short, they do what Karl Weick (1979, p. 261) prescribes for unblocking decision making: "Complicate yourself!" That is, generate more conceptual options. As Interaction Associates (1971, p. 15) explained:

> Flexibility in thinking is critical to good problem solving. A problem solver should be able to conceptually dance around the problem like a good boxer, jabbing and poking, without getting caught in one place or "fixated." At any given moment, a good problem solver should be able to apply a large number of strategies [for generating alternative definitions and solutions].

Moreover, a good problem solver is a person who has developed, through his understanding of strategies and experiences in problem solving, a sense of appropriateness of what is likely to be the most useful strategy at any particular time.

As a perusal through any bookstore will show, the number of books suggesting ways to enhance creative problem solving is enormous. We now present a few tools and hints that we have found to be especially effective and relatively simple for business executives and students to apply. Although some of them may seem game-like or playful, a sober pedagogical rationale underlies all of them. They help to unfreeze you from your normal skeptical, analytical approach to problems and increase your playfulness.

Methods for Improving Problem Definition

Problem definition is probably the most critical step in creative problem solving. Once a problem is properly defined, solving it is often relatively simple. However, Campbell (1952), Medawar (1967), and Schumacher (1977) point out that individuals tend to define problems in terms with which they are familiar. Medawar (1967, Introduction) notes, "Good scientists study the most important problems they think they can solve." When a problem is faced that is strange or does not appear to have a solution (Schumacher calls these "divergent problems"), the problem either remains undefined or is redefined in terms of something familiar. Unfortunately, new problems may not be the same as old problems, so relying on past definitions may impede the process of solving current problems, or lead to solving the wrong problem. Applying hints for creative problem definition can help individuals see problems in alternative ways so their definitions are less narrowly constrained. Three such hints for improving and expanding the definition process are discussed below.

Make the Strange Familiar and the Familiar Strange

One well-known technique for improving creative problem solving is called **synectics** (Gordon, 1961). The goal of synectics is to help you put something you don't know in terms of something you do know and vice versa. By analyzing what you know and applying it to what you don't know, you can develop new insights and perspectives.

First you form a definition of a problem (make the strange familiar). Then you try to make that definition out of focus, distorted, or transposed in some way (make the familiar strange). Use synectics—analogies and metaphors—to create this distortion. Postpone the original definition of the problem while you analyze the analogy or metaphor. Then impose the analysis on the original problem to see what new insights you can uncover.

For example, suppose you have defined a problem as low morale among members of your team. You may form an analogy or metaphor by answering questions such as the following about the problem: What does this remind me of? What does this make me feel like? What is this similar to? What isn't this similar to? (Your answers, for example, might be: This problem reminds me of trying to turn a rusty bolt. It makes me feel like I do when visiting a hospital ward. This is similar to the loser's locker room after a basketball game. And so on.) Metaphors and analogies should connect what you are less sure about (the original problem) to what you are more sure about (the metaphor). By analyzing the metaphor or analogy, you may identify attributes of the problem that were not evident before. New insights can occur.

Many creative solutions have been generated by such a technique. For example, William Harvey was the first to apply the "pump" analogy to the heart, which led to the discovery of the body's circulatory system. Niels Bohr compared the atom to the solar system and supplanted Rutherford's prevailing "raisin pudding" model of matter's building blocks. Creativity consultant Roger von Oech (1986) helped turn around a struggling computer company by applying a restaurant analogy to the company's operations. The real problems emerged when the restaurant, rather than the company, was analyzed. Major contributions in the field of organizational behavior have occurred by applying analogies to other types of organization, such as machines, cybernetic or open systems, force fields, clans, and so on. Probably the most effective analogies (called parables) were used by Jesus of Nazareth to teach principles that otherwise were difficult for individuals to grasp.

Some hints to keep in mind when constructing analogies are these: (1) Include action or motion in the analogy (e.g., driving a car, cooking a meal, attending a funeral); (2) include things that can be visualized or pictured in the analogy (e.g., stars, football games, crowded shopping malls); (3) pick familiar events or situations (e.g., families, kissing, bedtime); and (4) try to relate things that are not obviously similar (e.g., saying an organization is like a crowd is not nearly so rich a simile as saying an organization is like a psychic prison or a poker game).

Four types of analogies are recommended as part of synectics: **personal analogies,** where individuals try to identify themselves as the problem ("If I were the problem, how would I feel, what would I like, what could satisfy me?"); **direct analogies,** where individuals apply facts, technology, and common experience to the problem (e.g., Brunel solved the problem of underwater construction by watching a shipworm tunneling into a tube); **symbolic analogies,** where symbols or images are imposed on the problem (e.g., modeling the problem mathematically or diagramming the logic flow); and **fantasy analogies,** where individuals ask the question "In my wildest dreams, how would I wish the problem to be resolved?" (e.g., "I wish all employees would work with no supervision.").

Elaborate on the Definition

There are a variety of ways to enlarge, alter, or replace a problem definition once it has been specified. One way is to force yourself to generate at least two alternative hypotheses for every problem definition. That is, specify at least two plausible definitions of the problem in addition to the one originally accepted. Think in plural rather than singular terms. Instead of asking, "What is the problem?" "What is the meaning of this?" "What is the result?" ask instead questions such as: "What are the problems?" "What are the meanings of this?" "What are the results?"

As an example, look at Figure 6. Select the figure that is different from all the others. A majority of people select B first. If you did, you're right. It is the only figure that has all straight lines. On the other hand, quite a few people pick A. If you are one of them, you're also right. It is the only figure with a continuous line and no points of discontinuity. Alternatively, C can also be right, with the rationale that it is the only figure with two straight and two curved lines. Similarly, D is the only one with one curved and one straight line, and E is the only figure that is nonsymmetrical or partial. The

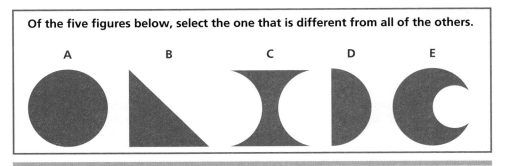

Of the five figures below, select the one that is different from all of the others.

A   B   C   D   E

Figure 6   The Five-Figure Problem

point is, there can often be more than one problem definition, more than one right answer, and more than one perspective from which to view a problem.

Another way to elaborate definitions is to use a question checklist. This is a series of questions designed to help individuals think of alternatives to their accepted definitions. Several creative managers have shared with us some of their most fruitful questions:

1. Is there anything else?

2. Is the reverse true?

3. Is there a more general problem?

4. Can it be stated differently?

5. Who sees it differently?

6. What past experience is this like?

As an exercise, take a minute now to think of a problem you are currently experiencing. Write it down so it is formally specified. Now manipulate that definition by answering each of the six questions in the checklist. If you can't think of a problem, try the exercise with this one: "I am not as attractive as I would like to be."

Reverse the Definition

A third tool for improving and expanding problem definition is to reverse the definition of the problem. That is, turn the problem upside down, inside out, or back to front. Reverse the way in which you think of the problem. For example, consider the following problem:

A tradition in Sandusky, Ohio, for as long as anyone could remember was the Fourth of July

Parade. It was one of the largest and most popular events on the city's annual calendar. Now, in 1988, the city mayor was hit with some startling and potentially disastrous news. The State of Ohio was mandating that liability insurance be carried on every attraction—floats, bands, majorettes—that participated in the parade. To protect against the possibility of injury or accident of any parade participant, each had to be covered by liability insurance.

The trouble, of course, was that taking out a liability insurance policy for all parade participants would require far more expense than the city could afford. The amount of insurance required for that large a number of participants and equipment made it impossible for the city to carry the cost. On the one hand, the mayor hated to cancel an important tradition that everyone in town looked forward to. On the other hand, to hold the event would break the city budget. If you were a consultant to the mayor, what would you suggest?

Commonly suggested alternatives in this problem include the following:

1. Try to negotiate with an insurance company for a lower rate. (However, the risk is merely being transferred to the insurance company.)

2. Hold fund raising events to generate enough money to purchase the insurance policy, or find a wealthy donor to sponsor the parade. (However, this may deflect potential donations away from, or may compete with, other community service agencies such as

United Way, Red Cross, or local churches who also sponsor fund raisers and require donations.)

3. Charge a "participation fee" to parade participants to cover the insurance expense. (However, this would likely eliminate most high school, junior high school, and elementary school bands and floats. It would also reduce the amount of money float builders and sponsoring organizations could spend on the actual float. Such a requirement would likely be a parade killer.)

4. Charge a fee to spectators of the parade. (However, this would require restricted access to the parade, an administrative structure to coordinate fee collection and ticketing, and the destruction of the sense of community participation that characterized this traditional event.)

Each of these suggestions is good, but each maintains a single definition of the problem. Each assumes that the solution to the problem is associated with solving the financial problem associated with the liability insurance requirement. Each suggestion, therefore, brings with it some danger of damaging the traditional nature of the parade or eliminating it altogether. If the problem is reversed, other answers normally not considered become evident. That is, the need for liability insurance at all could be addressed.

Here is an excerpt from a newspaper report of how the problem was addressed:

Sandusky, Ohio (AP) The Fourth of July parade here wasn't canceled, but it was immobilized by liability insurance worries. The band marched in place to the beat of a drum, and a country fair queen waved to her subjects from a float moored to the curb.

The Reverse Community Parade began at 10:00 a.m. Friday along Washington Row at the north end of the city and stayed there until dusk. "Very honestly, it was the issue of liability," said Gene Kleindienst, superintendent of city schools and one of the celebration's organizers. "By not having a mobile parade, we significantly reduced the issue of liability," he said.

The immobile parade included abut 20 floats and displays made by community groups. Games, displays, and food booths were in an adjacent park. Parade chairman Judee Hill said

some folks didn't understand, however. "Someone asked me if she was too late for the parade, and she had a hard time understanding the parade is here all day," she said.

Those who weren't puzzled seemed to appreciate the parade for its stationary qualities. "I like this. I can see more," said 67-year-old William A. Sibley. "I'm 80 percent blind. Now I know there's something there," he said pointing to a float.

Spectator Emmy Platte preferred the immobile parade because it didn't go on for "what seemed like miles," exhausting participants. "You don't have those little drum majorettes passing out on the street," she commented.

Baton twirler Tammy Ross said her performance was better standing still. "You can throw better. You don't have to worry about dropping it as much," she explained.

Mr. Kleindienst said community responses were favorable. "I think we've started a new tradition," he said.

By reversing the definition, Sandusky not only eliminated the problem without damaging the tradition and without shifting the risk to insurance companies or other community groups, it added a new dimension that allowed at least some people to enjoy the event more than ever.

This reversal is similar to what Rothenberg (1979) refers to as "Janusian thinking." Janus was the Roman god with two faces that looked in opposite directions. **Janusian thinking** means thinking contradictory thoughts at the same time: that is, conceiving two opposing ideas to be true concurrently. Rothenberg claimed, after studying 54 highly creative artists and scientists (e.g., Nobel Prize winners), that most major scientific breakthroughs and artistic masterpieces are products of Janusian thinking. Creative people who actively formulate antithetical ideas and then resolve them produce the most valuable contributions to the scientific and artistic worlds. Quantum leaps in knowledge often occur.

An example is Einstein's account (1919, p. 1) of having "the happiest thought of my life." He developed the concept that, "for an observer in free fall from the roof of a house, there exists, during his fall, no gravitational field . . . in his immediate vicinity. If the observer releases any objects, they will remain, relative to him, in a state of rest. The [falling] observer is therefore justified in considering his state as one of rest." Einstein concluded, in other words, that two seemingly contradictory states could be present simultaneously: motion and rest. This realization led to the development of his revolutionary general theory of relativity.

In another study of creative potential, Rothenberg (1979) found that when individuals were presented with a stimulus word and asked to respond with the word that first came to mind, highly creative students, Nobel scientists, and prize-winning artists responded with antonyms significantly more often than did individuals with average creativity. Rothenberg argued, based on these results, that creative people think in terms of opposites more often than do other people.

For our purposes, the whole point is to reverse or contradict the currently accepted definition in order to expand the number of perspectives considered. For instance, a problem might be that morale is too high instead of (or in addition to) too low in our team, or that employees need less motivation instead of more motivation to increase productivity. Opposites and backward looks often enhance creativity.

These three techniques for improving creative problem definition are summarized in Table 5. Their purpose is not to help you generate alternative definitions just for the sake of alternatives but to broaden your perspectives, to help you overcome conceptual blocks, and to produce more elegant (i.e., high-quality and parsimonious) solutions.

Ways to Generate More Alternatives

A common tendency is to define problems in terms of available solutions (i.e., the problem is defined as a solution already possessed or the first acceptable alternative, e.g., March & Simon, 1958). This tendency leads to consideration of a minimal number and narrow range of alternatives in problem solving. However, Guilford (1962), a pioneer in the study of creative problem solving, asserted that the primary characteristics of effective creative problem solvers are their fluency and their flexibility of thought. **Fluency** refers to the number of ideas or concepts produced in a given length of time. **Flexibility** refers to the diversity of ideas or concepts generated. While most problem solvers consider a few homogeneous alternatives, creative problem solvers consider many heterogeneous alternatives. The follow-

---

1. Make the strange familiar and the familiar strange.
2. Elaborate on the definition.
3. Reverse the definition.

Table 5   Techniques for Improving Problem Definition

---

ing techniques are designed to help you improve your ability to generate many varied alternatives when faced with problems. They are summarized in Table 6.

Defer Judgment

Probably the most common method of generating alternatives is the technique of **brainstorming** developed by Osborn (1953). This tool is powerful because most people make quick judgments about each piece of information or each alternative solution they encounter. This technique is designed to help people generate alternatives for problem solving without prematurely evaluating, and hence discarding, them. Four main rules govern brainstorming:

1. No evaluation of any kind is permitted as alternatives are being generated. Individual energy is spent on generating ideas, not on defending them.

2. The wildest possible ideas are encouraged. It is easier to tighten alternatives up than to loosen them.

3. The quantity of ideas takes precedence over the quality. Emphasizing quality engenders judgment and evaluation.

4. Participants should build on or modify the ideas of others. Poor ideas that are added to or altered often become good ideas.

---

1. Defer judgment.
2. Expand current alternatives.
3. Combine unrelated attributes.

Table 6   Techniques for Generating More Alternatives

Brainstorming techniques are best used in a group setting so individuals can stimulate ideas in one another. In fact, generating alternatives in a group setting produces more and better ideas than can be produced alone (Maier, 1967). One caution about brainstorming should be noted, however. Often, after a rush of alternatives is produced at the outset of a brainstorming session, the quantity of ideas rapidly subsides. But to stop there is an ineffective use of brainstorming. When no easily identifiable solutions are available, truly creative alternatives are often produced in brainstorming groups. So keep working!

The best way to get a feel for the power of brainstorming groups is to participate in one. Try the following exercise based on an actual problem faced by a group of students and university professors. Spend at least 20 minutes in a small group, brainstorming ideas.

A request had been made for a faculty member to design an executive education program for mid-level managers at a major automobile company. It was to focus on enhancing creativity and innovation among managers. The trouble was, the top human resource executive indicated that he did not want to approach the subject with "brain-teaser" examples. Instead, he wanted some other approaches that would help these managers become more creative personally and more effective at fostering innovation among others.

What ideas can you come up with for teaching this subject of creative problem solving to mid-level managers in an organization? How could you help them learn to be more creative? Generate as many ideas as you can following the rules of brainstorming. After at least 20 minutes, assess the fluency and flexibility of the ideas generated.

Expand Current Alternatives

Sometimes, brainstorming in a group is not possible or is too costly in terms of the number of people involved and hours required. Managers pursuing a hectic organizational life may sometimes find brainstorming an unusable alternative. Moreover, people sometimes need an external stimulus or blockbuster to help them generate new ideas. One useful and readily available technique for expanding alternatives is **subdivision,** or dividing a problem into smaller parts. March and

Simon (1958, p. 193) suggest that subdivision improves problem solving by increasing the speed with which alternatives can be generated and selected. As they explain,

The mode of subdivision has an influence on the extent to which planning can proceed simultaneously on the several aspects of the problem. The more detailed the factorization of the problem, the more simultaneous activity is possible, hence, the greater the speed of problem solving.

To see how subdivision helps develop more alternatives and speeds the process of problem solving, consider the problem, common in the creativity literature, of listing alternative uses for a familiar object. For example, in five minutes, how many uses can you list for a ping-pong ball? The more uses you list, the greater is your fluency in thinking. The more variety in the list, the greater is your flexibility in thinking. You might include the following in your list: bob for a fishing line, Christmas ornament, toy for a cat, gearshift knob, model for a molecular structure, wind gauge when hung from a string, head for a finger puppet, miniature basketball. Your list will be much longer.

After you generate your list, apply the technique of subdivision by identifying the specific characteristics of a ping-pong ball, that is, dividing it into its component attributes. For example, weight, color, texture, shape, porosity, strength, hardness, chemical properties, and conduction potential are all attributes of ping-pong balls that help expand the uses you might think of. By dividing an object mentally into more specific attributes, you can arrive at many more alternative uses (e.g., reflector, holder when cut in half, bug bed, ball for lottery drawing, and so on).

One exercise we have used with students and executives to illustrate this technique is to have them write down as many of their managerial strengths as they can think of. Most people list 10 or 12 attributes relatively easily. Then we analyze the various dimensions of the manager's role, the activities that managers engage in, the challenges that most managers face from inside and outside the organization, and so on. We then ask these same people to write down another list of their strengths as managers. The list is almost always twice as long or more. By identifying the subcomponents of any problem, far more alternatives can be generated than by considering the problem as a whole.

One final illustration. Divide the figure in Figure 7 into exactly four pieces equal in size, shape, and area. Try to do it in a minute or less. The problem is easy if you use subdivision. It is more difficult if you don't. One of the answers to the problem is in Appendix I.

Combine Unrelated Attributes

A third technique focuses on helping problem solvers expand alternatives by forcing the integration of seemingly unrelated elements. Research into creative problem solving has shown that an ability to see common relationships among disparate factors is a major factor differentiating creative from noncreative individuals (see Dellas & Gaier, 1970, for a review of the literature). Two ways to do this are through *morphological forced connections* (Koberg & Bagnall, 1974) and the *relational algorithm* (Crovitz, 1970).

With **morphological forced connections,** a four-step procedure is involved. First, the problem is written down. Second, attributes of the problem are listed. Third, alternatives to each attribute are listed. Fourth,

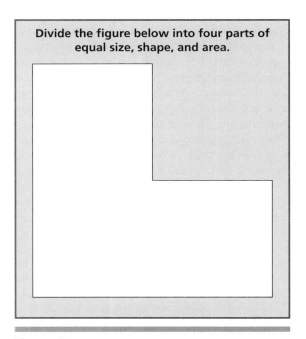

Divide the figure below into four parts of equal size, shape, and area.

Figure 7 Fractionation Problem

different alternatives from the attributes list are combined together.

To illustrate this procedure, suppose you are faced with the problem of a secretary who takes an extended lunch break almost every day despite your reminders to be on time. Think of alternative ways to solve this problem. The first solution that comes to mind for most people is to sit down and have a talk with (or threaten) the secretary. If that doesn't work, most of us would just fire or transfer the person. However, look at what other alternatives can be generated by using morphological connections (see Table 7).

You can see how many more alternatives come to mind when you force together attributes that aren't obviously connected. The matrix of attributes can create a very long list of possible solutions. In more complicated problems—for example, how to improve quality, how to serve customers better, how to improve the reward system—the potential number of alternatives is even greater, and, hence, more creativity is required to analyze them.

The second technique for combining unrelated attributes in problem solving, the **relational algorithm,** involves applying connecting words that force a relationship between two elements in a problem. For example, the following is a list of some relational words:

about	across	after
against	opposite	or
out	among	and
as	at	over
round	still	because
before	between	but
so	then	though
by	down	for
from	through	till
to	if	in
near	not	under
up	when	now
of	off	on
where	while	with

To illustrate the use of this technique, suppose you are faced with the following problem: Our customers are dissatisfied with our service. The two major elements in this problem are *customers* and *service*. They are connected by the phrase *are dissatisfied with*. With the relational algorithm technique, the relational words in the problem statement are removed and replaced with other

Step 1. Problem statement: The secretary takes extended lunch breaks every day with friends in the cafeteria.

Step 2. Major attributes of the problem:

Amount of time	*Start time*	*Place*	*With whom*	*Frequency*
More than 1 hour	12 noon	Cafeteria	Friends	Daily

Step 3. Alternative attributes:

Amount of time	*Start time*	*Place*	*With whom*	*Frequency*
30 minutes	11:00	Office	Coworkers	Weekly
90 minutes	11:30	Conference Room	Boss	Twice a Week
45 minutes	12:30	Restaurant	Management Team	Alternate Days

Step 4. Combining Attributes:

1. A 30-minute lunch beginning at 12:30 in the conference room with the boss once a week.
2. A 90-minute lunch beginning at 11:30 in the conference room with coworkers twice a week.
3. A 45-minute lunch beginning at 11:00 in the cafeteria with the management team every other day.
4. A 30-minute lunch beginning at 12:00 alone in the office on alternate days.

Table 7   Morphological Forced Connections

relational words to see if new ideas for alternative solutions can be identified. For example, consider the following connections where new relational words are used:

- Customers *among* service (e.g., Customers interact with service personnel).

- Customers *as* service (e.g., Customers deliver service to other customers).

- Customers *and* service (e.g., Customers and service personnel work together).

- Customers *for* service (e.g., Customer focus groups help improve our service).

- Service *near* customers (e.g., Change the location of the service).

- Service *before* customers (e.g., Prepare service before the customer arrives).

- Service *through* customers (e.g., Use customers to provide additional service).

- Service *when* customers (e.g., Provide timely service).

By connecting the two elements of the problem in different ways, new possibilities for problem solution can be formulated.

Hints for Applying Problem-Solving Techniques

Not every problem is amenable to these techniques and tools for conceptual blockbusting, of course. Our intent in presenting these six is to help you expand the number of options available to you for defining problems and generating additional potential solutions. They are most useful with problems that require a new approach or perspective. All of us have enormous creative potential, but the stresses and pressures of daily life, coupled with the inertia of conceptual habits, tend to submerge that potential. These hints are ways to help unlock it again.

Reading about techniques or wanting to be creative won't improve your creativity, of course. These techniques and tools are not magic in themselves. They depend on your ability to actually generate new ideas and to think different thoughts. Because that is so difficult for most of us, here are six practical hints to help prepare you to create more conceptual flexibility and better apply these techniques.

1. Give yourself some relaxation time. The more intense your work, the more your need for complete breaks. Break out of your routine sometimes. This

frees up your mind and gives room for new thoughts.

2. Find a place (physical space) where you can think. It should be a place where interruptions are eliminated, at least for a time. Reserve your best time for thinking.

3. Talk to other people about ideas. Isolation produces far fewer ideas than does conversation. Make a list of people who stimulate you to think. Spend some time with them.

4. Ask other people for their ideas about your problems. Find out what others think about them. Don't be embarrassed to share your problems, but don't become dependent on others to solve them for you.

5. Read a lot. Read at least one thing regularly that is outside your field of expertise. Keep track of new thoughts from your reading.

6. Protect yourself from idea-killers. Don't spend time with "black holes"—that is, people who absorb all of your energy and light but give nothing in return. Don't let yourself or others negatively evaluate your ideas too soon.

You'll find these hints useful not only for enhancing creative problem solving but for rational problem solving as well. Figure 8 summarizes the two problem-solving processes—rational and creative—and the factors you should consider when determining how to approach each type of problem. In brief, when you encounter a problem that is straightforward—that is, outcomes are predictable, sufficient information is available, and means-ends connections are clear—rational problem-solving techniques are most appropriate. You should apply the four distinct, sequential steps. On the other hand, when the problem is not straightforward—that is, information is ambiguous or unavailable and alternative solutions are not apparent—you should apply creative problem-solving techniques in order to improve problem definition and alternative generation.

Fostering Innovation

Unlocking your own creative potential is not enough, of course, to make you a successful manager. A major challenge is to help unlock it in other people as well. Fostering innovation and creativity among those with

whom you work is at least as great a challenge as increasing your own creativity. In this last section of the chapter, we briefly discuss some principles that will help you better accomplish the task of fostering innovation.

Management Principles

Neither Percy Spencer nor Spence Silver could have succeeded in his creative ideas had there not been a managerial support system present that fostered creative problem solving and the pursuit of innovation. In each case, certain characteristics were present in their organizations, fostered by managers around them, that made their innovations possible. In this section we will not discuss the macro-organizational issues associated with innovation (e.g., organization design, strategic orientation, and human resource systems). Excellent discussions of those factors are reviewed in sources such as Galbraith (1982), Kanter (1983), McMillan (1985), Tichy (1983), and Amabile (1988). Instead, we'll focus on activities in which individual managers can engage that foster innovation. Table 8 summarizes three management principles that help engender innovativeness and creative problem solving.

Pull People Apart; Put People Together

Percy Spencer's magnetron project involved a consumer product closeted away from Raytheon's main-line business of missiles and other defense-contract work. Spence Silver's new glue resulted when a polymer adhesive task force was separated from 3M's normal activities. The Macintosh computer was developed by a task force taken outside the company and given space and time to work on an innovative computer. Many new ideas come from individuals being given time and resources and allowed to work apart from the normal activities of the organization. Establishing bullpens, practice fields, or sandlots is as good a way to develop new skills in business as it has proven to be in athletics. Because most businesses are designed to produce the 10,000th part correctly or to service the 10,000th customer efficiently, they do not function well at producing the first part. That is why pulling people apart is often necessary to foster innovation and creativity.

On the other hand, forming teams (putting people together) is almost always more productive than having people work by themselves. Such teams should be characterized by certain attributes, though. For example,

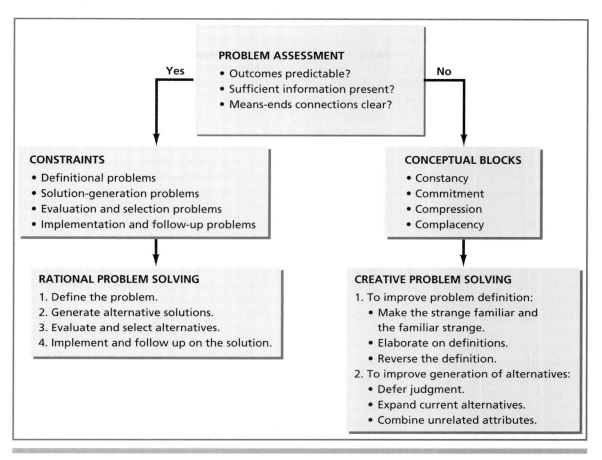

Figure 8   A Model of Rational and Creative Problem Solving

PRINCIPLE	EXAMPLES
1. Pull people apart; Put people together.	• Let individuals work alone as well as with teams and task forces. • Encourage minority reports and legitimize "devil's advocate" roles. • Encourage heterogeneous membership in teams. • Separate competing groups or subgroups.
2. Monitor and prod.	• Talk to customers. • Identify customer expectations both in advance and after the sale. • Hold people accountable. • Use "sharp-pointed" prods.
3. Reward multiple roles.	• Idea champion • Sponsor and mentor • Orchestrator and facilitator • Rule breaker

Table 8   Three Principles for Fostering Innovativeness

Nemeth (1986) found that creativity increased markedly when minority influences were present in the team, for example, when "devil's advocate" roles were legitimized, a formal minority report was always included in final recommendations, and individuals assigned to work on a team had divergent backgrounds or views. "Those exposed to minority views are stimulated to attend to more aspects of the situation, they think in more divergent ways, and they are more likely to detect novel solutions or come to new decisions" (Nemeth, 1986, p. 25). Nemeth found that those positive benefits occur in groups even when the divergent or minority views are wrong. Similarly, Janis (1971) found that narrow-mindedness in groups (dubbed "groupthink") was best overcome by establishing competing groups working on the same problem, participation in groups by outsiders, assigning a role of critical evaluator in the group, having groups made up of cross-functional participants, and so on. The most productive groups are those characterized by fluid roles, lots of interaction among members, and flat power structures.

Innovativeness can be fostered when individuals are placed in teams and when they are at least temporarily separated from the normal pressures of organizational life. Teams, however, are most effective at generating innovative ideas when they are characterized by attributes of minority influence, competition, heterogeneity, and interaction. You can help foster innovation among people you manage, therefore, by pulling people apart (e.g., giving them a bullpen) as well as putting people together (e.g., putting them on a team).

Monitor and Prod

Neither Percy Spencer nor Spence Silver was allowed to work on their projects with no accountability. Both men eventually had to report on the results they accomplished with their experimentation and imagination. At 3M, for example, people are expected to allocate 15 percent of their time away from company business to work on new, creative ideas. They can even appropriate company materials and resources to work on them. However, individuals are always held accountable for their decisions. They need to show results for their "play time."

Holding people accountable for outcomes, in fact, is an important motivator for improved performance. Two innovators in the entertainment industry captured this principle with these remarks: "The ultimate inspi-

ration is the deadline. That's when you have to do what needs to be done. The fact that twice a year the creative talent of this country is working until midnight to get something ready for a trade show is very good for the economy. Without this kind of pressure, things would turn to mashed potatoes" (von Oech, 1986, p. 119). One way Woody Morcott, DEO at Dana Corporation, holds people accountable for innovation is to require that each person in the company submit at least two suggestions for improvement each month. At least 70 percent of the new ideas must be implemented. Woody admitted that he stole the idea during a visit to a Japanese company where he noticed workers huddled around a table scribbling notes on how some ideas for improvement might work. At Dana, this requirement is part of every person's job assignment. Rewards are associated with such ideas as well. A plant in Chihuahua, Mexico, for example, rewards employees with $1.89 for every idea submitted and another $1.89 if the idea is used. "We drill into people that they are responsible for keeping the plant competitive through innovation," Morcott said (personal communication).

In addition to accountability, innovativeness is stimulated by what Gene Goodson at Johnson Controls called "sharp-pointed prods." After taking over the automotive group at that company, Goodson found that he could stimulate creative problem solving by issuing certain mandates that demanded innovativeness. One such mandate was, "There will be no more forklift trucks allowed in any of our plants." At first hearing, that mandate sounds absolutely outrageous. Think about it. You have a plant with tens of thousands of square feet of floor space. The loading docks are on one side of the building, and many tons of heavy raw materials are unloaded weekly and moved from the loading docks to work stations throughout the entire facility. The only way it can be done is with forklifts. Eliminating forklift trucks would ruin the plant, right? Wrong. This sharp-pointed prod demanded that individuals working in the plant find ways to move the work stations closer to the raw materials, to move the unloading of the raw materials closer to the work stations, or to change the size and amounts of material being unloaded. The innovations that resulted from eliminating forklifts saved the company millions of dollars in materials handling and wasted time, dramatically improved quality, productivity, and efficiency, and made it possible for Johnson Controls to capture some business from their Japanese competitors.

One of the best methods for generating useful prods is regularly to monitor customer preferences, expectations, and evaluations. Many of the most creative ideas have come from customers, the recipients of goods and services. Identifying their preferences in advance and monitoring their evaluations of products or services later are good ways to get ideas for innovation and to be prodded to make improvements. All employees should be in regular contact with their own customers, asking questions and monitoring performance.

By customers, we don't mean just the end-users of a business product or service. In fact, all of us have customers, whether we are students in school, members of a family, players on a basketball team, or whatever. Customers are simply those for whom we are trying to produce something or whom we serve. Students, for example, can count their instructors, class members, and potential employers as customers whom they serve. *A priori* and *post hoc* monitoring of their expectations and evaluations is an important way to help foster new ideas for problem solving. This monitoring is best done through one-on-one meetings (see Chapter 4, which discusses the Personal Management Interview Program), but it can also be done through follow-up calls, surveys, customer complaint cards, suggestion systems, and so on.

In summary, you can foster innovativeness by holding people accountable for new ideas and by stimulating them with periodic prods. The most useful prods generally come from customers.

Reward Multiple Roles

The success of the sticky yellow notes at 3M is more than a story of the creativity of Spence Silver. It also illustrates the necessity of people playing multiple roles in innovation and the importance of recognizing and rewarding those who play such roles. Without a number of people playing multiple roles, Spence Silver's glue would probably still be on a shelf somewhere.

Four crucial roles in the innovative process are the *idea champion* (the person who comes up with innovative problem solutions), the *sponsor* or *mentor* (the person who helps provide the resources, environment, and encouragement for the idea champion to work on his idea), the *orchestrator* or *facilitator* (the person who brings together cross-functional groups and necessary political support to facilitate implementation of creative ideas), and the *rule breaker* (the person who goes beyond organizational boundaries and barriers to ensure success of the innovation). Each of these roles is present in most important innovations in organizations, and all are illustrated by the Post-It Note example below.

This story has four major parts.

1. Spence Silver, while fooling around with chemical configurations that the academic literature indicated wouldn't work, invented a glue that wouldn't stick. Silver spent years giving presentations to any audience at 3M that would listen, trying to pawn off his glue on some division that could find a practical application for it. But nobody was interested.

2. Henry Courtney and Roger Merrill developed a coating substance that allowed the glue to stick to one surface but not to others. This made it possible to produce a permanently temporary glue, that is, one that would peel off easily when pulled but would otherwise hang on forever.

3. Art Fry found a problem that fit Spence Silver's solution. He found an application for the glue as a "better bookmark" and as a note pad. No equipment existed at 3M to coat only a part of a piece of paper with the glue. Fry therefore carried 3M equipment and tools home to his own basement, where he designed and made his own machine to manufacture the forerunner of Post-It Notes. Because the working machine became too large to get out of his basement, he blasted a hole in the wall to get the equipment back to 3M. He then brought together engineers, designers, production managers, and machinists to demonstrate the prototype machine and generate enthusiasm for manufacturing the product.

4. Geoffrey Nicholson and Joseph Ramsey began marketing the product inside 3M. They also submitted the product to the standard 3M market tests. The product failed miserably. No one wanted to pay $1.00 for a pad of scratch paper. But when Nicholson and Ramsey broke 3M rules by personally visiting test market sites and giving away free samples, the consuming public became addicted to the product.

In this scenario, Spence Silver was both a rule breaker and an idea champion. Art Fry was also an idea champion, but more importantly, he orchestrated the coming together of the various groups needed to get the innovation off the ground. Henry Courtney and Roger Merrill helped sponsor Silver's innovation by providing him with the coating substance that would allow his idea to work. Geoff Nicholson and Joe Ramsey were both rule breakers and sponsors in their bid to get the product accepted by the public. In each case, not only did all these people play unique roles, but they did so with tremendous enthusiasm and zeal. They were confident of their ideas and willing to put their time and resources on the line as advocates. They fostered support among a variety of constituencies, both within their own areas of expertise as well as among outside groups. Most organizations are inclined to give in to those who are sure of themselves, persistent in their efforts, and savvy enough to make converts of others.

Not everyone can be an idea champion. But when managers reward and recognize those who sponsor and orchestrate the ideas of others, innovation increases in organizations. Teams form, supporters replace competitors, and creativity thrives. Facilitating multiple role development is the job of the innovative manager.

Summary

In the last 15 years, the growth rate of new patent applications in this country has declined by 25 percent. Last year almost half of the patents issued in America were given to foreigners. One major U.S. corporation reported that five years ago over 70 percent of its licensing agreements consisted of patents it sold to other countries. Now it purchases over half its products using licensing agreements from foreign countries. America marketed 82 percent of the world's inventions 25 years ago, but it now ranks behind several other countries in new-product introductions. Despite the well-developed medical and pharmaceutical school system existing in the United States, Japan has still led the world in the introductions of new drugs for the last five years. One U.S. automobile manufacturer bragged of receiving over 30,000 suggestions for improvement from employees in one year; then a Japanese rival opened a plant 50 miles away and received over 3 million suggestions from employees in a single year. In short, the United States has experienced a decline in creativity and innovation in the last several years. Flexibility in thinking and effective management problem solving seem to have taken a nose-dive.

As we have pointed out, a well-developed model exists for solving problems. It consists of four separate and sequential stages: defining a problem; generating alternative solutions; evaluating and selecting the best solution; and implementing the chosen solution. This model, however, is mainly useful for solving straightforward problems. Many problems faced by managers are not of this type, and frequently managers are called on to exercise creative problem-solving skills. That is, they must broaden their perspective of the problem and develop alternative solutions that are not immediately obvious.

We have discussed and illustrated eight major conceptual blocks that inhibit most people's creative problem-solving abilities. Conceptual blocks are mental obstacles that artificially constrain problem definition and solution and that keep most people from being effective creative problem solvers. The four major conceptual blocks are summarized in Table 3.

Overcoming these conceptual blocks is a matter of skill development and practice in thinking, not a matter of innate ability. Everyone can become a skilled creative problem solver with practice. Becoming aware of these thinking inhibiters helps individuals overcome them. We also discussed three major principles for improving creative problem definition and three major principles for improving the creative generation of alternative solutions. Certain techniques were described that can help implement these six principles.

We concluded by offering some hints about how to foster creativity and innovativeness among other people. Becoming an effective problem solver yourself is important, but effective managers can also enhance this activity among their subordinates, peers, and superiors.

Behavioral Guidelines

Below are specific behavioral action guidelines to help your skill practice in problem solving, creativity, and fostering innovation.

1. Follow the four-step procedure outlined in Table 1 when solving straightforward problems. Keep the steps separate, and do not take shortcuts.

2. When approaching a difficult problem, try to overcome your conceptual blocks by consciously doing the following mental activities:

   ▶ Use lateral thinking in addition to vertical thinking.

- Use several thought languages instead of just one.

- Challenge stereotypes based on past experiences.

- Identify underlying themes and commonalities in seemingly unrelated factors.

- Delete superfluous information and fill in important missing information when studying the problem.

- Avoid artificially constraining problem boundaries.

- Overcome any unwillingness to be inquisitive.

- Use both right- and left-brain thinking.

3. When defining a problem, make the strange familiar and the familiar strange by using metaphor and analogy, first to focus and then to distort and refocus the definition.

4. Elaborate problem definitions by developing at least two alternative (opposite) definitions and by applying a checklist.

5. Reverse problem definitions by beginning with end results and working backwards.

6. In generating potential problem solutions, defer any judgment until many solutions have been proposed. Use the four rules of brainstorming:

- Do not evaluate.

- Encourage "wild ideas."

- Encourage quantity.

- Build on others' ideas.

7. Expand the list of current alternative solutions by subdividing the problem into its attributes.

8. Increase the number of possible solutions by combining unrelated problem attributes. Morphological connections and relational algorithms may be helpful.

9. Foster innovativeness among those with whom you work by doing the following:

- Find a "practice field" where individuals can experiment and try out ideas, and assign them responsibility for fostering innovation.

- Put people holding different perspectives in teams to work on problems.

- Hold people accountable for innovation.

- Use sharp-pointed prods to stimulate new thinking.

- Recognize, reward, and encourage the participation of multiple players, including idea champions, sponsors, orchestrators, and rule breakers.

Skill Analysis

Cases Involving Problem Solving

Admiral Kimmel's Failure at Pearl Harbor

In the summer of 1941, as relations between the United States and Japan were rapidly deteriorating, Admiral Kimmel, Commander in Chief of the Pacific Fleet, received many warnings concerning the imminence of war. During this period he worked out a plan in collaboration with his staff at Pearl Harbor, which gave priority to training key personnel and supplying basic equipment to U.S. outposts in the Far East. The plan took account of the possibility of a long, hard war with Japan and the difficulties of mobilizing scarce resources in manpower and material. At that time, Admiral Kimmel and his staff were keenly aware of the risks of being unprepared for war with Japan, as well as the high costs and risks involved in preparing for war. They appear to have been relatively optimistic about being able to develop a satisfactory military plan and about having sufficient time in which to implement it. In short, all the conditions were present for vigilance, and it seems likely that this coping pattern characterized their planning activity.

But during the late fall of 1941, as warnings became increasingly more ominous, a different pattern of coping behavior emerged. Admiral Kimmel and his staff continued to cling to the policy to which they had committed themselves, discounting each fresh warning and failing to note that more and more signs were pointing to Pearl Harbor as a possible target for a surprise air attack. They repeatedly renewed their decision to continue using the available resources primarily for training green sailors and soldiers and for supplying bases close to Japan, rather than instituting an adequate alert that would give priority to defending Pearl Harbor against enemy attack.

Knowing that neither their own sector nor the rest of the U.S. military organization was ready for a shooting war, they clung to an unwarranted set of rationalizations. The Japanese, they thought, would not launch an attack against any American possession; and if by some remote chance they decided to do so, it certainly wouldn't be at Pearl Harbor. Admiral Kimmel and his staff acknowledged that Japan could launch a surprise attack in any direction, but remained convinced that it would not be launched in their direction. They saw no reason to change their course. Therefore, they continued to give peacetime weekend leave to the majority of the naval forces in Hawaii and allowed the many warships in the Pacific Fleet to remain anchored at Pearl Harbor, as sitting ducks. Kimmel regularly discussed each warning with members of his staff. At times he became emotionally aroused and obtained reassurance from the members of his in-group. He shared with them a number of rationalizations that bolstered his decision to ignore the warnings. On November 27, 1941, for example, he received an explicit "war warning" from the chief of naval operations in Washington, which stirred up his concern but did not impel him to take any new protective action. This message was intended as a strong follow-up to an earlier warning, which Kimmel had received only three days earlier, stating that war with Japan was imminent and that "a surprise aggressive movement in any direction, including attack on Philippines or Guam, is a possibility." The new warning asserted that "an aggressive move by Japan is expected within the next few days" and instructed Kimmel to "execute appropriate defensive deployment" preparatory to carrying out the naval war plan.

The threat conveyed by this warning was evidently strong enough to induce Kimmel to engage in prolonged discussion with his staff about what should be done. But their vigilance seems to have been confined to paying careful attention to the way the warning was worded. During the meeting, members of the staff pointed out to Kimmel that Hawaii was not specifically mentioned as a possible target in either of the two war warnings, whereas other places—the Philippines, Malaya, and other remote areas—were explicitly named. Kimmel went along with the interpretation that the ambiguities they had detected in the wording must have meant that Pearl Harbor was not supposed to be regarded as a likely target, even though the message seemed to be saying that it was. The defensive quality that entered into this judgment is revealed by the fact that Kimmel made no effort to use his available channels of communication in Washington to find out what really had been meant. He ended up agreeing with the members of his advisory group that there was no chance of a surprise air attack on Hawaii at that particular time.

Since he judged Pearl Harbor not to be vulnerable, Kimmel decided that the limited-alert condition that had been instituted months earlier would be sufficient. He assumed, however, that all U.S. Army units in Hawaii had gone on full alert in response to this war warning, so that antiaircraft and radar units under army control would be fully activated. But, again, reflecting his defensive lack of interest in carrying out tasks that required acknowledging the threat, Kimmel failed to inquire of Army headquarters exactly what was being done. As a result, he did not discover until after the disaster on December 7 that the Army, too, was on only limited alert, designed exclusively to protect military installations against local sabotage.

On December 3, 1941, Kimmel engaged in intensive discussion with two members of his staff upon receiving a fresh warning from naval headquarters in Washington stating that U.S. cryptographers had decoded a secret message from Tokyo to all diplomatic missions in the United States and other countries, ordering them to destroy their secret codes. Kimmel realized that this type of order could mean that Japan was making last-minute preparations before launching an attack against the United States. Again, he and his advisors devoted considerable attention to the exact wording of this new, worrisome warning. They made much of the fact that the dispatch said "most" of the codes but not "all." They concluded that the destruction of the codes should be interpreted as a routine precautionary measure and not as a sign that Japan was planning to attack an American possession. Again, no effort was made to find out from Washington how the intelligence units there interpreted the message. But the lengthy discussions and the close attention paid to the wording of these messages imply that they did succeed in at least temporarily inducing decisional conflict.

By December 6, 1941, the day before the attack, Kimmel was aware of a large accumulation of extremely ominous signs. In addition to receiving the official war warnings during the preceding week, he had received a private letter three days earlier from Admiral Stark in Washington stating that both President Roosevelt and Secretary of State Hull now thought that the Japanese were getting ready to launch a surprise attack. Then on December 6, Kimmel received another message from Admiral Stark containing emergency war orders pertaining to the destruction of secret and confidential documents in American bases on outlying Pacific islands. On that same day, the FBI in Hawaii informed Kimmel that the local Japanese consulate had been burning its papers for the last two days. Furthermore, Kimmel's chief naval intelligence officer had reported to him that day, as he had on the preceding days, that despite fresh efforts to pick up Japanese naval signal calls, the whereabouts of all six of Japan's aircraft carriers still remained a mystery. (U.S. Naval Combat Intelligence had lost track of the Japanese aircraft carriers in mid-November, when they started to move toward Hawaii for the planned attack on Pearl Harbor.)

Although the various warning signs, taken together, clearly indicated that Japan was getting ready to launch an attack against the United States, they remained ambiguous as to exactly where the attack was likely to be. There was also considerable "noise" mixed in with the warning signals, including intelligence reports that huge Japanese naval forces were moving toward Malaya. But, inexplicably, there was a poverty of imagination on the part of Kimmel and his staff with regard to considering the possibility that Pearl Harbor itself might be one of the targets of a Japanese attack.

The accumulated warnings, however, were sufficiently impressive to Kimmel to generate considerable concern. On the afternoon of December 6, as he was pondering alternative courses of action, he openly expressed his anxiety to two of his staff officers. He told them he was worried about the safety of the fleet at Pearl Harbor in view of all the disturbing indications that Japan was getting ready for a massive attack somewhere. One member of the staff immediately reassured him that "the Japanese could not possibly be able to proceed in force against Pearl Harbor when they had so much strength concentrated in their Asiatic operations." Another told him that the limited-alert condition he had ordered many weeks earlier would certainly be sufficient and nothing more was needed. "We finally decided," Kimmel subsequently recalled, "that what we had [already] done was still good and we would stick to it." At the end of the discussion, Kimmel "put his worries aside" and went off to a dinner party.

Source: Janis & Mann, 1977, pp. 120–123.

Discussion Questions

1. What conceptual blocks are illustrated in this case?

2. Outline the problem-solving steps followed by Kimmel and his advisors. What steps in rational problem solving were skipped or short-circuited?

3. What kinds of conceptual blockbusters could have been useful to Kimmel? If you were his advisor, what would you have suggested to help his problem-solving processes?

4. If you knew then what you know now, how would you have redesigned Kimmel's structures and processes so that effective problem solving could occur?

The Sony Walkman

They had been disappointed at first, but it wasn't something that was going to keep them awake nights. Mitsuro Ida and a group of electronics engineers in Sony Corporation's Tape Recorder Division in Tokyo had tried to redesign a small, portable tape recorder, called "Pressman," so that it gave out stereophonic sounds. A year or so before, Ida and his group had been responsible for inventing the first Pressman, a wonderfully compact machine—ideal for use by journalists—which had sold very well.

But the sound in that tape machine was monaural. The next challenge for Sony's tape recorder engineers was to make a portable machine just as small, but with stereophonic sound. The very first stereo Pressman they made, in the last few months of 1978, didn't succeed. When Ida and his colleagues got the stereo circuits into the Pressman chassis (5.25 inches by 3.46 inches and only 1.14 inches deep), they didn't have any space left to fit in the recording mechanism. They had made a stereophonic tape recorder that couldn't record anything. Ida regarded this as a good first try but a useless product. But he didn't throw it away. The stereo Pressman was a nice little machine. So the engineers found a few favorite music cassettes and played them while they worked.

After Ida and his fellow designers had turned their nonrecording tape recorder into background music, they didn't entirely ignore it. They had frequent discussions about how to fit the stereo function and the recording mechanism into that overly small space. It was not an easy problem to solve, but that made it all the more fascinating and attractive to Ida and his group of inveterate problem solvers. Their focus on the problem of the stereo Pressman blinded them to the solution—to a different problem—that was in their hands.

"And then one day," said Takichi Tezuka, manager of product planning for the Tape Recorder Division, "into our room came Mr. Ibuka, our honorary chairman. He just popped into the room, saw us listening to this, and thought it was very interesting."

It is the province of honorary chairmen everywhere, because their status is almost invariably ceremonial, to putter about the plant looking in on this group and that, nodding over the latest incomprehensible gadget. To this mundane task, Masaru Ibuka brought an undiminished intelligence and an active imagination. When he happened into the Tape Recorder Division and saw Ida's incomplete tape recorder, he admired the quality of its stereophonic sound. He also remembered an entirely unrelated project going on elsewhere in the building, where an engineer named Yoshiyuki Kamon was working to develop lightweight portable headphones.

What if you combined them? asked Ibuka. At the very least, he said, the headphones would use battery power much more efficiently than stereo speakers. Reduce power requirements and you can reduce battery consumption. But another idea began to form in his mind. If you added the headphones, wouldn't you dramatically increase the quality of what the listener hears? Could you leave out the recorder entirely and make a successful product that just plays music?

In the world of tape recorders, Ibuka's thought was heresy. He was mixing up functions. Headphones traditionally were supposed to extend the usefulness of tape recorders, not be essential to their success. This idea was so well established that if Ibuka had not made an association between a defective tape recorder design and the unfinished headphone design, Walkman may well have remained a little byway in musical history. Design groups within Sony tend to be very close-knit and remain focused on short-term task completion. Even when things were less busy, there was never any reason for tape-recorder people to communicate with headphone people. They had nothing to do with each other. Tezuka, the man later described as "the secretariat of the Walkman project," said, "No one dreamed that a headphone would ever come in a package with a tape recorder. We're not very interested in what they do in the Headphone Division."

But, even without this insularity, there is no assurance that someone else at Sony would have made the connection that Ibuka made. To people today, the relationship between a cassette player and a set of headphones is self-evident. But to people at Sony, and at virtually every consumer electronics company, that connection was invisible in 1978.

Ibuka got a predictable response from the researchers in the electronics lab and from others in the Tape Recorder and Headphone Divisions. They were painfully polite but noncommittal. Ibuka might be right that the headphones would improve Pressman's efficiency, but nobody could guess how much of an improvement that would be. No one wanted to tell Ibuka that the idea of removing the speaker in favor of headphones was crazy. But it was! What if the owner of the device wanted to play back a tape so that more than one person could listen?

When Ibuka ventured further into illogic by suggesting a playback machine with no speaker and no recorder, he lost everybody. Who would want to buy such a thing? Who in Sony Corporation would support even 10 minutes of development on such a harebrained scheme?

In a way, they were right and Ibuka was wrong. This was an idea that violated most industries' well-established criteria for judging the natural increments of product development. It only makes sense that a new product prototype should be better than the previous generation of product. Ida's nonrecording prototype seemed worse. The idea had no support from the people who eventually would be responsible for funding its development, carrying out the research, and trying to sell it to a consumer market. The idea should have been killed. The system made sense and the people who worked within the system were making sense.

For Honorary Chairman Ibuka, the handwriting was on the wall. Even though he was a revered man at Sony, he had no authority to order such a project undertaken against the wishes of the division's leaders. It was clear that the only way to sell a bad idea to a group of cautious, reasonable businessmen was to find an ally. So, in his enthusiasm, his next step was straight to the office of his partner and friend, Akio Morita.

Source: Nayak and Ketteringham, 1986.

Discussion Questions

1. What principles of rational problem solving and creative problem solving were used in this case?

2. How was innovativeness fostered within Sony by top managers?

3. What roles were played by the various characters in the case that led to the success of the Walkman?

4. If you were a consultant to Sony, what would you advise to help foster this kind of innovation more frequently and more broadly throughout the company?

Skill Practice

Exercises for Applying Conceptual Blockbusting

Creative problem solving is most applicable to problems that have no obvious solutions. Most problems people face can be solved relatively easily with a systematic analysis of alternatives. But other problems are ambiguous enough that obvious alternatives are not workable; such problems require nontraditional approaches to find reasonable alternatives. Following are two such problems. They are real, not fictitious, and it probably characterizes your own college or university or public library and many local restaurants. Apply the principles of creative problem solving in the chapter to come up with realistic, cost-effective, creative solutions to these problems. Don't stop at the first solutions that come to mind because there are no obvious right answers.

Assignment

Form small groups to engage in the following problem-solving exercises. Each group should generate solutions to the cases. Each case is factual, not fictitious. Try to be as creative in your solutions as possible. The creativity of those solutions should be judged by an independent observer, and the best group's solution should be given recognition. In defining and solving the problems, use the following five steps. Do not skip steps.

1. Generate a single statement that accurately defines the problem. Make sure that all group members agree with the definition of the problem.

2. Propose alternative solutions to the problem. Write these down and prepare to report them to the larger group.

3. All small groups should report their top three alternatives to the large group. The top three are the ones that most group members agree would produce the best solution to the problem.

4. Now, in each small group, generate at least five plausible alternative definitions of the problem. Use any of the techniques for expanding problem definition discussed in the text. Each problem statement should differ from the others in its definition, not just in its attributions of causes of the problem.

5. After each group has agreed on the wording of the five statements, identify at least 10 new alternatives for solving the problems you have defined in step 4. Apply the techniques for expanding alternatives discussed in the text.

As a result of steps 4 and 5, your group should have identified some new alternatives as well as more alternatives than you did in steps 1 and 2. Report to the large group the three alternatives that your small group judges to be the most creative.

An observer should provide feedback on the extent to which each group member applied these principles effectively, using the Observer's Feedback Form in Appendix I.

The Bleak Future of Knowledge

Libraries throughout the world are charged with the responsibility of preserving the accumulated wisdom of the past and gathering information in the present. They serve as sources of information and resources, alternate schools, and places of exploration and discovery. No one would question the value of libraries to societies and cultures throughout the world. The materials housed there are the very foundation of civilization. But consider the following two problems.

1. In America alone (and the problem is much worse in Eastern Europe and the former Soviet-bloc countries), hundreds of thousands of books are in states of decay so advanced that when they are touched they fall into powder. Whereas parchments seem to survive better when they are handled, and books printed before 1830 on rag paper stay flexible and tough, books printed since the mid 19th century on wood-pulp paper are being steadily eaten away by natural acids. At the Library of Congress, about 77,000 books out of the stock of 13 million enter the endangered category every year. Fairly soon, about 40 percent of the books in the biggest research collections in America will be too fragile to handle. At the Bibliothèque Nationale in France, more than 600,000 books require treatment immediately. The largest library in England, the British Library, has a backlog of 1.6 million urgent cases.

2. The Library of Congress estimates that it will take 25 years to work through the backlog of cases. But of more concern is the fact that it costs about $200 in time and labor to treat a single volume. It costs more if it is to be put on another medium (e.g., microfiche, CD-ROM). The budget for most large libraries in the United States, including the Library of Congress, has been cut during the 1980s and 1990s, and with pressure to raise taxes to fund social programs ever present on a national level and the cost of higher education rising beyond the inflation rate in universities, it is doubtful that book preservation will receive high funding priority in the near future.

Source: The Economist, December 23, 1989.

Keith Dunn and McGuffey's Restaurant

Keith Dunn knew exactly what to expect. He knew how his employees felt about him. That's why he had sent them the questionnaire in the first place. He needed a shot of confidence, a feeling that his employees were behind him as he struggled to build McGuffey's Restaurants, Inc., beyond two restaurants and $4 million in annual sales.

Gathering up the anonymous questionnaires, Dunn returned to his tiny corporate office in Asheville, North Carolina. With one of his partners by his side, he ripped open the first envelope as eagerly as a Broadway producer checking the reviews on opening night. His eyes zoomed directly to the question where employees were asked to rate the three owners' performance on a scale of 1 to 10.

A zero. The employee had scrawled in a big, fat zero. "Find out whose handwriting this is," he told his partner, Richard Laibson.

He ripped open another: zero again. And another. A two. "We'll fire these people," Dunn said to Laibson coldly.

Another zero.

A one.

"Oh, go work for somebody else, you jerk!" Dunn shouted.

Soon he had moved to fire 10 of his 230 employees. "Plenty of people seemed to hate my guts," he says.

Over the next day, though, Dunn's anger subsided. "You think, I've done all this for these people and they think I'm a total jerk who doesn't care about them," he says. "Finally, you have to look in the mirror and think, 'Maybe they're right.' "

For Dunn, that realization was absolutely shattering. He had started the company three years earlier, in 1983, out of frustration over all the abuse he had suffered while working at big restaurant chains. If Dunn had one overriding mission at McGuffey's, it was to prove that restaurants didn't have to mistreat their employees.

He thought he had succeeded. Until he opened those surveys, he had believed that McGuffey's was a place where employees felt valued, involved, and appreciated. "I had no idea we were treating people so badly," he says. Somewhere along the way, in the day-to-day running of the business, he had lost his connection with them and left behind the employee-oriented company he thought he was running.

Dunn's 13-year odyssey through some big restaurant chains left him feeling as limp as a cheeseburger after a day under the heat lamps. Ponderosa in Georgia. Bennigan's in Florida and Tennessee. TGI Friday's in Texas, Tennessee, and Indiana. Within one six-month period at Friday's, he got two promotions, two bonuses, and two raises; then his boss left, and he got fired. That did it. Dunn was fed up with big chains.

In 1982, at the age of 29, he returned to Atlanta, where he had attended Emory University as an undergraduate and where he began waiting tables at a local restaurant.

There he met David Lynn, the general manager of the restaurant, a similarly jaded 29-year-old who, by his own admission, had "begun to lose faith." Lynn and Dunn started hatching plans to open their own place, where employees would enjoy working as much as customers enjoyed eating. They planned to target the smaller markets that the chains ignored. With financing from a friend, they opened McGuffey's in 1983.

True to their people-oriented goals, the partners tried to make employees feel more appreciated than they themselves had felt at the chains. They gave them a free drink and a meal at the end of every shift, let them give away appetizers and desserts, and provided them a week of paid vacation each year.

A special camaraderie developed among the employees. After all, they worked in an industry in which a turnover rate of 250 percent was something to aspire to. The night before McGuffey's opened, in October 1983, some 75 employees encircled the ficus tree next to the bar, joined hands, and prayed silently for two minutes. "The tree had a special energy," says Dunn.

Maybe so. By the third night of operation, the 230-seat McGuffey's had a waiting list. The dining room was so crowded that after three months the owners decided to add a 58-seat patio. Then they had to rearrange the kitchen to handle the volume. In its first three and a half months, McGuffey's racked up sales of about $415,000, ending 1983 just over $110,000 in the red, mostly because the partners paid back the bulk of their $162,000 debt right away.

Word of the restaurant's success reached Hendersonville, North Carolina, a town of 30,000 about 20 miles away. The managing agent of a mall there—*the* mall there—even stopped by to recruit the partners. They made some audacious requests, asking him to spend $300,000 on renovations, including the addition of a patio and upgraded equipment. The agent agreed. With almost no market research, they opened the second McGuffey's in April 1985; the first, in Asheville, was still roaring, having broken the $2 million mark in sales its first year, with a marginal loss of just over $16,000.

By midsummer, the 200-seat Hendersonville restaurant was hauling in $35,000 a week. "Gee, you guys must be getting rich," the partners heard all around town. "When are you going to buy your own jets?" "Everyone was telling us we could do no wrong," says Dunn. The Asheville restaurant, though, was developing some problems. Right after the Hendersonville McGuffey's opened, sales at Asheville fell 15 percent. But the partners shrugged it off; some Asheville customers lived closer to Hendersonville, so one restaurant was probably pulling some of the other's customers. Either way, the customers were still there. "We're just spreading our market a little thinner," Dunn told his partners. When Asheville had lost another 10 percent and Hendersonville 5 percent, Dunn blamed the fact that the drinking age had been raised to 21 in Asheville, cutting into liquor sales.

By 1985 the company recorded nearly $3.5 million in sales, with nominal losses of about $95,000. But the adulation and the expectation of big money and fancy cars were beginning to cloud the real reason they had started the business. "McGuffey's was born purely out of frustration," says Dunn. Now, the frustration was gone. "You get pulled in so many directions that you just lose touch," says Laibson. "There are things that you simply forget."

What the partners forgot, in the warm flush of success, were their roots.

"Success breeds ego," says Dunn, "and ego breeds contempt." He would come back from trade shows or real-estate meetings all pumped up. "Isn't this exciting?" he'd ask an employee. "We're going to open a new restaurant next year." When the employee stared back blankly, Dunn felt resentful. "I didn't understand why they weren't thrilled," he says. He didn't see that while his world was constantly growing and expanding, his employees' world was sliding downhill. They were still busing tables or cooking burgers and thinking, "Forget the new restaurant; you haven't said hello to me in months; and by the way, why don't you fix the tea machine?"

"I just got too good, and too busy, to do orientation," he says. So he decided to tape orientation sessions for new employees, to make a film just like the one he had been subjected to when he worked at Bennigan's. On tape, Dunn told new employees one of his favorite stories, the one about the customer who walks into a chain restaurant and finds himself asking questions of a hostess sign because he can't find a human. The moral: "McGuffey's will never be so impersonal as to make people talk to a sign." A film maybe, but never a sign.

Since Dunn wasn't around the restaurants all that much, he didn't notice that employees were leaving in droves. Even the departure of Tom Valdez, the kitchen manager in Asheville, wasn't enough to take the shine off his "glowing ego," as he calls it.

Valdez had worked as Dunn's kitchen manager at TGI Friday's. When the Hendersonville McGuffey's was opening up, Dunn recruited him as kitchen manager. A few months later, Valdez marched into Dunn's office and announced that he was heading back to Indianapolis. "There's too much b.s. around here," he blurted out. "You don't care about your people." Dunn was shocked. "As soon as we get this next restaurant opened, we'll make things the way they used to be," he replied. But Valdez wouldn't budge. "Keith," he said bitterly, "you are turning out to be like all the other companies." Dunn shrugged. "We're a big company, and we've got to do big-company things," he replied.

Valdez walked out, slamming the door. Dunn still didn't understand that he had begun imitating the very companies that he had so loathed. He stopped wanting to rebel against them; under the intense pressure of growing a company, he just wanted to master their tried-and-true methods. "I was allowing the company to become like the companies we hated because I thought it was inevitable," he says.

Three months later, McGuffey's two top managers announced that they were moving to the West Coast to start their own company. Dunn beamed, "Our employees learn so much," he would boast, "that they are ready to start their own restaurants."

Before they left, Dunn sat down with them in the classroom at Hendersonville. "So," he asked casually, "how do you think we could run the place better?" Three hours later, he was still listening. "The McGuffey's we fell in love with just doesn't exist anymore," one of them concluded sadly.

Dunn was outraged. How could his employees be so ungrateful? Couldn't they see how everybody was sharing the success? Who had given them health insurance as soon as the partners could afford it? Who had given them dental insurance this year? And who—not that anyone would appreciate it—planned to set up profit sharing next year?

Sales at both restaurants were still dwindling. This time, there were no changes in the liquor laws or new restaurants to blame. With employees feeling ignored, resentful, and abandoned, the rest rooms didn't get scrubbed as thoroughly, the food didn't arrive quite as piping hot, the servers didn't smile so often. But the owners, wrapped up in themselves, couldn't see it. They were mystified. "It began to seem like what made our company great had somehow gotten lost," says Laibson.

Shaken by all the recent defections, Dunn needed a boost of confidence. So he sent out the one-page survey, which asked employees to rate the owners' performance. He was crushed by the results. Out of curiosity, Dunn later turned to an assistant and asked a favor. Can you calculate our turnover rate? Came the reply: "220 percent, sir."

Keith Dunn figured he would consult the management gurus through their books, tapes, and speeches. "You want people-oriented management?" he thought. "Fine. I'll give it to you."

Dunn and Laibson had spent a few months visiting 23 of the best restaurants in the Southeast. Driving for hours, they'd listen to tapes on management, stop them at key points, and ask, "Why don't we do something like this?" At night, they read management books, underlining significant passages, looking for answers.

"They were all saying that people is where it's at," says Dunn. "We've got to start thinking of our people as an asset," they decided. "And we've got to increase the value of that asset." Dunn was excited by the prospect of forming McGuffey's into the shape of a reverse pyramid, with employees on top. Keeping employees, he now knew, meant keeping employees involved.

He heard consultant Don Beveridge suggest that smart companies kept managers involved by tying their compensation to their performance. McGuffey's had been handing managers goals every quarter; if they hit half the goals, they pocketed half their bonus. Sound reasonable? No, preached Beveridge, you can't reward managers for a halfhearted job. It has to be all or nothing. "From now on," Dunn told his managers firmly, "there's no halfway."

Dunn also launched a contest for employees. Competition, he had read, was a good way of keeping employees motivated.

So the CUDA (Customer Undeniably Deserves Attention) contest was born. At Hendersonville and Asheville, he divided the employees into six teams. The winning team would win $1,000, based on talking to customers, keeping the restaurant clean, and collecting special tokens for extra work beyond the call of duty.

Employees came in every morning, donned their colors, and dug in for battle. Within a few weeks, two teams pulled out in front. Managers also seemed revitalized. To Dunn, it seemed like they would do anything, *anything,* to keep their food costs down, their sales up, their profit margins in line. This was just what Tom Peters, Kenneth Blanchard, Don Beveridge, Zig Ziglar, and the others had promised.

But after about six months, only one store's managers seemed capable of winning those all-or-nothing bonuses. At managers' meetings and reviews, Dunn started hearing grumblings. "How come your labor costs are so out of whack?" he'd ask. "Heck, I can't win the bonus anyway," a manager would answer, "so why try?" "Look, Keith," another would say, "I haven't seen a bonus in so long, I've forgotten what they look like." Some managers wanted the bonus so badly that they worked understaffed, didn't fix equipment, and ran short on supplies.

The CUDA contest deteriorated into jealousy and malaise. Three teams lagged far behind after the first month or so. Within those teams people were bickering and complaining all the time: "We can't win, so what's the use?" The contest, Dunn couldn't help but notice, seemed to be having a reverse effect than the one he had intended. "Some people were really killing themselves," he says. About 12, to be exact. The other 100-plus were utterly demoralized.

Dunn was angry. These were the same employees who, after all, had claimed he wasn't doing enough for them. But OK, he wanted to hear what they had to say. "Get feedback," Tom Peters preached; "find out what your employees think." Dunn announced that the owners would hold informal rap sessions once a month.

"This is your time to talk," Dunn told the employees who showed up—all three of them. That's how it was most times, with three to five employees in attendance, and the owners dragging others away from their jobs in the kitchen. Nothing was sinking in, and Dunn knew it.

Source: Hyatt, 1989.

Skill Application

Activities for Solving Problems Creatively

Suggested Assignments

1. Teach someone else how to solve problems creatively. Record your experience in your journal.

2. Think of a problem that is important to you right now for which there is no obvious solution. Use the principles and techniques discussed in the chapter to work out a creative solution to that problem. Spend the time it takes to do a good job, even if several days are required. Describe the experience in your journal.

3. Help direct a group (your family, roommates, social club, church, etc.) in a creative problem-solving exercise using techniques discussed in the chapter. Record your experience in your journal.

4. Write a letter to a congressional representative, dean, or CEO identifying several alternative solutions to some perplexing problem facing his or her organization, community, or state right now. Write about an issue that you care about. Be sure to offer suggested solutions. This will require that you apply in advance the principles of problem solving discussed in the chapter.

Application Plan and Evaluation

The intent of this exercise is to help you apply this cluster of skills in a real-life, out-of-class setting. Now that you have become familiar with the behavioral guidelines that form the basis of effective skill performance, you will improve most by trying out those guidelines in an everyday context. Unlike a classroom activity, in which feedback is immediate and others can assist you with their evaluations, this skill application activity is one you must accomplish and evaluate on your own. There are two parts to this activity. Part 1 helps prepare you to apply the skill. Part 2 helps you evaluate and improve on your experience. Be sure to write down answers to each item. Don't short-circuit the process by skipping steps.

Part 1. Planning

1. Write down the two or three aspects of this skill that are most important to you. These may be areas of weakness, areas you most want to improve, or areas that are most salient to a problem you face right now. Identify the specific aspects of this skill that you want to apply.

2. Now identify the setting or the situation in which you will apply this skill. Establish a plan for performance by actually writing down a description of the situation. Who else will be involved? When will you do it? Where will it be done?

   Circumstances:

   Who else?

   When?

   Where?

3. Identify the specific behaviors you will engage in to apply this skill. Operationalize your skill performance.

4. What are the indicators of successful performance? How will you know you have been effective? What will indicate you have performed competently?

Part 2. Evaluation

5. After you have completed your implementation, record the results. What happened? How successful were you? What was the effect on others?

6. How can you improve? What modifications can you make next time? What will you do differently in a similar situation in the future?

7. Looking back on your whole skill practice and application experience, what have you learned? What has been surprising? In what ways might this experience help you in the long term?

Interpersonal Skills

Communicating Supportively

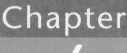

OBJECTIVES

- Differentiate between coaching and counseling problems

- Avoid defensiveness and disconfirmation by applying principles of supportive communication

- Improve work relationships by using personal management interviews

skill development

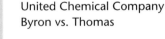

Skill Assessment

Diagnostic Surveys for Supportive Communication

Communicating Supportively

Step 1: Before you read the material in this chapter, please respond to the following statements by writing a number from the rating scale below in the left-hand column (Preassessment). Your answers should reflect your attitudes and behavior as they are now, not as you would like them to be. Be honest. This instrument is designed to help you discover your level of competency in communicating supportively so you can tailor your learning to your specific needs. When you have completed the survey, use the scoring key in Appendix I to identify the skill areas discussed in this chapter that are most important for you to master.

Step 2: After you have completed the reading and the exercises in this chapter and, ideally, as many as you can of the Skill Application assignments at the end of this chapter, cover up your first set of answers. Then respond to the same statements again, this time in the right-hand column (Postassessment). When you have completed the survey, use the scoring key in Appendix I to measure your progress. If your score remains low in specific skill areas, use the behavioral guidelines at the end of the Skill Learning section to guide further practice.

Rating Scale

1	Strongly disagree	4	Slightly agree
2	Disagree	5	Agree
3	Slightly disagree	6	Strongly agree

Assessment

Pre-   Post-   *In situations where I have to provide negative feedback or offer corrective advice:*

_____   _____   1. I understand clearly when it is appropriate to offer advice and direction to others and when it is not.

_____   _____   2. I help others recognize and define their own problems when I counsel them.

_____   _____   3. I am completely honest in the feedback that I give to others, even when it is negative.

_____   _____   4. I always give feedback that is focused on problems and solutions, not on personal characteristics.

_____   _____   5. I always link negative feedback to a standard or expectation that has been violated.

_____   _____   6. When I correct someone's behavior, our relationship is almost always strengthened.

_____   _____   7. I am descriptive in giving negative feedback to others. That is, I objectively describe events, their consequences, and my feelings about them.

_____   _____   8. I always suggest specific alternatives to those whose behavior I'm trying to correct.

_____ _____ 9. I reinforce other people's sense of self-worth and self-esteem in my communication with them.

_____ _____ 10. I convey genuine interest in the other person's point of view, even when I disagree with it.

_____ _____ 11. I don't talk down to those who have less power or less information than I.

_____ _____ 12. I convey a sense of flexibility and openness to new information when presenting my point of view, even when I feel strongly about it.

_____ _____ 13. I strive to identify some area of agreement in a discussion with someone who has a different point of view.

_____ _____ 14. My feedback is always specific and to the point, rather than general or vague.

_____ _____ 15. I don't dominate conversations with others.

_____ _____ 16. I take responsibility for my statements and point of view by saying, "I think" instead of "they think."

_____ _____ 17. When discussing someone's problem, I usually respond with a reply that indicates understanding rather than advice.

_____ _____ 18. When asking questions of others in order to understand their viewpoints better, I generally ask "what" questions instead of "why" questions.

_____ _____ 19. I hold regular, private meetings with people I work with and live with.

_____ _____ 20. I am clear about when I should coach someone and when I should provide counseling instead.

Communication Styles

This assessment instrument is divided into two parts.

In Part 1, four people complain about problems they face in their jobs. Following each complaint are five possible responses. Rank three of the responses you would be most likely to make, with 3 being your first choice, 2 being your second choice, and 1 being your third choice.

Part 2 of the assessment describes a particular situation. Several pairs of statements follow. Place a check mark next to the statement in each pair that you would mostly likely use in responding to that situation.

To score the Communication Styles instrument, turn to Appendix I to find the answer key and an interpretation of your scores.

Part 1

1. I've been in this job now for six months, and I hardly know anyone at all in the company. I just can't seem to make friends or to be accepted by other people. Most people are extremely busy and don't take time to socialize. I feel isolated and excluded from what's going on.

_____ a. Don't be concerned about not making friends so soon. Things will get better the longer you're with the company, you'll see.

_____ b. When you first meet people, what do you say? Are you the one to be friendly first?

_____ c. Because company employees are so busy, probably no one has time to get close socially. You shouldn't expect too much.

_____ d. So you're feeling that people haven't accepted you in the company?

_____ e. When I first joined the company it took me more than six months to get adjusted. I still don't know some of the people in several departments.

2. I can't stand my boss. He is the most autocratic, demanding person you can imagine. I've never worked around anyone who cared less for his employees than he does. His complete insensitivity and lack of humanity have made this a miserable place to work.

_____ a. You sound as if you're having difficulty dealing with rigid control and authority.

_____ b. I know how you feel because last year we had a woman in our department who would drive anybody crazy. She was the ultimate domineering boss.

_____ c. You're going to have problems unless you work this out. I think you should go to him and tell him how you feel.

_____ d. You really are having a hard time adjusting to your boss, aren't you?

_____ e. Why is it you feel so strongly about him?

3. What I want to know is, what happened on that last promotion decision? I thought I was in line for it. I'm sure no else in the department has my experience, and the scuttlebutt I heard indicated the job was mine for the asking. I'm really disappointed that you brought in someone from the outside over me. I don't think it's fair. What does it take to get promoted around here anyway?

_____ a. What was it that made you think this promotion was yours? Are you aware of the requirements of the job and what kind of person we were looking for?

_____ b. Don't be discouraged. Your work is good, and if you're patient I'm sure other chances will come along. I'll try to help you be ready the next time around.

_____ c. I think you have the wrong impression about this. The criteria were very clear for the new position, and the other person was just a better fit.

_____ d. In other words, you feel kind of puzzled about where you stand with the company.

_____ e. Are you interpreting this promotion decision as a challenge to your technical competence?

4. Hey, what's the idea of not approving my request for a new personal computer? I really need it in the office. We've got far more work to do than one machine can handle, and we're doing things manually that ought to be done on a spreadsheet. And don't give me that old story about tight company resources again. I've been in line for new equipment for a long time now.

_____ a. You sound really upset about not getting your request approved.

_____ b. Why do you need a new computer when you already have one? Can't you schedule work so that one system will handle your load? How about the possibility of borrowing one during the times you really feel the crunch?

_____ c. You know, several other offices are a lot worse off than yours is. Some of them don't have the trained personnel to operate the software. We're having a terrible time trying to get the necessary training accomplished for the existing machines.

_____ d. I know you're upset. But if you'll be patient, I'm sure I can work out a solution to your problem.

_____ e. I'm sorry, but it's true that resources are really tight. That's why we turned you down, so you're just going to have to make do.

Part 2

You are the manager of Carole Schulte, a 58-year-old supervisor who has been with the company for 21 years. She will retire at age 62, the first year she's eligible for a full pension. The trouble is, her performance is sliding, she is not inclined to go the extra mile by putting in extra time when required, and occasionally her work is even a little slipshod. Several line workers and customers have complained that she's treated them rather abruptly and without much sensitivity, even though superior customer service is a hallmark of your organization. She doesn't do anything bad enough to be fired, but she's just not performing up to levels you expect. Assume that you are having your monthly one-on-one meeting with her in your office. Which of the statements in each pair would you be most likely to use?

_____ 1. a. I've received complaints from some of your customers that you have not followed company standards in being responsive to their requests.

   b. You don't seem to be motivated to do a good job anymore, Carole.

_____ 2. a. I know that you've been doing a great job as supervisor, but there's just one small thing I want to raise with you about a customer complaint, probably not too serious.

   b. I have some concerns about several aspects of your performance on the job, and I'd like to discuss them with you.

_____ 3. a. When one of your subordinates called the other day to complain that you had criticized his work in public, I became concerned. I suggest that you sit down with that subordinate to work through any hard feelings that might still exist.

   b. You know, of course, that you're wrong to have criticized your subordinate's work in public. That's a sure way to create antagonism and lower morale.

_____ 4. a. I would like to see the following changes in your performance:

      _____ (1) (2) and (3).

   b. I have some ideas for helping you to improve; but first, what do you suggest?

_____ 5. a. I must tell you that I'm disappointed in your performance.

   b. Several of our employees seem to be unhappy with how you've been performing lately.

■ Skill Learning

The Importance of Effective Communication

Surveys have consistently shown that the ability to communicate effectively is the characteristic judged by managers to be most critical in determining promotability (see surveys reported by Randle, 1956; Bowman, 1964; Steil, Barker, & Watson, 1983; Brownell, 1986; Brownell, 1990). Frequently, the quality of communication between managers and their employees is fairly low (Schnake, Dumler, Cochran, & Barnett, 1990). This ability may involve a broad array of activities, from writing to speech-making to body language. Whereas skill in each of these activities is important, for most managers it is face-to-face, one-on-one communication that dominates all the other types in predicting managerial success. In a study of 88 organizations, both profit and nonprofit, Crocker (1978) found that, of 31 skills assessed, interpersonal communication skills, including listening, were rated as the most important. Thorton (1966, p. 237) summarized a variety of survey results by stating, "A manager's number-one problem can be summed up in one word: communication."

At least 80 percent of a manager's waking hours are spent in verbal communication, so it is not surprising that serious attention has been given to a plethora of procedures to improve interpersonal communication. Scholars and researchers have written extensively on communicology, semantics, rhetoric, linguistics, cybernetics, syntactics, pragmatics, proxemics, and canalization; and library shelves are filled with books on the physics of the communication process—encoding, decoding, transmission, media, perception, reception, and noise. Similarly, volumes are available on effective public-speaking techniques, making formal presentations, and the processes of organizational communication. Most colleges and universities have academic departments dedicated to the field of speech communication; most business schools provide a business communication curriculum; and many organizations have public communication departments and intra-organizational communication specialists such as newsletter editors and speech writers.

Even with all this available information about the communication process and the dedicated resources in many organizations for fostering better communication, most managers still indicate that poor communication is their biggest problem (Schnake, Dumler, Cochran, & Barnett, 1990). In a study of major manufacturing organizations undergoing large-scale changes, Cameron (1988) asked two key questions: (1) What is your major problem in trying to get organizational changes implemented? and (2) What is the key factor that explains your past success in effectively managing organizational change? To both questions, a large majority of managers gave the same answer: communication. All of them agreed that more communication is better than less communication. Most thought that overcommunicating with employees was more a virtue than a vice. It would seem surprising, then, that in light of this agreement by managers about the importance of communication, communication remains a major problem for managers. Why might this be?

One reason is that most individuals feel that they are very effective communicators. They feel that communication problems are a product of others' weaknesses, not their own (Brownell, 1990; Golen, 1990). Haney (1979, p. 219) reported on a survey of over 8,000 people in universities, businesses, military units, government agencies, and hospitals in which "virtually everyone felt that he or she was communicating at least as well as and, in many cases, better than almost everyone else in the organization. Most people readily admit that their organization is fraught with faulty communication, but it is almost always 'those other people' who are responsible." Thus, while most agree that proficiency in interpersonal communication is critical to managerial success, most individuals don't seem to feel a strong need to improve their own skill level.

Focus on Accuracy

Much of the writing on interpersonal communication focuses on the *accuracy* of the information being communicated. The emphasis is generally on making certain that messages are transmitted and received with little alteration or variation from original intent. The communication skill of most concern is the ability to transmit clear, precise messages. The following incidents illustrate problems that result from inaccurate communication:

A motorist was driving on the Merritt Parkway outside New York City when his engine stalled. He quickly determined that his battery was dead and managed to stop another driver who consented to push his car to get it started.

"My car has an automatic transmission," he explained, "so you'll have to get up to 30 or 35 miles an hour to get me started."

The second motorist nodded and walked back to his own car. The first motorist climbed back into his car and waited for the good Samaritan to pull up behind him. He waited—and waited. Finally, he turned around to see what was wrong.

There was the good Samaritan—coming up behind his car at about 35 miles an hour!

The damage amounted to $3,800 (Haney, 1979, p. 285).

A woman of 35 came in one day to tell me that she wanted a baby but had been told that she had a certain type of heart disease that, while it might not interfere with a normal life, would be dangerous if she ever had a baby. From her description, I thought at once of mitral stenosis. This condition is characterized by a rather distinctive rumbling murmur near the apex of the heart and especially by a peculiar vibration felt by the examining finger on the patient's chest. The vibration is known as the "thrill" of mitral stenosis.

When this woman had undressed and was lying on my table in her white kimono, my stethoscope quickly found the heart sounds I had expected. Dictating to my nurse, I described them carefully. I put my stethoscope aside and felt intently for the typical vibration which may be found in a small and variable area of the left chest.

I closed my eyes for better concentration and felt long and carefully for the tremor. I did not find it, and with my hand still on the woman's bare breast, lifting it upward and out of the way, I finally turned to the nurse and said: "No thrill."

The patient's black eyes snapped, and with venom in her voice, she said, "Well, isn't that just too bad! Perhaps it's just as well you don't get one. That isn't what I came for."

My nurse almost choked, and my explanation still seems a nightmare of futile words (Loomis, 1939, p. 47).

Because in England a billion is a million million, whereas in the United States and Canada a billion is a thousand million, it is easy to see how misunderstanding can occur regarding financial performance. Similarly, in an American meeting, if you "table" a subject, you postpone its discussion. In a British meeting, to "table" a topic means to discuss it now.

A Confucian proverb states: "Those who speak do not know. Those who know do not speak." It is not difficult to understand why Americans are often viewed as brash and unsophisticated in Asian cultures. A common problem for American business executives has been to announce, upon their return home, that a business deal has been struck, only to discover that no agreement was made at all. Usually it is because Americans assume that when their Japanese colleagues say "hai," the Japanese word for "yes," it means agreement. To the Japanese, it often means "Yes, I am trying to understand you (but I may not necessarily agree with you)."

When accuracy is the primary consideration, attempts to improve communication generally center on improving the mechanics: transmitters and receivers, encoding and decoding, sources and destinations, and noise.

Fortunately, much progress has been made recently in improving the transmission of accurate messages—that is, in improving their clarity and precision. Primarily through the development of a sophisticated information-based technology, major strides have been taken to enhance communication speed and accuracy in organizations. Computer networks with multimedia capabilities now enable members of an organization to transmit messages, documents, video images, and sound almost anywhere in the world. The technology that enables modern companies to share, store, and retrieve information has dramatically changed the nature of business in just a decade. Customers and employees routinely expect information technology to function smoothly and the information it manages to be reliable. Sound decisions and competitive advantage depend on such accuracy.

However, comparable progress has not occurred in the interpersonal aspects of communication. People still become offended at one another, make insulting statements, and communicate clumsily. The interpersonal aspects of communication involve the nature of the relationship between the communicators. Who says what to whom, what is said, why it is said, and how it is said all have an effect on the relationships between people. This has important implications for the effectiveness of the communication, aside from the accuracy of the statement. A statement Josiah Stamp made over 80 years ago illustrates this point.

> The government are very keen on amassing statistics. They collect them, add them, raise them to the nth power, take the cube root and prepare wonderful diagrams. But you must never forget that every one of these figures come in the first instance from the village watchman, who just puts down what he damn pleases.

Similarly, irrespective of the availability of sophisticated information technologies and elaborately developed models of communication processes, individuals still communicate pretty much as they please—often in abrasive, insensitive, and unproductive ways. More often than not, it is the interpersonal aspect of communication that stands in the way of effective message delivery rather than the inability to deliver accurate information (Golen, 1990).

Ineffective communication may lead individuals to dislike each other, be offended by each other, lose confidence in each other, refuse to listen to each other, and disagree with each other, as well as cause a host of other interpersonal problems. These interpersonal problems, in turn, generally lead to restricted communication flow, inaccurate messages, and misinterpretations of meanings. Figure 1 summarizes this process.

To illustrate, consider the following situation. Cal is introducing his new goal-setting program to the organization as a way to overcome some productivity problems. After Cal's carefully prepared presentation in the management council meeting, Jedd raises his hand. "In my opinion, this is a naive approach to solving our productivity issues. The considerations are much more complex than Cal seems to realize. I don't think we should waste our time by pursuing this plan any further." Jedd's opinion may be justified, but the manner in which he delivers the message will probably eliminate any hope of its being dealt with objectively. Instead, Cal will probably hear a message such as, "You're naive," "You're stupid," or "You're incompetent." We wouldn't be surprised if Cal's response were defensive or even hostile. Any good feelings between the two have probably been jeopardized, and their communication will probably be reduced to self-image protection. The merits of the proposal will be smothered by personal defensiveness. Future communication between the two will probably be minimal.

What Is Supportive Communication?

In this chapter, we focus on a kind of interpersonal communication that helps managers communicate accurately and honestly without jeopardizing interpersonal relationships—namely, **supportive communication.** Supportive communication is communication that seeks to preserve a positive relationship between the communicators while still addressing the problem at hand. Supportive communication has eight attributes, which

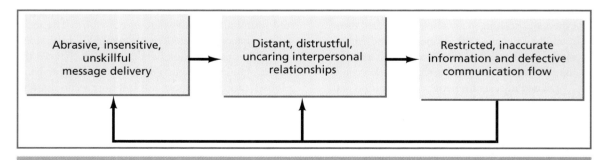

Figure 1 Relationships Between Unskillful Communication and Interpersonal Relationships

are summarized in Table 1. Later in the chapter we expand on each attribute. When supportive communication is used, not only is a message delivered accurately, but the relationship between the two communicating parties is supported, even enhanced, by the interchange. Positive interpersonal relationships result. The goal of supportive communication is not merely to be liked by other people or to be judged to be a nice person, however. Nor is it used merely to produce social acceptance. As pointed out in the introductory chapter, positive interpersonal relationships have practical, instrumental value in organizations. Researchers have found, for example, that organizations fostering these kinds of relationships enjoy higher productivity, faster problem solving, higher-quality outputs, and fewer conflicts and subversive activities than do groups and organizations where relationships are less positive. Moreover, delivering outstanding customer service is almost impossible without supportive communication. Customer complaints and misunderstandings frequently require supportive communication skills to resolve. Not only must managers be competent in using this kind of communication, therefore, but they must help their subordinates develop this competency as well.

One important lesson that American managers have been taught by foreign competitors is that good relationships among employees, and between managers and employees, produce bottom-line advantages (Ouchi, 1981; Peters, 1988). Hanson (1986) found, for example, that the presence of good interpersonal relationships between managers and subordinates was three times more powerful in predicting profitability in 40 major corporations over a five-year period than the four next most powerful variables—market share,

1. **Problem-Oriented, Not Person-Oriented** "How can we solve this problem?"	*Not*	"Because of you there is a problem."
2. **Congruent, Not Incongruent** "Your behavior really upset me."	*Not*	"Do I seem upset? No, everything's fine."
3. **Descriptive, Not Evaluative** "Here is what happened; here is my reaction; here is what I suggest that would be more acceptable to me."	*Not*	"You are wrong for doing what you did."
4. **Validating, Not Invalidating** "I have some ideas, but do you have any suggestions?"	*Not*	"You wouldn't understand, so we'll do it my way."
5. **Specific, Not Global** "You interrupted me three times during the meeting."	*Not*	"You're always trying to get attention."
6. **Conjunctive, Not Disjunctive** "Relating to what you just said, I'd like to discuss this."	*Not*	"I want to discuss this (regardless of what you want to discuss)."
7. **Owned, Not Disowned** "I've decided to turn down your request because . . ."	*Not*	"You have a pretty good idea, but they just wouldn't approve it."
8. **Supportive Listening, Not One-Way Listening** "What do you think are the obstacles standing in the way of improvement?"	*Not*	"As I said before, you make too many mistakes. You're just not doing the job."

Table 1   Eight Attributes of Supportive Communication

capital intensity, firm size, and sales growth rate—combined. Supportive communication, therefore, isn't just a "nice-person technique," but a proven competitive advantage for both managers and organizations.

Coaching and Counseling

The principles of supportive communication discussed in this chapter are best understood and most useful when they are applied to the interpersonal communication tasks commonly rated as the most challenging by managers: coaching and counseling subordinates (Ross, 1986). In coaching, managers pass along advice and information or set standards to help subordinates improve their work skills. In counseling, managers help subordinates recognize and address problems involving their state of mind, emotions, or personalities. Thus, coaching focuses on abilities, counseling on attitudes.

The chapter on Motivating Employees provides tools for analyzing and addressing employees' problems in ability and attitude. The current chapter focuses on the communication model and skills that will help you discuss problems with employees and set the stage to resolve them cooperatively. Thus, for example, when you study the six elements of an integrative motivation program in the chapter on Motivating Employees (see Table 1 in that chapter), the coaching and counseling models should be integral to considering how you would implement such a program.

The skills of coaching and counseling also apply to a broader array of activities, of course, such as handling customer complaints, passing critical or negative information upward, handling conflicts between other parties, negotiating for a certain position, and so on. However, coaching and counseling are almost universal managerial activities, and we will use them to illustrate and explain the behavioral principles involved.

Skillful coaching and counseling are especially important in (1) rewarding positive performance and (2) correcting problem behaviors or attitudes. Both of these activities are discussed in more detail in the chapter on Motivating Others. But in that chapter, we discuss the *content* of rewarding and correcting behavior (i.e., *what* to do), whereas in our present discussion we shall focus on the *processes* used by effective managers to coach and counsel employees (i.e., *how* to do it). Coaching and counseling are more difficult to perform effectively when employees are not performing up to expectations, when their attitudes are negative, when their behavior is disruptive, or when their personalities clash with others in the organization. Whenever managers have to help subordinates change their attitudes or behaviors, coaching or counseling is required. In these situations, managers face the responsibility of providing negative feedback to subordinates or getting them to recognize problems that they don't want to acknowledge. Managers must criticize and correct subordinates, but in a way that facilitates positive work outcomes, positive feelings, and positive relationships.

What makes coaching and counseling so challenging is the risk of offending or alienating subordinates. That risk is so high that many managers ignore completely the feelings and reactions of employees by taking a directive, hard-nosed, "shape up or ship out" approach to correcting behavior or attitudes. Or they soft-pedal, avoiding confrontations for fear of hurting feelings and destroying relationships—the "don't worry be happy" approach. The principles we describe in this chapter not only facilitate accurate message delivery in sensitive situations, but their effective use can produce higher levels of motivation, increased productivity, and better interpersonal relationships.

Of course, coaching and counseling skills are also required when negative feedback is not involved, such as when subordinates ask for advice, need someone to listen to their problems, or want to register complaints. Sometimes just listening is the most effective form of coaching or counseling. Although the risk of damaged relationships, defensiveness, or hurt feelings is not as likely as when negative feedback is given, these situations still require competent communication skills. Guidelines for how to implement supportive communication effectively in both negative and positive coaching and counseling situations are discussed in the rest of this chapter.

Consider the two following scenarios:

Tom Nielson is the manager of the division sales force in your firm, which makes and sells components for the aerospace industry. He reports directly to you. Tom's division consistently misses its sales projections, its revenues per salesperson are below the firm average, and Tom's monthly reports are almost always late. You make another appointment to visit with Tom after getting the latest sales figures, but he isn't in his office when you arrive. His secretary tells you that one of Tom's sales managers dropped by a few minutes ago to complain that some employees are coming in late for work in the morning and taking extra-long coffee breaks. Tom had immediately gone with the manager to his sales department to give the salespeople a "pep talk" and to remind them of performance expectations. You wait for 15 minutes until he returns.

Betsy Christensen has an MBA from a prestigious Big Ten school and has recently joined your firm in the financial planning group. She came with great recommendations and credentials. However, she seems to be trying to enhance her own reputation at the expense of others in her group. You have heard increasing complaints lately that Betsy acts arrogant, is self-promotional, and is openly critical of other group members' work. In your first conversation with her about her performance in the group, she denied that there is a problem. She said that, if anything, she was having a positive impact on the group by raising its standards. You schedule another meeting with Betsy after this latest set of complaints from her coworkers.

What are the basic problems in these two cases? How would you approach them so that the problems got solved and, at the same time, your relationships with your subordinates were strengthened? What would you say, and how would you say it, so that the best possible outcomes result? This chapter can help you improve your skill in handling such situations effectively.

Coaching and Counseling Problems

The two cases above help identify the two basic kinds of interpersonal communication problems faced by managers. In the case with Tom Nielson, the basic need is for **coaching.** Coaching situations are those in which managers must pass along advice and information or set standards for subordinates. Subordinates must be advised on how to do their jobs better and to be coached to better performance. Coaching problems are usually caused by lack of ability, insufficient information or understanding, or incompetence on the part of subordinates. In these cases, the accuracy of the information passed along by managers is important. The

subordinate must understand clearly what the problem is and how to overcome it.

In the Tom Nielson case, Tom was accepting upward delegation from his subordinates, and he was not allowing them to solve their own problems. In the chapter on Managing Stress, we learned that upward delegation is one of the major causes of ineffective time management. By not insisting that his subordinates bring recommendations for solutions to him instead of problems, and by intervening directly in the problems of his subordinate's subordinates, Tom became overloaded himself. He didn't allow his subordinates to do their jobs. Productivity almost always suffers in cases where one person is trying to resolve all the problems and run the whole show. Tom needs to be coached regarding how to avoid upward delegation and how to delegate responsibility as well as authority effectively. In the chapter on Motivating Employees, the section Diagnosing Work Performance Problems gives more specific guidelines for diagnosing the reasons for poor performance. Such diagnosis can then help guide the manager in coaching a subordinate.

The Betsy Christensen case illustrates a **counseling** problem. Managers need to counsel subordinates instead of coach them when the problem stems from attitudes, personality clashes, defensiveness, or other factors tied to emotions. Betsy's competency or skill is not a problem, but her unwillingness to recognize that a problem exists or that a change is needed on her part requires counseling by the manager. Betsy is highly qualified for her position, so coaching or giving advice would not be a useful approach. Instead, an important goal of counseling is to help Betsy recognize that a problem exists and to identify ways in which that problem might be addressed. Coaching applies to ability problems, and the manager's approach is, "I can help you do this better." Counseling applies to attitude problems, and the manager's approach is, "I can help you recognize that a problem exists."

Although many problems involve both coaching and counseling, it is important to recognize the difference between these two types of problems because a mismatch of problem with communication approach can aggravate, rather than resolve, a problem. Giving direction or advice (coaching) in a counseling situation often increases defensiveness or resistance to change. For example, advising Betsy Christensen about how to do her job or about the things she should not be doing (such as criticizing others' work) will probably only magnify her defensiveness because she doesn't perceive that she has a problem. Similarly, counseling in a situation that calls for coaching simply side-steps the problem and doesn't resolve it. Tom Nielson knows that a problem exists, for example, but he doesn't know how to resolve it. Coaching, not problem recognition, is needed.

The question that remains, however, is, "How do I effectively coach or counsel another person? What behavioral guidelines help me perform effectively in these situations?" Both coaching and counseling rely on the same set of key supportive communication principles summarized in Table 1, which we'll now examine more closely.

Defensiveness and Disconfirmation

If principles of supportive communication are not followed when coaching or counseling subordinates, two major obstacles result that lead to a variety of negative outcomes (Gibb, 1961; Sieburg, 1978; Brownell, 1986; Steil et al., 1983). These two obstacles are defensiveness and disconfirmation (see in Table 2).

Defensiveness is an emotional and physical state in which one is agitated, estranged, confused, and inclined to strike out (Gordon, 1988). Defensiveness arises when one of the parties feels threatened or punished by the communication. For that person, self-protection becomes more important than listening, so defensiveness blocks both the message and the interpersonal relationship. Clearly a manager's coaching or counseling will not be effective if it creates defensiveness in the other party. But defensive thinking may be pervasive and entrenched within an organization. Overcoming it calls for awareness by managers of their own defensiveness and vigorous efforts to apply the principles of supportive communication described in this chapter (Argyris, 1991).

The second obstacle, **disconfirmation,** occurs when one of the communicating parties feels put down, ineffectual, or insignificant because of the communication. Recipients of the communication feel that their self-worth is being questioned, so they focus more on building themselves up rather than listening. Reactions are often self-aggrandizing or show-off behaviors, loss of motivation, withdrawal, and loss of respect for the offending communicator.

The eight attributes of supportive communication, which we'll explain and illustrate in the following

Supportive communication engenders feelings of support, understanding, and helpfulness. It helps overcome the two main obstacles resulting from poor interpersonal communication:

Defensiveness
- One individual feels threatened or attacked as a result of the communication.
- Self-protection becomes paramount.
- Energy is spent on constructing a defense rather than on listening.
- Aggression, anger, competitiveness, and avoidance are common reactions.

Disconfirmation
- One individual feels incompetent, unworthy, or insignificant as a result of the communication.
- Attempts to reestablish self-worth take precedence.
- Energy is spent trying to portray self-importance rather than on listening.
- Showing off, self-centered behavior, withdrawal, and loss of motivation are common reactions.

Table 2 Two Major Obstacles to Effective Interpersonal Communication

pages, serve as behavioral guidelines for overcoming defensiveness and disconfirmation. Competent coaching and counseling depend on knowing and practicing these guidelines. They also depend on maintaining a balance among the guidelines, as we'll illustrate.

Principles of Supportive Communication

1. Supportive communication is problem-oriented, not person-oriented.

Problem-oriented communication focuses on problems and solutions rather than on personal traits. Person-oriented communication focuses on the characteristics of the individual, not the event. Problem-oriented communication is useful even when personal appraisals are called for because it focuses on behaviors and events, whereas person-oriented communication can send the message that the individual is inadequate.

Statements such as "You are dictatorial" and "You are insensitive" describe the person, while "I am not involved in decisions" and "We don't seem to see things the same way" describe problems. Imputing motives is person oriented ("It's because you want to control other people"), whereas describing overt behaviors is problem oriented ("You made several sarcastic comments in the meeting today").

One problem with person-oriented communication is that, while most people can change their behavior, few can change their basic personalities. Because nothing can generally be done to accommodate person-oriented communication, it leads to a deterioration in the relationship rather than to problem solving. Person-oriented messages often try to persuade the other individual that "this is how you should feel" or "this is what kind of person you are" (e.g., "You are an incompetent manager, a lazy worker, or an insensitive office mate"). But since most individuals accept themselves, their common reaction to person-oriented communication is to defend themselves against it or reject it outright. Even when communication is positive (e.g., "You are a wonderful person"), it may not be viewed as trustworthy if it is not tied to a behavior or an accomplishment. The absence of a meaningful referent is the key weakness in person-oriented communication.

In coaching and counseling, problem-oriented communication should also be linked to accepted standards or expectations rather than to personal opinions. Personal opinions are more likely to be interpreted as person-oriented and arouse defensiveness than statements in which the behavior is compared to an accepted standard. For example, the statement "I don't like the way you dress" is an expression of a personal opinion and will probably create resistance, especially if the listener does not feel that the communicator's opinions are any more legitimate than his or her own. On the other hand, "Your dress is not in keeping with the company dress code," or "Everyone is expected to wear a tie to work," are comparisons to external standards that have some legitimacy. Feelings of defensiveness are less likely to arise since the problem, not the person, is being addressed. In addition, other people are more likely to support a statement based on a common standard.

Effective supportive communicators need not avoid expressing personal opinions or feelings about the behavior or attitudes of others. But when doing so, they should keep in mind the following additional principles.

2. Supportive communication is based on congruence, not incongruence.

Rogers (1961), Dyer (1972), and Schnake et al. (1990) argue that the best interpersonal communications, and the best relationships, are based on **congruence,** that is, exactly matching the communication, verbally and nonverbally, to what an individual is thinking and feeling.

Two kinds of **incongruence** are possible: One is a mismatch between what one is experiencing and what one is aware of. For example, an individual may not even be aware that he or she is experiencing anger toward another person, even though the anger is really present. Therapists must frequently help individuals reach greater congruence between experience and awareness. A second kind of incongruence, and the one more closely related to supportive communication, is a mismatch between what one feels and what one communicates. For example, an individual may be aware of a feeling of anger but deny having that feeling.

When coaching and counseling subordinates, genuine, honest statements are always better than artificial or dishonest statements. Managers who hold back their true feelings or opinions, or who don't express what's really on their minds, create the impression that a hidden agenda exists. Subordinates sense that there is something else not being said. Therefore, they trust the communicator less and focus on trying to figure out what the hidden message is, not on listening or trying to improve. The chapter on Managing Stress discussed Covey's (1989) "emotional bank account" and the importance of mutual trust and respect in establishing collaborative relationships. Communication cannot be genuinely supportive unless it is based on trust and respect and is also *perceived* as trusting and respectful. Otherwise, false impressions and miscommunication result.

Rogers (1961, pp. 344–345) suggests that congruence in communication lies at the heart of a general law of interpersonal relationships.

The greater the congruence of experience, awareness, and communication on the part of one individual, the more the ensuing relationship will involve a tendency toward reciprocal communication with increasing congruence; a tendency toward more mutually accurate understanding of the communications; improved psychological adjustment and functioning in both parties; mutual satisfaction in the relationship.

Conversely, the greater the communicated incongruence of experience and awareness, the more the ensuing relationship will involve further communication with the same quality; disintegration of accurate understanding; less adequate psychological adjustment and functioning in both parties; mutual dissatisfaction in the relationship.

Congruence also relates to matching the content of your words to your manner and tone of voice. "What a nice day" can mean the opposite if muttered sarcastically. "I'm only concerned for your welfare" can mean the opposite if said without sincerity, especially if the history of the relationship suggests otherwise.

Striving for congruence, of course, does not mean that one should blow off steam immediately upon getting upset, nor does it mean that one cannot repress certain inappropriate feelings (e.g., anger, disappointment, aggression). Other principles of supportive communication must also be practiced, and achieving congruence at the expense of all other consideration is not productive. On the other hand, in problematic interactions, when reactive feedback must be given, individuals are more likely to express too little congruence than too much. This is because many people are afraid to respond in a completely honest way or are not sure how to communicate congruently without being offensive. Saying exactly what one feels can sometimes offend the other person.

Consider the problem of a subordinate who is not performing up to expectations and displays a nonchalant attitude when given hints that the division's rating is being negatively affected. What could the superior say that would strengthen the relationship with the subordinate and still resolve the problem? How can one express honest feelings and opinions and still remain problem-focused, not person-focused? How can one be completely honest without offending another person? Other principles of supportive communication provide some guidelines.

3. Supportive communication is descriptive, not evaluative.

Evaluative communication makes a judgment or places a label on other individuals or on their behavior: "You are doing it wrong," "You are incompetent." Such evaluation generally makes the other person feel under attack and respond defensively. Probable responses are, "I'm not doing it wrong," or "I am as competent as you are." Arguments, bad feelings, and a weakening of the interpersonal relationship result.

The tendency to evaluate others is strongest when the issue is emotionally charged or when a person feels personally threatened. Sometimes people try to resolve their own bad feelings or anxieties by placing a label on others: "You are bad" implies "I am good. Therefore, I feel better." They may have such strong feelings that they want to punish the other person for violating their expectations or standards: "What you've done deserves to be punished. You deserve what's coming to you."

The problem with evaluative communication is that it is likely to be self-perpetuating. Placing a label on another generally leads that person to place a label on *you*, which makes you defensive in return. The accuracy of the communication and quality of the relationship deteriorate. Arguments ensue.

An alternative to evaluation is **descriptive communication.** Because it is difficult to avoid evaluating other people without some alternative strategy, descriptive communication reduces the tendency to evaluate and perpetuate a defensive interaction. Descriptive communication involves three steps, summarized in Table 3.

First, *describe objectively the event that occurred or the behavior that needs to be modified.* This description should identify elements of the behavior that could be confirmed by another person. Behavior, as mentioned before, should be compared to accepted standards rather than to personal opinions or preferences. Subjective impressions or attributions to the motives of another person should be avoided. The description "You have finished fewer projects this month than anyone else in the division" can be confirmed by an objective record. It relates strictly to the behavior and to an objective standard, not to the motives or personal characteristics of the subordinate. There is less likelihood of the subordinate's feeling unfairly treated, since no evaluative label is placed on the behavior or the person. Describing a behavior, as opposed to evaluating a behavior, is relatively neutral, as long as the manager's manner is congruent with the message.

Second, *describe reactions to the behavior or its consequences.* Rather than projecting onto another person the cause of the problem, focus on the reactions or consequences the behavior has produced. This requires that communicators be aware of their own reactions and able

> **Step 1:** Describe objectively the event, behavior, or circumstance.
> - Avoid accusations.
> - Present data or evidence.
>
> *Example:* Three clients have complained to me this month that you have not responded to their requests.
>
> **Step 2:** Focus on the behavior and your reaction, not on the other person's attributes.
> - Describe your reactions and feelings.
> - Describe the objective consequences that have resulted or will result.
>
> *Example:* I'm worried because each client has threatened to go elsewhere if we aren't more responsive.
>
> **Step 3:** Focus on solutions.
> - Avoid discussing who's right or wrong.
> - Suggest an acceptable alternative.
> - Be open to other alternatives.
>
> *Example:* We need both to win back their confidence and to show them you are responsive. For example, you could do a free analysis of their systems.

Table 3   Descriptive Communication

to describe them. Using one-word descriptions for feelings is often the best method: "I'm *concerned* about our productivity." "Your level of accomplishment *frustrates* me." Similarly, the consequences of the behavior can be pointed out: "Profits are off this month," "Department quality ratings are down," or "Two customers have called in to express dissatisfaction." Describing feelings or consequences also lessens the likelihood of defensiveness since the problem is framed in the context of the communicator's feelings or objective consequences, not the attributes of the subordinate. If those feelings or consequences are described in a non-accusing way, the major energies of the communicators can be focused on problem solving rather than on defending against evaluations.

Third, *suggest a more acceptable alternative.* This helps the other person save face (Goffman, 1955) and feel valued (Sieburg, 1978) by separating the individual from the behavior. The self-esteem of the person is preserved; it is just the behavior that should be modified. Care should be taken not to give the message, "I don't like the way things are, so what are you going to do about it?" The change need not be the responsibility of only one of the communicating parties. Rather, the emphasis should be on finding a solution that is acceptable to both, not on deciding who is right and who is wrong or who should change and who shouldn't: "I'd like to suggest that we meet regularly to help you complete six more projects than last month," or "I would like to help you identify the things that are standing in the way of higher performance."

One concern that is sometimes expressed regarding descriptive communication is that these steps may not work unless the other person knows the rules, too. For example, the other person might say, "I don't care how you feel," or "I have an excuse for what happened, so it's not my fault," or "It's too bad if this annoys you. I'm not going to change." Any such lack of concern or a defensive stance now becomes the priority problem, because the problem of low performance will be very difficult to address as long as the more important interpersonal problem between the manager and the subordinate is blocking progress. In effect, the focus has shifted from coaching to counseling, from focusing on ability to focusing on attitude. If the manager and the subordinate cannot work on the problem together, no amount of communication about the consequences of poor performance will be productive. Instead, the focus of the communication should be shifted to the obstacles that inhibit working together to improve performance. Staying focused on the problem, remaining congruent, and using descriptive language become critical.

Effective managers do not abandon the three steps. They simply switch the focus. They might respond, "I'm surprised to hear you say that you don't care how I feel about this problem (step 1). Your response concerns me, and I think it might have important implications for the productivity of our team (step 2). I suggest we spend some time trying to identify the obstacles you feel might be inhibiting our ability to work together on this problem (step 3)."

It has been our experience that few individuals are completely recalcitrant about wanting to improve, and few are completely unwilling to work on problem solving when they believe that the communicator has their interests at heart. A common criticism of American managers, however, is that compared to their Asian competitors, many do not believe in these assumptions. They do not accept the fact that employees are "doing the best that they can" and that "people are motivated by opportunities for improvement." These are core Theory Y assumptions (McGregor, 1960), as opposed to Theory X assumptions such as "employees are to be mistrusted" and "it takes a sharp stick to motivate change." In our experience, however, most people want to do better, to perform successfully, and to be contributors. When managers use supportive communication principles not as manipulative devices but as genuine techniques to foster development and improvement, we have seldom found that people will not accept these genuine, congruent expressions.

It is important to keep in mind, however, that the steps of descriptive communication do not imply that one person should do all the changing. Frequently a middle ground must be reached on which both individuals are satisfied (e.g., one person becomes more tolerant of deliberate work, and the other person becomes more conscious of trying to work faster).

It is important to follow up coaching and counseling sessions with monitoring discussions. A subordinate's performance problems, for example, may stem from poor work habits developed over time. Such habits are not likely to change abruptly even if the coaching sessions goes especially well. If the subordinate doesn't show reasonable improvement, in subsequent coaching discussions the manager may need to be more directive.

When it is necessary to make evaluative statements, the evaluations should be made in terms of some established criteria (e.g., "Your behavior does not meet the prescribed standard"), probable outcomes (e.g., "Continuation of your behavior will lead to worse consequences"), or less appropriate behavior by the same individual (e.g., "This behavior is not as good as your past behavior"). The important point is to avoid disconfirming the other person or arousing defensiveness.

4. Supportive communication validates rather than invalidates individuals.

Communication can be destructive. Barnlund (1968, p. 618) observed:

> People do not take time, do not listen, do not try to understand, but interrupt, anticipate, criticize, or disregard what is said; in their own remarks they are frequently vague, inconsistent,

verbose, insincere, or dogmatic. As a result, people often conclude conversations feeling more inadequate, more misunderstood, and more alienated than when they started.

Validating communication helps people feel recognized, understood, accepted, and valued. Communication that is invalidating arouses negative feelings about self-worth, identity, and relatedness to others. It denies the presence, uniqueness, or importance of other individuals (Sieburg, 1978). Especially important are communications that invalidate people by conveying superiority, rigidity, indifference, and imperviousness (Sieburg, 1978; Galbraith, 1975; Gibb, 1961; Brownell, 1986; Steil et al., 1983).

Communication that is **superiority oriented** gives the impression that the communicator is informed while others are ignorant, adequate while others are inadequate, competent while others are incompetent, or powerful while others are impotent. It creates a barrier between the communicator and those to whom the message is sent.

Superiority-oriented communication can take the form of put-downs, in which others are made to look bad so that the communicator looks good. Or it can take the form of "one-upmanship," in which the communicator tries to elevate himself or herself in the esteem of others. One form of one-upmanship is withholding information, either boastfully ("If you knew what I knew, you would feel differently") or coyly to trip people up ("If you had asked me, I could have told you the executive committee would disapprove of your proposal"). Another common form of superiority-oriented communication is the use of jargon, acronyms, or words used in such a way as to exclude others or to create barriers in a relationship. Doctors, lawyers, government employees, and many other professionals are well known for their use of jargon or acronyms to exclude others or to elevate themselves rather than to clarify a message. Speaking a foreign language in the presence of individuals who don't understand it may also be done to create the impression of superiority. In most circumstances, using words or language that a listener can't understand is bad manners because it invalidates the other person.

Rigidity in communication is the second major type of invalidation: The communication is portrayed as absolute, unequivocal, or unquestionable. No other opinion or point of view could possibly be considered.

Individuals who communicate in dogmatic, "know-it-all" ways often do so in order to minimize others' contributions or to invalidate others' perspectives. It is possible to communicate rigidity, however, in ways other than just being dogmatic. Rigidity is also communicated by:

- Reinterpreting all other viewpoints to conform to one's own.

- Never saying, "I don't know," but having an answer for everything.

- Appearing unwilling to tolerate criticisms or alternative points of view.

- Reducing complex issues to simplistic definitions or generalizations.

- Placing exclamation points after statements so the impression is created that the statement is final, complete, or unqualified.

Indifference is communicated when the other person's existence or importance is not acknowledged. A person may do this by using silence, by making no verbal response to the other's statements, by avoiding eye contact or any facial expression, by interrupting the other person frequently, by using impersonal words ("one should not" instead of "you should not"), or by engaging in unrelated activity during a conversation. The communicator appears not to care about the other person and gives the impression of being impervious to the other person's feelings or perspectives.

Imperviousness (Sieburg, 1978) means that the communicator does not acknowledge the feelings or opinions of the other person. They are either labeled illegitimate—"You shouldn't feel that way" or "Your opinion is incorrect"—or they are labeled as naive—"You don't understand," "You've been misinformed," or (worse yet) "Your opinion is uninformed."

Communication is invalidating when it denies the other person an opportunity to establish a mutually satisfying relationship or when contributions cannot be made by both parties. When one person doesn't allow the other to finish a sentence, adopts a competitive, win-or-lose stance, sends confusing messages, or disqualifies the other person from making a contribution, communication is invalidating and, therefore, dysfunctional for effective problem solving.

Invalidation is even more destructive in coaching and counseling than criticism or disagreement because criticism and disagreement validate the other person by recognizing that what was said or done is worthy of correction, response, or at least notice (Jacobs, 1973). As William James (1965) stated, "No more fiendish punishment could be devised, even were such a thing physically possible, than that one could be turned loose in a society and remain absolutely unnoticed by all the members thereof." **Validating communication,** on the other hand, helps people feel recognized, understood, accepted, and valued (see also Chapter 8, Empowering and Delegating). It has four attributes: It is egalitarian, flexible, two-way, and based on agreement.

Respectful communication (the opposite of superiority-oriented communication) is especially important when a manager coaches or counsels a subordinate. When a hierarchical distinction exists between coaches or counselors and subordinates, it is easy for subordinates to feel invalidated since they have access to less power and information than their manager. Supportive communicators, however, help subordinates feel that they have a stake in identifying problems and resolving them by communicating an egalitarian stance. They treat subordinates as worthwhile, competent, and insightful and emphasize joint problem solving rather than projecting a superior position. One way they do this is by using flexible (rather than rigid) statements.

Flexibility in communication is the willingness of the coach or counselor to accept that additional data and other alternatives may exist and other individuals may be able to make significant contributions both to the problem solution and to the relationship. It means communicating genuine humility—not self-abasement or weakness—and openness to new insight. As Benjamin Disraeli noted, "To be conscious that you are ignorant is a first great step toward knowledge."

Perceptions and opinions are not presented as facts in flexible communication, but are stated provisionally. No claim is made for the truthfulness of opinions or assumptions. Rather, they are identified as being changeable if more data should become available. Flexible communication conveys a willingness to enter into joint problem solving rather than to control the other person or to assume a master-teacher role. Being flexible is not synonymous with being wishy-washy. "Gee, I can't make up my mind" is wishy-washy, whereas "I have my own opinions, but what do you think?" suggests flexibility.

Two-way communication is an implied result of respectfulness and flexibility. Individuals feel validated when they are asked questions, given "air time" to express their opinions, and encouraged to participate actively in the coaching and counseling process. Two-way interchange communicates the message that subordinates are valued by the manager and that coaching and counseling are best accomplished in an atmosphere of teamwork.

Finally, the manager's communication validates the subordinate when it identifies **areas of agreement** and joint commitment. One way to express validation based on agreement is to identify positive behaviors and positive attitudes as well as negative ones during the process of coaching and counseling. The manager should point out important points made by the subordinate before pointing out trivial ones, areas of agreement before areas of disagreement, advantages of the subordinate's statements before disadvantages, compliments before criticisms, and positive next steps before past mistakes. The point is, validating other people helps create feelings of self-worth and self-confidence that can translate into self-motivation and improved performance. Invalidation, on the other hand, seldom produces such positive outcomes, yet it is a common form of management response to subordinates.

5. Supportive communication is specific (useful), not global (useless).

In general, the more specific a statement is, the more useful it is. For example, the statement "You have trouble managing your time" is too general to be useful, whereas "You spent an hour scheduling meetings today when that could have been done by your assistant" provides specific information that can serve as a basis for behavioral change. "Your communication needs to improve" is not nearly as useful as a more specific "In this role play, you used evaluative statements 60 percent of the time and descriptive statements 10 percent of the time."

Specific statements avoid extremes and absolutes. The following are extreme statements that lead to defensiveness or disconfirmation:

A: "You never ask for my advice."
B: "Yes, I do. I always consult you before making a decision."
A: "You have no consideration for others' feelings."
B: "I do so. I am completely considerate."
A: "This job stinks."
B: "You're wrong. It's a great job."

Another common type of global communication is the either-or statement, such as "You either do what I say or I'll fire you," "Life is either a daring adventure or nothing" (Helen Keller), and "If America doesn't reduce its national debt, our children will never achieve the standard of living we enjoy today."

The problem with extreme and either-or statements is that they deny any alternatives. The possible responses of the recipient of the communication are severely constrained. To contradict or deny it generally leads to defensiveness and arguments. A statement by Adolf Hitler in 1933 illustrates the point: "Everyone in Germany is a National Socialist; the few outside the party are either lunatics or idiots."

Specific statements are more useful in coaching and counseling because they focus on behavioral events and indicate gradations in positions. More useful forms of the examples above are the following:

A: "You made that decision yesterday without asking for my advice."
B: "Yes, I did. While I generally like to get your opinion, I didn't think it was necessary in this case."
A: "By using sarcasm in your response to my request, you gave me the impression you don't care about my feelings."
B: "I'm sorry. I know I am often sarcastic without thinking how it affects others."
A: "The pressure to meet deadlines affects the quality of my work."
B: "Since deadlines are part of our work, let's consider ways to manage the pressure."

Specific statements may not be useful if they focus on things over which another person has no control. "I hate it when it rains," for example, may relieve some personal frustration, but nothing can be done to change the weather. Similarly, communicating the message (even implicitly) "The sound of your voice bothers me" only proves frustrating for the interacting individuals. Such a statement is usually interpreted as a personal attack. Specific communication is useful to the extent that it focuses on an identifiable problem or behavior about which something can be done (e.g., "It bothers me when you talk so loudly in the hall that it disturbs others' concentration").

6. Supportive communication is conjunctive, not disjunctive.

Conjunctive communication is joined to previous messages in some way. It flows smoothly. **Disjunctive communication** is disconnected from what was stated before.

Communication can become disjunctive in at least three ways. First, there can be a lack of equal opportunity to speak. When one person interrupts another, when someone dominates by controlling "air time," or when two or more people try to speak at the same time, the communication is disjunctive. The transitions between exchanges do not flow smoothly. Second, extended pauses are disjunctive. When speakers pause for long periods in the middle of their speeches or when there are long pauses before responses, the communication is disjunctive. Pauses need not be total silence; the space may be filled with "umm," "aaah," or a repetition of something stated earlier, but the communication does not progress. Third, topic control can be disjointed. When one person decides unilaterally what the next topic of conversation will be (as opposed to having it decided bilaterally), the communication is disjunctive. Individuals may switch topics, for example, with no reference to what was just said, or they may control the other person's communication topic by directing what should be responded to. Sieburg (1969) found that more than 25 percent of the statements made in small-group discussions failed to refer to or even acknowledge prior speakers or their statements.

These three factors—taking turns speaking, management of timing, and topic control—contribute to what

Wiemann (1977) calls "interaction management." They have been found to be critical to effective supportive communication. In an empirical study of perceived communication competence, Wiemann (1977, p. 104) found that "the smoother the management of the interaction [of the three factors above], the more competent the communicator was perceived to be." In fact, interaction management was concluded to be the most powerful determinant of perceived communication competence in his experimental study. Individuals who used conjunctive communication were rated as being significantly more competent in interpersonal communication than were those whose communication was disjunctive.

This suggests that skilled coaches and counselors use several kinds of behaviors in managing communication situations so they are conjunctive rather than disjunctive. For example, they foster conjunctive communication in an interaction by asking questions that are based directly on the subordinate's previous statement, by waiting for a sentence to be completed before beginning a response (e.g., not finishing a sentence for someone else), and by saying only two or three sentences at a time before pausing to give the other person a chance to add input. In addition, they avoid long pauses; their statements refer to what has been said before; and they take turns speaking. Figure 2 illustrates the continuum of conjunctive and disjunctive statements.

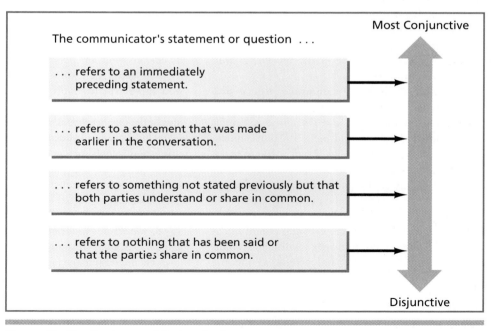

Figure 2   The Continuum of Conjunctive Statements

By using conjunctive communication, managers confirm the worth of the other person's statements, thereby helping to foster joint problem solving and teamwork.

7. Supportive communication is owned, not disowned.

Taking responsibility for one's statements and acknowledging that the source of the ideas is oneself and not another person or group is **owning communication.** Using first-person words, such as "I," "me," "mine," indicates owning communication. **Disowning communication** is suggested by use of third-person or first-person-plural words: "We think," "They said," or "One might say." Disowned communication is attributed to an unknown person, group, or to some external source (e.g., "Lots of people think"). The communicator avoids taking responsibility for the message and therefore avoids investing in the interaction. This conveys the message that the communicator is aloof or uncaring about the receiver or is not confident enough in the ideas expressed to take responsibility for them.

Glasser (1965) based his approach to mental health—reality therapy—on the concept of taking responsibility for, or owning, communication and behavior. According to Glasser, mental health depends on accepting responsibility for one's statements and behaviors. According to reality therapy, taking responsibility for one's communication builds self-confidence and a sense of self-worth in the communicator. It also builds trust in the receiver of the communication.

One result of disowning communication is that the listener is never sure whose point of view the message represents: "How can I respond if I don't know to whom I am responding?" "If I don't understand the message, whom can I ask?" Moreover, an implicit message associated with disowned communication is, "I want to keep distance between you and me." The speaker communicates as a representative rather than as a person, as a message-conveyer rather than an interested individual. Owning communication, on the other hand, indicates a willingness to invest oneself in a relationship and to act as a colleague or helper.

This last point suggests that the coach or counselor encourage the subordinate also to own his or her statements. The manager can do this by example but also by asking the subordinate to restate disowning statements, as in this exchange:

SUBORDINATE: Everyone else says my work is fine.
MANAGER: So no one besides me has ever expressed dissatisfaction with your work or suggested how to improve it?
SUBORDINATE: Well . . . Mark complained that I took shortcuts and left him to clean up after me.
MANAGER: Was his complaint fair?
SUBORDINATE: Yeah, I guess so.
MANAGER: Why did you take shortcuts?
SUBORDINATE: My work was piling up, and I felt I had too much to do.
MANAGER: Does this happen often, that your work builds up and you look for shortcuts?
SUBORDINATE: More than I'd like.

Here the manager has used conjunctive questions to guide the subordinate away from disowning responsibility toward acknowledging a behavior that may be affecting the subordinate's performance.

8. Supportive communication requires listening, not one-way message delivery.

The previous seven attributes of supportive communication all focus on message delivery, where a message is initiated by the coach or counselor. But another aspect of supportive communication—that is, listening and responding effectively to someone else's statements—is at least as important as delivering supportive messages. As Maier, Solem, and Maier (1973, p. 311) stated: "In any conversation, the person who talks the most is the one who learns the least about the other person. The good supervisor therefore must become a good listener." Haas and Arnold (1995) found that about one-third of the characteristics that people in the workplace use to judge communication competence have to do with listening. In short, good listeners are more likely to be seen as skillful communicators.

In a survey of personnel directors in 300 businesses and industries conducted to determine what skills are most important in becoming a manager, Crocker (1978) reported that effective listening was ranked highest. Despite its importance in managerial success, however, and despite the fact that most people spend at least 45 percent of their communication time listening, most people have underdeveloped listening skills. Tests have shown, for example, that individuals are usually about 25 percent effective in listening (Huseman,

Lahiff, & Hatfield, 1976), that is, they listen to and understand only about a fourth of what is being communicated. When asked to rate the extent to which they are skilled listeners, 85 percent of all individuals rate themselves as average or worse. Only 5 percent rate themselves as highly skilled (Steil, 1980). It is particularly unfortunate that listening skills are often poorest when people interact with those closest to them, such as family members and coworkers. They interrupt and jump to conclusions more frequently (i.e., they stop listening) with people close to them than with others.

When individuals are preoccupied with meeting their own needs (e.g., saving face, persuading someone else, winning a point, avoiding getting involved), when they have already made a prior judgment, or when they hold negative attitudes toward the communicator or the message, they can't listen effectively. Because a person listens at the rate of 500 words a minute but speaks at a normal rate of only 125 to 250 words a minute, the listener's mind can dwell on other things half the time. Therefore, being a good listener is neither easy nor automatic. It requires developing the ability to hear and understand the message sent by another person, while at the same time helping to strengthen the relationship between the interacting parties.

Rogers and Farson (1976, p. 99) suggest that this kind of listening conveys the idea that, "I'm interested in you as a person, and I think what you feel is important. I respect your thoughts, and even if I don't agree with them, I know they are valid for you. I feel sure you have a contribution to make. I think you're worth listening to, and I want you to know that I'm the kind of person you can talk to."

People do not know they are being listened to unless the listener makes some type of **response.** Competent managers who must coach and counsel select carefully from a repertoire of response alternatives that clarify the communication as well as strengthen the interpersonal relationship. The mark of a supportive listener is the competence to select appropriate responses to others' statements.

The appropriateness of a response depends largely on whether the focus of the interaction is primarily coaching or counseling. Of course, seldom can these two activities be separated from one another completely—effective coaching often involves counseling and effective counseling sometimes involves coaching—and attentive listening involves the use of a variety of responses. But some responses are more appropriate under certain circumstances than others.

Figure 3 lists four major response types and arranges them on a continuum from most directive and closed to most nondirective and open. Closed responses eliminate discussion of topics and provide direction to

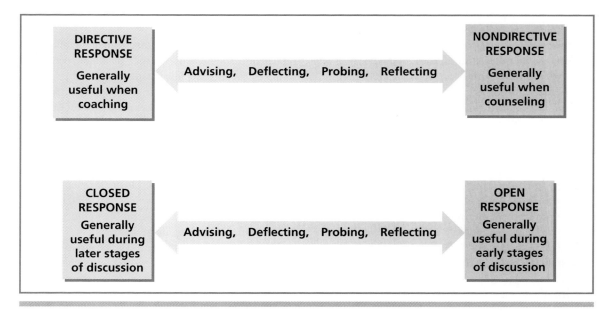

Figure 3   Responsive Types in Supportive Listening

individuals. They represent methods by which the listener can control the topic of conversation. Open responses, on the other hand, allow the communicator, not the listener, to control the topic of conversation. Each of these response types has certain advantages and disadvantages, and none is appropriate all the time under all circumstances.

Most people get in the habit of relying heavily on one or two response types, and they use them regardless of the circumstances. Moreover, most people have been found to rely first and foremost on evaluative or judgmental responses (Rogers, 1961). That is, when they encounter another person's statements, most people tend to agree or disagree, to pass judgment, or to immediately form a personal opinion about the legitimacy or veracity of the statement. On the average, about 80 percent of most people's responses have been found to be evaluative. Supportive listening, however, avoids evaluation and judgment as a first response. Instead, it relies on flexibility in response types and the appropriate match of responses to circumstances. The four response types follow.

Advising. An **advising response** provides direction, evaluation, personal opinion, or instructions. Such a response imposes on the communicator the point of view of the listener, and it creates listener control over the topic of conversation. The advantages of an advising response are that it helps the communicator understand something that may have been unclear before, it helps identify a problem solution, and it can provide clarity about how the communicator should feel or act in the future. It is most appropriate when the listener has expertise that the communicator doesn't possess or when the communicator is in need of direction. Supportive listening sometimes means that the listener does the talking, but this is usually appropriate only when advice or direction is specifically requested. Most listeners have a tendency to offer much more advice and direction than is appropriate.

One problem with advising is that it can produce dependence. Individuals get used to having someone else generate answers, directions, or clarifications. They are not permitted to figure out issues and solutions for themselves. A second problem is that advising also creates the impression that the communicator is not being understood by the listener. Rogers (1961) found that most people, even when they seem to be asking for advice, mainly desire understanding and acceptance, not advice. They want the listener to share in the communication but not take charge of it. The problem with advising is that it removes from the communicator control of the conversation. A third problem with advising is that it shifts focus from the communicator's issue to the listener's advice. When listeners feel advising is appropriate, they concentrate more on the legitimacy of the advice or on the generation of alternatives and solutions than on simply listening attentively. When listeners are expected to generate advice and direction, they may focus more on their own experience than on the communicator's. A fourth potential problem with advising is that it can imply that communicators don't have sufficient understanding, expertise, insight, or maturity and that they need help because of their incompetence.

One way to overcome the disadvantages of advising in coaching and counseling is to avoid giving advice as a first response. It should follow other responses that allow communicators to have control over the topics of conversation, that show understanding and acceptance, and that encourage self-reliance on the part of communicators. In addition, advice should either be connected to an accepted standard or should be tentative. An accepted standard means that communicators and listeners both acknowledge that the advice will lead to a desired outcome and that it is inherently good, right, or appropriate. When this is impossible, the advice should be communicated as the listener's opinion or feeling, and as only one option (i.e., with flexibility), not as the only option. This permits communicators to accept or reject the advice without feeling that the advisor is being invalidated or rejected if the advice is not accepted.

Deflecting. A **deflecting response** switches the focus from the communicator's problem to one selected by the listener. The listener changes the subject. Listeners may substitute their own experience for that of the communicator (e.g., "Let me tell you something similar that happened to me") or introduce an entirely new topic (e.g., "That reminds me of [something else]"). The listener may think the current problem is unclear to the communicator and that the use of examples or analogies will help. Or the listener may feel that the communicator needs to be reassured that others have experienced the same problem and that support and understanding are available.

Deflecting responses are most appropriate when a comparison or reassurance is needed. They can provide empathy and support by communicating the message "I understand because of what happened to me (or someone else)." They can also convey the assurance "Things will be fine. Others have also had this experience." Deflection is also often used to avoid embarrassing either the communicator or the listener. Changing the subject when either party gets uncomfortable and answering a question other than the one asked are common examples.

The disadvantages of deflecting responses, however, are that they can imply that the communicator's message is not important or that the experience of the listener is more significant than that of the communicator. It may produce competitiveness or feelings of being one-upped by the listener. Deflection can be interpreted as, "My experience is more worthy of discussion than yours." Or it may simply change the subject from something that is important and central to the communicator to a topic that is not important.

Deflecting responses are most effective when they are conjunctive—that is, when they are clearly connected to what the communicator just said, when the listener's response leads directly back to the communicator's concerns, and when the reason for the deflection is made clear. That is, deflecting can produce desirable outcomes in coaching and counseling if the communicator feels supported and understood, not invalidated, by the change in topic focus.

Probing. A **probing response** asks a question about what the communicator just said or about a topic selected by the listener. The intent of a probe is to acquire additional information, to help the communicator say more about the topic, or to help the listener foster more appropriate responses. For example, an effective way to avoid being evaluative and judgmental and to avoid triggering defensive reactions is to continue to ask questions. Questioning helps the listener adopt the communicator's frame of reference so that in coaching situations suggestions can be specific (not global) and in counseling situations statements can be descriptive (not evaluative). Questions tend to be more neutral in tone than direct statements.

Questioning, however, can sometimes have the unwelcome effect of switching the focus of attention from the communicator's statement to the reasons behind it. The question "Why do you think that?" for example, might force the communicator to justify a feeling or a perception rather than just report it. Similarly, probing responses can serve as a mechanism for escaping discussion of a topic or for maneuvering the topic around to one the listener wants to discuss (e.g., "Instead of discussing your feelings about your job, tell me why you didn't respond to my memo"). Probing responses can also allow the communicator to lose control of the conversation, especially when difficult subjects need to be addressed (e.g., "I'll talk about only those things you ask me").

Two important hints should be kept in mind to make probing responses more effective. One is that "why" questions are seldom as effective as "what" questions. "Why" questions lead to topic changes, escape, and speculation more often than to valid information. For example, the question "Why do you feel that way?" can lead to statements such as "Because my id is not sufficiently controlled by my ego" or "Because my father was an alcoholic and my mother beat me." These are extreme, even silly, examples, but they illustrate how ineffective "why" questions can be. "What do you mean by that?" is likely to be more fruitful.

A second hint is to tailor the probes to fit the situation. For example, Supplement B in this book summarizes four types of probes that are useful in interviewing. When the communicator's statement does not contain enough information, or part of the message is not understood, an **elaboration probe** should be used (e.g., "Can you tell me more about that?"). When the message is not clear or is ambiguous, a **clarification probe** is best (e.g., "What do you mean by that?"). A **repetition probe** works best when the communicator is avoiding a topic or hasn't answered a previous question (e.g., "Once again, what do you think about that?"). A **reflective probe** is most effective when the communicator is being encouraged to keep pursuing the same topic in greater depth (e.g., "You say you are discouraged?"). Probing responses are especially effective in turning hostile or conflictive conversations into supportive conversations. Asking questions can often turn attacks into consensus, evaluations into descriptions, general statements into specific statements, disowning statements into owning statements, or person-focused declarations into problem-focused declarations. In other words, probes can often be used to help others use supportive communication when they have not been trained in advance to do so.

Reflecting. The primary purpose of the **reflecting response** is to mirror back to the communicator the message that was heard and to communicate understanding and acceptance of the person. Reflecting the message *in different words* allows the speaker to feel listened to, understood, and free to explore the topic in more depth. Reflective responding involves paraphrasing and clarifying the message. Instead of simply mimicking the communication, supportive listeners contribute meaning, understanding, and acceptance to the conversation while still allowing communicators to pursue topics of their choosing. Athos and Gabarro (1978), Brownell (1986), Steil et al. (1983), and others argue that this response should be used most of the time in coaching and counseling since it leads to the clearest communication and the most supportive relationships.

A potential disadvantage of reflective responses is that communicators can get an impression opposite from the one intended. That is, they can get the feeling that they are not being understood or listened to carefully. If they keep hearing reflections of what they just said, their response might be, "I just said that. Aren't you listening to me?" Reflective responses, in other words, can be perceived as an artificial "technique" or as a superficial response to a message.

The most effective listeners keep the following rules in mind when using reflective responses.

1. Avoid repeating the same response, such as "You feel that . . . ," "Are you saying that . . . ?" or "What I heard you say was. . . ."

2. Avoid an exchange in which listeners do not contribute equally to the conversation, but serve only as mimics. (One can use understanding or reflective responses while still taking equal responsibility for the depth and meaning of the communication.)

3. Respond to the personal rather than the impersonal. For example, to a complaint by a subordinate about close supervision and feelings of incompetence and annoyance, a reflective response would focus on personal feelings rather than on supervision style.

4. Respond to expressed feelings before responding to content. When expressed, feelings are the most important part of the message to the person and may stand in the way of the ability to communicate clearly.

5. Respond with empathy and acceptance. Avoid the extremes of complete objectivity, detachment, or distance on the one hand or over-identification (accepting the feelings as one's own) on the other.

6. Avoid expressing agreement or disagreement with the statements. Use reflective listening and other listening responses to help the communicator explore and analyze the problem. Later you can draw on this information to help fashion a solution.

The Personal Management Interview

Not only are the eight attributes of supportive communication effective in normal discourse and problem-solving situations, but they can be most effectively applied when specific interactions with subordinates are planned and conducted frequently. One important difference between effective and ineffective managers is the extent to which they provide their subordinates with opportunities to receive regular feedback, to feel supported and bolstered, and to be coached and counseled. Providing these opportunities is difficult, however, because of the tremendous time demands most managers face. Many managers want to coach, counsel, and train subordinates, but they simply never find the time. Therefore, one important mechanism for applying supportive communication and for providing subordinates with development and feedback opportunities is to implement a personal management interview program.

A **personal management interview program** is a regularly scheduled, one-on-one meeting between a manager and his or her subordinates. In a study of the performance of intact departments and teams in a variety of organizations, Boss (1983) found that effectiveness increased significantly when managers conducted regular, private meetings with subordinates on a biweekly or monthly basis. These meetings were referred to as "personal management interviews." Figure 4 compares the performance effectiveness of teams and departments that implemented the program versus those that did not.

Instituting a personal management interview program consists of two steps. First, a role-negotiation session is held in which expectations, responsibilities, standards of evaluation, reporting relationships, and so on, are clarified. Unless such a meeting is held, most subordinates do not have a clear idea of exactly what is expected of them or on what basis they will be evaluated. In our own experiences with managers and executives, few have expressed confidence that they know precisely what is expected of them or how they are being evaluated in their jobs. In a role-negotiation session, that uncertainty is overcome; the manager and subordinate negotiate all job-related issues that are not prescribed by policy or by mandate. A written record should be made of the agreements and responsibilities that result from the meeting that can serve as an infor-

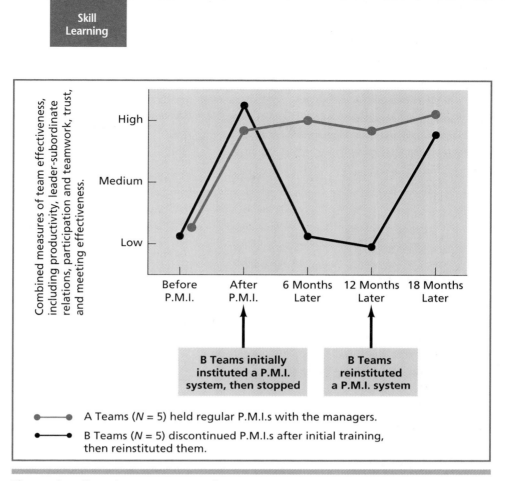

Figure 4 Effects of an Ongoing Personal Management Interview Program
Source: Bass, 1983.

mal contract between the manager and the subordinate. The goal of a role-negotiation session is to obtain clarity between both parties regarding what each expects from the other. Because this role negotiation is not adversarial but rather focuses on supportiveness and team-building, the eight supportive communication principles should characterize the interaction.

The second, and most important, step in a personal management interview plan is a program of ongoing, one-on-one meetings of the manager with each subordinate. These meetings are regular (not just when a mistake is made or a crisis arises) and private (not overheard by others) for good reason. This meeting provides managers with the opportunity to coach and counsel subordinates and to help them improve their own skills and job performance. Therefore, each meeting should last from 45 minutes to an hour and focus on items such as the following: (1) managerial and organizational problems, (2) information sharing, (3) interpersonal issues, (4) obstacles to improvement, (5) training in manage-

ment skills, (6) individual needs, (7) feedback on job performance, and (8) personal concerns or problems.

The meeting always leads toward action items to be accomplished before the next meeting, some by the subordinate and others by the manager. Both parties prepare for the meeting, and both bring items to be discussed. It is not a formal appraisal session called by the manager, but a development and improvement session in which both the manager and subordinate have a stake. It is a chance for subordinates to have personal time with the manager to work out issues and report information; consequently, it helps eliminate unscheduled interruptions and long, inefficient group meetings. At each subsequent meeting, action items are reviewed from previous meetings, so that continuous improvement is encouraged. Table 4 summarizes the characteristics of the personal management interview program.

Boss's research found that a variety of benefits resulted in teams that instituted this program. It not only increased their effectiveness, but improved individual

1. The interview is regular and private.

2. The major intent of the meeting is continuous improvement in personal, interpersonal, and organizational performance, so the meeting is action oriented.

3. Both the manager and the subordinate prepare agenda items for the meeting. It is a meeting for both of them, not just for the manager.

4. Sufficient time is allowed for the interaction, usually about an hour.

5. Supportive communication is used so that joint problem solving and continuous improvement result (in both task accomplishment and interpersonal relationships).

6. The first agenda item is a follow-up on the action items generated by the previous meeting.

7. Major agenda items for the meeting might include:
   - Managerial and organizational problems
   - Organizational values and vision
   - Information sharing
   - Interpersonal issues
   - Obstacles to improvement
   - Training in management skills
   - Individual needs
   - Feedback on job performance
   - Personal concerns and problems

8. Praise and encouragement are intermingled with problem solving.

9. A review of action items generated by the meeting occurs at the end of the interview.

Table 4 Characteristics of a Personal Management Interview Program

accountability, department meeting efficiency, and communication flows. Managers actually found more discretionary time available because the program reduced interruptions and unscheduled meetings. Furthermore, participants defined it as a success experience in itself. When correction or negative feedback had to be communicated, and when coaching or counseling was called for (which is typical of almost every manager-subordinate relationship at some point), supportive communication helped strengthen the interpersonal relationship at the same time that problems were solved and performance improved. In summary, setting aside time for formal, structured interaction between managers and their subordinates in which supportive communication played a part produced markedly improved bottom-line results in those organizations that implemented the program.

Summary

The most important barriers to effective communication in organizations are interpersonal. Much technological progress has been made in the last two decades in improving the accuracy of message delivery in organizations, but communication problems still persist between managers and their subordinates and peers. A major reason for these problems is that the communication does not support a positive interpersonal relationship. Instead, it frequently engenders distrust, hostility, defensiveness, and feelings of incompetence and low self-esteem.

Such dysfunctional communication is seldom associated with situations in which compliments are given, congratulations are made, a bonus is awarded, or other positive interactions occur. Most people have little trouble communicating effectively in such situations. However, potentially harmful communication patterns are most likely to emerge when one is giving feedback on poor performance, saying "no" to a proposal or request, resolving a difference of opinion between two subordinates, correcting problem behaviors, receiving criticism from others, or facing other negative interactions. These situations also arise frequently in the context of coaching and counseling subordinates. Handling these situations in a way that fosters interpersonal growth and a strengthening of relationships is one mark of an effective manager.

In this chapter, we have pointed out that effective communicators adhere to the principles of supportive communication, thus ensuring greater clarity and understanding of messages while making other persons feel accepted, valued, and supported. Of course, it is possible to become overly concerned with technique in trying to incorporate these principles and thereby defeat the goal of being supportive. One can become artificial, or incongruent, by focusing on technique alone, rather than on honest, caring communication. But if the principles are practiced and consciously implemented in everyday interactions, they can be important tools for improving your communication competence.

Behavioral Guidelines

The following behavioral guidelines will help you practice supportive communication:

1. Differentiate between coaching situations, which require giving advice and direction to help foster behavior change, and counseling situations, in which understanding and problem recognition are the desired outcomes.

2. Use problem-oriented statements rather than person-oriented statements, that is, behavioral referents or characteristics of events, not attributes of the person.

3. Communicate congruently by acknowledging your true feelings without acting them out in destructive ways.

4. Use descriptive, not evaluative, statements. Describe objectively what occurred; describe your reactions to events and their objective consequences; and suggest acceptable alternatives.

5. Use validating statements that acknowledge the other person's importance and uniqueness; communicate an investment in the relationship by demonstrating your respect and flexibility; foster two-way interchanges; and identify areas of agreement or positive characteristics before pointing out areas of disagreement or negative characteristics.

6. Use specific rather than global (either-or, black-or-white) statements, and focus on things that can be controlled.

7. Use conjunctive statements that flow smoothly from what was said previously; ensure equal speaking opportunities for all; don't cause long pauses; don't completely control the topic; and acknowledge what was said before.

8. Own your statements, and encourage the other person to do likewise. Use personal words ("I") rather than impersonal words ("management").

9. Demonstrate supportive listening: Use a variety of responses to others' statements, depending on whether you are coaching or counseling someone else, but with a bias toward reflecting responses.

10. Implement a personal management interview program characterized by supportive communication, in order to coach, counsel, and foster personal development among subordinates.

Skill Analysis

Cases Involving Coaching and Counseling

Find Somebody Else

Ron Davis, the relatively new general manager of the machine tooling group at Parker Manufacturing, was visiting one of the plants. He scheduled a meeting with Mike Leonard, a plant manager who reported to him.

RON: Mike, I've scheduled this meeting with you because I've been reviewing performance data, and I wanted to give you some feedback. I know we haven't talked face-to-face before, but I think it's time we review how you're doing. I'm afraid that some of things I have to say are not very favorable.

MIKE: Well, since you're the new boss, I guess I'll have to listen. I've had meetings like this before with new people who come in my plant and think they know what's going on.

RON: Look, Mike, I want this to be a two-way interchange. I'm not here to read a verdict to you, and I'm not here to tell you how to do your job. There are just some areas for improvement I want to review.

MIKE: OK, sure, I've heard that before. But you called the meeting. Go ahead and lower the boom.

RON: Well, Mike, I don't think this is lowering the boom. But there are several things you need to hear. One is what I noticed during the plant tour. I think you're too chummy with some of your female personnel. You know, one of them might take offense and level a sexual harassment suit against you.

MIKE: Oh, come on. You haven't been around this plant before, and you don't know the informal, friendly relationships we have. The office staff and the women on the floor are flattered by a little attention now and then.

RON: That may be so, but you need to be more careful. You may not be sensitive to what's really going on with them. But that raises another thing I noticed—the appearance of your shop. You know how important it is in Parker to have a neat and clean shop. As I walked through this morning, I noticed that it wasn't as orderly and neat as I would like to see it. Having things in disarray reflects poorly on you, Mike.

MIKE: I'll stack my plant up against any in Parker for neatness. You may have seen a few tools out of place because someone was just using them, but we take a lot of pride in our neatness. I don't see how you can say that things are in disarray. You've got no experience around here, so who are you to judge?

RON: Well, I'm glad you're sensitive to the neatness issue. I just think you need to pay attention to it, that's all. But regarding neatness, I notice that you don't dress like a plant manager. I think you're creating a substandard impression by not wearing a tie, for example. Casualness in dress can be used as an excuse for workers to come to work in really grubby attire. That may not be safe.

MIKE: Look, I don't agree with making a big separation between the managers and the employees. By dressing like people out on the shop floor, I think we eliminate a lot of barriers. Besides, I don't have the money to buy clothes that might get oil on them every day. That seems pretty picky to me.

RON: I don't want to seem picky, Mike. But I do feel strongly about the issues I've mentioned. There are some other things, though, that need to get corrected. One is the appearance of the reports you send into division headquarters. There are often mistakes, misspellings, and, I suspect, some wrong numbers. I wonder if you are paying attention to these reports. You seem to be reviewing them superficially.

MIKE: If there is one thing we have too much of, it's reports. I could spend three-quarters of my time filling our report forms and generating data for some bean counter in headquarters. We have reports coming out our ears. Why don't you give us a chance to get our work done and eliminate all this paperwork?

RON: You know as well as I do, Mike, that we need to carefully monitor our productivity, quality, and costs. You just need to get more serious about taking care of that part of your responsibility.

MIKE: OK. I'm not going to fight about that. It's a losing battle for me. No one at headquarters will ever decrease their demand for reports. But, listen, Ron, I also have one question for you.

RON: OK. What's that?

MIKE: Why don't you go find somebody else to pick on? I need to get back to work.

Discussion Questions

1. What principles of supportive communication and supportive listening are violated in this case?

2. How could the interaction have been changed to produce a better outcome?

3. Categorize each of the statements by naming the rule of supportive communication that is either illustrated or violated.

4. What should Ron do in his follow-up meeting with Mike?

Rejected Plans

The following dialogue occurred between two employees in a large firm. The conversation illustrates several characteristics of supportive communication.

ELLEN: How did your meeting go with Mr. Peterson yesterday?

BOB: Well, uh, it went . . . aaah . . . it was no big deal.

ELLEN: It looks as if you're pretty upset about it.

BOB: Yeah, I am. It was a totally frustrating experience. I, uh, well, let's just say I would like to forget the whole thing.

ELLEN: Things must not have gone as well as you had hoped they would.

BOB: I'll say! That guy was impossible. I thought the plans I submitted were very clear and well thought out. Then he rejected the entire package.

ELLEN: You mean he didn't accept any of them?

BOB: You got it.

ELLEN: I've seen your work before, Bob. You've always done a first-rate job. It's hard for me to figure out why your plans were rejected by Peterson. What did he say about them?

BOB: He said they were unrealistic and too difficult to implement, and . . .

ELLEN: Really?

BOB: Yeah, and when he said that I felt he was attacking me personally. But, on the other hand, I was also angry because I thought my plans were very good, and, you know, I paid close attention to every detail in those plans.

ELLEN: I'm certain that you did.

BOB: It just really ticks me off.

ELLEN: I'll bet it does. I would be upset, too.

BOB: Peterson must have something against me.

ELLEN: After all the effort you put into those plans, you still couldn't figure out whether Peterson was rejecting you or your plans, right?

BOB: Yeah. Right. How could you tell?

ELLEN: I can really understand your confusion and uncertainty when you felt Peterson's actions were unreasonable.

BOB: I just don't understand why he did what he did.

ELLEN: Sure. If he said your plans were unrealistic, what does that mean? I mean, how can you deal with a rationale like that? It's just too general—meaningless, even. Did he mention anything specific? Did you ask him to point out some problems or explain the reasons for his rejection more clearly?

BOB: Good point, but, uh, you know . . . I was so disappointed at the rejection that I was kinda like in outer space. You know what I mean?

ELLEN: Yeah. It's an incapacitating experience. You have so much invested personally that you try to divest as fast as you can to save what little self-respect is left.

BOB: That's it all right. I just wanted to get out of there before I said something I would be sorry for.

ELLEN: Yet, in the back of your mind, you probably figured that Peterson wouldn't risk the company's future just because he didn't like you personally. But then, well . . . the plans were good! It's hard to deal with that contradiction on the spot, isn't it?

BOB: Exactly. I knew I should have pushed him for more information, but, uh, I just stood there like a dummy. But what can you do about it now? It's spilled milk.

ELLEN: I don't think it's a total loss, Bob. I mean, from what you have told me—what he said and what you said—I don't think that a conclusion can be reached. Maybe he doesn't understand the plans, or maybe it was just his off day. Who knows? It could be a lot of things. What would you think about pinning Peterson down by asking for his objections, point by point? Do you think it would help to talk to him again?

BOB: Well, I would sure know a lot more than I know now. As it is, I wouldn't know where to begin revising or modifying the plans. And you're right, I really don't know what Peterson thinks about me or my work. Sometimes I just react and interpret with little or no evidence.

ELLEN: Maybe, uh . . . maybe another meeting would be a good thing, then.

BOB: Well, I guess I should get off my duff and schedule an appointment with him for next week. I am curious to find out what the problem is, with the plans, or me. (Pause) Thanks, Ellen, for helping me work through this thing.

Discussion Questions

1. Categorize each statement in the case according to the supportive communication characteristic or type of response it represents. For example, the first statement by Bob obviously is not very congruent, but the second one is much more so.

2. Which statements in the conversation were most helpful? Which do you think would produce defensiveness or close off the conversation?

3. What are the potential disadvantages of giving outright advice for solving Bob's problem? Why doesn't Ellen just tell Bob what he ought to do? Is it incongruent to ask Bob what he thinks is the best solution?

Skill Practice

Exercises for Diagnosing Communication Problems and Fostering Understanding

United Chemical Company

The role of manager encompasses not only one-on-one coaching and counseling with an employee but also frequently entails helping other people understand coaching and counseling principles for themselves. Sometimes it means refereeing interactions and, by example, helping other people learn about correct principles of supportive communication. This is part of the task in this exercise. In a group setting, coaching and counseling become more difficult because multiple messages, driven by multiple motives, interact. Skilled supportive communicators, however, help each group member feel supported and understood in the interaction, even though the solution to an issue may not always be the one he or she would have preferred.

Assignment

In this exercise you should apply the principles of supportive communication you have read about in the chapter. First, you will need to form groups of four people each. Next, read the case and assign the following roles in your group: Max, Sue, Jack, and an observer. Assume that a meeting is being held with Max, Sue, and Jack immediately after the end of the incidents in the following case. Play the roles you have been assigned and try to resolve the problems. The observer should provide feedback to the three players at the end of the exercise. An Observer's Form to assist in providing feedback is in Appendix I.

The Case

The United Chemical Company is a large producer and distributor of commodity chemicals, with five production plants in the United States. The main plant in Baytown, Texas, is not only a production plant but also the company's research and engineering center.

The process design group consists of eight male engineers and their supervisor, Max Kane. The group has worked together steadily for a number of years, and good relationships have developed among all the members. When the workload began to increase, Max hired a new design engineer, Sue Davis, a recent master's degree graduate from one of the foremost engineering schools in the country. Sue was assigned to a project that would expand the capacity of one of the existing plant facilities. Three other design engineers were assigned to the project along with Sue: Jack Keller (age 38, 15 years with the company), Sam Sims (age 40, 10 years with the company), and Lance Madison (age 32, 8 years with the company).

As a new employee, Sue was very enthusiastic about the opportunity to work at United. She liked her work very much because it was challenging and it offered her a chance to apply much of the knowledge she had gained in her university studies. On the job, Sue kept mostly to herself and her design work. Her relations with her fellow project members were friendly, but she did not go out of her way to have informal conversations with them during or after working hours.

Sue was a diligent employee who took her work seriously. On occasions when a difficult problem arose, she would stay after hours in order to come up with a solution. Because of her persistence, coupled with her more current education, Sue usually completed her portion of the various project stages several days ahead of her colleagues. This was somewhat irritating to her because on these occasions she had to go to Max to ask for additional work to keep her busy until her coworkers caught up to her. Initially, she had offered to help Jack, Sam, and Lance with their assignments, but each time she was abruptly turned down.

About five months after Sue had joined the design group, Jack asked to see Max about a problem the group was having. The conversation between Max and Jack went as follows:

MAX: Jack, I understand you want to discuss a problem with me.

JACK: Yes, Max, I don't want to waste your time, but some of the other design engineers want me to discuss Sue with you. She is irritating everyone with her know-it-all, pompous attitude. She's just not the kind of person we want to work with.

MAX: I can't understand that, Jack. She's an excellent worker, and her design work is always well done and usually flawless. She's doing everything the company wants her to do.

JACK: The company never asked her to disrupt the morale of the group or to tell us how to do our work. The animosity in our group could eventually result in lower-quality work for the whole unit.

MAX: I'll tell you what I'll do. Sue has a meeting with me next week to discuss her six-month performance. I'll keep your thoughts in mind, but I can't promise an improvement in what you and the others believe is a pompous attitude.

JACK: Immediate improvement in her behavior is not the problem; it's her coaching others when she has no right to. She publicly shows others what to do. You'd think she was lecturing an advance class in design with all her high-powered, useless equations and formulas. She'd better back off soon, or some of us will quit or transfer.

During the next week, Max thought carefully about his meeting with Jack. He knew that Jack was the informal leader of the design engineers and generally spoke for the other group members. On Thursday of the following week, Max called Sue into his office for her mid-year review. One portion of the conversation went as follows:

MAX: There is one other aspect I'd like to discuss with you about your performance. As I just related to you, your technical performance has been excellent; however, there are some questions about your relationships with the other workers.

SUE: I don't understand. What questions are you talking about?

MAX: Well, to be specific, certain members of the design group have complained about your apparent "know-it-all-attitude" and the manner in which you try to tell them how to do their job. You're going to have to be patient with them and not publicly call them out about their performance. This is a good group of engineers, and their work over the years has been more than acceptable. I don't want any problems that will cause the group to produce less effectively.

SUE: Let me make a few comments. First of all, I have never publicly criticized their performance to them or to you. Initially, when I finished ahead of them, I offered to help them with their work but was bluntly told to mind my own business. I took the hint and concentrated only on my part of the work. What you don't understand is that after five months of working in this group I have come to the conclusion that what is going on is a rip-off of the company. The other engineers are goldbricking; they're setting a work pace much slower than they're capable of. They're more interested in the music from Sam's radio, the local football team, and the bar they're going to go to for TGIF. I'm sorry, but this is just not the way I was raised or trained. And finally, they've never looked on me as a qualified engineer, but as a woman who has broken their professional barrier.

Source: Szilagyi & Wallace, 1983, pp. 204–205.

Byron vs. Thomas

Effective one-on-one coaching and counseling are skills that are required in many settings in life, not just in management. It is hard to imagine a parent, roommate, Little League coach, room mother, or good friend who would not benefit from training in supportive communication. Because there are so many aspects of supportive communication, however, it is sometimes difficult to remember all of them. That is why practice, with observation and feedback, is so important. These attributes of supportive communication can become a natural part of your interaction approach as you conscientiously practice and receive feedback from a colleague.

Assignment

In the following exercise, one individual should take the role of Hal Byron, and another should take the role of Judy Thomas. To make the role-play realistic, do not read each other's role descriptions. When you have finished reading, role-play a meeting between Hal Byron and Judy Thomas. A third person should serve as the observer. An Observer's Form to assist in providing feedback is in Appendix I.

Hal Byron, Department Head

You are Hal Byron, head of the operations group—the "back room"—in a large bank corporation. This is your second year on the job, and you have moved up rather quickly in the bank. You enjoy working for this firm, which has a reputation for being one of the finest in the region. One reason is that outside opportunities for management development and training are funded by the bank. In addition, each employee is given an opportunity for a personal management interview each month, and these sessions are usually both productive and developmental.

One of the department members, Judy Thomas, has been in this department for 19 years, 15 of them in the same job. She is reasonably good at what she does, and she is always punctual and efficient. She tends to get to work earlier than most employees in order to peruse the *American Banker* and *U.S.A. Today.* You can almost set your watch by the time Judy visits the rest room during the day and by the time she makes her phone call to her daughter every afternoon.

Your feeling about Judy is that although she is a good worker, she lacks imagination and initiative. This has been indicated by her lack of merit increases over the last five years and by the fact that she has had the same job for 15 years. She's content to do just what is assigned, nothing more. Your predecessor must have given hints to Judy that she might be in line for a promotion, however, because Judy has raised this with you more than once. Because she has been in her job so long, she is at the top of her pay range, and without a promotion, she cannot receive a salary adjustment above the basic cost-of-living increase.

The one thing Judy does beyond the basic minimum job requirements is to help train young people who come into the department. She is very patient and methodical with them, and she seems to take pride in helping them learn the ropes. She has not been hesitant to point out this contribution to you. Unfortunately, this activity does not qualify Judy for a promotion, nor could she be transferred into the training and development department. Once you suggested that she take a few courses at the local college, paid for by the bank, but she matter-of-factly stated that she was too old to go to school. You surmise that she might be intimidated because she doesn't have a college degree.

As much as you would like to promote Judy, there just doesn't seem to be any way to do that in good conscience. You have tried putting additional work under her control, but she seems to be slowing down in her productivity rather than speeding up. The work needs to get done, and expanding her role just puts you behind schedule.

This interview coming up is probably the time to level with Judy about her performance and her potential. You certainly don't want to lose her as an employee, but there is not going to be a change in job assignment for a long time unless she changes her performance dramatically.

Judy Thomas, Department Member

You are a member of the operations group in a large bank corporation. You have been with the bank now for 19 years, 15 of them in the same job. You enjoy the company because of its friendly climate and because of its prestigious image in the region. It's nice to be known as an employee of this firm. However, lately you have become more dissatisfied as you've seen person after person come into the bank and get promoted ahead of you. Your own boss, Hal Byron, is almost 20 years your junior. Another woman who joined the bank the same time you did is now a senior vice president. You can't understand why you've been neglected. You are efficient and accurate in your work, you have a near-perfect attendance record, and you consider yourself to be a good employee. You have gone out of your way on many occasions to help train and orient young people who are just joining the bank. Several of them have written letters later telling you how important your help was in getting them promoted. A lot of good that does you!

The only thing you can figure out is that there is a bias against you because you haven't graduated from college. On the other hand, others have moved up without a diploma. You haven't taken advantage of any college courses paid for by the bank, but after a long day at work, you're not inclined to go to class for another three hours. Besides, you only see your family in the evenings, and you don't want to take time away from them. It doesn't take a college degree to do your job, anyway.

Your monthly personal management interview is coming up with your department head, Hal Byron, and you've decided the time has come to get a few answers. Several things need explaining. Not only haven't you been promoted, but you haven't even received a merit increase for five years. You're not getting any credit for the extra contributions you make with new employees, nor for your steady, reliable work. Could anyone blame you for being a little bitter?

Skill Application

Activities for Communicating Supportively

Suggested Assignments

1. Tape-record an interview with someone such as a coworker, friend, or spouse. Focus on the issues or challenges faced right now by that person. Try to serve as a coach or counselor. Categorize your statements in the interview on the basis of the supportive communication principles in the chapter. (The Rejected Plans case provides an example of such an interview.)

2. Teach someone you know the concepts of supportive communication and supportive listening. Provide your own explanations and illustrations so the person understands what you are talking about. Describe your experience in your journal.

3. Think of an interpersonal problem you share with someone, such as a roommate, parent, friend, or instructor. Discuss the problem with that person, using supportive communication. Write up the experience in as much detail as possible. Concentrate on the extent to which you and the other person used the eight principles of supportive communication. Record and describe areas in which you need to improve.

4. Write two mini-case studies. One should recount an effective coaching or counseling situation. The other should recount an ineffective coaching or counseling situation. The cases should be based on a real event, either from your own personal experience or from the experience of someone you know well. Use all the principles of supportive communication and listening in your cases.

Application Plan and Evaluation

The intent of this exercise is to help you apply this cluster of skills in a real-life, out-of-class setting. Now that you have become familiar with the behavioral guidelines that form the basis of effective skill performance, you will improve most by trying out those guidelines in an everyday context. Unlike a classroom activity, in which feedback is immediate and others can assist you with their evaluations, this skill application activity is one you must accomplish and evaluate on your own. There are two parts to this activity. Part 1 helps prepare you to apply the skill. Part 2 helps you evaluate and improve on your experience. Be sure to write down answers to each item. Don't short-circuit the process by skipping steps.

Part 1. Planning

1. Write down the two or three aspects of this skill that are most important to you. These may be areas of weakness, areas you most want to improve, or areas that are most salient to a problem you face right now. Identify the specific aspects of this skill that you want to apply.

2. Now identify the setting or the situation in which you will apply this skill. Establish a plan for performance by actually writing down a description of the situation. Who else will be involved? When will you do it? Where will it be done?

   Circumstances:

   Who else?

   When?

   Where?

3. Identify the specific behaviors you will engage in to apply this skill. Operationalize your skill performance.

4. What are the indicators of successful performance? How will you know you have been effective? What will indicate you have performed competently?

Part 2. Evaluation

5. After you have completed your implementation, record the results. What happened? How successful were you? What was the effect on others?

6. How can you improve? What modifications can you make next time? What will you do differently in a similar situation in the future?

7. Looking back on your whole skill practice and application experience, what have you learned? What has been surprising? In what ways might this experience help you in the long term?

Gaining Power and Influence

OBJECTIVES

▶ Enhance personal and position power

▶ Use influence to accomplish exceptional work

▶ Neutralize inappropriate influence attempts

skill development

Skill Assessment

Diagnostic Surveys for Gaining Power and Influence

Gaining Power and Influence

Step 1: Before you read this chapter, please respond to the following statements by writing a number from the rating scale below in the left-hand column (Preassessment). Your answers should reflect your attitudes and behavior as they are now, not as you would like them to be. Be honest. This instrument is designed to help you discover your level of competency in gaining power and influence so you can tailor your learning to your specific needs. When you have completed the survey, use the scoring key in Appendix I to identify the skill areas discussed in this chapter that are most important for you to master.

Step 2: After you have completed the reading and the exercises in this chapter and, ideally, as many as you can of the Skill Application assignments at the end of this chapter, cover up your first set of answers. Then respond to the same statements again, this time in the right-hand column (Postassessment). When you have completed the survey, use the scoring key in Appendix I to measure your progress. If your score remains low in specific skill areas, use the behavioral guidelines at the end of the Skill Learning section to guide further practice.

Rating Scale

1	Strongly disagree	4	Slightly agree
2	Disagree	5	Agree
3	Slightly disagree	6	Strongly agree

Assessment

Pre-   Post-   *In a situation where it is important to obtain more power:*

_____ _____ 1. I constantly strive to become highly proficient in my line of work.

_____ _____ 2. I always express friendliness, honesty, and sincerity toward those with whom I work.

_____ _____ 3. I always put forth more effort and take more initiative than expected in my work.

_____ _____ 4. I strongly support organizational ceremonial events and activities.

_____ _____ 5. I form a broad network of relationships with people throughout the organization at all levels.

_____ _____ 6. I find something in which I can specialize that helps meet others' needs.

_____ _____ 7. I consistently send personal notes to others when they accomplish something significant or when I pass along important information to them.

_____ _____ 8. In my work I consistently strive to generate new ideas, initiate new activities, and minimize routine tasks.

_____ _____ 9. I consistently try to find ways to be an external representative for my unit or organization.

_____ _____ 10. I am continually upgrading my skills and knowledge.

_____ _____ 11. I strive very hard to enhance my personal appearance.

_____ _____ 12. I always work harder than most coworkers.

_____ _____ 13. I strongly encourage new members to support important organizational values by both their words and their actions.

_____ _____ 14. I work hard to get access to important information by becoming central in communication networks.

_____ _____ 15. I constantly strive to maintain some part of my work that is unique to me; others don't duplicate it.

_____ _____ 16. I constantly strive to find opportunities to make reports about my work, especially to senior people.

_____ _____ 17. I work hard to maintain variety in the tasks that I do.

_____ _____ 18. I strive hard to keep my work connected to the central mission of the organization.

When trying to influence someone for a specific purpose:

_____ _____ 19. I consistently emphasize reason and factual information.

_____ _____ 20. I feel comfortable using a variety of different influence techniques, matching them to specific circumstances.

_____ _____ 21. I work hard to reward others for agreeing with me, thereby establishing a condition of reciprocity.

_____ _____ 22. I always use a direct, straightforward approach rather than an indirect or manipulative one.

_____ _____ 23. I always avoid using threats or demands to impose my will on others.

When resisting an inappropriate influence attempt directed at me:

_____ _____ 24. I use resources and information I control to equalize demands and threats.

_____ _____ 25. I refuse to bargain with individuals who use high-pressure negotiation tactics.

_____ _____ 26. I explain why I can't comply with reasonable-sounding requests by pointing out how the consequences would affect my responsibilities and obligations.

When trying to influence those above me in the organization:

_____ _____ 27. I help determine the issues to which they pay attention by effectively selling the importance of those issues.

_____ _____ 28. I convince them that the issues on which I want to focus are compatible with the goals and future success of the organization.

_____ _____ 29. I help them solve problems that they didn't expect me to help them solve.

_____ _____ 30. I work as hard to make them look good and be successful as I do working for my own success.

Using Influence Strategies

Indicate, by writing the appropriate number in the blank, how often you use each of the following strategies for getting others to comply with your wishes. Choose from a scale of 1 to 5, with 1 being "rarely," 3 being "sometimes," and 5 being "always." After you have completed the survey, use the scoring key in Appendix I to tabulate your results. Information on these strategies is shown in Tables 7, 8, and 9.

1. "If you don't comply, I'll make you regret it."

2. "If you comply, I will reward you."

3. "These facts demonstrate the merit of my position."

4. "Others in the group have agreed; what is your decision?"

5. "People you value will think better (worse) of you if you do (do not) comply."

6. "The group needs your help, so do it for the good of us all."

7. "I will stop nagging you if you comply."

8. "You owe me compliance because of past favors."

9. "This is what I need; will you help out?"

10. "If you don't act now, you'll lose this opportunity."

11. "I have moderated my initial position; now I expect you to be equally reasonable."

12. "This request is consistent with other decisions you've made."

13. "If you don't agree to help out, the consequences will be harmful to others."

14. "I'm only requesting a small commitment [now]."

15. "Compliance will enable you to reach a personally important objective."

Skill Learning

Building a Strong Power Base and Using Influence Wisely

Newspaper columnist James Kilpatrick once noted, "The name of the game is power. Nothing else. Who has power, how he gets it, how power is delegated, how power is restrained, how power is exercised—these are the questions that absorb us" (Kipnis, 1976, p. 2).

This sentiment was echoed by Mary Cunningham, the highest-ranking female (V. P. for Corporate Public Affairs) at Bendix, who was forced to resign at the age of 28 because of her "inappropriate public behavior" with William Agee, Bendix's chairman. Reflecting on this experience, she commented, "In business school they taught us about cash flow, not about corporate politics; about return on equity, not about egos and pride. My experience taught me that [courses on power] should have been every bit as much a part of the core curriculum as Production, Marketing, and Finance" (*Powerplay,* 1984, p. 283).

Professor John Kotter of Harvard University, who teaches a course on power, agrees with this assessment. "It makes me sick to hear economists tell students that their job is to maximize shareholder profits," he says. "Their job is going to be managing a whole host of constituencies: bosses, underlings, customers, suppliers, unions, you name it. Trying to get cooperation from different constituencies is an infinitely more difficult task than milking your business for money" (*Newsweek,* September 16, 1985, p. 56).

Bogdan J. Dawidowicz, a young senior systems analyst at General Motors, is grateful he took Professor Kotter's course during his Harvard MBA program. He credits it for his ability to handle extremely delicate assignments. For example, when he was told to evaluate product scheduling at a GM plant, he knew that plant management would not take kindly to an outsider disrupting their routine, demanding information, and critiquing their performance. So he called the plant superintendent and enlisted his support. Following an extended discussion, the superintendent took the lead in scheduling appointments with his staff and compil-

ing all the necessary information prior to the visit (*Business Week,* August 26, 1985, p. 54).

A Balanced View of Power

It should come as no surprise that many authorities argue that the effective use of power is the most critical element of management. One such authority, Warren Bennis, seeking the quintessential ingredients of effective leaders, interviewed 90 individuals who had been nominated by peers as the most influential leaders in all walks of our society. Bennis found that these individuals shared one significant characteristic: they made *others* feel powerful. These leaders were powerful because they had learned how to build a strong power base in their organizations or institutions. They were influential because they used their power to help peers and subordinates accomplish exceptional tasks. It requires no particular power, skill, or genius to accomplish the ordinary. But it is difficult to do the truly unusual without political clout (Bennis & Nanus, 1985).

Lack of Power

Unfortunately, for many people power is a "four-letter word" connoting vulgar and distasteful activities that they feel uncomfortable discussing. It conjures up images of vindictive, domineering bosses and manipulative, cunning subordinates (Zaleznik, 1970). It is associated with dirty office politics engaged in by ruthless individuals who use as their handbooks for corporate guerrilla warfare books such as *Winning Through Intimidation* and who subscribe to the philosophy of Heinrich von Treitschke: "Your neighbor, even though he may look upon you as a natural ally against another power which is feared by you both, is always ready, at the first opportunity, as soon as it can be done with safety, to better himself at your expense. . . . Whoever fails to increase his power, must decrease it, if others increase theirs" (Korda, 1975, p. 4).

Those with a distaste for power argue that teaching managers and prospective managers how to increase their power is tantamount to sanctioning the use of primitive forms of domination. They support this argument by noting the nasty political fight between Lewis Glucksman and Peter Peterson for control of Lehman Brothers that cost Lehman its independence, the conflict between cofounders Steven Jobs and John Sculley that turned Apple Computer into a battleground, and the firing of Frank Biondi, the president of Viacom, by its power-hungry chairperson Sumner Redstone.

This, however, is a narrow view of power. Robert Dilenschneider, president and CEO of a leading public relations firm, states: "The use of influence is itself not negative. It can often lead to a great good. Like any powerful force—from potent medicine to nuclear power—it is the morality with which influence is used that makes all the difference" (Dilenschneider, 1990, p. xviii). Power need not be associated with aggression, brute force, craftiness, or deceit. Power can also be viewed as a sign of personal efficacy. It is the ability to mobilize resources to accomplish productive work. People with power shape their environment, whereas the powerless are molded by theirs. Rollo May, in *Power and Innocence* (1972), suggests that those who are unwilling to exercise power and influence are condemned to experience unhappiness throughout their lives.

There is nothing more demoralizing than feeling you have a creative new idea or a unique insight into a significant organizational problem and then come face to face with your organizational impotence. This face of power is seen by many young college graduates, who annually flood the corporate job market. They are energetic, optimistic, and supremely confident that their "awesome" ability, state-of-the-art training, and indefatigable energy will rocket them up the corporate ladder. However, many soon become discouraged and embittered. They blame "the old guard" for protecting their turf and not being open to new ideas. Their feelings of frustration prompt many to look for greener pastures of opportunity in other companies—only to be confronted anew with rejection and failure. One such "victim" stated dejectedly, "Hell is knowing you have a better solution than someone else but not being able to get the votes."

These individuals learn quickly that only the naive believe that the best recommendation always gets selected, the most capable individual always gets the promotion, and the deserving unit gets its fair share of the budget. These are political decisions heavily influenced by the interests of the powerful.

Astute managers understand that in the long run no one benefits from lopsided distributions of power. One seasoned veteran of organizational power games summarized his experience: "Powerless members of an organization either get angry and try to tear down the system, or they become apathetic and withdraw. Either way, everyone loses."

Rosabeth Kanter (1979) has pointed out that powerful managers not only can accomplish more personally, but can also pass on more information and make more resources available to subordinates. For this reason, people tend to prefer bosses with "clout." Subordinates tend to feel that they have higher status in an organization and their morale is higher when they perceive that their boss has considerable upward influence. In contrast, Kanter argues, powerlessness tends to foster bossiness, rather than true leadership. "In large organizations, at least," she notes, "it is powerlessness that often creates ineffective, desultory management and petty, dictatorial, rules-minded managerial styles" (p. 65).

Kanter (1979) has identified several indicators of a manager's upward and outward power in an organization. These are shown in Table 1. In some respects, these serve as a set of behavioral objectives for our discussion of power and influence.

Powerful managers can
- intercede favorably on behalf of someone in trouble.
- get a desirable placement for a talented subordinate.
- get approval for expenditures beyond the budget.
- get items on and off the agenda at policy meetings.
- get fast access to top decision makers.
- maintain regular, frequent contact with top decision makers.
- acquire early information about decisions and policy shifts.

Table 1 Indicators of a Manager's Upward and Outward Power
Source: Kanter, 1979.

Abuse of Power

But what about Lord Acton's well-known dictum, "Power corrupts, and absolute power corrupts absolutely"? Hardly a week goes by that new evidence of this seemingly ageless observation isn't reflected in news headlines. Doesn't that suggest that effective managers should avoid power because "abuse of office," with a likely fall from power, will inevitably follow?

This certainly appears to be an ageless lesson of history. In the Greek plays of Sophocles, for instance, the viewer is confronted with the image of great and powerful rulers transformed by their prior success so that they are filled with a sense of their own worth and importance—with *hubris*—which causes them to be impatient of the advice of others and unwilling to listen to opinions different from their own. Yet in the end they are destroyed by events that they discover, to their anguish, they cannot control. Oedipus is destroyed soon after the crowds say (and he believes) that "he is almost like a God"; King Creon, at the zenith of his political and military power, is brought down as a result of his unjust and unfeeling belief in the infallibility of his judgments.

Perhaps the most blatant modern-day example of such hubris is the "slash and burn" management style of Al Dunlap at Scott Paper and Sunbeam Electric. He takes pride in being responsible for thousands of employees losing their jobs while he takes home multimillion dollar bonuses (De George, 1996). Another example is Archer Daniels Midland chairperson and CEO Dwayne Andreas, who was fined a record $100 million for price fixing citric acid and lysine. His act of hubris may shake the foundation of this family dynasty (Greenwald, 1996). Similarly, the blind ambition of Bausch and Lomb chairperson and CEO Daniel Gill resulted in some questionable ethics in the sales of contact lenses to distributors. He no longer leads Bausch and Lomb (Moremont, 1995).

Sophocles warns us never to be envious of the powerful until we see the nature of their endings. Too often arrogance, bred of power, finally causes its own defeat and unhappy ending (Kipnis, 1976, p. 169). Support for the modern-day relevance of this warning is reflected in the results of a study of both successful and failed corporate executives (McCall & Lombardo, 1983). Scholars at the Center for Creative Leadership identified approximately 20 executives who had risen to the top of their firms and matched them with a sim-

- Insensitive to others; abrasive and intimidating
- Cold, aloof, and arrogant
- Betraying others' trust
- Overly ambitious; playing politics and always trying to move up
- Unable to delegate to others or to build a team
- Overdependent on others (e.g., a mentor)

Table 2 Characteristics That Derail Managers' Careers
Source: McCall & Lombardo, 1983.

ilar group of 20 executives who had failed to reach their career aspirations. Earlier, both groups had entered their respective organizations with equal promise. There were no noticeable differences in their preparation, expertise, education, and so forth. However, over time, the second group's careers had become "derailed" by the personal inadequacies shown in Table 2.

It is sobering to note how many of these problems relate to the ineffective use of power in interpersonal relationships. In general, this group tends to support Lord Acton's dictum as well as the warnings of Sophocles. They were given a little authority, and they failed the test of worthy stewardship.

Evolving Definition of Power

Having established the importance of building a strong base of power, let us take a step back and look at what we mean when we talk of power. Traditionally power has been defined as having control over the behavior of others, as bosses have control over their subordinates or parents have control over their children. However, in today's business world, the definition of power is changing. Several trends in organizations are shifting the definition of power from "having authority over others" to "being able to get things done."

- Organizations are becoming less hierarchical, or flatter, as they downsize layers of management (especially middle managers) and as they outsource work that can be done more cheaply by someone else. Rather than adding to their full-time employment ranks, many organizations are choosing to grow through the use of temporary and part-time workers who can more easily be let go during tough economic times. These leaner organizations are staffed by fewer managers who must learn to yield influence to lower-level employees in order to get the work of the organization done (Stewart, 1992).

▶ Information technology such as computers are helping to decentralize the flow of information to lower levels of the organizational hierarchy. This not only gives lower-level employees more influence, but also increases their flexibility. Today, more and more workers are telecommuting, or working out of their homes but staying linked to the organization through the use of computers, faxes, and phones. When employees are off-site, managers must cede more decision-making control and discretion to them.

▶ Traditional boundaries within and between organizations are becoming blurred. The "boundaryless" organization is becoming in vogue as we see evidence of the virtual organization composed of a network of different entities (Tully, 1993). Such an organization will exist only for the life of a project (say, a motion picture) and then disband

upon its completion. These structural changes shift the nature of authority relationships as well.

Each of these changes is contributing to the evolution of the role of the typical manager from director to coach and mentor. Under these conditions, power is likely to come less from someone's formal position in the organization than from one's ability to perform. The conditions make the notion of empowerment particularly important for your effectiveness in today's organizations.

Empowerment

Like the 90 successful leaders interviewed by Warren Bennis, the 20 executives who did not derail used their power to empower others and accomplish exceptional organizational objectives. As they applied their influence in positive ways, they gained more power and formal organizational authority, creating a positive, upward spiral that carried them up the organizational career ladder.

In this chapter, we focus on how managers themselves can gain and use power effectively. In Chapter 8, on the other hand, we will focus on the skill of em-

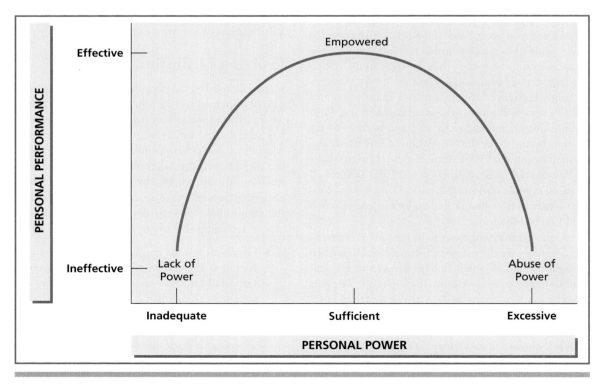

Figure 1   Personal Power: Stepping-Stone or Stumbling Block

powerment and provide guidelines that will enable managers to help others gain and use power.

The relationship between power and personal effectiveness we have described is depicted in Figure 1. Both lack of power and the abuse of power are equally debilitating and counterproductive. In contrast, empowerment uses sufficient amounts of personal power to achieve high levels of effectiveness.

The purpose of this chapter is to help managers "stay on top of the power curve," as represented by the indicators of organizational power reported by Kanter in Table 1. This is accomplished with the aid of two specific management skills:

▶ gaining power (overcoming feelings of powerlessness)

▶ converting power effectively into interpersonal influence in ways that avoid the abuse of power

Strategies for Gaining Organizational Power

Two basic factors determine a person's power in an organization: personal attributes and position characteristics. Naturally, the importance of each factor varies depending on the organizational context. For example, position title is extremely important in a strong hierarchical system, such as the military or civil service. The saying "Rank has its privileges" illustrates the fact that in these organizations rewards are allocated more on the basis of position title than personal performance. In contrast, in a small business where the organization's survival depends on good customer relations, imaginative ideas for new products, and favorable financial agreements with banks, personal characteristics are often the predominant source of power. The work of each employee is highly visible and the unique contribution of the aggressive salesperson or the problem-solving engineer will likely be recognized and rewarded. This may be why we see more and more MBAs choosing to forego employment with Blue Chip firms for smaller entrepreneurial ventures (Labich, 1995).

There are differences of opinion among organizational scholars regarding the relative importance of these two sources of power: *who* you are versus *where* you are (Pfeffer, 1981, 1992; Kanter, 1979; Kotter, 1977). We recommend a balanced view. During the course of their careers, individuals find themselves in organizational sit-

uations that are more or less responsive to each source of power. However, both sources generally must be developed if one is to build a strong power base. A person occupying a dominant position in an organization who doesn't have the personal skills necessary to capitalize on this strategic advantage will not realize the full potential for power inherent in that position. Conversely, an individual who has the requisite attributes to be a powerful, persuasive powerholder, but is in an isolated position doing meaningless work, is also not likely to realize his or her full potential. Therefore, in our discussions of power we will argue that managers seeking influence should try to enhance both their personal attributes and the characteristics of their position.

Sources of Personal Power

Four personal characteristics are important sources of power. As Table 3 shows, these are *expertise, personal attraction, effort,* and *legitimacy.* Expertise reflects knowledge and capabilities; personal attraction involves affective appeal; effort suggests personal commitment and motivation; and legitimacy conveys credibility.

Expertise

Expertise is an important source of power in an era of technological sophistication. It can result from formal training and education or from on-the-job experience. Expertise is especially salient in business organizations because of their preference for a highly rationalized decision-making process (Pfeffer, 1977). In an environment in which choices are supposed to be made by objectively considering information supporting each alternative, a person possessing knowledge readily accrues

CHARACTERISTIC	DESCRIPTION
Expertise	Task-relevant knowledge or experience
Personal attraction	Desirable characteristics associated with friendship
Effort	Higher-than-expected commitment of time
Legitimacy	Behavior consistent with key organizational values

Table 3   Determinants of Personal Power

power. This can become problematic when subordinates have more expertise than their bosses. The skillful subordinate makes knowledge available to the superior in a manner that does not threaten the boss's right to make the final decision but at the same time reinforces the subordinate's position as an expert.

Expertise provides a strong base of power in large, technologically sophisticated, rapidly changing organizations. In this environment, the technical specialist is especially powerful because top management is so far removed from the core work activities of the organization. Management is often less aware of new breakthroughs in basic research, the latest production innovations introduced by competitors, or the changing interests of the workforce. Consequently, responsibility for monitoring these areas is typically delegated to staff specialists, who develop a monopoly on knowledge in their field. Staff specialists can include accountants, human resource administrators, computer consultants, and legal staff. Research and Development professionals may also possess expert power. The proverbial executive secretary who has outlasted four presidents and is the only one in the company who knows where important documents have been filed and how much has actually been spent in the president's expense budget is in a key role to gain influence over others.

That staff specialists gain power by virtue of their expertise points out the importance of examining both position and personal sources of power. If you examined only the position-power of staff specialists, you might conclude that they have very little power. Their role in the organization is not very visible, compared to line management; their jobs are often routine; and their tasks, by themselves, are generally not linked to the most central objectives and concerns of the firm. However, a staff specialist can compensate for weak position-power by developing expertise in a particular aspect of organizational life. This might involve a new accounting system, tax loopholes, safety and pollution regulations, or recent legal precedents in acquisitions.

There is, however, a Catch-22 associated with expert power. Becoming an expert on a subject typically requires considerable time and effort. As a result, it is easy to become typecast as a specialist in one field. If you are interested in moving up in the general management hierarchy, the label of specialist is a hindrance. The increasing boundarylessness of today's organizations may especially devalue over-specialization. Given the dynamic environment facing today's organizations,

over-specialization may be a recipe for obsolescence. Aspiring young managers must be careful not to limit advancement opportunities by focusing their attention on very narrow aspects of a business's activities. This is tempting for individuals who are overly anxious to establish a power base. There are always small niches in an organization to which power-hungry novices can quickly lay claim. Only when they have fallen into the specialist trap do they recognize the value of building a broad base of knowledge about a wide variety of organizational activities to enhance their long-term attractiveness for promotion.

Personal Attraction

Personal attraction is manifested in a variety of ways: "When she makes a presentation in a management meeting, her presence is so powerful any message sounds good"; "His magnetic personality enables him to attract the most qualified and dedicated people to his department—everyone wants to work for him." There are basically three sources of personal attraction: agreeable behavior, impression management, and attractive physical appearance.

Social psychologists who have done research on interpersonal attraction have isolated several critical behaviors that determine what they call "likability." These behaviors are the kind one would normally associate with friendship. Indeed, much of this research has been motivated by a desire to understand the essential ingredients of friendships. Studies of this type have identified several major factors that foster interpersonal attraction. Some of these are shown in Table 4 (Canfield & LaGaipa, 1970).

How can we relate this information on friendship to the supposedly hard-nosed world of management? Does this imply that you must become good friends with your coworkers, subordinates, or boss? Not necessarily. Very often, people choose to work with others because of their demonstrated expertise, even when they know they will have difficulty getting along with them. Furthermore, it is often inappropriate to establish a close friendship with someone in your office. Thus, one need not become friends with everyone at work, but people who possess personality characteristics that are attractive to their coworkers (the kind that, if circumstances permitted, would likely lead to a strong friendship) will likely feel empowered (Mechanic, 1962).

We like people when we have reason to believe
they will

• support an open, honest, and loyal relationship.
• foster intimacy by being emotionally accessible.
• provide unconditional, positive regard and
  acceptance.
• endure some sacrifices if the relationship should
  demand them.
• provide social reinforcement in the form of
  sympathy or empathy.
• engage in the social exchanges necessary to sustain
  a relationship.

Table 4   Characteristics of Likable People
Source: Adapted from Canfield & LaGaipa, 1970.

This proposition has been corroborated by an impressive amount of evidence. For example, individuals making persuasive arguments are more likely to be effective if they are liked by their audience. This stems from the fact that likable individuals are viewed as more trustworthy and impartial than disliked individuals. Subordinates who are liked by their supervisor also tend to be given the benefit of the doubt in performance appraisals. This benevolent orientation is also manifest in the fact that bosses use rewards, rather than coercion, to influence subordinates they like (Tedeschi, 1974).

We don't want to overemphasize this point, nor do we mean to suggest that "good guys" always win, but there is an impressive amount of evidence that individuals with agreeable personalities become more influential than those with disagreeable personalities. Their arguments are given more credence, their influence attempts are less likely to evoke resistance, and coworkers seem less threatened if they are promoted. In general, given a strong cultural distrust of individuals with power, leaders with likable personalities tend to put others at ease and, in so doing, gain greater trust and influence.

The third basis for interpersonal attraction—physical appearance—operates independently of personality, or even behavior. Studies have shown that people judged to have an attractive appearance are also judged to have socially desirable personality characteristics and to lead highly successful lives. It is further assumed that they hold prestigious jobs and are highly successful marriage partners and parents. In addition, attractive

individuals are judged to be masters of their own fate—pursuing their own goals, imbued with a sense of mission—rather than being buffeted by environmental forces (Dion, Bersheid, & Walster, 1972). In general, it appears that people assume attractive individuals are also virtuous and efficacious.

There is considerable evidence that these are not merely fanciful attributions. In some respects, attractive people are more successful. A 1993 Associated Press survey found that, on the average, physically attractive people are paid more than their counterparts in organizations. Attractive students are assumed by teachers to be intelligent and disinclined to get into mischief. In a work setting, the written work of attractive people is more likely to be judged of high quality, and attractive people are more likely to receive high performance appraisals from their supervisors than are other people (Bersheid & Walster, 1974; Ross & Ferris, 1981).

Thus far, researchers have been unable to validate the attributed connection between physical attractiveness and socially desirable personality characteristics. However, there is some indirect evidence for this. It has been demonstrated that an important source of unpleasant social behavior is low self-esteem. When people who have been judged attractive or unattractive are asked to describe themselves, attractiveness tends to be highly correlated with self-esteem. Attractive people are more likely to feel good about themselves and to have high self-confidence than unattractive people (Keats & Davis, 1970).

Findings on personal attraction are obviously the most difficult to transform into concrete suggestions for personal development. There is not much one can do as an adult to transform radically one's basic appearance. However, this information is still highly relevant for managers for two reasons. First, one can make modest changes to enhance one's attractiveness by being sensitive to principles of good grooming, dress, and posture. At an extreme, more and more people are resorting to plastic surgery and other artificial forms of physical enhancement to boost their self-confidence (Berton, 1997; Fornham, 1996). One can also emphasize those aspects of one's personality that are consistent with the social norms prevalent in a given organizational context. Second, one can become more sensitive to the way others form impressions and make evaluations. If you suspect you do not measure up very well in this category, despite your best efforts at "accentuating the positive," it is a good idea to compensate by emphasizing other sources of power. If, indeed, self-confidence is the primary mechanism for transforming personal attractiveness into organizational power, then other personal and positional characteristics can contribute in a similar manner to one's self-confidence.

Effort

In a seminal article entitled "Sources of Power of Lower Participants," David Mechanic (1962) described several ways members of organizations can obtain more power than is warranted by their position in the hierarchy. One strategy he discussed is based on the premise that because senior members of an organization are unable to attend to all their important business, they are forced to rely on junior members to perform many tasks critical to the goals of the organization. The senior officers thus become highly dependent on their subordinates. If subordinates do not perform well, it reflects poorly on their boss's judgment and ability to supervise. As a result, subordinates are in a position to increase their power by working hard on these vital assignments, thereby gaining favor with their supervisors.

In addition to creating a sense of personal obligation, a high level of effort can enhance other personal characteristics. For example, individuals who work hard at a task tend to increase their knowledge of the subject. Therefore, they are more likely to be sought out for their advice on that topic. They are also more apt to gather information that is relevant to other members of the organization. This information often can be the key to reducing another person's uncertainty.

The efficacy of personal effort is borne out in the career of Gordon McGovern, CEO of Campbell Soup and erstwhile President of Pepperidge Farms. During the 1960s, when he was a young executive rising through the ranks at Pepperidge Farms, McGovern liked to get up before dawn and hop aboard one of the company's bread delivery trucks. "I'd talk to the distributors and to the store managers to see what people were buying," he recalls. In addition, as a trainee, he learned how to mix bread in 10-quart bowls and knead it by hand. This extra effort gave McGovern personal knowledge of the production process, the distribution system, and customers' preferences (Miller, 1985). Similarly, Herb Kelleher, CEO of Southwest Airlines, is known for his Management By Walking Around. He frequently serves customers on flights and visits baggage handlers and gate agents to listen to their concerns.

A high level of personal effort can also result in increased responsibility and opportunity through a process known as *cognitive dissonance reduction*. A fundamental principle of psychology is that individuals strive to reduce inconsistencies between their own personal beliefs and personal behavior and between their expectations of others and the behavior of others. Applied to our discussion of effort, this principle has an important implication. When individuals exert more effort to perform their jobs than is expected, according to organizational policy or office norms, an inconsistency exists. Since the person's rewards are based on completion of the amount of work normally expected, the inconsistency can be eliminated only by reduced effort or increased responsibility. While it is quite common for "rate-busters" in blue-collar jobs to be informed by their coworkers that their extra effort is unacceptable because it makes the rest of the group look bad, this approach to dissonance reduction is less common in managerial ranks. At that level, extraordinary effort is viewed as a sign of commitment and dedication and should be encouraged and rewarded. This is reflected in the increasing number of evening and weekend hours that employees are expected to put into their jobs. This has profound effects on an employee's ability to maintain a normal family life (Morris, 1997). Extraordinary effort by a manager is likely to be interpreted positively if it is focused on enhancing the organization's goals rather than on personal self-aggrandizement. Power accrues, in other words, when individuals are viewed as contributors to the good of the group. On the other hand, if their efforts are seen as costly to others personally, or inimical to the general welfare of the group, dissonance occurs, which leads to resistance.

Legitimacy

Values play an important role in organizations. They confer legitimacy and guide the behavior of the members who adhere to them. Organizational leaders are vigilant in defending core organizational values and in socializing newcomers to proper modes of thinking and acting. Often, new members or outsiders fail to understand the critical role an organization's culture plays in articulating, and defending, its raison d'être. Conventional thinking may appear peculiar or arbitrary until it is examined from both an historical and a strategic perspective.

Managers understand that a precondition for their organization's becoming a market leader is to be perceived as a unique player in the market (e.g., not just another computer company). They strive to create a distinctiveness that merits attention from the financial community, potential employees, and customers. This may involve placing a premium on quality, economy, value, service, loyalty to employees, or civic involvement. This uniqueness is the basis for internal organizational pride and external projections of excellence. It is often referred to as the organization's *distinctive competence* or *core competency.*

This perspective is initially articulated as the vision of a dominant leader (often the founder) and institutionalized as the organization's culture (Schein, 1991; Peters, 1978; Deal & Kennedy, 1982). It typically focuses on the "hows" and "whys" of doing business the "right" way. Values are proclaimed via the insistent message of a strong leader. For example, Harold Geneen at ITT stressed, "Search for the unshakable facts"; Tom Jones at Northrop emphasized, "Everybody at Northrop is in marketing"; John DeButts at AT&T drummed into employees, "The system is the solution"; Ed Rust at State Farm frequently asked colleagues, "How would a good neighbor handle this?"

Actions that are congruent with the prevailing value system are deemed credible, or legitimate, by other organizational members. They are taken for granted, rather than challenged or scrutinized. Therefore, legitimacy increases acceptance, and acceptance is a key to personal influence.

New members of an organization are taught what is acceptable behavior through stories (the engineer who worked for 72 hours straight to save a project), rites (graduation or promotion ceremonies), and symbols (uniforms, no private offices for managers). The savvy newcomer looks beyond formal position statements, probing for answers to questions such as "What are the organization's 'sacred cows'?" "What's the quickest way to get into trouble?" "What is the source of organizational pride?" "Who are the corporate heroes?" "What are the revered traditions?"

Many required organizational practices make sense only when viewed as symbolic support for fundamental values. For example, a large insurance firm stipulates that no one can be promoted above a certain level in any department unless he or she has completed the requirements for insurance industry professional certification (i.e., Certified Life Underwriter). Young employees in data processing, accounting, or personnel who chafe under the edict to take classes on the details of the insurance business miss the symbolic meaning of this requirement. The founders of the firm felt that the organization's key to success was a work force deeply committed to delivering the best product and backing it with the best service. They further believed that the natural tendency for some individuals to identify more closely with their department's interests than with the insurance business undermined this corporate objective. They feared organizational factions would lose sight of the overarching goal. Therefore, commitment to taking insurance courses has become synonymous with commitment to the organization's mission, and organizational commitment is a litmus test for organizational advancement.

This doesn't mean that a nonconformist can't get ahead in the corporate world. It simply suggests that he or she will be held to a higher standard in terms of other sources of personal power, such as expertise and effort. A conversation during a promotion review meeting in a major corporation reflects this attitude: "I don't trust the SOB, but he is so blasted smart and he works so darn hard, we have no choice but to promote him."

Such an outcome appears less sinister and more rational when one considers that organizations abhor uncertainty, both in their environment and internally. Espoused values and beliefs help reduce uncertainty. They provide a framework for interpreting the behavior of others, communicate a consistent set of priorities, and increase the efficiency of the interpersonal transactions. Individuals who fail to conform with these organizational expectations create "noise" in the system. Their inconsistency makes communication and interaction problematic, because, in common parlance, colleagues "don't know where they're coming from." Consequently, these individuals tend to become bypassed and isolated. In fact, Jack Welch, CEO of General Electric, has proclaimed that managers at GE who "make their numbers" but who do not espouse the value system of GE will not be promoted as they have been in the past.

Many organizations reward team players who fit in without attracting unusual attention. For example, Morgan Stanley, a large financial institution, screens out applicants who appear highly competitive and individualistic. Then they rotate new employees through several units during a probation period so they can be scrutinized by a variety of managers. In addition, major decisions are made by teams, and rewards are influenced by individual contributions to team accomplishments. The purpose of this intense socialization process is to bond new members to the organization's core values of cooperation and loyalty.

Before leaving the subject of organizational culture and personal legitimacy, it is important to note that the discussion so far has been descriptive rather than normative. That is, we have described what it takes to become empowered in an organization, especially one with strong cultural values. That doesn't mean that strict conformity is morally right or that it is necessarily in the best long-term interests of the firm. In fact, in the chapter entitled "Managing Conflict" we will present evidence that highly inbred, rigid companies have a high rate of failure. In the introductory chapter we stressed the paradoxical nature of management. This is one of those paradoxes (Pascale, 1985). Successful organizations have members who are both capable of gaining power by fitting in and of using that power to challenge the prevailing belief system that, in some sense, has been responsible for their gaining power. Unchallenged organizational beliefs often interfere with a company's necessary adaptation to changing competitive and regulatory conditions. However, challenges are most successful when mounted by members whose commitment to the organization has been the most loyal. "Paying your dues" creates legitimacy, and legitimacy is a prerequisite for effective criticism.

Sources of Position Power

Not all power stems from personal characteristics. In addition, the nature of one's position and task assign-

ments play an important role. Five important characteristics of a position account for its power potential: **centrality, criticality, flexibility, visibility,** and **relevance.** These are shown in Table 5.

Centrality and Criticality

One of the most important ways of gaining power in an organization is by establishing a broad network of task and interpersonal relationships (Pfeffer, 1992). Networks are critical to effective performance for one compelling reason: Except for routine jobs, no one has all the necessary information and resources to accomplish what's expected of him or her. Indeed, one investigation of the determinants of effective management performance concluded that a key factor distinguishing high and low performers was the ability to establish informal relationships via networks. Isolates in informal networks were unable to gather the information, resource commitments, and personal support necessary to accomplish unusual, important tasks (Kaplan & Mazique, 1983). On the other hand, those who have extensive diverse social networks in their work earn higher salaries and are more successful than those with extensive but narrow contact with others (Pfeffer & Konrad, 1991).

Power is accrued via horizontal and vertical network relationships by virtue of one's location and function in the network. Horizontal networks link positions with similar levels of authority, whereas vertical networks include positions with different levels of authority. The more central a position is to the flow of information throughout a network, and the more critical the function is to the performance of others in a network, the more power will be accrued. This view of organizational power is referred to as "strategic contingencies" (Hickson, Hinings, Lee, Schneck, & Pennings, 1971). It argues that the reason for the uneven distribution of

CHARACTERISTIC	DESCRIPTION
Centrality	Access to information in a communication network
Criticality	Impact on tasks performed in a work flow
Flexibility	Amount of discretion vested in a position
Visibility	Degree to which task performance is seen by influential people in the organization
Relevance	Alignment of assigned tasks and organizational priorities

Table 5 Determinants of Position Power

power in organizations is that units and positions differ in their ability to control strategic contingencies (e.g., the securing of information, expertise, financing) critical to the effective performance of others. Few important activities occur in isolation; what happens in one unit affects another. It follows that the more pervasive the effect of a position's activities throughout the organization, the greater is its power base.

Increasing the power of a position by increasing its centrality in a communication network and its criticality (i.e., uniqueness) in a work-flow system represents a very different approach from conventional strategies. Typically, young aspiring members of an organization think only in terms of increasing their power by moving up the organizational career ladder. They mistakenly assume that power is the exclusive right of hierarchical position. If they are not promoted as fast as they'd like, they assume their ability to accomplish the unusual is thereby curtailed. Inexperienced, ineffective organizational members grumble about not having enough formal power to get work done, and they covet the influence wielded on higher levels. In contrast, savvy organizational members realize that informal network power is available to individuals at all levels. Furthermore, they understand that informal personal power generally precedes, rather than follows from, formal organizational power. A promotion is simply a formal recognition by senior management that an individual has demonstrated the ability to get work done using informal networks.

The merits of building a horizontal power base became clear to Alan Brewer, a business manager in the medical supplies division of Hewlett-Packard (HP) when his initiatives were blocked by senior managers. He suggested to a manager in the medical instruments division that the reusable electrodes on HP electrocardiograph machines be replaced with disposable electrodes, which were becoming much more popular. The reply was, "It's too expensive to make the switch." Alan had done enough research to know this wasn't true. Further investigation revealed the real problem. The man who had helped develop the disposable electrodes was abrasive, and he had alienated members of the instruments division. Now, members were unwilling to take any action that would make this person look good.

Alan overcame this problem by asking people in his division to develop a new electrode—one that would not be burdened by association with an unpopular executive. During the development stage, he actively served as a mediator, keeping colleagues in other divisions abreast of his progress. Several suggestions for enhancements were incorporated during this phase. After building a broad base of support for the new product throughout the organization, he had no difficulty getting the second request approved (*Newsweek,* September 16, 1985, p. 56).

The twin concepts of network centrality and criticality suggest some specific guidelines for expanding your power base horizontally.

First, become a central actor in the broadest possible communication network. One of the biggest mistakes individuals make at the outset of their management careers is to become isolated. Such people assume that getting ahead in their department is sufficient for getting ahead in the organization. As a result, they concentrate all their attention on building strong relations with their immediate coworkers. If you reconsider organizations in terms of horizontal structures, you will see how isolated a communication network in a single department is. It is important to become a central actor in the organization's communication network, not just the department's. This can be done by going to lunch with people in other departments, reading the annual reports of all the divisions, volunteering for interdepartmental task forces, and seeking out boundary-spanning positions that require you to work with other departments.

Second, increase the criticality of your task assignments. A simple diagnostic question for determining the criticality of your position responsibilities is, "If I were absent for a week, how much of a problem would that create for the organization?" The answer to this question depends on several factors: (1) how dependent others are on the work performed by your position; (2) the level of technical skills and specialized knowledge required to perform your position; and (3) the number of other individuals performing essentially the same tasks. Following this logic, general-purpose positions performed by several individuals have less power than those with exclusive responsibility for specific, highly technical, functions. For example, secretaries in a steno pool have less power than do private secretaries, as evidenced by the fact that absences in a steno pool are easily covered, whereas a private secretary's prolonged illness can cause havoc. The criticality of a position can be increased by taking on functions essential for the performance of other activities, by reducing redundancy through combining several positions, or by increasing the level of technical knowledge required to perform assigned tasks.

In addition to the location of a position in the organization's communication network and work-flow structure, other characteristics of a position influence the amount of power its occupant is likely to garner. In her research on the determinants of power in business organizations, Kanter (1979) identified three additional critical characteristics: flexibility, visibility, and relevance.

Flexibility

A critical requirement for building a power base is flexibility, or discretion—that is, freedom to exercise one's judgment. A person who has no latitude to improvise, to innovate, or to demonstrate initiative, will find it extremely difficult to become powerful (except in unusual situations in which meticulous obedience to rules disrupts the system, as in the case of air traffic controllers' slowdowns). Power can be lost because circumstances often change more readily than people or their jobs can change to keep up with the new times (Pfeffer, 1992). A flexible position has few rules or established routines governing how work should be done. In addition, when a manager needs to make a nonroutine decision, it is not necessary to seek a senior manager's approval. Flexibility tends to be associated with certain types of work assignments, particularly tasks that are high in variety and novelty (Hinings, Hickson, Pennings, & Schneck, 1974). People in such positions are assigned several types of activities, each of which requires the use of considerable judgment. The more routine the work and the fewer the tasks assigned a person, the easier it is to preprogram the job to eliminate the need for discretion.

Flexibility is also correlated with the life cycle of a position. New tasks are much more difficult to routinize than old ones. Similarly, the number of rules governing a position tends to be positively correlated with the number of individuals who have previously occupied it. Since the intention of rules is to expose exceptions, the longer a position has been in existence, the more likely it is that exceptions have been discovered.

The same logic applies to the life cycle of a decision-making process. The longer a group has been meeting to discuss an issue, the more difficult it is to have any significant amount of influence over its deliberations, unless the decision-making process becomes hopelessly stalemated. The critical decisions about how discussions will be conducted, what evidence should be examined, and which alternatives are germane are all made early in a group's history. To make a difference, therefore, it is important to be a participant from the beginning.

One indication of the amount of flexibility inherent in a position is the reward system governing it. If people occupying a position are rewarded for being reliable and predictable, that suggests the organization will penalize people who use discretion. On the other hand, if people are rewarded for unusual performance and innovation, discretion is encouraged. A "reliable performance" reward system uses as its performance criterion conformity to a set of prescribed means for performing a task, such as a detailed procedure for assembling an electronic circuit. In contrast, an "unusual performance" reward system eschews consistency in favor of initiative. For example, a company may teach salespeople how to close a deal but at the same time encourage them to figure out better ways to do the task. Individuals with a high need for power should avoid a job that is governed by the reliable performance criterion, no matter how attractive it might appear in other aspects, because it will strip them of a necessary prerequisite of power.

Visibility

A sage corporate executive once counseled a young, aspiring MBA, "The key formula for promotion is excellent performance multiplied by visibility." Obviously, a highly visible, poor performance will not lead to promotion, but the real message of this advice is that an excellent, but obscure, performance won't either. This advice is supported by a Chicago consultant, Karolus Smejda, who is frequently brought into organizations to coach "competent but invisible" young managers. "The boss will say to me, 'Karolus, this guy is a wonderful worker, but he's just not visible enough.' My job is to make that person aware of the need to become well connected," he says (*Newsweek,* September 16, 1985, p. 56).

One measure of visibility is the number of people with whom you normally interact in your organization. This helps explain why *people-oriented* positions tend to be more powerful than *task-oriented* positions. Of course, contacts with some members of an organization are more important than with others. It is critical that a position foster frequent contact with senior officials. This can be accomplished through participation in company or outside programs, meetings, and conferences. Many a young career has been secured by a strong presentation at a trade association convention or board meeting.

Recognizing this point, an enterprising junior executive in a large Chicago conglomerate seized on a chance occurrence to impress the chairman of the board. By a strange set of circumstances, the young executive was asked to fill in for the secretary of the board of directors and take notes at a stockholders' meeting. Making sure that he arrived early, he greeted every person who entered the boardroom and then introduced that person to every other member in the room. The fact that this young man was able to put everyone at ease (not to mention remember the names of a large number of strangers) so impressed the chairman that he subsequently provided several opportunities for him to advance rapidly in the organization.

This example points out an important distinction between centrality and visibility. The purpose of becoming central in a broad communication network is to tap into a rich flow of information so you can satisfy the information needs of others. In contrast, from the point of view of visibility, being in a position that allows you to interact with a large number of influential people increases your power by making your accomplishments more evident to the people who allocate resources, such as desirable assignments and promotions.

The value of visibility is clearly demonstrated in the position of an executive secretary. For example, Jean C. Jones, executive secretary to the Chairman of Intel Corporation, decided each day how many of the 125 telephone calls would gain Gordon Moore's ear and how much of the 30-inch stack of mail he would see. The power inherent in this gatekeeping role is also reflected in the fact that Kathleen Kallmer parlayed her job as executive secretary to Beatrice Company's Chairman James L. Dutt into an assistant vice-presidency in four years (*Business Week,* April 26, 1986, p. 84).

By far, the best way to gain visibility is by means of direct contact, and face-to-face communication is the most influential means to accomplish this. Inexperienced managers often assume that credit for writing an excellent report automatically goes to the author. Unfortunately for good writers, this is not always the case. If one member of a group composes a very good report and another member gives a very good presentation of the report to an executive committee, the presenter will likely receive a disproportionately large share of the credit for the work. Busy executives tend to be more impressed by what they see in a meeting than by what they read in their offices. They have fewer distractions in meetings (no stacks of other reading material or interruptions by phone calls), and a slightly positive personal evaluation of a presentation can be transformed into a very strong positive evaluation by the approving nods and smiles of other executives in the meeting.

Another important opportunity for gaining visibility is participation in problem-solving task forces. Being asked to serve in this capacity conveys to others that you have valuable expertise. More importantly, if the task force's report is received well by senior officials, your name will be associated with the group responsible for the "breakthrough." Using the language of the strategic contingencies model, problem solvers gain power by helping others cope with uncertainty. For example, those heads of government whose accomplishments stand out dramatically in a historical perspective are those who proposed remedies during major crises. Consider that Winston Churchill is credited with helping Britain survive World War II. On the smaller scale of a business firm, this truism is equally reliable. The visibility of a person's performance is directly proportional to the significance of the tasks performed and the popularity of the causes championed.

An additional source of visibility is name recognition. Elected officials recognize the value of keeping their names before the electorate, so they place signs at state and city boundaries and entrances to public transportation terminals welcoming travelers. In organizations there are analogous opportunities for enhancing your visibility. For example, if your office regularly sends information to the public or other departments, try enclosing a signed cover note. If you are new to an organization, introduce yourself to other members. If you have a good idea, formally communicate it to the appropriate parties in person, as well as in a follow-up memo. If someone has recently accomplished something significant, send a note expressing congratulations and appreciation.

Relevance

This leads us to the fifth critical characteristic of powerful positions identified by Kanter. Powerful figures in an organization are generally associated with activities that are directly related to central objectives and issues (Salancik & Pfeffer, 1977). This accounts for the power attributed to problem solvers, mentioned earlier. But this maxim also holds during periods of normalcy, when there are no major crises to resolve. As one manager put it, "My peers are responsive to me because the functions that I manage are the lifeblood of the organization. I manage the people who provide readings on their vital signs; consequently, my presence in their office implies that there's a vital concern of one sort or another that needs to be dealt with" (Kaplan & Mazique, 1983, p. 10).

A noted organizational sociologist, Charles Perrow (1970), argues that, in an advanced consumer-products-oriented economy, sales and marketing represent the central concerns of most businesses. Because other activities in the organization are dependent on revenues from sales, the work performed by sales personnel is most relevant to the central concern of organizational survival.

Refining this general proposition, Paul Lawrence and Jay Lorsch (1969) identified the "dominant competitive issue" for companies using different types of technology. The dominant competitive issue is the organizational activity that most accounts for the firm's ability to compete effectively with other members of its industry. Companies using a flow-process form of technology, such as oil refineries and chemical plants, were found to be most dependent on effective marketing because of their sizable capital investment and small range of product alternatives. In contrast, companies using a standard mass-production (assembly-line) form of technology, with a stable line of products and established customers, were most dependent on the efficiency of their production process. Finally, high-tech firms, or companies producing custom-designed products, were most successful when they had strong R&D departments.

This general principle accounts for a significant recent shift in the power of the human resources department in large corporations. In the past, human resources executives occupied the outer circle in the corporate power structure. They ran a staff of personnel specialists, occupying the lower floors of the headquarters building. Today, a great many report directly to the CEO and play a key role in strategic decisions. The reason for this dramatic change is that with the increase in acquisitions, mergers, and divestments, corporations must base strategic decisions on human resources considerations. These include matching high-priced skills with critical jobs, keeping key personnel after a merger, solving human-resources problems that arise from introducing new technology or closing a plant, and formulating agreements with the unions of an acquired firm.

According to business authorities, "The rise of the human resources function is the most dramatic change in managerial function since financial executives rose to power in the 1960s during the 'conglomerate era,' when asset management was the pressing problem in corporations" (*Business Week,* December 2, 1985, p. 58).

These results have significant implications for task relevance. An individual who seeks influential positions must be sensitive to the relevance of his or her department's activities for the company. For example, a design engineer who works for an oil company is less likely to become influential than one who works for an electronics firm, and operations researchers will have more influence in companies with established product lines and an assembly-line production process. Computer scientists are more likely to feel empowered in a software development firm than if they are working for an insurance company or a public utility. In the latter organization, computer programming is viewed as a support function, with only an indirect effect on profitability.

There are other indications of the relevance of assigned activities besides their relationship to the firm's dominant competitive issue. For example, the role of representative or advocate is powerful because it enables a person to become identified with important causes. Another key role is that of evaluator. Positions designated by the organization as checkpoints become powerful by virtue of the fact that they create dependence. The approval controlled by people in these positions is highly relevant to those individuals who must receive it to obtain organizational rewards.

The role of trainer or mentor to new members of a work unit is another powerful position. It places you in a critical position to reduce uncertainty for newcomers and substantially enhance their performance. Newcomers are generally apprehensive, and they will appreciate your showing them the ropes. Also, successful performance in this developmental role earns you the respect and admiration of those colleagues who stand to benefit from your effective training.

To summarize, we have discussed five aspects of organizational positions that are critical to the achievement of power. Centrality and criticality derive from the location of a position in work communication and work flow networks. A position that is both central and critical is powerful because its occupants have access to information and resources and can influence their flow.

Criticality is associated with relevance in that a relevant task tends to be viewed as more critical, but the two terms differ in their power-generating mechanisms. In the case of criticality, power stems from the relationship between the tasks performed by a person and the tasks performed by other individuals. When a task is attached to only one position in a work-flow process, that uniqueness makes the individual performing the task critical to others in the work group. In contrast, relevance refers to the relationship between a task and the value placed on activities in an organization: for example, the dominant competitive issue. Powerful positions are those in which individuals perform tasks closely aligned with the vital interests of the organization.

As Table 5 shows, centrality, criticality, and relevance encourage the gaining of power through horizontal relationships. That is, a position's potential for power is based on its relationship to other lateral positions and activities in the organization. On the other hand, visibility and flexibility are linked to hierarchical power. Flexibility reflects the amount of discretion vested in a position by superiors. Positions that are closely supervised provide a poor vantage point for establishing a power base. A highly visible position has close ties with higher levels of authority, so a noteworthy performance in a visible position receives more recognition, which is an important prerequisite for an individual's upward mobility in an organization.

Transforming Power Into Influence

Having discussed the skill of gaining power, we now turn our attention to converting power into influence. This concept requires an understanding of the difference between power and influence. As indicated at the beginning of the chapter, many popular books on this subject suggest that power is an end in itself. They bring to mind the old commercials about "98-pound weaklings" who take up body building to punish bullies for stealing their girlfriends.

Our goal here is not to help people gain power for its own sake. When the weak seek power simply because they are tired of being pushed around, tyranny generally follows their ascension. Our interest, instead, is in helping people accomplish the exceptional in organizations, recognizing that this generally requires political clout. The well-meaning but politically naive seldom make major contributions to organizations. Consequently, our focus is on how you can become influential as well as powerful.

However, we can't talk about influence without first understanding power, since power is a necessary precondition for influence. Influential people have power, but not all powerful people have influence. Influence entails actually securing the consent of others to work with you in accomplishing an objective. Many powerful people cannot do that, as evidenced by the chronic inability of American presidents to convince Congress to pass what the president considers to be essential legislation. The skill of transforming power into influence hinges on securing the consent of others in ways that minimize their resistance and resentment.

Influence Strategies: The Three Rs

Power is converted into influence when the target individual consents to behave according to the desires of the power holder. The influence strategies used by managers to obtain compliance fall into three broad categories: **retribution, reciprocity,** and **reason** (Kipnis, 1987; Kipnis, Schmidt, & Wilkinson, 1980; Allen et al., 1979). Table 6 lists these strategies and the corresponding direct and indirect approaches. Specific examples of these strategies are shown in Table 7 (Marwell & Schmitt, 1967; Cialdini, 1988).

STRATEGIES	INDIRECT APPROACH	DIRECT APPROACH
Force others to do what you say	1. Intimidation (pressure)	2. Coercion (threaten)
Make others *want* to do what you say	3. Ingratiation (obligate)	4. Bargaining (exchange)
Help others to see why they *should* do what you say	5. Appeal to personal values (apply general principles)	6. Present facts (stress merits and needs)

Table 6 Influence Strategies

RETRIBUTION (COERCION AND INTIMIDATION)	
General form:	"If you don't do X, you will regret it!"
Threat:	"If you do not comply, I will punish you."
Social pressure:	"Others in your group have agreed; what's your decision?"
Had enough?:	"I will stop nagging you if you comply."
Perceived scarcity and time pressure:	"If you don't act now, you'll lose this opportunity/cause problems for others."
Avoid causing pain to others:	"If you don't agree, others will be hurt/disadvantaged."

RECIPROCITY (EXCHANGE AND INTEGRATION)	
General form:	"If you do X, you'll receive Y."
Promise:	"If you comply, I will reward you."
Esteem:	"People you value will think better (worse) of you if you do (do not) comply."
Pregiving:	"I will do something you like for you; then will you do this for me?"
Obligation:	"You owe me compliance because of past favors." ("Even though I implied there would be no future obligation.")
Reciprocal compromise:	"I have lowered my initial offer/price, and now I expect you to reciprocate" (no matter how unreasonable my initial position was).
Escalation of commitment:	"I'm only interested in a small commitment." ("But I'll be back later for more.")

REASON (PERSUASION BASED ON FACTS, NEEDS, OR PERSONAL VALUES)	
General form:	"I want you to do X, because it's consistent with/good for/necessary to . . ."
Evidence:	"These facts/experts' opinions demonstrate the merits of my position/request."
Need:	"This is what I need; will you help out?"
Goal attainment:	"Compliance will enable you to reach a personally important objective."
Value congruence:	"This action is consistent with your commitment to X."
Ability:	"This endeavor would be enhanced if we could count on your ability/experience."
Loyalty:	"Because we are friends/minorities, will you do this?"
Altruism:	"The group needs your support, so do it for the good of us all."

Table 7   Examples of Influence Strategies

You may have mixed reactions to these lists. Some strategies will probably strike you as particularly effective; others may seem inappropriate or even manipulative or dishonest. Our purpose in listing these is not to imply that all strategies within a category ought to be used. Rather, the full arsenal of influence strategies is presented so that you can informatively choose those with which you feel most comfortable and so that you can be aware when others are attempting to influence you.

These three influence strategies rely on different mechanisms for obtaining compliance. Fear of **retribution** is based on personal threat, which typically stems from formal authority. The direct form of this approach involves an explicit threat to impose sanctions if the manager's will is not obeyed. Recognizing their vulnerability to sanctions controlled by the boss, subordinates generally comply reluctantly. The threat usually involves either the denial of expected rewards or the imposition of punishment.

Intimidation is an indirect form of retribution because the threat is only implied. Behind the manager's forceful request is the possibility of organizationally based sanctions for noncompliance, but the dominant feature of the demand is an intimidating interpersonal style. Intimidation can take many forms: A manager publicly criticizes a subordinate's report, a member of a management committee is systematically ignored during meetings, or junior executives are given impossible tasks by insecure senior executives.

Acts of intimidation are generally accompanied by special emphasis on the authority of the power holder. Assignments are typically given in the boss's office, in a highly formal manner, with reference to the vulnerability of the target (e.g., mentioning his junior grade or short tenure with the organization). This sets the stage for an implicit threat (e.g., "If people aren't willing to work overtime on this project, corporate headquarters is going to pull the plug on our budget and a number of younger employees will get hurt").

Intimidation can also occur through peer pressure. Managers who know that a majority of their subordinates support a controversial action can use group dynamics to secure the compliance of the minority. This is done by telling the majority that a decision must be unanimous and it's their responsibility to demonstrate leadership by securing the commitment of all members. Or, the manager can apply pressure directly to the holdout members of the group by stressing the need for harmony, mutual support, and working for the common good.

One form of intimidation was used by the Ohio Bell Telephone Company in the late 1970s (Mescon, Albert, & Khedouri, 1977). Employees were shown a film of a fictional newscast set in 1984, in which reports explained that Congress was about to nationalize the telephone system because Ohio Bell was unable to provide adequate service and was going broke. As a result, countless Bell employees were about to lose their jobs. The newscaster concluded with a theme he said would have saved the company had it been heeded years ago: "A full day's work for a full day's pay." Bell calculated that the increased productivity resulting from showing this film saved the company $29 million over the next three years.

The second strategy extracts compliance from others by invoking the norm of **reciprocity.** Reciprocity operates on the principle of satisfying the self-interest of both parties. The direct form of this approach is straightforward bargaining in which each party gains something from the exchange. In bargaining, both parties are aware of the costs and benefits associated with striking a deal, and their negotiations focus on reaching an agreement that is satisfactory to both. Ingratiation, on the other hand, is more subtle. It involves using friendliness and favors to incur social obligations. When compliance is required or support is needed, previous benefactors are then reminded of their debts.

Reciprocity is used in many ways in organizations. These include striking deals with influential opinion leaders to support a new program, asking subordinates to work overtime in exchange for an extended weekend, doing small favors for the boss so one can take longer lunch hours occasionally, and formally negotiating with staff members to get them to accept undesirable assignments (Cohen & Bradford, 1991).

Although the retribution and reciprocity strategies are both grounded in the manager's control of outcomes valued by others, the dynamics of these strategies are different. Retribution strategies exploit a subordinate's natural desire to avoid pain or unpleasantness, while strategies of reciprocity are used to make the outcomes desired by the manager seem desirable and attractive to the subordinate. Retribution strategy ignores the rights of others and the norm of fairness, whereas reciprocity strategy honors both. An emphasis on retribution leads to ignoring the quality of the ongoing relationship between the parties, while reciprocity implies a recognition of the value of strengthening their interdependence.

The third approach is based on the manager's persuasive ability. Instead of seeking compliance by making the instrumental nature of their relationship salient to the target person, this approach appeals to **reason.** The manager argues that compliance is warranted because of the inherent merits of the request. Here the focus is on helping others to see why your ideas make sense. This is most likely to occur if the manager is perceived as knowledgeable on the subject and if his or her personal characteristics are attractive to the target person. The direct approach to persuasion relies on the compelling nature of the facts supporting the case. A convincing statement is made, coupled with a specific request. For example, "If your shift doesn't work overtime tonight, we will lose $5,000 worth of product. Will you pitch in and help us solve this problem?" In the indirect form, the manager appeals to the other person's personal values or goals. These might include being altruistic, a loyal team member, respected as an expert, helping keep the plant nonunion, or keeping customers satisfied.

Because persuasion is sometimes confused with manipulation, it is important here to distinguish between the two. A *persuasive appeal* is explicit and direct, while a *manipulative act* is implicit and deceptive. The persuader respects the autonomy of decision makers and trusts their ability to judge evidence effectively. In contrast, a manipulator has low regard for the abilities of decision makers and doesn't trust them to make good decisions. Manipulators have the same objectives as authoritarian leaders—they simply use more subtle tactics. Manipulative managers, therefore, often appear to the casual observer to be using a democratic leadership style. In fact, they are actually "illusory democrats" because, while their actions may appear democratic, they have no inclination to share power. They use a democratic style only because it makes others less defensive and therefore more vulnerable to their power initiatives (Dyer, 1972).

As Table 8 notes, each approach has advantages and limitations (Cuming, 1981; Mulder et al., 1986). The retribution strategy produces immediate action, and work is performed exactly according to the manager's specifications. But the retribution strategy comes with high costs. Of the three strategies, it is the most likely to engender resistance. Most people do not like to be forced to do something. Effective managers use this approach sparingly, generally reserving it for crises or as a last resort when the other strategies have failed. It is best suited to situations in which the goals of the parties are competing or independent. This approach is effective only when the target person perceives that the manager has both the power and the will to follow through on his or her threat. Otherwise, the person being influenced may be tempted to call the manager's bluff. Also, the threatened sanctions must be sufficiently severe that disobedience is unthinkable.

When used repeatedly, the retribution approach produces resentment and alienation that frequently generate overt or covert opposition. Consequently, it should be used extensively only when the ongoing commitment of the target person is not critical, when opposition is acceptable (the target person can be replaced if necessary), and when extensive surveillance is possible. Because these conditions tend to stifle initiative and innovative behavior—even when individual compliance is obtained—organizational performance is likely to suffer because affected individuals have lit-

tle incentive to bring emerging problems resulting from changing conditions to their supervisor's attention.

The reciprocity strategy allows the manager to obtain compliance without causing resentment, since both parties benefit from the agreement. Also, because of the instrumental nature of the exchange, it is not necessary to take time to justify the manager's actions. It is most appropriate when each party controls some outcomes valued by the other party and established rules govern the transaction, including provisions for adjudication of grievances. Even under these conditions, such exchanges—especially agreements that are not formally documented—require some degree of trust. If individuals have reneged on past agreements, their credibility as negotiating partners becomes suspect. Reciprocity is also best suited to situations in which the power holder needs the target person to perform specific unambiguous assignments. Consequently, neither a long-term commitment to general goals and values nor the extensive use of personal judgment is required. An agreement to perform certain tasks according to specified terms is sufficient.

The chief disadvantage of this approach, when used frequently, is that it engenders a highly instrumental view of work. The other person begins to expect that every request is open for negotiation and that every completed assignment will generate a reward of equal value. In its extreme form, this approach undercuts internalized commitment as members take on a highly calculative orientation and downplay the value of working hard to achieve organizational goals, regardless of personal gain.

The assets and liabilities of the third approach—reason—are more complicated. The objective of the rational strategy is a higher form of compliance, that is, internalized commitment. While the focus of compliance is acceptable behavior, commitment requires shared understanding. Commitment relies on teaching correct principles and explaining legitimate needs and then trusting the good intent and sound judgment of subordinates to act appropriately. In its ideal form, commitment decreases the need for surveillance based on accountability and enhances the subordinate's initiative, commitment, and creativity. This approach works best when the worst thing the other person can do is turn down the request, since he or she has little incentive to hurt the manager. Also, the target person should feel there is little potential for the manager to cause harm, as is typically the case when the target person is the manager's coworker or

INFLUENCE STRATEGY	WHEN TO USE IT	POSSIBLE ADVANTAGES	POSSIBLE DISADVANTAGES	POSSIBLE COMPLAINTS
Retribution	• Unequal power, in influencer's favor • Commitment and quality not important • Tight time constraints • Serious violation • Issue not important to target • If issue is important, retribution not likely • Specific, unambiguous request • Resistance to request is likely	• Quick, direct action	• Stifles commitment, creativity • Insecurity of boss • Engenders resentment • Must increase seriousness of threats to maintain pressure	• Violation of rights • Ethical violations
Reciprocity	• Parties mutually dependent • Each party has resources valued by other • Adequate time for negotiating • Established exchange norms exist • Parties viewed as trustworthy • Commitment to broad goals and values not critical • Needs are specific and short-term	• Low incidence of resentment • Justification for request not required	• Engenders instrumental view of work (expectation of specific rewards for specific actions) • Encourages people to feel that the terms of assignments are open for negotiation	• Unfairness, dashed expectations, manipulation
Reason	• Adequate time for extensive discussion • Common goals/values • Parties share mutual respect/ credibility • Parties share ongoing relationship	• Need for surveillance enhanced	• Considerable time required to build trust (time increases as number of people increases) • Requires common goals and values	• Difference of opinions, conflicting perceptions of priorities

Table 8   Comparisons Among Influence Strategies

superior. On the other hand, when the target person is a subordinate, the manager must demonstrate his or her unwillingness to rely on coercion and intimidation in seeking compliance.

The principal disadvantage of the rational, or reason, approach is the amount of time required to build the trust and mutual understanding required to make it operate effectively. This time increases as the number of involved individuals expands. Also, because the success of this strategy requires congruence of goals and values (rather than the rewards or sanctions a person controls), this approach is difficult to implement when the parties have dissimilar backgrounds, subscribe to competing philosophies, or are assigned conflicting responsibilities, such as maintaining quality versus meeting deadlines.

Recent research provides compelling evidence supporting the superior benefits of the approach based on reason (Schmidt & Kipnis, 1987). Individuals who rely primarily on reason and logic to influence others are rated as highly effective by their bosses, and they report low levels of job-related stress and high levels of job satisfaction (Kipnis & Schmidt, 1988). In contrast, individuals who persistently use any other approach to get their way tend to receive lower performance ratings and experience higher levels of personal stress and job dissatisfaction.

Although the evidence is not clear-cut, it does appear that a more general rule can be proposed. Higher-numbered strategies in Table 6 are more effective than lower-numbered strategies. This ordering reflects the overall value system portrayed in this book: Direct is better than indirect; open is better than closed; exchange is better than intimidation; and sincere requests are better than guile.

In general, managers are more effective when they assume others are reasonable, well-meaning, and motivated. Unfortunately, in some cases, these assumptions are proven false. When this happens, it is important to be prepared to protect ourselves from unwanted, inappropriate efforts by others to influence our actions.

Acting Assertively: Neutralizing Influence Attempts

Not only is it important to learn how to influence others effectively, but we must also understand how to protect ourselves against the undesirable attempts of others to influence us. As we discussed earlier, one-sided dependence is the antithesis of empowerment. Recalling Figure 1, feelings of lack of power are just as harmful to personal performance as flagrant, excessive use of power. Therefore, it is just as important to be skillful at resisting unwanted influence attempts as it is to influence the behavior of others effectively and appropriately. This skill is especially important in work

situations where maintaining personal initiative is difficult in the face of strong countervailing pressures.

Table 7 contains an impressive arsenal of influence strategies. Is it possible to neutralize the impact of such a highly developed, well-conceived set of tools? Many people fall prey to these influence attempts, either because they are unaware of the social dynamics affecting their decisions or because they feel compelled to give in without offering any resistance. To avoid this plight, it is important to develop the skill of resisting inappropriate influence. Assertiveness increases self-determination by thwarting exploitation by overpowering bosses, manipulative sales personnel, and high-pressured negotiators (Cialdini, 1988).

Neutralizing Retribution Strategies Used by Others

Coercive and intimidating actions are intended to create a power imbalance by substituting dependence for interdependence. This is the most detrimental form of influence, and therefore it should be resisted most vigorously and directly. You can use several approaches. These tend to form a hierarchy of responses, as follows (begin with the first and progress to the others if the initial response fails):

1. **Use countervailing power to shift dependence to interdependence.** The primary reason individuals (particularly bosses) rely heavily on the threat of retribution as an influence strategy is because they perceive an inequality in power. Obviously, the boss in an organization has the final say, but the larger the perceived discrepancy in power, the greater the temptation to exploit the powerless. The first half of this chapter outlined several techniques for increasing your power base. However, when exploitation occurs, the time for planning how to increase your power base has passed. Ideally, you are in a position to focus your boss's attention on your mutual dependence, that is, your interdependence. Point out the negative consequences of failing to respect your rights and acting cooperatively. As part of this discussion, it may be appropriate to discuss more acceptable means of satisfying the boss's demands.

2. **Confront the exploiting individual directly.** All individuals, no matter what their job or or-

ganizational status, must protect their personal rights. One of those rights is to be treated as an intelligent, mature, responsible adult. In the Managing Conflict chapter, we discuss how to initiate a complaint effectively. Key elements include describing the problem in terms of behaviors, consequences, and feelings, persisting until understood, and making specific suggestions. These techniques can be used in this situation to stress the seriousness of your concerns. If necessary, you should specify actions you are willing to take to stop coercive behavior. For example, whistle-blowing involves registering a complaint with an external governing body.

3. **Actively resist.** As a last resort, you should consider "fighting fire with fire." This is obviously a sensitive matter, but there are some individuals who will keep pushing others until they meet resistance. A work slowdown, deliberate disobedience to orders, or reporting the problem to a senior manager might be necessary. Again, this step should be pursued only after all other efforts to counter unwanted threats and demands have failed.

Neutralizing Reciprocity Strategies by Others

Many of the persuasion strategies used in sales and advertising fall into this category. In the marketplace, your concern is to avoid being duped. In the workplace, your concern is to avoid being manipulated. The following hierarchically arranged actions should be helpful in either situation. Once again, begin with the first response and follow with others if necessary.

1. **Examine the intent of any gift or favor-giving activity.** When a favor or gift is offered, you should consider the motives of the person, the appropriateness of the behavior, and the probable consequences. You should ask yourself questions such as "Is the giver likely to profit from this?" "Is this transaction inappropriate, unethical, or illegal?" "Is there a stated or implied expectation of reciprocation, and would I feel good about complying if the gift or favor were not offered?" In brief, when in doubt about a benefactor's motives, ask questions or decline the gift.

2. **Confront individuals who are using manipulative bargaining tactics.** Common ploys used in these situations are escalating commitments ("I'm only interested in a small commitment [now])" and reciprocal compromises ("I've lowered my [extreme] initial position; now I expect you [in the spirit of fair play] to also offer a compromise"). Simply drawing attention to these attempts at manipulation will enhance your power in the relationship. State that you do not approve of the manipulative strategy; then propose an alternative exchange, with emphasis on the merits of the case or the true value of the product rather than on the craftiness of the negotiators. You will thus be able to reshape the exchange process and avoid being manipulated.

3. **Refuse to bargain with individuals who use high-pressure tactics.** If steps 1 and 2 have failed, refuse to continue the discussion unless high-pressure tactics, such as imposing unrealistic time constraints or emphasizing the limited supply of the commodity or service, are dropped. If you suspect that the dynamics of the negotiation process may be clouding your judgment about the value of the object or the importance of the issue, ask yourself, "Would I be interested in this item if there were an unlimited supply and no decision-making deadline?" If the answer is negative, either disengage from the negotiation process or focus your attention on its inequality. By shifting attention from content to process, you neutralize the advantage of a more experienced or powerful bargainer. By refusing to continue unless artificial constraints of time and supply are removed, you can establish fairer terms of trade.

Neutralizing Reason Strategies by Others

Although strategies based on reason are the most egalitarian of influence attempts, they can still create or exacerbate conditions of inequity. The following ordered guidelines should help you avoid these situations.

1. **Explain the effects of compliance on performance.** Often, others' pressing priorities are your incidentals. Just because someone can present a legitimate, convincing case does not mean

you should comply with the request. For example, a request may be reasonable, but its timing bad; compliance would mean your having to miss important personal deadlines or neglect your customers. You should discuss these concerns with the influencer. By acknowledging the other person's need, explaining your concerns about personal compliance, and then helping to find alternatives, you avoid becoming overcommitted without giving offense.

2. **Defend your personal rights.** If you have used step 1 and your petitioner persists, focus the discussion on your personal rights. If individuals frequently come to you for help because they mismanage their time or resources, appeal to their sense of fairness. Ask if it is right to ask you to get behind in your own work in order to bail them out of their predicaments. Coworkers have the right to request your help in a pinch, but you also have the right to say no when even reasonable requests place you at a serious disadvantage or when they stem from the negligence or overdependence of others.

3. **Firmly refuse to comply with the request.** If your efforts to explain why you are unable to comply have not worked, you should firmly restate your refusal and terminate the discussion. Some people feel their case is so compelling, they have difficulty believing others won't comply. If your coworker still "won't take no for an answer," it's probably because your no wasn't firm enough. As a last resort, you may have to seek the support of a higher authority.

Increasing Your Influence With Higher Level Authorities

To become influential, you must avoid abusing your power or being abused by those with more power. Thus far, our discussion of transforming power into influence has focused on avoiding the pitfalls of power. We have described influence strategies that are least likely to elicit negative reactions and have discussed ways to rebuff unwanted attempts to influence you.

Our focus thus far has been on influencing those at peer or subordinate levels in the organization. Perhaps even more important, however, is the ability to influence one's boss, or others in higher level organizational positions. In order to wield power and influence effec-

tively, it is crucially important to (1) defend oneself against abuses of power from above, and (2) develop the ability to be proactive in "influencing upward."

There are two general strategies for influencing upward that can augment or enlarge the authority your superiors extend to you. These are issue selling and benefiting the boss. If you are effective at **issue selling,** you can draw your boss's attention to those issues or problems that concern you, notwithstanding the numerous other issues that compete for his or her time and attention. The issues that draw a boss's attention are those that are perceived as most consequential. Effectively influencing upward, therefore, means that you are able to convince your boss that a particular issue you espouse is important enough to deserve attention.

Benefiting your boss means that you enhance your influence by helping your boss achieve more than he or she could achieve without you. It means going beyond developing criticality in your position, as discussed earlier, and assisting your boss in ways that may not be requested or expected, but that increase his or her success.

Issue Selling

Capturing the attention of senior executives in a company is no easy task. But by so doing, you can have significant influence over the strategic direction of the organization, as well as the kinds of decisions that are made. To illustrate, imagine that you work for the world's largest company, General Motors. Assume, further, that you are convinced that a recently departed vice president has stolen important company documents about future products and factory designs. If you feel strongly that the company should pursue the matter, how do you get the attention of senior management?

Consider what you are up against. Senior management is faced with an unrelenting cacophony of "special issues"—environmental pollution standards, safety regulations, supplier relationships, union contracts, Japanese transplants, foreign trade policy, investment in the city of Detroit, local politics, public image, homelessness, sponsorship of basic research, antitrust legislation, new technologies, health care legislation, literacy education, drug abuse, communications technology, and many others—that demand time and attention over and above that devoted to the basic managerial tasks of overseeing production and delivering service to customers. Senior management simply cannot deal with all of these issues in depth. Inevitably, these realities will impact upon the case of corporate espionage you think you have uncovered. This issue may be important to you, but in order to influence upper management to pay attention to this situation and allocate sufficient resources to resolve it, you will have to "sell your issue" effectively. If you prove ineffective in doing so, you may lose credibility and, consequently, the ability to influence upward in the future. But if you succeed in selling this issue effectively, your influence in the company should increase markedly.

The issues that capture senior managers' attention determine an organization's future direction, resource allocations, and long-term strategy. Furthermore, the personal careers of many people may be enhanced or hurt by those selections. Entire units have been downsized in companies, for example, when top managers changed priorities. Individuals have been made into heros—or, conversely, "blackballed"—depending on their degree of success in representing "their" issues to senior management. As pointed out by Dutton and Ashford (1993, p. 402):

> For individuals, strategic issues are part of the currency through which their careers are made or broken. . . . There are career consequences of issue selling[;] . . . important outcomes accrue to individuals who successfully promote strategic issues.

Thus, being the champion or representative of an issue and getting it on the agenda of top management enhances your influence and, potentially, your career success. It makes you more visible, expands your interpersonal network by providing an opportunity to discuss "your" issue with others you may not have met before, and increases the likelihood that action will be taken on the issue. Such sponsorship could eventually lead to your being put in charge of an important company priority. Thus, issue selling is a potential vehicle for markedly increasing your influence.

But how can an issue best be sold? How can you capture the attention of the boss or other top managers? Several researchers (Dutton & Ashford, 1993; Dutton & Duncan, 1987) have investigated the issue-selling process; Table 9 summarizes the most effective strategies for capturing managers' attention. These 12 prescriptions point out ways in which you can influence upward through issue selling.

1. **Congruence.** Select an issue that is congruent with your own position and interests. A person in

PRINCIPLE	EXPLANATION
Congruence	The issue must be congruent with your position or role.
Credibility	The issue must be presented in an honest, open, nonself-serving manner.
Communication	The issue must be communicated through a broad communication network.
Compatibility	The issue must be compatible with company culture.
Solvability	The issue must be solvable.
Payoff	The payoff from addressing the issue must be clear.
Expertise	The expertise to resolve the issue must be identified.
Responsibility	The responsibility of top management for addressing the issue must be made clear.
Presentation	The issue must be presented succinctly, in emotional terms, with supporting data, and with novel information.
Bundling	The issue must be bundled with similar issues.
Coalitions	The issue must be sponsored by other people.
Visibility	The issue must be presented in a public forum.

Table 9 Ways to Sell Issues Upward

the marketing department trying to sell an issue relating to computers would be less effective than would an information specialist.

2. **Credibility.** Maintain credibility by being honest and straightforward and by demonstrating that your interest in the issue is not mere personal gain. Issues that seem self-serving are more difficult to sell.

3. **Communication.** Gain or maintain access to a broad communication network. Use multiple communication channels, including face-to-face conversations, written memos, E-mail, conferences, news clippings, and so on.

4. **Compatibility.** Select issues that are in harmony with key principles of the organization. Avoid issues that contradict company culture.

5. **Solvability.** Make it clear that the issue can be resolved. Show that solution alternatives are available. Unresolvable issues don't capture attention.

6. **Payoff.** Point out the long-term payoff, for the organization or the manager, of addressing the issue. The higher the potential payoff appears to be, the more likely the issue will receive attention.

7. **Expertise.** Identify the expertise needed to solve the problem. Issues are more likely to capture attention if it is clear that the expertise necessary to resolve them resides in the organization, or better still, under the purview of the top manager or boss.

8. **Responsibility.** Point out the responsibility that top managers have to address the issue. Emphasize the negative consequences associated with ignoring the issue or leaving it unresolved.

9. **Presentation.** Ensure that the issue is presented succinctly, in emotionally positive terms, with supporting data and novel information. Complex and convoluted information does not capture attention, so the issue must be explained in precise, simple terms. Couching the issue in the form of a personal story or emotional experience and presenting it in a novel way, with good supporting data, will help capture attention.

10. **Bundling.** Bundle the issue together with other important issues that interest top managers. Point out the relationship between your issue and other issues already being addressed.

11. **Coalitions.** Bring others on board to help sell the issue. Building coalitions of supporters makes the issue hard to ignore.

12. **Visibility.** Sell the issue in a public forum rather than in a private meeting. The more individuals who hear about the issue, the more likely it is to reach the boss's agenda.

The point of these 12 steps in issue selling is to influence the agenda of your boss. By being effective at issue selling, you can shape the agenda of those above you and, potentially, the entire organization. That agenda not only helps determine the ultimate performance of the organization, but also plays an important role in determining which managers are called upon to take leading roles in the organization's future. Issue selling, therefore, is an important aspect of managing upward in order to gain and use power more effectively. You will notice that all of these 12 steps rely on reason, rather than reciprocity or retribution.

Benefiting the Boss

A second aspect of influencing upward is benefiting your boss: in particular, providing benefits that are neither requested nor expected. In the literature on customer satisfaction, customer loyalty, and total quality management, it has been discovered that individuals develop lifelong loyalty to those who provide "surprises and delights" in their products or services. When a provider gives a customer more value than he or she expected or requested, long-lasting feelings of commitment and loyalty are engendered in the customer. Think of the last time someone "went the extra mile" for you when you didn't expect it and never would have requested it. How do you feel about that person? In all likelihood, your loyalty, commitment, and gratitude toward that person probably increased.

Similar outcomes result from benefiting your boss. Your influence and power expand, not because you are trying to become more powerful, but because you are trying to help your boss become more successful. Your power increases as you are vigilant in understanding your boss's needs and lightening his or her responsibilities.

Based on intensive examination of effective boss-subordinate relationships in major corporations, Gabarro and Kotter (1980) suggested several guidelines for directing efforts to the benefit of your boss. As shown in

Table 10, these include understanding your boss's pressures and priorities, as well as assessing your own needs and strengths. Add to those suggestions several more garnered from the literature on developing customer loyalty (Berry, Parasuraman, & Zeithaml, 1994), and you will see several options for successfully achieving influence by benefiting your boss. Following are 10 guidelines for treating your boss as your most important customer.

1. **Problem solving.** Ask yourself, "What ongoing problems does my boss face that he or she doesn't expect me or anyone else to solve? What can I do to remove or resolve these problems?"

2. **Understanding.** Get as much understanding as you can of what your boss's job entails, sources of information, major frustrations or roadblocks, and what your boss considers to be his or her biggest challenges.

3. **Diagnosing.** Diagnose your boss's strengths, weaknesses, and preferred style as a manager. Where are his or her blind spots? In what areas might problems arise? In what ways can you protect an unguarded flank?

4. **Self-awareness.** Where do your own talents and expertise lie? How can they complement those of your boss? Determine ways you can supplement and create additional value to your boss's leadership.

5. **Communicating.** Keep your boss informed of your own activities and of problems that arise. Be sure to pass along helpful information that he or she may not normally receive. Expand the amount of relevant information available, but be careful not to overload or inundate your boss with trivia.

6. **Trustworthiness.** Avoid secretiveness and hidden agendas. Become relied upon by your boss by being dependable, consistent, and honest. Do your own work well, then consider ways in which you can go the extra mile for your boss.

7. **Protecting.** Help protect your boss from unwanted or unimportant matters. Volunteer to take care of such items without being asked. Help your boss free up time for reflection, planning, and analysis.

8. **Listening.** Listen carefully to multiple perspectives—for example, customers, peers, lower-level employees—as well as to your boss. Be able to provide a broadly informed perspective when discussing issues with your boss. Be able to represent not only your own opinion but those of others as well.

9. **Timeliness.** Be faster than expected. Deliver results, information, or responses in less time than requested.

10. **Creativity.** Be on the lookout for new ideas, new perspectives, and improvements that can assist your boss. Give credit to others when it is due, but help your boss become aware of new ideas, regardless of the source. Strive for continuous small improvements in your own work and that of your boss, but constantly look for ways to help in substantial, creative ways.

In contrast to issue selling, this set of strategies relies more on reciprocity than on retribution or reason. You will notice that in dealing with higher level authorities, retribution is rarely going to be an effective influence strategy.

Make sure you understand your boss, including
- your boss's goals and objectives.
- the pressures on him or her.
- your boss's strengths, weaknesses, blind spots.
- his or her preferred work style.

Assess yourself, including
- your own strengths and weaknesses.
- your personal style.
- your predisposition toward dependence on authority figures.

Develop and maintain a relationship that
- fits the needs and styles of you both.
- is characterized by mutual expectations.
- keeps your boss informed.
- is based on dependability and honesty.
- selectively uses your boss's time and resources.

Table 10 Managing the Relationship With Your Boss
Source: Gabarro & Kotter, 1980.

Summary

In Figure 2, the two skills discussed in this chapter—gaining power and translating power into influence—are highlighted. We began by discussing sources of power, such as personal attributes and position characteristics. Both of these must be developed if one is to maximize one's potential as a power holder. A strong person in a weak position and a weak person in a strong position are both at a disadvantage. Ideally, one should become a strong person in a strong position.

A manager must establish a power base in order to get work accomplished and obtain commitments to important objectives. But power without influence is not sufficient. Consequently, we discussed how to translate power into influence by selecting an appropriate influence strategy and implementing it in such a way that resistance is minimized. In general, this is most likely to occur when managers use the higher-numbered strategies in Table 6. Persuasion tends to build trust and encourage internalized commitment, while coercion and intimidation erode trust, produce only superficial compliance, and encourage servility.

The unbridled use of power tends to increase resistance among subordinates, which in turn erodes the manager's power base. It also transforms the nature of the manager's stewardship over subordinates. The more a manager dominates subordinates, the more dependent they become on management's initiatives. As a result, managers tend to overvalue their contribution to their workers' job-performance activities ("Without me, they would be lost"). This inflated sense of self-importance encourages abuse of power that weakens the manager's influence and may even lead others to demand the manager's resignation. Thus, the abuse of power is both organizationally and personally destructive.

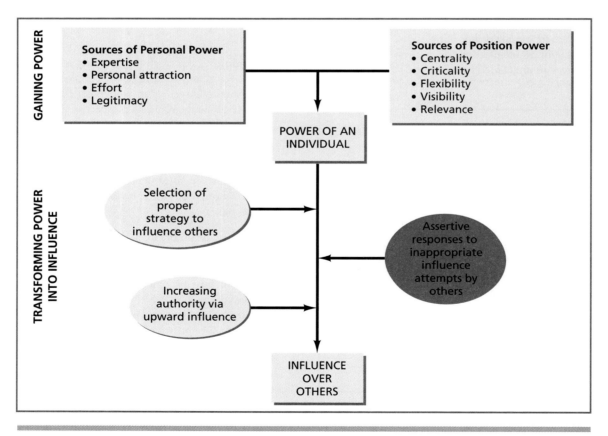

Figure 2 Model of Power and Influence

Power need not be abused, however. Managers, by definition, are located somewhere above the midpoint in the range of organizational levels (from the CEO at the top to hourly employees at the bottom). Managers who shun initiative and refuse to take responsibility for their actions see themselves as the "janitors" for the management pyramid above them. Their job, as they see it, is to clean up messes and carry out orders. Their attitude and demeanor reflect that of their bosses. In contrast, managers characterized by high initiative, personal responsibility, and influence see themselves as presidents of the organizational pyramid below them. They work within acknowledged constraints, but they figure out ways to do things right. They take full responsibility for their subordinates' performance, as well as for their commitment to their work and their membership in the organization.

Translating power into influence should not only be directed downward—that is, toward organizational subordinates, but also upward—that is, toward organizational superiors. Incompetent attempts to influence upward can quickly derail a manager's career, while competent upward influence can markedly enhance it. By helping to set the agenda of senior managers (issue selling) and by working for senior management's success (benefiting the boss), a manager's influence can increase significantly. When applying these two principles, however, managers should be motivated, not by a thirst for mere self-aggrandizement, but by an honest desire to benefit their company and strengthen their boss's position.

The counsel of the late A. Bartlett Giamatti, former President of Yale University and Commissioner of Major League Baseball, serves as a particularly fitting conclusion to this discussion: "Far better to conceive of power as consisting in part of the knowledge of when not to use all the power you have. . . . Whoever knows how to restrain and effectively release power finds . . . that power flows back to him" (1981, p. 169).

Behavioral Guidelines

Effective management within an organization includes both gaining power and exercising influence wisely. Key guidelines for gaining power include:

1. Enhance your *personal power* in the organization by:

   ▶ developing an area in which you are the acknowledged expert.

   ▶ cultivating critical skills.

   ▶ fostering the attributes of friendship (genuineness, intimacy, acceptance, validation of self-worth, tolerance, and social exchange).

   ▶ enhancing your personal appearance.

   ▶ putting forth more effort than expected.

   ▶ reinforcing core organizational values; using stories and ceremonies to socialize new members.

2. Increase the *centrality* and *criticality* of your position by:

   ▶ expanding your network of communication contacts.

   ▶ having information routed through you.

   ▶ making at least part of your job responsibilities unique.

   ▶ taking on tasks critical to the work flow.

   ▶ increasing the technical sophistication of your work.

   ▶ combining positions to reduce redundancy.

3. Increase the *latitude* and *flexibility* of your job by:

   ▶ reducing the percentage of routine activities.

   ▶ expanding task variety and novelty.

   ▶ initiating new ideas.

   ▶ getting involved in new projects.

   ▶ participating in the early stages of decision-making processes.

   ▶ seeking unusual and design-oriented jobs, rather than those that are repetitive and maintenance-oriented.

4. Increase the *visibility* of your job performance by:

   ▶ expanding the number of contacts you have with senior people.

   ▶ making oral presentations of written work.

   ▶ participating in problem-solving task forces.

   ▶ inviting senior managers to help you recognize important accomplishments within your work group.

   ▶ sending personal notes of congratulations or cover notes accompanying reports or useful information.

5. Increase the *relevance* of your tasks to the organization by:

   ▶ becoming an internal coordinator or external representative.

   ▶ providing services and information to other units.

   ▶ monitoring and evaluating activities within your own unit.

   ▶ expanding the domain of your work activities.

   ▶ becoming involved in activities central to the organization's top priorities.

   ▶ becoming a trainer or mentor for new members.

The general guidelines for influencing others effectively involve matching your influence strategy to specific situations, acting assertively when others attempt to influence you inappropriately, and empowering others. In general, use reason strategies more often than reciprocity strategies, and reciprocity more than threats of retribution. Use open, direct approaches in preference to indirect, manipulative approaches.

6. Use *reason* strategies when:

   ▶ there are few time constraints.

   ▶ initiative and innovation are vital.

   ▶ interpersonal trust is high.

   ▶ the relationship is long-term.

   ▶ interpersonal conflict is not high.

   ▶ personal goals are congruent and/or respected by both parties.

   ▶ it is important for the other person to understand why the request is being made.

7. Use *reciprocity* strategies when:

   ▶ the parties are mutually dependent.

   ▶ there are clearly specified rules governing interpersonal transactions.

   ▶ long-term commitment to common goals and values is not important.

   ▶ there is sufficient time to reach satisfactory agreements.

8. Use *retribution* strategies when:

   ▶ there is a substantial imbalance of power between the parties.

   ▶ the ongoing commitment of the other person is not critical.

   ▶ quality and innovation are not important.

   ▶ opposition is acceptable (e.g., when personnel replacement is possible, if necessary).

   ▶ extensive surveillance is possible.

   ▶ no other alternatives exist.

9. To neutralize *reason* influence strategies of others:

   ▶ explain the negative consequences of compliance.

   ▶ defend your rights.

   ▶ firmly refuse to comply with request.

10. To neutralize *reciprocal* influence strategies of others:

    ▶ examine the context of any gift- or favor-giving activity.

    ▶ confront individuals using escalating or compromising tactics.

    ▶ refuse to bargain with individuals using high-pressure tactics.

11. To neutralize *retribution* influence strategies of others:

    ▶ use countervailing power to shift dependence to interdependence.

    ▶ confront the exploitative individual directly.

    ▶ actively resist.

12. To *sell issues* to senior managers:

    ▶ select issues that are congruent with your position or role.

    ▶ present the issue honestly and without being self-serving.

    ▶ communicate the issue broadly.

    ▶ select an issue that is compatible with the culture.

    ▶ select a solvable issue.

▶ clarify the payoff to be achieved.

▶ identify the needed expertise.

▶ point out senior managers' responsibility for the issue.

▶ be succinct, use emotional imagery, and provide supporting data and novel information.

▶ bundle the issue with other similar important issues.

▶ find like-minded supporters.

▶ use public forums.

13. To *benefit your boss:*

▶ solve problems whose solutions aren't expected or requested.

▶ develop an understanding of your boss's job.

▶ diagnose your boss's strengths, weaknesses, and management style.

▶ know your own talents, inclinations, and operating style.

▶ keep your boss informed.

▶ maintain trustworthiness.

▶ protect your boss from unwanted or unimportant matters.

▶ listen to multiple perspectives from multiple sources.

▶ be faster than expected.

▶ generate new, creative ideas for your boss.

Skill Analysis

Cases Involving Power and Influence

John DeLorean: Why I Quit General Motors

It was a shocking experience for me "upstairs." After eight years of running car divisions, I suddenly found myself in the fall of 1972 with no direct operating responsibilities and a nonjob as a group executive. I had no business to manage directly. Where I had been a quarterback for eight years, I now was watching the game from the sidelines. I still wanted to play in the games. On the field. These feelings of occupational emptiness were complicated by personalities.

At the time in my career when I was just one of the corporate boys spending my working and nonworking hours with General Motors people or the company suppliers, I had a tightly knit group of corporate friends, and I obeyed the corporate dictates in behavior and dress. But as I grew, it dawned on me that all of us were becoming too inbred. We were losing contact with America. With our customers. In addition, while I enjoyed work, I've always placed enjoying life higher on my list of priorities. So I made a habit of widening my circle of friends and broadening my tastes. This awareness precipitated a seemingly endless chain of personality conflicts, the most difficult of which was with Roger M. Kyes, who was my boss while I was running the Pontiac and Chevrolet divisions. He made life unbearable for me, and he was dedicated to getting me fired; he told me so, many times. Fortunately, I had the protection of my ability as I ran those two divisions to fend off Kyes. But I remember vividly my conflicts with him, especially when he was irritated by my style of dress. The corporate rule was dark suits, light shirts, and muted ties. I followed the rule to the letter, only I wore stylish Italian-cut suits, wide-collared off-white shirts, and wide ties.

My hair length was ear-length, with sideburns. I felt both my clothes and hair style were contemporary but not radical. . . .

The fact that I had been divorced, was a health nut, and dated generally younger actresses and models didn't set well with the corporate executives or their wives either. And neither did my general disappearance from the corporate social scene. . . .

I thought all of this was an improper intrusion into my personal life, but I did not pay much attention to it, which I guess perpetuated the problem. I figured I was loyal and dedicated to GM. I did my job and did it well. The company had a right to know how I was spending my business life, but it had no right to know how I was spending my private and nonbusiness life.

Nevertheless, my clothing and lifestyle were increasingly rattling the cages of my superiors, as was the amount of publicity my personal and business lives were generating. I was being resented because my style of living violated an unwritten but widely revered precept that said no personality could outshine General Motors. The executives were supposed to be just as gray and almost as lifeless as the corporate image.

The resentments toward me festered and grew to great proportions without my knowledge. I knew some people disliked me. But since I didn't play the corporate political game, I was not wired into the underground flow of information which would have given me better knowledge about those who viewed themselves as my corporate enemies. . . .

It bothered me when Tom Murphy, my boss during my term at Chevrolet, many times said to me, "You know, John, everybody said I was going to have a helluva lot of trouble with you. But I would really have to say that this is untrue. As far as I am concerned you do the best job of running your division of anyone. You keep me informed of the important things. I know what you are doing. Far and away I have less trouble with you than anybody in the divisions."

Those were kind words from Murphy, the only top manager with whom I felt I had a good rapport. However, the warnings he was getting from other members of management that I was "trouble" indicated to me now that my papers were being "graded upstairs" by something other than my test scores. But my support from Murphy suddenly ended. It was a sinister occurrence that terminated it.

Greenbrier Incident

In November 1972, the corporation was staging a massive management meeting of the top 700 GM executives in Greenbrier, West Virginia. These were infrequent gatherings, at least three years apart, which were designed to discuss in total all of the corporation's problems and exchange ideas on how to solve them. Many of The Fourteenth-Floor executives were given broad subjects on which to address the conference. As a group executive, I was given the topic of "Product Quality." I prepared a tough talk which in essence said the only way we can remain a success and grow is to deliver real value to the customer. I said that I felt the emphasis at General Motors had switched from this goal to one of taking the last nickel out of every part to improve profits in the short run. I singled out specific products and programs for criticism. The talk was both critical and constructive. It was the kind of talk that was for corporate ears and none other.

As is the required practice, we submitted early drafts of our talks to top management through the public relations department. Management then made corrections and generally edited the draft along the lines it felt was proper. In the process, an executive could wind up writing a speech four or five times or more. After each new draft was prepared, all the copies of the previous version were destroyed. My final draft was toned by management and edited to complement the speeches of the other executives.

Just prior to the conference, my Greenbrier talk turned up in the hands of Bob Irvin, automotive writer for the *Detroit News.* And he printed it. It was not the final version that he wrote about. It was one of the earlier drafts. The only people who had copies of that version were me, the public relations staff, and top management. I hadn't leaked it. Nothing in the world could do me more harm personally and internally than to leak this type of a speech. My job was to sell our cars, not criticize them publicly. I was trying, with the talk, to impress people in the corporation with the need for drastic improvement in product quality to counter the growing wave of consumer unrest, fulfill our responsibility to our customers, and restore our tarnished image.

The leak destroyed the Greenbrier conference for me and was probably the single thing that hurt me most in the corporation. I could tell that my solid image in Murphy's eyes began to diminish from the day the newspaper story appeared. I was shocked and sick. So was my staff. It was obvious that someone who wanted to give me a good shot to the gut, did.

A short time later, a friend of mind lunching in a downtown Detroit restaurant ran across a private investigator who knew GM's operations and who told him that the speech was leaked by a man on the GM public relations staff.

If I was having my doubts about staying with the corporation, and I was, it was quite obvious that some people in the corporation were taking steps to see that I couldn't stay. . . .

Fourteenth Floor

I balked at becoming a group executive when the job was first offered to me in September. . . . Nevertheless, after two weeks of ceaseless pressure from my bosses, I relented and went "upstairs." A non-Chevrolet man was named to the post I was departing. It was not very long before I realized that I had made a horrible mistake. On my second day on the new job my boss, Richard Terrell, who succeeded Kyes as executive vice-president for Car and Truck, Body and Assembly, called me into his office. I had heard very little from him when I was running Chevrolet. Not once did we get into a serious discussion about the division's business. I suspect this was his choice since, until he succeeded Kyes, Terrell's entire 36-year GM career was spent in nonautomotive businesses, first with the Electronics Division and then the Frigidaire Division. He, therefore, knew little directly about GM's automotive operations. This was my first meeting with Terrell in my new capacity. He is moderately tall, with thin gray hair, steel-rimmed glasses, a perpetual smile that looks more like a smirk, and a manner that often gives a false sense of authority to what he says.

I walked into his office and sat down in front of his desk. Terrell pushed a button under the cabinet behind his desk, which closed the office door, leaned forward in his chair, looked sternly across his desk, and said to me in steely tones, "I want you to disappear into the wallpaper up here. I don't want to see you in the newspaper."

Those were not his exact words. He couched his message in terms of "team play," "good of the corporation," and how "no man is above the corporation." But the point of Terrell's message was as obvious to me as the dark suit and white shirt he wore.

"DeLorean, disappear into the boondocks."

I was shocked. And I knew that, while I hadn't heard from Terrell when I was running Chevrolet, I was going to be hearing a lot from him in the secretive quarters of The Fourteenth Floor because I was not protected by my ability and performance as I had been when I ran the car divisions. Up here I had nothing to operate to show that ability. I thought to myself: "Dealing with Terrell is going to be the Kyes situation all over again."

About a week or so later, I was in the office of Elliott M. (Pete) Estes, who was executive vice-president of operations. I was talking to him about some of my doubts about the business in general and life upstairs, and he said, "I've always told them that it's good for GM to have someone like you in the ranks. It shows how democratic we are."

I am sure Pete didn't realize the impact on me of his comment. He didn't say anything about how well I'd managed my business, the people I had developed, or what I'd contributed to the corporation in terms of quality products and substantial profit. All he said was I was sort of a weirdo. Until then, I guess I had deluded myself into thinking I was held in high esteem by my superiors, even if they didn't like me personally, because I was a business success. I had risen faster in the corporation than any of them, and I thought for that reason that I at least had their professional respect.

So I was tragically shocked to realize that this was not the case. Just as the corporation at the time had token blacks, token women, and token Chicanos, I was viewed as their token hippie. I just didn't fit in. When I thought over the meetings with Terrell and Estes, I began to realize once again that I could no longer stay with General Motors. I agonized over the prospect of leaving.

The Greenbrier incident made it obvious that someone in the corporation was making an effort to hurt my business reputation. . . . I then began a campaign to leave the corporation that was going to culminate tomorrow morning when I officially resigned. Late Sunday night, I went to sleep. . . .

At about 9:30 a.m., I arrived at the General Motors Building at 59th Street and Fifth Avenue. A minute or so later I walked into the office of Chairman Richard Gerstenberg on the twenty-fourth floor. In the room were Gerstenberg, Murphy—by now the vice-chairman—and Kenneth C. MacDonald, who was secretary of the board's bonus and salary committee. . . .

Resignation

The atmosphere in Gerstenberg's office was neither friendly nor bitter. It was strictly businesslike. The meeting lasted less than twenty minutes. I signed the document of resignation, effective May 31, 1973, which was prepared by the corporation. We all shook hands, and I left the room and headed for the bank of elevators.

Once on the main floor, I walked out into Fifth Avenue. For the first time in a quarter of a century I was out of work in the auto industry. There was a slight feeling of relief because the struggle was over. Bill Finelli took me back to LaGuardia and a flight to Detroit.

The board met that afternoon and approved my resignation. The public relations department prepared a news release—which was made public later in the month—announcing my resignation in which Gerstenberg praised my contributions to General Motors and wished me well in my new ventures. Once back in Detroit I drove home.

As I ate dinner quietly at home that night with my wife, Christina, and my son, Zachary, I fully realized I had done what few top executives have ever done in the automobile industry. I had quit General Motors.

Source: Wright, 1980, pp. 9–17.

Discussion Questions

1. Identify the sources of positional and personal power held by DeLorean in this case. How did DeLorean's views of power differ from others' at GM?

2. What impact did DeLorean's promotion from being the manager of an operating division to a senior executive at corporate headquarters have on his power at GM?

3. John DeLorean argues that managers at GM must totally subjugate their individuality to the corporate image. He complains that there was no place for the unique expression of personal style. The more he expressed his individuality, the less power he appeared to have in the organization. What is the relationship between conformity and power?

John DeLorean: Wild Ride for DeLorean Motors

He might have become president of General Motors. By the age of 49, he had raced up the ladder of the giant corporation and, as a group executive, was just one step from the top. But frustrated with a management system that he considered backward, he quit and launched a project that many considered impossible, to build a new car company from the ground up. He put his reputation on the line by thumbing his nose at his former colleagues in Detroit. He declared that he would show the rest of the auto industry how to build cars and that his company would produce an "ethical" car that U.S. buyers could afford. He identified closely with the product, putting his name on the company (DeLorean Motor Company) and the car, and his picture in the advertising. "Live the Dream" was the first ad slogan for the luxury auto, a stainless-steel two-seater with distinctive gull-wing doors.

Early Promise and Accomplishments

Despite the fact that a new car company had not been formed in the U.S. for over 50 years, DeLorean began his new venture like a man possessed, and his early achievements suggested he might prove his critics wrong. From 1975 to 1980, he raised $200 million in capital for his new venture from the British government, investors, and dealers. He established an advanced manufacturing plant in Belfast, Northern Ireland, employing 1,500 employees that provided a symbol of unity for Catholics and Protestants in a strife-torn, economically depressed area. He established an extensive dealers' network in the United States, which gave him potential economic clout equal to the fourth largest car producer in the United States—American Motors. In 1981, U.S. dealers had a year-long waiting list for the car, and the $25,000 car was being informally offered at a premium price of $33,900 for those desiring immediate delivery.

John DeLorean himself was viewed by many people as a political symbol, proof that the failures of big American business and government were not inevitable. Life could be changed for the better in the United States if, as DeLorean said, "everyone could just cut through the baloney and get on with the job."

However, this surprising upstart enterprise, the darling of the investment community and the jet-setters, soon encountered serious problems. In spite of the $200 million raised by DeLorean, most of the funds were tied up in research and development and manufacturing equipment. Given the long gestation period involved in building a car from scratch, the project developed a voracious appetite for capital.

Within a year, Cinderella's coach turned into a pumpkin. In 1981, a recession in the world auto market reduced sales and further aggravated working capital requirements. In this depressed economy, and against the advice of the company's manufacturing, marketing, and engineering chiefs, DeLorean ordered that car production in Belfast be doubled. He did so because of his confidence that his new product—by then profitable—would be scooped up by buyers. But the increased output quickly exceeded sales, and the company was plunged into a cash squeeze.

In February 1982, the Belfast manufacturing operation went into voluntary receivership in a desperate effort to keep the plant running after the British government refused to increase its $150 million investment in the facility. This was part of a series of frantic efforts initiated by DeLorean to salvage his dream. A deal with a New York real estate executive Peter Kalikow failed when Kalikow would not agree on final terms with the British receivers. Other alleged buyers, widely discussed by DeLorean in the press, including a major oil company, a European automaker, and a big investment firm, all failed to materialize.

Troubled by news of financial distress, BankAmerica Corp. lost faith in DMC's repaying abilities and moved to repossess the company's inventory of cars on piers on the East and West coasts. Meanwhile, the financial ills had begun to affect U.S. dealers as they complained about lack of reimbursement for warranty work and delays in delivery of spare parts.

Observers at this stage noted signs of stress in the former GM auto executive, including mood swings and contradictory statements. During this time, DeLorean was working at a hectic pace, meeting with 50 to 60 investors at once, in an effort to raise the required money to satisfy impatient creditors. Things came to a head when DeLorean was arrested in October 1982 and arraigned on eight counts of conspiring to peddle large amounts of cocaine and heroin. Officials called it a last-ditch effort to generate large amounts of capital to keep the fledgling car company afloat.

Although DeLorean was acquitted on all eight counts in a jury decision at Los Angeles in August 1984, and he was subsequently acquitted of fraud and misappropriation charges in another jury decision in Detroit in late 1986, the car project would never recover from these blows. In 1987, a bankruptcy court awarded a favorable deal to DeLorean that allowed him to retain a substantial portion of his personal assets. DeLorean was still optimistic about starting another sporting car project, completely different from the earlier one. However, in 1988, a British court decision, later upheld by a U.S. district judge, made him personally liable to pay $53 million to the principal investor in the car project—the British government.

What Went Wrong?

Critics of DeLorean blame him for the company's downfall, citing three serious personal and managerial shortcomings. First, they point to his lavish lifestyle and lack of interest in the company's operations. They argue that he preferred to be in New York most of the time, where he could be in the limelight, selling the project to the media and the investing public, and in the process attending the large number of parties thrown by the New York social set. He visited his factory about once a month. As one of his executives said, "John hated talking to dealers, production people, and investors. The only thing that interested him was self-promotion."

His absence from Belfast, coupled with his unwillingness to delegate authority, meant there was no one in control of the day-to-day operations. Thus, when the project began encountering delays, or when the car developed quality problems, there were no timely, coordinated responses. Furthermore, because he had hired two teams of designers, his presence was needed to mediate conflicts.

Second, when DeLorean was in Belfast, his colleagues complained that he was very autocratic. Morale that had been sky-high at the beginning of the project soon sank to a record low. DeLorean refused to listen to anybody who opposed him. When Bill Haddad, the company's chief public relations person, warned DeLorean that his attempts at pressuring the British government to come up with more money would play badly with the press, DeLorean ignored his advice. Robert Dowey resigned in August 1978 as the company's first chief financial officer because of an argument over money matters that ended with DeLorean saying, "You do things my way or leave." After that, the company had two other CFOs. In total, more than 10 ranking executives were fired or quit.

Critics cite as further evidence of DeLorean's disregard for the interests of his staff the fact that he decided not to honor stock option commitments. Most senior managers left lucrative jobs at prestigious firms, lured by the challenge of increased responsibilities in the new company along with the promise of generous stock options. Later, DeLorean decided to establish a new holding company that would own DMC, a move that made worthless the stock options issued to executives, because stock in the original company would never be issued. Haddad's open outrage at this move was an important factor in his ultimate removal from the company.

A third factor cited for the demise of DMC was the alleged financial improprieties. DeLorean paid himself half a million dollars, and paid his senior executives salaries that were excessive by industry standards. Further, he personally traveled on the Concorde between New York and London and stayed in the most expensive hotels, such as the Claridge in London, even after the company had gone into receivership. The office of DMC in New York was located in a penthouse suite at 280 Park Avenue, just across from the Waldorf Astoria. It was purchased from Xerox and appeared to be unusually expensive for a start-up company.

Critics also claim that he diverted resources from the company for his personal use. A former DeLorean official alleged that one company executive spent most of his time working on projects related to a snow-grooming ski-resort equipment company owned by John. His secretary, Marian Gibson, reported that he exaggerated losses to the company's plant from rioting in Belfast and used some of this money in personal purchases of real estate. She also stated that instead of $4 million he said he had invested in the company, DeLorean actually invested only $750,000.

Responses to Critics

DeLorean vigorously denied these charges, arguing that Bill Haddad carried on a personal vendetta against him and that Marian Gibson's accusations were instigated by Haddad. He counters that Haddad submitted documents to the British government purporting that he was a homosexual and circulated fake memos in the company to make him look bad. He defends his dismissal of other executives, saying that some were done on grounds of misappropriation of funds. In similar fashion, he dismisses the charges of acting autocratically and capriciously. "The tales of victimization of officers are baloney."

In response to the characterization of being an absentee CEO, he counters that he had to do the unenviable job of being fund-raiser, diplomat, and cheerleader, all in one. Furthermore, the reason he didn't turn over operational control to his staff was because the senior managers were specialists from other car companies, none of them possessing his level of general management experience. Moreover, he defends the problems of quality control, saying that the defects in his car were less than those encountered for the new Jaguar. He argues that his decision to double production in 1981 was sound because he had the orders to back it up. He claims that the back orders for the car, even when they closed production, were worth two years of production.

DeLorean also points out a number of "conspiring" external factors that exacerbated the normal cash-flow problems experienced by new companies. These included: (1) In 1981, the U.S. dollar increased in value, causing his car's price to shoot up from $18,000 to $25,000, and therefore to compare unfavorably with the Corvette, its main competitor, which sold for about $16,000. (2) He alleges that the British government refused to advance him further loans under pressure from GM. (After the closure of the company, GM opened a car project in Northern Ireland, investing and employing at a level similar to DMC. Earlier they had been against investing in Northern Ireland.) (3) During the early 1980s, the American auto industry experienced its worst slump in 40 years. Industry sales rates dropped from 8 million to 5 million a year. This recession forced automakers to cut off lines of credit for their dealers. Since 75 percent of DMC's dealers were GM and Ford dealers, cutting off dealer financing meant they couldn't pay for the cars they had already ordered from DeLorean, many of which were already on ships or in production.

Sources: Kolen, Simison, & Kempe, 1982; Fallon & Srodes, 1983; DeLorean, 1985.

Discussion Questions

1. In the book *On a Clear Day You Can See General Motors*, John DeLorean complains bitterly about the alleged abuse of executive privilege at GM. He viewed this behavior as counterproductive and personally insulting. Later, his subordinates at DeLorean Motor Co. made similar accusations about his management style. Is abuse of power inevitable among senior executives?

2. DeLorean's life seems to be characterized by a tragic pattern of sudden successes followed by spectacular failures. What role did his use of influence play in his roller-coaster management career?

3. Suppose you were a senior executive at DMC and you were the target of DeLorean's inappropriate use of influence. What could you have done to neutralize his actions?

John DeLorean: Reflections

Toward the end of his 1985 autobiography, John DeLorean reflected on his life—his ups and downs at General Motors (GM) and DeLorean Motor Company (DMC), his jet-set lifestyle, his failed marriage to model Christina Ferrari, and his time spent in jail on drug charges.

Recognizing that during the decade of the 1980s notoriety had replaced infamy, he started searching for truthful answers to the problems in his troubled life. He concluded that his life had been marred by pride and arrogance. Looking back over his career, he realized that he had consistently rationalized his actions, believing that his objectives and motivations were noble. For example, while starting DMC he had emphasized his desire to help the Irish people, but later he admitted that deep down he was doing it for himself.

Reflecting on his days at GM, DeLorean noticed a pattern in his policy confrontations with older executives: He would champion a principle that would be difficult politically for them to attack (e.g., minority hiring), thus forcing his colleagues to reluctantly support his positions. In retrospect, he could see this as a form of taunting his colleagues. Irrespective of the merits of the issue, getting attention was his driving motive.

He also saw his marriage to a beautiful woman as part of a strategy to make others envious of his glamorous lifestyle. He knew they would never know the problems in his marriage; they would feel only disappointment that they had to live with women who were less attractive and desirable.

DeLorean noted the similarities between his experiences at GM and DMC and those of the Nixon Administration. In particular, he identified with John Dean, who characterized his crimes against the public as having been committed in the name of "blind ambition." DeLorean recognized that his fight to build his own company was driven by "blind pride." He wanted to build a car that he could be proud of and that might successfully compete with GM cars. But in retrospect, he realized that he had inadequate money for the project and was constantly trying to catch up with DMC's debt. In reflecting on that era, he observed that although he should have temporarily abandoned the project, pride kept him going. "Too many people had said I couldn't succeed. Pride said I had to prove them wrong. What drove me to the brink of destruction was pride, not my faith in the future, not a rational appraisal of the actions I was taking. I could not fail. I was going to have a successful company, seemingly at all costs."

At the conclusion of his autobiography, DeLorean noted that it wasn't until he was alone in a prison cell that he finally faced the truth about himself and his career. He concluded, "Stripped of my business, my friends, my money, and my power, there was no more reason to be proud. By trying to walk alone, to live a life of foolish arrogance in pursuit of selfish personal goals, I had lost everything."

Discussion Questions

1. How does the view of empowerment discussed in this chapter differ from DeLorean's view of power? How have his views on the subject evolved over time?

2. DeLorean blames his personal inadequacies for the failure of his firm. It is common after a firm has failed to blame the owner. What other factors influenced this outcome? What role did DeLorean's personal failings play?

3. What are the two or three basic principles regarding the relationship of power and influence to managerial effectiveness that are illustrated in the DeLorean cases?

⬡ Skill Practice

Exercise for Gaining Power

Repairing Power Failures in Management Circuits

Rosabeth Kanter (1979) argues that much of what is labeled "poor management" in organizations is simply individuals protecting their diminished power bases. Instead of criticizing these managers as incompetent, she proposes that we bolster their feelings of personal power. If we solve the real problem of perceived lack of power, the undesirable symptoms of poor leadership often evaporate. This point of view is consistent with the principles discussed in this chapter.

Assignment

In this exercise, you are asked to give advice to individuals who feel powerless. For each of the situations below, form groups to explore opportunities for enhancing the power base of these three individuals. Prepare to report your recommendations.

Situation 1: First-Line Supervisor

Kate Shalene has been a first-line supervisor for six months. She was proud of her new promotion but surprised to discover she felt increasingly powerless. Instead of being a stepping-stone, this position was feeling more and more like a dead end. Managers above her were about her age and the hoped-for company expansion never materialized. She was not a central part of the organization, and she felt that no one ever noticed her unless she messed up. She was expected to be supportive of her subordinates, but they never returned the favor. She was expected to absorb their flack without support from above. In general, she felt as though she was constantly "getting it from both ends." Her job was extremely rule bound, so she had little discretion in what she did or how she did it. She had only modest control over the pay or benefits of her subordinates, because their union agreement left very little flexibility. So she felt powerless to reward them or punish them in ways that really mattered.

As a result, she found she was more and more apt to impose rules to get subordinates to do what she wanted. She became increasingly jealous of any successes and recognition achieved by her subordinates, so she tended to isolate them from people higher up in the organization and from complete information. She lost her penchant for informality and became increasingly rigid in following standard operating procedures. Predictably, her subordinates were becoming more resentful and less productive.

Situation 2: Staff Professional

Shawn Quinn came to the organization a year ago as a staff professional. He believed it might be a way for him to achieve considerable visibility with the top brass, but instead he felt isolated and forgotten. As a staff officer, he had almost no decision-making authority except in his narrow area of expertise. Most of what went on in the organization occurred without his involvement. Innovation and entrepreneurial activity were completely out of his realm. While some of the line officers were given opportunities for professional development, no one seemed to care about his becoming more experienced and capable. They saw him only as a specialist. Because his job didn't require that he work with others, he had little opportunity to cultivate relationships that might lead to contacts with someone near the top.

What hurt was that a consultant had been hired a few times to work on projects that were part of his area. If consultants could be brought in to do his work, he thought, he must not be very important to the organization.

Shawn found himself being more and more turf conscious. He didn't want others encroaching on his area of expertise. He tried to demonstrate his competence to others, but the more he did so, the more he became defined as a specialist, outside the mainstream of the organization. Overall, he felt that he was losing ground in his career.

Situation 3: Top Executive

May Phelps has been a top executive for three years now. When she obtained the position, she felt that her ultimate career goal had been achieved. Now she was not so sure. Surprisingly, she discovered myriad constraints limiting her discretion and initiative. For example, the job had so many demands and details associated with it that she never had time to engage in any long-term planning. There always seemed to be one more crisis that demanded her attention. Unfortunately, most of the constraints were from sources she couldn't control, such as government regulations, demands for greater accountability made by the board of directors and by stockholders, union relationships, equal opportunity statutes, and so on. She had built her reputation as a successful manager on being entrepreneurial, creative, and innovative, but none of those qualities seemed appropriate for the demands of her current work. Furthermore, because she was so mired in operations, she had become more and more out of touch with the information flow in the organization. Some things had to remain confidential with her, but her secrecy made others unwilling to share information with her. She had assistants who were supposed to be monitoring the organization and providing her with information, but she often felt they only told her what she wanted to hear.

May had begun to hear rumors that certain special-interest groups were demanding her removal from the top job. She responded by becoming more dictatorial and defensive, with the result that the organization was becoming more control-oriented and conservative. She felt that she was on a downward spiral, but she couldn't find a way to reverse the trend. "I always thought the saying 'It's lonely at the top' was just a metaphor," she mused.

Exercise For Using Influence Effectively

Managers are given formal power in an organization by virtue of their position of authority. However, they often find that this authority does not readily translate into actual influence. Particularly when they are working with peers, they find it necessary to develop informal relationships through making deals, persuasive arguments, and so forth. These relationships form the basis of real influence in an organization.

Assignment

After reading the following case, assume the roles of Ann's staff members. Divide into small groups and conduct an informal staff discussion in which you design a plan for influencing Ann's colleagues and superiors to support her proposal. First, decide which general influence strategy (or combination of strategies) is most appropriate for this situation. Second, using Table 7, recommend specific actions for implementing your general strategy. Prepare to present your suggestions, including justifications.

Ann Lyman's Proposal

Ann Lyman was recently hired by the Challenge Products Corporation (CPC) as a senior marketing executive for the electronic housewares division. Her previous experience at Pearces, a major competitor, had earned her a reputation for being a creative and hard-working manager. Her department at Pearces had increased in sales at least 15 percent per year over the past five years, and she had been featured in a lead article in *Contemporary Management*. This combination of competence and visibility was what attracted the attention of John Dilworth, the CEO of Challenge. John was troubled about the two-quarter decline in electronic sales. This was the core of CPC's business, and he could not risk losing market share.

In the past, CPC's products had dominated such a large share of their markets that, ironically, marketing wasn't considered very important. Production touted its high quality and low costs, purchasing emphasized its contribution to keeping costs low, and engineering stressed the durability of its designs. CPC products, it was argued by many, "sold themselves."

But that was before the cheaper, "look-alike" products from Asia flooded the discount stores. No longer could CPC expect high customer loyalty simply because it was the oldest, best known, most reliable name brand on the shelf. Ann was convinced that in order for CPC to stay competitive, the company needed to expand its product line, offering more options at different price levels. She felt they also needed to branch out into "trend designs" that appealed to the contemporary lifestyle of young adults. These options would require finding new channels of distribution, such as specialty mail-order catalogs, as well as manufacturing generic products for department stores' private labels.

These changes had far-reaching ramifications for other departments at CPC. For one thing, they meant that engineering would have to shorten its design cycle, provide support for a broader range of products, and emphasize customer-oriented, rather than functional, features. These changes would obviously not sit well with the production department, which jealously protected its long production runs based on standard orders and relatively few model changes. They also stressed ease of fabrication and assembly. In addition, purchasing would be required to find new sourcing alternatives for nonstandard parts, which would make it more difficult to get volume discounts and ensure quality.

After three months on the job, Ann felt she was ready to make her proposal to John. She pushed her staff hard to add the finishing touches before John left on his two-week vacation to

Lake Tahoe. She wasn't disappointed—he thought it was a winner. He was excited and ready to "sign on." But he was also realistic about the difficulty they faced convincing others that these changes were necessary. Ann's counterparts in production, purchasing, and engineering would certainly object. "It'll be a hard sell, but I think you have some good ideas," he concluded. "While I'm away, I'd like you to design a plan for getting the cooperation of the other departments. You can count on me for general support, but the culture in this organization isn't consistent with sending out an edict. You'll have to figure out how to get their support some other way."

Exercises for Neutralizing Unwanted Influence Attempts

An important aspect of becoming empowered and influential is reducing inappropriate dependence. Obviously, social and work interdependence are integral parts of organizational life. Most forms of interdependence are natural and healthy. However, sometimes individuals attempt to turn interdependence into dependence by exercising inappropriate influence. Their objective is to increase their power over us by creating a significant imbalance of power.

Assignment

Following are two role-play exercises. In each case, assume the role of the person who needs to resist unwanted influence (Betty or Pat). Prior to the beginning of the role play, review the relevant behavioral guidelines (see the Observer's Feedback Form in Appendix I), determine which combination is most appropriate, and plan your strategy for dealing with this problem. Do not read the other role descriptions (Bill or Lynn). Following the role-play, an assigned observer will give you feedback using the Observer's Feedback Form as a guide.

Cindy's Fast Foods

Betty, Assistant Manager

You are the assistant manager of Cindy's, a fast-food franchise in a college town. You are one of the few student employees who has stayed on after graduation. You weren't ready to move on, and there weren't that many good jobs in elementary education, anyway. The spring before graduation, the owner offered you the job of assistant manager. The timing was perfect because the offer would relieve the pressure on you to pursue teaching jobs in which you really weren't interested. Your work at Cindy's had sparked your interest in business, and your student-teaching experience had not been very successful. Even though your parents weren't too pleased about paying four years' tuition at an expensive private liberal-arts college to have you end up "cooking hamburgers" for a career, their feelings mellowed when you explained the opportunities you would have to advance and possibly purchase a franchise. "Besides," you told them, "I'll only be in this position for three years, and then I can decide whether I want to apply for a manager's position or try again for a teaching job."

It's hard to believe it's been two years since graduation. Your manager, Bill, has done a conscientious job helping you learn the ropes as a manager. He has worked you hard, but trained you well. You feel indebted to him for his help. You have become quite close friends, although his occasional dirty jokes and sexist comments with the guys on break in the back room make you feel uncomfortable.

One night you are finishing your book work for the day, after the rest of the crew has gone home. These late nights are the one really bad feature of your job. Just as you are about to turn out the lights, Bill comes in. It is not unusual for him to stop by at closing. He is single, likes to bowl after work, and sometimes drops by later on his way home. You are just putting on your coat when he asks you to come into his office. He shuts the door, and pulls up a chair next to you. "Betty, I've been watching your performance very closely. You're a hard worker. The employees enjoy your management style. And I've taken a liking to you as well. I think I have a good shot at transferring to a much larger store in Cincinnati. I'll be glad to get out of this one-horse town and gain more visibility closer to corporate headquarters."

You start getting a little nervous as he moves his chair closer to yours. "I think you would be a really good replacement for me, but you haven't completed your full term as assistant. So I'll need to ask for a special exception to the corporate policy. And I'll have to put in a good word for you with the owner. However, there's some risk involved for me, because the regional manager is a real stickler on rules, and I've asked him to recommend me for the Cincinnati job. But I'd be willing to take that risk under certain conditions." As he waits for a response, you know very well where this conversation is headed.

Bill, Manager

You have been attracted to Betty for some time. You find her very attractive, and you enjoy her company. You have several times manufactured excuses to have personal chats with her or to be alone with her. You think Betty finds you attractive, also. It seems that she has been extra friendly lately. You figure she's either bucking for your job or sending you signals that she'd like to expand your relationship beyond strictly business—or both. Besides, you feel she owes you something. You have worked extra hard to train her, and you've been dropping hints to the owner that you think Betty might be ready to move up.

9:00 to 7:30

Pat Simpson, Loan Officer

You are a member of a small consumer-loan company. The staff consists of you, another loan officer, and a secretary. Last month, a larger financial institution acquired your firm and made some personnel changes. The other loan officer, with whom you had worked for four years, was replaced by Lynn Jones. Having entered the company at about the same time, you and Lynn have known each other for years. In fact, you worked in the Ann Arbor office together for a year. During that time, you were both single, and together you enjoyed the night life of Detroit. You learn that Lynn is still single and "living the life of Riley." In contrast, you have been married for about three years. You looked forward to working with Lynn again but wondered if your lack of interest in the local night scene would affect your relationship. Lynn has the reputation of being capable but lazy. She's known for taking in lots of loan applications and then striking bargains with or cajoling coworkers into helping out with the dreaded credit-checking process. You wonder if this practice has anything to do with the fact that her uncle was a founding partner in the bank.

After Lynn arrives, you are shocked at the difference in your work attitudes and lifestyles. "Boy, what a difference three years makes!" you think to yourself. You and your previous office mate, Jim, were both married, and both of you favored a vigorous working tempo from 9:00 to 5:15, taking lunch when convenient. You and Jim had a great working relationship, and the loan volume in your office increased steadily. There was even some discussion of expanding the size of the staff. In contrast, Lynn prefers leisurely mornings that begin in earnest around 10:30, luncheons as long as Mexican siestas, and a flurry of activity between 4:00 and 7:30 P.M.

You and your spouse are experiencing some marital turbulence, and you feel it is very important to be home in the evenings. Your spouse has begun attending night classes and leaves for school at 8:00 P.M. The educational program is an extremely intense three-year ordeal. Unfortunately, the stress level already seems unbearable. When you stay at the office late, you not only miss dinner together but you don't even see each other until after class, when you are both so tired there is no opportunity for quality time. It seems as though most weekends are devoted to homework.

Because the office staff is so small, the difference in workday rhythms is creating a serious hardship on you. Lynn doesn't function very well in the morning and has begun expressing irritation when you rush out the door at closing time. Lately, your relationship has become strained. You handle most of the walk-in business early in the morning, eat lunch at your desk, and have your paperwork done by 5:30 at the latest. In contrast, Lynn is just getting into high gear about 4:00. Because company rules require checking each others' loan approvals, Lynn becomes testy when you say you can't stay after 5:30 to check her work. Some evenings you have relented and stayed until 7:00 or 8:00, but your spouse got very upset. When you don't stay late, you are greeted by a stack of paperwork on your desk in the morning, which makes it difficult for you to meet with new customers. Several times Lynn has tried to get you to do the credit checks on her loan applications, saying that the press of new business was too great.

Something has got to change! You decide to go to lunch with Lynn today and tell her how you feel.

Lynn Johnson, Loan Officer

You have worked for this firm for 10 years, and you are very good at your work. During that time, you have passed up offers from larger financial institutions because you like the flexibility of working in a small office. Besides, your family is well-to-do, so you aren't concerned about making a lot of money.

In every other office, your coworkers have been willing to accommodate your work style. They recognize that you are one of the top loan officers in the company—and having the right last name doesn't hurt any—so they make allowances for your idiosyncrasies.

But your new office mate (and, you thought, old friend) is an exception. Since you arrived, the relationship has been testy because of your different schedules. You don't understand why there can't be more tolerance for your work style. After all, you get the job done, and that's what counts. Besides, your requests for assistance are not that unreasonable; other coworkers have always been willing to comply.

Thinking about the impending discussion, you realize how important it is for you to get Pat to change her work habits to conform with yours. You certainly hope you can convince Pat to pitch in and help you when you get behind. "I mean, that's what coworkers (and old friends) are for, right?" you muse on the way to work. During the discussion, you plan to stress the reasonableness of your requests. Others have never objected strenuously; why should Pat? If that doesn't work, you plan to try and work out a bargain. Maybe you could put in a good word for Pat with your uncle, a founder of the company. Pat's career hasn't exactly skyrocketed, and she is probably itching to move to a larger office in a metropolitan city. Possibly, her title could be upgraded to Senior Loan Officer.

Skill Application

Activities for Gaining Power and Influence

Suggested Assignments

1. Select a friend or associate who has complained to you about feeling powerless in an organizational position. This might be a person who holds a relatively insignificant leadership position in a campus organization or a low-level position in a work organization. Perhaps the individual feels his or her personal abilities do not command respect in that position. Sit down with this person and teach him or her the guidelines for gaining power in an organization. (You might use the Assessment Survey at the beginning of the chapter as a diagnostic instrument.) As part of this conversation, design a specific plan of action for increasing both the positional and personal bases of power. Discuss the outcomes of this plan with your friend and report on his or her success.

2. Using the guidelines for gaining power, develop a plan for increasing your power in an organizational setting. Describe the setting, including the factors you feel account for your feelings of powerlessness. Use your score on the Assessment Survey as a diagnostic aid. Formulate a detailed strategy for increasing your positional and personal power. Report on your results and describe the benefits of becoming more empowered.

3. Over time, analyze your efforts to influence other people. Use the "Three Rs" model to catalog your strategies. Consider why you used each strategy. Did you repeatedly rely on one or two strategies, or did you vary your approach according to circumstances? Keep track of the outcome of each attempt. Did you seem to have more success with one of the strategies? Next, select a person you have attempted to influence, one with whom you have a close, ongoing relationship. Discuss the alternative influence strategies with that person and ask him or her what effect the frequent use of each approach might have on your relationship.

4. Watch at least two realistic dramas (movies, plays, TV). Observe the influence strategies used by various characters. Which form of influence did they use most frequently, and why? Did certain people demonstrate a preference for a particular strategy? If so, was this based on personality traits, sex roles, authority relationships, or other situational factors? How successful were these influence attempts, and what impact did they have on ongoing relationships?

5. Identify a specific relationship in which you are regularly asked to do things that you feel are inappropriate. Using the relevant guidelines for resisting unwanted influence, formulate a strategy for assertively responding to the next attempt. Role-play this approach with a friend or coworker and incorporate his or her suggestions. After you implement your plan, report on the outcome. What was the reaction? Were you successful in communicating your position? Was an understanding reached regarding future interactions that is more fair? Based on this experience, examine other relationships for which this approach might be appropriate.

6. Review the guidelines for empowering others presented in the chapter. Make a list of specific actions you could take that would empower others in a work, civic, educational, or family setting. Implement your plan for a period of time and then report on your results. What was the most difficult aspect of the assignment? What were the benefits to you and others? Based on this experience, formulate plans for expanding these actions to other relationships.

Application Plan and Evaluation

The intent of this exercise is to help you apply this cluster of skills in a real-life, out-of-class setting. Now that you have become familiar with the behavioral guidelines that form the basis of effective skill performance, you will improve most by trying out those guidelines in an everyday context. Unlike a classroom activity, in which feedback is immediate and others can assist you with their evaluations, this skill application activity is one you must accomplish and evaluate on your own. There are two parts to this activity. Part 1 helps prepare you to apply the skill. Part 2 helps you evaluate and improve on your experience. Be sure to write down answers to each item. Don't short-circuit the process by skipping steps.

Part 1. Planning

1. Write down the two or three aspects of this skill that are most important to you. These may be areas of weakness, areas you most want to improve, or areas that are most salient to a problem you face right now. Identify the specific aspects of this skill that you want to apply.

2. Now identify the setting or the situation in which you will apply this skill. Establish a plan for performance by actually writing down a description of the situation. Who else will be involved? When will you do it? Where will it be done?

   Circumstances:

   Who else?

   When?

   Where?

3. Identify the specific behaviors you will engage in to apply this skill. Operationalize your skill performance.

4. What are the indicators of successful performance? How will you know you have been effective? What will indicate you have performed competently?

Part 2. Evaluation

5. After you have completed your implementation, record the results. What happened? How successful were you? What was the effect on others?

6. How can you improve? What modifications can you make next time? What will you do differently in a similar situation in the future?

7. Looking back on your whole skill practice and application experience, what have you learned? What has been surprising? In what ways might this experience help you in the long term?

Chapter

6

Motivating Employees

OBJECTIVES

▶ Diagnose work-performance problems

▶ Develop employee abilities

▶ Foster a motivating and rewarding work environment

skill development

◀ Skill Assessment

Diagnosing Poor Performance and Enhancing Motivation
Work Performance Assessment

■ Skill Learning

Increasing Motivation and Performance
Diagnosing Work Performance Problems
Enhancing Individuals' Abilities
Fostering a Motivating and Rewarding Work Environment
Elements of an Effective Motivation Program
Summary
Behavioral Guidelines for Improving Performance

⬗ Skill Analysis

Electro Logic

⬡ Skill Practice

Joe Chaney
Work Performance Assessment
Shaheen Matombo

● Skill Application

Suggested Assignments
Application Plan and Evaluation

Skill Assessment

Diagnostic Surveys for Motivating Others

Diagnosing Poor Performance and Enhancing Motivation

Step 1: Before you read the material in this chapter, please respond to the following statements by writing a number from the rating scale below in the left-hand column (Preassessment). Your answers should reflect your attitudes and behavior as they are now, not as you would like them to be. Be honest. This instrument is designed to help you discover your level of competency in motivating others so you can tailor your learning to your specific needs. When you have completed the survey, use the scoring key in Appendix I to identify the skill areas discussed in this chapter that are most important for you to master.

Step 2: After you have completed the reading and the exercises in this chapter and, ideally, as many as you can of the Skill Application assignments at the end of this chapter, cover up your first set of answers. Then respond to the same statements again, this time in the right-hand column (Postassessment). When you have completed the survey, use the scoring key in Appendix I to measure your progress. If your score remains low in specific skill areas, use the behavioral guidelines at the end of the Skill Learning section to guide further practice.

Rating Scale

1	Strongly disagree	4	Slightly agree
2	Disagree	5	Agree
3	Slightly disagree	6	Strongly agree

Assessment

Pre-   Post-   *When another person needs to be motivated:*

_____   _____   1. I always approach a performance problem by first establishing whether it is caused by a lack of motivation or ability.

_____   _____   2. I always establish a clear standard of expected performance.

_____   _____   3. I always offer to provide training and information, without offering to do tasks myself.

_____   _____   4. I am honest and straightforward in providing feedback on performance and assessing advancement opportunities.

_____   _____   5. I use a variety of rewards to reinforce exceptional performances.

_____   _____   6. When discipline is required, I give specific suggestions for improvement.

_____   _____   7. I design task assignments to make them interesting and challenging.

_____   _____   8. I strive to provide the rewards that each person values.

_____ _____ 9. I make sure that people feel fairly and equitably treated.

_____ _____ 10. I make sure that people get timely feedback from those affected by task performance.

_____ _____ 11. I carefully diagnose the causes of poor performance before taking any remedial or disciplinary action.

_____ _____ 12. I always help people establish performance goals that are challenging, specific, and time bound.

_____ _____ 13. Only as a last resort do I attempt to reassign or release a poorly performing individual.

_____ _____ 14. Whenever possible, I make sure valued rewards are linked to high performance.

_____ _____ 15. I consistently discipline when effort is below expectations and below capabilities.

_____ _____ 16. I try to combine or rotate assignments so that people can use a variety of skills.

_____ _____ 17. I try to arrange for an individual to work with others in a team, for the mutual support of all.

_____ _____ 18. I make sure that people use realistic standards for measuring fairness.

_____ _____ 19. I provide immediate compliments and other forms of recognition for meaningful accomplishments.

_____ _____ 20. I always determine if a person has the necessary resources and support to succeed in a task.

Work Performance Assessment

Respond to the following statements, based on your current (or recent) work situation. Then turn to Appendix I for the scoring key.

Rating Scale

1 Strongly disagree   4 Agree

2 Disagree   5 Strongly agree

3 Neutral

_____ 1. My supervisor and I agree on the quality of my performance.

_____ 2. I feel I have adequate training to perform my current job assignments.

_____ 3. I believe that my native skills and abilities are matched very well with my job responsibilities.

_____ 4. I believe that I have adequate resources and supplies to do my job well.

_____ 5. I understand my boss's expectations and generally feel they are realistic.

_____ 6. I believe that rewards are distributed fairly, on the basis of performance.

_____ 7. The rewards and opportunities available to me if I perform well are attractive to me personally.

_____ 8. My supervisor indicates that I am not performing as well as I should, but I disagree.

_____ 9. I could do a much better job if I had more training.

	10.	I believe that my job is too difficult for my ability level.
	11.	I believe that my job performance is hindered by a lack of supplies and resources.
	12.	I believe my boss's expectations are unclear and unrealistic.
	13.	I believe my boss plays favorites in allocating rewards.
	14.	I do not find the rewards and opportunities available to high performers very appealing.

■ Skill Learning

Increasing Motivation and Performance

I can't understand why we have such poor luck with Directors of Engineering. The man in there before Haverstick was technically well qualified. He'd been a good designer for us before we promoted him to be the first head of engineering. But he took to drinking heavily, and we had to relieve him of the responsibility. Then Haverstick seemed so promising. They say he is doing well in his new job at the Beta Company. But they operate much differently from the way we do. Then, Steve Spencer—he seemed to have all the qualifications we needed. And he certainly was a gentleman. But he never could get things done. Apparently he couldn't gain the respect of the design boys. So, here we are, looking for another replacement. I'm beginning to wonder whether we'll ever find the right one.

So ends a classic case of organizational design, "Higgins Equipment Company" (Dalton, Lawrence, & Lorsch, 1970, p. 81). The comments of the company president reflect the frustration he has experienced trying to staff a key position in the organization. He had filled the position three times with individuals of experience and high promise, but their performance was consistently disappointing. A close reading of the case reveals myriad structural obstacles facing any occupant of this position. Several subunits in the engineering division perform production and marketing activities. The director is both the head of engineering

and the director of a subunit called Engineering Services, which coordinates engineering and production activities. Finally, one of the department heads in engineering was one of the founders of the firm and has informal direct access to the president.

Diagnosing Work Performance Problems

A Chinese proverb states, "For every hundred men hacking away at the leaves of a diseased tree, only one man stoops to inspect the roots." The first part of this chapter examines how to identify correctly the underlying causes of performance problems. The second part presents a six-step process for creating a highly motivating work environment.

A good diagnostician needs to have a model to guide the inquiry process. Vroom (1964; see also, Steers, Porter, & Bigley, 1996) has summarized the determinants of task performance as follows:

$$Performance = Ability \times Motivation\ (Effort)$$

where

$$Ability = Aptitude \times Training \times Resources$$

$$Motivation = Desire \times Commitment$$

According to these formulas, **performance** is the product of ability multiplied by motivation, **ability** is the product of aptitude multiplied by training and resources, and **motivation** is the product of desire and commitment. The multiplicative function in these formulas suggests that all elements are essential. For example, workers who have 100 percent of the motivation and 75 percent of the ability required to perform a task can perform at an above-average rate. However, if these individuals have only 10 percent of the ability required, no amount of motivation will enable them to perform satisfactorily.

Aptitude refers to the native skills and abilities a person brings to a job. These involve physical and mental capabilities, but for many people-oriented jobs, they also include personality characteristics, such as those discussed in Chapter 1, Developing Self-Awareness. Most of our inherent abilities can be enhanced by education and training. Indeed, much of what we call native ability in adults can be traced to previous skill-enhancement experiences, such as modeling the social skills of parents or older siblings. Nevertheless, it is useful to consider training as a separate component of ability, since it represents an important mechanism for improving employee performance. Ability should be assessed during the job-matching process by screening applicants against the skill requirements of the job. If an applicant has minor deficiencies in skill aptitude but many other desirable characteristics, an intensive training program can be used to increase the applicant's qualifications to perform the job.

Our definition of ability is broader than most. We are focusing on the ability to perform, rather than the performer's ability. Therefore, our definition includes a third, situational component: adequate resources. Frequently, highly capable and well-trained individuals are placed in situations that inhibit job performance. Specifically, they aren't given the resources (technical, personnel, political) to perform assigned tasks effectively.

Motivation represents an employee's desire and commitment to perform and is manifested in job-related effort. Some people want to complete a task but are easily distracted or discouraged. They have high desire but low commitment. Others plod along with impressive persistence, but their work is uninspired. These people have high commitment but low desire.

The first diagnostic question that must be asked by the supervisor of a poor performer is whether the person's performance deficiencies stem from lack of ability or lack of motivation. Managers need four pieces of information in order to answer this question (Michener, Fleishman, & Vaske, 1976):

1. How difficult are the tasks being assigned to the individual?

2. How capable is the individual?

3. How hard is the individual trying to succeed at the job?

4. How much improvement is the individual making?

Low ability is generally associated with very difficult tasks, overall low individual ability, evidence of strong effort, and lack of improvement over time.

The answer to the question "Is this an ability or motivation problem?" has far-reaching ramifications for manager-subordinate relations. Research on this topic has shown that managers tend to apply more pressure to a person if they feel that the person is deliberately not performing up to expectations, rather than not performing effectively due to external, uncontrollable forces. Managers sometimes justify their choice of a forceful influence strategy on the grounds that the subordinate has a poor attitude, is hostile to authority, or lacks dedication.

Unfortunately, if the manager's assessment is incorrect and poor performance is related to ability rather than motivation, the response of increased pressure will worsen the problem. If poor performers feel that management is insensitive to their problems—that they lack resources, adequate training, or realistic time schedules—they may respond counterproductively to any tactics aimed at increasing their effort. Quite likely they will develop a motivational problem—that is, their desire and commitment will decrease—in response to management's insensitive, "iron-fisted" actions. Seeing this response, management will feel that their original diagnosis is confirmed, and they will use even stronger forms of influence to force compliance. The resulting vicious cycle is extremely difficult to break and underscores the high stakes involved in accurately diagnosing poor performance problems.

In this chapter, we will examine the two components of performance in more detail. We'll discuss manifestations of low ability and poor motivation, their causes, and some proposed remedies. We'll devote more attention to motivation, since motivation is more central to day-to-day manager-subordinate interactions. While ability tends to remain stable over long periods of time, motivation fluctuates; therefore, it requires closer monitoring and frequent recharging.

Enhancing Individuals' Abilities

A person's lack of ability might inhibit good performance for several reasons. Ability may have been assessed improperly during the screening process prior to employment, the technical requirements of a job may have been radically upgraded, or a person who performed very well in one position may be promoted into a higher-level position that is too demanding. (The Peter Principle states that people are typically promoted one position above their level of competence.) In addition, human and material resource support may have been reduced because of organizational budget cutbacks.

As noted by Quick (1977), managers should be alert for individuals who show signs of ability deterioration. Following are three danger signals for management positions:

Taking refuge in a specialty. Managers show signs of insufficient ability when they respond to situations not by managing, but by retreating to their technical specialty. This often occurs when general managers who feel insecure address problems outside their area of expertise and experience. Anthony Jay, in *Management and Machiavelli* (1967), dubs this type of manager "George I," after the King of England who, after assuming the throne, continued to be preoccupied with the affairs of Hanover, Germany, whence he had come.

Focusing on past performance. Another danger sign is measuring one's value to the organization in terms of past performance or on the basis of former standards. Some cavalry commanders in World War I relied on their outmoded knowledge of how to conduct successful military campaigns and, as a result, failed miserably in mechanized combat. This form of obsolescence is common in organizations that fail to shift their mission in response to changing market conditions.

Exaggerating aspects of the leadership role. Managers who have lost confidence in their ability tend to be very defensive. This often leads them to exaggerate one aspect of their managerial role. Such managers might delegate most of their responsibilities because they no longer feel competent to perform them well. Or they might become nuts-and-bolts administrators who scrutinize every detail to an extent far beyond its practical value. Still others become "devil's advocates," but rather than stimulating creativity, their negativism thwarts efforts to change the familiar.

Strategies for Improving Abilities

Five principal tools are available for overcoming poor performance problems due to lack of ability: *resupply, retrain, refit, reassign,* and *release.* We will discuss these in the order in which a manager should consider them.

Once a manager has ascertained that lack of ability is the primary cause of someone's poor performance, a performance review interview should be scheduled to explore these options, beginning with resupplying and retraining. Unless the manager has overwhelming evidence that the problem stems from low aptitude, it is wise to assume initially that it is due to a lack of resources or training. This gives the subordinate the benefit of the doubt and reduces the likely defensive reaction to an assessment of inadequate aptitude.

The **resupply** option focuses on the support needs of the job, including personnel, budget, and political clout. Asking, "Do you have what you need to perform this job satisfactorily?" allows the subordinate to express his or her frustration related to inadequate support. Managers should be cautioned that poorly performing subordinates typically blame external causes (Staw, McKechnie, & Puffer, 1983). Therefore, one should explore the subordinate's complaints about lack of support in detail to determine their validity. Even if employees exaggerate their claims, starting your discussion of poor performance in this manner signals your willingness to help them solve the problem from their perspective rather than to find fault from your perspective.

The next least threatening option is to **retrain.** Each year, the U.S. private sector spends approximately $50 billion on training for about 40 million employees—almost one-third of the civilian labor force (Lee, 1991). This is a sizeable expenditure for American corporations, but the reasons for these expenditures are clear. First of all, technology is changing so quickly that employees' skills can soon become obsolete. It has been said that 25-year-old engineering graduates will need to be reeducated eight times within their 40-year careers (Lusterman, 1985). Second, employees will typically fill a number of different positions throughout their careers, each demanding different proficiencies. Finally, demographic changes in our society will lead to an increasingly older workforce. In order for companies to remain competitive, more and more of them must retrain their older employees.

Training programs can take a variety of forms. For example, many firms are using computer technology more in education. This can involve interactive technical instruction and business games that simulate problems likely to be experienced by managers in the organization. More traditional forms of training include subsidized university courses and in-house technical or management seminars. Some companies have experimented with company sabbaticals to release managers or senior technical specialists from the pressures of work so they can concentrate on retooling.

In many cases, resupplying and retraining are insufficient remedies for poor performance. When this happens, the next step should be to explore **refitting** poor performers to their task assignments. While the subordinates remain on the job, the components of their work are analyzed, and different combinations of tasks and abilities that accomplish organizational objectives and provide meaningful and rewarding work are explored. For example, an assistant may be brought in to handle many of the technical details of a first-line supervisor's position, freeing up more time for the supervisor to focus on people development or to develop a long-term plan to present to upper management.

If a revised job description is unworkable or inadequate, the fourth alternative is to **reassign** the poor performer, either to a position of less responsibility or to one requiring less technical knowledge or interpersonal skills. For example, a medical specialist in a hospital who finds it increasingly difficult to keep abreast of new medical procedures but has demonstrated management skills might be shifted to a full-time administrative position.

The last option is to **release.** If retraining and creative redefinition of task assignments have not worked and if there are no opportunities for reassignment in the organization, the manager should consider releasing the employee from the organization. This option is generally constrained by union agreements, company policies, seniority considerations, and government regulations. Frequently, however, chronic poor performers

who could be released are not because management chooses to sidestep a potentially unpleasant task. Instead, the decision is made to set these individuals "on the shelf," out of the mainstream of activities, where they can't cause any problems. Even when this action is motivated by humanitarian concerns ("I don't think he could cope with being terminated"), it often produces the opposite effect. Actions taken to protect an unproductive employee from the embarrassment of termination just substitute the humiliation of being ignored. Obviously, termination is a drastic action that should not be taken lightly. However, the consequences for the unproductive individuals and their coworkers of allowing them to remain after the previous four actions have proven unsuccessful should be weighed carefully in considering this option.

This approach to managing ability problems is reflected in the philosophy of Wendell Parsons, CEO of Stamp-Rite. He argues that one of the most challenging aspects of management is helping employees recognize that job enhancements and advancements are not always possible. Therefore, he says, "If a long-term employee slows down, I try to turn him around by saying how much I value his knowledge and experience, but pointing out that his production has slipped too much. If boredom has set in and I can't offer the employee a change, I encourage him to face the fact and consider doing something else with his life" (*Nation's Business,* March 1988, p. 25).

Fostering a Motivating and Rewarding Work Environment

The second component of employee performance is motivation. While it is important to see to the training and the support needs of subordinates and to be actively involved in the hiring and the job-matching processes to ensure adequate aptitude, the influence of a manager's actions on the day-to-day motivation of subordinates is equally vital. Effective managers devote considerable time to gauging and strengthening their subordinates' motivation, as reflected in their effort and concern.

In one of the seminal contributions to management thought, Douglas McGregor (1960) introduced the term "Theory X" to refer to a management style characterized by close supervision. The basic assumption of this theory is that people really do not want to work hard or assume responsibility. Therefore, in order to get the job done, managers must coerce, intimidate, manipulate, and closely supervise their employees. In contrast, McGregor espoused a "Theory Y" view of workers. He argued that workers basically want to do a good job and assume more responsibility. Therefore, he argued, management's role is to assist workers to reach their potential by productively channeling their motivation to succeed. Unfortunately, McGregor believed, most managers subscribe to Theory X assumptions about workers' motives.

The alleged prevalence of the Theory X view brings up an interesting series of questions about motivation. What is the purpose of teaching motivation skills to managers? Should managers learn these skills so they can help employees reach their potential? Or are we teaching these skills to managers so they can more effectively manipulate their employees' behavior? These questions naturally lead to a broader set of issues regarding employee-management relations. Assuming a manager feels responsible for maintaining a given level of productivity, is it also possible to be concerned about the needs and desires of employees? In other words, are concerns about employee morale and company productivity compatible, or are they mutually exclusive?

Contemporary research, as well as the experience of highly acclaimed organizational motivation programs (Steers, Porter, & Bigley, 1996), supports the position that concerns about morale and performance can coexist. As Figure 1 shows, effective motivational programs not only can, but must, focus on increasing both satisfaction and productivity. A high emphasis on satisfaction with a low emphasis on performance represents an irresponsible view of the role of management. Managers are hired by owners to look after the owners' interests. This entails holding employees accountable for producing satisfactory results. Managers who emphasize satisfaction to the exclusion of performance will be seen as nice people, but their **indulging** management style undermines the respect of their subordinates. It is easy to imagine an organizational climate that is so satisfaction-oriented that management becomes overly responsive to employees' requests and the resulting country-club-like atmosphere hinders good performance.

A strong emphasis on performance to the exclusion of satisfaction is equally ineffective. This time, instead of indulging, the manager is **imposing.** In this situation, managers have little concern for how employees feel about their jobs. The boss issues orders, and the employees must follow them. Exploited employees are unhappy employees, and unhappy employees may seek employment with the competition. Thus, while exploitation may increase productivity in the short run, its long-term effects generally decrease productivity through increased absenteeism, employee turnover, and in some cases, even sabotage and violence.

When managers emphasize neither satisfaction nor performance, they are **ignoring** their responsibilities and the facts at hand. The resulting neglect reflects a lack of management. There is no real leadership, in the sense that employees receive neither priorities nor direction. Paralyzed between what they consider to be mutually exclusive options of emphasizing performance or satisfaction, managers choose neither. The

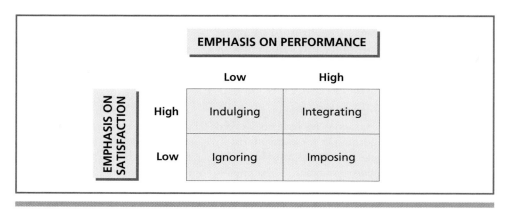

Figure 1 Relationship Between Satisfaction and Performance

resulting neglect, if allowed to continue, may ultimately lead to the failure of the work unit.

The **integrating** motivation strategy emphasizes performance and satisfaction equally. Effective managers are able to combine what appear to be competing forces into integrative, synergistic programs. Instead of accepting the conventional wisdom that says competing forces cancel each other out, they capitalize on the tension between the combined elements to forge new approaches creatively. However, this does not mean that both objectives can be fully satisfied in every specific case. Some tradeoffs occur naturally in ongoing work situations. However, in the long run, both objectives should be given equal consideration.

The integrative view of motivation proposes that while the importance of employees feeling good about what they are doing and how they are being treated cannot be downplayed, this concern should not overshadow management's responsibility to hold people accountable for results. Managers should avoid the twin traps of working to engender high employee morale for its own sake or pushing for short-term results at the expense of long-term commitment. The best managers have productive people who are also satisfied with their work environment (Kotter, 1996).

This view of management is reflected in David Bradford and Allan Cohen's popular management guide, *Managing for Excellence* (1984). "Excellence requires budget and control systems, formalized ways to appraise, reward, and promote, long-range planning and forecasting systems, and division of labor and job descriptions. The dilemma for the manager, then, is not whether control needs to be exercised, but how to see that it is exercised without weakening the motivation of those with energy and enthusiasm" (p. 21).

Elements of an Effective Motivation Program

The remainder of this chapter lays out a step-by-step program for creating an integrative, synergistic motivational program grounded in the belief that employees can simultaneously be high performers and personally satisfied. Table 1 shows the basic components of a motivational program that integrates performance and satisfaction.

The key assumptions underlying these six elements are:

1. Employees frequently start out motivated. Therefore, a lack of motivation is a learned response, often fostered by misunderstood or unrealistic expectations.

---

1. Establish moderately difficult goals that are understood and accepted.
   Ask: "Do subordinates understand and accept my performance expectations?"

2. Remove personal and organizational obstacles to performance.
   Ask: "Do subordinates feel it is possible to achieve this goal or expectation?"

3. Use rewards and discipline appropriately to extinguish unacceptable behavior and encourage exceptional performance.
   Ask: "Do subordinates feel that being a high performer is more rewarding than being a low or average performer?"

4. Provide salient internal and external incentives.
   Ask: "Do subordinates feel the rewards used to encourage high performance are worth the effort?"

5. Distribute rewards equitably.
   Ask: "Do subordinates feel that work-related benefits are being distributed fairly?"

6. Provide timely rewards and honest feedback on performance.
   Ask: "Are we getting the most out of our rewards by administering them on a timely basis as part of the feedback process?"
   Ask: "Do subordinates know where they stand in terms of current performance and long-term opportunities?"

Table 1 Six Elements of an Integrative Motivation Program

2. The role of management is to create a supportive, problem-solving work environment in which necessary resources to perform a task are provided.

3. Rewards should encourage high personal performance that is consistent with management objectives.

4. Motivation works best when it is based on self-governance.

5. Individuals should be treated fairly.

6. Individuals deserve timely, honest feedback on work performance.

Clear Performance Goals

Managers should begin assessing the motivational climate of their work environment by asking, "Do subordinates understand and accept my performance expectations?" The foundation of an effective motivation program is proper **goal setting** (Locke & Latham, 1990). The salience of goal setting is so well recognized that it has been incorporated in several formal management tools, such as management by objectives (MBO). Effective goal setting has three critical components: goal-setting process, goal characteristics, and feedback.

A common theme in this book is, "The way you do things is very often as important as what you do." Applied to goal setting, this means that the process used to set goals must be considered carefully. The critical consideration regarding the goal-setting process is that goals must be understood and accepted if they are to be effective. Subordinates are more likely to "buy into" goals if they feel they were part of the goal-setting process (Earley & Kanfer, 1985). This is especially important if the work environment is unfavorable for goal accomplishment (Latham, Erez, & Locke, 1988). For example, a goal might be inconsistent with accepted practice, require new skills, or exacerbate poor management-employee relations. To be sure, if working conditions are highly conducive to goal accomplishment, subordinates may be willing to commit themselves to the achievement of goals in whose formulation they did not participate. However, such acceptance usually occurs only when management demonstrates an overall attitude of understanding and support (Latham & Locke, 1979). When

management does not exhibit a supportive attitude, the imposed goals or task assignments are likely to be viewed as unwelcome demands. As a result, subordinates will question the premises underlying the goals or assignments and will comply only reluctantly with the demands.

Sometimes it is difficult to implement these process guidelines. A manager frequently is given directions regarding new tasks or assignment deadlines that must be passed on. However, if subordinates believe management is committed to involving them in all discretionary aspects of the governance of their work unit, they are more willing to accept top-down directions regarding the nondiscretionary aspects of work assignments. For example, a computer programming unit may not have any say about which application programs are assigned to the group or what priority is assigned each incoming assignment. However, the manager can still involve unit members in deciding how much time to allocate to each assignment ("What is a realistic goal for completing this task?") or who should receive which job assignment ("Which type of programs would you find challenging?").

Shifting from process to content, research has shown that **goal characteristics** significantly affect the likelihood that the goal will be accomplished (Locke & Latham, 1990). Effective goals are *specific, consistent,* and *appropriately challenging.*

Specific goals are measurable, unambiguous, and behavioral. Specific goals reduce misunderstanding about what behaviors will be rewarded. Admonitions such as "be dependable," "work hard," "take initiative," or "do your best" are too general and too difficult to measure and are therefore of limited motivational value. In contrast, when a new vice president of operations was appointed at a major midwestern steel factory, he targeted three goals: Reduce finished product rejection by 15 percent (quality); reduce average shipment period by two days (customer satisfaction); and respond to all employee suggestions within 48 hours (employee involvement).

Goals should also be **consistent.** An already hardworking assistant vice president in a large metropolitan bank complains that she cannot increase both the number of reports she writes in a week and the amount of time she spends "on the floor," visiting with employees and customers. Goals that are inconsistent—in the sense that they are logically impossible to accomplish simultaneously—or incompatible—in the sense that they both require so much effort that they can't be accomplished at the same time—create frustration and alienation. When subordinates complain that goals are incompatible or inconsistent, managers should be flexible enough to reconsider their expectations.

One of the most important characteristics of goals is their level of **challenge** (Wood, Mento, & Locke, 1987). Simply stated, hard goals are more motivating than easy goals. One explanation for this is called "achievement motivation" (Atkinson & Raynor, 1974). According to this perspective, workers size up new tasks in terms of their chances for success and the significance of the anticipated accomplishment.

Based only on perceived likelihood of success, one would predict that those who seek success would choose an easy task to perform because the probability for success is the highest. However, these individuals also factor into their decisions the significance of completing the task. To complete a goal that anyone can reach is not rewarding enough for highly motivated individuals. In order for them to feel successful, they must believe that an accomplishment represents a meaningful achievement. Given their desire for success and achievement, it is clear that these workers will be most motivated by challenging, but reachable, goals.

Although there is no single standard of difficulty that fits all people, it is important to keep in mind that high expectations generally foster high performance. As one experienced manager said, "We get about what we expect." Warren Bennis, author of *The Unconscious Conspiracy: Why Leaders Can't Lead,* agrees. "In a study of school teachers, it turned out that when they held high expectations of their students, that alone was enough to cause an increase of 25 points in the students' IQ scores" (Bennis, 1984).

In addition to selecting the right type of goal, an effective goal program must also include **feedback.** Feedback provides opportunities for clarifying expectations, adjusting goal difficulty, and gaining recognition. Therefore, it is important to provide benchmark opportunities for individuals to determine how they are doing. These along-the-way progress reports are particularly critical when the time required to complete an assignment or reach a goal is very long. For example, feedback is very useful for projects such as writing a large computer program or raising a million dollars for a local charity. In these cases, feedback should be linked to accomplishing intermediate stages or completing specific components.

Managerial Support and Encouragment

One of the key ingredients of an effective goal program is a supportive work environment. After setting goals, the manager should shift focus to facilitating successful accomplishment. This can be done by asking, "Do subordinates feel it is possible to achieve this goal?" Help from management must come in many forms, including making sure the worker has the required abilities for the job, providing the necessary training, securing needed resources, and encouraging cooperation and support from other work units. It is the manager's job to make the paths leading toward the targeted goals easier for the subordinate to travel.

This management philosophy can be illustrated readily with examples from sports. Instead of assuming the role of the star quarterback who expects the rest of the team to make him look good, the facilitative manager is more like the blocking fullback or the pulling guard who specializes in downfield blocking and punching holes in the opposition's defenses. In a basketball example, this type of leader is like the player who takes more pride in his number of assists than in the number of points he has scored.

This view is reflected in the management philosophy of Stew Leonard, star of management films on effective motivation, Dale Carnegie ads, and one of 11 businessmen honored at the White House. His dairy sells $100 million worth of food a year—the largest sales volume per square foot in the grocery business. When asked for his management philosophy, Stew downplays gimmicks and high pressure in favor of "genuine caring" for customers and employees. This involves overcoming the natural tendency to worry about "What's in it for me?" The man who helped make Paul Newman's salad dressing famous offers this management advice: "Don't go into business to get rich. Do it to enrich people. It will come back to you." Stew Leonard understands that the more we focus on our rewards, the less rewarding our focus becomes (*Champaign, Illinois, News-Gazette,* January 20, 1987, p. 6).

However, as with all general management guidelines, effective results follow from sensitive, informed implementation tailored to specific circumstances. In this case, the manner in which this enabling, facilitative role should be implemented varies considerably among individuals, organizational settings, and tasks. When subordinates believe that strong management support is needed, leaders who are not aware of the obstacles to performance, or not assertive enough to remove them, probably will be perceived as part of the employee's problem, rather than the source of solutions. By the same token, when management intervention is not needed or expected, managers who are constantly involved in the details of subordinates' job performance will be viewed as meddling and unwilling to trust. This view of management is incorporated in the "path goal" theory of leadership (House & Mitchell, 1974; see also, Shamir, House, & Arthur, 1993), shown in Figure 2. The key question it addresses is, "How much help should a manager provide?" In response, the model proposes that the level of involvement should vary according to how much subordinates need to perform a specific task; how much they expect, in general; and how much support is available to them from other organizational sources.

The key task characteristics of the path-goal model are structure and difficulty. A task that is highly structured, as reflected in the degree of built-in order and direction, and relatively easy to perform does not require extensive management direction. If managers offer too

much advice, they will come across as controlling, bossy, or nagging, because from the nature of the task itself, it is already clear to the subordinates what they should do. On the other hand, for an unstructured and difficult task, management's direction and strong involvement in problem-solving activities will be seen as constructive and satisfying.

The second factor that influences the appropriate degree of management involvement is the expectations of the subordinates. Three distinct characteristics influence expectations: desire for autonomy, experience, and ability. Individuals who prize their autonomy and independence prefer managers with a highly participative, unobtrusive, leadership style because it gives them more latitude for controlling what they do. In contrast, people who prefer the assistance of others in making decisions, establishing priorities, and solving problems prefer greater management involvement.

The connection between a worker's ability and experience levels and preferred management style is straightforward. Capable and experienced employees feel they need less assistance from their managers because they are adequately trained, know how to obtain the necessary resources, and can handle political entanglements with their counterparts in other units. They appreciate managers who "give them their head"

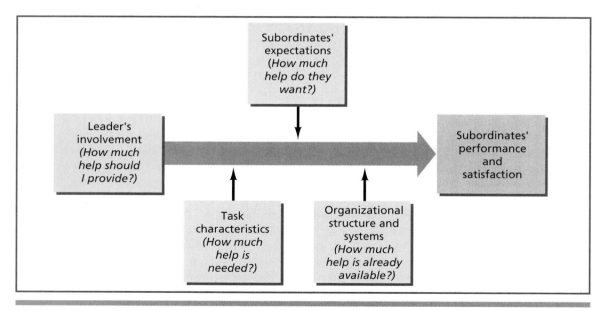

Figure 2   Leader Involvement and Subordinate Performance

but periodically check to see if further assistance is required. On the other hand, it is frustrating for relatively new employees, or those with marginal skills, to feel that their manager has neither the time nor interest to listen to basic questions.

An important concept in the path-goal approach to leadership is that management involvement should complement, rather than duplicate, organizational sources of support. Specifically, managers should provide more "downfield blocking" in situations where work-group norms governing performance are not clear, organizational rewards for performance are insufficient, and organizational controls governing performance are inadequate.

One of the important lessons from this discussion of the path-goal model is that managers must tailor their management style to specific conditions, such as those shown in Table 2. Although managers should focus on facilitating task accomplishment, their level of direct involvement should be calibrated to the nature of the work, the availability of organizational support, as well as the ability and experience of the individuals. If managers are insensitive to these contingencies, they probably will be perceived by some subordinates as interfering with their desires to explore their own way, while others will feel lost.

This conclusion underscores how important it is that managers understand the needs and expectations of their subordinates. Bill Dyer, a leading business con-

sultant, has observed that effective managers regularly ask their subordinates three simple questions: "How is your work going?" "What do you enjoy the most/least?" "How can I help you succeed?" Asking these questions communicates a supportive style; hearing the answers allows managers to fine-tune their facilitative actions.

The wisdom of this approach is supported by a recent analysis of the challenges facing manufacturing firms in the United States. Barry A. Stein, president of Goodmeasure, Inc., a Cambridge, Massachusetts, consulting firm, argues that one key to breathing new life into ailing "smokestack industries" involves redefining the role of the shop foreman. "They can't control people anymore. They have to coach them, help do the planning, approve organizational direction, and make sure the directions are clear. [They must redefine their role as] an enabling function, rather than a control function" (*Business Week,* April 25, 1983, p. 74).

Performance–Reward Linkages

Once clear goals have been established and the path to goal completion has been cleared by management, the next step in an effective motivational program is to encourage goal accomplishment by linking performance to outcomes (rewards and discipline). The relevant diagnostic question is, "Do subordinates feel that being

CONTINGENCIES	CONDITIONS APPROPRIATE FOR **HIGH** MANAGEMENT INVOLVEMENT	CONDITIONS APPROPRIATE FOR **LOW** MANAGEMENT INVOLVEMENT
Task structure	Low	High
Task mastery	Low	High
Subordinate's desire for autonomy	Low	High
Subordinate's experience	Low	High
Subordinate's ability	Low	High
Strength of group norms	Low	High
Effectiveness of organization's controls and rewards	Low	High

Table 2   Factors Influencing Management Involvement
Source: Adapted from House & Mitchell, 1974.

a high performer is more rewarding than being a low or average performer?"

Our discussion of this important element of an effective motivational program is based on two related principles: (1) In general, managers should link rewards to performance, rather than seniority or membership. (2) Managers should use discipline to extinguish counterproductive behaviors and use rewards to reinforce constructive behaviors.

If an organization rewards all people identically or on some basis other than performance, then high performers are likely to feel they are receiving less than they deserve. Obviously, the most important individuals in any organization are its high performers. Therefore, motivational schemes should be geared to keeping this employee group satisfied. This observation has led some organizational consultants to use the performance ratings of individuals leaving an organization as an index of the organization's motivational climate.

The principle under discussion here points to a need for caution regarding the practice in some organizations of minimizing distinctions between workers. Some "progressive" organizations have received considerable publicity for motivational programs that include providing recreational facilities, library services, day care, and attractive stock option programs for all employees. These organizations work hard to reduce status distinctions by calling everyone "associates" or "partners," eliminating reserved parking places, and instituting a company uniform. Although there are obvious motivational benefits to employees who feel they are receiving basically the same rewards regardless of seniority or level of authority, this motivational philosophy, when carried to an extreme or implemented indiscriminately, eventually demotivates high performers. In an era of egalitarianism, managers often overlook the vital link between performance and rewards and as a consequence find it difficult to attract and retain strong performers (Pfeffer, 1994).

Fortunately, many firms recognize this pitfall. In a survey, 42 percent of 125 organizations contacted indicated they had made changes in their compensation plan during the previous three years to achieve a better link between pay and performance (Murlis & Wright, 1985). These respondents reported that an interesting set of pressures were prompting them to move in this direction. Hard-charging, typically younger managers were insisting on tighter control over employee performance; executives were determined to "get more bang for the buck" during periods of shrinking resources; personnel managers were trying to reduce the number of grievances focusing on "unfair" pay decisions; and employees were trying to eliminate what they considered to be discrimination in the workplace.

Technological constraints sometimes make it difficult to link rewards and individual performance perfectly. For example, people working on an automobile assembly line or chemists working on a group research project have little control over their personal productivity. In these situations, rewards linked to the performance of the work group will foster group cohesion and collaboration and partially satisfy the individual members' concerns about fairness (Lawler, 1988). When it is not possible to assess the performance of a work group (work shift, organizational department), it is advisable to consider an organization-wide performance bonus. While the merits and technical details of various group and organizational reward systems are beyond the scope of this chapter, managers should link valued rewards and good performance at the most appropriate level of aggregation (Steers, Porter, & Bigley, 1996).

Appropriate Managerial Responses

An effective motivational program goes beyond the design of the organizational reward system. Managers must also recognize that their daily interactions with subordinates constitute an important source of motivation. It is difficult for even highly sensitive and aware managers to understand fully the impact of their actions on the behavior and attitudes of subordinates. Unfortunately, some managers don't even try to monitor these effects. The danger of this lack of awareness is that it may lead to managerial actions which actually reinforce undesirable behaviors in their subordinates. This has been called "the folly of rewarding A while hoping for B" (Kerr, 1995). For example, a vice president of R&D with a low tolerance for conflict and uncertainty may unwittingly undermine the company's avowed objective of developing highly creative products by punishing work groups that do not exhibit unity or a clear, consistent set of priorities. Further, while avowing the virtue of risk, the manager may punish failure; while stressing creativity, he or she may kill the spirit of the idea champion. These actions will encourage a work group to avoid challenging projects, suppress debate, and routinize task performance.

One of the common laments among management veterans is, "I can't get my people to take enough initiative. They have a very narrow view of their responsibilities, and they are hesitant to exceed those self-imposed boundaries. Why are these individuals unwilling to do more than the bare minimum?" The answer is clear to Raymond I. Mirashiro, President and CEO of Trans Hawaiian in Honolulu. The head of this $26 million-a-year firm, which moves people and luggage to and from airports and provides a variety of tourist services, including 650,000 leis a year, recalls the problem he was having "acting like a dictator but expecting his 1,000 employees to respond like they were in a democracy." He was persuaded by a vice president to participate in an intensive course of Zen. During this experience, he learned that he was, to a large extent, responsible for his subordinates' actions. "If a subordinate did not follow through on something he was supposed to do, before I would have called the employee 'stupid.' Now I ask myself if I gave the employee proper instructions." Furthermore, he has come to understand, "It is extremely important that I know that the other person is truly receptive to what I'm say-

ing. If he is not, then I will become the cause of the error if something goes wrong. I'm as much to blame as him" (*Nation's Business,* March 1988, p. 3).

The do's and don'ts for encouraging subordinates to assume more initiative, shown in Table 3, demonstrate the power of managers' actions in shaping behavior. Actions and reactions that might appear insignificant to the boss often have strong reinforcing or extinguishing effects on subordinates. Hence the truism, "Managers get what they reward, not what they want" and its companion, "People do what is *inspected,* not what is *expected.*" Indeed, the reinforcing potential of managers' reactions to subordinates' behaviors is so strong that it has been argued, "The best way to change an individual's behavior in a work setting is to change his or her manager's behavior" (Thompson, 1978, p. 52). Given the considerable leverage managers have over their subordinates' motivation to reach optimal performance, it is important that they learn how to use rewards and punishments effectively to produce positive, intended results consistently.

Psychologists call the process of linking rewards and punishments with behaviors in such a manner that the behaviors are more or less likely to persist "op-

DO	DON'T
Ask "How are we going to do this? What can I contribute to this effort? How will we use this result?", thus implying your joint stake in the work and results.	Imply that the task is the employees' total responsibility, that they hang alone if they fail. Individual failure means organizational failure.
Use an interested, exploring manner, asking questions designed to bring out factual information.	Play the part of an interrogator, firing questions as rapidly as they can be answered. Also, avoid asking questions that require only "yes" or "no" replies.
Keep the analysis and evaluation as much in the employees' hands as possible by asking for their best judgment on various issues.	React to their presentations on an emotional basis.
Present facts about organization needs, commitments, strategy, and so on, which permit them to improve and interest them in improving what they propose to do.	Demand a change or improvement in a peremptory tone of voice or on what appears to be an arbitrary basis.
Ask them to investigate or analyze further if you feel that they have overlooked some points or overemphasized others.	Take their planning papers and cross out, change dates, or mark "no good" next to certain activities.
Ask them to return with their plans after factoring these items in.	Redo their plans for them unless their repeated efforts show no improvement.

Table 3   Guidelines for Fostering Subordinate Initiative
Source: Kellogg, 1979, p. 121.

erant conditioning" (Komaki, Coombs, & Schepman, 1996). This approach uses a wide variety of motivational strategies that involve the presentation or withdrawal of positive or negative reinforcers or the use of no reinforcement whatsoever. Although there are important theoretical and experimental differences in these strategies, such as between negative reinforcement and punishment, for the purposes of our discussion we will focus on three types of management responses to employee behavior: no response (ignoring), negative response (disciplining), and positive response (rewarding).

The trickiest strategy to transfer from the psychologist's laboratory to the manager's work environment is "no response." Technically, what psychologists refer to as "extinction" is defined as a behavior followed by no response whatsoever. However, in most managerial situations, people develop expectations about what is likely to follow their actions based upon their past experience, office stories, and so forth. Consequently, what is intended as a nonresponse, or a neutral response, generally is interpreted as either a positive or negative response. For example, if a subordinate comes

into your office complaining bitterly about a coworker, and you attempt to discourage this type of behavior by changing the subject or responding in a low, unresponsive monotone voice, the subordinate may view this as a form of rejection. If your secretary sheepishly slips a delinquent report on your desk, and you ignore her behavior because you are busy with other business, she may be so relieved at not being reprimanded for her tardiness that she actually feels reinforced.

These simple examples underscore an important point: Any behavior that is repeatedly exhibited in front of a boss is being rewarded, regardless of the boss's intention ("I don't want to encourage that type of behavior, so I'm purposely ignoring it"). By definition, if a behavior persists, it is being reinforced. Thus, if an employee is chronically late or continually submits sloppy work, the manager must ask where the reinforcement for this behavior is coming from. Consequently, while extinction plays an important role in the learning process when conducted in strictly controlled laboratory conditions, it is a less useful technique in organizational settings because the interpretation of a supposedly neutral response is impossible

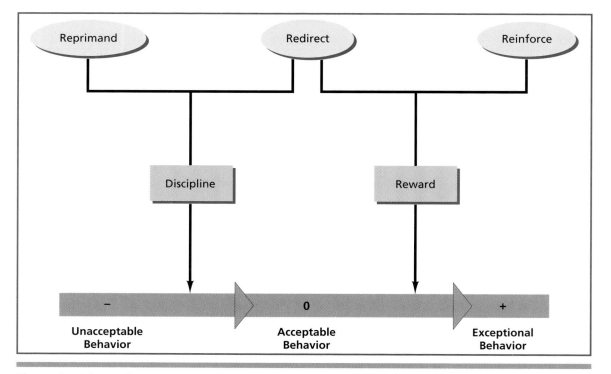

Figure 3   Behavior-Shaping Strategies

to control. Thus the focus of our discussion will be on the proper use of disciplining and rewarding strategies, as Figure 3 shows.

The **disciplining** approach involves responding negatively to an employee's behavior with the intention of discouraging future occurrences of that behavior. For example, if an employee is consistently late, a supervisor may reprimand him with the hope that this action will decrease the employee's tardiness. Nagging subordinates for their failure to obey safety regulations is another example.

The **rewarding** approach consists of linking desired behaviors with employee-valued outcomes. When a management trainee completes a report in a timely manner, the supervisor praises his promptness. If a senior executive takes the initiative to solve a thorny, time-consuming problem on her own, she could be given some extra time to enjoy a scenic location at the conclusion of a business trip. The value of positive reinforcement, according to Tom Peters and Bob Waterman, two prominent management consultants, is that it keeps the management-subordinate dialogue focused on "nudging good things onto the agenda, rather than ripping bad things off the agenda" (1982, p. 69).

Disciplining and rewarding are both viable and useful techniques and each has its place in the effective manager's motivational repertoire. However, as Figure 3 shows, each technique is associated with different behavior-modification goals. Discipline should be used to extinguish unacceptable behaviors. However, once an individual's behavior has reached an acceptable level, negative responses will not push the behavior up to the exceptional level. It is difficult to encourage employees to perform exceptional behaviors through nagging, threatening, or related forms of discipline. The left-hand side of Figure 3 shows that subordinates work to remove an aversive response rather than to gain a desired reward. Only through positive reinforcement do employees have control over achieving what they want and, therefore, the incentive to reach a level of exceptional performance.

The emphasis in Figure 3 on matching discipline and rewards with unacceptable and acceptable behaviors, respectively, highlights two common misapplications of reinforcement principles. First, it helps us better understand why top performers frequently get upset because they feel "management is too soft on those guys who are always screwing things up." Thinking that it is

good management practice to always be upbeat and optimistic and to discourage negative interactions, some managers try to downplay the seriousness of mistakes by ignoring them, by trying to temper the consequences by personally fixing errors, or by encouraging the high performers to be more tolerant and patient. Other managers feel so uncomfortable with confronting personal performance problems that they are willing to overlook all but the most egregious mistakes.

Although there is a lot to be said for managers having a positive attitude and giving poor performers the benefit of the doubt, their failure to reprimand and redirect inappropriate behaviors leads to two undesirable outcomes: the work unit's morale is seriously threatened, and the poor performer's behaviors are not improved.

Just as some managers find it unpleasant to issue reprimands for poor performance, other managers have difficulty praising exceptional performance. As a result, subordinates complain, "Nothing ever satisfies him." This second misapplication of the negative-response behavior-shaping strategy is just as dysfunctional as the indiscriminate use of praise. These managers mistakenly believe that the best way to motivate people is by always keeping expectations a little higher than their subordinates' best performance and then chiding them for their imperfection. In the process, they run the risk of burning out their staff or inadvertently encouraging lower performance ("We'll get chewed out anyway, so why try so hard?"). Furthermore, the irony is that this method creates a competitive, self-defeating situation in which subordinates look forward to the boss's making mistakes—the bigger the better!

Unfortunately, many managers genuinely believe that this is the best way to manage in all situations. They define their role as that of a "sheep dog," circling the perimeter of the group, nipping at the heels of those who begin to stray. They establish a fairly broad range of acceptable behaviors and then limit their interactions with employees to barking at those who exceed the boundaries. This negative, desultory style of management creates a demoralizing work environment and does not foster exceptional performance. Instead, workers are motivated to stay out of the boss's way and to avoid doing anything unusual or untried. Innovation and involvement are extinguished, and mundane performance becomes not only acceptable but desirable.

Having looked at the consequences of misapplying rewards and discipline, we will now turn our attention to the proper use of behavior-shaping techniques.

Modifying Behaviors

The mark of exceptional managers is their ability to foster exceptional behavior in their subordinates. This is best accomplished by using a nine-step behavior-shaping process, which can be applied to the full range of subordinates' behaviors. They can be used either to make unacceptable behaviors acceptable or to transform acceptable behaviors into exceptional ones. They are designed to avoid the harmful effects typically associated with the improper use of discipline discussed in the previous section (Wood & Bandura, 1989). They also ensure the appropriate use of rewards.

Table 4 shows the nine steps for improving behaviors. These are organized into three broad initiatives: **reprimand, redirect,** and **reward.** As shown in Figure 3, Steps 1–6 (reprimand and redirect) are used to extinguish unacceptable behaviors and replace them with acceptable ones. Steps 4–9 (redirect and reward) are used to transform acceptable behaviors into exceptional behaviors.

An important principle to keep in mind regarding the use of reprimands is that discipline should immediately follow the offensive behavior and focus exclusively on the specific problem. This is not an appropriate time to dredge up old concerns or make general, unsubstantiated accusations. The focus of the discussion should be on eliminating a problem behavior, not on making the subordinate feel bad. This approach increases the likelihood that the employee will associate the negative response with a specific act rather than viewing it as a generalized negative evaluation, which will reduce the hostility typically engendered by being reprimanded. (See the guidelines for initiating a complaint in Chapter 7, Managing Conflict, for more information on this topic.)

Second, inappropriate behaviors should be redirected into appropriate channels. It is important that people being reprimanded understand how they can receive rewards in the future. The process of redirection reduces the despair that occurs when people feel they are likely to be punished no matter what they do. If expected behaviors are not made clear, then workers may stop the inappropriate behavior but feel lost, not knowing how to improve. Keep in mind that the ultimate goal of any negative feedback should be to transform inappropriate behaviors into appropriate behaviors, in contrast to simply punishing a person for causing a problem or making the boss look bad. The lingering negative effects of a reprimand will quickly wear off if the manager is able to reward desirable behaviors shortly thereafter. This goal can be achieved only if workers know how they can receive positive outcomes.

Experienced managers know it is just as difficult to transform acceptable behaviors into exceptional ones. Helping an "OK, but uninspired" subordinate catch the vision of moving up to a higher level of desire and commitment can be very challenging. This process begins at Step 4 (redirect) by first clearly describing the goal or target behavior. The goal of skilled managers is to avoid having to administer any negative responses and especially to avoid trial-and-error learning among new subordinates. This is done by clearly laying out their expectations and collaboratively establishing work objectives. In addition, it is a good idea to provide an experienced mentor, known for exceptional performance, as a sounding board and role model.

Reprimand

1. Identify the specific inappropriate behavior. Give examples. Indicate that the action must stop.
2. Point out the impact of the problem on the performance of others, on the unit's mission, and so forth.
3. Ask questions about causes and explore remedies.

Redirect

4. Describe the behaviors or standards you expect. Make sure the individual understands and agrees that these are reasonable.
5. Ask if the individual will comply.
6. Be appropriately supportive. For example, praise other aspects of their work, identify personal and group benefits of compliance; make sure there are no work-related problems standing in the way of meeting your expectations.

Reward

7. Identify rewards that are salient to the individual.
8. Link the attainment of desirable outcomes with incremental, continuous improvement.
9. Reward (including using praise) all improvements in performance in a timely and honest manner.

Table 4 Guidelines for Improving Behaviors

Making Rewards Salient

Having established a link between performance and outcomes (through rewards and discipline) as part of an integrative motivational program, it is now important to focus on the salience, or personal value, of various outcomes. (To simplify the discussion, we will focus only on rewards.) It stands to reason that performance will be enhanced only to the extent that the rewards attached to it are personally valued by the recipient. The diagnostic question, then, is, "Do subordinates feel the rewards used to encourage high performance are worth the effort?"

One of the biggest mistakes that can be made in implementing a reward system is assuming that managers understand their subordinates' preferences. The manager's lament, "What does Joe expect, anyway? I gave him a bonus, and he's still complaining to other members of the accounting department that I don't appreciate his superior performance," indicates an apparent miscalculation of what Joe really values.

The difficulty many managers have in predicting what rewards will be most attractive to their subordinates is illustrated in Table 5. This table shows the results of a study consisting of two phases: First, data-processing analysts were asked to rank-order various rewards in terms of their perceived personal value; second, the analysts' managers were asked to estimate the order in which the workers would rank the rewards. Their responses indicate a very low correlation between workers' actual priorities and the priorities attributed to them by their bosses. It is especially interesting to note that the employees surveyed tended to focus primarily on rewards controlled by their immediate supervisors, while the managers assumed their subordinates were motivated by organizationally mediated outcomes. Managers, in general, vastly underestimate their potential for directly influencing the behavior of subordinates.

The broad tendency for managers to miscalculate subordinates' reward preferences usually takes two forms: (1) assuming that all subordinates value the same outcomes; and (2) assuming that the manager's outcome preferences are shared by subordinates. The individuals responding to the survey summarized in Table 5 were computer programmers. If advertising executives, secretaries, or pharmaceutical sales personnel had been given the survey, their rank-ordered preferences probably would have been different. In addition, within this sample of programmers, their preferences were undoubtedly affected by their age, seniority, educational level, marital status, and so forth.

Recognizing the diversity of most work groups, many organizations, including those as diverse as Morgan Stanley investment bank and American Can, are experimenting with "cafeteria-style" incentive systems (Lawler, 1987). Employees receive a certain number of work credits based on performance, seniority, or task difficulty, and they are allowed to trade those in for a variety of benefits, including upgraded insurance packages, financial planning services, disability income plans, extended vacation benefits, tuition reimbursement for educational programs, and so forth. By giving employees an opportunity to select from a benefits menu, these organizations are maximizing the motivational value of these outcomes to each individual employee.

A flexible reward system helps managers avoid the second common motivational mistake: projecting their own preferences onto subordinates. Ineffective managers don't spend enough quality time with their workers to understand their personal needs and goals. Under these circumstances, it is natural for managers to assume that their subordinates share their views regarding the attractiveness of various job outcomes.

Job Factors	Survey of Employees	Survey of Bosses
Full appreciation of work done	1	8
Feeling of being in on things	2	10
Sympathetic help on personal problems	3	9
Job security	4	2
Good wages	5	1
Interesting work	6	5
Promotional growth in organization	7	3
Personal loyalty to employees	8	6
Good working conditions	9	4
Tactful disciplining	10	7

Table 5 Order of Importance of Various Job Factors
Source: A. I. LeDue, Jr., 1980.

This error is reflected in the case of a stockbroker who was promoted to office manager because upper management in the home office felt he was "the most qualified and most deserving." Unfortunately, they failed to ask him if he wanted the promotion. They assumed that because they enjoyed their management positions, all their subordinates shared similar views. Two weeks after receiving his "reward" for good performance, the supersalesman-turned-manager was in the hospital with a bleeding ulcer.

Effective managers overcome the egocentric bias reflected in this example through frequent, personal, and supportive discussions with their subordinates. Such informal exchanges should focus on career opportunities, life goals, and personal priorities. Another technique used by managers is discussing with subordinates recent significant changes in the careers of common acquaintances. Subordinates' responses to changing circumstances affecting others' responsibilities, pay, personal time, travel requirements, and so forth, often provide useful insights into their own personal preferences.

Managers should be particularly sensitive to the dynamic quality of human needs. Clay Alderfer (1977) has argued that needs are organized in a hierarchy, with three broad categories, or levels. At the most basic level, individuals begin with "existence" (basic life-sustaining) needs and then proceed to "relatedness" (social) needs, finally reaching the level of "growth" (self-actualizing) needs. Further, he proposed that as individuals fulfill a specific need, they shift their focus to the next-highest hierarchical level (E → R → G). Satisfied needs become dormant until a dramatic shift in circumstances increases their salience. For example, a middle-level executive who is fired during a hostile takeover may suddenly find that her interest in personal growth is overwhelmed by a pressing need for security. Other major events that may shift an individual's need priority include a birth or death in the family, marriage or divorce, job transfer or job obsolescence, promotion, or demotion. Effective managers are sensitive to shifts in their subordinates' needs and accommodate those shifts by implementing flexible organizational reward systems.

Enhancing Work Design

All of the outcomes shown in Table 5, except for "interesting work," are called **external motivators** because they are controlled by someone other than the worker, typically the immediate supervisor. The supervisor can show appreciation for a job well done, offer job security, show personal loyalty to employees, and provide good working conditions. It is a slightly different story for interesting work. Although managers control the components of a job, they have no direct control over whether a specific subordinate finds a job interesting. The outcomes associated with an interesting job come from **internal motivators,** which are factors inherent in the job itself, not from any particular actions of the manager.

Effective motivators understand that the person-job interface has a strong impact on how an employee performs his job. No matter how many externally controlled rewards managers use, if their subordinates find their jobs uninteresting and unfulfilling, performance will suffer. Attention to internal motivators is particularly critical in situations where managers have relatively little control over the organizational incentive system. In these cases it is often possible to compensate for lack of control over external factors by fine-tuning the person-job fit.

Work design is the process of matching job characteristics and workers' skills and interests. One popular work-design model proposes that particular job dimensions cause workers to experience specific psychological reactions called "states." In turn, these psychological reactions produce specific personal and work outcomes. Figure 4 shows the relationship between the core job dimensions, the critical psychological states they produce, and the resulting personal and work outcomes (Hackman & Oldham, 1980). A variety of empirical research has found that the five core job dimensions—**skill variety, task identity, task significance, autonomy,** and **feedback**—are positively related to job satisfaction.

The more variety in the skills a person can use in performing work, the more the person perceives the task as meaningful or worthwhile. Similarly, the more an individual can perform a complete job from beginning to end (task identity) and the more the work has a direct effect on the work or lives of other people (task significance), the more the employee will view the job as meaningful. On the other hand, when the work requires few skills, only part of a task is performed, or there seems to be little effect on others' jobs, experienced meaningfulness is low.

The more autonomy in the work (freedom to choose how and when to do particular jobs), the more responsibility workers feel for their successes and failures. Increased responsibility results in increased commitment to one's work. Autonomy can be increased by instituting flexible work schedules, decentralizing decision making, or selectively removing formalized con-

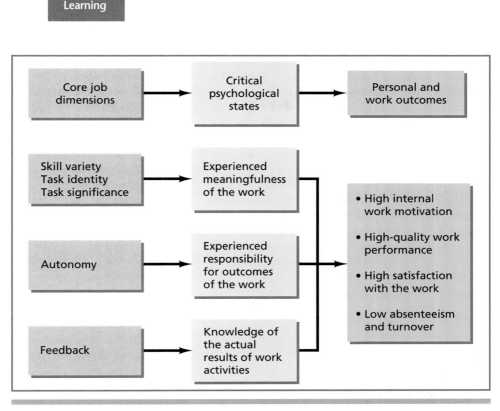

Figure 4   Designing Highly Motivating Jobs
Source: Hackman & Oldham, 1980.

trols, such as the ringing of a bell to indicate the beginning and end of a work day.

Finally, the more feedback individuals receive about how well their jobs are being performed, the more knowledge of results they have. Knowledge of results permits workers to understand the benefits of the jobs they perform. Employees' knowledge of results may be enhanced by increasing their direct contact with clients or by giving them feedback on how their jobs fit in and contribute to the overall operation of the organization.

By enhancing the core job dimensions and increasing critical psychological stages, employees' job fulfillment is increased. Job fulfillment (high internal work motivation) is associated with other outcomes valued by management. These include high-quality work performance, high employee satisfaction with their jobs, and low absenteeism and turnover. Employees who have well-designed jobs enjoy doing them because they are intrinsically satisfying.

This discussion of work design suggests five managerial action guidelines that can help increase desirable personal and work outcomes. The first one is to *combine tasks*. A combination of tasks is by definition a more

challenging and complex work assignment. It requires workers to use a wider variety of skills, which makes the work seem more challenging and meaningful. Telephone directories at the former Indiana Bell Telephone company used to be compiled in 21 steps along an assembly line. Through job redesign, each worker was given responsibility for compiling an entire directory.

A related managerial principle is to *form identifiable work units* so that task identity and task significance can be increased. Clerical work in a large insurance firm was handled by 80 employees organized by functional task (e.g., opening the mail, entering information into the computer, sending out statements). Work was assigned, based on current work load, by a supervisor over each functional area. To create higher levels of task identity and task significance, the firm reorganized the clerical staff into eight self-contained groups. Each group handled all business associated with specific clients.

The third guideline for enhancing jobs is *establishing client relationships*. A client relationship involves an ongoing personal relationship between an employee (the producer) and the client (the consumer). The establishment of this relationship can increase autonomy, task identity, and feedback. Take, for example, research and design (R&D) employees. While they may be the ones who design a product, feedback on customer satisfaction generally is routed through their managers or a separate customer-relations unit. At Caterpillar, Inc., members of each division's R&D group are assigned to make regular contacts with their major clients.

The fourth suggestion, *load jobs vertically,* refers to granting more authority for making job-related decisions to workers. When we speak here of "vertical," we refer to the distribution of power between a subordinate and a boss. As supervisors delegate more authority and responsibility, their subordinates' perceived autonomy, accountability, and task identity increase. Historically, workers on auto assembly lines have had little decision-making authority. However, in conjunction with increased emphasis on quality, many plants now allow workers to adjust their equipment, reject faulty materials, and even shut down the line if a major problem is evident.

The final managerial suggestion is to *open feedback channels.* Workers need to know how well or how poorly they are performing their jobs if any kind of improvement is expected. Thus it is imperative that they receive timely and consistent feedback, which allows them to make appropriate adjustments in their behavior so they can receive desired rewards. The traditional approach to quality assurance in American industry is to "inspect it in." A separate quality assurance group is assigned to check the production team's quality. The emerging trend is to give producers responsibility for checking their own work. If it doesn't meet quality standards, they immediately fix the defect. Following this procedure, workers receive immediate feedback on their performance.

Although this management tool, like others, involves tradeoffs, the record of job redesign interventions is impressive. Depending on the approach taken, firms typically report a substantial increase in productivity, work quality, and worker satisfaction (reflected in lower rates of absenteeism). The Social Security Administration increased productivity 23.5 percent among a group of 50 employees; General Electric realized a 50 percent increase in product quality as a result of a job-redesign program; and the absenteeism rate among data-processing operators at Travelers Insurance decreased 24 percent (Kopelman, 1985).

In summary, this section on external and internal rewards contains two important lessons for managers.

First, managers should ensure there are enough reward options available for subordinates so they can personally select salient outcomes. The motivational potential of an effective goal-setting process and a supportive, obstacle-removing management style is dissipated if employees feel that high performance will not lead to personally attractive outcomes.

Second, managers should recognize that both external and internal outcomes are necessary ingredients of effective motivational programs. In particular, ignoring internal outcomes can significantly undermine a manager's efforts to motivate. Most people desire interesting and challenging work activities. Good wages and job security will do little to overcome the negative effects of individuals' feeling that their abilities are being underutilized (Staw, 1986).

Insuring Equitable Rewards

Once appropriate rewards have been determined for each employee, managers must then consider how to distribute those rewards (Cropanzano & Folger, 1996). This brings us to concerns about equity. Any positive benefits of salient rewards will be negated if workers feel they are not receiving their fair share. The relevant diagnostic question here is, "Do subordinates feel that work-related benefits are distributed fairly?" (As in the previous section, we will focus here only on rewards. However, the same principles also apply to the equitable use of discipline.)

Equity refers to workers' perceptions of the fairness of rewards. Evaluations of equity are based on a social comparison process in which workers individually compare what they are getting out of the work relationship (outcomes) to what they are putting into the work relationship (inputs). Outcomes include such items as pay, fringe benefits, increased responsibility, and prestige, while inputs may include hours worked and work quality, as well as education and experience. The ratio of outcomes to inputs is then compared to corresponding ratios of other individuals, judged to be an appropriate comparison group. The outcome of this comparison is the basis for beliefs about fairness.

If workers experience feelings of inequity, they will behaviorally or cognitively adjust their own, or fellow workers', inputs and/or outputs. In some cases, this may lead to a decrease in motivation and performance. For example, if employees believe that they are underpaid, they have a number of options. Cognitively, they may rationalize that they really are not working as hard as they thought they were; thus, they reduce the perceived value of their own inputs. Alternatively, they might convince themselves that coworkers are actually working harder than they thought they were. Behaviorally, workers can request a pay raise (increase their outcomes), or they can decrease their inputs by leaving a few minutes early each day, decreasing their effort, deciding not to complete an optional training program, or finding excuses not to accept difficult assignments.

The significance of this aspect of motivation underscores the need for managers to monitor closely subordinates' perceptions of equity (Kerr, 1996). In some cases, these conversations may uncover faulty comparison processes. For example, employees might misunderstand the value placed on various inputs, for example, experience versus expertise or quantity versus quality; or they might have unrealistic views of their own or others' performance. A recent survey reported that 75 percent of the respondents felt their leadership skills were better than those of 75 percent of the population.

However, just as often these discussions uncover real inequities. For example, the hourly rate of a worker may not be keeping up with recent skill upgrades or increased job responsibilities. The act of identifying and correcting legitimate inequities generates enormous commitment and loyalty. For example, a manager in the computer industry felt he had been unfairly passed over for promotion by a rival. Utilizing the company's open-door policy, he took his case to a higher level in the firm. After a thorough investigation, the decision was reversed and the rival reprimanded. The individual's response was, "After they went to bat for me, I could never leave the company."

The important thing to keep in mind about equity and fairness is that we are dealing with perceptions. Consequently, whether they are accurate or distorted, legitimate or ill-founded, they are both accurate and legitimate in the mind of the perceiver until proven otherwise. A basic principle of social psychology states: "That which is perceived as being real is real in its consequences." Therefore, effective managers should constantly perform "reality checks" on their subordinates' perceptions of equity, using questions such as: "What criteria for promotions, pay raises, and so on do you feel management should be placing more/less emphasis on?" "Relative to others similar to you in this organization, do you feel your job assignments, promotions, and so on are appropriate?" "Why do you think Alice was recently promoted over Jack?"

Insuring Timely Rewards and Accurate Feedback

This leads us to the final elements in an integrative motivation program: minimizing the time lag between behaviors and feedback and providing accurate feedback. The last diagnostic question contains two parts. The first is, "Are we getting the most out of our rewards by administering them on a timely basis as part of the feedback process?"

Up to this point, we have emphasized that employees need to understand and accept performance standards; they should feel that management is working hard to help them reach their performance goals; they should feel that available internal and external rewards are personally attractive; they should believe that rewards and reprimands are distributed fairly; and they should feel that these outcomes are administered primarily on the basis of performance.

All these elements are necessary for an effective motivational program, but they alone are not sufficient. Rewards, even highly valued ones, lose their motivating potential unless they are given at the correct time. It is the timing of reinforcements that lets employees know which behaviors are being encouraged. Giving a reward at the wrong time can inadvertently increase an undesirable behavior. For example, giving a long overdue, fully warranted raise to a subordinate during an interview in which she or he is complaining about the unfairness of the reward system may reinforce complaining rather than good work performance. Moreover, failure to give a reward when a desired behavior occurs will make it even more difficult to increase that behavior in the future. If the owners of a new business have delayed the implementation of a promise to grant stock options for the core start-up cadre as compensation for their low wages and 70- to 80-hour work weeks, the workers' willingness to sustain such a pace on promises and dreams alone may begin to wane.

The importance of timing becomes obvious when one considers that all the research findings supporting the value of operant conditioning as a motivational system assume that outcomes immediately follow behaviors. Imagine how little we would know about behavior-shaping processes if, in the experiments with birds and rats described in psychology textbooks, the food pellets were dropped into the cage several minutes after the desired behavior occurred.

Unfortunately, although timing is a critical aspect of reinforcement, it is frequently ignored in everyday management practice. The formal administrative apparatus of many organizations often delays for months the feedback on the consequences of employee performance. It is customary practice to restrict in-depth discussions of job performance to formally designated appraisal interviews, which generally take place every 6 or 12 months. ("I'll have to review this matter officially later, so why do it twice?") Delay between performance and feedback dilutes the effectiveness of any rewards or discipline dispensed as a result of the evaluation process.

In contrast, effective managers understand the importance of immediate, spontaneous rewards. They use the formal performance evaluation process to discuss long-term trends in performance, solve problems inhibiting performance, and set performance goals. But they don't expect these infrequent general discussions to provide much motivation. For this, they rely on brief, frequent, highly visible performance feedback. At least once a week they seek some opportunity to praise desirable work habits among their subordinates.

Peters and Waterman, in their classic book *In Search of Excellence* (1982), stress the importance of immediacy by relating the following amusing anecdote:

> At Foxboro, a technical advance was desperately needed for survival in the company's early days. Late one evening, a scientist rushed into the president's office with a working prototype. Dumbfounded at the elegance of the solution and bemused about how to reward it, the president bent forward in his chair, rummaged through most of the drawers in his desk, found something, leaned over the desk to the scientist, and said, "Here!" In his hand was a banana, the only reward he could immediately put his hands on. From that point on, the small "gold banana" pin has been the highest accolade for scientific achievement at Foxboro. (pp. 70–71)

The implication for effective management is clear: Effective rewards are spontaneous rewards. Reward programs that become highly routinized, especially those linked to formal performance appraisal systems, lose their immediacy. A related problem occurs with established reward programs: overused incentives lose their salience. If people feel that "Everyone has gotten it," then "it" loses appeal.

There is a second critical aspect of reinforcement timing: the consistency of reward administration. Administering a reward every time a behavior occurs is called continuous reinforcement. Administering rewards on an intermittent basis (the same reward is always used but is not given every time it is warranted) is referred to as partial, or intermittent, reinforcement. Neither approach is clearly superior; both approaches have tradeoffs. Continuous reinforcement represents the fastest way to establish new behavior. For example, if a boss consistently praises a subordinate for writing reports using the manager's preferred format, the subordinate will readily adopt that style in order to receive more and more contingent rewards. However, if the boss suddenly takes an extended leave of absence, the learned behavior will be highly vulnerable to extinction because the reinforcement pattern is broken. In contrast, while partial reinforcement results in very slow learning, it is very resistant to extinction. The persistence associated with gambling behavior illustrates the addictive nature of a partial reinforcement schedule. Not knowing when the next payoff may come preserves the myth that the jackpot is only one more try away.

This information about reinforcement timing derived from experimental research has important implications for effective management. First, it is important to realize that continuous reinforcement systems are very rare in organizations unless they are mechanically built into the job, as in the case of the piece-rate pay plan. Seldom are individuals rewarded every time they make a good presentation or effectively handle a customer's complaint. When we recognize that most nonassembly-line work in an organization is typically governed by a partial reinforcement schedule, we gain new insights into some of the more frustrating aspects of a manager's role. For example, it helps explain why new employees seem to take forever to catch on to how the boss wants things done. It also suggests why it is so difficult to extinguish outdated behaviors, particularly in older employees.

Second, given how difficult it is for one manager to reinforce consistently the desired behaviors in a new employee (or an employee who is going through a reprimand, redirect, reward cycle), it is generally a good idea to use a team effort. By sharing your developmental objectives with other individuals who interact with the target employee, you increase the likelihood of the desired behaviors being reinforced during the critical early stages of improvement. For example, if a division head is trying to encourage a new member of her staff to become more assertive, she might encourage other staff members to respond positively to the newcomer's halting efforts in meetings or private conversations.

Improving the Quality of Feedback

Before concluding this discussion of feedback, a note about the message itself is warranted. The second diagnostic question related to feedback is, "Do subordinates know where they stand in terms of current performance and long-term opportunities?" In addition to the timing of feedback, the content of that feedback, and the motivation guiding the feedback process, can have a powerful impact on the target individual's willingness and ability to improve. If the content is inaccurate, improvement is frustratingly difficult. If the message is masked in subterfuge and obscured by mixed signals, the credibility of the entire motivational system is undermined.

It is important to be honest and open with subordinates regarding their current performance and future opportunities. The time-worn excuses, "We don't want to run the risk of discouraging marginal performers" and "We shouldn't tell people their future promotion opportunities are in jeopardy because upper management doesn't like their 'style,' "generally constitute efforts to cloak managers' feelings of discomfort under the guise of doing what's best for the subordinate.

When managers are reluctant to share unflattering or unhopeful feedback, it is often because they are unwilling to spend sufficient time with individuals receiving negative feedback to help them thoroughly understand their shortcomings, put them in perspective, consider options, and explore possible remedies. It is sometimes easier to pass on an employee with a poor performance record or unrealistic expectations to the next supervisor than it is to confront the problem directly, provide honest and constructive feedback, and help the individual respond appropriately. Therefore, many individuals feel that supportive communication of negative performance information is the management skill which is most difficult to master—and therefore the one most highly prized.

Summary

Our discussion of enhancing work performance has focused on specific analytical and behavioral management skills. We first introduced the fundamental distinction between ability and motivation. Then we discussed several diagnostic questions for determining whether inadequate performance was due to insufficient ability. A five-step process for handling ability problems (resupply, retrain, refit, reassign, and release) was outlined. We introduced the topic of motivation by stressing the need for placing equal emphasis on concerns for satisfaction and performance. The remainder of the chapter focused on the second skill by presenting six elements of an integrative approach to motivation.

The summary model shown in Figure 5 (and its "diagnostic" version shown later in Figure 7) encompasses our discussions of ability and motivation. This flowchart depiction of the factors impacting performance and satisfaction underscores the interdependence among the various components. Skilled managers incorporate all components of this model into their motivational efforts rather than concentrating only on a favorite subset. There are no shortcuts to effective management. All elements of the motivation process must be included in a total, integrated program for improving performance and satisfaction.

The flowchart shows effort as the beginning point for the model. Recall that motivation is manifested as work effort and that effort consists of desire and commitment. Motivated employees have the desire to initiate a task and the commitment to do their best. Whether their motivation is sustained over time depends on the remaining elements of the model, which are organized into two major segments: (1) the effort → performance link and (2) the outcomes → satisfaction link. These two crucial links in the motivational process can best be summarized as questions pondered by individuals asked to work harder, change their work routine, or strive for a higher level of quality: First, "If I put forth more effort, am I likely to be able to perform up to expectations?" and second, "Am I likely to find being a high performer personally rewarding?"

Beginning on the left side of the model, we see that the combination of goals and ability determines the extent to which effort is successfully transformed into performance. In the path-goal theory of leadership, the importance of fitting the right job to the right person

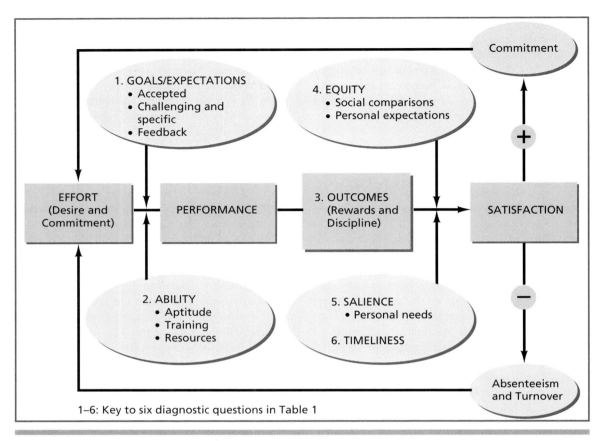

Figure 5 Integrative Model of Motivation Enhancement

and providing necessary resources and training are emphasized. These factors must be combined with effective goal setting (understanding and accepting moderately difficult goals) if increased effort is to result in increased performance.

Proceeding to the outcomes → satisfaction segment of the model, the importance of perceived equity and reward salience stand out. Individuals must believe that the rewards offered are appropriate, not only for their personal performance level but also in comparison to the rewards achieved by "similar" others. The subjective value that individuals attach to incentives for performance reflects their personal relevance, or salience. Rewards with little personal value have low motivational potential. These subjective factors combine with the timeliness and accuracy of feedback to determine the overall motivational potential of rewards.

Based upon their perceptions of outcomes, workers will experience varying degrees of satisfaction or dissatisfaction. Satisfaction creates a positive feedback loop, increasing the individual's motivation, as manifested by increased effort. Dissatisfaction, on the other hand, results in decreased effort and, therefore, lower performance and rewards. If uncorrected, this pattern may ultimately result in absenteeism or turnover.

Behavioral Guidelines for Improving Performance

This discussion is organized around key diagnostic models and questions that serve as the basis for enhancing the following skills: (1) properly diagnosing performance problems; (2) initiating actions to enhance individuals' abilities; and (3) strengthening the motivational aspects of the work environment.

Table 1 summarizes the process for properly diagnosing the causes of poor work performance in the form of six diagnostic questions. (A "decision tree" version of these questions is included in the Skill Practice section.) The guideline to thoroughly investigate work performance is:

- Separate ability from motivational problems.

- Agree on a program for improving performance.

- Release a poor performer only as a last resort.

The key guidelines for enhancing ability and creating a highly motivating work environment are:

1. Clearly define an acceptable level of overall performance or specific behavioral objective.

    - Make sure the individual understands what is necessary to satisfy your expectations.

    - Formulate goals and expectations collaboratively, if possible.

    - Make goals as challenging and specific as possible.

2. Help remove all obstacles to reaching the objective.

    - Make sure the individual has adequate technical resources, personnel, and political support.

    - If a lack of ability appears to be hindering performance, use the resupply, retrain, refit, reassign, or release series of remedies.

3. Make rewards and discipline contingent on high performance or drawing nearer to the behavioral objective.

    - Carefully examine the behavioral consequences of your nonresponses. (Ignoring a behavior is rarely interpreted as a neutral response.)

- Consistently discipline individuals whose effort is below your expectations and their capabilities.

4. When discipline is required, treat it as a learning experience for the individual.

    - Specifically identify the problem and explain how it should be corrected.

    - Use the reprimand and redirect guidelines in Table 4.

5. Transform acceptable into exceptional behaviors.

    - Reward each level of improvement.

    - Use the redirect and reward guidelines in Table 4.

6. Use reinforcing rewards that appeal to the individual.

    - Allow flexibility in individual selection of rewards.

    - Provide appealing external rewards as well as satisfying and rewarding work (intrinsic satisfaction).

    - To maintain salience, do not overuse rewards.

7. Periodically check subordinates' perceptions regarding the equity of reward allocations.

    - Correct misperceptions related to equity comparisons.

8. Minimize the time lag between behaviors and feedback on performance, including the administration of rewards or reprimands. (Spontaneous feedback shapes behavior best.)

    - Provide honest and accurate assessments of current performance and long-range opportunities.

Skill Analysis

Case Involving Motivation Problems

Electro Logic

Electro Logic (EL) is a small R&D firm located in a midwestern college town adjacent to a major university. Its primary mission is to perform basic research on, and development of, a new technology called "Very Fast, Very Accurate" (VFVA). Founded four years ago by Steve Morgan, an electrical engineering professor and inventor of the technology, EL is primarily funded by government contracts, although it plans to market VFVA technology and devices to non-governmental organizations within the year.

The government is very interested in VFVA, as it will enhance radar technology, robotics, and a number of other important defense applications. EL recently received the largest small-business contract ever awarded by the government to research and develop this or any other technology. Phase I of the contract has just been completed, and the government has agreed to Phase II contracting as well.

The organizational chart of EL is shown in Figure 6. Current membership is 75, with roughly 88 percent in engineering. The hierarchy of engineering titles and requirements for each are listed in Table 6. Heads of staff are supposedly appointed based on their knowledge of VFVA technology and their ability to manage people. In practice, the president of EL hand-picks these people based on what some might call arbitrary guidelines: Most of the staff leaders were or are the president's graduate students. There is no predetermined time frame for advancement up the hierarchy. Raises are, however, directly related to performance appraisal evaluations.

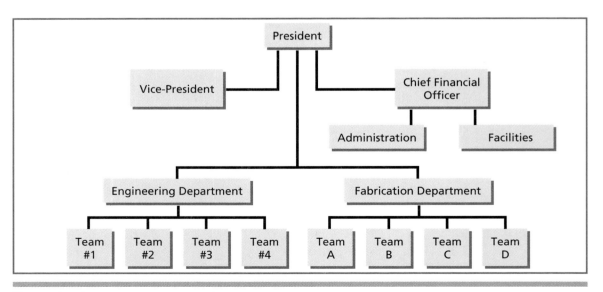

Figure 6 Electro Logic Organization Chart

TITLE	REQUIREMENT
Member of Technical Staff	BSEE, MSEE
Senior Member of Technical Staff	PhD, MSEE with 2 years of industrial experience; BSEE with 5 years of industrial experience
Research Engineer	PhD with 2 years of industrial experience BSEE or MSEE with 7 years of industrial experience
Research Scientist	PhD with appropriate experience in research
Senior Research Scientist	PhD with appropriate industrial and research experience

Table 6 Engineering Titles and Requirements

Working directly with the engineers are the technicians. These people generally have a high-school degree, although some also have college degrees. They are trained on the job, although some have gone through a local community college's program on microtechnology fabrication. The technicians perform the mundane tasks of the engineering department: running tests, building circuit boards, manufacturing VFVA chips, and so on. Most are full-time hourly employees.

The administrative staff is composed of the staff head (with an MBA from a major university), accountants, personnel director, graphic artists, purchasing agent, project controller, technical writers/editors, and secretaries. Most of the people in the administrative staff are women. All are hourly employees except the staff head, personnel director, and project controller. The graphic artists and technical writer/editor are part-time employees.

The facilities staff is composed of the staff head and maintenance personnel. EL is housed in three different buildings, and the primary responsibility of the facilities staff is to ensure that the facilities of each building are in good working order. Additionally, the facilities staff is often called upon to remodel parts of the buildings as the staff continues to grow.

EL anticipates a major recruiting campaign to enhance the overall staff. In particular, it is looking for more technicians and engineers. Prior to this recruiting campaign, however, the president of EL hired an outside consultant to assess employee needs as well as the morale and overall effectiveness of the firm. The consultant has been observing EL for about three weeks and has written up some notes of her impressions and observations of the company.

Consultant's Notes From Observations of Electro Logic

Facilities: Electro Logic (EL) is housed in three different buildings. Two are converted houses, and one is an old school building. Senior managers and engineers are in the school, and others are scattered between the houses.

Meetings: Weekly staff meetings in the main building are held to discuss objectives and to formulate and review milestone charts.

Social interaction: A core group of employees interact frequently on a social basis, for example, sports teams, parties. The administration staff celebrate birthdays at work. The president occasionally attends.

Work allocation: Engineers request various tasks from the support staff, which consists of technicians and administrative unit personnel. There is obviously some discretion used by the staff in assigning priorities to the work requests, based on rapport and desirability of the work.

Turnover: The highest turnover is among administration personnel and technicians. Exit interviews with engineers indicate they leave because of the company's crisis-management style, better opportunities for career advancement and security in larger organizations, and overall frustration with EL's "pecking order." Engineers with the most responsibility and authority tend to leave.

Salary and benefits: In general, wages at EL are marginal by national and local standards. A small group of scientists and engineers do make substantial salaries and have a very attractive benefits package, including stock options. Salaries and benefits for new engineers tend to be linked to the perceived level of their expertise.

Offices and facilities: Only EL's president, vice-president, and chief financial officer have their own offices. Engineers are grouped together in "pods" by project assignment. There is very little privacy in these work areas, and the noise from the shared printer is distracting. The head of administration shares a pod with the personnel director, facilities head, and the project controller. One to three secretaries per building are located in or near the reception areas. The large building has an employee lounge with three vending machines. There is also a coffee and tea station. The smaller buildings have only a pop machine in the reception area.

Consultant's Interviews With Employees

After making these observations, the consultant requested interviews with a cross-section of the staff for the purpose of developing a survey to be taken of all employees. Presented below are excerpts from those interviews.

Pat Klausen, Senior Member of the Technical Staff

CONSULTANT: What is it about Electro Logic (EL) that gives you the most satisfaction?

PAT: I really enjoy the work. I mean, I've always liked to do research, and working on VFVA is an incredible opportunity. Just getting to work with Steve (EL's president and VFVA's inventor) again is exciting. I was his graduate student about six years ago, you know. He really likes to work closely with his people—perhaps sometimes too closely. There have been times when I could have done with a little less supervision.

CONSULTANT: What's the least satisfying aspect of your work?

PAT: Probably the fact that I'm never quite sure that we'll be funded next month, given the defense budget problems and the tentativeness of our research. I've got a family to consider, and this place isn't the most stable in terms of its financial situation. Maybe it'll change once we get more into commercial production. Who knows?

CONSULTANT: You've offered some general positives and negatives about EL. Can you be more specific about day-to-day dealings? What's good and bad about working here on a daily basis?

PAT: You're sure this isn't going to get back to anyone? OK. Well, in general I'm not satisfied with the fact that too often we end up changing horses in the middle of the stream, if you know what I mean. In the past seven months, three of my engineers and four of my techs have been pulled off my project onto projects whose deadlines were nearer than mine. Now I'm faced with a deadline, and I'm supposed to be getting more staff. But I'll have to spend so much time briefing them that it might make more sense for me to just finish the project myself. On the other hand, Steve keeps telling me that we have to be concerned with EL's overall goals, not just our individual concerns—you know, we have to be "team players," "good members of the family." It's kind of hard to deal with that, though, when deadlines are bearing down and you know your butt's on the line, team player or not. But if you go along with this kind of stuff and don't complain, the higher-ups treat you well. Still, it seems to me there's got to be a better way to manage these projects.

CONSULTANT: What are the positive aspects of your daily work?

PAT: Well, the people here are all great to work with. They know their stuff or can learn quickly. I tend to be a social person and I really like socializing with these people. We play softball and basketball together and do happy hours and stuff. I like that. I've got some good friends here, which helps get my work orders filled quickly, if you know what I mean.

Bob Christensen, Member of the Technical Staff

CONSULTANT: You said earlier that Steve was your advisor for your MS. So you've known him a long time.

BOB: Yes, that's right. I've known Professor Morgan—Steve—for about eight years. I had him for a few undergraduate classes; then, of course, he was my advisor for my two-year Master's program, and now I've worked at Electro Logic (EL) for two years.

CONSULTANT: It seems as if you enjoy working with Steve.

BOB: Oh, yeah. But I really don't get to work directly with him anymore. I'll see him at meetings and such, but that's about it.

CONSULTANT: So he's not your immediate supervisor?

BOB: No, but for the amount of time I spend with my supervisor, Steve might as well be. My boss and I meet maybe once every three weeks for about an hour to see if all is well. And that's it. The rest of the time, I'm on my own. I used to talk to Steve when I had questions, but he's gotten so busy now that it's hard to see him—you need to make an appointment a few days in advance.

CONSULTANT: Do you think your supervisor treats all his staff this way?

BOB: To be honest, I have heard some complaints. In fact, about six months ago, the situation was so bad, some other people and I had a meeting with him. He promised that he would be more available to us and was, for about a month. Then we got involved in a new proposal, so he made himself scarce again. So nothing's really changed. We're coming up on finalizing the proposal now, and it's important that I see him, ask him questions. The last few drafts I've submitted to him, he's returned, rewritten in his own way, and with no explanation of the changes. Sometimes I think he treats me like somebody who doesn't know anything, as if I had no training whatsoever. I realize his neck is on the line with this project, but sometimes it seems that he uses being busy to avoid talking to me.

Chris Chen, Research Scientist

CONSULTANT: What kind of characteristics should a person have if he/she wants to work as a research scientist at Electro Logic (EL)?

CHRIS: Well, certainly technical knowledge is important. When I've interviewed recent college grads for entry-level positions, I am always concerned with their GPA. I like to see straight-A averages, if possible. But for experienced research scientists, technical knowledge shows up in their publication records, mostly. So I'll read their papers. I also think a research scientist has to be highly self-motivated, not look to others for praise and such. Particularly here. If you want someone to tell you you've done a good job, you'll be waiting a long time.

It's not clear to me that research scientists really get the support we need from the rest of the staff here. Work orders are often lost or put off for one reason or another. Senior members seem to get more techs than scientists do, and they certainly get more attention from Steve. The rumor is that these guys also get higher raises than the scientists; allegedly, this is to keep pay at an equitable rate—you know, they're supposedly more valuable to the company. Of course, everybody knows that most of the senior members are Steve's old graduate students, and so he takes care of them really well. One of the things that really galls me is that I need to keep up my publication record to maintain my career options. But publishing is frowned on because it takes time away from your work. I've even been told that my work can't be published because of proprietary rights or that the defense department considers the information classified. However, if somebody important is working with me and needs the publication, then it's full steam ahead.

CONSULTANT: You sound pretty disgruntled with your work.

CHRIS: It's not my work so much. I'm really very happy doing this work—it's cutting-edge, after all. The problem is that I'm never quite sure where the work is going. I do my part of a project, and unless I go out of my way to talk to other people, I never find out the final results of the total project. That's just something you learn to live with around here—being part of a system that's not particularly open.

Meg Conroy, Assistant to the Head of Administration

CONSULTANT: You've only been here a short time, is that correct?

MEG: That's right—just a little over a year.

CONSULTANT: Why did you take the job?

MEG: Well, I was in my last semester of college and was looking for a job, like most college seniors. My fiancé at the time—now he's my husband—was already working for Electro Logic (EL) and found out that there was an opening. So I applied.

CONSULTANT: So you were a business major in school?

MEG: Oh, no. I was a history major.

CONSULTANT: Do you like your job?

MEG: It has a lot to offer. I get paid pretty well for what I'm doing. And I'm learning a lot. I just wish the company would let me take some classes in administration, like accounting. The auditors ask some pretty tough questions. Steve says we should hire that expertise, but I'd still be responsible for supervising the people.

CONSULTANT: Is there any particular aspect about your job that you really find satisfying?

MEG: Well, let me think. I guess I like the fact that I get to do a lot of different tasks so that things don't get so boring. I would hate to have to do the same thing, day in and day out. A lot of times, I go to the library to do research on different things, and that's nice because it gets me out of the office.

CONSULTANT: What don't you like about your job?

MEG: Well, I often get the feeling that administration isn't taken seriously. You know, the engineers could get along without us quite nicely, or so they seem to think. The whole structure of the department shows that we're the catch-all department: If you don't fit anywhere else, they put you in here. Perhaps some of that is because our department is primarily women—in fact, I've been told that 95 percent of all the female employees are in administration. Sometimes it's hard to work with the engineers because they treat you like you don't know anything, and they always want things to be done their way. Clearly, the engineers get the money and consideration and yet, well, we do contribute quite a lot to the whole team, as Steve would say. But words of praise just aren't as impressive as actions. Sure, we get our birthday parties, but that still seems to be a little patronizing. We rarely get to see what's going on in the research area. I've asked a number of engineers specific questions, and they just kind of look at me with a blank stare and give me some really simplified answer. It seems to me if you want to build a family, like the president says, you can't treat administration like a bad relation.

P. J. Ginelli, Technician

CONSULTANT: I gather you've just been through your semiannual performance appraisal. How did it go?

P. J.: Like I expected. No surprises.

CONSULTANT: Do you find these appraisals useful?

P. J.: Sure. I get to find out what he thinks of my work.

CONSULTANT: Is that all?

P. J.: Well, I suppose it's a nice opportunity to understand what my supervisor wants. Sometimes he's not so clear during the rest of the year. I suppose he's been given specific goals from higher-ups before he talks with me, so he's clear and then I'm clear.

CONSULTANT: Do you like what you're doing?

P. J.: Oh yeah. The best part is that I'm not at the main building and so I don't have to put up with the "important" people, you know? I've heard from other techs that those guys can be a real pain—trying to be nice and all, but really just being a bother. I mean, how can you get your stuff done when the president's looking over your shoulder all the time? On the other hand, if the president knows your name, I suppose that's a good thing when it comes to raises and promotions. But my boss sticks up for his techs; we get a fair deal from him.

CONSULTANT: Do you think you'll be able to get ahead at Electro Logic (EL)?

P. J.: Get ahead? You mean become an engineer or something? No, and I really don't want to do that. Everyone around here keeps pushing me to move up. I'm afraid to tell people how I really feel for fear they'll decide I don't fit into this high-tech environment. I don't want to be the "black sheep of the family." I like where I am, and if the raises keep coming, I'll keep liking it. One of my kids is starting college next year, and I need the money to help her out. I get a lot of overtime, particularly when contract deadlines are near. I suppose the rush toward the end of contracts gives some people big headaches, but for me, I don't mind. The work is pretty slow otherwise, and so at least I'm working all the time and then some. But my family wishes my schedule was more predictable.

CONSULTANT: Do you think you'll continue working for EL?

P. J.: I'm not sure I want to answer that. Let's just say that my ratings on the performance appraisal were good, and I expect to see an improvement in my pay. I'll stay for that.

Chalida Montgomery, Technician

CONSULTANT: In general, what are your feelings about the work you do for Electro Logic (EL)?

CHALIDA: Well, I feel my work is quite good, but I also feel that I perform rather boring, tedious tasks. From what my supervisor says, the kinds of things I do are what electrical engineering students do in their last year of classes. I gather their final project is to make a circuit board, and that's what I do, day in and day out.

CONSULTANT: What is it that you would like to do?

CHALIDA: Well, it would be nice to be able to offer some input into some of the designs of these boards. I know I don't have a Ph.D. or anything, but I do have lots of experience. But because I'm a tech, the engineers don't really feel I've got much to offer—even though I build the boards and can tell from the design which one will do what the designer wants it to do.

I also would like to maybe supervise other technicians in my department. You know, some kind of advancement would be nice. As it is, lots of techs ask me how to do things, and of course I help, but then they get the credit. Around here, you have to have a piece of paper that says you're educated before they let you officially help other people.

Discussion Questions

1. Using the behavioral guidelines and Figure 5 as diagnostic aids, what are the strengths and weaknesses of Electro Logic (EL) from a motivational perspective?

2. What are the high-priority action items you would include in a consulting report to Steve Morgan, president of EL? Focus on specific actions that he could initiate that would better use the abilities of the staff and foster a more motivating work environment.

Skill Practice

Exercises for Diagnosing Work Performance Problems

Proper diagnosis is a critical aspect of effective motivation management. Often managers become frustrated because they don't understand the causes of observed performance problems. They might experiment with various "cures," but the inefficiency of this trial-and-error process often only increases their frustration level. In addition, the accompanying misunderstanding adds extra strain to the manager-subordinate relationship. This generally makes the performance problem even more pronounced, which in turn prompts the manager to resort to more drastic responses, and a vicious downward spiral ensues.

The performance diagnosis model in Figure 7 offers a systematic way for managers and subordinates to pinpoint collaboratively the causes of dissatisfaction and performance problems. It assumes that employees will work hard and be good performers if the work environment encourages these actions. Consequently, rather than jumping to conclusions about poor performance stemming from deficiencies in personality traits or a bad attitude, this diagnostic process helps managers focus their attention on improving the selection, job design, performance evaluation, and reward-allocation systems. In this manner, the specific steps necessary to accomplish work goals and management's expectations are examined to pinpoint why a worker's performance is falling short.

The manager and low-performing subordinate should follow the logical discovery process in the model, step by step. They should begin by examining the current perceptions of performance as well as the understanding of performance expectations and then proceed through the model until the performance problems have been identified. The model focuses on seven of these problems.

A. **Perception Problem:** "Do you agree your performance is below expectations?" A perception problem suggests that the manager and subordinate have different views of the subordinate's current performance level. Unless this disagreement is resolved, it is futile to

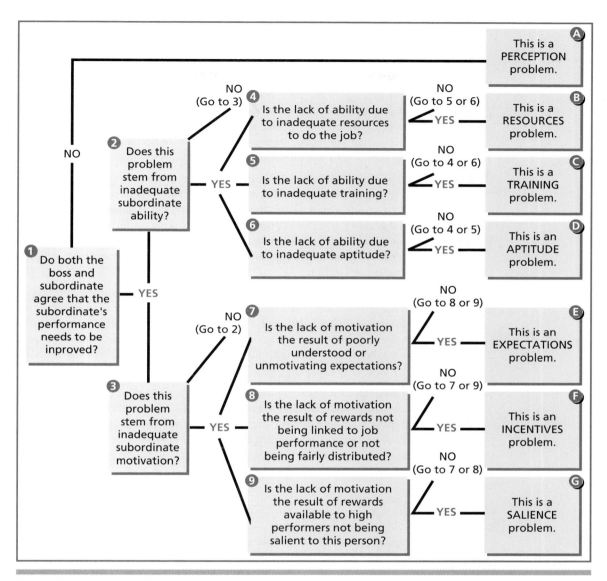

Figure 7 Performance Diagnosis Model

continue the diagnostic process. The entire problem-solving process is based on the premise that both parties recognize the existence of a problem and are interested in solving it. If agreement does not exist, the manager should focus on resolving the discrepancy in perceptions, including clarifying current expectations (Problem E).

B. **Resources Problem:** "Do you have the resources necessary to do the job well?" Ability has three components, and these should be explored in the order shown in the model. This order reduces a subordinate's defensive reactions. Poor performance may stem from a lack of resource support. Resources include material and personnel support as well as cooperation from interdependent work groups.

C. **Training Problem:** "Is a lack of training interfering with your job performance?" Individuals may be asked to perform tasks that exceed their current skill or knowledge level. Typically, this problem can be overcome through additional training or education.

D. **Aptitude Problem:** "Do you feel this is the right job/blend of work assignments for you?" This is the most difficult of the three ability problems to resolve because it is the most basic. If the *resupply* (providing additional resources) and *retraining* solutions have been explored without success, then more drastic measures may be required. These include *refitting* the person's current job requirements, *reassigning* him or her to another position, or, finally, *releasing* him or her from the organization.

E. **Expectations Problem:** "What are your performance expectations for this position? What do you think my expectations are?" This problem results from poor communication regarding job goals or job requirements. In some cases, the stated goals may be different from the desired goals. In other words, the employee is working toward one goal while the supervisor desires another. This often occurs when subordinates are not sufficiently involved in the goal- or standard-setting process. When this results in unrealistic, imposed expectations, motivation suffers.

F. **Incentives Problem:** "Do you believe rewards are linked to your performance in this position?" Either the individual does not believe that "performance makes a difference" or insufficient performance feedback and reinforcement have been given. The manager should also ask, "Do you feel rewards are being distributed equitably?" This provides an opportunity to discuss subordinates' criteria for judging fairness. Often, unrealistic standards are being used.

G. **Salience Problem:** "Are the performance incentives attractive to you?" Salience refers to the importance an individual attaches to available rewards. Oftentimes, the incentives offered to encourage high performance aren't highly valued by a particular individual. Managers need to be creative in generating a broad range of rewards and flexible in allowing subordinates to choose among rewards.

Assignment

Option 1: Read the case, "Joe Chaney," and privately use the diagnostic model (see Figure 7) to pinpoint plausible performance problems. Next, discuss in small groups your individual assessments and list specific questions you should ask Joe to accurately identify, from his point of view, the obstacles to his high performance. Finally, brainstorm ideas for plausible solutions. Prepare to represent your group in role-playing a problem-solving interview with Joe.

Option 2: Administer the Work Performance Assessment survey to several employees. Using the scoring key in Appendix I, categorize the obstacles to high performance and satisfaction reported by the respondents. Then get together in small groups, with each group assuming the role of a management task force charged with the responsibility to analyze this employee survey data. Discuss the patterns in the data as well as possible remedies for these problems, using the behavioral guidelines and motivational models in the chapter as guides. Prepare a report on your analysis and recommendations for specific changes.

Joe Chaney

Joe Chaney joined your architectural firm two years ago as a draftsman. He is 35 years old and has been a draftsman since graduating from a two-year technical school right after high school. He is married and has four children. He has worked for four architectural firms in 12 years.

Joe came with mediocre recommendations from his previous employer, but you hired him anyway because you needed help desperately. Your firm's workload has been extremely high due to a local construction boom. The result is that a lot of the practices that contribute to a supportive, well-managed work environment have been overlooked. For instance, you can't remember the last time you conducted a formal performance review or did any career counseling. Furthermore, the tradition of closing the office early on Friday for a social hour was dropped long ago. Unfortunately, the tension in the office runs pretty high some days due to unbearable time pressures and the lack of adequate staff. Night and weekend work have become the norm rather than the exception.

Overall, you have been pleasantly surprised by Joe's performance. Until recently, he worked hard and consistently produced high-quality work. Furthermore, he frequently volunteered for special projects, made lots of suggestions for improving the work environment, and has demonstrated an in-depth practical knowledge of architecture and the construction business. However, during the past few months, he has definitely slacked off. He doesn't seem as excited about his work, and several times you have found him daydreaming at his desk. In addition, he has gotten into several heated arguments with architects about the specifications and proper design procedures for recent projects.

After one of these disagreements, you overheard Joe complaining to his officemate, "No one around here respects my opinion. I'm just a lowly draftsman. I know as much as these hotshot architects, but because I don't have the degree, they ignore my input, and I'm stuck doing the grunt work. Adding insult to injury, my wife has had to get a job to help support our family. I must be the lowest-paid person in this firm." In response to a question from a coworker regarding why he didn't pursue a college degree in architecture, Joe responded, "Do you have any idea how hard it is to put bread on the table, pay a Seattle mortgage, work overtime, be a reasonably good father and husband, plus go to night school? Come, on, be realistic!"

Work Performance Assessment

Respond to the following statements, based on your current work situation.

Rating Scale

1	Strongly disagree	4	Agree
2	Disagree	5	Strongly agree
3	Neutral		

_____ 1. My supervisor and I agree on the quality of my performance.

_____ 2. I feel I have adequate training to perform my current job assignments.

_____ 3. I believe that my native skills and abilities are matched very well with my job responsibilities.

_____ 4. I believe that I have adequate resources and supplies to do my job well.

_____ 5. I understand my boss's expectations and generally feel they are realistic.

_____ 6. I believe that rewards are distributed fairly, on the basis of performance.

_____ 7. The rewards and opportunities available to me if I perform well are attractive to me personally.

_____ 8. My supervisor indicates that I am not performing as well as I should, but I disagree.

	9.	I could do a much better job if I had more training.
_____	10.	I believe that my job is too difficult for my ability level.
_____	11.	I believe that my job performance is hindered by a lack of supplies and resources.
_____	12.	I believe my boss's expectations are unclear and unrealistic.
_____	13.	I believe my boss plays favorites in allocating rewards.
_____	14.	I do not find the rewards and opportunities available to high performers very appealing.

Exercise for Reshaping Unacceptable Behaviors

Shaheen Matombo

One of the most challenging aspects of management is transforming inappropriate behaviors into appropriate behaviors. Managers commonly take insufficient action to transform negative actions into positive ones. Some of these insufficient responses include assuming that ignoring an employee's shortcomings will make them go away; praising positive aspects of an individual's performance in hopes that this will encourage him or her to rechannel unproductive energies; discussing problems in vague, general terms in a group meeting, in hopes that the unproductive person will "take a hint" and change; and getting upset with an individual and demanding that he or she "shape up."

Assignment

Assume the role of Andre Tate in the following case. After reading the case, review the applicable behavioral guidelines shown on the Observer's Feedback Form in Appendix I. In small groups, discuss how you would resolve this problem. Prepare to role-play your discussion with Shaheen Matombo. After the discussion, assigned observers will provide feedback on your performance, using the Observer's Form as a guide. Unless you are assigned to play her role, do not read the role instructions for Shaheen prior to the interview.

Andre Tate, Manager

Shaheen has been a member of your staff for only three months. You don't know much about her other than that she is a single parent who has recently entered the workforce after a difficult divorce. She is often 10 to 20 minutes late for work in the morning. You are the manager of a very hectic customer relations office for a utility company. The phones start ringing promptly at 8:00. When she is late for work, you have to answer her phone, and this interrupts your work schedule. This morning, you are particularly annoyed. She is 25 minutes late, and the phones are ringing like crazy. Because you have been forced to answer them, it will be difficult for you to complete an important assignment by the noon deadline. You are getting more upset by the minute.

    While you are in the middle of a particularly unpleasant phone conversation with an irate customer, you look out your window and see Shaheen bounding up the steps to the building. You think to yourself, "This is ridiculous, I've got to put a stop to her tardiness. Maybe I should just threaten to fire her unless she shapes up." Upon further reflection, you realize that would be impractical, especially during this period of retrenchment after the rate hike was turned down. Given the rumors about a possible hiring freeze, you know it may be difficult to refill any vacancies.

Also, Shaheen is actually a pretty good worker when she is there. She is conscientious and has a real knack with cranky callers. Unfortunately, it has taken her much longer than expected to learn the computer program for retrieving information on customer accounts. She frequently has to put callers on hold while she asks for help. These interruptions have tended to increase an already-tense relationship with the rest of the office staff. She has had some difficulty fitting in socially; the others are much younger and have worked together for several years. Shaheen is the first new hire in a long time, so the others aren't used to breaking someone in. Three of your staff have complained to you about Shaheen's constant interruptions. They feel their productivity is going down as a result. Besides, she seems to expect them to drop whatever they are doing every time she has a question. They had expected their workload to be lighter when a new person was hired, but now they are having second thoughts. (In the past, you have had enough time to train new hires, but your boss has had you tied up on a major project for almost a year.)

Shaheen enters the office obviously flustered and disheveled. She has "I'm sorry" written all over her face. You motion for her to pick up the blinking phone line and then scribble a note on a tablet while you complete your call: "See me in my office at 12:00 sharp!" It's time you got to the bottom of Shaheen's disruptive influence on an otherwise smooth-flowing operation.

Shaheen Matombo, Staff Member

Boy, what a morning! Your babysitter's father died during the night, and she called you from the airport at 6:30 A.M. saying she would be out of town for three or four days. You tried three usually available backups before you finally found someone who could take Keen, your three-year-old. Then Shayla, your seventh-grader, went through five outfits before she was satisfied that she had just the right look for her first yearbook picture. It's a miracle that Buddy, your oldest, was able to pull himself out of bed after getting only five hours of sleep. On top of football and drama, he's now joined the chess team, and they had their first tournament last night. Why did it have to fall on the night before his final in physics? This morning you wished you had his knack for juggling so many activities. By the time you got the kids delivered, you were already 10 minutes behind schedule. Then there was this incredible accident on the expressway that slowed traffic to a crawl.

As you finally pull off the downtown exit ramp, you notice you're almost 20 minutes late for work. "My kingdom for a car phone!" you groan. "Although by now I probably couldn't get an open line into the office, anyway." As you desperately scan the side streets for a parking space, you begin to panic. "How am I going to explain this to Andre? He'll be furious. I'm sure he's upset about my chronic lateness. On top of that, he's obviously disappointed with my lack of computer skills, and I'm sure the others complain to him about having to train a newcomer." You're sure that one of the reasons you got the job was that you had completed a computer class at the local community college. Unfortunately, there hadn't been much carryover to the incredibly complex computer program you use at work. (It seems to defy every convention of logic.)

"What am I going to tell him about my being late for work so often?" Unfortunately, there isn't an easy answer. "Maybe it will get better as the kids and I get used to this new routine. It's just very difficult to get the kids to the bus stop and the sitter, commute 20 minutes, and arrive precisely at 8:00. I wonder if he would allow me to come in at 8:30 and only take a half-hour lunch. Staying late wouldn't work because they close down the computers at 5:00, unless there was some paperwork I could do for half an hour."

Then what about the problems with the computer and the other staff members? "Sooner or later he's going to get on my case about those things. Is it my fault I don't think like a computer? Some people might be able to sit down and figure this program out in a couple of hours, but not me. So is that my fault or should someone be giving me more training? I wish the others weren't so cliquish and unwilling to help me out. I wonder why that's the case. It's like they're afraid I'll become as good as they are if they share their experience with me. I wish Andre had more time to help me learn the ropes, but he seems to always be in meetings."

"Well, I'm probably going to catch it this morning. I've never been this late. Maybe I'll be back home full-time sooner than I expected."

Skill Application

Activities for Motivating Others

Suggested Assignments

1. Identify a situation in which you have some responsibility for another person whose performance is significantly below your expectation. Using the Work Performance Assessment Survey included in the Skill Practice section, collect information on the individual's perceptions of the situation. Using the diagnostic model (decision tree) in that section, specifically identify the perceived performance problems. Compare these results with your own views of the situation. Conduct an interview with the individual and discuss the results, highlighting areas of disagreement. Based on this discussion, formulate a plan of action that both parties accept. If inadequate ability is a problem, follow the resupply, retrain, refill, reassign, and release remedial steps. If insufficient effort is a problem, use the steps for reprimanding, redirecting, and rewarding discussed in the chapter as a resource for this discussion. Implement this plan for a period of time and then report on the results.

2. Focus on some aspect of your own work in which you feel performance is below your (or others') expectations. Using the Work Performance Assessment Survey, identify the specific obstacles to improved performance. Then formulate a plan for overcoming these obstacles, including getting commitments from others. Discuss your plan with individuals affected by it and arrive at a set of actions all parties accept. Implement the plan for a period of time and report on your results. How successful were you in making the changes? Did your performance improve as expected? Based on this experience, identify other aspects of your work that you could improve in a similar fashion.

3. Identify four or five situations in which you are typically provoked to exhibit punishing behavior. These might involve friends, family members, or work associates. Examine these situations and identify one where punishment (discipline) is not working. Using the guidelines for reprimanding, redirecting, and rewarding, design a specific plan for shaping the other person's behaviors so you can begin rewarding positive

actions. Report on your results. Based on this experience, consider how you might be able to use this strategy in other similar situations.

4. Using the six-step model for creating a motivating work environment (see Table 1), design a specific plan for managing a new relationship (e.g., a new subordinate) or a new phase in an old relationship (e.g., friend, family member, or subordinate about to begin work on a new project). Write down specific directions for yourself for implementing each of the six steps. Discuss your plan with this individual and ask for suggestions for improvement. Make sure your perceptions of the key aspects of the plan are consistent with his or hers. Implement your plan for a period of time and then report on the consequences. Based on this experience, identify changes that would be appropriate in similar settings.

Application Plan and Evaluation

The intent of this exercise is to help you apply this cluster of skills in a real-life, out-of-class setting. Now that you have become familiar with the behavioral guidelines that form the basis of effective skill performance, you will improve most by trying out those guidelines in an everyday context. Unlike a classroom activity, in which feedback is immediate and others can assist you with their evaluations, this skill application activity is one you must accomplish and evaluate on your own. There are two parts to this activity. Part 1 helps prepare you to apply the skill. Part 2 helps you evaluate and improve on your experience. Be sure to write down answers to each item. Don't short-circuit the process by skipping steps.

Part 1. Planning

1. Write down the two or three aspects of this skill that are most important to you. These may be areas of weakness, areas you most want to improve, or areas that are most salient to a problem you face right now. Identify the specific aspects of this skill that you want to apply.

2. Now identify the setting or the situation in which you will apply this skill. Establish a plan for performance by actually writing down a description of the situation. Who else will be involved? When will you do it? Where will it be done?

   Circumstances:

   Who else?

   When?

   Where?

3. Identify the specific behaviors you will engage in to apply this skill. Operationalize your skill performance.

4. What are the indicators of successful performance? How will you know you have been effective? What will indicate you have performed competently?

Part 2. Evaluation

5. After you have completed your implementation, record the results. What happened? How successful were you? What was the effect on others?

6. How can you improve? What modifications can you make next time? What will you do differently in a similar situation in the future?

7. Looking back on your whole skill practice and application experience, what have you learned? What has been surprising? In what ways might this experience help you in the long term?

Chapter

7

Managing Conflict

OBJECTIVES

▶ Diagnose the sources of conflict

▶ Understand the impact of culture and diversity on managing conflict

▶ Select the appropriate conflict-management strategy

▶ Manage interpersonal confrontations

skill development

Skill Assessment

Diagnostic Surveys for Managing Conflict

Managing Interpersonal Conflict

Step 1: Before you read this chapter, please respond to the following statements by writing a number from the rating scale below in the left-hand column (Preassessment). Your answers should reflect your attitudes and behavior as they are now, not as you would like them to be. Be honest. This instrument is designed to help you discover your level of competency in managing conflict so you can tailor your learning to your specific needs. When you have completed the survey, use the scoring key in Appendix I to identify the skill areas discussed in this chapter that are most important for you to master.

Step 2: After you have completed the reading and the exercises in this chapter and, ideally, as many as you can of the Skill Application assignments at the end of this chapter, cover up your first set of answers. Then respond to the same statements again, this time in the right-hand column (Postassessment). When you have completed the survey, use the scoring key in Appendix I to measure your progress. If your score remains low in specific skill areas, use the behavioral guidelines at the end of the Skill Learning section to guide further practice.

Rating Scale

1	Strongly disagree	4	Slightly agree
2	Disagree	5	Agree
3	Slightly disagree	6	Strongly agree

Assessment

Pre-   Post-   *When I see someone doing something that needs correcting:*

_____ _____ 1. I avoid making personal accusations and attributing self-serving motives to the other person.

_____ _____ 2. When stating my concerns, I present them as my problems.

_____ _____ 3. I succinctly describe problems in terms of the behavior that occurred, its consequences, and my feelings about it.

_____ _____ 4. I specify the expectations and standards that have been violated.

_____ _____ 5. I make a specific request, detailing a more acceptable option.

_____ _____ 6. I persist in explaining my point of view until it is understood by the other person.

_____ _____ 7. I encourage two-way interaction by inviting the respondent to express his or her perspective and to ask questions.

_____ _____ 8. When there are several concerns, I approach the issues incrementally, starting with easy and simple issues and then progressing to those that are difficult and complex.

When someone complains about something I've done:

_____ _____   9. I look for our common areas of agreement.

_____ _____ 10. I show genuine concern and interest, even when I disagree.

_____ _____ 11. I avoid justifying my actions and becoming defensive.

_____ _____ 12. I seek additional information by asking questions that provide specific and descriptive information.

_____ _____ 13. I focus on one issue at a time.

_____ _____ 14. I find some aspects of the complaint with which I can agree.

_____ _____ 15. I ask the other person to suggest more acceptable behaviors.

_____ _____ 16. I strive to reach agreement on a remedial plan of action.

When two other people are in conflict and I am the mediator:

_____ _____ 17. I acknowledge that conflict exists and treat it as serious and important.

_____ _____ 18. I help create an agenda for a problem-solving meeting by identifying the issues to be discussed, one at a time.

_____ _____ 19. I do not take sides, but remain neutral.

_____ _____ 20. I help focus the discussion on the impact of the conflict on work performance.

_____ _____ 21. I keep the interaction focused on problems rather than on personalities.

_____ _____ 22. I make certain that neither party dominates the conversation.

_____ _____ 23. I help the parties generate multiple alternatives.

_____ _____ 24. I help the parties find areas on which they agree.

Strategies for Handling Conflict

Indicate how often you use each of the following by writing the appropriate number in the blank. Choose a number from a scale of 1 to 5, with 1 being "rarely," 3 being "sometimes," and 5 being "always." After you have completed the survey, use the scoring key in Appendix I to tabulate your results. (Information on these five strategies is shown in Table 3 later in this chapter.)

_____   1.   I argue my position tenaciously.

_____   2.   I try to put the needs of others above my own.

_____   3.   I try to arrive at a compromise both parties can accept.

_____   4.   I try not to get involved in conflicts.

_____   5.   I strive to investigate issues thoroughly and jointly.

_____   6.   I try to find fault in other persons' positions.

_____   7.   I strive to foster harmony.

_____	8.	I negotiate to get a portion of what I propose.
_____	9.	I avoid open discussions of controversial subjects.
_____	10.	I openly share information with others in resolving disagreements.
_____	11.	I enjoy winning an argument.
_____	12.	I go along with the suggestions of others.
_____	13.	I look for a middle ground to resolve disagreements.
_____	14.	I keep my true feelings to myself to avoid hard feelings.
_____	15.	I encourage the open sharing of concerns and issues.
_____	16.	I am reluctant to admit I am wrong.
_____	17.	I try to help others avoid "losing face" in a disagreement.
_____	18.	I stress the advantages of "give and take."
_____	19.	I encourage others to take the lead in resolving controversy.
_____	20.	I state my position as only one point of view.

■ Skill Learning

Interpersonal Conflict Management

In an era of ever-increasing and ever-bigger mergers, a remarkable number—somewhere between one-half and two-thirds—simply don't work. Why? One prominent reason is that key executives in the merging firms can't agree on their respective roles, status, perks, and so on. These tensions are compounded by disagreements over which operating procedures to use and whose "corporate culture" will dominate. The inability or willingness to resolve these conflicts unravels an otherwise attractive business marriage. (Abstracted from "Do Mergers Really Work?" _Business Week,_ June 3, 1985, pp. 88–100)

One of the leading causes of business failure among major corporations is too much agreement among top management. They have similar training and experience, which means they tend to view conditions the same way and pursue similar goals. This problem is compounded by Boards of Directors failing to play an aggressive oversight role. They avoid conflict with the internal management team who appear unified on key issues and very confident of their positions. (Abstracted from J. Argenti, _Corporate Collapse: The Causes and Symptoms._ New York: Wiley, 1976)

In 1984 Ross Perot, an outspoken self-made billionaire, sold Electronic Data Systems [EDS] to General Motors [GM] for $2.5 billion and immediately became GM's largest stockholder and member of the board. GM needed EDS's expertise to coordinate its massive information system. Roger Smith, GM's chairman, also hoped that Perot's fiery spirit would reinvigorate GM's bureaucracy. Almost immediately, Perot became a severe critic of GM policy and practice. He noted that it takes longer for GM to produce a car than it took the country to win WWII. He was especially critical of GM's bureaucracy, claiming it fostered conformity at the expense of getting results. By December 1986, Roger Smith had apparently had enough of Perot's "reinvigoration." Whether his criticisms were true, or functional, the giant automaker paid nearly twice the market value of his stock ($750 million) to silence him and arrange his resignation from the board. (Adapted from "The GM System Is Like a Blanket of Fog," *Fortune,* February 15, 1988, pp. 48–49)

As reflected in these brief vignettes, interpersonal conflict is an essential, ubiquitous part of organizational life. In fact, given the current business trends toward workforce diversity, globalization, and joint ventures, how managers from different organizations and cultures deal with conflict is an increasingly important question (Seybolt, Derr, & Nielson, 1996). Organizations in which there is little disagreement generally fail in competitive environments. Members are either so homogeneous that they are ill-equipped to adapt to changing environmental conditions or so complacent that they see no need to improve the status quo. Conflict is the lifeblood of vibrant, progressive, stimulating organizations. It sparks creativity, stimulates innovation, and encourages personal improvement (Wanous & Youtz, 1986; Pascale, 1990).

This view is clearly in line with the management philosophy of Andrew Grove, president of Intel. "Many managers seem to think it is impossible to tackle anything or anyone head-on, even in business. By contrast, we at Intel believe that it is the essence of corporate health to bring a problem out into the open as soon as possible, even if this entails a confrontation. Dealing with conflicts lies at the heart of managing any business. As a result, confrontation—facing issues about which there is disagreement—can be avoided only at the manager's peril. Workplace politicking grows quietly in the dark, like mushrooms; neither can stand the light of day" (*Fortune,* July 23, 1984, p. 74).

These introductory quotes, however, point out that not all conflict produces beneficial results. Some people have a very low tolerance for disagreement. Whether this is the result of family background, cultural values, or personality characteristics, a high level of interpersonal conflict saps their energy and demoralizes their spirit. Also, some types of conflicts, regardless of frequency, generally produce dysfunctional outcomes. These include petty personality conflicts and arguments over things that can't be changed. This is especially the case when conflict is stimulated for self-serving purposes. For example, some managers feel so unsure of their qualifications and support that they continually stir up conflicts between subordinates. This reduces the threat of a coalition forming to challenge the boss's rule, creates situations that reaffirm the boss's superior position (e.g., when conflicts occur that only he or she can resolve), and provides an opportunity for the boss to berate subordinates for quarreling like children. This is a classic case of using a natural, legitimate organizational process for contrived, illegitimate personal purposes. Fortunately, it appears to be the exception, not the rule, in management practice.

As Figure 1 shows, most scholars agree that some conflict is both inevitable and beneficial in effective organizations (Brown, 1983). However, a well-known psychologist, Abraham Maslow (1965), has observed a high degree of ambivalence in our society regarding the value of conflict. On the one hand, he notes that managers intellectually appreciate the value of conflict and competition. They agree it is a necessary ingredient of the free-enterprise system. However, their actions demonstrate a personal preference for avoiding conflicts whenever possible.

The tension between intellectual acceptance of a principle and emotional rejection of its enactment was illustrated in a classic study of decision making (Boulding, 1964). Several groups of managers were formed to solve a complex problem. They were told their performance would be judged by a panel of experts in terms of the quantity and quality of solutions generated. The groups were identical in size and composition, with the exception that half of them included a "confederate." Before the experiment began, the researcher instructed this person to play the role of "devil's advocate." This person was to challenge the group's conclusions, forcing the others to examine critically their assumptions and the logic of their arguments. At the end of the problem-solving period, the recommendations made by both sets

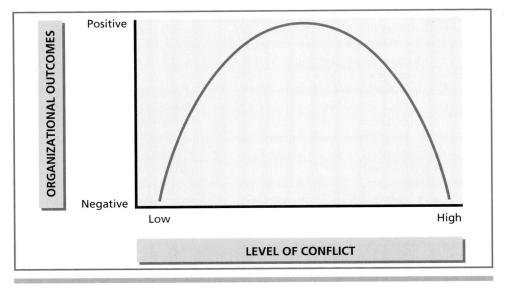

Figure 1   Relationship Between Level of Conflict and Organizational Outcomes

of groups were compared. The groups with the devil's advocates had performed significantly better on the task. They had generated more alternatives, and their proposals were judged as superior. After a short break, the groups were reassembled and told that they would be performing a similar task during the next session. However, before they began discussing the next problem, they were given permission to eliminate one member. In every group containing a confederate, he or she was the one asked to leave. The fact that every high-performance group expelled their unique competitive advantage because that member made others feel uncomfortable demonstrates a widely shared reaction to conflict: "I know it has positive outcomes for the performance of the organization as a whole, but I don't like how it makes me feel personally."

We believe that much of the ambivalence toward conflict stems from a lack of understanding of the causes of conflict and the variety of modes for managing it effectively, and from a lack of confidence in one's personal skills for handling the tense, emotionally charged environment typical of most interpersonal confrontations. It is natural for an untrained or inexperienced person to avoid threatening situations, and it is generally acknowledged that conflict represents the most severe test of a manager's interpersonal skills. The task of the effective manager, therefore, is to maintain

an optimal level of conflict, while keeping conflicts focused on productive purposes (Robbins, 1974; Kelly, 1970; Thomas, 1976).

With today's international business environment and increasingly diverse workforce, this requires four sets of skills. First, managers must be able to diagnose accurately the causes of conflict. Second, managers must understand how cultural differences and other diversity issues may be affecting the conflict situation. Third, having identified the sources of conflict and taken into account the context and personal preferences for dealing with conflict, managers must be able to select an appropriate conflict management strategy. Fourth, skillful managers must be able to settle interpersonal disputes effectively so that underlying problems are resolved and the relationship between disputants is not damaged.

Diagnosing the Sources of Interpersonal Confrontations

Managers often behave as though serious interpersonal confrontations are the result of personality defects. They label people who are frequently involved in conflicts "troublemakers" or "bad apples" and attempt to transfer or dismiss them as a way of resolving conflict. While some individuals seem to have a propensity for making trouble and appear to be cantankerous under even the best of circumstances, "sour dispositions" actually account for only a small percentage of organizational conflicts (Schmidt & Tannenbaum, 1965; Hines, 1980).

This proposition is supported by research on performance appraisals (Latham & Wexley, 1981). It has been shown that managers generally attribute poor performance to personal deficiencies in workers, such as laziness, lack of skill, or lack of motivation. However, when workers are asked the causes of their poor performance, they generally explain it in terms of problems in their environment, such as insufficient supplies or uncooperative coworkers. While some face-saving is obviously involved here, this line of research suggests that managers need to guard against the reflexive tendency to assume that bad behaviors imply bad people. In fact, aggressive or harsh behaviors sometimes observed in interpersonal confrontations often reflect the frustrations of people who have good intentions but are unskilled in handling intense, emotional experiences.

In contrast to the personality-defect theory of conflict, we propose four sources of interpersonal conflict in Table 1. These are **personal differences, informational deficiency, role incompatibility,** and **environmental stress.** Individuals bring different backgrounds to their roles in organizations. Their values and needs have been shaped by different socialization processes, depending on their cultural and family traditions, level of education, breadth of experience, and so forth. As a result, their interpretations

of events and their expectations about relationships with others in the organization will vary considerably. Conflicts stemming from incompatible personal values and needs are some of the most difficult to resolve. They often become highly emotional and take on moral overtones. A disagreement about who is factually *correct* easily turns into a bitter argument over who is morally *right*.

Such a conflict occurred in a major industrial company between a 63-year-old white executive vice-president and a 35-year-old Chinese member of the corporate legal department who was exiled in 1989 following Tiananmen Square. They disagreed vehemently over whether the company should accept a very attractive offer from the Chinese government to build a manufacturing facility. The vice-president felt the company had a responsibility to its stockholders to pursue every legal opportunity to increase profits. In contrast, the lawyer felt that collaborating with the Chinese government was tantamount to condoning its morally repugnant disregard for human rights.

Conflicts may also result from deficiencies in the organization's information system. An important message may not be received, a boss's instructions may be misinterpreted, or decision-makers may arrive at different conclusions because they use different databases. Conflicts based on misinformation or misunderstanding tend to be factual; hence, clarifying previous messages or obtaining additional information generally resolves the dispute. This might entail rewording the boss's instructions, reconciling contradictory sources of data, or redistributing copies of misplaced messages. This type of conflict is common in organizations, but it is also easy to resolve. Because value systems are not challenged, such confrontations tend to be less emotional. Once the breakdown in the information system is repaired, disputants are generally able to resolve their disagreement with a minimum of resentment.

For example, UOP, Inc., made an agreement with Union Carbide in 1987 that doubled its workforce. Conflicts over operating procedures surfaced immediately between original employees and new employees from Union Carbide. This, combined with traditional conflicts between functional groups in the organization, led UOP to begin a new training program in which groups of employees met to discuss quality improvements. "We discovered that the main problem had been a lack of communication," said one senior official. "No one had any idea what other groups were

SOURCES OF CONFLICT	FOCUS OF CONFLICT
Personal differences	Perceptions and expectations
Informational deficiency	Misinformation and misrepresentation
Role incompatibility	Goals and responsibilities
Environmental stress	Resource scarcity and uncertainty

Table 1 Sources of Conflict

up to, so they all assumed that their way was best" (Caudron, 1992, p. 61).

The complexity inherent in most organizations tends to produce conflict between members whose tasks are interdependent but whose roles are incompatible. This type of conflict is exemplified by the classic goal conflicts between line and staff, production and sales, marketing and R&D. Each unit has different responsibilities in the organization, and as a result each places different priorities on organizational goals (e.g., customer satisfaction, product quality, production efficiency, compliance with government regulations). It is also typical of firms whose multiple product lines compete for scarce resources.

During the early days at Apple Computer, the Apple II division accounted for a large part of the company's revenue. It viewed the newly created Macintosh division as an unwise speculative venture. The natural rivalry was made worse when a champion of the Macintosh referred to the Apple II team as "the dull and boring product division." Since this type of conflict stems from the fundamental incompatibility of the job responsibilities of the disputants, it can often be resolved only through the mediation of a common superior.

Role incompatibility conflicts may overlap with those arising from personal differences or information deficiencies. The personal differences members bring to an organization generally remain dormant until they are triggered by an organizational catalyst, such as interdependent task responsibilities. One reason members often perceive that their assigned roles are incompatible is that they are operating from different bases of information. They communicate with different sets of people, are tied into different reporting systems, and receive instructions from different bosses.

Another major source of conflict is environmentally induced stress. Conflicts stemming from personal differences and role incompatibilities are greatly exacerbated by a stressful environment. When an organization is forced to operate on an austere budget, its members are more likely to become embroiled in disputes over domain claims and resource requests. Scarcity tends to lower trust, increase ethnocentrism, and reduce participation in decision making. These are ideal conditions for incubating interpersonal conflict (Cameron, Kim, & Whetten, 1987).

When a large Eastern bank announced a major downsizing, the threat to employees' security was so severe that it disrupted long-time, close working rela- tionships. Even friendships were not immune to the effects of the scarcity-induced stress. Long-standing golf foursomes and car pools were disbanded because tension among members was so high.

Another environmental condition that fosters conflict is uncertainty. When individuals find it difficult to predict what is going to happen to them from month to month, they become very anxious and prone to conflict. This type of "frustration conflict" often stems from rapid, repeated change. If task assignments, management philosophy, accounting procedures, and lines of authority are changed frequently, members find it difficult to cope with the resulting stress, and sharp, bitter conflicts can easily erupt over seemingly trivial problems. This type of conflict is generally intense, but it dissipates quickly once a change becomes routinized and individuals' stress levels are lowered.

When a major pet-food manufacturing facility announced that one-third of its managers would have to support a new third shift, the feared disruption of personal and family routines prompted many managers to think about sending out their résumés. In addition, the uncertainty of who was going to be required to work at night was so great that even routine management work was disrupted by posturing and infighting.

These four sources of conflict are illustrated in problems at First Boston, one of the top seven investment banks dominating the New York capital market. This venerable firm became embroiled in conflict between two important revenue divisions: trading and investment banking. After the stock market crash in 1987, the trading division, which accounted for the bulk of First Boston's profits in the 1980s through mergers and acquisitions, asked that resources be diverted from trading (an unprofitable line) to investment banking. They also asked for allocation of computer costs on the basis of usage instead of splitting the costs in half, since investment banking did not use computers very much.

A review committee, including the CEO (a trader by background) reviewed the problem and finally decided to reject the investment banking proposals. This led to the resignations of the head of the investment division and several of the senior staff, including seven leveraged buyout specialists.

This problem was exacerbated by increasing frictions between competing subcultures within the firm. In the 1950s, when First Boston began, it was "WASPish" in composition, and its business came chiefly through the "old-boy network." In the 1970s,

First Boston recruited a number of innovative "whiz kids"—mostly Jews, Italians, and Cubans. These individuals generated innovative ways to package mergers and acquisitions, which are now the mainstay of the current business in the investment area. These were less-aristocratic people, many even wearing jeans to the office. The tension between the new "high flyers" and the "old guard" colored many decisions (*The Economist,* April 23, 1988, pp. 88–90).

The Impact of Culture and Diversity on Managing Conflict

Increased interdependence and interactions across national, organizational, and departmental borders create multiple opportunities not only for improved decision making, creativity, and innovation, but also for miscommunication, misunderstanding, misperceptions, and loss of productivity. In resolving conflicts, diversity of conflict management styles leads to a variety of approaches and resolutions that, in turn, have the potential for both conflict escalation and de-escalation (Rubin, Pruitt, & Kim, 1991; Seybolt et al., 1996; Tjosvold, 1991). As we suggest in our overview model of managing conflict (see Figure 5 on page 345), before we can consider alternative conflict strategies, we must recognize the disputants' personal preferences for handling conflict, as well as the context in which the conflict occurs. In the business environment of the 1990s, culture and workforce diversity are critical elements of the context and influencing factors of preferences for managing conflict.

Managing diversity has become an important component of managerial activities. **Managing diversity** can be defined as the planning and implementation of organizational systems, policies, and practices to manage people so that the potential advantages of diversity are maximized while potential disadvantages are minimized (Cox, 1994). Diversity theorist Taylor Cox Jr. posits that by managing diversity in their workforces, organizations are satisfying three types of goals: (1) ethical or social responsibility goals; (2) legal obligations; and (3) economic performance goals (Cox, 1994). First, managing diversity demonstrates organizational willingness to provide equal opportunities and fairness for all employees regardless of gender, race, age, or any other differentiating

characteristic other than performance. Second, certain aspects of managing diversity are mandated by law. Neglect of these laws often results in significant lawsuits and financial losses to settle cases of discrimination. Federal funds may also be reduced via affirmative action laws if a representative amount of diversity does not exist in a company's workforce. Third, managing diversity actually affects an organization's bottom-line results of economic performance. Cox developed a model—the Interactional Model of Cultural Diversity (IMCD), shown in Figure 2—that supplies the rationale for how diversity influences organizational effectiveness.

The main points of the IMCD model are the following: (1) the model demonstrates the influence of diversity on multiple levels—the individual, the group, and the organization; (2) the diversity climate of the organization is determined by the extent to which differences are valued in the workplace and the extent to which members of minority groups are respected and integrated into both the formal and informal power structure of the organization; (3) the diversity climate impacts individual career outcomes, both affective (e.g., job satisfaction) and tangible (e.g., promotions); (4) organizational outcomes are affected directly by the nature of the diversity climate and indirectly by the way individuals feel about their careers and the organization.

Cox and other scholars who adhere to the "value in diversity" perspective offer considerable evidence for the performance benefits of a diverse workforce when managed effectively (e.g., Cox, Lobel, & McLeod, 1991; Mandell & Kohler-Gray, 1990; Morrison, 1996). From recent studies of diversity (Cox & Blake, 1991; Morrison, 1996), some of the consistently cited economic benefits of managing diversity include:

- obtaining and maintaining increased market share

- cost savings from reducing turnover rates among minority employees

- improved creativity and problem-solving capabilities due to the broader range of perspectives and cultural mindsets

- perceptions of fairness and equity in the workplace

- increased flexibility that positively affects motivation and minimizes conflict between work and nonwork demands (e.g., family, personal interest, leisure)

Given this relatively brief discussion of the impact of diversity on business organizations, we now consider

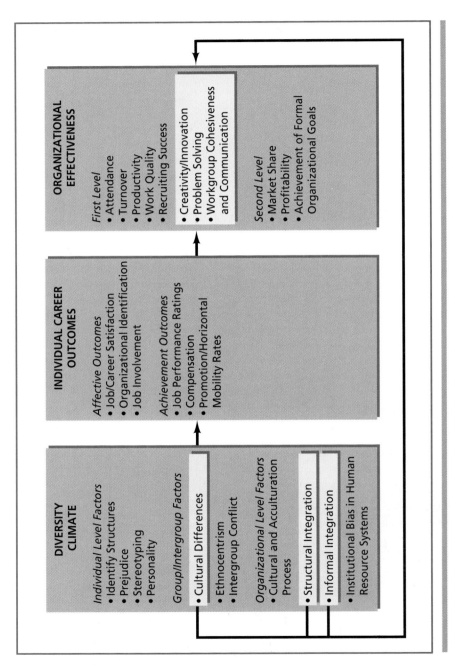

Figure 2 A Model of the Impact of Diversity on Career Outcomes and Organizational Effectiveness

Source: Cox (1994).

how diversity and cultural differences influence the management of conflict. Cox's IMCD model suggests that both interpersonal and intergroup conflict can affect the diversity climate in the organization, with subsequent implications for the overall effectiveness of the organization. One factor to consider in conflict management is the cultural differences of the participants involved. Are both participants from the majority culture of the organization? If one is from a minority culture, to what extent is the diversity climate in the organization positive or negative? Has this particular minority group or individual had a history of conflict within this organization? These questions are important in evaluation the context of the conflict situation.

Personal preferences for handling conflict are an additional consideration when thinking about conflict management. Because conflict is a culturally defined event (Hocker & Wilmot, 1991; Sillars & Weisberg, 1987; Weldon & Jehn, 1995), cultural differences can have a significant impact on conflict management preferences. They not only influence choices of how to respond in conflict situations, but culture can also affect the sources of conflicts that we have previously presented. For example, much of our perceptions and expectations related to work and business organizations are culturally learned. Conflicts between individuals from different cultural groups frequently stem from personal differences inherent in not understanding one another's cultural values. Another example is the role of uncertainty that is an environmental source of stress and conflict. One of the four primary dimensions revealed in the seminal cultural research by Geert Hofstede (1980) is the extent to which uncertainty is tolerated or avoided. Some cultures, such as in Japan, have a high uncertainty avoidance. An environment high in uncertainty would be likely to lead to more conflict for a Japanese individual than for an American individual (lower than average score on Hofstede's uncertainty avoidance dimension). Teams in U.S. organizations often experience significant initial conflict due to role incompatibilities. One of the reasons for this is a cultural value of individualism, which Hofstede found to be higher in the United States than in any of the other 39 countries that were investigated.

To be more effective as managers in business organizations of the future, we must take into account diversity and culture when managing conflict situations. Cross-cultural conflict management is an important consideration in any discussion of conflict management. We can no longer afford to separate out differences in culture, gender, or other areas of diversity as isolated topics. We must begin to see these areas as parts of an integrated whole in a global economy. While much more might have been said here about the impact of culture on conflict in business organizations, we included sufficient information to underscore our main points. Other books (e.g., Trompenaars, 1994; Adler, 1991) provide more comprehensive insights into the role of culture on important management activities.

Conflict Response Alternatives

Now that we have examined typical causes of conflict and explored the potential impact of diversity and culture on the conflict management process, we will discuss common responses to conflict situations. After discussing those response alternatives, we will briefly demonstrate how selection of conflict responses is influenced by the individual's culture and, to a lesser extent, the individual's gender.

As revealed in the Assessment survey, people's responses to interpersonal confrontations tend to fall into five categories: forcing, accommodating, avoiding, compromising, and collaborating (Filley, 1975, 1978; Robbins, 1974). These responses can be organized along two dimensions, as shown in Figure 3 (Ruble & Thomas, 1976). These five approaches to conflict reflect different degrees of cooperativeness and assertiveness. A cooperative response is intended to satisfy the needs of the interacting person, whereas an assertive response focuses on the needs of the focal person. The cooperativeness dimension reflects the importance of the relationship, whereas the assertiveness dimension reflects the importance of the issue.

The **forcing response** (assertive, uncooperative) is an attempt to satisfy one's own needs at the expense of the other individual's. This can be done by using formal authority, physical threats, manipulation ploys, or by ignoring the claims of the other party. The blatant use of the authority of one's office ("I'm the boss, so we'll do it my way.") or a related form of intimidation is generally evidence of a lack of tolerance or self-confidence. The use of manipulation or feigned ignorance is a much more subtle reflection of an egoistic leadership style. Manipulative leaders often appear to be democratic by proposing that conflicting proposals be referred to a committee for further investigation. However, they

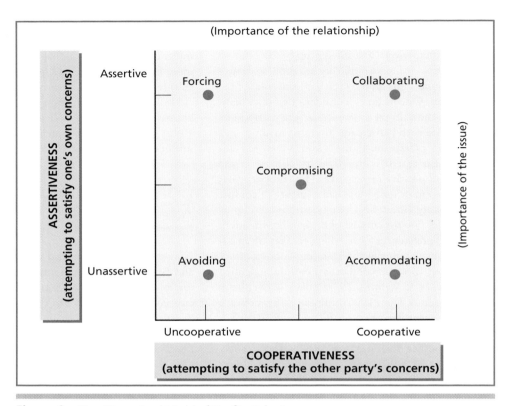

Figure 3 Two-Dimensional Model of Conflict Behavior
Source: Adapted from Ruble & Thomas, 1976, p. 145.

ensure that the composition of the committee reflects their interests and preferences so that what appears to be a selection based on merit is actually an authoritarian act. A related ploy some managers use is to ignore a proposal that threatens their personal interests. If the originator inquires about the disposition of his or her memo, the manager pleads ignorance, blames the mail clerk or new secretary, and then suggests that the proposal be redrafted. After several of these encounters, subordinates generally get the message that the boss isn't interested in their ideas.

The problem with the repeated use of this conflict-management approach is that it breeds hostility and resentment. While observers may intellectually admire authoritarian or manipulative leaders because they appear to accomplish a great deal, their management styles generally produce a backlash in the long run as people become unwilling to absorb the emotional costs.

The **accommodating approach** (cooperative, unassertive) satisfies the other party's concerns while ne-

glecting one's own. Unfortunately, as in the case of boards of directors of failing firms who neglect their interests and responsibilities in favor of accommodating the wishes of management, this strategy generally results in both parties "losing." The difficulty with the habitual use of the accommodating approach is that it emphasizes preserving a friendly relationship at the expense of critically appraising issues and protecting personal rights. This may result in others taking advantage of you, which lowers your self-esteem as you observe yourself being used by others to accomplish their objectives while you fail to make any progress toward your own.

As demonstrated in the Ross Perot example, the **avoiding response** (uncooperative, unassertive) neglects the interests of both parties by sidestepping the conflict or postponing a solution. This is often the response of managers who are emotionally ill-prepared to cope with the stress associated with confrontations. Or, it might reflect recognition that a relationship is not strong enough to absorb the fallout of an intense conflict. The repeated use of this approach causes considerable frustration for others because issues never seem to get resolved, really tough problems are avoided because of their high potential for conflict, and subordinates engaging in conflict are reprimanded for undermining the harmony of the work group. Sensing a leadership vacuum, people from all directions rush to fill it, creating considerable confusion and animosity in the process.

The **compromising response** is intermediate between assertiveness and cooperativeness. A compromise is an attempt to obtain partial satisfaction for both parties, in the sense that both receive the proverbial "half loaf." To accommodate this, both parties are asked to make sacrifices to obtain a common gain. While this approach has considerable practical appeal to managers, its indiscriminate use is counterproductive. If subordinates are continually told to "split the difference," they may conclude that their managers are more interested in resolving disputes than solving problems. This creates a climate of expediency that encourages game playing, such as asking for twice as much as you need.

A common mistake made in mergers is trying to appear fair to both parties by compromising on competing corporate policies and practices as well as on which redundant staff members get laid off. When decisions are made on the basis of "spreading the pain evenly" or "using half of your procedures and half of ours," rather than on the basis of merit, then harmony takes priority over value. Ironically, actions taken in the name of "keeping peace in the merged families" often end up being so illogical and impractical that the emerging union is doomed to operate under a pall of constant internal turmoil and conflict.

The **collaborating approach** (cooperative, assertive) is an attempt to address fully the concerns of both parties. It is often referred to as the "problem-solving" mode. In this mode, the intent is to find solutions to the cause of the conflict that are satisfactory to both parties rather than to find fault or assign blame. In this way, both parties can feel that they have "won." This is the only win-win strategy among the five. The avoiding mode results in a lose-lose outcome and the compromising, accommodating, and forcing modes all represent win-lose outcomes. Although the collaborative approach is not appropriate for all situations, when used appropriately, it has the most beneficial effect on the involved parties. It encourages norms of collaboration and trust while acknowledging the value of assertiveness. It encourages individuals to focus their disputes on problems and issues rather than on personalities. Finally, it cultivates the skills necessary for self-governance, so that effective problem solvers feel empowered.

The collaborative approach to problem solving and conflict resolution works best in an environment supporting openness, directness, and equality. In an interview with Steven Jobs, the editors of *Inc.* magazine quizzed the man they heralded as the "entrepreneur of the decade" regarding the perils of being a celebrity boss. ("It must help you in attracting the best minds to your new computer firm [NeXT], but once they're there, aren't they intimidated, working for a legend?")

It all depends on the culture. The culture at NeXT definitely rewards independent thought, and we often have constructive disagreements—at all levels. It doesn't take a new person long to see that people feel fine about openly disagreeing with me. That doesn't mean I can't disagree with them, but it does mean that the best ideas win. Our attitude is that we want the best. Don't get hung up on who owns the idea. Pick the best one, and let's go. (April 1989, p. 123)

Table 2 shows a comparison of the five conflict-management approaches. Research on conflict management styles reports that culture and in some cases gender significantly affect the preferred use of the five response styles we have just discussed (Seybolt et al., 1996; Weldon & Jehn, 1995). Among the cultural differences that appear on a generally consistent basis is that Asian cultures prefer nonconfrontational styles of accommodating and avoiding more than Western cultures (Rahim & Blum, 1994; Ting-Toomey et al., 1991). Americans and South Africans prefer a more forcing response than Asian cultures (Rahim & Blum, 1994; Seybolt et al., 1996). Compromise is the most commonly preferred style across cultures (Seybolt et al., 1996), possibly because compromising may be viewed as the least costly alternative and the style that most quickly reaches acceptable levels of fairness to both parties. Most cross-cultural research of conflict management strategies has involved Asian and American cultures (for more comprehensive reviews, see Rahim & Blum, 1994; Weldon & Jehn, 1995). Also, a frequent criticism of much of this line of research is that most of the studies have applied Western conflict

APPROACH	OBJECTIVE	YOUR POSTURE	SUPPORTING RATIONALE	LIKELY OUTCOME
I. Forcing	Get your way.	"I know what's right. Don't question my judgment or authority."	It is better to risk causing a few hard feelings than to abandon an issue you are committed to.	You feel vindicated, but other party feels defeated and possibly humiliated.
II. Avoiding	Avoid having to deal with conflict.	"I'm neutral on that issue." "Let me think about it." "That's someone else's problem."	Disagreements are inherently bad because they create tension.	Interpersonal problems don't get resolved, causing long-term frustration manifested in a variety of ways.
III. Compromising	Reach an agreement quickly.	"Let's search for a solution we can both live with so we can get on with our work."	Prolonged conflicts distract people from their work and engender bitter feelings.	Participants become conditioned to seek expedient, rather than effective, solutions.
IV. Accommodating	Don't upset the other person.	"How can I help you feel good about this encounter?" "My position isn't so important that it is worth risking bad feelings between us."	Maintaining harmonious relationships should be our top priority.	The other person is likely to take advantage of you.
V. Collaborating	Solve the problem together.	"This is my position. What is yours?" "I'm committed to finding the best possible solution." "What do the facts suggest?"	The positions of both parties are equally important (though not necessarily equally valid). Equal emphasis should be placed on the quality of the outcome and the fairness of the decision-making process.	The problem is most likely to be resolved. Also, both parties are committed to the solution and satisfied that they have been treated fairly.

Table 2   A Comparison of Five Conflict-Management Approaches

models to non-Western cultures. Whether the five response alternative discussed in this section are equally relevant in other cultures remains unclear.

Additional debate exists about the impact of gender on conflict management responses. Some studies report that males prefer a forcing response more than females, while females tend to select compromising more than males (Kilmann & Thomas, 1977; Ruble & Schneer, 1994). Other studies found gender to have little influence on an individual's preferred responses to conflict (Korabik, Baril, & Watson, 1993). From a review of the growing literature on conflict styles and gender, Keashly (1994) draws five conclusions:

▷ there is little evidence of gender differences in abilities and skills related to conflict management

▷ evidence suggests that sex-role expectations appear to influence behavior and perceptions of behavior in particular conflict situations

▷ influences and norms other than sex-role expectations may affect and influence conflict and behavior

▷ the experience and meaning of conflict may differ for women and men

▷ there is a persistence of beliefs in gender-linked behavior even when these behaviors are not found in research.

In summary despite recent research finding to the contrary, perceptions still exist that gender difference do occur in conflict management styles within and between cultures.

Negotiation Strategies

Recently, a number of organizational scholars have noted the similarities between conflict management and **negotiation strategies** (Savage, Blair, & Sorenson, 1989; Smith, 1987). Negotiation strategies are commonly divided into two types: integrative and distributive. Negotiators who focus on dividing up a "fixed pie" use **distributive** bargaining techniques, whereas parties interested in **integrative** outcomes search for collaborative ways of "expanding the pie" by avoiding fixed, incompatible positions (Bazerman & Neale, 1992). Distributive negotiators assume an adversarial, competitive posture. They assume that one of the par-

ties can improve only at the other party's expense. In contrast, integrative bargainers use problem-solving techniques to find "win-win" outcomes. They are interested in finding the best solution rather than forcing a choice between the parties' preferred solutions (Fisher & Brown, 1988; Bazerman, 1986; Pruitt, 1983).

As Table 3 shows, four of the five conflict-management strategies are distributive in nature. One or both parties must sacrifice something in order for the conflict to be resolved. Compromising, forcing, accommodating, and avoiding are considered distributive solutions. Compromise occurs when both parties make sacrifices in order to find a common ground. Compromisers are generally more interested in finding an expedient solution than they are in finding an integrative solution. Forcing and accommodating demand that one party give up its position in order for the conflict to be resolved. When parties to a conflict avoid resolution, they do so because they assume that the costs of resolving the conflict are so high that they are better off not even attempting resolution. The "fixed pie" still exists, but the individuals involved view attempts to divide it as threatening, so they avoid decisions regarding the allocation process altogether.

Unfortunately, distributive negotiation strategies are consistent with the natural inclination of many individuals to approach conflicts from a "tough-guy" or an "easy-touch" or a "split-the-difference" perspective. The problem with the frequent use of these negotiation strategies is that they engender competition, exploitation, or irresponsibility.

The forcing approach to negotiations, in particular, has intuitive appeal. Many observers equate effective negotiators with a tough, highly combative, and even

Negotiation Strategies	Distributive	Integrative
Conflict-Management Strategies	Compromising Forcing Accommodating Avoiding	Collaborating

Table 3 Comparison Between Negotiation and Conflict-Management Strategies

ruthless approach. Research has clearly demonstrated that this "end-justifies-the-means" view of negotiation is generally ineffective and frequently counterproductive, however. This is illustrated by one of the most shocking labor conflicts in the 1980s, when 11,500 air traffic controllers walked off their jobs on August 3, 1981. Pointing to a law that forbade strikes by federal employees, the Reagan Administration insisted on no negotiations. Instead of open and constructive bargaining, there were threats, hostility, and disruptive actions. During a 48-hour window in which the controllers could return to their jobs, only a handful did return. The conflict ended with the remaining air traffic controllers quitting their jobs and then being fired by the president. There were no apparent winners as a result of the conflict. Air travelers were stranded for days, airline schedules were in chaos for months, the air traffic controllers lost their jobs, and the government had to hire and train new controllers (Bowers, 1983).

Later we will discuss the limited circumstances under which all forms of conflict management are appropriate. However, as a general-purpose strategy, the integrative approach is far superior. When adopted as an organizing framework, the following integrative negotiation strategies have been shown to foster collaboration (Northcraft & Neale, 1990).

Establish superordinate goals. In order to foster a climate of collaboration, both parties need to focus on what they share in common. Making more salient their shared goals of increased productivity, of lower costs, of reduced design time, or of improved relations between departments sensitizes the parties to the merits of resolving their differences to avoid jeopardizing their mutual goals. The step is characterized by the general question, "What common goals provide a context for these discussions?"

Separate the people from the problem. Having clarified the mutual benefits to be gained by successfully concluding a negotiation, it is useful to focus attention on the real issue at hand: solving a problem. Negotiations are more likely to result in mutual satisfaction if the parties depersonalize the discussions. Integrative negotiators suppress their personal desires for revenge or one-upmanship. The other party is viewed as the advocate of a point of view, rather than as a rival. The integrative bargainer would say, "That is an unreasonable position" rather than, "You are an unreasonable person."

Focus on interests, not positions. Positions are demands the negotiator makes. Interests constitute the reason behind the demands. Experience shows that it is easier to establish agreement on interests, given that they tend to be broader and multifaceted. This step involves redefining and broadening problems to make them more tractable. When a variety of issues are examined, parties are better able to understand each other's point of view and place their own views in perspective. A characteristic integrative statement is, "Help me understand why you advocate that position."

Invent options for mutual gains. This step also involves creativity, although this time it is focused on generating unusual solutions. Although it is true that some negotiations may necessarily be distributive, it is a mistake for negotiators to adopt a win-lose posture automatically. By focusing both parties' attention on brainstorming alternative, mutually agreeable, solutions, the negotiation dynamics naturally shift from competitive to collaborative. In addition, the more options and combinations there are to explore, the greater the probability of reaching an integrative solution. The integrative negotiator proposes, "Now that we better understand each others' underlying concerns and objectives, let's brainstorm ways of satisfying both our needs."

Use objective criteria. No matter how integrative both parties may be, there are bound to be some incompatible interests. Rather than seizing on these as opportunities for testing wills, it is far more productive to determine what is fair. This requires both parties to examine how fairness should be judged. A shift in thinking from "getting what I want" to "deciding what makes most sense" fosters an open, reasonable attitude. It encourages parties to avoid overconfidence or overcommitment to their initial position. This approach is characterized by asking, "What is a fair way to evaluate the merits of our arguments?"

Define success in terms of gains, not losses. If a manager seeks a 10 percent raise and receives only 6 percent, that outcome can be viewed as either a 6 percent improvement or as a 40 percent shortfall. The first interpretation focuses on gains, the second on losses (in this case, unrealized expectations). The outcome is the same, but the manager's satisfaction with it varies substantially. It is important to recognize that our satisfaction with an outcome is affected by the standards we use to judge it. Recognizing this, the integrative negotiator facilitates resolution by judging the value of proposed solutions against reasonable standards. The integrative approach to assessing proposals is, "Does this outcome constitute a meaningful improvement over current conditions?"

An example of the integrative approach to negotiations can be found in an examination of the 1978 Camp David Accords (Fisher & Ury, 1981). When Egypt and Israel first sat down to discuss possession of the Sinai Peninsula, a collaborative agreement seemed impossible. Both countries demanded at least partial possession of the land that Israel had occupied since the 1967 Middle East War. An attempt at compromise—giving each country a portion of the land—was rejected by both sides. When framed in terms of the amount of land each country would occupy, potential solutions could only be distributive. Egypt wanted 100 percent, Israel was demanding at least some portion of the land, and neither would be satisfied with any less.

But by reframing this seemingly single-issue conflict through examining the underlying interests behind the demands, a collaborative solution emerged. Israel wanted the land for reasons of security, while Egypt wanted sovereignty over it. By providing a demilitarized zone and allowing Israeli air bases in the Sinai—thereby assuring Israeli security—Egypt regained control of the Peninsula. Both sides "won."

This negotiation was successful because both parties agreed to play by the same set of integrative bargaining rules. What happens if you are trying to collaborate and the other party is using combative, high-pressure negotiation tactics? Should you simply persist, hoping the other party will eventually follow suit, while at the same time risking the other party's taking advantage of your noncombative posture or risking the possibility that you will eventually become so frustrated that you'll join the fracas?

In these situations, it is useful to review the guidelines for resisting inappropriate influence attempts presented in the chapter on Gaining Power and Influence, as well as the initiator's guidelines presented later in this chapter. In essence, these guidelines suggest shifting the focus of the discussion from "content" to "process" in these situations. By presenting your frustration, you are able to draw attention to the unsatisfactory negotiation process. In the course of this type of conversation the other party's underlying reasons for using a particular negotiation style often surface, and the resulting information about time pressure, or lack

of trust, or unrealistic constituent expectations can be used to build a more collaborative mode of interaction. ("How can we work together to resolve our concerns about process so they don't impair the outcome of our discussion?")

Selecting the Appropriate Approach

A comparison of alternative approaches inevitably leads to the question, "Which one is best?" While the collaborative approach produces the fewest negative side-effects, each approach has its place. The appropriateness of a management strategy depends on its congruence with both personal style and situational demands.

It should be obvious that the five modes of handling conflict discussed here are not equally attractive to all individuals. Each of us tends to have a preferred strategy that is consistent with the value we place on conflict and with our dominant personality characteristics (Cummings, Harnett, & Stevens, 1971; Porter, 1973). This research identifies three distinct personality profiles. The **altruistic-nurturing** personality seeks gratification through promoting harmony with others and enhancing their welfare, with little concern for being rewarded in return. This personality type is characterized by trust, optimism, idealism, and loyalty. The **assertive-directing** personality seeks gratification through self-assertion and directing the activities of others with a clear sense of having earned rewards. Individuals with this personality characteristic tend to be self-confident, enterprising, and persuasive. The **analytic-autonomizing** personality seeks gratification through the achievement of self-sufficiency, self-reliance, and logical orderliness. This personality type is cautious, practical, methodical, and principled.

When altruistic-nurturing individuals encounter conflict, they tend to press for harmony by accommodating the demands of the other party. In contrast, the assertive-directing personality tends to challenge the opposition by using the forcing approach. The analyzing-autonomizing personality becomes very cautious when encountering conflict. Initially, this personality attempts to resolve the problem rationally. However, if the conflict intensifies, analyzing-autonomizing individuals will withdraw and break contact.

While there appears to be a strong link between dominant personality characteristics and preferred modes of handling conflict, managers who can adopt different strategies depending on the nature of the conflict are likely to be most effective (Savage, Blair, & Sorenson, 1989). This general principle has been borne out in research on conflict management.

In one study, 25 executives were asked to describe two conflict situations—one with bad results and one with good (Phillips & Cheston, 1979). These incidents were then categorized in terms of the conflict-management approach used. As Figure 4 shows, there were 23 incidents of forcing, 12 incidents of problem solving, 5 incidents of compromise, and 12 incidents of avoidance. Admittedly, this was a very small sample of managers, but the fact that there were almost twice as many incidents of forcing as problem solving and nearly five times as many

as compromising is noteworthy. It is also interesting that the executives indicated that forcing and compromising were equally as likely to produce good as bad results, whereas problem solving was always linked with positive outcomes, and avoidance generally led to negative results.

It is striking that, despite the fact that forcing was as likely to produce bad as good results, it was by far the most commonly used conflict-management mode. Since this approach is clearly not superior in terms of results, one wonders why these senior executives reported a propensity for using it.

A likely answer is expediency. Evidence for this supposition is provided by a study of the preferred influ-

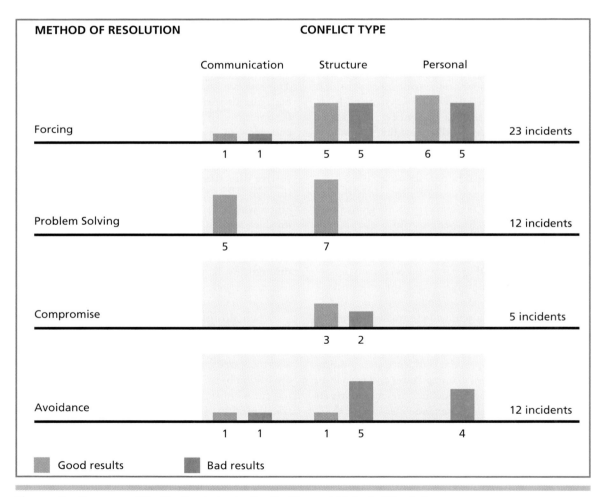

Figure 4   Outcomes of Conflict Resolution by Conflict Type and Method of Resolution
Source: Phillips & Cheston, 1979, p. 79.

ence strategies of over 300 managers in three countries (Kipnis & Schmidt, 1983). This study reports that when subordinates refuse or appear reluctant to comply with a request, managers become directive. When resistance in subordinates is encountered, managers tend to fall back on their superior power and insist on compliance. So pervasive was this pattern that the authors of this study proposed an "Iron Law of Power: The greater the discrepancy in power between influence and target, the greater the probability that more directive influence strategies will be used" (p. 7).

A second striking feature of this figure is that some conflict-management approaches were never used for certain types of issues. In particular, the managers did not report a single case of problem solving or compromising when personal problems were the source of the conflict. These approaches were used primarily for managing conflicts involving incompatible goals and conflicting reward systems between departments. Two conclusions can be drawn from this study. First, no one approach is most effective for managing every type of conflict. Second, managers are more effective in dealing with conflicts if they feel comfortable using a variety of approaches. These conclusions point out the need to understand the conditions under which each conflict-management technique is most effective. This knowledge allows one to match the characteristics of a conflict incident with the management techniques best suited for those characteristics. The salient situational factors to consider are summarized in Table 4.

The forcing approach is most appropriate when a conflict of values or perspectives is involved and one feels compelled to defend the "correct" position; when a superior-subordinate relationship is involved; when maintaining a close, supportive relationship is not critical; and

when there is a sense of urgency. An example of such a situation might be a manager's insisting that a summer intern follow important company safety regulations.

The accommodating approach is most appropriate when the importance of maintaining a good working relationship outweighs all other considerations. While this could be the case regardless of your formal relationship with the other party, it is often perceived as being the only option for subordinates of powerful bosses. The nature of the issues and the amount of time available play a secondary role in determining the choice of this strategy. Accommodation becomes especially appropriate when the issues are not vital to your interests and the problem must be resolved quickly.

Trying to reach a compromise is most appropriate when the issues are complex and moderately important, there are no simple solutions, and both parties have a strong interest in different facets of the problem. The other essential situational requirement is adequate time for negotiation. The classic case is a bargaining session between representatives of management and labor to avert a scheduled strike. While the characteristics of the relationship between the parties are not essential factors, experience has shown that negotiations work best between parties with equal power who are committed to maintaining a good long-term relationship.

The collaborating approach is most appropriate when the issues are critical, maintaining an ongoing supportive relationship between peers is important, and time constraints are not pressing. Although collaboration can also be an effective approach for resolving conflicts between a superior and subordinate, it is important to point out that when a conflict involves peers, the collaborative mode is more appropriate than either the forcing or accommodating approaches.

SITUATIONAL CONSIDERATIONS		CONFLICT-MANAGEMENT APPROACH			
	FORCING	ACCOM-MODATING	COMPRO-MISING	COLLABO-RATING	AVOIDING
Issue Importance	High	Low	Med	High	Low
Relationship Importance	Low	High	Med	High	Low
Relative Power	High	Low	Equal-High	Low-High	Equal-High
Time Constraints	Med-High	Med-High	Low	Low	Med-High

Table 4   Matching the Conflict-Management Approach With the Situation

The avoidance approach is most appropriate when one's stake in an issue is not high and there is not a strong interpersonal reason for getting involved, regardless of whether the conflict involves a superior, subordinate, or peer. A severe time constraint becomes a contributing factor because it increases the likelihood of using avoidance, by default. While one might prefer other strategies, such as compromise and collaboration, that have a good chance of resolving problems without damaging relationships, these are ruled out because of time pressure.

Resolving Interpersonal Confrontations Using the Collaborative Approach

It should now be clear that part of the skill of effective conflict management is choosing an appropriate approach based on a thoughtful assessment of the situation. One characteristic of unsuccessful conflict managers is their habitual reliance on one or two strategies regardless of changing circumstances. A second characteristic of ineffective conflict managers is their inability to implement the collaborative approach effectively. In the study by Kipnis and Schmidt (1983) discussed earlier, most managers expressed general support for the collaborative approach, but when it appeared things weren't going their way, they reverted back to a directive approach.

One reason for this pattern is that the collaborative approach to conflict management is the most difficult to implement successfully. It requires much more skill than accommodating or forcing, for example. It is a fairly simple matter for managers to either give in or impose their will, but resolving differences in a truly collaborative manner is a complicated and taxing process. As a result, when situational conditions indicate that the collaborative approach is most appropriate, unskilled managers will often opt for less challenging approaches. To help you gain proficiency in using the collaborative approach, the remainder of this chapter describes behavioral guidelines for effectively resolving interpersonal confrontations.

These guidelines are derived from principles presented in the chapters on Communicating Supportively and Gaining Power and Influence. These chapters present general principles pertaining to the interplay between language and influence; the merits of a collaborative problem-solving process; the long-term negative effects of specific acts of exploitation or unreasonableness; and the value of increasing information inputs in order to improve the quality of decision making. The behavioral guidelines discussed next constitute specific applications of these proven management principles.

The guidelines for collaborative conflict management also draw upon the negotiation literature discussed earlier. However, although general negotiation strategies and conflict management approaches are similar in concept, specific negotiation tactics and conflict management guidelines tend to diverge. This is because the nature of the issues are generally different. Although there is obviously some overlap in content, negotiations tend to focus on substantive issues (e.g., responsibility for the distribution of a new product), whereas interpersonal conflicts are more likely to be triggered by an emotional confrontation (e.g., a sexual harassment complaint). Because interpersonal confrontations involving complaints and criticisms have been shown to be the most difficult to manage in a collaborative manner, they are the focus of this section.

We will treat conflict management as a problem-solving process with four phases: (1) problem identification, (2) solution generation, (3) action plan formulation and agreement, and (4) implementation and follow-up. In the midst of a heated discussion, the first two phases are the most critical steps, as well as the most difficult to manage effectively. In addition, they are the only ones a party to a dispute can control. If you initiate a complaint, you can control how you state it and whether you request a change in behavior. However, you cannot control whether the other party agrees to change or, having agreed, actually follows up. Therefore, we will primarily focus on phases one and two during our skill training. Because disputants' orientations are discrepant during the early phases of a confrontation, we shall examine the role of each participant separately.

A dyadic confrontation involves two actors, an **initiator** and a **responder.** For example, a subordinate might complain about not being given a fair share of opportunities to work overtime; or the head of production might complain to the head of sales about frequent changes in order specifications. A dyadic conflict represents a greater challenge for responders because they have responsibility for transforming a complaint into a problem-solving discussion. This requires considerable patience and self-confidence, since unskilled initiators will generally begin the discussion by blaming the responder for the problem. In this situation, an unskilled responder will naturally become defensive and look for an opportunity to "even the score."

If these lose-lose dynamics persist, a **mediator** is generally required to cool down the participants, reestablish constructive communication, and help the parties reconcile their differences. The presence of a mediator removes some pressure from the responder because an impartial referee provides assistance in moving the confrontation through the problem-solving phases.

The following guidelines provide a model for acting out the initiator, responder, and mediator roles in such a way that problem solving can occur. In our discussion of each role, we will assume that other participants in the conflict are not behaving according to their prescribed guidelines.

Initiator

Maintain personal ownership of the problem. It is important to recognize that when you are upset and frustrated, this is *your* problem, not the other person's. You may feel that your boss or coworker is the source of your problem, but resolving your frustration is your immediate concern. The first step in addressing this concern is acknowledging accountability for your feelings. Suppose someone enters your office with a smelly cigar without asking if it is all right to smoke. The fact that your office is going to stink for the rest of the day may infuriate you, but the odor does not present a problem for your smoking guest. One way to determine ownership of a problem is to identify whose needs are not being met. In this case, your need for a clean working environment is not being met, so the smelly office is *your* problem.

The advantage of acknowledging ownership of a problem when registering a complaint is that it reduces defensiveness (Adler, 1977). In order for you to get a problem solved, the respondent must not feel threatened by your initial statement of that problem. By beginning the conversation with a request that the responder help solve your problem, you immediately establish a problem-solving atmosphere. For example, you might say, "Bill, do you have a few minutes? I have a problem I need to discuss with you."

Succinctly describe your problem in terms of behaviors, consequences, and feelings. A useful model for remembering how to state your problem effectively has been prescribed by Gordon (1970): "I have a problem. When you do X, Y results, and I feel Z." While we don't advocate the memorization of set formulas for improving communication skills, keeping this model in mind will help you implement three critical guidelines.

First, describe the specific *behaviors* (X) that present a problem for you. This will help you avoid the reflexive tendency when you are upset to give feedback that is evaluative and not specific. One way to do this is to specify the expectations or standards that have been violated. For example, a subordinate may have missed a deadline for completing an assigned task, your boss may gradually be taking over tasks previously delegated to you, or a colleague in the accounting department may have repeatedly failed to provide you with data required for an important presentation.

Second, outline the specific, *observable consequences* (Y) of these behaviors. Simply telling others that their actions are causing you problems is often sufficient stimulus for change. In fast-paced work environments, people generally become insensitive to the impact of their actions. They don't intend to cause offense, but they become so busy meeting deadlines associated with "getting the product out the door" that they tune out subtle negative feedback from others. When this occurs, bringing to the attention of others the consequences of their behaviors will often prompt them to change.

Unfortunately, not all problems can be resolved this simply. At times, offenders are aware of the negative consequences of their behaviors, yet they persist in them. In such cases, this approach is still useful in stimulating a problem-solving discussion because it presents concerns in a nonthreatening manner. Possibly the responders' behaviors are constrained by the expectations of their boss or by the fact that the department is currently understaffed. Responders may not be able to change these constraints, but this approach will encourage them to discuss them with you so you can work on the problem together.

Third, describe the *feelings* (Z) you experience as a result of the problem. It is important that the responder understand that the behavior is not just inconvenient. You need to explain how it is affecting you personally by engendering feelings of frustration, anger, or insecurity. Explain how these feelings are interfering with your work. They may make it more difficult for you to concentrate, to be congenial with customers, to be supportive of your boss, or to be willing to make needed personal sacrifices to meet deadlines.

You should use this three-step model as a guide rather than as a formula. The order of the components may vary, and you should not use the same words every time. Obviously, it would get pretty monotonous if everyone in a work group initiated a discussion about an interpersonal issue with the words, "I have a problem." Observe how the key elements in the model are used in different ways in the following examples from Adler (1977, p. 223):

> I have to tell you that I get upset [feelings] when you make jokes about my bad memory in front of other people [behavior]. In fact, I get so angry that I find myself bringing up your faults to get even [consequences].

> I have a problem. When you say you'll be here for our date at six and don't show up until after seven [behavior], the dinner gets ruined, we're late for the show we planned to see [consequences], and I feel hurt because it seems as though I'm just not that important to you [feelings].

> The employees want to let management know that we've been having a hard time lately with the short notice you've been giving when you need us to work overtime [behavior]. That probably explains some of the grumbling and lack of cooperation you've mentioned [consequences]. Anyhow, we wanted to make it clear that this policy has really got a lot of the workers feeling pretty resentful [feeling].

Avoid drawing evaluative conclusions and attributing motives to the respondent. When exchanges between two disputing parties become vengeful, each side often has a different perspective about the justification of the other's actions. Typically, each party believes that it is the victim of the other's aggression. In international conflicts, opposing nations often believe they are acting defensively rather than offensively. Similarly, in smaller-scale conflicts each side may have distorted views of its own hurt and the motives of the "offender" (Kim & Smith, 1993). Therefore, in presenting your problem, avoid the pitfalls of making accusations, drawing inferences about motivations or intentions, or attributing the responder's undesirable behavior to personal inadequacies. Statements such as, "You are always interrupting me," "You haven't been fair to me since the day I disagreed with you in the board meeting," and "You never have time to listen to our problems and suggestions because you manage your

time so poorly," are good for starting arguments but ineffective for initiating a problem-solving process.

Another key to reducing defensiveness is to delay proposing a solution until both parties agree on the nature of the problem. When you become so upset with someone's behavior that you feel it is necessary to initiate a complaint, it is often because the person has seriously violated your ideal role model. For example, you might feel that your manager should have been less dogmatic and listened more during a goal-setting interview. Consequently, you might express your feelings in terms of prescriptions for how the other person should behave and suggest a more democratic, or sensitive, style.

Besides creating defensiveness, the principal disadvantage to initiating problem solving with a suggested remedy is that it hinders the problem-solving process. Before completing the problem-articulation phase, you have immediately jumped to the solution-generation phase, based on the assumption that you know all the reasons for, and constraints on, the other person's behavior. You will jointly produce better, more acceptable, solutions if you present your statement of the problem and discuss it thoroughly before proposing potential solutions.

Persist until understood. There are times when the respondent will not clearly receive or acknowledge even the most effectively expressed message. Suppose, for instance, that you share the following problem with a coworker (Adler, 1977, p. 228):

> I've been bothered by something lately and I want to share it with you. To be honest, I'm uncomfortable [feeling] when you use so much profanity [behavior]. I don't mind an occasional "damn" or "hell," but the other words are hard for me to accept. Lately I've found myself avoiding you [consequences], and that's no good either, so I wanted to let you know how I feel.

When you share your feelings in this nonevaluative way, it's likely that the other person will understand your position and possibly try to change behavior to suit your needs. On the other hand, there are a number of less-satisfying responses that could be made to your comment:

> Listen, these days everyone talks that way. And besides, you've got your faults, too, you know!" [Your coworker becomes defensive, rationalizing and counter-attacking.]

Yeah, I suppose I do swear a lot. I'll have to work on that some day. [Gets the general drift of your message but fails to comprehend how serious the problem is to you.]

Listen, if you're still angry about my forgetting to tell you about that meeting the other day, you can be sure that I'm really sorry. I won't do it again." [Totally misunderstands.]

Speaking of avoiding, have you seen Chris lately? I wonder if anything is wrong with him. [Is discomfited by your frustration and changes the subject.]

In each case, the coworker does not understand or does not wish to acknowledge the problem. In these situations, you must repeat your concern until it has been acknowledged as a problem to be solved. Otherwise, the problem-solving process will terminate at this point and nothing will change. Repeated assertions can take the form of restating the same phrase several times or reiterating your concern with different words or examples that you feel may improve comprehension. To avoid introducing new concerns or shifting from a descriptive to an evaluative mode, keep in mind the "X, Y, Z" formula for feedback. Persistence is most effective when it consists of "variations *on* a theme," rather than "variation *in* themes."

Encourage two-way discussion. It is important to establish a problem-solving climate by inviting the respondent to express opinions and ask questions. There may be a reasonable explanation for another's disturbing behavior; the person may have a radically different view of the problem. The sooner this information is introduced into the conversation, the more likely the issue will be resolved. As a rule of thumb, the longer the initiator's opening statement, the longer it will take the two parties to work through their problem. This is because the lengthier the problem statement, the more likely it is to encourage a defensive reaction. The longer we talk, the more worked up we get, and the more likely we are to violate principles of supportive communication. As a result, the other party begins to feel threatened, starts mentally outlining a rebuttal or counterattack, and stops listening empathetically to our concerns. Once these dynamics enter the discussion, the collaborative approach is usually discarded in favor of the accommodation or forcing strategies, depending on the circumstances. When this

occurs, it is unlikely that the actors will be able to reach a mutually satisfactory solution to their problem without third-party intervention.

Manage the agenda: Approach multiple or complex problems incrementally. One way to shorten your opening statement is to approach complex problems incrementally. Rather than raising a series of issues all at once, focus initially on a simple or rudimentary problem. Then, as you gain greater appreciation for the other party's perspective and share some problem-solving success, you can discuss more challenging issues. This is especially important when trying to resolve a problem with a person who is important to your work performance but does not have a long-standing relationship with you. The less familiar you are with the other's opinions and personality, as well as the situational constraints influencing his or her behaviors, the more you should approach a problem-solving discussion as a fact-finding and rapport-building mission. This is best done by focusing your introductory statement on a specific manifestation of a broader problem and presenting it in such a way that it encourages the other party to respond expansively. You can then use this early feedback to shape the remainder of your agenda. For example, "Bill, we had difficulty getting that work order processed on time yesterday. What seemed to be the problem?"

Focus on commonalities as the basis for requesting a change. Once a problem is clearly understood, the discussion should shift to the solution-generation phase. Most disputants share at least some personal and organizational goals, believe in many of the same fundamental principles of management, and operate under similar constraints. These commonalities can serve as a useful starting point for generating solutions. The most straightforward approach to changing another's offensive behavior is making a request. The legitimacy of a request will be enhanced if it is linked to common interests. These might include shared values, such as treating coworkers fairly and following through on commitments, or shared constraints, such as getting reports in on time and operating within budgetary restrictions. This approach is particularly effective when the parties have had difficulty getting along in the past. In these situations, pointing out how a change in the respondent's behavior would positively affect your shared fate will reduce defensiveness: "Jane, one of the things we have all worked hard to build in this audit team is mutual support. We are all pushed to the limit getting this job completed by the third-quarter deadline next week, and the rest of the team members find it difficult to accept your unwillingness to work overtime during this emergency. Because the allocation of next quarter's assignments will be affected by our current performance, would you please reconsider your position?"

Responder

Now we shall examine the problem-identification phase from the viewpoint of the person who is supposedly the source of the problem. In a work setting, this could be a manager who is making unrealistic demands, a new employee who has violated critical safety regulations, or a coworker who is claiming credit for ideas you generated. The following guidelines for dealing with someone's complaint show how to shape the initiator's behavior so you can have a productive problem-solving experience.

Establish a climate for joint problem solving by showing genuine interest and concern.
When a person complains to you, do not treat that complaint lightly. While this may seem self-evident, it is often difficult to focus your attention on someone else's problems when you are in the middle of writing an important project report or concerned about preparing for a meeting scheduled to begin in a few minutes. Consequently, unless the other person's emotional condition necessitates dealing with the problem immediately, it is better to set up a time for another meeting if your current time pressures will make it difficult to concentrate.

In most cases, the initiator will be expecting you to set the tone for the meeting. You will quickly undermine collaboration if you overreact or become defensive. Even if you disagree with the complaint and feel it has no foundation, you need to respond empathetically to the initiator's statement of the problem. This is done by conveying an attitude of interest and receptivity through your posture, tone of voice, and facial expressions.

One of the most difficult aspects of establishing the proper climate for your discussion is responding appropriately to the initiator's emotions. Sometimes you may need to let a person blow off steam before trying to address the substance of a specific complaint. In some cases, the therapeutic effect of being able to express negative emotions to the boss will be enough to

satisfy a subordinate. This occurs frequently in high-pressure jobs where tempers flare easily as a result of the intense stress.

However, an emotional outburst can be very detrimental to problem solving. If an employee begins verbally attacking you or someone else, and it is apparent that the individual is more interested in getting even than in solving an interpersonal problem, you may need to interrupt and interject some ground rules for collaborative problem solving. By explaining calmly to the other person that you are willing to discuss a genuine problem but that you will not tolerate personal attacks or scapegoating, you can quickly determine the initiator's true intentions. In most instances, he or she will apologize, emulate your emotional tone, and begin formulating a useful statement of the problem.

Seek additional information about the problem.
Untrained initiators typically present complaints that are both general and highly evaluative. They make generalizations about your motives and your personal strengths and weaknesses from a few specific incidents. If the two of you are going to transform a personal complaint into a joint problem, you must redirect the conversation from general and evaluative accusations to descriptions of specific behaviors.

To do this, ask for details about specific actions that form the basis for the evaluation. You might find it useful to phrase your questions so they reflect the "X, Y, Z" model described in the initiator's guidelines: "Can you give me a specific example of my behavior that concerns you?" "When I did that, what were the specific consequences for your work?" "How did you feel when that happened?" When a complaint is both serious and complex, it is especially critical for you to understand it completely. In these situations, check your level of understanding by summarizing the initiator's main points and asking if your summary is correct.

Sometimes it is useful to ask for additional complaints: "Are there any other problems in our relationship you'd like to discuss?" If the initiator is just in a griping mood, this is not a good time to probe further; you don't want to encourage this type of behavior. But if the person is seriously concerned about improving your relationship, your discussion to this point has been helpful, and you suspect that the initiator is holding back and not talking about the really serious issues, you should probe deeper. Often, people begin by complaining about a minor problem to "test the waters." If you blow up, the conversation is terminated, and the critical issues aren't discussed. However, if you are responsive to a frank discussion about problems, the more serious issues are likely to surface.

Agree with some aspect of the complaint. This is an important point that is difficult for some people to accept because they wonder how it is possible to agree with something they don't believe is true. They may also be worried about reinforcing complaining behavior. In practice, this step is probably the best test of whether a responder is committed to using the collaborative approach to conflict management rather than the avoiding, forcing, or accommodating approaches. People who use the forcing mode will grit their teeth while listening to the initiator, just waiting to find a flaw they can use to launch a counterattack. Or they will simply respond, "I'm sorry, but that's just the way I am. You'll simply have to get used to it." Accommodators will apologize profusely and ask for forgiveness. People who avoid conflicts will acknowledge and agree with the initiator's concerns, but only in a superficial manner because their only concern is how to terminate the awkward conversation quickly.

In contrast, collaborators will demonstrate their concerns for both cooperation and assertiveness by looking for points in the initiator's presentation with which they can genuinely agree. Following the principles of supportive communication, you will find it possible to accept the other person's viewpoint without conceding your own position. Even in the most blatantly malicious and hostile verbal assault (which may be more a reflection of the initiator's insecurity than evidence of your inadequacies), there is generally a grain of truth. A few years ago, a junior faculty member in a business school who was being reviewed for promotion received a very unfair appraisal from one of his senior colleagues. Since the junior member knew that the critic was going through a personal crisis, he could have dismissed the criticism as irrelevant and tendentious. However, one particular phrase, "You are stuck on a narrow line of research," kept coming back to his mind. There was something there that couldn't be ignored. As a result of turning a vindictive reproach into a valid suggestion, the junior faculty member made a major career decision that produced very positive outcomes. Furthermore, by publicly giving the senior colleague credit for the suggestion, he substantially strengthened the interpersonal relationship.

There are a number of ways you can agree with a message without accepting all of its ramifications (Adler, 1977). You can find an element of truth, as in the incident related above. Or you can agree in principle with the argument: "I agree that managers should set a good example" or "I agree that it is important for sales clerks to be at the store when it opens." If you can't find anything substantive with which to agree, you can always agree with the initiator's perception of the situation: "Well, I can see how you would think that. I have known people who deliberately shirked their responsibilities." Or, you can agree with the person's feelings: "It is obvious that our earlier discussion greatly upset you."

In none of these cases are you necessarily agreeing with the initiator's conclusions or evaluations, nor are you conceding your position. You are trying to understand: to foster a problem-solving, rather than argumentative, discussion. Generally, initiators prepare for a complaint session by mentally cataloguing all the evidence supporting their point of view. Once the discussion begins, they introduce as much evidence as necessary to make their argument convincing; that is, they keep arguing until you agree. The more evidence that is introduced, the broader the argument becomes and the more difficult it is to begin investigating solutions. Consequently, establishing a basis of agreement is the key to culminating the problem-identification phase of the problem-solving process.

Ask for suggestions of acceptable alternatives. Once you are certain you fully understand the initiator's complaint, move on to the solution-generation phase by asking the initiator for recommended solutions. This triggers an important transition in the discussion by shifting attention from the negative to the positive and from the past to the future. It also communicates your regard for the initiator's opinions. This step is a key element in the joint problem-solving process. Some managers listen patiently to a subordinate's complaint, express appreciation for the feedback, say they will rectify the problem, and then terminate the discussion. This leaves the initiator guessing about the outcome of the meeting. Will you take the complaint seriously? Will you really change? If so, will the change resolve the problem? It is important to eliminate this ambiguity by agreeing on a plan of action. If the problem is particularly serious or complex, it is useful to write down specific agreements, including assignments and deadlines, as well as providing for a follow-up meeting to check progress.

Mediator

Frequently, it is necessary for managers to mediate a dispute (Karambayya & Brett, 1989; Kressel & Pruitt, 1989; Northcraft & Neale, 1994). While this may occur for a variety of reasons, we will assume in this discussion that the manager has been invited to help the initiator and responder resolve their differences. While we will assume that the mediator is the manager of both disputants, this is not a necessary condition for the guidelines we shall propose. For example, a hair stylist in a college-town beauty salon complained to the manager about the way the receptionist was favoring other beauticians who had been there longer. Since this allegation, if true, involved a violation of the manager's policy of allocating walk-in business strictly on the basis of beautician availability, the manager felt it necessary to investigate the complaint. In doing so, she discovered considerable animosity between the two employees, stemming from frequent disagreements regarding the amount of work the stylist had done on a given day. The stylist felt that the receptionist was keeping sloppy records, while the receptionist blamed the problem on the stylist's forgetting to hand in her credit slip when she finished with a customer. The problems between the stylist and the receptionist appeared serious enough to the participants and broad enough in scope that the manager decided to call both parties into her office to help them resolve their differences. The following guidelines are intended to help mediators avoid the common pitfalls associated with this role shown in Table 5.

Acknowledge that a conflict exists and propose a problem-solving approach for resolving it.
It is vital that the mediator take seriously the problems between conflicting parties. If they feel they have a serious problem, the mediator should not belittle its significance. Remarks such as, "I'm surprised that two intelligent people like you have not been able to work out your disagreement. We have more important things to do here than get all worked up over such petty issues" will make both parties defensive and interfere with any serious problem-solving efforts. While you might wish that your subordinates could have worked out their disagreement without bothering you, this is not the time to lecture them on self-reliance. Inducing guilt feelings by implying personal failure during an al-

1. After you have listened to the argument for a short time, begin to nonverbally communicate your discomfort with the discussion (e.g., sit back, begin to fidget).
2. Communicate your agreement with one of the parties (e.g., through facial expressions, posture, chair position, reinforcing comments).
3. Say that you shouldn't be talking about this kind of thing at work or where others can hear you.
4. Discourage the expression of emotion. Suggest that the discussion would better be held later after both parties have cooled off.
5. Suggest that both parties are wrong. Point out the problems with both points of view.
6. Suggest part-way through the discussion that possibly you aren't the person who should be helping solve this problem.
7. See if you can get both parties to attack you.
8. Minimize the seriousness of the problem.
9. Change the subject (e.g., ask for advice to help you solve one of your problems).
10. Express displeasure that the two parties are experiencing conflict (e.g., imply that it might undermine the solidarity of the work group).

Table 5   Ten Ways to Fail as a Mediator
Source: Adapted from Morris & Sashkin, 1976.

ready-emotional experience tends to distract the participants from the substantive issues at hand. Seldom is this conducive to problem solving.

One early decision a mediator has to make is whether to convene a joint problem-solving session or meet separately with the parties first. The diagnostic criteria shown in Table 6 should help you weigh the tradeoffs. First, what is the current position of the disputants? Are both aware a problem exists? Are they equally motivated to work on solving the problem? The more similar the awareness and motivation of the parties, the more likely it is that a joint session will be productive. If there is a serious discrepancy in awareness and motivation, the mediator should work to reduce that discrepancy through one-on-one meetings before bringing the disputants together.

Second, what is the current relationship between the disputants? Does their work require them to interact

FACTORS	HOLD JOINT MEETINGS	HOLD SEPARATE MEETINGS FIRST
Awareness and Motivation		
• Both parties are aware of the problem.	Yes	No
• They are equally motivated to resolve the problem.	Yes	No
• They accept your legitimacy as a mediator.	Yes	No
Nature of the Relationship		
• The parties hold equal status.	Yes	No
• They work together regularly.	Yes	No
• They have an overall good relationship.	Yes	No
Nature of the Problem		
• This is an isolated (not a recurring) problem.	Yes	No
• The complaint is substantive in nature and easily verified.	Yes	No
• The parties agree on the root causes of the problem.	Yes	No
• The parties share common values and work priorities.	Yes	No

Table 6 Choosing a Format for Mediating Conflicts

frequently? Is a good working relationship critical for their individual job performance? What has their relationship been in the past? What is the difference in their formal status in the organization? As we discussed earlier, joint problem-solving sessions are most productive between individuals of equal status who are required to work together regularly. This does not mean that joint meetings should not be held between a supervisor and subordinate, only that greater care needs to be taken in preparing for such a meeting. Specifically, if a department head becomes involved in a dispute between a worker and a supervisor, the department head should make sure that the worker does not feel this meeting will serve as an excuse for two managers to gang up on an hourly employee.

Separate fact-finding meetings with the disputants prior to a joint meeting are particularly useful when the parties have a history of recurring disputes, especially if these disputes should have been resolved without a mediator. Such a history often suggests a lack of conflict management or problem-solving skills on the part of the disputants, or it might stem from a broader set of issues that are beyond their control. In these situations, individual coaching sessions prior to a joint meeting will increase your understanding of the root causes and improve the individuals' abilities to resolve their differences. Following up these private meetings with a joint problem-solving session, in which the mediator coaches the disputants through the process for resolving their conflicts, can be a positive learning experience.

Third, what is the nature of the problem? Is the complaint substantive in nature and easily verifiable? If the problem stems from conflicting role responsibilities and the actions of both parties in question are common knowledge, then a joint problem-solving session can begin on a common information and experimental base. However, if the complaint stems from differences in managerial style, values, personality characteristics, and so forth, bringing the parties together immediately following a complaint may seriously undermine the problem-solving process. Complaints that are likely to be interpreted as threats to the self-image of one or both parties (Who am I? What do I stand for?) warrant considerable individual discussion before a joint meeting is called. To avoid individuals' feeling as though they are being ambushed in a meeting, you should discuss serious personal complaints with them ahead of time, in private.

In seeking out the perspective of both parties, maintain a neutral posture regarding the disputants—if not the issues. Effective mediation requires impartiality. If a mediator shows strong personal bias in favor of one party in a joint problem-solving session, the other party may simply walk out. However, such personal bias is more likely to emerge in private conversations with the disputants. Statements such as "I can't believe he really did that!" and "Everyone seems to be having trouble working with Charlie these days" imply that the mediator is taking sides, and any attempt to appear impartial in a joint meeting will seem like mere window dressing to appease the other party. No matter how well-intentioned or justified these comments might be, they destroy the credibility of the mediator in the long run. In contrast, effective mediators respect both parties' points of view and make sure that both perspectives are expressed adequately.

Occasionally it is not possible to be impartial on issues. One person may have violated company policy, engaged in unethical competition with a colleague, or broken a personal agreement. In these cases, the challenge of the mediator is to separate the offense from the offender. If a person is clearly in the wrong, the inappropriate behavior needs to be corrected, but in such a way that the individual doesn't feel his or her image and working relationships have been permanently marred. This can be done most effectively when correction occurs in private.

Manage the discussion to insure fairness. Keep the discussion issue-oriented, not personality-oriented.   It is important that the mediator maintain a problem-solving atmosphere throughout the discussion. This is not to say that strong emotional statements don't have their place. People often associate effective problem solving with a calm, highly rational discussion of the issues and associate a personality attack with a highly emotional outburst. However, it is important not to confuse *affect* with *effect*. Placid, cerebral discussions may not solve problems, and impassioned statements don't have to be insulting. The critical point about process is that it should be centered on the issues and the consequences of continued conflict on performance. Even when behavior offensive to one of the parties obviously stems from a personality quirk, the discussion of the problem should be limited to the behavior. Attributions of motives or generalizations from specific events to personal proclivities distract participants from the problem-solving process. It is important that the mediator establish and maintain these ground rules.

It is also important for a mediator to ensure that neither party dominates the discussion. A relatively even balance in the level of inputs improves the quality of the final outcome. It also increases the likelihood that both parties will accept the final decision, because there is a high correlation between feelings about the problem-solving process and attitudes about the final solution. If one party tends to dominate a discussion, the mediator can help balance the exchange by asking the less talkative individual direct questions: "Now that we have heard Bill's view of that incident, how do you see it?" "That's an important point, Brad, so let's make sure Brian agrees. How do you feel, Brian?"

Facilitate exploration of solutions rather than assess responsibility for the problem.   When parties must work closely and have a history of chronic interpersonal problems, it is often more important to teach problem-solving skills than to resolve a specific dispute. This is done best when the mediator adopts the posture of facilitator. The role of judge is to render a verdict regarding a problem in the past, not to teach people how to solve problems in the future. While some disputes obviously involve right and wrong actions, most interpersonal problems stem from differences in perspective. In these situations it is important that the mediator avoid being seduced into "rendering a verdict" by comments such as "Well, you're the boss; tell us which one is right," or more subtly, "I wonder if I did what was right?" The problem with a mediator's assuming the role of judge is that it sets in motion processes antithetical to effective interpersonal problem solving. The parties focus on persuading the mediator of their innocence and the other party's guilt rather than striving to improve their working relationship with the assistance of the mediator. The disputants work to establish facts about what happened in the past rather than to reach an agreement about what ought to happen in the future. Consequently, a key aspect of effective mediation is helping disputants explore multiple alternatives in a nonjudgmental manner.

Explore options by focusing on interests, not positions.   Often, conflict resolution is hampered by the perception that incompatible positions necessarily entail irreconcilable differences. Mediation of such conflicts can best be accomplished by examining the interests (goals and concerns) behind the positions. It is these interests that are the driving force behind the positions, and these interests are ultimately what people want satisfied.

It is the job of the mediator to discover where interests meet and where they conflict. Interests often remain unstated because they are unclear to the participants. In order to flesh out each party's interests, ask "why" questions: "Why have they taken this position?" "Why does this matter to them?" Understand that there is probably no single, simple answer to these questions. Each side may represent a number of constituents, each with a special interest.

After each side has articulated its underlying interests, help the parties identify areas of agreement and reconcilability. It is common for participants in an intense conflict to feel that they are on opposite sides of *all* issues—that they have little in common. Helping them recognize that there are areas of agreement and reconcilability often represents a major turning point in resolving long-standing feuds.

Make sure all parties fully understand and support the solution agreed upon, and establish follow-up procedures.   The last two phases of the problem-solving process are: (1) agreement on an action plan; and (2) follow-up. These will be discussed here within the context of the mediator's role, but they are equally relevant to the other roles.

A common mistake of ineffective mediators is terminating discussions prematurely, on the supposition that once a problem has been solved in principle, the disputants can be left to work out the details on their own. Or, a mediator may assume that because one party has recommended a solution that appears reasonable and workable, the second disputant will be willing to implement it. It is important when serving as a mediator to insist on a specific plan of action both parties are willing to implement. If you suspect any hesitancy on

the part of either disputant, this needs to be explored explicitly ("Tom, I sense that you are somewhat less enthusiastic than Sue about this plan. Is there something that bothers you?") When you are confident that both parties support the plan, check to make sure they are aware of their respective responsibilities and then propose a mechanism for monitoring progress. You might schedule another formal meeting, or you might stop by both individuals' offices to get a progress report.

Summary

Conflict is a difficult and controversial topic. In our culture, it has negative connotations. We place a high value on getting along with people by being kind and friendly. Although many people intellectually understand the value of conflict, they feel uncomfortable when confronted by it. Their discomfort may result from a lack of understanding of the conflict process as well as from a lack of training in how to handle interpersonal confrontations effectively. In this chapter, we have addressed these issues by introducing both analytical and behavioral skills.

A summary model of conflict management, shown in Figure 5, contains three phases: diagnosing sources of conflict; selecting an appropriate conflict-management strategy; and implementing the strategy, using specific problem-solving techniques, to resolve interpersonal disputes effectively. The first two phases comprise the

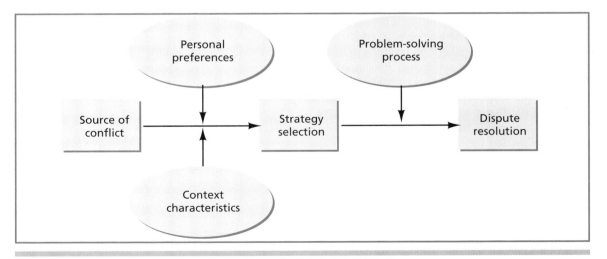

Figure 5   Summary Model of Conflict Management

diagnostic and analytical aspects of conflict management. Understanding the "why's" behind confrontations is a key to deciding "how" to respond appropriately. But skillful implementation is of little value if the wrong approach has been selected. The third phase focuses on the behavioral component of conflict management. The overall philosophy guiding our discussion of conflict is reflected in the implementation segment of the model. We argue that conflict plays an important role in effective organizations. Therefore, the operational component of this model focuses on successful resolution of specific disputes, not on eliminating or preventing all conflict.

Conflict can be produced by a variety of circumstances: irreconcilable personal differences, discrepancies in information, role incompatibilities, and environmentally induced stress. These causes, and the resulting conflicts, differ in both frequency and intensity. Information-based conflicts occur frequently, but they are easily resolved because disputants have low personal stakes in the outcome. In contrast, conflicts grounded in differences of perceptions and expectations are generally intense and difficult to defuse.

Before selecting a conflict response, consider the diversity and cultural context. Conflicts that escalate tensions between majority and minority groups in organizations can negatively impact the performance and effectiveness of individuals, work groups, and the entire organization. Once again, we are not advocating the elimination of conflict, but rather more effective management of conflict. Cultural differences also impact individual preferences for dealing with conflict. In a global business environment, we are likely to have increasing conflicts with individuals from other cultures, and differences in how individuals think about and prefer to resolve conflict needs to be better understood.

There are five approaches to handling conflict: avoiding, compromising, collaborating, forcing, and accommodating. These reflect different degrees of assertiveness and cooperativeness. There is no single best way to handle all conflicts. Instead, in choosing a response mode, managers should consider the quality and duration of the ongoing relationship between the actors, the nature and seriousness of their problem, as well as their personal preferences. Successful strategies are congruent with salient contextual factors and the overall philosophy and personality of the implementor.

The collaborative approach, like the integrative negotiation strategy, generally produces the highest-quality solutions and has the least detrimental effect on relationships. When it is used effectively, the parties tend to be most satisfied with the outcome. Unfortunately, the collaborative approach is the most difficult to implement successfully in a highly emotional situation. It takes little skill to impose your authority on another person, to withdraw from a confrontation, to split the difference between opponents, or to abandon your position at the slightest sign of opposition. Therefore, the behavioral guidelines for resolving an interpersonal confrontation involving complaints and criticisms by using a problem-solving approach have been described in detail. These guidelines incorporate integrative negotiation tactics for managing conflict.

Behavioral Guidelines

Effective conflict management involves both analytic and behavioral elements. First, it is important to understand the true causes of a conflict and to select the appropriate conflict-management or negotiation approach. Second, it is necessary to implement the approach effectively.

Behavioral guidelines for the diagnostic aspects of conflict management include the following:

1. Collect information on the sources of conflict. Identify the source by examining the focus of the dispute. The four sources (and their respective focuses) are: personal differences (perception and expectations); information deficiency (misinformation and misinterpretation); role incompatibility (goals and responsibilities); and environmental stress (resource scarcity and uncertainty).

2. Utilize the collaborative approach for managing conflict, including integrative negotiation tactics, unless specific conditions dictate the use of an alternative approach.

3. Use the forcing approach only when the issue is extremely important to you; a close, ongoing relationship is not necessary; you have much more power than the other person; and there is a high sense of urgency.

4. Use the accommodating approach only when the issue is not important to you; a close, ongoing relationship is critical; you have no other option (low power); and time is not a factor.

5. Use the compromising approach only when the issue is very complex and of moderate importance to both parties (and the parties feel strongly about different aspects of the issues); the relationship is of moderate importance; the parties have relatively equal power; and time constraints are low.

6. Use the avoiding approach only when the issue is not important to you; the relationship is not critical; your relative power is equal to, or greater than that of the other person; and time is not a significant factor.

Behavioral guidelines for implementing effectively the collaborative (problem-solving) approach to conflict management are summarized below. These are organized according to three roles. Guidelines for the problem-identification and solution-generation phases of the problem-solving process are specified for each role. Guidelines for the action plan and follow-up phases are the same for all three roles.

Initiator

Problem Identification

1. Succinctly describe your problem in terms of behaviors, consequences, and feelings ("When you do X, Y happens, and I feel Z.")

   Maintain personal ownership of the problem.

   ▶ Use a specific incident to illustrate the expectations or standards violated.

   ▶ Stick to the facts. Avoid drawing evaluative conclusions and attributing motives to the respondent.

2. Persist until understood; encourage two-way discussion.

   ▶ Restate your concerns or give additional examples.

   ▶ Avoid introducing additional issues or letting frustration sour your emotional tone.

   ▶ Invite the respondent to ask questions and express another perspective.

3. Manage the agenda carefully.

   ▶ Approach multiple problems incrementally, proceeding from simple to complex, easy to difficult, concrete to abstract.

▶ Don't become fixated on a single issue. If you reach an impasse, expand the discussion to increase the likelihood of an integrative outcome.

Solution Generation

4. Make a request.

   ▶ Focus on those things you share in common (principles, goals, constraints) as the basis for recommending preferred alternatives.

Responder

Problem Identification

1. Establish a climate for joint problem solving.

   ▶ Show genuine concern and interest. Respond empathetically, even if you disagree with the complaint.

   ▶ Respond appropriately to the initiator's emotions. If necessary, let the person "blow off steam" before addressing the complaint.

2. Seek additional information about the problem.

   ▶ Ask questions that channel the initiator's statements from general to specific and from evaluative to descriptive.

3. Agree with some aspect of the complaint.

   ▶ Signal your willingness to consider making changes by agreeing with facts, perceptions, feelings, or principles.

Solution Generation

4. Ask for recommendations.

   ▶ To avoid debating the merits of a single suggestion, brainstorm multiple alternatives.

Mediator

Problem Identification

1. Acknowledge that a conflict exists.

   ▶ Select the most appropriate setting (one-on-one conference versus group meeting) for coaching and fact finding.

- Propose a problem-solving approach for resolving the dispute.

2. Maintain a neutral posture.

- Assume the role of facilitator, not judge. Do not belittle the problem or berate the disputants for their inability to resolve their differences.

- Be impartial toward disputants and issues (provided policy has not been violated).

- If correction is necessary, do it in private.

3. Manage the discussion to ensure fairness.

- Focus discussion on the conflict's impact on performance and the detrimental effect of continued conflict.

- Keep the discussion issue-oriented, not personality-oriented.

- Do not allow one party to dominate the discussion. Ask directed questions to maintain balance.

Solution Generation

4. Explore options by focusing on the interests behind stated positions.

- Explore the "why's" behind disputants' arguments or claims.

- Help disputants see commonalities among their goals, values, and principles.

- Use commonalities to generate multiple alternatives.

- Maintain a nonjudgmental manner.

All Roles

Action Plan and Follow-Up

1. Ensure that all parties support the agreed-upon plan.

- Verify understanding of, and commitment to, specific actions.

2. Establish a mechanism for follow-up.

- Create benchmarks for measuring progress and ensuring accountability.

- Encourage flexibility in adjusting the plan to meet emerging circumstances.

Skill Analysis

Case Involving Interpersonal Conflict

Educational Pension Investments

Educational Pension Investments (EPI), located in New York, invests pension funds for educational institutions. In 1988 it employed approximately 75 people, 25 of whom were responsible for actual investment activities. The company managed about $1.2 billion of assets and derived an income of about $2.5 million.

The firm was incorporated in 1960 by a group of academic professionals who wanted to control the destiny of their retirement years. They solicited pension funds under the assumption that their investments would be consistent and safe. Through their nearly three decades in the business, they have weathered rapid social and technological change as well as economic volatility. Through it all, they have resisted opportunities to "make it big" and instead stayed with less-profitable, but relatively secure, investments.

Dan Richardson has an MBA from Wharton and is one of the original founders of EPI. He started out working in the research department and has worked in every department since then. The other partners, comfortable with Dan's conservative, yet flexible, nature, elected him to the position of CEO in the spring of 1975. After that, Dan became known as "the great equalizer." He worked hard to make sure that all the partners were included in decisions and that strong relations were maintained. Over the years, he became the confidant of the other seniors and the mentor of the next generation. He took pride in his "people skills," and EPI's employees looked to Dan for leadership and direction.

Dan's management philosophy is built on the concept of loyalty—loyalty to the organization, loyalty to its members, and loyalty to friends. As he is fond of saying, "My dad was a small town banker. He told me, 'Look out for the other guys and they'll look out for you.' Sounds corny, I know, but I firmly believe in this philosophy."

Dan, bolstered by the support of the other founding members of EPI, continued the practice of consistent and safe investing. This meant maintaining low-risk investment portfolios with moderate income. However, EPI's growth has increasingly not kept pace with other investment opportunities. As a result, Dan has reluctantly begun to consider the merits of a more aggressive investment approach. This consideration was further strengthened by the expressions of several of the younger analysts who were beginning to refer to EPI as "stodgy." Some of them were leaving EPI for positions in more aggressive firms.

One evening, Dan talked about his concern with his racquetball partner and long-time friend, Mike Roth. Mike also happened to be an investment broker. After receiving his MBA from the University of Illinois, Mike went to work for a brokerage firm in New York, beginning his career in the research department. His accomplishments in research brought him recognition throughout the firm. Everyone respected him for his knowledge, his work ethic, and his uncanny ability to predict trends. Mike knew what to do and when to do it. After only two years on the job, he was promoted to the position of portfolio manager. However, he left that firm for greener pastures and had spent the last few years moving from firm to firm.

When Mike heard Dan's concerns about EPI's image and need for an aggressive approach, he suggested to his friend that what EPI needed was some fresh blood, someone who could infuse enthusiasm into the organization. Someone like him. He told Dan, "I can help you get things moving. In fact, I've been developing some concepts that would be perfect for EPI."

Dan brought up the idea of hiring Mike at the next staff meeting, but the idea was met with caution and skepticism. "Sure, he's had a brilliant career on paper," said one senior partner. "But he's never stayed in one place long enough to really validate his success. Look at his résumé. During the past seven years, he's been with four different firms, in four different positions."

"That's true," said Dan, "but his references all check out. In fact, he's been described as a rising star, aggressive, productive. He's just what we need to help us explore new opportunities."

"He may have been described as a comer, but I don't feel comfortable with his apparent inability to settle down," said another. "He doesn't seem very loyal or committed to anyone or anything."

Another partner added, "A friend of mine worked with Mike a while back and said that while he is definitely good, he's a real maverick—both in terms of investment philosophy and lifestyle. Is that what we really want at EPI?"

Throughout the discussion, Dan defended Mike's work record. He repeatedly pointed out Mike's impressive performance. He deflected concerns about Mike's reputation by saying that he was a loyal and trusted friend. Largely on Dan's recommendation, the other partners agreed, although somewhat reluctantly, to hire Mike. When Dan offered Mike the job, he promised Mike the freedom and flexibility to operate a segment of the fund as he desired.

Mike took the job and performed his responsibilities at EPI in a superior manner. Indeed, he was largely responsible for increasing the managed assets of the company by 150 percent. However, a price was paid for this increase. From the day he moved in, junior analysts enjoyed working with him very much. They liked his fresh, new approach, and were encouraged by the spectacular results. This caused jealousy among the other partners, who thought Mike was pushing too hard to change the tried-and-true traditions of the firm. It was not uncommon for sharp disagreements to erupt in staff meetings, with one or another partner coming close to storming out of the room. Throughout this time, Dan tried to soothe ruffled feathers and maintain an atmosphere of trust and loyalty.

Mike seemed oblivious to all the turmoil he was causing. He was optimistic about potential growth opportunities. He believed that computer chips, biotechnology, and laser engineering were the "waves of the future." Because of this belief, he wanted to direct the focus of his portfolio toward these emerging technologies. "Investments in small firm stocks in these industries, coupled with an aggressive market timing strategy, should yield a 50 percent increase in performance." He rallied support for this idea not only among the younger members of EPI but also with the pension fund managers that invested with EPI. Roth championed his position and denigrated the merits of the traditional philosophy. "We should compromise on safety and achieve some real growth while we can," Roth argued. "If we don't, we'll lose the investors' confidence and ultimately lose them."

Most of the senior partners disagreed with Roth, stating that the majority of their investors emphasized security above all else. They also disagreed with the projected profits, stating that "We could go from 8 to 12 percent ROI; then again, we could drop to 4 percent. A lot depends on whose data you use." They reminded Roth, "The fundamental approach of the corporation is to provide safe and moderate-income mutual funds for academic pension funds to invest in. That's the philosophy we used to solicit the investments originally, and that's the approach we are obligated to maintain."

Many months passed, and dissension among the managers grew. Roth's frustration over the lack of support among the senior partners began to undermine the day-to-day operations of EPI. He began to criticize detractors in discussions with younger EPI employees. In addition, he assigned research department employees tasks related to technological investments, distracting them from investigating more traditional alternatives. He gradually implemented his ideas within his portfolio, which accounted for approximately 35 percent of EPI's revenues. This disrupted the operations of other managers in EPI because the performance of their funds relied on the timely input of the researchers and other support staff. The other managers bristled when the research staff began tracking the ROI of the various investments on a chart prominently displayed on the conference room wall.

Amidst a rapidly spreading undercurrent of tension, one of the founding partners, Tom Watson, approached Dan one day. Conservative in his ways, Watson is the partner who walks the office and always has time to stop and chat. He began the conversation.

"Dan, I speak for most of the senior staff when I say that we are very troubled by Mike's approach. We've expressed ourselves well enough for Mike to understand, but his actions defy everything we've said. He's a catastrophe just waiting to happen."

"I can understand your concern, Tom," replied Dan. "I'm troubled, too. We have an opportunity to attract new business with some of Mike's new ideas. And the younger staff love working on his projects. But he has stirred up a lot of turmoil."

Tom agreed. "The real issue is that EPI is no longer presenting a unified image. Mike is willfully defying the stated objectives of our organization. And some of our oldest clients don't like that."

"That's true, Tom. On the other hand, some of our newer clients are really encouraged by Mike's approach—and his track record is extremely impressive."

"Come on, Dan. You and I both know that many experts feel the market is overheating. Mike's paper profits could quickly be incinerated if the budget and trade deficits don't turn around. We can't stake the reputation of the firm on a few high-flying technology stocks. Dan, the other senior partners agree. Mike must either conform to the philosophy and management practices of this organization or else resign."

Reflecting on the situation, Dan realized he faced the most difficult challenge of his career. He felt a strong personal investment in helping Mike succeed. Not only had he hired Mike over the objections of several colleagues; he had personally helped him "learn the ropes" at EPI. Beyond that, Dan was haunted by his promise to Mike that he would have the freedom and flexibility to perform the requirements of the position as he pleased. However, this flexibility had clearly caused problems within EPI.

Finally, bowing to the pressure of his peers, Dan called Mike in for a meeting, hoping to find some basis for compromise.

DAN: I gather you know the kinds of concerns the senior partners have expressed regarding your approach.

MIKE: I guess you've talked with Tom. Well, we did have a small disagreement earlier this week.

DAN: The way Tom tells it, you're willfully defying corporate objectives and being insubordinate.

MIKE: Well, it's just like Watson to see progressive change as an attempt to take away his power.

DAN: It's not quite that simple, Mike. When we founded EPI, we all agreed that a conservative stance was best. And right now, with the economic indicators looking soft, many experts agree that it may still be the best alternative.

MIKE: Dan, what are you going to rely on—predictions or performance? These concerns are just smokescreens to deflect attention away from the sub-par records of other portfolio managers. Old views need to be challenged and ultimately discarded. How else are we going to progress and keep up with our competitors?

DAN: I agree we need to change, Mike—but gradually. You have great ideas and terrific instincts, but you can't change a 30-year-old firm overnight. You can help me promote change, but you're pushing so fast, others are digging in their heels. The rate of change is just as important as the direction.

MIKE: You're telling me. And at this rate, it doesn't make much difference which direction we're headed in.

DAN: Come on, Mike. Don't be so cynical. If you'd just stop rubbing people's noses in your performance record and try to see things from their perspective, we could calm things down around here. Then maybe we could start building consensus.

Mike's emotions betray his impatience with the pace of the organization; he becomes agitated.

MIKE: I've always admired your judgment, and I value your friendship, but I honestly think you're kidding yourself. You seem to think you can get this firm to look like it's progressive—shrugging off its stodgy image—without taking any risks or ruffling any feathers. Are you interested in appearance or substance? If you want appearance, then hire a good PR person. If you want substance, then back me up and we'll rewrite the record book. Get off the fence, Dan, before your butt's full of slivers.

DAN: Mike, it simply isn't that easy. I'm not EPI, I'm simply its caretaker. You know we make decisions around here by consensus; that's the backbone of this organization. To move ahead, the confidence of the others has to be won, especially the confidence of the seniors. Frankly, your reputation as a maverick makes it hard to foster confidence in, and loyalty to, your plans.

MIKE: You knew my style when you hired me. Remember how you made it a point to promise me flexibility and autonomy? I'm not getting that any more, Dan. All I'm getting is grief, even though I'm running circles around your conservative cronies.

DAN: Well, that may be true. But your flamboyance . . .

MIKE: Oh, yeah. The sports car, the singles lifestyle, the messy office. But, again, that's appearance, Dan, not substance. Performance is what counts. That's what got me this far, and that's my ticket out. You know I could walk into any firm in town and write my own plan.

DAN: Well, there's no reason to be hasty.

MIKE: Do you honestly believe this can be salvaged? I think not. Maybe it's time for me to be moving on. Isn't that why you called me in here anyway?

Dan, feeling uncomfortable, breaks eye contact and shifts his gaze to the New York skyline. After a long pause, he continues, still gazing out of the window.

DAN: I don't know, Mike. I feel I've failed. My grand experiment in change has polarized the office; we've got two armies at war out there. On the other hand, you really have done a good job here. EPI will no doubt lose a good part of its customer base if you leave. You have a loyal following, with both customers and staff. If you go, so do they—along with our shot at changing our image.

MIKE: It's just like you, Dan, to take this problem personally. Blast it, you take everything personally. Even when I beat you at racquetball. Your heart's in the right place—you just can't ever seem to make the cut-throat hit. You know and I know that EPI needs a change in image. But it doesn't appear to be ready for it yet. And I'm certainly not willing to move slowly.

DAN: Yeah. Maybe. It's just hard to give up . . . [long pause]. Well, why don't we talk more about this after the reception tonight? Come on over and see Joanie and the kids. Besides, I'm dying to show off my new boat.

MIKE: What you see in sailing is beyond me. It's a waste of time, lazily drifting on gentle breezes . . .

DAN: Save it for later, "Speed King." I've got to get ready for tonight.

Discussion Questions

1. What are the sources of conflict in this case?

2. What approaches to conflict management are used by the actors in this situation? How effective was each?

3. Based on the behavioral guidelines for the collaborative approach, how could Dan have managed this conflict more effectively?

Skill Practice

Exercise in Diagnosing Sources of Conflict

SSS Software Management Problems

In order to manage conflict between others effectively, it is important to be aware of early warning signs. It is also important to understand the underlying causes of disagreements. Conflict that is unmanaged, or managed ineffectively, interferes with work-group performance. A key to managing conflict effectively is recognizing it in its early stages and understanding its roots.

Assignment

Reread the memos, faxes, voice mail, and E-mail messages in the SSS Software exercise in the Introduction. As you examine each of these documents, look for evidence of organizational conflicts. Identify the two conflicts that you think are most significant for you to address in your role as Chris Perillo. Begin your analysis of these conflicts by identifying their likely sources or causes. Use the list below to guide your thinking. Prepare to present your analysis, along with supporting evidence from the memos. Also, share your ideas regarding how this analysis of the causes of conflict would influence your approach to resolving the conflict.

Source of Conflict	Focus of Conflict
1. Personal differences	Perception and expectations
2. Informational deficiency	Misinformation and misinterpretation
3. Role incompatibility	Goals and responsibilities
4. Environmental stress	Resource scarcity and uncertainty

Exercises in Selecting an Appropriate Conflict-Management Strategy

Not all conflicts are alike; therefore, they cannot all be managed in exactly the same way. Effective managers are able to assess accurately the true causes of conflict and to match each type of conflict with an appropriate management strategy.

SITUATIONAL CONSIDERATION	CONFLICT-MANAGEMENT APPROACH				
	FORCING	ACCOM- MODATING	COMPRO- MISING	COLLABO- RATING	AVOIDING
Issue Importance	High	Low	Med	High	Low
Relationship Importance	Low	High	Med	High	Low
Relative Power	High	Low	Equal-High	Low-High	Equal-High
Time Constraints	Med-High	Med-High	Low	Low	Med-High

Table 7   Matching the Conflict-Management Approach With the Situation

Assignment

For each of the following brief scenarios, select the most appropriate conflict management strategy. Refer to Table 7 for assistance in matching situational factors with strategies.

Bradley's Barn

You have decided to take your family out to the local steak house, Bradley's Barn, to celebrate your son's birthday. You are a single parent, so getting home from work in time to prepare a nice dinner is very difficult. On entering the restaurant, you ask the hostess to seat you in the non-smoking section because your daughter, Shauna, is allergic to tobacco smoke. On your way to your seat, you notice that the restaurant seems crowded for a Monday night.

After you and your children are seated and have placed your orders, your conversation turns to family plans for the approaching holiday. Interspersed in the general conversation is a light banter with your son about whether or not he is too old to wear "the crown" during dinner—a family tradition on birthdays.

Suddenly you become aware that your daughter is sneezing and her eyes are beginning to water. You look around and notice a lively group of business people seated at the table behind you; all of them are smoking. Your impression is that they are celebrating some type of special occasion. Looking back at Shauna, you realize that something has to be done quickly. You ask your son to escort Shauna outside while you rush to the front of the restaurant and find the hostess.

Discussion Questions

1. What are the salient situational factors?

2. What are the most appropriate conflict-management strategy?

Avocado Computers

When the head of Avocado Computers ran into production problems with his automated production facility, he hired you away from a competitor. It meant a significant increase in pay and the opportunity to manage a state-of-the-art production facility. What's more, there were very few other female production managers in Silicon Valley. Now you've been on the job a year, and it's been exciting to see your staff start working together as a team to solve problems, improve quality, and finally get the plant up to capacity. In general, Bill, the owner, has also been a plus. He is energetic, fair, and a proven industry leader. You feel fortunate to be in a coveted position, in a "star" firm, in a growth industry.

However, there is one distraction that bugs you. Bill is a real stickler about cleanliness, order, and appearance. He wants the robots all painted the same color, the components within the computer laid out perfectly on a grid, the workers wearing clean smocks, and the floor "clean enough to eat off." You are troubled by this compulsion. "Sure," you think, "it might impress potential corporate clients when they tour the production facility, but is it really that important? After all, who's ever going to look at the inside of their computer? Why should customers care about the color of the robot that built their computers? And who, for Pete's sake, would ever want to have a picnic in a factory?"

Today is your first yearly performance appraisal interview with Bill. In preparation for the meeting, he has sent you a memo outlining "Areas of Strength" and "Areas of Concern." You look with pride at the number of items listed in the first column. It's obvious that Bill likes your work. But you are a bit miffed at the single item of concern: "Needs to maintain a cleaner facility, including employee appearance." You mull over this "demerit" in your mind, wrestling with how to respond in your interview.

Discussion Questions

1. What are the salient situational factors?

2. What is the most appropriate conflict-management strategy?

Phelps, Inc.

You are Philip Manual, the head of sales for an office products firm, Phelps, Inc. Your personnel sell primarily to small businesses in the Los Angeles metropolitan area. Phelps is doing about average for this rapidly growing market. The firm's new president, Jose Ortega, is putting a lot of pressure on you to increase sales. You feel that a major obstacle is the firm's policy on extending credit. Celeste, the head of the credit office, insists that all new customers fill out an extensive credit application. Credit risks must be low; credit terms and collection procedures are tough. You can appreciate her point of view, but you feel it is unrealistic. Your competitors are much more lenient in their credit examinations; they extend credit to higher risks; their credit terms are more favorable; and they are more lenient in collecting overdue payments. Your sales personnel frequently complain that they aren't "playing on a level field" with their competition. When you brought this concern to Jose, he said he wanted you and Celeste to work things out. His instructions didn't give many clues to his priorities on this matter. "Sure, we need to increase sales, but the small business failure in this area is the highest in the country, so we have to be careful we don't make bad credit decisions."

You decide it's time to have a serious discussion with Celeste. A lot is at stake.

Discussion Questions

1. What are the salient situational factors?

2. What is the most appropriate conflict-management strategy?

Exercises in Resolving Interpersonal Disputes

The heart of conflict management is resolving intense, emotionally charged confrontations. We have discussed guidelines for utilizing the collaborative (problem-solving) approach to conflict management in these situations. Assuming that the collaborative approach is appropriate for a particular situation, the general guidelines can be used by an initiator, a responder, or a mediator.

Assignment

Following are three situations involving interpersonal conflict and disagreement. After you have finished reading the assigned roles, review the appropriate behavioral guidelines (see the Observer's Feedback Form in Appendix I). Do not read any of the role descriptions except those assigned to you.

In the first exercise, practice applying the guidelines for the initiator's role. In the second incident, which focuses on proper responses to emotional accusations, you will play the respondent's role. In the third exercise, you will practice mediating conflicts between subordinates. An observer will be assigned to give you feedback on your performance, using the Observer's Form as a guide.

Freida Mae Jones: Racism in Organizations

Freida Mae Jones, Assistant Manager, Branch Operations

Reprinted with permission of the author, Martin R. Moser, Ph.D., Associate Professor of Management, College of Management, University of Lowell, Lowell, Massachusetts.

Freida Mae Jones was born in her grandmother's Georgia farmhouse on June 1, 1949. She was the sixth of George and Ella Jones's 10 children. Mr. and Mrs. Jones moved to New York City when Freida was four because they felt that the educational and career opportunities for their children would be better in the North. With the help of some cousins, they settled in a five-room apartment in the Bronx. George worked as a janitor at Lincoln Memorial Hospital, and Ella was a part-time housekeeper in a nearby neighborhood. George and Ella were conservative, strict parents. They kept a close watch on their children's activities and demanded they be home by a certain hour. The Joneses believed that because they were black, the children would have to perform and behave better than their peers to be successful. They believed that their children's education would be the most important factor in their success as adults.

Freida entered Memorial High School, a racially integrated public school, in September 1963. Seventy percent of the student body was Caucasian, 20 percent black, and 10 percent Hispanic. About 60 percent of the graduates went on to college, of which 4 percent were black, Hispanic, and male. In her senior year, Freida was the top student in her class. Following school regulations, Freida met with her guidance counselor to discuss plans upon graduation. The counselor advised her to consider training in a "practical" field such as housekeeping, cooking, or sewing, so that she could find a job.

George and Ella Jones were furious when Freida told them what the counselor had advised. Ella said, "Don't they see what they are doing? Freida is the top-rated student in her whole class and they are telling her to become a manual worker. She showed that she has a fine mind and can work better than any of her classmates and still she is told not to become anybody in this world. It's really not any different in the North than back home in Georgia, except that they don't try to hide it down South. They want her to throw away her fine mind because she is a black girl and not a white boy. I'm going to go up to her school tomorrow and talk to the principal."

As a result of Mrs. Jones's visit to the principal, Freida was assisted in applying to 10 Eastern colleges, each of which offered her full scholarships. In September 1966, Freida entered Werbley College, an exclusive private women's college in Massachusetts. In 1970, Freida graduated summa cum laude in history. She decided to return to New York to teach grade school in the city's public school system. Freida was unable to obtain a full-time position, so she substituted. She also enrolled as a part-time student in Columbia University's Graduate School of Education. In 1975 she had attained her Master of Arts degree in Teaching from Columbia but could not find a permanent teaching job. New York City was laying off teachers and had instituted a hiring freeze because of the city's financial problems.

Feeling frustrated about her future as a teacher, Freida decided to get an MBA. She thought that there was more opportunity in business than in education. Churchill Business School, a small, prestigious school located in upstate New York, accepted Freida into its MBA program.

Freida completed her MBA in 1977 and accepted an entry-level position at the Industrialist World Bank of Boston in a fast-track management development program. The three-year program introduced her to all facets of bank operations, from telling to loan training and operations management. She was rotated to branch offices throughout New England. After completing the program she became an assistant manager for branch operations in the West Springfield branch office.

During her second year in the program, Freida had met James Walker, a black doctoral student in business administration at the University of Massachusetts. Her assignment to West Springfield precipitated their decision to get married. They originally anticipated that they would marry when James finished his doctorate and could move to Boston. Instead, they decided he would pursue a job in the Springfield-Hartford area.

Freida was not only the first black but also the first woman to hold an executive position in the West Springfield branch office. Throughout the training program Freida felt somewhat uneasy although she did very well. There were six other blacks in the program, five men and one woman, and she found support and comfort in sharing her feelings with them. The group spent much of their free time together. Freida had hoped that she would be located near one or more of the group when she went out into the "real world." She felt that although she was able to share her feelings about work with James, he did not have the full appreciation or understanding of her coworkers. However, the nearest group member was located 100 miles away.

Freida's boss in Springfield was Stan Luboda, a 55-year-old native New Englander. Freida felt that he treated her differently than he did the other trainees. He always tried to help her and took a lot of time (too much, according to Freida) explaining things to her. Freida felt that he was treating her like a child and not like an intelligent and able professional.

"I'm really getting frustrated and angry about what is happening at the bank," Freida said to her husband. "The people don't even realize it, but their prejudice comes through all the time. I feel as if I have to fight all the time just to start off even. Luboda gives Paul Cohen more responsibility than me and we both started at the same time with the same amount of training. He's meeting customers alone and Luboda has accompanied me to each meeting I've had with a customer."

"I run into the same thing at school," said James. "The people don't even know that they are doing it. The other day I met with a professor on my dissertation committee. I've known and worked with him for over three years. He said he wanted to talk with me about a memo he had received. I asked him what it was about and he said that the records office wanted to know about my absence during the spring semester. He said that I had to sign some forms. He had me confused with Martin Jordan, another black student. Then he realized that it wasn't me, but Jordan he wanted. All I could think was that we all must look alike to him. I was angry. Maybe it was an honest mistake on his part, but whenever something like that happens, and it happens often, it gets me really angry."

"Something like that happened to me," said Freida. "I was using the copy machine, and Luboda's secretary was talking to someone in the hall. She had just gotten a haircut and was saying her hair was now like Freida's—short and kinky—and that she would have to talk to me about how to take care of it. Luckily, my back was to her. I bit my lip and went on with my business. Maybe she was trying to be cute, because I know she saw me standing there, but comments like that are not cute, they are racist."

"I don't know what to do," said James. "I try to keep things in perspective. Unless people interfere with my progress, I try to let it slide. I only have so much energy and it doesn't make sense to waste it on people who don't matter. But that doesn't make it any easier to function in a racist environment. People don't realize that they are being racist. But a lot of times their expectations of black people or women, or whatever, are different because of skin color or gender. They expect you to be different, although if you were to ask them they would say that they don't. In fact, they would be highly offended if you implied that they were racist or sexist. They don't see themselves that way."

"Luboda is interfering with my progress," said Freida. "The kinds of experiences I have now will have a direct effect on my career advancement. If decisions are being made because I am black or a woman, then they are racially and sexually biased. It's the same kind of attitude that the guidance counselor had when I was in high school, although not as blatant." In September 1980, Freida decided to speak to Luboda about his treatment of her. She met with him in his office. "Mr. Luboda, there is something that I would like to discuss with you, and I feel a little uncomfortable because I'm not sure how you will respond to what I am going to say."

Stan Luboda, Manager, Branch Operations

Stan Luboda is a 55 year-old native New Englander who has managed the Springfield Branch for over a decade and has extensive ties to a tightly knit western Massachusetts community. Stan feels that he is a liberal and open minded, and is proud that he recruited Frieda Mae Jones, one of only two African-American females in the Industrialist World Bank of Boston management development program. Stan feels that his working relationship with all of his assistant Branch managers is cordial and working smoothly. He has structured the work so that each Assistant Branch Manager is specialized in one part of the business.

He has assigned Paul Cohen to some established accounts as well as having him work on securing new customers, while he has Frieda Mae Jones managing the important processing department and supervising a staff of clerical and accounting personnel. While having lunch with Garland Smith, his boss who was visiting from the Boston head office, the subject of why Stan had assigned Cohen the more visible customer contact assignments, while assigning Jones to the back-room operations role, came up.

"Look Garland, you know I'm not a naïve person, and I'm very open minded, which is why I'm so pleased to have Frieda Mae on my staff," said Luboda. "You know the way the world works. There are some things that need to be taken more slowly than others. There are some assignments for which Cohen has been given more responsibility, and there are some assignments for which Jones is given more responsibility than Cohen."

"Don't you think Cohen's career will advance more quickly than Jones's because of the assignments that he gets?" Smith replied.

"That is not true," said Luboda. "Jones's career will not be hurt because she is getting different responsibilities than Cohen. Both of them need the different kinds of experiences they are getting. And you have to face the reality of the banking business. We are in a conservative business. When we speak to customers we need to gain their confidence, and we put the best people for the job in the positions to achieve that end. If we don't get their confidence they can go down the street to our competitors and do business with them. Their services are no different than ours. It's a competitive business in which you need every edge you have. It's going to take time for people to change some of their attitudes about whom they borrow money from or where they put their money. I can't change the way people feel. I am running a business, but believe me I won't make any decisions that are detrimental to the bank."

Assignment

Two people will play the roles of Frieda Mae Jones and Stan Luboda as they discuss the assignments that Frieda Mae has been assigned. A third person should be assigned the role of being an observer to provide feedback at the end of the meeting, using the Observer's Feedback Form in Appendix I as a guide. Frieda Mae Jones initiates the meeting by saying "Mr. Luboda, there is something that I would like to discuss with you, and I feel a little uncomfortable because I'm not sure how you will respond to what I'm going to say." After the role-play, the following Discussion Questions should be examined.

Discussion Questions

1. Do you think that the Joneses were being realistic or overly sensitive in their belief that their children would have to work harder to be successful because they were black? Explain your answer.

2. If you were Freida, what else could you have done? If you were Luboda, what else could you have done?

3. Do you think that Luboda was discriminating against Freida? Why or why not?

4. Does Freida have legal grounds to sue the bank for discrimination? Why or why not?

5. What role did the bank's upper management play in the managing diversity process? What could they have done differently?

6. Luboda's arguments for his decisions about Freida's responsibilities seemed to be based on the idea that the bank's customers might be uncomfortable with a black female in a position of authority. Is this a valid argument? Why or why not?

Can Larry Fit In?

Melissa, Office Manager

You are the manager of an auditing team sent to Bangkok, Thailand, to represent a major international accounting firm headquartered in New York. You and Larry, one of your auditors, were sent to Bangkok to set up an auditing operation. Larry is about seven years older than you and has five more years seniority in the firm. Your relationship has become very strained since you were recently designated as the office manager. You feel you were given the promotion because you have established an excellent working relationship with the Thai staff as well as a broad range of international clients. In contrast, Larry has told other members of the staff that your promotion simply reflects the firm's heavy emphasis on affirmative action. He has tried to isolate you from the all-male accounting staff by focusing discussions on sports, local night spots, and so forth.

You are sitting in your office reading some complicated new reporting procedures that have just arrived from the home office. Your concentration is suddenly interrupted by a loud knock on your door. Without waiting for an invitation to enter, Larry bursts into your office. He is obviously very upset, and it is not difficult for you to surmise why he is in such a nasty mood.

You recently posted the audit assignments for the coming month, and you scheduled Larry for a job you knew he wouldn't like. Larry is one of your senior auditors, and the company norm is that they get the choice assignments. This particular job will require him to spend two weeks away from Bangkok in a remote town, working with a company whose records are notoriously messy.

Unfortunately, you have had to assign several of these less-desirable audits to Larry recently because you are short of personnel. But that's not the only reason. You have received several complaints from the junior staff (all Thais) recently that Larry treats them in a condescending manner. They feel he is always looking for an opportunity to boss them around, as if he were their supervisor instead of an experienced, supportive mentor. As a result, your whole operation works more smoothly when you can send Larry out of town on a solo project for several days. It keeps him from coming into your office and telling you how to do your job, and the morale of the rest of the auditing staff is significantly higher.

Larry slams the door and proceeds to express his anger over this assignment.

Larry, Senior Auditor

You are really ticked off! Melissa is deliberately trying to undermine your status in the office. She knows that the company norm is that senior auditors get the better jobs. You've paid your dues, and now you expect to be treated with respect. And this isn't the first time this has happened. Since she was made the office manager, she has tried to keep you out of the office as much as possible. It's as if she doesn't want her rival for leadership of the office around. When you were asked to go to Bangkok, you assumed that you would be made the office manager because of your seniority in the firm. You are certain that the decision to pick Melissa is yet another indication of reverse discrimination against white males.

In staff meetings, Melissa has talked about the need to be sensitive to the feelings of the office staff as well as the clients in this multicultural setting. "Where does she come off preaching about sensitivity! What about my feelings, for heaven's sake?" you wonder. This is nothing more than a straightforward power play. She is probably feeling insecure about being the only female accountant in the office and being promoted over someone with more experience. "Sending me out of town," you decide, "is a clear case of 'out of sight, out of mind.'"

Well, it's not going to happen that easily. You are not going to roll over and let her treat you unfairly. It's time for a showdown. If she doesn't agree to change this assignment and apologize for the way she's been treating you, you're going to register a formal complaint with her boss in the New York office. You are prepared to submit your resignation if the situation doesn't improve.

Meeting at Hartford Manufacturing Company

Hartford Manufacturing Company is the largest subsidiary of Connecticut Industries. Since the end of World War I, when it was formed, Hartford Manufacturing has become an industrial leader in the Northeast. Its sales currently average approximately $25 million a year, with an annual growth of approximately 6 percent. There are over 850 employees in production, sales and marketing, accounting, engineering, and management.

Lynn Smith is general manager. He has held his position for a little over two years and is well respected by his subordinates. He has the reputation of being firm but fair. Lynn's training in college was in engineering, so he is technically minded, and he frequently likes to walk around the production area to see for himself how things are going. He has also been known to roll up his sleeves and help work on a problem on the shop floor. He is not opposed to rubbing shoulders with even the lowest-level employees. On the other hand, he tries to run a tight company, and employees pretty well stick to their assigned tasks. He holds high expectations for performance, especially from individuals in management positions.

Richard Hooton is the director of production at Hartford Manufacturing. He has been with the company since he was 19 years old, when he worked on the dock. He has worked himself up through the ranks and now, at age 54, is the oldest of the management personnel. Hooton has his own ideas of how things should be run in production, and he is reluctant to tolerate any intervention from anyone, even Lynn Smith. Because he has been with the company so long, he feels he knows it better than anyone else, and he believes he has had a hand in making it the success that it is. His main goal is to keep production running smoothly and efficiently.

Barbara Price is the director of sales and marketing. She joined the company about 18 months ago, after completing her MBA at Dartmouth. Before going back to school for a graduate degree, she held the position of assistant manager of marketing at Connecticut Industries. Price is a very conscientious employee and is anxious to make a name for herself. Her major objective, which she has never hesitated to make public, is to be a general manager some day. Sales at Hartford Manufacturing have increased in the past year to near-record levels under her guidance.

Chuck Kasper is the regional sales director for the New York region. He reports directly to Barbara Price. The New York region represents the largest market for Hartford Manufacturing, and Chuck is considered the most competent salesperson in the company. He has built personal relationships with several major clients in his region, and it appears that some sales occur as much because of Chuck Kasper as because of the products of Hartford Manufacturing. Chuck has been with the company for 12 years, all of them in sales.

This is Friday afternoon, and tomorrow Lynn Smith leaves for Copenhagen at noon to attend an important meeting with potential overseas investors. He will be gone for two weeks. Before he leaves, there are several items in his in-basket that must receive attention. He calls a meeting with Richard Hooton and Barbara Price in his office. Just before the meeting begins, Chuck Kasper calls and asks if he may join the meeting for a few minutes, since he is in town and has something important to discuss that involves both Lynn Smith and Richard Hooton. Smith gives permission for him to join the meeting, since there may not be another chance to meet with Kasper before the trip. The meeting convenes, therefore, with Smith, Hooton, Price, and Kasper all in the room.

Assignment

Groups of four individuals should be formed. Each person should take the role of one of the characters in the management staff of Hartford Manufacturing Company. A fifth person should be assigned to serve as an observer to provide feedback at the end of the meeting, using the Observer's Feedback Form in Appendix I as a guide. The letters described in the case that were received by Lynn Smith are shown in Figures 6, 7, and 8. Only the person playing the role of Lynn Smith should read the letters, and no one should read the instructions for another staff member's role. (The letters will be introduced by Lynn Smith during the meeting.)

Lynn Smith, General Manager

Three letters arrived today, and you judge them to be sufficiently important to require your attention before you leave on your trip. Each letter represents a problem that requires immediate action, and you need commitments from key staff members to resolve these problems. You are concerned about this meeting because these individuals don't work as well together as you'd like.

For example, Richard Hooton is very difficult to pin down. He always seems suspicious of the motives of others and has a reputation for not making tough decisions. You sometimes wonder how a person could become the head of production in a major manufacturing firm by avoiding controversial issues and blaming others for the results.

In contrast, Barbara Price is very straightforward. You always know exactly where she stands. The problem is that sometimes she doesn't take enough time to study a problem before making a decision. She tends to be impulsive and anxious to make a decision, whether it's the right

T. J. Koppel, Inc.
General Accountants
8381 Spring Street
Hartford, Connecticut 06127

February 10, 199-

Mr. Lynn Smith
General Manager
Hartford Manufacturing Company
7450 Central Avenue
Hartford, CT 06118

Dear Mr. Smith:

As you requested last month, we have now completed our financial audit of Hartford Manufacturing Company. We find accounting procedures and fiscal control to be very satisfactory. A more detailed report of these matters is attached. However, we did discover during our perusal of company records that the production department has consistently incurred cost overruns during the past two quarters. Cost per unit of production is approximately 5 percent over budget. While this is not a serious problem given the financial solvency of your company, we thought it wise to bring it to your attention.

Respectfully,

T. J. Koppel

TJK: srw

Figure 6

one or not. Her general approach to resolving disagreements between departments is to seek expedient compromises. You are particularly disturbed by her approach to the sales-incentive problem. You felt strongly that something needed to be done to increase sales during the winter months. You reluctantly agreed to the incentive program because you didn't want to dampen her initiative. But you aren't convinced this is the right answer, because, frankly, you're not yet sure what the real problem is.

Chuck Kasper is your typical, aggressive, "take no prisoners" sales manager. He is hard-charging and uncompromising. He is great in the field because he gets the job done, but he sometimes ruffles the feathers of the corporate staff with his uncompromising, "black-and-white"

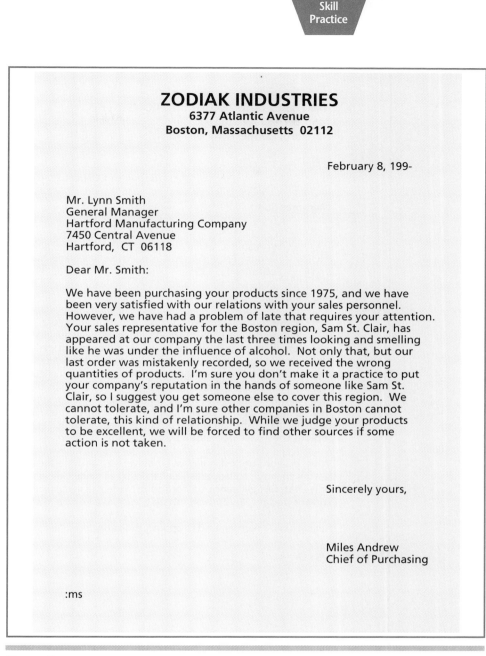

ZODIAK INDUSTRIES
6377 Atlantic Avenue
Boston, Massachusetts 02112

February 8, 199-

Mr. Lynn Smith
General Manager
Hartford Manufacturing Company
7450 Central Avenue
Hartford, CT 06118

Dear Mr. Smith:

We have been purchasing your products since 1975, and we have been very satisfied with our relations with your sales personnel. However, we have had a problem of late that requires your attention. Your sales representative for the Boston region, Sam St. Clair, has appeared at our company the last three times looking and smelling like he was under the influence of alcohol. Not only that, but our last order was mistakenly recorded, so we received the wrong quantities of products. I'm sure you don't make it a practice to put your company's reputation in the hands of someone like Sam St. Clair, so I suggest you get someone else to cover this region. We cannot tolerate, and I'm sure other companies in Boston cannot tolerate, this kind of relationship. While we judge your products to be excellent, we will be forced to find other sources if some action is not taken.

Sincerely yours,

Miles Andrew
Chief of Purchasing

:ms

Figure 7

style. He is also fiercely loyal to his sales staff, so you're sure he'll take the complaint about Sam St. Clair hard.

In contrast to the styles of these others, you have tried to use an integrating approach to problem solving: focusing on the facts, treating everyone's inputs equally, and keeping conversations about controversial topics problem-focused. One of your goals since taking over this position two years ago is to foster a "team" approach within your staff.

[*Note:* For more information about how you might approach the issues raised by these letters in your staff meeting, review the collaborating approach in Table 2 as well as the mediator's behavioral guidelines at the end of the Skill Learning section of this chapter.]

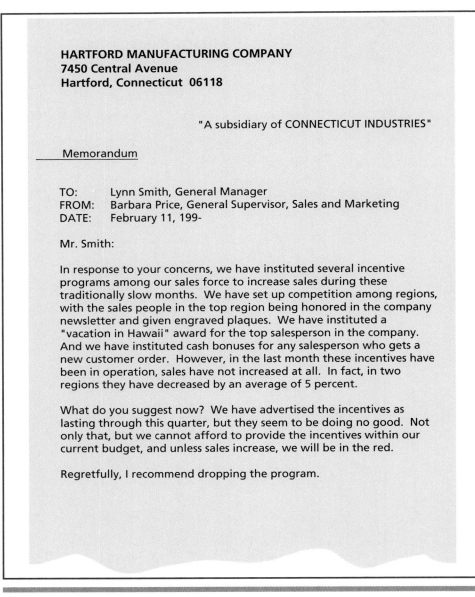

HARTFORD MANUFACTURING COMPANY
7450 Central Avenue
Hartford, Connecticut 06118

"A subsidiary of CONNECTICUT INDUSTRIES"

Memorandum

TO: Lynn Smith, General Manager
FROM: Barbara Price, General Supervisor, Sales and Marketing
DATE: February 11, 199-

Mr. Smith:

In response to your concerns, we have instituted several incentive programs among our sales force to increase sales during these traditionally slow months. We have set up competition among regions, with the sales people in the top region being honored in the company newsletter and given engraved plaques. We have instituted a "vacation in Hawaii" award for the top salesperson in the company. And we have instituted cash bonuses for any salesperson who gets a new customer order. However, in the last month these incentives have been in operation, sales have not increased at all. In fact, in two regions they have decreased by an average of 5 percent.

What do you suggest now? We have advertised the incentives as lasting through this quarter, but they seem to be doing no good. Not only that, but we cannot afford to provide the incentives within our current budget, and unless sales increase, we will be in the red.

Regretfully, I recommend dropping the program.

Figure 8

Richard Hooton, Director of Production

The backbone of Hartford Manufacturing is production. You have watched the company grow from a small, struggling shop to a firm with a real impact on the region because of its outstanding production processes. Your own reputation among those who know manufacturing is a good one, and you are confident that you have been a major factor in the success of Hartford Manufacturing. You have passed up several job offers over the years because you feel loyal to the company, but sometimes the younger employees don't seem to afford you the respect that you think you deserve.

The only times you have had major problems in production are when the young know-it-alls fresh from college have come in and tried to change things. With their scientific management concepts coupled with fuzzy-headed human relations training, they have more often made a mess of things than helped to improve matters. The best production methods have been practiced for years in the company, and you have yet to see anyone who could improve on your system.

On the other hand, you have respect for Lynn Smith as the general manager. Because he has experience, the right kind of training, and is involved in the production part of the organization, he often has given you good advice and has shown special interest. He mostly lets you do what you feel is best, however, and he seldom dictates specific methods for doing things.

Your general approach to problems is to avoid controversy. You feel uncomfortable when production is made the scapegoat for problems in the company. Because this is a manufacturing business, it seems as if everyone tries to pin the blame for problems on the production department. You've felt for years that the firm was getting away from what it does best: mass producing a few standard products. Instead, the trend has been for marketing and sales to push for more and more products, shorter lead times, and greater customization capability. These actions have increased costs and caused significant production delays as well as higher rejection rates.

[*Note:* During the upcoming meeting, you should adopt the avoidance approach shown in Table 2. Defend your turf, place blame on others, defer taking a stand, and avoid taking responsibility for making a controversial decision.]

Barbara Price, Director of Sales and Marketing

You are anxious to impress Lynn Smith because you have your eye on a position that is opening up at the end of the year in the parent company, Connecticut Industries. It would mean a promotion for you. A positive recommendation from Lynn Smith would carry a lot of weight in the selection process. Given that both Hartford Manufacturing and Connecticut Industries are largely male-dominated, you are pleased with your career advancement so far, and you are hoping to keep it up.

One current concern is Lynn Smith's suggestion some time ago that you look into the problem of slow sales during the winter months. You implemented an incentive plan that was highly recommended by an industry analyst at a recent trade conference. It consists of three separate incentive programs: (1) competition among regions in which the salesperson in the top region would have his or her picture in the company newsletter and receive an engraved plaque, (2) a vacation in Hawaii for the top salesperson in the company, and (3) cash bonuses for salespeople who obtained new customer orders. Unfortunately, these incentives haven't worked. Not only have sales not increased for the company as a whole, but sales for two regions are down an average of 5 percent. You have told the sales force that the incentives will last through this quarter, but if sales don't improve, your budget will be in the red. You haven't budgeted for the prizes, since you expected the increased sales to more than offset the cost of the incentives.

Obviously, this was a bad idea—it isn't working—and it should be dropped immediately. You are a bit embarrassed about this aborted project. But it is better to cut your losses and try something else rather than continue to support an obvious loser.

In general, you are very confident and self-assured. You feel that the best way to get work done is through negotiation and compromise. What's important is making a decision quickly and efficiently. Maybe everyone doesn't get exactly what he or she wants, but at least they can get on with their work. There are no black and whites in this business—only "grays" that can be traded off to keep the management process from bogging down with "paralysis by analysis." You are impatient over delays caused by intensive studies and investigations of detail. You agree with Tom Peters: Action is the hallmark of successful managers.

[*Note:* During this meeting, use the compromise approach shown in Table 2. Do whatever is necessary to help the group make a quick decision so you can get on with the pressing demands of your work.]

Chuck Kasper, Regional Sales Director

You don't get back to company headquarters often because your customer contacts take up most of your time. You regularly work 50 to 60 hours a week, and you are proud of the job you do. You also feel a special obligation to your customers to provide them with the best product available in the timeliest fashion. This sense of obligation comes not only from your commitment to the company but also from your personal relationships with many of the customers.

Lately, you have been receiving more and more complaints about late deliveries of Hartford Manufacturing's products to your customers. The time between their ordering and delivery is increasing, and some customers have been greatly inconvenienced by the delays. You have made a formal inquiry of production to find out what the problem is. They replied that they are producing as efficiently as possible, and they see nothing wrong with past practices. Richard Hooton's assistant even suggested that this was just another example of the sales force's unrealistic expectations.

Not only will sales be negatively affected if these delays continue, but your reputation with your customers will be damaged. You have promised them that the problem will be quickly solved and that products will begin arriving on time. Since Richard Hooton is so rigid, however, you are almost certain that it will do no good to talk with him. His subordinate probably got his negative attitude from Hooton.

In general, Hooton is a 1960s production worker who is being pulled by the rest of the firm into the new age of the 1990s. Competition is different, technology is different, and management is different, but Richard is reluctant to change. You need shorter lead times, a wider range of products, and the capacity to do some customized work. Sure, this makes production's work harder, but other firms are providing these services with the use of just-in-time management processes, robots, and so forth.

Instead of getting down to the real problems, the home office, in their typical high-handed fashion, announced an incentives plan. This implies that the problem is in the field, not the factory. It made some of your people angry to think they were being pressed to increase their efforts when they weren't receiving the back-up support in Hartford to get the job done. Sure, they liked the prizes, but the way the plan was presented made them feel as if they weren't working hard enough. This isn't the first time you have questioned the judgment of Barbara, your boss. She certainly is intelligent and hard-working, but she doesn't seem very interested in what's going on out in the field. Furthermore, she doesn't seem very receptive to "bad news" about sales and customer complaints.

[*Note:* During this meeting, use the forcing approach to conflict management and negotiations shown in Table 2. However, don't overplay your part, because you are the senior regional sales manager, and if Barbara continues to move up fast in the organization, you may be in line for her position.]

Skill Application

Activities for Managing Conflict

Suggested Assignments

1. Select a specific conflict with which you are very familiar. Using the framework for identifying the sources of conflict discussed in this chapter, analyze this situation carefully. It might be useful to compare your perceptions of the situation with those of informed observers. What type of conflict is this? Why did it occur? Why is it continuing? Next, using the guidelines for selecting an appropriate conflict management strategy, identify the general approach that would be most appropriate for this situation. Consider both the personal preferences of the parties involved and the relevant situational factors. Is this the approach that the parties have been using? If not, attempt to introduce a different perspective into the relationship and explain why you feel it would be more productive. If the parties have been using this approach, discuss with them why it has not been successful thus far. Share information on specific behavioral guidelines or negotiation tactics that might increase the effectiveness of their efforts.

2. Select three individuals that you know who are from diverse cultural backgrounds and have experience working in American companies. Discuss with them the sources (especially the personal differences) of previous conflicts they have experienced at work. Ask them about their preferences in dealing with conflict situations. What strategies do they prefer to use? How do they generally attempt to resolve disputes? What relevant situational factors influence the way they manage conflict situations with individuals from other cultures and with individuals of their own cultures? With the help of these three persons, identify specific behavioral guidelines for managing conflict more effectively with other persons from their respective cultures.

3. Identify a situation in which another individual is doing something that needs to be corrected. Using the respondent's guidelines for collaborative problem solving, construct a plan for discussing your concerns with this person. Include specific language designed to state your case assertively without causing a defensive reaction. Role-play this interaction with a friend and incorporate any suggestions for improvement. Make your presentation to the individual and report on your results. What was the reaction? Were you successful in balancing assertiveness with support and responsibility? Based on this experience, identify other situations you feel need to be changed and follow a similar procedure.

4. Volunteer to serve as a mediator to resolve a conflict between two individuals or groups. Using the guidelines for implementing the collaborative approach to mediation, outline a plan of action prior to your intervention. Be sure to consider carefully whether or not private meetings with the parties prior to your mediation session are appropriate. Report on the situation and your plan. How did you feel? What specific actions worked well? What was the outcome? What would you do differently? Based on this experience, revise your plan for use in related situations.

5. Identify a difficult situation involving negotiations. This might involve transactions at work, at home, or in the community. Review the guidelines for integrative bargaining and identify the specific tactics you plan to use. Write down specific questions and responses to likely initiatives from the other party. In particular, anticipate how you might handle the possibility of the other party's using a distributive negotiation strategy. Schedule a negotiation meeting with the party involved and implement your plan. Following the session, debrief the experience with a coworker or friend. What did you learn? How successful were you? What would you do differently? Based on this experience, modify your plan and prepare to implement it in related situations.

Application Plan and Evaluation

The intent of this exercise is to help you apply this cluster of skills in a real-life, out-of-class setting. Now that you have become familiar with the behavioral guidelines that form the basis of effective skill performance, you will improve most by trying out those guidelines in an everyday context. Unlike a classroom activity, in which feedback is immediate and others can assist you with their evaluations, this skill application activity is one you must accomplish and evaluate on your own. There are two parts to this activity. Part 1 helps prepare you to apply the skill. Part 2 helps you evaluate and improve on your experience. Be sure to write down answers to each item. Don't short-circuit the process by skipping steps.

Part 1. Planning

1. Write down the two or three aspects of this skill that are most important to you. These may be areas of weakness, areas you most want to improve, or areas that are most salient to a problem you face right now. Identify the specific aspects of this skill that you want to apply.

2. Now identify the setting or the situation in which you will apply this skill. Establish a plan for performance by actually writing down a description of the situation. Who else will be involved? When will you do it? Where will it be done?

   Circumstances:

   Who else?

   When?

   Where?

3. Identify the specific behaviors you will engage in to apply this skill. Operationalize your skill performance.

4. What are the indicators of successful performance? How will you know you have been effective? What will indicate you have performed competently?

Part 2. Evaluation

5. After you have completed your implementation, record the results. What happened? How successful were you? What was the effect on others?

6. How can you improve? What modifications can you make next time? What will you do differently in a similar situation in the future?

7. Looking back on your whole skill practice and application experience, what have you learned? What has been surprising? In what ways might this experience help you in the long term?

Group Skills

Empowering and Delegating

OBJECTIVES

▶ Empower others

▶ Empower yourself

▶ Delegate effectively

Skill Assessment

Diagnostic Surveys for Empowering and Delegating

Effective Empowerment and Delegation

Step 1: Before you read the material in this chapter, please respond to the following statements by writing a number from the rating scale below in the left-hand column (Preassessment). Your answers should reflect your attitudes and behavior as they are now, not as you would like them to be. Be honest. This instrument is designed to help you discover your level of competency in empowering and delegating so you can tailor your learning to your specific needs. When you have completed the survey, use the scoring key in Appendix I to identify the skill areas discussed in this chapter that are most important for you to master.

Step 2: After you have completed the reading and the exercises in this chapter and, ideally, as many as you can of the Skill Application assignments at the end of this chapter, cover up your first set of answers. Then respond to the same statements again, this time in the right-hand column (Postassessment). When you have completed the survey, use the scoring key in Appendix I to measure your progress. If your score remains low in specific skill areas, use the behavioral guidelines at the end of the Skill Learning section to guide further practice.

Rating Scale

1	Strongly disagree	4	Slightly agree
2	Disagree	5	Agree
3	Slightly disagree	6	Strongly agree

Assessment

Pre-   Post-   *In situations where I have an opportunity to empower others:*

_____   _____   1. I help people develop personal mastery in their work by involving them first in less complex tasks, and then in more difficult tasks.

_____   _____   2. I help people feel competent in their work by recognizing and celebrating their small successes.

_____   _____   3. I try to demonstrate successful task accomplishment.

_____   _____   4. I point out other successful people who can serve as role models.

_____   _____   5. I frequently praise, encourage, and express approval of other people.

_____ _____ 6. I provide regular feedback and needed support.

_____ _____ 7. I try to foster friendships and informal interaction.

_____ _____ 8. I highlight the important impact that a person's work will have.

_____ _____ 9. I try to provide all the information that people need to accomplish their tasks.

_____ _____ 10. As I become aware of it, I pass along relevant information to people on a continuous basis.

_____ _____ 11. I ensure that people have the necessary resources (equipment, space, and time) to succeed.

_____ _____ 12. I help people get access to needed resources that I may not have available personally.

_____ _____ 13. I help people become involved in teams in order to increase their participation.

_____ _____ 14. I let teams make decisions and implement their own recommendations.

_____ _____ 15. I foster confidence by being fair and equitable in my decisions.

_____ _____ 16. I exhibit caring and personal concern for each person with whom I have dealings.

When delegating work to others:

_____ _____ 17. I specify clearly the results I desire.

_____ _____ 18. I specify clearly the level of initiative I want others to take (e.g., wait for directions, do part of the task and then report, do the whole task and then report, etc.).

_____ _____ 19. I allow participation by those accepting assignments regarding when and how work will be done.

_____ _____ 20. I make certain that the amount of authority I give matches the amount of responsibility I give for producing results.

_____ _____ 21. I work within existing organizational structures when delegating assignments, and I never bypass someone without informing him or her.

_____ _____ 22. I identify constraints and limitations that people will face but also provide needed support.

_____ _____ 23. I maintain accountability for results, not for methods used.

_____ _____ 24. I delegate consistently—not just when I'm overloaded.

_____ _____ 25. I avoid upward delegation by asking people to recommend solutions, rather than merely asking for advice or answers, when a problem is encountered.

_____ _____ 26. I make clear the consequences of success and failure.

Personal Empowerment Assessment

This instrument helps identify the extent to which you are empowered in your own work. You should respond to the items based on your own job, or, if you are in school, the work you do as a student. The items listed below describe different orientations people can have with respect to their work roles. Using the following scale, indicate the extent to which you believe each is true of you.

Rating Scale

1	Very strongly disagree	5	Agree
2	Strongly disagree	6	Strongly agree
3	Disagree	7	Very strongly agree
4	Neutral		

Assessment

_____ 1. The work that I do is very important to me.

_____ 2. I am confident about my ability to do my work.

_____ 3. I have significant autonomy in determining how I do my job.

_____ 4. I have significant impact on what happens in my work unit.

_____ 5. I trust my coworkers to be completely honest with me.

_____ 6. My work activities are personally meaningful to me.

_____ 7. My work is within the scope of my competence and capabilities.

_____ 8. I can decide how to go about doing my own work.

_____ 9. I have a great deal of control over what happens in my work unit.

_____ 10. I trust my coworkers to share important information with me.

_____ 11. I care about what I do in my work.

_____ 12. I am confident in my capabilities to successfully perform my work.

_____ 13. I have considerable opportunity for independence and freedom in how I do my work.

_____ 14. I have significant influence over what happens in my work unit.

_____ 15. I trust my coworkers to keep the promises they make.

_____ 16. The work I do has special meaning and importance to me.

_____ 17. I have mastered the skills necessary to do my work.

_____ 18. I have a chance to use personal initiative in carrying out my work.

_____ 19. My opinion counts in my work unit's decision making.

_____ 20. I believe that my coworkers care about my well-being.

Skill Learning

Empowering and Delegating

Many management-skills books are oriented toward helping managers know how to control others' behavior. They focus on how managers can increase employees' performance, engender conformity, or motivate employees to achieve certain objectives.

This book, too, includes skills that will help you motivate people to do what you want them to do (see Chapter 6) or achieve power and influence over them (see Chapter 5). The present chapter, however, focuses on a skill called **empowerment** and on a special form of empowerment called **delegation**.

Empowerment is based on a set of assumptions that are in contrast to those normally made by managers. Empowerment means providing freedom for people to do successfully what *they* want to do, rather than getting them to do what *you* want them to do. Managers who empower people remove controls, constraints, and boundaries for them instead of motivating, directing, or stimulating their behavior. Rather than being a "push" strategy, in which managers induce employees to respond in desirable ways through incentives and influence techniques, empowerment is a "pull" strategy. It focuses on ways that managers can design a work situation so that it energizes and provides intrinsic encouragement to employees. In the context of such a strategy, workers accomplish tasks because they are intrinsically attracted by them, not because of an extrinsic reward system or influence technique.

Empowering others, however, can lead to dilemmas. On the one hand, evidence shows that empowered employees are more productive, more satisfied, and more innovative, and that they create higher-quality products and services than nonempowered employees (Sashkin, 1982, 1984; Kanter, 1983; Greenberger & Stasser, 1991; Spreitzer, 1992). Organizations are more effective when an empowered workforce exists (Conger & Kanungo, 1988; Gecas, 1989; Thomas & Velthouse, 1990). On the other hand, empowerment means giving up control and letting others make decisions, set goals, accomplish results, and receive rewards. It means that other people probably will get credit for success. Managers with high needs for power and control (see McClelland, 1975) face a challenge when they are expected to sacrifice their needs for someone else's gain. They may ask themselves: "Why should others get the goodies when I am in charge? Why should I allow others to exercise power, and even facilitate their acquiring more power, when I naturally want to receive rewards and recognition myself?"

The answer is that although empowering others is neither easy nor natural (we aren't born knowing how to do it), it need not actually require a great amount of self-sacrifice. You don't need to sacrifice desired rewards, recognition, or effectiveness in order to be a skillful empowering manager. On the contrary, through real empowerment, managers actually multiply their own effectiveness. They and their organizations become more effective than they could have been otherwise. Nevertheless, for most managers, empowerment is a skill that must be developed and practiced, because despite the high visibility of the concept of empowerment in popular literature, its actual practice is all too rare in modern management.

Evidence for this assertion comes from a national survey by the Louis Harris organization, reported in *Business Week* for January 18, 1993. According to this survey, feelings of powerlessness and alienation among workers have risen sharply in recent years. The percentage of workers answering yes to the questions in Table 1 illustrates this trend.

In this chapter, we begin by discussing the core dimensions of empowerment and, in particular, how to effectively accomplish empowerment. In the second part of this section, we discuss a special situation in which empowerment is essential: the delegation of responsibility. We conclude with a summary model of empowerment and delegation and a list of behavioral guidelines for successfully empowering and delegating to others.

QUESTION	1972	1985	1992
What I think doesn't count very much anymore.	50%	62%	62%
Most people with power take advantage of people like myself.	43	65	71
The people in charge don't really care what happens to me.	46	65	71
I'm left out of things going on around me.	25	48	48

Table 1 Powerlessness and Alienation Survey

A Management Dilemma Involving Empowerment

One of the most well-researched findings in organization and management science over the last four decades has shown that when environments are predictable and stable, organizations can function as routine, controlled, mechanistic units. Under such conditions, workers can be expected to follow rules and procedures and to engage in standardized, formalized behavior. Managers can maintain control and issue top-down mandates regarding the strategy and direction to be pursued by the organization. However, the modern business environment is often described using terms such as *hyper-turbulence, complexity, speed, competition,* and *revolutionary change.* Under such conditions, prescriptions for organizational and management effectiveness call for a flexible, autonomous, entrepreneurial workforce (Peters, 1992; Drucker, 1988), rather than one that relies on management for direction and control. Less-centralized decision making, less top-down direction, and less-autocratic leadership are all prescribed as prerequisites for high-performing modern organizations.

When environments are unstable and unpredictable—when they change a lot or in unpredictable ways—organizations must be more flexible and organic. Workers are expected to be adaptable and self-managing. Managers must involve others in decision making and facilitate broad participation and accountability (Eisenhart, 1993; Lawrence & Lorsch, 1967). The workers' flexibility must match the flexibility of the environment (Ashby, 1956).

Our own research has shown, however, that instead of becoming adaptable, flexible, autonomous, and self-managing, individuals in rapidly changing, complex environments tend to behave in opposite ways than they should in order to succeed. Both managers and employees tend to become less flexible, less adaptable, less autonomous, less self-managing, more stable, more rigid, and more defensive when they face turbulence and change (Cameron, Whetten, & Kim, 1987; Cameron, Kim, & Whetten, 1987).

In our research on how organizations are managed when they face decline, turbulence, downsizing, and change, we have identified 12 negative attributes or attitudes, which we label "the dirty dozen." Table 2 summarizes these negative attitudes.

The Dirty Dozen

Among the dirty dozen attributes is a "threat-rigidity" response (Staw, Sandelands, & Dutton, 1981; Weick, 1993), in which people become conservative. They hunker down and become self-protective and increasingly rely on old, first-learned habits and past behaviors. In reaction to a perceived threat, they do that which they know how to do best or that which has worked best in the past. Despite new circumstances in which old behaviors may not be effective, there is an escalating commitment to habitual behavior. People consider fewer options, look for information that confirms their previous biases, and become more narrow-minded in their perspectives. In addition, less communication occurs among workers. When individuals in organizations are divulging information, they become vulnerable by putting their personal expertise or untested ideas at risk. This sense of vulnerability magnifies the feeling of uncertainty brought about by changing conditions. Under such circumstances, people are less likely to become contributing team mem-

ATTRIBUTE	EXPLANATION
Centralization	Decision making is pulled toward the top of the organization. Less power is shared.
Threat-rigidity response	Conservative, self-protective behaviors predominate. Old habits persist. Change is resisted.
Loss of innovativeness	Trial-and-error learning stops. Low tolerance for risk and creativity occurs.
Decreasing morale	In-fighting and a mean mood permeate the organization. It isn't fun.
Politicized environment	Special-interest groups organize and become vocal. Everything is negotiated.
Loss of trust	Leaders lose the confidence of subordinates. Distrust predominates among employees.
Increased conflict	In-fighting and competition occur. Self-centeredness predominates over the good of the organization.
Restricted communication	Only good news is passed upward. Information is not widely shared and is held close to the vest.
Lack of teamwork	Individualism and disconnectedness inhibit teamwork. Lack of coordination occurs.
Loss of loyalty	Commitment to the organization and to the leader erodes. Focus is on defending oneself.
Scapegoating leaders	Leadership anemia occurs as leaders are criticized, priorities become blurred, and a siege mentality occurs.
Short-term perspective	A crisis mentality is adopted. Long-term planning and flexibility are avoided.

Table 2   The Dirty Dozen: Outcomes of Stress in Organizations
Source: Adapted from Cameron et al. (1987).

bers and to try out new, innovative ideas. Fear and conflict increase, while trust, morale, and productivity decrease. A "mean mood" is typical of most interactions, as loyalty and commitment to the organization erode. The tendency in such circumstances is for most important decisions to be made at the top of the organizational hierarchy because managers at the top feel an increasing need to be in control and to be closer to decisions. On the other hand, people at lower organizational levels become hesitant to make decisions without getting approval from a superior.

How can we ever expect a workforce in the modern, changing environment to develop the prescribed characteristics for effectiveness—that is, to be adaptable, flexible, autonomous, and self-managing? If people become more rigid and resistant in uncertain times rather than more independent, how can we ever foster effective performance?

The answer to these questions is to use empowerment. If managers are skilled at empowering workers, the inertia that drives organizations toward dysfunctional dirty dozen attitudes is counteracted. Workers become more effective, even in the face of trying times. Empowerment is a key to unlocking the potential of a successful workforce in an era of chaotic change and escalating competitive conditions.

But what is empowerment? What does it mean to be an empowered worker? What is the set of management skills associated with empowerment?

The Meaning of Empowerment

To empower means to enable; it means to help people develop a sense of self-confidence; it means to help people overcome feelings of powerlessness or helplessness; it means to energize people to take action; it means to mobilize intrinsic motivation to accomplish a task.

Empowered people not only possess the wherewithal to accomplish something, but they also think of themselves differently than they did before they were empowered.

Empowerment is different from merely giving power to someone. Like empowerment, power connotes the ability to get things done (see the chapter on Gaining Power and Influence). But power and empowerment are not the same thing. Table 3 contrasts the concepts of power and empowerment so as to highlight their differences. People may both have power and be empowered. However, although one can *give* someone else power, one must *accept* empowerment for oneself. You cannot empower me; you can only create the circumstances in which I can empower myself.

As explained in the chapter on Gaining Power and Influence, the acquisition of power is based on several personal factors and certain position attributes. In each case, other people need to acknowledge your power, follow your lead, and acquiesce to your influence in order for you to have power. The underlying source of your power is other people. In the case of empowerment, however, an individual can be empowered even if no one acknowledges his or her personal attributes or position. Victor Frankl, Nelson Mandela, and Mahatma Gandhi are examples of individuals who, despite the absence of the attributes of power, maintained complete empowerment in dismal circumstances (i.e., in prison and in a bigoted environment). This is because the source of empowerment is internal. One accepts it for oneself. In addition, if I become more powerful, that generally means you become less powerful. If I have the power to get someone to do what I want, but that differs from what you want, my power and your power come into conflict. That's why, ultimately, relatively few people have power and why it tends to lead toward conflict. Power games become a clash of wills or a battle to see who will win and reign supreme. On the other hand, every person can be empowered without affecting any other person's position or stature. It merely leads to each of us being enabled to accomplish what we choose.

Historical Roots of Empowerment

The word empowerment has been in vogue in the 1980s and 1990s. The concept of empowerment has been referred to in many books and articles in the last few years, and it has become popular to use the term to refer to everything from team-building to decentralized structures. In fact, the word has been so overused that its precise meaning may have become obscured. It may be helpful, therefore, to provide a brief background of the roots of empowerment because it is by no means a new concept. This should help us avoid confusing empowerment with other related management behaviors.

Empowerment has roots in the disciplines of psychology, sociology, and theology dating back for decades—even centuries. In the field of psychology, Adler (1927) developed the concept of "mastery motivation," emphasizing the striving that people have for competence in dealing with their world. Similar concepts introduced several decades ago include "effectance motivation," an intrinsic motivation to make things happen (White, 1959); "psychological reactance," which refers to seeking freedom from constraints (Brehm, 1966); "competence motivation," a striving to encounter and master challenges (Harter, 1978); and "personal causation," a drive to experience

POWER	EMPOWERMENT
External source	Internal source
Ultimately, few people have it	Ultimately, everyone can have it
The capacity to have others do what you want	The capacity to have others do what they want
To get more implies taking it away from someone else	To get more does not affect how much others have
Leads to competition	Leads to cooperation

Table 3 The Difference Between Power and Empowerment

free agency (DeCharms, 1979). In each of these studies, the root concepts are similar to the notion of empowerment discussed in this chapter: that is, the inclination of people to experience self-control, self-importance, and self-liberation.

In sociology, notions of empowerment have been fundamental to most "rights" movements (e.g., Civil Rights, Women's Rights, Gay Rights) (see Solomon, 1976; Bookman & Morgan, 1988), in which people campaign for freedom and control of their own circumstances. Moreover, much of the writing attacking societal problems through social change has centered fundamentally on the empowerment of groups of people (Marx, 1844; Alinsky, 1971). That is, people seek social change in order to increase their access to an empowered condition.

In theology, debates about free will versus determinism, self-will versus submissiveness, predestination versus faith and works, and humanism versus positivism have been hotly debated for centuries. At their root, they are all variations on a theme of empowerment versus helplessness. The more recent literature on "liberation theology" (Friere & Faundez, 1989) emphasizes the empowerment of individuals to take charge of their own destinies, rather than relying solely and completely on the dictates of an all-controlling, supernatural force. This does not mean that people who believe in a Supreme Being cannot feel empowered; rather empowered people couple a sense of self-mastery and self-determination with their faith in a higher power.

Empowerment is not a new concept. It has appeared in various forms throughout modern management literature. In the 1950s, for example, management literature was filled with prescriptions that managers should be friendly to employees (human relations); in the 1960s, that managers should be sensitive to the needs and motivations of people (sensitivity training); in the 1970s, that managers should ask employees for help (employee involvement); and, in the 1980s, that managers should form teams and hold meetings (quality circles) (see Byham, 1988). The continuation of these themes in the 1990s and beyond suggests that managers should learn how to foster empowerment. But despite the continuing emphasis on various versions of employee involvement and empowerment, the ability to empower employees is still not common in most managers' repertoire of skills. Empowerment is more rarely seen than prescribed.

Inhibitors to Empowerment

In his book on managerial empowerment, Peter Block (1987, p. 154) noted that empowerment is very difficult to accomplish:

> Many, increasingly aware of the price we pay for too many controls, have had the belief that if some of these controls were removed, a tremendous amount of positive energy in service of the organization would be released. While in many cases this has happened, too often our attempts at giving people more responsibility have been unwelcome and met with persistent reluctance. Many managers have tried repeatedly to open the door of participation to their people, only to find them reluctant to walk through it. [In a study of managers who were offered total responsibility for their work areas], about 20 percent of the managers took the responsibility and ran with it, about 50 percent of the managers cautiously tested the sincerity of the offer and then over a period of six months began to make their own decisions. The frustrating part of the effort was that the other 30 percent absolutely refused to take the reins. They clutched tightly to their dependency and continued to complain that top management did not really mean it, they were not given enough people or resources to really do their job, and the unique characteristics of their particular location made efforts at participative management unreasonable.

As Block noted, many managers and employees are reluctant to accept empowerment, but they are even more reluctant to offer empowerment. One reason for this is the personal attitudes of managers. Several management surveys, for example, have examined the reasons managers have for not being willing to empower their employees (Newman & Warren, 1977; Preston & Zimmerer, 1978; Byham, 1988). These reasons can be organized into three broad categories.

1. **Attitudes about subordinates.** Managers who avoid empowering others often believe their subordinates are not competent enough to accomplish the work, aren't interested in taking on more responsibility, are already overloaded and unable to accept more responsibility, would require too much time to train, or shouldn't be

involved in tasks or responsibilities typically performed by the boss. They feel that the problem of nonempowerment lies with the employees, not with themselves. The rationale is: *I'm willing to empower my people, but they just won't accept the responsibility.*

2. **Personal insecurities.** Some managers fear they will lose the recognition and rewards associated with successful task accomplishment if they empower others. They are unwilling to share their expertise or "trade secrets" for fear of losing power or position. They have an intolerance for ambiguity which leads them to feel that they personally must know all the details about projects assigned to them. They prefer working on tasks by themselves rather than getting others involved, or they are unwilling to absorb the costs associated with subordinates making mistakes. The rationale is: *I'm willing to empower people, but when I do, they either mess things up or try to grab all the glory.*

3. **Need for control.** Nonempowering managers also often have a high need to be in charge and to direct and govern what is going on. They presume that an absence of clear direction and goals from the boss and a slackening of controls will lead to confusion, frustration, and failure on the part of employees. They feel that direction from the top is mandatory. Moreover, they often see short-lived, disappointing results from pep talks, work teams, suggestion systems, job enrichment programs, and other fix-it activities ("We tried that, and it didn't work"). The rationale is: *I'm willing to empower people, but they require clear directions and a clear set of guidelines; otherwise, the lack of instructions leads to confusion.*

The rationale associated with each of these inhibitors may be partially true, but they nevertheless inhibit managers from achieving the success associated with skillful empowerment. Even if managers demonstrate the willingness and courage to empower others, success still requires skillful implementation. Incompetent empowerment, in fact, can undermine rather than enhance the effectiveness of an organization and its employees. For example, such incompetent empowerment as giving employees freedom without clear directions or resources has been found to lead to psychological casualties among individuals, as manifested by increased depression (Alloy, Peterson, Abrahamson, & Seligman, 1984), heightened stress (Averill, 1973), decreased performance and job satisfaction (Greenberger, Stasser, Cummings, & Dunham, 1989), lowered alertness, and even in-

creased mortality (Langer & Rodin, 1976). Of course, these negative consequences are not solely associated with incompetent empowerment. But they have been noted, nevertheless, in situations where attempted empowerment was ineffective and unskillful. For example, when managers associated empowerment with behaviors such as "simply letting go," refusing to clarify expectations, abdicating responsibility, having an absence of ground-rules, or giving inflexible or inconsistent directions—none of which are consistent with skillful empowerment—the results were not only unsuccessful, but even harmful. Because of the negative psychological and physiological consequences for workers resulting from nonempowerment or from incompetent empowerment, Sashkin (1984) labelled skillful empowerment "an ethical imperative" for managers.

Dimensions of Empowerment

In one of the best empirical studies of empowerment to date, Spreitzer (1992) identified four dimensions of empowerment. We have added one dimension to her model, based on the research of Mishra (1992). In this section, we explain these five key dimensions of empowerment. In order for managers to empower others successfully, they must engender these five qualities in those they intend to empower. Skillful empowerment means producing (1) a sense of *self-efficacy,* (2) a sense of *self-determination,* (3) a sense of *personal consequence,* (4) a sense of *meaning,* and (5) a sense of *trust* in other people (see Table 4). When managers are able to foster these five attributes in others, they have successfully empowered them. We suggested earlier that empowered people not only can accomplish tasks, but that they also think differently about themselves. These five dimensions describe that difference. After explaining the five dimensions, we provide guidelines for engendering each of them.

Self-Efficacy

When people are empowered, they have a sense of self-efficacy, or the feeling that they possess the capability and competence to perform a task successfully. Empowered people not only feel *competent,* they feel *con-*

DIMENSION	EXPLANATION
Self-efficacy	A sense of personal competence
Self-determination	A sense of personal choice
Personal consequence	A sense of having impact
Meaningfulness	A sense of value in activity
Trust	A sense of security

Table 4   Five Core Dimensions of Empowerment

fident that they can perform adequately. They feel a sense of personal mastery and believe they can learn and grow to meet new challenges (see Bennis & Nanus, 1985; Conger & Kanungo, 1988; Bandura, 1989; Gecas, 1989; Zimmerman, 1990). Some writers believe that this is the most important element in empowerment because having a sense of self-efficacy determines whether people will try and persist in attempting to accomplish a difficult task.

> The strength of people's conviction in their own effectiveness is likely to affect whether they would even try to cope with given situations. . . . They get involved in activities and behave assuredly when they judge themselves capable of handling situations that would otherwise be intimidating. . . . Efficacy expectations determine how much effort people will expend and how long they will persist in the face of obstacles and aversive experiences (Bandura, 1977, pp. 193–194).

A great deal of research has been done on the consequences of self-efficacy and its opposite, powerlessness, especially in relation to physical and psychological health. For example, self-efficacy has been found to be a significant factor in overcoming phobias and anxieties (Bandura, 1986), alcohol and drug abuse (Seeman & Anderson, 1983), eating disorders (Schneider & Agras, 1985), smoking addiction (DiClemente, 1985), depression (Seligman, 1975), as well as increasing tolerance for pain (Neufeld & Thomas, 1977). Recovery from illness and injury, as well as coping with job loss or disruptions, is more effective and more rapid among people who have developed a strong sense of self-efficacy, because they are more physically and psychologically resilient and are bet-

ter able to change negative behaviors (Schwalbe & Gecas, 1988; Gecas, Seff, & Ray, 1988).

Bandura (1977) suggested that three conditions are necessary for people to feel a sense of self-efficacy: (1) a belief that they have the ability to perform a task, (2) a belief that they are capable of putting forth the necessary effort, and (3) a belief that no outside obstacles will prevent them from accomplishing the task. In other words, people feel empowered when they develop a sense of self-efficacy by having a basic level of competence and capability, a willingness to put forth effort to accomplish a task, and the absence of overwhelming inhibitors to success.

Self-Determination

Empowered people also have a sense of self-determination. Whereas self-efficacy refers to a sense of competence, self-determination refers to feelings of *having a choice.* "To be self-determining means to experience a sense of choice in initiating and regulating one's own actions" (Deci, Connell, & Ryan, 1989, p. 580). People feel self-determined when they can voluntarily and intentionally involve themselves in tasks, rather than being forced or prohibited from involvement. Their actions are a consequence of personal freedom and autonomy. Empowered individuals have a sense of responsibility for and ownership of their activities (Rappoport, Swift, & Hess, 1984; Rose & Black, 1985; Staples, 1990; Zimmerman, 1990). They see themselves as proactive self-starters. They are able to take initiative on their own accord, make independent decisions, and try out new ideas (Conger & Kanungo, 1988; Thomas & Valthouse, 1990; Vogt & Murrell,

1990). Rather than feeling that their actions are predetermined, externally controlled, or inevitable, they experience themselves as the locus of control.

In the chapter on Developing Self-Awareness, we discussed the difference between an internal and external locus of control. People who feel a sense of empowerment are most likely to have an internal locus of control: that is, they feel that they control what happens to them.

Research shows that a strong sense of self-determination is associated with less alienation in the work environment (Seeman, 1982), more work satisfaction (Organ & Green, 1974), higher levels of work performance (Anderson, Hellriegel, & Slocum, 1977), more entrepreneurial and innovative activity (Hammer & Vardi, 1981), high levels of job involvement (Runyon, 1973), and less job strain (Gennill & Heisler, 1972). In medical research, recovery from severe illness has been found to be associated with having the patient "reject the traditional passive role and insist on being an active participant in his own therapy" (Gecas, 1989, p. 298). People who are helped to feel that they can have personal impact on what happens to them, even with regard to the effects of disease, are more likely to experience positive outcomes than those who lack this feeling.

Self-determination is associated most directly with having choices about the *methods* used to accomplish a task, the amount of *effort* to be expended, the *pace* of the work, and the *time frame* in which it is to be accomplished. Empowered individuals have a feeling of ownership for tasks because they can determine how they are accomplished, when they are accomplished, and how quickly they are completed. Having a choice is the critical component of self-determination.

Personal Consequence

Empowered people have a sense of personal control over outcomes. They believe that they can make a difference by influencing the environment in which they work or the outcomes being produced. Personal consequence is "an individual's beliefs at a given point in time in his or her ability to effect a change in a desired direction" (Greenberger, Stasser, Cummings, & Dunham, 1989, p. 165). It is the conviction that through one's own actions, a person can influence what happens. A sense of personal consequence, then, refers to a perception of *impact*.

Empowered individuals do not believe that obstacles in the external environment control their actions; rather, they believe that those obstacles can be controlled. They have a feeling of "active control"—which allows them to bring their environment into alignment with their wishes—as opposed to "passive control"—in which their wishes are brought into alignment with environmental demands (see Rothbaum, Weisz, & Snyder, 1982; Rappoport, Swift, & Hess, 1988; Zimmerman & Rappoport, 1988; Greenberger & Stasser, 1991; Thomas & Velthouse, 1990). Instead of being reactive to what they see around them, people with a sense of personal consequence try to maintain command over what they see.

Having a sense of personal consequence is closely related to a sense of self-control. For individuals to feel empowered, they must not only feel that what they do produces an effect, but that they can produce the effect themselves. That is, they must feel that they are in control of producing the consequence in order for that consequence to be associated with a sense of empowerment.

Research on personal control suggests that people are intrinsically motivated to seek personal control (White, 1959). They fight to maintain a sense of control of themselves and their situations. Prisoners of war, for example, have been known to do strange things such as refusing to eat certain foods, not walking in a certain place, or developing secret communication codes, in order to maintain a sense of personal control. A certain amount of personal control is necessary for people to maintain psychological and physical well-being. When people lose personal control over themselves, we usually label them as insane and psychopathic.

Even small losses of personal control can be harmful physically and emotionally. For example, loss of control has been found to lead to depression, stress, anxiety, low morale, loss of productivity, burnout, learned helplessness, and even increased death rates (see Langer, 1983; Greenberger & Stasser, 1991). Having a sense of personal control, then, appears necessary for health as well as for empowerment. On the other hand, even the most empowered people are not able to control totally everything that happens to them. No one is in complete control of the outcomes in his or her life. Nevertheless, empowerment helps people increase the number of personal outcomes that they can control. Often, this is as much a matter of identifying areas in which personal consequence is possible as it is of manipulating or changing the external environment to increase control over it.

Meaning

Empowered people have a sense of meaning. They value the purpose or goals of the activity in which they are engaged. Their own ideals and standards are perceived as consistent with what they are doing. The activity "counts" in their own value system. Empowered individuals believe in and care about what they produce. They invest psychic or spiritual energy in the activity, and they feel a sense of personal significance from their involvement. They experience personal connectedness and personal integrity as a result of engaging in the activity (Rappoport, 1981; Bennis & Nanus, 1985; Block, 1987; Conger & Kanungo, 1988; Manz & Sims, 1989). Meaningfulness, then, refers to a perception of *value*.

Activities infused with meaning create a sense of purpose, passion, or mission for people. They provide a source of energy and enthusiasm, rather than draining energy and enthusiasm from people. Merely getting paid, helping an organization earn money, or just doing a job does not create a sense of meaning for most people. Something more fundamental, more personal, and more value-laden must be linked to the activity. It must be associated with something more human.

Acquiring personal benefit does not guarantee meaning. For example, service to others may bring no personal reward, yet it may be far more meaningful than work that produces a hefty paycheck. Involvement in activities without meaning, on the other hand, creates dissonance and annoyance, and produces a sense of disengagement from the work. People become bored or exhausted. Other incentives—such as rules, supervision, or extra pay—are required to get people to invest in the work. Unfortunately, these extra incentives are costly to organizations and represent nonvalue-added expenses that constrain organizational efficiency and effectiveness. It costs companies a lot of money to require work that has little or no meaning to workers. Self-estrangement results from lack of meaning; vigor and stimulation result from meaningful work (see Hackman & Oldham, 1980; Brief & Nord, 1990; Kahn, 1990; Thomas & Velthouse, 1990).

Research on meaningfulness in work has found that when individuals engage in work which they feel is meaningful, they are more committed to it and more involved in it. They have a higher concentration of energy and are more persistent in pursuing desired goals than when a sense of meaningfulness is low. People feel more excitement and passion for their work and have a greater sense of personal significance and self-worth because of their association with activity that is meaningful. Individuals empowered with a sense of meaningfulness also have been found to be more innovative, upwardly influential, and personally effective than those with low meaningfulness scores (Kanter, 1968; Bramucci, 1977; Nielson, 1986; Deci & Ryan, 1987; Vogt & Murrell, 1990; Spreitzer, 1992).

Trust

Finally, empowered people have a sense of trust. They are confident that they will be treated fairly and equitably. They maintain an assurance that even if they are in subordinate positions, the ultimate outcome of their actions will be justice and goodness as opposed to harm or hurt. Usually, this means they have confidence that those holding authority or power positions will not harm or injure them, and that they will be treated impartially. However, even in circumstances where individuals holding power positions do not demonstrate integrity and fairness, empowered people still maintain a sense of personal assurance. Trust means, in other words, having a sense of personal *security*. Trust also implies that individuals place themselves in a position of vulnerability (Zand, 1972). Yet empowered individuals have faith that, ultimately, no harm will come to them as a result of that trust (Deutsch, 1973; Luhmann, 1979; Barber, 1983; Mishra, 1992).

How can a person maintain trust and a sense of security even when caught in a circumstance that seems unfair, inequitable, or even dangerous? In his attempts to gain independence for India, for example, Gandhi determined that he would burn the passes that the British government required be carried by all native Indians but not by British citizens. Gandhi called a meeting and publicly announced his intent to resist this law by burning the passes of each of his Indian supporters. In a now famous incident, after Gandhi burned several of the passes, the British police intervened by clubbing him with nightsticks. Despite the beating, Gandhi continued to burn passes. Where is the security in this case? In what did Gandhi have trust? Was Gandhi empowered or not? Gandhi's sense of security came not from the British authorities but from his faith in the principles that he espoused. His sense of security was associated with his belief that doing the right thing always leads, ultimately, to the right consequence.

Research on trust has found that trusting individuals are more apt to replace superficiality and facades with directness and intimacy; they are more apt to be open, honest, and congruent rather than deceptive or shallow. They are more search-oriented and self-determining, more self-assured and willing to learn. They have a larger capacity for interdependent relationships, and they display a greater degree of cooperation and risk-taking in groups than do those with low trust. Trusting people are more willing to try to get along with others and to be a contributing part of a team. They are also more self-disclosing, more honest in their own communication, and more able to listen carefully to others. They have less resistance to change and are better able to cope with unexpected traumas than are those with low levels of trust. Individuals who trust others are more likely to be trustworthy themselves and to maintain high personal ethical standards (see Gibb & Gibb, 1969; Golembiewski & McConkie, 1975; Mishra, 1992).

Because "trusting environments allow individuals to unfold and flourish" (Golembiewski & McConkie, 1975, p. 134), empowerment is closely tied to a sense of trust. Having a feeling that the behavior of others is consistent and reliable, that information can be held in confidence, and that promises will be kept all are a part of developing a sense of empowerment in people. Trusting others allows people to act in a confident and straightforward manner, without wasting energy on self-protection, trying to uncover hidden agendas, or playing politics. In brief, a sense of trust empowers people to feel secure.

Review of Empowerment Dimensions

The main point of our discussion thus far is to show that fostering the five attributes of empowerment in individuals—*self-efficacy* (a sense of competence), *self-determination* (a sense of choice), *personal consequence* (a sense of impact), *meaning* (a sense of value), and *trust* (a sense of security)—produces very positive outcomes. Research findings associated with each of the five dimensions of empowerment indicate that both personal and organizational advantages result when people feel empowered. Negative consequences occur, on the other hand, when people experience the opposite of empowerment, such as powerlessness, helplessness, and alienation. Helping people feel a certain way about themselves and their work helps them to be more effective in the behaviors they display. Some authors have gone so far as to claim that helping others develop this feeling of empowerment is at the very root of managerial effectiveness. Without it, they claim, neither managers nor organizations can be successful in the long term (Kanter, 1983; Bennis & Nanus, 1985; Block, 1987; Conger, 1989). As a psychological state, however, empowerment is never under the complete control of a manager. Individuals can refuse to feel empowered. Still, a sense of empowerment can be influenced significantly by the conditions in which people find themselves. For that reason, the next section of this chapter discusses specific actions managers can take to empower others.

How to Develop Empowerment

People are most in need of empowerment when they are faced with situations they perceive to be threatening, unclear, overly controlled, coercive, or isolating; when they experience inappropriate feelings of dependency or inadequacy; when they feel stifled in their ability to do what they would like to do; when they are uncertain about how to behave; when they feel that some negative consequence is imminent; and when they feel unrewarded and unappreciated.

Ironically, most large organizations engender these kinds of feelings in people, because, as Block (1987) noted, bureaucracy encourages dependency and submission. Rules, routines, and traditions define what can be done, stifling and supplanting initiative and discretion. In such circumstances, the formal organization—not the individual—is the recipient of empowerment. Therefore, in large organizations, empowerment is especially needed.

But empowerment is also key in environments outside of vast bureaucracies. For example, studies demonstrate positive effects of empowerment on child development, learning in school, coping with personal stress, and changing personal habits (see Ozer & Bandura, 1990).

Despite the applicability of empowerment in many different contexts, our discussion considers ways in which managers can empower their employees. We focus on empowerment mainly as a *management* skill, even though people in other roles, such as parents, teachers, coaches, tutors, and friends, can also benefit by developing the skills of empowerment.

Research by Kanter (1983), Bandura (1986), Hackman and Oldham (1980), and others has produced at least nine specific prescriptions for fostering empowerment, that is, producing a sense of competence, choice, impact, value, and security. These include (1) articulating a clear vision and goals, (2) fostering personal mastery experiences, (3) modeling, (4) providing support, (5) creating emotional arousal, (6) providing necessary information, (7) providing necessary resources, (8) connecting to outcomes, and (9) creating confidence. Each of these prescriptions is discussed below. Figure 1 illustrates their relationships to the five core dimensions of empowerment.

Some of these prescriptions are similar to the guidelines found in the chapters on Communicating Supportively, Gaining Power and Influence, and Motivating Employees. Because a completely separate and unique set of managerial skills does not exist for communicating with, influencing, and motivating others, some commonality and overlap is inevitable. On the other hand, the context of empowerment sheds a different light on some of the guidelines you have read about before.

Articulating a Clear Vision and Goals

Creating an environment in which individuals can feel empowered requires that they be guided by a clearly articulated vision of where the organization is going and how they can contribute as individuals. All of us desire to know the purpose of the activities in which we engage, what the ultimate objective is, and how we fit into that objective. The worst circumstance we can

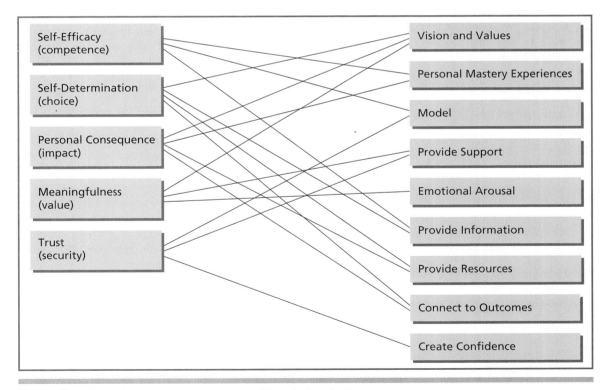

Figure 1   Relationships Between Dimensions and Prescriptions for Empowerment

experience is one with a total lack of direction, where people do whatever comes to mind, or where no common objective or goal is evident. This is the classical condition—labeled *anomie*—that leads to anarchy, chaos, and even death (Durkheim, 1963). To avoid such chaotic conditions, a clear vision and an established set of goals must be articulated so that behavior remains congruent with organizational purposes.

Cameron and Quinn (1998), Martin et al. (1983), and others have reported that several studies confirm that the most effective way to articulate a vision in a clear and energizing way is by using word pictures, stories, metaphors, and real-life examples. That is, individuals are more likely to understand a vision if it has both right brain (intuitive, pictorial, story-based) as well as left brain (logical, reasonable, performance-based) elements associated with it. Not only do people understand communication more clearly when it contains stories and examples as well as descriptions, but they develop more of a sense of self-determination ("I can see the alternatives available"), a sense of personal consequence ("I can see how I can influence the outcomes"), and a sense of meaning ("I can see why this is so important").

Empowerment is also enhanced as specific behavioral goals are identified that help guide individuals' behavior as they work on their tasks. Goals specify desired outcomes as well as accountability. Locke and Latham (1990) identified the attributes of the most effective goals, and the acronym "SMART goals" best summarizes these attributes.

Specific goals—those that are identifiable, behavioral, and observable.

Measurable goals—those that have outcome criteria associated with them, that can be assessed objectively, and where the degree of successful accomplishment can be determined. One can evaluate the accomplishment of measurable goals.

Aligned goals—those that are congruent with the overall purposes and vision of the organization. Their accomplishment contributes to the broader good.

Reachable goals—realistic goals, those that are not so far above the capacity of the individual that they become discouraging at best and considered nonsense at worst. Reachable does not mean easily achieved, because research is clear that difficult goals are better motivators of behavior and predict higher levels of accomplishment than do easy goals (Locke & Latham, 1990).

Time-bound goals—that is, a time for accomplishing the goals is specified. Goals that have no ending point are not effective; a deadline for achievement is clear.

The point is individuals are empowered as they are provided a clear vision of the future and some specific, behavioral goals that help clarify how they can get there.

Fostering Personal Mastery Experiences

Bandura (1986) found that the single most important thing a manager can do to empower other people is to help them experience personal mastery over some challenge or problem. By successfully accomplishing a task, defeating an opponent, or resolving a problem, people develop a sense of mastery. Personal mastery can be fostered by providing people with the opportunity to accomplish successively more difficult tasks which eventually lead to the accomplishment of desirable goals. The key is to start with easy tasks and then progress by small steps to more difficult tasks until the person experiences a sense of mastery over an entire complex of problems.

Managers can help workers feel increasingly empowered by helping them develop an awareness that they can succeed. One way to do this is by breaking apart large tasks and giving workers only one part at a time. The manager watches for small successes achieved by workers and then highlights and celebrates them. Jobs can be expanded incrementally so that tasks becomes broader and more complex as workers master the basic elements. Employees are given further problem-solving responsibility as they succeed in resolving rudimentary difficulties. Managers can also provide opportunities for employees to direct or lead others in a project, task force, or committee.

When managers adopt a *small-wins strategy,* individuals get opportunities to succeed in small ways, even though an overall challenge may be formidable (Weick, 1979). Small wins can occur when large problems are divided up into limited units that can be attacked individually. Small wins may seem insignificant by themselves, but they generate a sense of movement, progress, and success. The recognition and celebration of small wins generates momentum that leads people to feel empowered and capable.

Lee Iacocca used this strategy to turn around a failing Chrysler Corporation in the early 1980s. An analysis of his speeches to the top management team at Chrysler over a period of five years reveals that even though Chrysler was losing money, costs were too high, and quality was a major problem, Iacocca continued to celebrate small successes. For example, he regularly announced that a certain amount of money was saved, a particular improvement was produced, a certain executive was hired away from the competition, or a compliment was received from a Wall Street analyst, even though the firm was losing a billion dollars a year. A great deal of emphasis was placed on succeeding at small things, all of which were aimed at eventually toppling the much larger challenge of company survival. In this case, continual small wins led to a big achievement.

Modeling

Another way to empower people is to model or demonstrate the correct behavior that they are to perform. Observing someone else succeed at challenging activities, Bandura (1977) found, provides a forceful impetus for others to believe that they, too, can succeed. It helps people presume that a task is do-able, that a job is within their capabilities, and that success is possible.

The manager may serve as the role model by demonstrating desired behaviors. On the other hand, it may not be possible for a manager to model desired behaviors personally for every single employee. The manager may not see an employee often enough to show him or her how to accomplish work or to frequently demonstrate success. Alternatively, however, managers may be able to draw their employees' attention to other people who have been successful in similar circumstances. They might make it possible for employees to associate with senior or visible people who could serve as role models, and they could provide opportunities for workers to be coached by these successful people. They can partner employees with mentors who can discuss their own past experiences that were similar to the employee's.

In other words, empowering people involves making available examples of past success. This is consistent with the learning model upon which this book is based. The Skill Analysis step of the learning model exemplifies appropriate and inappropriate behavior engaged in by others. It provides a model of people who have succeeded in accomplishing the desired skill. This modeling function helps foster a sense of empowerment in individuals who are trying to develop and improve management skills by showing ways in which such skills can be showcased successfully.

Think of what happens when a barrier is broken. In track and field athletics, for example, once John Thomas broke the seven-foot high jump mark and Roger Bannister broke the four-minute mile record, a host of other athletes quickly exceeded that standard. But before the first person broke those barriers, they were considered insurmountable. It took someone to demonstrate that the standard could be exceeded in order for others to experience the empowerment necessary to replicate the accomplishment themselves.

Providing Support

A fourth technique for helping others experience empowerment is providing them with social and emotional support. If people are to feel empowered, managers should praise them, encourage them, express approval of them, back them, and reassure them. Kanter (1983) and Bandura (1986) each found that a crucial part of empowerment is having responsive and supportive managers. Managers seeking to empower their subordinates should find ways to praise their performance regularly. They can write letters or notes to workers, to members of their unit, or even to their family indicating that the employee's good work has been noticed. They can provide feedback to workers about their abilities and competencies. They can arrange for opportunities where workers can receive social support from others by becoming part of a team or social unit. They can express confidence in employees by supervising them less closely or by allowing longer time intervals to elapse before requiring them to report results. Managers can hold regular ceremonies where employees' achievements are recognized. It may simply be a matter of listening to employees and trying to understand their feelings and points of view.

Managers can empower others, then, by engendering a feeling that they are accepted, that they are a valued asset, and that they are an integral part of the overall organizational mission or objective. This support can come from either the manager or coworkers.

Cameron, Freeman, and Mishra (1991), for example, described a variety of support activities undertaken by a highly effective manager who was forced to lay off workers due to a corporate downsizing mandate. Understandably, the layoffs resulted in undermined employee trust, increased skepticism, and an escalated sense of powerlessness. Because the announcement came down from the parent company, workers felt that they had lost the ability to control their own destinies. In short, they felt unempowered. Following the layoff, the manager held personal meetings with each remaining employee to reaffirm his or her value to the organization. People were told in a straightforward manner that they were considered valuable human resources, not human liabilities, to the company. A special "Build with Pride" week was held in which outsiders—the press, government officials, family members, school classes—were invited to tour the facility and provide feedback (which, by the way, consistently took the form of praise) to the employees for the products and services they were producing. An impromptu hot dog roast was held one lunch hour to recognize and celebrate the extra-mile efforts of one group of employees in the facility. People were assured that counseling, training, and assistance would be provided when job assignments changed or positions were merged as a result of the downsizing. In general, this notable manager attempted to re-empower his workforce by providing social and emotional support in a variety of ways. He helped provide the assistance people needed to cope with the uncertainty resulting from this uncontrollable event. Predictably, both organizational and individual performance results did not deteriorate after downsizing. Instead, contrary to what happens in most organizations that downsize, performance actually improved.

Emotional Arousal

Emotional arousal means replacing negative emotions such as fear, anxiety, or crabbiness with positive emotions such as excitement, passion, or anticipation. To empower people, managers help make the work environment fun and attractive. They ensure that the purpose behind the work is clear. They ensure that people's right brain (the side that controls emotions and passions) is involved in the work as well as their left brain (the side that controls logic and analysis). Bandura (1977) found that the absence of positive emotional arousal makes it difficult, if not impossible, for individuals to feel empowered.

The visible celebrations of employee accomplishments and motivational events in marketing firms such as Mary Kay Cosmetics, Shacklee Products, and Amway are well known. However, emotional arousal doesn't simply mean tooting horns, increasing the decibel levels, listening to speeches, or superficially creating excitement. Instead, emotional arousal occurs more likely when what individuals are doing is connected to values they hold dear. To feel a sense of empowerment, workers must see how what they are doing every day is associated with their basic beliefs. Employees can get more excited, for example, about working for the betterment of humankind, for the improvement of the quality of people's lives, and for personal growth and development, than they can for a 10 percent return to institutional investors. This is not to say that revenue for stockholders is unimportant. But emotional arousal is associated more with personal values than with organizational profitability.

Managers can also increase workers' sense of empowerment by holding periodic social gatherings to foster friendships among coworkers. In their official communications, they can occasionally include a joke or lighthearted message to relieve tension. They can use superlatives in providing feedback or describing successes (e.g., say "terrific" instead of "good"; "awesome" instead of "acceptable"). They can make sure that employees are clear about how their work will affect the company's customers. They can help identify external threats or challenges that need to be met.

Successful emotional arousal is often associated with athletic teams. Chuck Coonradt (1985) observed that "people are willing to pay for the privilege of working harder than they will work when they are paid." That is, individuals will actually pay money in order to work at a more demanding level than the level at which they work when they are receiving a salary. Here is one example.

> In the frozen food business, people are hired to work in refrigerated warehouses in terrible working conditions at near-zero temperatures. But the

unions and OSHA have done much to make conditions bearable. Companies are required to provide insulated clothing and boots. They are required to provide hot drinks within so many feet of cold work areas. Workers must have a ten-minute break every hour. It's tough to get people to work in those kinds of conditions. Yet, whenever a winter snowstorm passes over . . . the mountains, followed by clearing skies and plunging temperatures, there is a sudden jump in employee absenteeism, particularly among young workers. Instead of staying home to avoid the freezing temperatures, they migrate up the local canyons to test the new and famous powder snow. . . . Equipped with hundreds of dollars of equipment, they gladly take a reduction in pay for the day off and a chance to buy a $40 pass to spend the day outside in subfreezing temperatures. There are no hot-drink vending machines on the slopes, nor does anyone demand a ten-minute break every hour (Coonradt, 1985, p. 1).

Thus, people actually end up working harder, in worse conditions—and paying for the privilege—than when they are at work getting paid. Why is this so? Why does recreation produce such energy, such commitment, and such sense of empowerment?

Part of the explanation relates to the emotional arousal that results from several characteristics of sports. For example, all recreation has a clear *goal* (e.g., winning, exceeding a personal best). Without a clearly defined goal, no one gets excited. That goal is always pitted against a standard that people care about (e.g., winning the NCAA championship, bowling a 300 game). In recreation, the *scorekeeping* and *feedback* systems are objective, self-administered, and continuous. In a basketball game, for example, everyone knows that a free throw always counts one point, that the winner is the team that makes the most baskets, and that there is never a time when everyone can't find out the exact score of the game. One reason why people get so excited watching athletic events is because of the scorekeeping and feedback systems. In recreation, the *out-of-bounds* is clearly identified. Everyone knows the consequence of kicking a soccer ball over the end line, of hitting a ball to the left side of third base, or of stepping over the end of the takeoff board in the long jump. They are all out-of-bounds, and everyone knows that out-of-bounds behavior stops action.

Managers can help empower people through emotional arousal, not just by being a cheerleader, delivering charismatic speeches, and keeping the work climate fun, but also by capitalizing on some of the principles of recreation that create excitement: clear goals; objective, self-administered, and continuous scorekeeping and feedback; and clearly defined out-of-bounds behavior.

Providing Information

Kanter (1983) identified information as one of the most crucial managerial "power tools." Acquiring information, particularly information that is viewed as central or strategic in an organization, can be used to build a power base and to make oneself indispensable and influential in that organization. On the other hand, when managers provide their people with more, rather than less information, those people gain a sense of empowerment and are more likely to work productively, successfully, and in harmony with the manager's wishes. The manager actually enhances his or her power base by involving others in the pursuit of desirable outcomes. With more information, people tend to experience more self-determination, personal control, and trust. The resulting sense of empowerment enhances the probability that they will not resist the manager, defend against his or her power, or work at protecting themselves. Rather, they are likely to collaborate with the empowering manager.

Therefore, a manager who wishes to increase an employee's sense of empowerment will make sure that the employee is given all task-relevant information needed to carry out an assignment. The empowering manager will make available, on an ongoing basis, pertinent technical information and data collected by others.

Such a manager keeps workers informed about what is happening in other areas of the organization that might affect what the worker is doing. Managers will keep employees informed of policy-making meetings and senior-level discussions related to their area of responsibility. Workers can be given access to sources closest to the information they need: for example, senior level people in the organization, customers, or the market research staff. Historical or "context" information can be shared, in order to give the worker as broad a background as possible. Managers should make certain that employees have information about the effects of their own behavior on others and on the organization's goals.

To be sure, it is possible to overload people with information and to create anxiety and burnout with too much data. But our experience has been that most people suffer from too little information instead of too much. Furthermore, if the operative terms *relevant information* are applied in this context, overload is less likely to occur. Spreitzer (1992) found, for example, that people who received relevant information about costs, customers, and strategy felt significantly more empowered than those who did not. Block (1987, p. 90) argued:

> Sharing as much information as possible is the opposite of the military notion that only those who "need to know" should be informed. Our goal is to let people know our plans, ideas, and changes as soon as possible. . . . If we are trying to create the mindset that everyone is responsible for the success of this business, then our people need complete information.

Our own research further confirms the importance of providing information to enhance empowerment (Cameron, Freeman, & Mishra, 1993). In one study, for example, we interviewed CEOs of large, well-known companies every six months to assess organizational changes and strategies they were using to cope with declining revenues. In one firm, not much progress was being made in improving the financial outlook. The CEO was very careful to share information on financial, productivity, cost, and climate indicators in the company only with his senior management team. No one else in the firm had access to that information. A change of CEO, however, led to a dramatic change in information-sharing policy. The new CEO began to provide information to every single employee in the firm who desired it. No data were treated as the sole possession of senior management. The sweepers had the same access as the vice-presidents. The resulting empowerment that employees experienced led to dramatic results. Employee-initiated improvements increased markedly, morale and commitment surged, and the resulting financial turnaround made the CEO look like a genius. He attributed his success to his willingness to empower employees by sharing the information they needed to know to improve.

Providing Resources

In addition to providing information, empowerment is also fostered by providing people with other kinds of resources that help them accomplish their tasks. In this sense, managers who empower others act more like blocking backs on a football team than quarterbacks. They are less directors and commanders than they are resource providers (creating time to throw a pass or make a handoff) and obstacle eliminators (blocking on-rushing defensive linemen). One of the primary missions of empowering managers, then, is to help others accomplish their objectives.

Managers attempting to enhance employees' empowerment by providing them with needed resources will ensure that workers receive adequate and ongoing training and development experiences. Sufficient technical and administrative support will be provided to ensure success. Managers will give employees space, time, or equipment that may not be readily available otherwise. They will ensure that workers have access to communication or interpersonal networks that will make their jobs easier. Workers can also be given discretion to spend monies or commit resources to activities that they consider important.

It is unrealistic, of course, to assume that everyone can have everything he or she desires. Very few successful organizations have excess resources to be distributed at will. On the other hand, the most important resources that empowering managers can provide are those that help people achieve control over their own work and lives; that is, foster a sense of self-efficacy and self-determination. When individuals feel that they have what they need to be successful and that they have the freedom to pursue what they want to accomplish, performance is significantly higher than when these types of resources are not available (Spreitzer, 1992).

One of the best examples of using resources to empower comes from Carl Sewell, one of the most successful car salesmen in the United States, who described his approach to empowerment through providing resources:

> Not many people get to see our service repair shop—our insurance company wants to keep traffic there to a minimum—but those who do always comment on its cleanliness. And, in fact, it's immaculate. Why? Because, while customers rarely see it, our technicians do. They live and work there every day. Where would you like to spend your day—in a place that's dirty or one that's spotless? But it's more than just aesthetics. If we make the technicians' work environment more professional, more pleasant, more efficient,

if we provide them with the very best equipment and tools, we're going to be able to hire the best technicians. . . . All this gives them another reason for working for us instead of our competition (Sewell, 1990, p. 53).

One reason Carl Sewell has been so dramatically successful is that he provides each individual with everything necessary to accomplish desired goals. This is true whether Sewell is dealing with mechanics or top salespersons, and whether his company is selling Cadillacs and Lexuses or Hyundais and Geos. It is not only *need*-to-have resources that Sewell provides, but also some *nice*-to-have resources. The point is: "Resources lead to empowerment."

Connecting to Outcomes

One of the important lessons learned by U.S. manufacturing companies as a result of the Japanese invasion of the North American automobile and consumer electronics industries in the late 1970s and 1980s is that workers experience more empowerment when they can see the outcomes of their work. It was often a surprise to U.S. companies, for example, that their Japanese counterparts regularly visited customers in their homes or place of business, regularly observed how the products that the workers produced were used, and regularly received feedback directly from end users. This connection to the ultimate customer helped workers feel more empowered as well as provided a valuable source of improvement ideas. The importance of connecting workers with customers was confirmed, as mentioned in Chapter 6, by Hackman and Oldham's (1980) research on job design and job enrichment. Those investigators found that people are motivated at work when they can interact with ultimate customers in order to see the effects of their work.

A related idea is to provide employees with the authority to resolve problems on the spot. Studies at IBM, Ford Motor Company, Carl Sewall's auto dealerships, and other companies indicated that allowing employees to address customer concerns at the time the complaint was registered positively affected both employee and customer. When employees were given discretion to resolve a problem, respond immediately to a customer's complaint, fix the error instantly, or commit a certain level of company resources in pursuing customer satisfaction, not only was customer satisfaction dramatically increased (an average improvement of 300 percent), but workers felt far more empowered as well. Employees were given the necessary *authority* to go along with their *responsibility* for customer satisfaction, and they were provided with an opportunity to affect outcomes directly.

Hackman, Oldham, Janson, and Purdy (1975) suggested that another of the highly effective ways to enhance employee motivation and satisfaction is to create *task identity*, that is, the opportunity to accomplish a whole task. Individuals become frustrated and lack a sense of empowerment when they work on only part of a task, never see the end result of their work, and are blocked from observing the impact that their job creates. One of us has a colleague who quit a very lucrative job in a prestigious Wall Street firm because he became frustrated with his inability to see the results of his work. He was regularly given assignments to accomplish the first few steps in a complicated job and then had to hand the work off to a senior executive who completed the work and received most of the recognition. Not only was this colleague denied deserved rewards, but more important to him, he was unable to feel that he had completed a whole job. Task identity and the resulting sense of empowerment were completely lacking.

Having task identity implies that individuals can plan, implement, and evaluate the success of their efforts. The effects of what is accomplished can be assessed as well as the outcome. To feel empowered, in other words, I want to know whether I successfully completed my assigned job as well as whether that job made any difference to the overall success of my work unit. The more clear that connection is, the more I will feel empowered.

In sum, clarifying the connections between individuals' work and their outcomes and effects fosters empowerment by helping others develop a sense of *self-efficacy* (they feel more capable and competent) and a sense of *personal consequence* (a sense of having personal impact).

Creating Confidence

The final technique for engendering empowerment is to create a sense of confidence among workers in the trustworthiness of the manager. Rather than being on-guard and suspicious, workers are secure in their feeling that the manager and the organization are honorable. This confidence helps drive out uncertainty, insecurity, and ambiguity in the relationships between employees and the manager.

There are at least two reasons why individuals feel more empowered as they develop greater confidence in their manager. First, the wasteful, unproductive behaviors associated with mistrust and suspicion are avoided. When people distrust one another, they don't listen, they don't communicate clearly, they don't try hard, and they don't collaborate. On the other hand, when trust exists, individuals are free to experiment, to learn, and to contribute without fear of retribution. Second, individuals who are admirable and honorable always create positive energy for others and make them feel more capable. Not without reason do universities trumpet the number of Nobel Prize winners on their faculties, the past Heisman trophy winners on their football teams, the number of outstanding faculty members in their business schools, and the notable achievements of their best students. Although other members of the university may have nothing to do with the achievements being publicized, they gain an enhanced self-image and a sense of empowerment because they are affiliated with the same organization. For the same reasons, creating confidence in a manager helps employees develop a sense of empowerment.

In creating such a sense of confidence and trustworthiness, five factors are especially important: (1) *reliability,* (2) *fairness,* (3) *caring,* (4) *openness,* and (5) *competence.* Managers create confidence, and thereby engender empowerment in others, as they display these five characteristics which are associated with being honorable.

Reliability. Managers who wish their employees to develop confidence in them need to exhibit reliability. The managers' behavior must be consistent, dependable, and stable. Their actions are congruent with their words and attitudes.

Fairness. Good managers also need to be fair and must not take wrongful advantage of anyone. They are equitable in their actions. Workers are clear about the criteria used by the manager in making judgments as well as how the manager applies those criteria. Managers must make clear the standards by which workers will be judged and ensure that those standards are applied in an unbiased way.

Caring. Managers must show a sense of personal concern for workers and help each one feel important to the manager. Managers validate the points of view of their workers and avoid denigrating them as individuals. When correction is needed, caring

managers focus on the mistake or the behavior, not on the worker's personal characteristics.

Openness. Confidence-building managers are open in their relationships. No harmful secrets exist, and relevant information is shared openly and honestly with employees. This does not suggest that a manager cannot keep confidences. But it does mean that workers should not have to worry about hidden agendas that could negatively affect them because their manager is straightforward and honest.

Competence. Workers should be made aware of their manager's competence. Employees need to be assured that their manager has the necessary ability, experience, and knowledge to perform tasks and to solve problems. Without flaunting their expertise, skillful managers inspire a feeling on the part of employees that their confidence in the expertise and proficiency of their leader is not misplaced.

The power of creating confidence in employees is illustrated by several CEOs who were interviewed regarding their keys to successful organizational change. Each CEO had managed a downsizing or redesign of his organization and was attempting to maintain a healthy, productive workforce in the midst of turmoil. The key role of trust and confidence in management is hard to miss (see Cameron, Freeman, & Mishra, 1993; Mishra, 1992).

> If they don't believe what I'm telling them, if they think it's all a bunch of bull, don't expect them to go out there and work a little harder. They won't work a little different. They're not going to be receptive to change unless they understand and trust the things that we're talking about are true. I think trust is the biggest single issue.

> I had a boss one time who said, "What you do speaks so much louder than what you say." I've always stuck that in the back of my mind. I believe that. The people watch very closely what you do. And, boy, you cannot underestimate that.

> What's most important in my organization is this: being truthful. Don't b.s. anyone. Tell them what it is. Right or wrong or different. Tell them the truth.

> My people are all 150 percent dedicated to helping one another. Because no one of them can do it alone, they need each other badly. But

here comes the openness and trust. You have to talk about those things. I don't think you can go in and accomplish things without talking about what the barriers are going to be in trying to make a change or set a new direction.

Successful managers create confidence in themselves among their employees. They are authentic, honorable, and trustworthy.

Review of Empowerment Principles

Table 5 summarizes the list of actions that we have discussed on the previous pages in relation to the nine prescriptions for empowerment. It provides a list of things managers can do to empower their employees. Not all of these suggestions are relevant in every circumstance or with every person, of course, but developing the skill

---

Articulate a Clear Vision and Goals
- Create a picture of a desired future.
- Use word pictures and emotional language to describe the vision.
- Identify specific targets and strategies that will lead to the vision.
- Establish SMART goals.
- Associate the vision and goals with personal values.

Foster Personal Mastery Experiences
- Break apart large tasks and assign one part at a time.
- Assign simple tasks before difficult tasks.
- Highlight and celebrate small wins.
- Incrementally expand job responsibilities.
- Give increasingly more responsibility to solve problems.

Model Successful Behaviors
- Demonstrate successful task accomplishment.
- Point out other people who have succeeded.
- Facilitate interaction with other role models.
- Find a coach.
- Establish a mentor relationship.

Provide Support
- Praise, encourage, express approval for, and reassure.
- Send letters or notes of praise to family members or coworkers.
- Regularly provide feedback.
- Foster informal social activities to build cohesion.
- Supervise less closely and provide time-slack.
- Hold recognition ceremonies.

Arouse Positive Emotions
- Foster activities to encourage friendship formation.
- Periodically send lighthearted messages.
- Use superlatives in giving feedback.
- Highlight compatibility between important personal values and organizational goals.

- Clarify impact on the ultimate customer.
- Foster attributes of recreation in work: clear goals, effective scorekeeping and feedback systems, and out-of-bounds behavior.

Provide Information
- Provide all task-relevant information.
- Continuously provide technical information and objective data.
- Pass along relevant cross-unit and cross-functional information.
- Provide access to information or people with senior responsibility.
- Provide access to information from its source.
- Clarify effects of actions on customers.

Provide Resources
- Provide training and development experiences.
- Provide technical and administrative support.
- Provide needed time, space, or equipment.
- Ensure access to relevant information networks.
- Provide more discretion to commit resources.

Connect to Outcomes
- Provide a chance to interact directly with customers.
- Provide authority to resolve problems on the spot.
- Provide immediate, unfiltered, direct feedback on the results.
- Create task identity—that is, the opportunity to accomplish a complete task.
- Clarify and measure effects as well as direct outcomes.

Create Confidence
- Exhibit reliability and consistency.
- Exhibit fairness and equity.
- Exhibit caring and personal concern.
- Exhibit openness and honesty.
- Exhibit competence and expertise.

Table 5 Practical Suggestions for Empowering Others

of empowerment at least partly depends on knowing what alternatives are available to empower people as well as knowing how to implement them. This list is not comprehensive; other activities may be equally effective in empowering people. But the nine prescriptions and the suggestions associated with each of them represent actions that you will want to practice as you try to improve your competence in the skill of empowerment. The Skill Practice section of this chapter provides an opportunity for you to do this.

Research suggests that empowered individuals are most inclined to empower others. For that reason, we included an Assessment instrument at the beginning of this chapter that measures the extent to which you experience empowerment in your own work. Your scores on the instrument entitled Personal Empowerment Assessment indicate how much your own work is empowering for you in terms of self-efficacy, self-determination, personal control, meaning, and trust. Knowing what provides a sense of empowerment for you can be helpful as you consider ways in which you, in turn, can empower others. The other instrument that you completed in the Skill Assessment section (Effective Empowerment and Delegation) identifies the extent to which you behave in ways that empower people with whom you work and the extent to which you delegate work effectively. How much you actually engage in the behaviors discussed above is assessed, as well as the extent to which you are an effective delegator. We now turn to the topic of delegation.

Delegating Work

The situation in which empowerment is most needed is when other people must become involved in accomplishing work. Obviously, if a person is doing a task alone, knowing how to empower others is largely irrelevant. On the other hand, it is impossible for a manager to perform all the work needed to carry out an organization's mission, so work and the responsibility to carry it out must be delegated to others. All managers, therefore, are required to empower their employees if they are to accomplish the tasks of the organization. Without delegation and the empowerment that must accompany it, no organization and no manager can enjoy long-term success. Delegation involves the assignment of work to other people, and it is an activity inherently associated with all managerial positions.

In this section, we discuss the nature of delegation as well as ways in which delegation can be most effectively empowered. Delegation normally refers to the assignment of a task. It is work focused. Empowerment, on the other hand, focuses on individuals' feelings. It relates to the way people think about themselves. We have previously discussed ways in which managers can affect people's sense of being empowered. We will now discuss ways in which managers can get work accomplished effectively through *empowered delegation.*

We begin by pointing out that although delegation is commonly practiced by managers, it is by no means always competently performed. In fact, one of the grand masters of management, Lester Urwick (1944, p. 51), claimed that the "lack of courage to delegate properly, and of knowledge of how to do it, is one of the most general causes of failures in organizations." Moreover, as pointed out by Leana (1987), researchers have paid little attention to delegation, and less is known about the relationships between delegation and management effectiveness than many other common management skills (Locke & Schweiger, 1979).

Advantages of Empowered Delegation

Learning to become a competent delegator who can simultaneously empower others has several important advantages for managers. It obviously helps managers accomplish more work than they could accomplish otherwise and can be used as a time-management tool to free up discretionary time. On the other hand, if delegation occurs only when managers are overloaded, those receiving the delegated tasks may feel resentful and sense that they are being treated only as objects to meet the managers' ends. In such cases, they will experience a sense of disempowerment. However, skillful use of empowered delegation can provide significant benefits to organizations, managers, and individuals receiving assigned tasks. Table 6 summarizes these advantages.

Empowered delegation can help develop subordinates' capabilities and knowledge so that their effectiveness is increased. It can be a technique to encourage personal mastery experiences. Delegation also can be used to demonstrate trust and confidence in the person receiving the assignment. Mishra (1992) and Gambetta (1988) summarized research showing that individuals who felt trusted by their managers were significantly

ADVANTAGE	EXPLANATION
Time	Increases the manager's discretionary time
Development	Develops delegates' knowledge and capabilities
Trust	Demonstrates trust and confidence in delegates
Commitment	Enhances commitment of delegates
Information	Improves decision making with better information
Efficiency	Enhances efficiency and timeliness of decisions
Coordination	Fosters work integration by manager coordination

Table 6   Advantages of Delegation

more effective than those who didn't feel that way. Empowered delegation can be used to enhance the commitment of individuals receiving work. Beginning with the classic study of participation by Coch and French (1948), research has consistently demonstrated a positive relationship between having an opportunity to participate in work and subsequent satisfaction, productivity, commitment, acceptance of change, and desire for more work. Empowered delegation also can be used to improve the quality of decision making by bringing to bear more information, closer to the source of the problem, than the manager has alone. Delegating tasks to those who have direct access to relevant information can enhance efficiency (i.e., require less time and fewer resources) as well as effectiveness (i.e., result in a better decision). Finally, empowered delegation can increase the coordination and integration of work by funneling information and final accountability through a single source. Empowering managers, in other words, can ensure that no cross-purposes occur in delegation and that different tasks are not producing contradictory effects. Competently administered, empowered delegation can produce all five dimensions of empowerment: a sense of competence, choice, impact, value, and security.

On the other hand, when delegation is ineffectively performed, several negative consequences can result that not only inhibit empowerment but also subvert the ability to get work accomplished at all. For example, instead of freeing up time, ineffective delegation may require even more time to supervise, evaluate, correct, and arbitrate disagreements among employees. Employees may find themselves spending a longer time to accomplish a task because of lack of

know-how, experience, or information. Stress levels and interpersonal conflict may increase when tasks, accountability, or expectations are unclear. Managers may find themselves out of touch with what is really going on with employees, may lose control, and may find goals being pursued that are incompatible with the rest of the organization. Chaos, rather than coordination, can result. Subordinates may also begin to expect that they should be involved in all decisions and that any decision the manager makes alone is autocratic and unfair.

In this section, we identify ways in which the positive outcomes of delegation can be cultivated and the potential negative outcomes of poor delegation avoided. Empowerment and delegation must be linked in the accomplishment of work. We will present guidelines for deciding *when* to delegate, *to whom* to delegate, and, finally, *how* to delegate.

Deciding When to Delegate

Empowered delegating involves deciding, first of all, when to delegate tasks to others and when to perform them oneself. When should subordinates be assigned to design and perform work or make decisions? To determine when delegation is most appropriate, managers should ask five basic questions (Vroom & Yetton, 1973; Vroom & Jago, 1974). Research indicates that when delegation occurs based on these questions, successful results are almost four times more likely than when these questions are not considered. These questions are equally applicable whether assigned work is to be delegated to a team or to a single subordinate.

1. **Do subordinates have the necessary (or superior) information or expertise?** In many cases, subordinates may actually be better qualified than their managers to make decisions and perform tasks because they are more familiar with customer preferences, hidden costs, work processes, and so forth, due to being closer to actual day-to-day operations.

2. **Is the commitment of subordinates critical to successful implementation?** Participation in the decision-making process increases commitment to the final decision. When employees have some latitude in performing a task (i.e., what work they do, and how and when they do it), they generally must be involved in the decision-making process to ensure their cooperation. Whereas participation usually will increase the time required to make a decision, it will substantially decrease the time required to implement it.

3. **Will subordinates' capabilities be expanded by this assignment?** Delegation can quickly get a bad name in a work team if it is viewed as a mechanism used by the boss to get rid of undesirable tasks. Therefore, delegation should be consistent, not just when overloads occur. It should reflect an overall management philosophy emphasizing employee development. Enhancing the abilities and interests of subordinates should be a central motive in delegating tasks.

4. **Do subordinates share with management and each other common values and perspectives?** If subordinates do not share a similar point of view with one another and with their manager, unacceptable solutions, inappropriate means, and outright errors may be perpetuated. In turn, this produces a need for closer supervision and frequent monitoring. Articulating a clear mission and objective for subordinates is crucial. In particular, managers must be clear about *why* the work is to be done. Coonradt (1985) found that important people are always told why, but less important people are merely told *what, how,* or *when.* Telling subordinates why the work is meaningful creates a common perspective.

5. **Is there sufficient time to do an effective job of delegating?** It takes time to save time. To avoid misunderstanding, managers must spend sufficient time explaining the task and discussing acceptable procedures and options. Time must be available for adequate training, for questions and answers, and for opportunities to check on progress.

Empowered delegation depends on a positive answer to each of the preceding questions. If any of these conditions is not present when delegation is being considered, the probability is greater that it will not be effective. More time will be required, lower quality will result, more frustration will be experienced, and less empowerment will occur. However, a negative answer to any of the preceding questions does not necessarily mean that effective delegation is forever precluded because managers can change situations so that subordinates get more information, develop common perspectives, have adequate time to receive delegation, and so forth.

Deciding to Whom to Delegate

Having decided to delegate a task, managers must then consider whether to involve only a single individual or a team of subordinates. If the decision is made to form a team, it is also important to decide how much authority to give the members of the team. For example, managers should determine if the team will only investigate the problem and explore alternatives or if it will make the final decision. Managers must also outline whether or not they will participate in the team's deliberations. Figure 2 presents a model for helping managers decide who should receive delegated tasks—individuals or teams—and whether the manager should be an active participant in a team if it is formed.

Figure 2 is constructed as a "tree diagram" that allows a manager to ask questions and, as a result of the answer to each question, move along a path until a final alternative is selected (Huber, 1980; Vroom & Jago, 1974). Here is how it works.

If you were a manager determining whether to involve others in accomplishing a task or making a decision, you should look over the considerations below the question, "Should I involve others in the task or the decision?" If you decide that subordinates do not possess relevant information or skills, that their acceptance is not important, that no personal development can occur for members of the team, that time is tight, or that conflicts will arise among subordinates, you should answer "no" to this question. The tree then prescribes that you perform the task or make the decision yourself. However, if you answer "yes" to this question, you then move on to the next question:

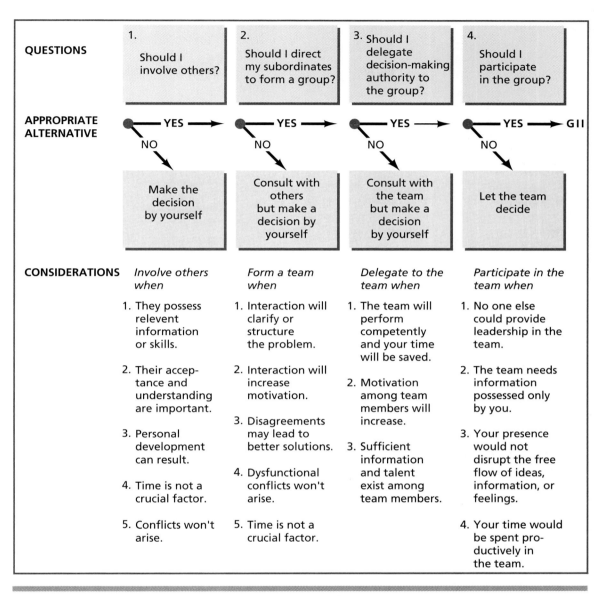

Figure 2 A Model for Deciding When to Delegate to an Individual or to a Team

"Should I direct my subordinates to form a team?" Look over the five considerations below that question and then continue through the model. Any of the considerations below a question can result in a "no" answer. The most participative and empowering alternative is to delegate work to a team and then participate as an equal member of the team. The least empowering response, of course, is to do the work yourself.

Deciding How to Delegate Effectively

When a decision has been made to delegate a task, and the appropriate recipients of the delegation have been identified, empowered delegation has just begun. Positive outcomes of empowered delegation are contingent upon managers following 10 proven principles throughout the process.

1. Begin with the end in mind.   Managers must articulate clearly the desired results intended from the delegated task. Being clear about what is to be accomplished and why it is important is a necessary prerequisite for empowered delegation. If fact, unless people know why a task is important and what is to be achieved by performing it, they are unlikely to act at all. No voluntary action ever persists unless these two elements are present. We don't stick with work, school, assignments, or other activities unless we have an idea of the purposes and intended outcomes involved. At a minimum, recipients of delegation will infer or fabricate a purpose or desired outcome, or the task will not be performed at all. To ensure that the ends desired by a manager are likewise perceived as desirable by others, the manager should point out the personal benefits to be achieved, the connection of task accomplishment to the organization's mission, or the important values represented by the task (e.g., service, learning, growth).

2. Delegate completely.   In addition to the desired ends, managers must clearly specify the constraints under which the tasks will be performed. Every organization has rules and procedures, resource constraints, or boundaries that limit the kind of action that can be taken. These should be clarified when the task is delegated. In particular, managers must be clear about deadlines and the time frame for reporting back. When should the task be completed, who should receive the report, and to whom is accountability being assigned? No empowerment can occur without employees knowing what these boundaries are.

Managers also must specify precisely the level of initiative expected. No other oversight in the delegation process causes more confusion than the failure to delineate expectations regarding the level of initiative expected or permitted. At least five levels of initiative are possible, each of which may vary in terms of the amount of empowerment available to subordinates. These initiative levels differ in terms of the amount of control permitted over the timing and content of the delegated task. The five alternatives are:

- *Wait to be told what to do.* Take action only after specific directions are given. This is the least empowering form of delegation because it permits no initiative on the part of the subordinate. There is no control over timing, that is, when the task is to be accomplished, or content, that is, what is to be done.

- *Ask what to do.* Some discretion is provided to subordinates in that they have some control over the timing of the task, but not its content. Subordinates may formulate ideas for approaching the task, but because no action can be taken until the manager gives approval, empowerment is highly constrained.

- *Recommend, then take action.* This alternative is more empowering because subordinates are given some freedom over both the timing and the content of the delegated task. However, at least three different types of recommendations are possible, each with a different level of empowerment. One is for subordinates to simply gather information, present it to the manager, and let him or her decide what needs to be done. Another is for subordinates to determine alternative courses of action for each part of the task, leaving the manager to choose which course will be followed. Still another possibility is to outline a course of action for accomplishing the entire task and have the whole package approved at once. Progressively more empowerment is associated with each of these three recommendation types.

- *Act, then report results immediately.* Subordinates are given the freedom to act on their own initiative, but they are required to report to the manager immediately upon completion to ensure that their actions are correct and compatible with other organizational work. Subordinates may be permitted to perform only one part of a task at a time, reporting the results of each individual step. Or, they may be given the discretion to perform the entire task, reporting only when the final result has been accomplished. The latter alternative, of course, is the most empowering. But it may not be possible unless subordinates possess the necessary ability, information, experience, or maturity.

- *Initiate action, and report only routinely.* Subordinates receive complete control over timing and over content of the tasks assigned. Reporting occurs only in a routine fashion to maintain coordination. With sufficient ability, information, experience, and maturity among subordinates, this level of initiative is not only the most empowering but also the likeliest to produce high satisfaction and motivation among subordinates (Hackman & Oldham, 1980).

The important point for managers to remember is that they must be very clear about which of these levels of initiative they expect of their subordinates.

3. Allow participation in the delegation of assignments.

Subordinates are more likely to accept delegated tasks willingly, perform them competently, and experience empowerment when they help decide what tasks are to be delegated to them and when. Often, managers cannot give subordinates complete choice about such matters, but providing opportunities to decide when tasks will be completed, how accountability will be determined, when work will begin, or what methods and resources will be used in task accomplishment increases employees' empowerment. Such participation should not be manipulative; that is, opportunities for participation should not be provided merely to convince subordinates of decisions already made. Rather, managers should promote participation when task requirements allow it and when acceptance and personal development can result.

Bernard (1938) formulated an "acceptance theory of authority" in which he proposed that people will accept and fulfill assignments only if four conditions are met. First, subordinates must *understand* what they are being asked to do. Second, subordinates must perceive that the assignment is *consistent* with the purpose of the organization. Third, subordinates must believe that the assignment is *compatible* with their own interests. Fourth, subordinates must be *able* to perform the assignment.

Bernard's theory underscores the importance of two-way communication during the delegation process. Not only should subordinates be encouraged to ask questions and seek information regarding delegated assignments, but they should also feel free to express ideas about the parameters of the work to be delegated. Expecting subordinates to seek answers to questions or providing guidance on every aspect of the delegated assignment can perpetuate overdependence if the manager answers every detailed question or provides continual advice. On the other hand, managers who remain available for consultation and idea interchange, foster two-way communication, and encourage a climate of openness and sharing make the delegation process empowering.

4. Establish parity between authority and responsibility.

The oldest and most general rule of thumb in delegation is to match the amount of responsibility given with the amount of authority provided. Commonly, managers assign responsibility for work to subordinates without furnishing a corresponding amount of discretion to make decisions and authority to implement those decisions. If subordinates are to be successful, they must have as much authority as they need to accomplish the tasks assigned to them. An important part of developing a sense of self-determination and a sense of personal control—both critical dimensions of empowerment—is ensuring this match. Of course, managers also must take care not to delegate more authority than responsibility, thereby giving subordinates more authority, discretion, resources, or information than they can use. Such a mismatch leads to lack of accountability, potential abuses of power, and confusion on the part of subordinates. For example, without the necessary responsibility, providing a child with a loaded gun, or a $50 bill in a candy shop, could result in actions that would not lead to desirable outcomes.

Although managers cannot delegate *ultimate* accountability for delegated tasks, they can delegate *prime* accountability. This means that "the buck stops," eventually, at the manager's desk. Final blame for failure cannot be given away. This is *ultimate* accountability. On the other hand, managers can delegate prime accountability, which means that subordinates can be given responsibility for producing desired short-term results. Their accountability is to the manager who delegated to them. Giving subordinates prime accountability is an important part of empowered delegation.

5. Work within the organizational structure.

Another general rule of empowered delegation is to delegate to the lowest organizational level at which a job can be done. The people who are closest to the actual work being performed or the decision being made should be involved. They are usually the ones with the largest, most accurate fund of information. By definition, this increases efficiency (lower labor and information collection costs), and it frequently increases effectiveness (better understanding of problems). Whereas managers have a broader overall view of problems, the detailed knowledge needed to accomplish many tasks is most likely to reside with those who are lower in the organizational hierarchy.

In delegating a task down more than one level in an organization, it is important that the organizational chain of command be followed. In other words, delegation must occur *through* subordinates, not *around* them. If a senior manager circumvents the formal hierarchy, bypassing a manager to communicate directly with that manager's subordinate, the manager becomes unempowered. The subordinate now becomes accountable to the senior manager, not the manager with direct responsibility for the subordinate. The entire accountability system is thus destroyed. Following the chain of command by involving those at affected levels of the hierarchy in delegation is important for empowered delegation.

All individuals affected by a decision must be informed that it has been delegated. This applies to cross-functional coordination as well as hierarchical coordination. If a subordinate has been delegated responsibility, others who may have needed information, who may influence the results, or who may implement the recommendations must be notified of the delegation. If delegation occurs but no one knows about it, authority is essentially nullified.

6. Provide adequate support for delegated tasks.

When authority is delegated to subordinates, managers must provide as much support to them as possible. As discussed earlier, this involves making public announcements and presenting clearly stated expectations. It also means continuously providing relevant information and resources to help subordinates accomplish tasks. Reports, recent news clippings, customer data, articles, and even random thoughts that pertain to the delegated task should be passed on as they become available. This support not only aids task accomplishment but also communicates interest and concern for subordinates. Managers should help subordinates learn where to acquire needed resources, since the manager alone cannot be the sole source of all the support that subordinates will need.

Agreeing on the limits of resource use is also important. Since unlimited access to resources is never possible, managers must be clear about the limit beyond which no further resources can be used. Formulating a budget or establishing a set of specifications is a common way to specify limits.

Another form of support that managers can provide is to bestow credit—but not blame—publicly. Even though prime accountability has been delegated, pointing out mistakes or faults in front of others embarrasses workers, creates defensiveness, fosters the impression that the manager is trying to pass the buck and get rid of final accountability, and guarantees that workers will be less willing to initiate action on their

own in the future. Correcting mistakes, critiquing work, and providing negative feedback on task performance of subordinates should be done in private, where the probability of problem solving and training can be enhanced.

7. Focus accountability on results.

Once tasks are delegated and authority is provided, managers generally should avoid closely monitoring the way in which subordinates accomplish tasks. Excessive supervision of methods destroys the five dimensions of empowerment: self-efficacy, self-determination, personal control, meaningfulness, and trust. Successful accomplishment of a task, after all, rather than use of the manager's preferred procedures, is the primary goal of delegation. To be sure, harmful or unethical means for accomplishing tasks cannot be tolerated, nor can methods be used that obstruct other employees or subvert organizational rules. For the most part, though, managers should focus primarily on results achieved by subordinates, rather than on the techniques used to achieve those results.

In order for accountability to be maintained, there must be agreement on acceptable levels of performance. Managers must clearly specify what level of performance is expected, what constitutes unacceptable performance, and what requirements are associated with the result. Without such specifications, it becomes difficult for managers not to worry about means as well as ends. By allowing subordinates to exercise initiative regarding how to tackle a task, their sense of empowerment is enhanced, and innovation and originality are more likely as well.

8. Delegate consistently.

The time for managers to delegate is before they have to. Sometimes, when managers have time to do work themselves, they do just that, even though that work could and should be delegated. Two problems result. First, delegation becomes simply a method for relieving the manager's workload and stress. A primary reason for delegation— empowering subordinates—is forgotten. Employees begin to feel that they are merely "pressure valves" for managers rather than valued team members. Secondly, when delegation occurs only under pressure, there is no time for training, providing needed information, or engaging in two-way discussions. Clarity of task assignments may be impaired. Workers' mistakes and failures increase, and managers are tempted to perform tasks alone, in order to ensure quality. When managers delay delegating until they are overloaded, they create pressure on themselves to perform delegatable tasks personally, thereby increasing their own overload.

Another key to consistent delegation is for managers to delegate both pleasant and unpleasant tasks. Sometimes managers keep for themselves the tasks they like to perform and pass less-desirable work along to subordinates. It is easy to see the detrimental consequences this has on morale, motivation, and performance. When individuals feel that they are being used only to perform "dirty work," follow-through on delegated tasks is less likely. On the other hand, managers must not be afraid to share difficult or unpleasant tasks with subordinates. Playing the role of martyr by refusing to involve others in disagreeable tasks or drudgery creates unrealistic expectations for employees and isolates managers. Consistency of delegation, then, means that managers delegate tasks continuously, not just when overworked, and that they delegate both pleasant and unpleasant tasks.

9. Avoid upward delegation. Although it is crucial for subordinates to participate in the delegation process in order to become empowered, managers must conscientiously resist all so-called upward delegation, in which subordinates seek to shift responsibility for delegated tasks back onto the shoulders of the superior who did the initial delegating. Managers who fail to forestall upward delegation will find their time being tied up doing subordinates' work rather than their own.

Suppose a worker comes to a manager after delegation has occurred and says, "We have a problem. This assignment just isn't turning out very well. What do you suggest I do?" If the manager replies, "Gee, I'm not sure. Let me think about it, and I'll get back to you," the original delegated task has now been shifted from the employee back to the manager. Note that the manager has promised to report to the employee, that is, to maintain prime accountability, and the employee is now in a position to follow up on the manager's commitment, that is, supervising the manager. Thus, the subordinate has become the manager, and the manager the subordinate. Managers, in the hope of being helpful to, and supportive of their subordinates, often get caught in the trap of upward delegation.

One way to avoid upward delegation is to insist that workers always take the initiative for developing their own solutions. Instead of promising the subordinate a report on the manager's deliberations, a more appropriate response would have been, "What do you recommend?" "What alternatives do you think we should consider?" "What have you done so far?" "What do you think would be a good first step?" Rather than sharing problems and asking for advice, subordinates should be required to share *proposed solutions* or to ask permission to implement them. Managers should refuse to solve delegated tasks. That is why specifying the expected level of initiative (see Rule 2) is so important. Not only does this avoid upward delegation, but it also helps managers train employees to become competent problem solvers and to avoid working on tasks for which someone else has prime accountability. Yielding to upward delegation does not empower subordinates but, rather, makes them more dependent.

10. Clarify consequences. Subordinates should be made aware of the consequences of the tasks being delegated to them. They are more likely to accept delegation and be motivated to take initiative if it is clear what the rewards for success will be, what the opportunities might be, what the impact on the ultimate customer or the organization's mission can be, and so on. In particular, managers should help employees understand the connection between successful performance and financial rewards, opportunities for advancement, learning and developmental opportunities, informal recognition, and so forth. Most specific delegated assignments do not result in a direct payoff from the formal reward system, of course. But associating some desirable consequence—as minor as a pat on the back or a congratulatory mention in a staff meeting or as major as a financial bonus or incentive—enhances successful delegation.

Clarifying consequences also can help ensure an understanding that delegation not only implies task accomplishment, but enhancement of interpersonal relationships as well. Relationships with others in the organization, on the team, or with the manager individually should be strengthened as a result of task accomplishment. Accomplishing assignments in the course of damaging or destroying relationships creates more long-term costs than any organization can bear. Therefore, a desirable consequence of any delegation experience is the enhancement of interpersonal relationships and a strengthening of the organization.

Review of Delegation Principles

The 10 principles summarizing *how* to delegate, preceded by the five criteria for determining *when* to delegate, and the four questions for identifying *to whom* to delegate, provide guidelines for ensuring not only that subordinates will experience a sense of empowerment but that other positive consequences will result as well. In particular, research results clearly show that empowered delegation leads to the following consequences:

1. Delegated tasks are readily accepted by subordinates.

2. Delegated tasks are successfully completed.

3. Morale and motivation remain high.

4. Workers' problem-solving abilities are increased.

5. Managers have more discretionary time.

6. Interpersonal relationships are strengthened.

7. Organizational coordination and efficiency are enhanced.

Figure 3 summarizes the relationships among these principles.

Summary

Empowerment means helping to develop in others a sense of self-efficacy, self-determinism, personal control, meaning, and trust. The current business environment is not particularly compatible with the principles of managerial empowerment. Because of the turbulent, complex, competitive circumstances that many organizations face, managers frequently ex-

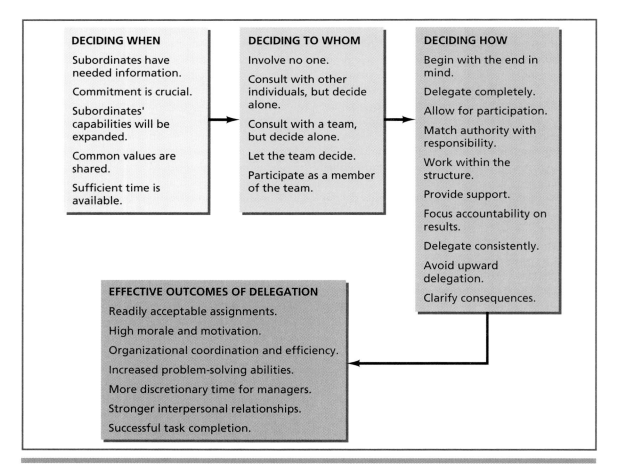

Figure 3 Relationships Among Principles of Effective Delegation

perience a tendency to be less, rather than more, empowering. When managers feel threatened, they become rigid and seek more control over their employees, not less. However, without empowered employees, organizations cannot succeed in the long run. Learning how to be a competent empowering manager is therefore a critical skill for individuals who probably will face a predilection not to practice empowerment.

Nine prescriptions that managers can use to empower others were discussed. We also offered a series of principles and criteria for ensuring empowered delegation, which results in better acceptance of delegated tasks by subordinates, enhanced motivation and morale, improved coordination and efficiency, better development of subordinates, increased discretionary time, strengthened relationships, and successful task performance. Producing a sense of empowerment in others and delegating in a way that empowers subordinates also brings desirable outcomes for organizations as well as employees. Empowered employees are more productive, psychologically and physically healthy, proactive and innovative, persistent in work, trustworthy, interpersonally effective, intrinsically motivated, and have higher morale and commitment than employees who are not empowered. Figure 4 illustrates the relationships among the various elements of empowerment and delegation.

Behavioral Guidelines

As you practice empowering others and carry out empowered delegating, you will want to use the following guidelines as cues.

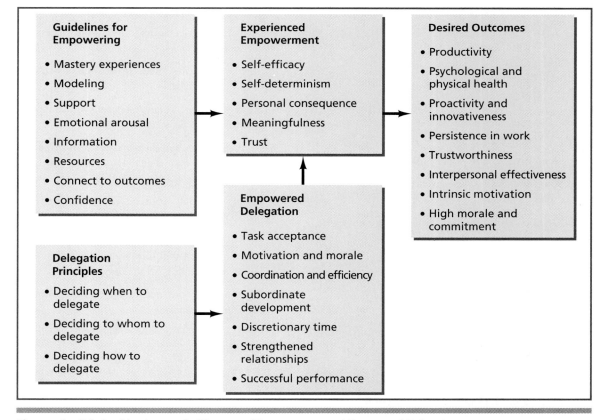

Figure 4   Relationships Among the Elements of Empowerment and Empowered Delegation

To ensure empowerment in others, follow these guidelines.

1. Articulate a *clear vision and goals* for others by:
   - Creating a picture of a desired future.
   - Using word pictures and emotional language to describe the vision.
   - Identifying specific targets and strategies that will lead to the vision.
   - Establishing SMART goals.
   - Associating the vision and goals with personal values.
2. Foster personal *mastery experiences* for others by:
   - Breaking apart large tasks and helping the person do one part at a time.
   - Involving people in simple tasks before difficult tasks.
   - Highlighting and celebrating small wins that others accomplish.
   - Incrementally expanding others' job responsibilities.
   - Giving increasingly more responsibility to others to solve problems.
3. Successfully *model* the behaviors you want others to achieve by:
   - Demonstrating successful task accomplishment.
   - Pointing out other people who have succeeded at the same task.
   - Facilitating interaction with other people who can serve as role models.
   - Finding a coach or tutor for the person.
   - Establishing a mentor relationship with the person.
4. Provide needed *support* to other people by:
   - Praising, encouraging, expressing approval for, and reassuring others when they perform well.
   - Writing letters or notes of praise to employees, as well as to their family members and coworkers, in recognition of noteworthy accomplishments.
   - Providing regular feedback to people.
   - Fostering informal social activities in order to build cohesion among people.
   - Supervising less closely and providing more time between reports on results.
   - Holding formal and informal recognition ceremonies.
5. Arouse *positive emotions* among others by:
   - Fostering activities to encourage formation of friendships.
   - Periodically sending lighthearted messages to people to keep the climate fun and interesting.
   - Using superlatives in giving positive feedback.
   - Highlighting compatibility between important personal values held by your employees and the organization's goals.
   - Clarifying the impact of outcomes on ultimate customers.
   - Fostering attributes of recreation in work by clarifying goals, instituting effective scorekeeping and feedback systems, and specifying out-of-bounds behavior.
6. Provide *information* needed by others to accomplish their work by:
   - Providing all information relating to the accomplishment of a task.
   - Continuously providing technical information and objective data that may come to you from time to time.
   - Passing along relevant cross-unit and cross-functional information to which others may not have access.
   - Providing access to information or to people with senior responsibility in the organization.
   - Providing access to first-hand rather than second-hand information.
   - Clarifying the effects of employees' actions on customers.
7. Provide *resources* needed for others to accomplish their work by:
   - Providing training and development experiences or information about where they can be obtained.

- Providing technical and administrative support or information about where they can be obtained.

- Providing needed time, space, or equipment, or information about where they can be obtained.

- Ensuring access to relevant information networks.

- Providing discretion to others to commit resources that will help accomplish ultimate objectives.

8. *Connect* others' work to outcomes and effects by:

- Providing a chance to interact directly with customers.

- Providing authority to resolve problems on the spot.

- Providing immediate, unfiltered, direct feedback on the results.

- Creating task identity—that is, the opportunity to accomplish a complete task.

- Clarifying and measuring effects as well as direct outcomes.

9. Create *confidence* among others by:

- Being reliable and consistent in your behavior toward others.

- Being fair and equitable in all your decisions and judgments.

- Exhibiting caring and personal concern for others.

- Being open and honest in your communications.

- Exhibiting competence and expertise with regard to objectives to be achieved.

To effectively achieve empowered delegation, follow these guidelines.

1. Determine *when* to delegate work to others by addressing five key criteria:

- Do subordinates have the information or expertise necessary to perform a task? Are they closer to the relevant information than you are?

- Is the commitment of subordinates critical to successful implementation? Can subordinates subvert task accomplishment?

- Will subordinates' capabilities be expanded by this assignment? Will it help others to develop themselves?

- Do subordinates share a set of common values and perspectives? Are there likely to be conflicting points of view?

- Does sufficient time exist to do an effective job of delegating? Can adequate information and training be provided?

2. Determine *to whom* work should be delegated by using the decision tree in Figure 2. Decide whether you should do the task yourself, consult with individual subordinates, consult with a team of subordinates, or participate as an equal member of a team of subordinates by analyzing the characteristics of the subordinates listed in the figure.

3. To delegate work effectively, follow these 10 guidelines:

- Begin with the end in mind. Specify desired results.

- Delegate completely. Identify the level of initiative to be taken by subordinates.

- Allow participation, especially regarding how and when tasks will be accomplished.

- Match levels of authority with levels of responsibility. Maintain balance.

- Work within the structure. When delegating work at lower levels, delegate through subordinates, not around them.

- Provide support for tasks being delegated. Identify resource limitations.

- Maintain accountability for results. Avoid overly close monitoring of methods.

- Delegate consistently. Do not delegate merely because you are overloaded.

- Avoid upward delegation. Ask subordinates to recommend solutions rather than asking for assistance or advice.

- Clarify consequences. Identify important effects of successful task accomplishment.

Cases Involving Empowerment and Delegation

Minding the Store

On January 1, Ruth Cummings was formally named branch manager for the Saks Fifth Avenue store in a suburb of Denver. Her boss, Ken Hoffman, gave her this assignment on her first day: "Ruth, I'm putting you in charge of this store. Your job will be to run it so that it becomes one of the best stores in the system. I have a lot of confidence in you, so don't let me down."

One of the first things Ruth did was to hire an administrative assistant to handle inventories. Because this was such an important part of the job, she agreed to pay her assistant slightly more than the top retail clerks were making. She felt that having an administrative assistant would free her to handle marketing, sales, and personnel matters—areas she felt were crucial if the store was to be a success.

Within the week, however, she received a call from Hoffman: "Say, Ruth, I heard that you hired an administrative assistant to handle inventories. Don't you think that is a bit risky? Besides, I think paying an assistant more than your top sales clerk is damaging to morale in the store. I wish you had cleared this with me before you made the move. It sets a bad precedent for the other stores, and it makes me look like I don't know what is going on in the branches."

Three weeks later, Ruth appeared on a local noontime talk show to discuss new trends in fashion. She had worked hard to make contact with the hosts of the show, and she felt that public exposure like this would increase the visibility of her store. Although the TV spot lasted only 10 minutes, she was pleased with her performance and with the chance to get public exposure.

Later that night at home, she received another phone call from Hoffman: "Don't you know the policy of Saks? Any TV appearances made on behalf of the store are to be cleared through the main office. Normally, we like to have representatives from the main store appear on these kinds of shows because they can do a better job of plugging our merchandise. It's too bad that you didn't notify someone of your intentions. This could be very embarrassing for me."

Just before Easter, Ruth was approached in the store by one of the sales clerks. A customer had asked to charge approximately $3,000 worth of china as a gift for his wife. He had been a customer of the store for several years and Ruth had seen him on several occasions, but store rules indicated that no charge could be made for more than $1,000 for any reason. She told the customer that she was not authorized to okay a charge of that amount, but that if he would visit the main store in Denver, maybe arrangements could be made.

Later in the day, an irate Hoffman called again: "What in the world are you thinking about, Ruth? Today we had a customer come into the main store and say that you wouldn't make a sale to him because the charge was too much. Do you know how long he has been a customer of ours? Do you know how much he spends in the store every year? I certainly hope we have not lost him as a customer because of your blunder. This makes me very upset. You've just got to learn to use your head."

Ruth thought about the conversation for several days and finally decided that she needed to see Ken Hoffman. She called his secretary to schedule an appointment for the following day.

Discussion Questions

1. What guidelines related to empowerment were violated by Ken Hoffman? By Ruth Cummings?

2. What guidelines related to delegation were violated by Ken Hoffman? By Ruth Cummings?

3. What should Ruth Cummings and Ken Hoffman discuss in their meeting? Identify specific agenda items that should be raised.

4. What are the questions that Ruth should ask Ken to help her acquire the necessary elements of empowerment? What questions should Ken ask Ruth to be better able to ensure her success?

5. If you were an outside consultant attending the meeting, what advice would you give Ken? What advice would you give Ruth?

Changing the Portfolio

You are head of a staff unit reporting to the vice president of finance. He has asked you to provide a report on the firm's current portfolio, including recommendations for changes in the current selection criteria. Doubts have been raised about the efficiency of the existing system given the current market conditions, and there is considerable dissatisfaction with prevailing rates of return.

You plan to write the report, but at the moment you are perplexed about the approach to take. Your own specialty is the bond market, and it is clear to you that detailed knowledge of the equity market, which you lack, would greatly enhance the value of the report. Fortunately, four members of your staff are specialists in different segments of the equity market. Together, they possess a vast amount of knowledge about the intricacies of investment. However, they seldom agree on the best way to achieve anything when it comes to investment philosophy and strategy.

You have six weeks before the report is due. You have already begun to familiarize yourself with the firm's current portfolio and have been provided by management with a specific set of constraints that any portfolio must satisfy. Your immediate problem is to come up with some alternatives to the firm's present practices and to select the most promising for detailed analysis in your report.

Discussion Questions

1. Should this decision be made by you alone? Why or why not?

2. If you answered the question, "Should I involve others?" affirmatively, which alternative in Figure 2 should be used in making a decision? Justify your choice.

3. What are the most important considerations in deciding whom to involve in this task?

4. If others are to become involved, how much empowerment should they have? What would you do specifically to achieve the appropriate level of empowerment?

Skill Practice

Exercises for Empowerment

Executive Development Associates

Assume that you are Mary Ann O'Connell, General Manager at Executive Development Associates. Your firm provides outplacement, training and development, career planning, and head-hunting services for a large number of Fortune 500 companies. You have been at the corporate board meeting for the last three days in the Rocky Mountains, and you relied on your secretary to screen out all but the most important or urgent messages. You slipped into the office on the way home from the airport Monday evening, just to check your electronic messages and your mail. Aside from a host of phone calls to return, here is the collection of messages that your secretary retrieved from your E-mail file and mail box.

Assignment

1. For each message, outline specifically the plan you will implement to empower others effectively to solve these problems. Determine who should be involved, what level of initiative should be taken, what actions you can take to ensure empowerment, how accountability should be maintained, and so on.

2. Write out the actions you'd take in response to each item. A worksheet has been provided to remind you of what you should consider as you record your responses.

3. After you have completed your own responses, form a team of fellow students and share your plans. Provide feedback to one another on what is especially good, what could be improved, and what could be added to each action plan. In particular, what principles of empowerment are included, which are omitted, and which are contradicted?

Interoffice Memorandum
Data Processing Center

DATE: 15 June 1997
TO: Mary Ann O'Connell, General Manager
FROM: Roosevelt Monroe, for the Data Processing Staff

After looking over last quarter's audit, it is clear that the number of complaints our group is receiving from individuals throughout the company is escalating. The problem is an obvious one to us. It is, simply, that several incompatible software systems have evolved over the last several years in various departments, and it is becoming increasingly difficult to coordinate across units. As you know, some data have to be retyped two or three times into different systems because of these incompatibilities.

Our own employees, not to mention our customers, are becoming increasingly impatient with our slow turnaround time. They focus squarely on our group as the bottleneck. We think the rising complaint numbers in the quarterly audit are misleading, however, and divert us from the real cause of the problem.

We're writing this memo to you collectively to urge you to address this issue as soon as possible. At a minimum, it should be discussed at our upcoming staff meeting on Tuesday. So far, the data processing staff is taking the blame for not getting data processed fast enough, yet it is really the fault of the system, not our unit.

We'll look forward to hearing from you on Tuesday.

Interoffice Memorandum
Human Resources Department

DATE: 15 June 1997
TO: Mary Ann
FROM: Lucy

I was excited by your speech at the senior management meeting last week in which you established a new challenge for all senior executives. With the new competitive environment that we face, the vision that you articulated for our future is both exciting and challenging and, I think, an important step forward. It really makes clear the key success factors that should drive our business.

In particular, I think your directive for all senior executives to disseminate the vision to their own subordinates throughout the organization is a good way to get the message delivered. However, in your speech you made a statement that troubled me. You said: "We used to pay you on the basis of new accounts generated, quarterly earnings, customer satisfaction ratings, and new product designs. Our new barometer is going to be how you're doing in disseminating the vision throughout your own units."

Frankly, I'm perplexed as to how we'll ever measure this directive. As the person responsible for administering the appraisal and compensation systems, I'm not sure what criteria we'll look for or what indicators we'll use to determine success. I'm afraid that we'll create dissatisfaction if we don't have something specific outlined. Our people, especially those who may not perform, will think it is purely arbitrary. Do you really mean to have us change the appraisal and compensation systems to include this new criterion? How do you propose that we measure effective performance? What would you like me to do to support your statement? Did you mean to make the statement that you did?

This is rather urgent because I have a staff meeting Tuesday afternoon, and I promised to have a response by then. I've already stalled until I had a chance to talk to you.

Midwest State University

24 May 1997

Dear Ms. O'Connell:

I am happy to be joining Executive Development Associates after several years at Midwest State University. As you know, leaving Midwest State has been quite traumatic for me, and that is what motivated me to make a request of you. I'm convinced that the reason I didn't receive tenure at Midwest State is because the expectations were never clear about what my responsibilities were and what the criteria for success were.

I know your company is very professional and employees are pretty much on their own, but I'm feeling a need to get some specific performance requirements outlined for me. I'm sure that I can be a good addition to your company, but I want to be clear about what your expectations are.

I have set a meeting with you on Tuesday through your secretary. Would you please outline a specific set of responsibilities and expectations for my job as instructor in the training and development department? If possible, I'd like it in writing to avoid any misunderstanding. Regardless, I'll look forward to talking to you Tuesday.

Thank you for your consideration.

Sincerely,

Lester Frost

Lester Frost

Interoffice Memorandum
Training and Development

DATE: Monday, A.M.
TO: Mary Ann
FROM: Pam
RE: Tom Kinnir's Jury Duty

I know you're just getting back, but we've got an emergency on our hands.

I was just notified this morning by Tom that he has been selected for jury duty and that (can you believe it) he is being sequestered! Holy cow, Mary Ann, this couldn't have come at a worse time. As our expert on activity-based costing, Tom's the only guy we have who can teach the topic. So what's the trouble, you say? The trouble is that we have over 100 corporate trainers showing up here for a seminar on Friday, and the seminar isn't prepared yet. Tom said that he has some notes and a few transparencies on his desk, but he had planned to spend this entire week designing and preparing it. Not only don't any of us know the topic very well, but we're not even sure what information we need, what data still need to be gathered, who's got what, and how we go about filling in. Help! We're counting on this seminar to make budget this quarter, and we're feeling a little ticked-off at Tom for waiting until the last minute. What do we do next?

By the way, how were the Rocky Mountains???

Interoffice Memorandum
Outplacement Department

DATE: Monday, A.M.
TO: Mary Ann O'Connell
FROM: Aneil Mishra
RE: Pending Plant Closure

You may have missed the news over the weekend. It was announced in the paper that Detroit Manufacturing has filed for Chapter 11 protection and that they're closing their Toledo plant. That means about 4,000 people will be out of work.

If we want the business, we've got to get moving right away. They will be looking at proposals from outplacement firms next week. We've got to get our proposal together, identify staff, determine a budget, and prepare a presentation in the next day or two.

Sounds like a great opportunity. I'll stop by tomorrow when you get back.

Worksheet: Executive Development Associates

For each message, write out your plan of action, taking into consideration the questions listed below. Most, but not all questions are relevant to each message, and they can guide your action plan. After you have formed your own responses, form a team of fellow students and share your plans. Provide feedback to one another on what is especially good, what could be improved, and what could be added to each action plan.

1. Who should be involved in resolving this issue? Will you form a team?

2. What kinds of personal mastery experiences can be provided for those who will be involved? Can you model successful behavior?

3. What kinds of support, information, and resources can be given?

4. How will you create emotional arousal and create confidence in others?

5. What are the main considerations in deciding if you should delegate each task?

6. If you opt for delegation, what will you do to include the following?

Begin with the end in mind.

Delegate completely.

Allow participation.

Match authority with responsibility.

Work within the structure.

Provide support.

Maintain accountability.

Ensure consistency of delegation.

Avoid upward delegation.

Clarify consequences.

Hillside Oaks Advertizing Company

In this exercise, you will participate in one of three different teams, which constitute Hillside Oaks Advertizing Company. The Top Team consists of two people, the Middle Team has three people, and the Bottom Team includes five people. Each team has its own responsibilities, described below. You will be assigned randomly to one of the three teams. An observer will also be assigned to each team to evaluate its overall functioning.

The object of this exercise is to satisfy the customer. You should try, therefore, not only to deliver what is expected, but actually to exceed customer expectations. The customer is a distributor of new, cutting-edge products that have not yet become established in the marketplace. Your advertising organization has been requested to create as many creative and exciting television commercials as you can for each product in this portfolio. The customer wants to choose among several different options for each product, so you need to generate an array of choices. At the end of the exercise, only one advertising team will be selected.

The products in the customer's portfolio are:

A new kind of soft drink that contains fruit juice and extra nutrients

A new hand-held, color photocopying machine

A new light bulb that lasts twice as long as regular bulbs and is recyclable

Your task is to create, in written form, as many television commercials as you can for each product. You will be given 35 minutes. Your ideas will be evaluated by the customer based on innovativeness, excitement, perceived effectiveness, and cost. Your costs are associated with script writing, filming, actors, and location. Using well-known personalities, lots of people, and exotic locations increases your costs.

Top Team members have the following responsibilities:

▶ Task assignments for organization members

▶ Organization design

▶ Reward and recognition system

▶ Control over production resources (e.g., paper, pens, Post-It notes)

▶ Determine if product is of sufficient quality to be shown to the customer

Middle Team members have the following responsibilities:

- Supervising the work of the Bottom Team
- Evaluating quality
- Serving as liaisons between the Top and Bottom Teams
- Carrying out assignments from the Top Team
- Determining whether the commercials are high, moderate, or low cost
- Passing products to the Top Team

Bottom Team members have the following responsibilities:

- Generating ideas for commercials
- Outlining the scripts
- Passing products to the Middle Team

The Observer has the following responsibilities:

- Evaluating the extent to which each team performed its responsibilities
- Completing the Observer's Feedback Form (see Appendix I)

At the end of the exercise, each team will have 5 minutes to describe its products. Presentations, therefore, must be brief and to the point. The "customer" will consist of other members of the class who will rate the product portfolio using the form below. Individuals may not evaluate their own organization's products. Each class member will complete a Customer Scoring Sheet (see Appendix I) for each organization. Those scoring sheets, along with the evaluation given on the Observer's Feedback Form, will determine which organization receives the highest point total. The organization that obtains the highest score will be hired.

Discussion Questions

1. What principles of empowerment were most successful in this organization?
2. What tendencies exist to maintain power differentials among teams?
3. What kinds of resistance to cooperation and teamwork did you experience?
4. What methods of organizing work were most effective?
5. How effective was the delegation?
6. How could empowerment have been improved? What advice would you give others?

Skill Application

Activities for Empowerment and Delegation

Suggested Assignments

1. Teach someone else (your spouse, a colleague, your boss) how to empower others and delegate effectively. Include the principles in Table 5 in your discussion. Use your own examples and illustrations.

2. Interview a manager about his or her empowerment practices. Try to determine what is especially effective, what doesn't work, what comes off as condescending, and what motivates people to perform. Identify the extent to which the manager knows and uses the principles discussed in the Skill Learning section of this chapter.

3. Think of a situation you now face with which you would like some help. It may be a task you want to accomplish, a tough decision you need to make, or a team you want to form. Make sure you think of something that requires the involvement of other people. Write down specific things you can do to empower other people to help you. How can you help them do what they want to do, while simultaneously have them do what you want them to do?

4. Schedule a meeting with a manager who is not very good at empowerment. (Finding such a person shouldn't be difficult, because most leaders tend to be more authoritarian and bureaucratic than empowering.) As a student who has learned about and practiced empowerment and delegation, share what you have learned and offer suggestions which could help this manager improve.

Application Plan and Evaluation

This exercise is intended to help you apply this cluster of skills in a real-life, out-of-class setting. Now that you have become familiar with the behavioral guidelines that form the basis of effective skill performance, you will improve most by trying out those guidelines in an everyday context. Unlike a classroom activity, in which feedback is immediate and others can assist you with their evaluations, this skill application activity is one you must accomplish and evaluate on your own. There are two parts to this activity. Part 1 assists in preparing you to apply the skill. Part 2 helps you evaluate and improve on your experience. Be sure to write down answers to each item. Don't short-circuit the process by skipping steps.

Part 1. Planning

1. Write down the two or three aspects of this skill that are most important to you. These may be areas of weakness, areas you most want to improve, or areas that are most salient to a current problem. Identify the specific aspects of this skill that you want to apply.

2. Now identify the setting or the situation in which you will apply this skill. Establish a plan for performance by actually writing down a description of the situation. Who else will be involved? When will you do it? Where will it be done?

Circumstances:

Who else?

When?

Where?

3. Identify the specific behaviors you will engage in to apply this skill. Operationalize your skill performance.

4. What are the indicators of successful performance? How will you know you have been effective? What will indicate you have performed competently?

Part 2. Evaluation

5. After you have completed your implementation, record the results. What happened? How successful were you? What was the effect on others?

6. How can you improve? What modifications can you make next time? What will you do differently in a similar situation in the future?

7. Looking back on your whole skill practice and application experience, what have you learned? What has been surprising? In what ways might this experience help you in the long term?

Building Effective Teams

skill development

Skill Assessment

Diagnostic Surveys for Building Effective Teams

Team Development Behaviors

Step 1: Before you read the material in this chapter, please respond to the following statements by writing a number from the rating scale below in the left-hand column (Preassessment). Your answers should reflect your attitudes and behavior as they are now, not as you would like them to be. Be honest. This instrument is designed to help you discover your level of competency in building effective teams so you can tailor your learning to your specific needs. When you have completed the survey, use the scoring key in Appendix I to identify the skill areas discussed in this chapter that are most important for you to master.

Step 2: After you have completed the reading and the exercises in this chapter and, ideally, as many as you can of the Skill Application assignments at the end of this chapter, cover up your first set of answers. Then respond to the same statements again, this time in the right-hand column (Postassessment). When you have completed the survey, use the scoring key in Appendix I to measure your progress. If your score remains low in specific skill areas, use the behavioral guidelines at the end of the Skill Learning section to guide further practice.

Rating Scale

1	Strongly disagree	4	Slightly agree
2	Disagree	5	Agree
3	Slightly disagree	6	Strongly agree

Assessment

Pre-	Post-	*When attempting to build and lead an effective team:*
1		1. I am knowledgeable about the different stages of development that teams can go through in their life cycles.
6		2. I make certain that all team members are introduced to one another when a team first forms.
5		3. I provide directions, answer team members' questions, and clarify goals, expectations, and procedures when the team first comes together.
5		4. I help team members establish a foundation of trust among one another and between themselves and me.
5		5. I ensure that standards of excellence—not mediocrity or mere acceptability—characterize the team's work.
4		6. I provide a great deal of feedback to team members regarding their performance.
4		7. I encourage team members to balance individual autonomy with interdependence among themselves.

_3_   ____   8. I help team members become at least as committed to the success of the team as to their own personal success.

_5_   ____   9. I help members learn to play roles that assist the team in accomplishing its tasks as well as building strong interpersonal relationships.

_6_   ____   10. I articulate a clear, exciting, value-laden vision of what the team can achieve.

_6_   ____   11. I help team members become committed to the team vision.

_6_   ____   12. I encourage a win/win philosophy in the team: that is, when one member wins, every member wins.

_3_   ____   13. I help the team avoid groupthink, or making the group's cohesion and survival more important than accomplishing its goal.

_2_   ____   14. I use process management procedures to help the group become more efficient and more productive, and to prevent errors.

_5_   ____   15. I encourage team members to represent the team's vision, goals, and accomplishments to outsiders.

_5_   ____   16. I diagnose and capitalize on the team's core competencies.

_5_   ____   17. I encourage the team to achieve dramatic breakthrough innovations as well as small continuous improvements.

_4_   ____   18. I help the team work toward preventing mistakes, not just correcting them after-the-fact.

_5_   ____   19. I manage difficult team members effectively through supportive communication, collaborative conflict management, and empowerment.

Diagnosing the Need for Team Building

Teamwork has been found to dramatically affect organizational performance. Some managers have credited teams with helping them to achieve incredible results. On the other hand, teams don't work all the time in all organizations. Therefore, managers must decide when teams should be organized. To determine the extent to which teams should be built in your organization, complete the instrument below.

Think of an organization in which you participate (or will participate) that produces a product or service. Answer these questions with that organization in mind. Write a number from a scale of 1 to 5 in the blank at the left; 1 indicates that there is little evidence; 5 indicates there is a lot of evidence.

_1_   1.   Production or output has declined or is lower than desired.

_3_   2.   Complaints, grievances, or low morale are present or increasing.

_2_   3.   Conflicts or hostility between members is present or increasing.

_1_   4.   Some people are confused about assignments, or their relationships with other people are unclear.

_1_   5.   Lack of clear goals and lack of commitment to goals exist.

_2_   6.   Apathy or lack of interest and involvement by members is in evidence.

3	7.	Insufficient innovation, risk taking, imagination, or initiative exists.
2	8.	Ineffective and inefficient meetings are common.
2	9.	Working relationships across levels and units are unsatisfactory.
1	10.	Lack of coordination among functions is apparent.
1	11.	Poor communication exists; people are afraid to speak up; listening isn't occurring; and information isn't being shared.
3	12.	Lack of trust exists among members and between members and senior leaders.
2	13.	Decisions are made that some members don't understand, or with which they don't agree.
1	14.	People feel that good work is not rewarded or that rewards are unfairly administered.
1	15.	People are not encouraged to work together for the good of the organization.
4	16.	Customers and suppliers are not part of organizational decision making.
1	17.	People work too slowly and there is too much redundancy in the work being done.
3	18.	Issues and challenges that require the input of more than one person are being faced.
3	19.	People must coordinate their activities in order for the work to be accomplished.
2	20.	Difficult challenges that no single person can resolve or diagnose are being faced.

Source: Adapted from Dyer, 1987.

Skill Learning

Developing Teams and Teamwork

Near the home of one of the authors of this book, scores of Canada geese spend the winter. They fly over the house to the nature pond nearby almost every morning. What is distinctive about these flights is that the geese always fly in a V pattern. The reason for this pattern is that the flapping wings of the geese in front create an up-draft for the geese that follow. This V pattern increases the range of the geese collectively by 71 percent compared to flying alone. On long flights, after the lead goose has flown at the front of the V for awhile, it drops back to take a place in the V where the flying is easier. Another goose then takes over the lead

position, where the flying is most strenuous. If a goose begins to fly out of formation, it is not long before it returns to the V because of the resistance it experiences when not supported by the other geese's wing flapping.

Another noticeable feature of these geese is the loud honking that occurs when they fly. Canada geese never fly quietly. One can always tell when they are in the air because of the noise. The reason for the honking is not random, however. It occurs among geese in the rear of the formation in order to encourage the lead goose. The leader doesn't honk—just those who are supporting and urging on the leader.

If a goose is shot, becomes ill, or falls out of formation, two geese break ranks and follow the wounded or ill goose to the ground. There they remain, nurturing their companion, until it is either well enough to return to the flock or dies.

This remarkable phenomenon serves as an apt metaphor for our chapter on teamwork. The lessons garnered from the flying V formation help highlight important attributes of effective teams and skillful teamwork. For example:

▶ Effective teams have interdependent members. Like geese, the productivity and efficiency of an entire unit is determined by the coordinated, interactive efforts of all its members.

▶ Effective teams help members be more efficient working together than alone. Like geese, effective teams outperform even the best individual's performance.

▶ Effective teams function so well that they create their own magnetism. Like geese, team members desire to affiliate with a team because of the advantages they receive from membership.

▶ Effective teams do not always have the same leader. As with geese, leadership responsibility often rotates and is shared broadly in skillfully led teams.

▶ In effective teams, members care for and nurture one another. No member is devalued or unappreciated. All are treated as an integral part of the team.

▶ In effective teams, members cheer for and bolster the leader, and vice versa. Mutual encouragement is given and received by each member.

▶ In effective teams, there is a high level of trust among members. Members are interested in others' success as well as their own.

Because any metaphor can be carried to extremes, we don't wish to overemphasize the similarities between Canada geese and work teams. But these seven points, which are the focus of this chapter, are among the important attributes of teams. Learning how to foster effective team processes, team roles, team leadership, and positive relationships among team members are among the most important team-building skills discussed in this chapter. Our intent is to help you improve your skill in managing teams, both as a leader and as a team member.

The Advantages of Teams

Whether one is a manager, a subordinate, a student, or a homemaker, it is almost impossible to avoid being a member of a team. Some form of teams and teamwork permeate our everyday lives. What we discuss in this chapter, therefore, is applicable to team activity in many settings outside the workplace. However, our focus here is limited primarily to teams and teamwork in employing organizations rather than in homes, classrooms, or in the world of sports.

According to the *Wall Street Journal,* the first work team ever formed in an organization was established in Filene's department store in Boston in 1898. This innovation was slow to catch on, however, because the Industrial Revolution emphasized work processes and production techniques predicated on individualized tasks and specialized roles. Mass production focused on a "one-person/one-job" philosophy. However, a 1993 survey of 1,293 U.S. organizations by the American Society for Quality Control (ASQC) and the Gallup Organization found that over 80 percent of respondents reported some form of work-team activity, mainly problem-solving teams. Typically, two or more teams were found per company, but almost all teams were of recent origin, the median lifespan being only five years. Two-thirds of full-time employees indicated that they participate in teams, and 84 percent participate in more than one team (ASQC, 1993). Teams and teamwork, in other words, have begun to permeate modern organizational life.

One reason this is the case is that increasing amounts of data show improvements in productivity, quality, and morale when teams are utilized. For example, a noted management consultant, Tom Peters (1987, p. 306) asserts:

> Are there any limits to the use of teams? Can we find places or circumstances where a team structure doesn't make sense? Answer: No, as far as I can determine. That's unequivocal, and meant to be. Some situations may seem to lend themselves more to team-based management than others. Nonetheless, I observe that the power of the team is so great that it is often wise to violate apparent common sense and force a team structure on almost anything.

Many companies have attributed their improvements in performance directly to the institution of teams in the workplace (Wellins et al., 1991). For example, by using teams:

▶ Shenandoah Life Insurance Company in Roanoke, Virginia, saved $200,000 annually because of reduced staffing needs, while increasing its volume 33 percent.

▶ Westinghouse Furniture Systems increased productivity 74 percent in three years.

▶ AAL increased productivity by 20 percent, cut personnel by 10 percent, and handled 10 percent more transactions.

▶ Federal Express cut service errors by 13 percent.

▶ Carrier reduced unit turnaround time from two weeks to two days.

▶ Volvo's Kalamar facility reduced defects by 90 percent.

▶ General Electric's Salisbury, North Carolina, plant increased productivity by 250 percent compared to other GE plants producing the same product.

▶ Corning cellular ceramics plant decreased defect rates from 1,800 parts per million to 9 parts per million.

▶ AT&T's Richmond operator service increased service quality by 12 percent.

▶ Dana Corporation's Minneapolis valve plant trimmed customer lead time from six months to six weeks.

▶ General Mills plants are 40 percent more productive than plants operating without teams.

Other more scientific and systematic studies of the impact of teams have found equally impressive results. Literally thousands of studies have been conducted on groups and teams and their impact on various performance outcomes. One of the first and most well-known studies ever conducted on teams was undertaken by Coch and French (1948) in the Harwood Company, a manufacturer of men's shirts, shorts, and pajamas. Faced with the necessity of responding to competitors' lower prices, Harwood decided to speed up the line and make other process changes. Workers had responded badly, however, to previous changes in the production process, and they resisted the threat of further changes. To im-

plement these planned changes, Harwood management used three different types of strategies.

One group of employees received an explanation of the new standards to be imposed, the proposed changes in the production process to be implemented, and why the changes were needed. A question-answer period followed the explanation. A second group of employees was presented the problem, asked to discuss it and reach agreement on solutions, and then elect representatives to generate the new standards and procedures. In a third group, every member was asked to discuss and become involved in establishing and implementing the new standards and procedures. All members participated fully as a team.

The results of this comparison were dramatic. Despite having their jobs simplified, members of the first group showed almost no improvement in productivity; hostility toward management escalated; and, within 40 days, 17 percent of the employees had left the company. Members of the second group regained their previous levels of productivity within 14 days and improved slightly thereafter. Morale remained high and no employee left the company. Members of the third group, on the other hand, who fully participated as a team, regained earlier productivity levels by the second day and improved 14 percent over that level within the month. Morale remained high, and no one left the company.

Other classic studies of coal miners, pet food manufacturers, and auto workers revealed similar advantages of teams (e.g., Trist, 1969; Walton, 1965). More recently, one of the most comprehensive surveys ever conducted on employee involvement in teams was carried out among the Fortune 1000 companies by Lawler, Mohrman, and Ledford (1992). They found that employee involvement in teams had a strong positive relationship with several dimensions of organizational and worker effectiveness. Table 1 shows the percent of organizations reporting improvement and positive impact as a result of team involvement. In general, Lawler and his colleagues found that among firms that were actively using teams, both organizational and individual effectiveness were above average and improving in virtually all categories of performance. In firms without teams or in which teams were infrequently used, effectiveness was average or low in all categories.

In studies of self-directed teams, Near and Weckler (1990) found that individuals in self-directed teams scored significantly higher than individuals in traditional work structures on innovation, information sharing, employee involvement, and task significance.

PERFORMANCE CRITERIA	PERCENT INDICATING IMPROVEMENT
Changed management style to more participatory	78
Improved organizational processes and procedures	75
Improved management decision making	69
Increased employee trust in management	66
Improved implementation of technology	60
Elimination of layers of management supervision	50
Improved safety and health	48
Improved union-management relations	47

PERFORMANCE CRITERIA	PERCENT INDICATING POSITIVE IMPACT
Quality of products and services	70
Customer service	67
Worker satisfaction	66
Employee quality of work life	63
Productivity	61
Competitiveness	50
Profitability	45
Absenteeism	23
Turnover	22

Table 1 Impact of Involvement in Teams on Organizations and Workers (N = 439 of the *Fortune* 1000 firms)
Source: Lawler et al. (1992).

Macy et al. (1990) reported that the use of self-directed teams correlated highly with increases in organizational effectiveness, heightened productivity, and reduced defects. Wellins et al. (1991) reported that two-thirds of companies that implemented self-directed work teams could run their companies with fewer managers, and in 95 percent of the cases, a reduced number of managers was reported to be beneficial to company performance. The results of other well-known studies have produced similar outcomes (Ancona & Caldwell, 1992; Hackman, 1990; Gladstein, 1984).

Many of the reasons for these positive outcomes of teams have been known for years. Maier (1967), for example, in a classic description of the conditions under which teams are more effective than individuals acting alone, and vice versa, pointed out that teams:

▶ Produce a greater number of ideas and pieces of information than individuals acting alone, so decision making and problem solving are more informed and are of higher quality.

▶ Improve understanding and acceptance among individuals involved in problem solving and decision making due to team members' participation in the process.

▶ Have higher motivation and performance levels than individuals acting alone because of the effects of "social facilitation": that is, people are more energized and active when they are around other people.

▶ Offset personal biases and blind spots that inhibit effective problem analysis and implementation but that are not noticed by single individuals.

▶ Are more likely to engage in a "risky shift"—that is, to entertain risky alternatives and to take innovative action—than individuals acting alone.

In addition, teams are usually more fun. Consider, for example, the two advertisements that appeared next to one another in a metropolitan newspaper, both seeking to fill the same type of position. They are reproduced in Figure 1. While neither advertisement is negative or inappropriate, they are substantially different. Which job would you rather take? Which firm would you rather work for? The team-focused job seems more desirable, doesn't it?

On the other hand, teams are not a panacea for everything that ails organizations, nor do they represent a magic potion that managers can use to accomplish their objectives. Just getting people together and calling them a team by no means makes them a team. A leading expert on teams, Richard Hackman (1993), pointed out that mistakes are common in team building and team management. Rewarding and recognizing individuals instead of the team, not maintaining stability of membership over time, not providing teams with autonomy, not fostering interdependence among team members, using the team to make all de-

cisions instead of having individuals make decisions when appropriate, failing to orient all team members, having too many members on the team, not providing appropriate structure for the team, and not providing the team with needed resources are all common mistakes Hackman found in his studies of teams. Moreover, a team is not always an appropriate mechanism for dealing with a challenge facing an organization. For example, simple, routine, or highly formalized work is not well-suited for teams. Verespei (1990) observed:

All too often corporate chieftains read the success stories and ordain their companies to adopt work teams—NOW. Work teams don't always work and may even be the wrong solution to the situation in question.

Our Team Needs One Good Multiskilled Maintenance Associate

Our team is down one good player. Join our group of multiskilled Maintenance Associates who work together to support our assembly teams at American Automotive Manufacturing.

We are looking for a versatile person with skills in one or more of the following: ability to set up and operate various welding machinery, knowledge in electric arc and M.I.G. welding, willingness to work on detailed projects for extended time periods, and general overall knowledge of the automobile manufacturing process. Willingness to learn all maintenance skills a must. You must be a real team player, have excellent interpersonal skills, and be motivated to work in a highly participative environment.

Send qualifications to :

American Automotive Manufacturing
P.O. Box 616
Ft. Wayne, Indiana 48606
Include phone number. We respond to all applicants.

Maintenance Technician/Welder

Leading automotive manufacturer looking for Maintenance Technician/Welder. Position requires the ability to set up and operate various welding machinery and a general knowledge of the automobile production process. Vocational school graduates or 3-5 years of on-the-job experience required. Competitive salary, full benefits, and tuition reimbursement offered.

Interviews Monday, May 6, at the Holiday Inn South, 3000 Semple Road, 9:00 a.m. to 7:00 p.m. Please bring pay stub as proof of last employment.

National Motors Corporation
5169 Blane Hill Center
Springfield, Illinois 62707

Figure 1 A Team-Oriented and a Traditional Advertisement for a Position

Teams, in other words, can be very powerful tools for managers in producing organizational success, but they are by no means a "sure thing." The Assessment instrument, Diagnosing the Need for Team Building, helps identify the extent to which teams will help an organization improve its performance. Teams can take too long to make decisions; they may drive out effective action with groupthink; and they can create confusion and frustration for their members. All of us have been irritated by being members of an inefficient team, a team dominated by one member, or having to take responsibility for the output of a team that compromised on excellence in order to get agreement from everyone. "A camel," it is said, "is a horse designed by a team."

Teams can be incredibly effective as they develop certain attributes of high performance. It is well-established, for example, that teams perform better than even the most competent individuals performing alone when certain attributes are present. An examination of high-performing teams reveals at least 16 attributes that distinguish them from teams that perform less well (Petrock, 1991). Consider, for example, a World Cup soccer team, an NBA basketball team, a world-class string quartet, or a jazz orchestra. The attributes listed below are among the most crucial for ensuring high performance. Helping you learn how to establish these attributes is an important purpose of this chapter.

Clear goals. Sports and music performance are motivating to team members because the goals are clear and are constantly emphasized.

Goals that are known by all. Every team member can give the same answer to the question: "What are we trying to accomplish?"

Goals achieved in small steps. Large goals are achieved in small steps, such as innings, downs, holes, frames, sections, bars, and sets—each with subobjectives.

Standards of excellence. All performance is measured against a standard of excellence, and mediocrity is never acceptable.

Feedback of results. All team members get immediate feedback on how they are doing and how the team is doing.

Skills and knowledge used. All team members have an opportunity to use all their skills and abilities when they participate.

Continuous training. Because constant improvement is expected, all team members are being trained continuously, on and off the playing field or stage.

Equipment and facilities. Adequate resources are provided for the team to succeed at its job.

Autonomy. Team members can exercise self-initiative and can make their own decisions on how they will perform.

Performance-based rewards. Rewards are based on accomplishments—not title, effort, or politics.

Competition. The risk of losing is always possible, and competition occurs not only against an opponent but against personal past performance.

Praise and recognition. Praise is greatest among team members themselves but comes from many sources and is continuous.

Team commitment. Team members are committed to the success of one other and to the team, so that when one fails, all feel a sense of failure.

Plans and tactics. Every team member is aware of the strategy to be used to accomplish the team's objective, and no competition is entered without advance planning.

Rules and penalties. Rules and penalties are known in advance by everyone, and they are fair, consistent, and immediate.

Performance measures. Many aspects of performance are measured: for example, batting averages, hits in scoring position, singles, doubles, triples, home runs, on-base percentages, runs-batted-in, power ratings, percent hits versus left- and right-handed pitchers are all measured for baseball hitters; pitch, tone quality, flow, mistakes, dynamics, precision, blend, sight-reading are all measured for quartets.

Team failure is common, so how can success in teams be assured? How can managers ensure the effectiveness of the teams in which they are involved? What should one learn to become a skillful team leader and team member? Because of the rapid growth of teams, as well as the potential positive impact teams can have on organizations' success, it is clear that understanding teams and teamwork is a prerequisite for any effective manager in modern organizations. We now turn, therefore, to the key management skills of team building and teamwork.

Stages of Team Development

In effective teams, team members' behavior is interdependent, and personal goals are subservient to the accomplishment of the team goal. A commitment to, and desire for team membership is present. Even though individuals may be formally designated as a team, if they act so as to bring exclusive credit to themselves, to accomplish their own objectives instead of the team's objective, or to maintain independence from others, they are not truly a team, regardless of their name. A key challenge, then, is to determine how to build the elements of a team into an independent group of individuals who have no prior commitment to one another or to a common task.

To effectively build, lead, or participate in a team one must understand the stages of development that teams follow as they form and carry out their functions. Effective managers are skillful at helping teams be successful as they progress from early stages of development—when a team is still struggling to become a coherent entity—to a more mature stage of development—when the team has become a highly effective, smoothly functioning organization. This chapter focuses on helping you improve your skill in diagnosing and leading each phase of team development.

Evidence of a predictable pattern of team development has been available since the early part of this century. Beginning with Dewey's (1933) emphasis on five (cognitive) stages of learning and Freud's (1921) analysis of children's (affective) responses to authority figures, research has proliferated on the cognitive and affective changes that occur in groups and teams over time. In fact, several thousand studies of groups and teams have appeared in just the last decade. Researchers have studied a wide variety of types of groups and teams with varying compositions and attributes. Problem-solving teams, quality circles, therapy groups, task forces, interpersonal growth groups, student project teams, and many other types have been studied extensively. Studies have ranged from teams meeting for just one session to teams with working lives extending over several years. Membership in teams has varied widely, ranging from children to aged people, top executives to line workers, students to instructors, volunteers to prison inmates, professional athletes to playground children, and so on. The analyses have focused on dynamics such as team-member roles, unconscious cognitive processes, group dynamics, problem-solving strategies, communication patterns, leadership actions, interpersonal needs, decision-making quality, innovativeness, and productivity.

Despite the variety in composition, purpose, and longevity across teams being investigated, the stages of group and team development emerging from these studies have been strikingly similar. For a review and summary of a dozen or so team-stage development models, see Cameron and Whetten (1981), Cameron and Whetten (1984), and Quinn and Cameron (1983). Teams tend to develop through four separate stages. These stages were first labeled by Tuckman (1965) as *forming, conforming, storming,* and *performing.* Because of their rhyme and parsimony, these labels are still widely used today. Table 2 summarizes the four main stages of team development. (The ordering of stages 2 and 3 are reversed from Tuckman's original model as a result of research conducted by Quinn & Cameron, 1988; Cameron & Whetten, 1981; and Greiner, 1972.)

In order for teams to be effective and for team members to benefit most from team membership, teams must progress through the first three stages of development to achieve Stage 4. In each separate stage, particular challenges and issues predominate, and it is by successfully managing these issues and overcoming the challenges that a team matures and becomes more effective. Skillful managers, whether serving as team leaders or team members, help the team progress to the next stage of development. Table 3 summarizes these challenges and issues.

To explain each stage and identify ways in which skilled managers assist teams in moving forward toward increasingly high performance and effectiveness, we discuss the dominant *team member questions, interpersonal relationships, task issues,* and *effective leader behaviors* that characterize each stage. Being able to diagnose the stage of a team's development and adopt appropriate leader behaviors is a skill that separates the most effective managers from those who are less effective.

The Development of a Team

To illustrate the development of a real team over these four stages, we will look at what turned out to be one of the highest-performing teams in history: the one formed to plan and carry out logistical support for soldiers in the Persian Gulf War (Pagonis, 1993). This team was organized in 1990 as a result of President Bush's announcement that the United States would

STAGE	EXPLANATION
Forming	The team is faced with the need to become acquainted with its members, its purpose, and its boundaries. Relationships must be formed and trust established. Clarity of direction is needed from team leaders.
Conforming	The team is faced with creating cohesion and unity, differentiating roles, identifying expectations for members, and enhancing commitment. Providing supportive feedback and fostering commitment to a vision are needed from team leaders.
Storming	The team is faced with disagreements, counterdependence, and the need to manage conflict. Challenges include violations of team norms and expectations and overcoming groupthink. Focusing on process improvement, recognizing team achievement, and fostering win/win relationships are needed from team leaders.
Performing	The team is faced with the need for continuous improvement, innovation, speed, and capitalizing on core competencies. Sponsoring team members' new ideas, orchestrating their implementation, and fostering extraordinary performance are needed from the team leaders.

Table 2   Four Stages of Team Development

STAGE	CATEGORY	CHARACTERISTICS
Forming	Team Member Questions	• Who are these other people? • What is going to happen? • What is expected of me? • Where are we headed and why? • Who is the leader? • What are our goals? • How do I fit in? • How much work will this involve?
	Interpersonal Relationships	• Silence • Self-consciousness • Dependence • Superficiality • Reactivity • Uncertainty
	Task Issues	• Orient members. • Become comfortable with team membership. • Establish trust. • Establish relationships with the leaders. • Establish clarity of purpose. • Deal with feelings of dependence.
	Effective Leader Behaviors	• Make introductions. • Answer questions. • Establish a foundation of trust. • Model expected behaviors. • Clarify goals, procedures, rules, and expectations.

Table 3   Typical Attributes of the Four Stages of Team Development

STAGE	CATEGORY	CHARACTERISTICS
Conforming	Team Member Questions	• What are the norms and expectations? • How much should I conform? • What role can I perform? • Will I be supported? • Where are we headed? • How much should I invest and commit?
	Interpersonal Relationships	• Cooperativeness • Ignoring disagreements • Conformity to standards and expectations • Obedience to leader directions • Heightened interpersonal attraction • Commitment to a team vision
	Task Issues	• Maintain unity and cohesion. • Differentiate and clarify roles. • Determine levels of personal investment. • Clarify the future. • Decide on levels of commitment to the team's future.
	Effective Leader Behaviors	• Facilitate role differentiation among team members. • Show support to team members. • Provide feedback. • Articulate a vision of the future for the team. • Help generate commitment to the vision.
Storming	Team Member Questions	• How will we handle disagreements? • How will we communicate negative information? • Can the team be changed? • How can we make decisions amidst disagreement? • Do we really need this leader? • Do I want to maintain my membership in the team?
	Interpersonal Relationships	• Polarization of team members • Coalitions or cliques being formed • Competition among team members • Disagreement with the leader • Challenging others' points of view • Violating team norms
	Task Issues	• Manage conflict. • Legitimize productive expressions of individuality. • Overcome groupthink. • Examine key work processes of the team. • Turn counterdependence into interdependence.
	Effective Leader Behaviors	• Identify a common enemy and reinforce the vision. • Generate commitment among team members. • Turn students into teachers. • Be an effective mediator. • Provide individual and team recognition. • Foster win/win thinking.

Table 3 *(continued)*

STAGE	CATEGORY	CHARACTERISTICS
Performing	Team Member Questions	• How can we continuously improve? • How can we foster innovativeness and creativity? • How can we build on our core competence? • What improvements can be made to our processes? • How can we maintain a high level of energy and commitment to the team?
	Interpersonal Relationships	• High mutual trust • Unconditional commitment to the team • Multifaceted relationships among team members • Mutual training and development • Entrepreneurship • Self-sufficiency
	Task Issues	• Capitalize on core competence. • Foster continuous improvement. • Anticipate needs of customers and respond in advance of requests. • Enhance speed and timeliness. • Encourage creative problem solving.
	Effective Leader Behaviors	• Foster innovation and continuous improvement simultaneously. • Advance the quality culture of the team. • Provide regular, ongoing feedback on team performance. • Play sponsor and orchestrator roles for team members. • Help the team avoid reverting back to earlier stages.

Table 3   *(continued)*

send troops to Saudi Arabia in order to confront Iraqi aggression in Kuwait.

The tasks of this team were daunting. It was charged with transporting over half a million people and their personal belongings to the other side of the world, on short notice. But transporting the people was only part of the challenge. Supporting them once they arrived, moving them into position for a surprise attack, supporting their battle plans, and then getting them and their equipment back home were even greater challenges. Over 122 million meals had to be planned, moved, and served—approximately the number eaten by all the residents of Wyoming and Vermont in three months. Fuel (1.3 billion gallons) had to be pumped—about the same amount used in Montana, North Dakota, and Idaho in a year—in order to support sol-

diers driving 52 million miles. Tanks, planes, ammunition, carpenters, cashiers, morticians, social workers, doctors, and a host of support personnel had to be transported, coordinated, fed, and housed. More than 500 new traffic signs had to be constructed and installed in order to help individuals speaking several different languages navigate the relatively featureless terrain of Saudi Arabia. Five hundred tons of mail had to be sorted and processed each day. Over 70,000 contracts with suppliers had to be negotiated and executed. All green-colored equipment—over 12,000 tracked vehicles and 117,000 wheeled vehicles—had to be repainted desert brown and then repainted green when shipped home. Soldiers had to be trained to fit in with an unfamiliar culture that was intolerant of typical soldier-relaxation activity. Supplies had to be distributed at a moment's notice to several different locations, some of them behind enemy lines, in the heat of battle. Traffic control was monumental, as evidenced by one key checkpoint near the front where 18 vehicles per minute passed, seven days a week, 24 hours a day, for six weeks. Over 60,000 enemy prisoners of war had to be transported, cared for, and detained. Because the war ended far sooner than anyone predicted, most of the equipment, ammunition, and supplies had to be brought back home—but only after thorough scrubbing to remove microorganisms or pests and shrinkwrapping. Since large, bulk containers had been broken up into smaller units during the war, it took twice as long to gather and ship materials out of Saudi Arabia as it did to ship them in. In short, this team was faced with a set of tasks that had never before been accomplished on that scale and in a time frame that would have been laughable if it weren't factual. The team assigned to accomplish these tasks had to be assembled and guided from the very first stage through the final stage of team development.

The various stages of this team's development can be found in the 1993 book *Moving Mountains,* written by General Pagonis, leader of the logistics support team. Pagonis was awarded a third star during Desert Storm for providing outstanding logistical support. He helped plan and execute the famous "end run" that took Saddam Hussein's army completely by surprise. Most observers now agree that it was the success of the logistics team that really won the Persian Gulf War for the United States.

To better understand how General Pagonis' logistics team could reach such a high level of effectiveness—a level where enormously complicated activities were coordinated flawlessly and precisely without a single leader standing up front barking out directions—it is necessary to understand the aspects of each of the four stages of team development. Each stage is explained in some detail below, with the required management and leadership behaviors given special attention.

The Forming Stage

Team member questions, interpersonal relationships, and task issues.   Most performers know that at the beginning of a concert, the audience is "cold." Because people are not initially very responsive, major performers use a warm-up act to get the au-

dience "in-tune" or to "become one" with the performer. Similarly, when team members first come together, they are much like an audience at the outset of a concert. They are not a team, but an aggregation of individuals sharing a common setting. Something must happen for them to feel that they are a cohesive unit. Recall an instance in which you met with a group of people for the first time. It may have been at the outset of a semester in school, in a committee or task force meeting, in a church or professional group, or on an intramural sports team. When you first came together with other potential team members, you probably did not feel integrated into a cohesive unit. In fact, you likely had several *questions* on your mind such as:

- Who are these other people?
- What is going to happen?
- What is expected of me?
- Where are we headed and why?
- Who is the leader?
- What are our goals?
- How do I fit in?
- How much work will this involve?

The questions uppermost in the minds of participants in a new team have to do with establishing a sense of security and direction, getting oriented, and becoming comfortable with the new situation. Sometimes, new team members can articulate these questions, while at other times they are little more than general feelings of discomfort or disconnectedness. Uncertainty and ambiguity tend to predominate as individuals seek some type of understanding and structure. Because there is no shared history with the team, there is no unity among members. Thus, the typical *interpersonal relationships* that predominate in this stage are:

- Silence
- Self-consciousness
- Dependence
- Superficiality
- Reactivity
- Uncertainty

Even though some individuals may enter a team situation with great enthusiasm and anticipation, they are usually hesitant to demonstrate their emotions to others until they begin to feel at ease. Moreover, without knowing the rules and boundaries, it feels risky to speak out or to even ask questions. Seldom are new members willing to actively query a leader when a team first meets together, even though uncertainty prevails. When the leader asks questions of team members, rarely does someone jump at the chance to answer them. When answers are given, they are likely to be brief. Little interaction occurs among team members themselves, most communication is targeted at the team leader or person in charge, and each individual is generally thinking more of himself or herself than of the team. Interactions tend to be formal and guarded. Congruent behaviors are masked in the interest of self-protection.

Individuals cannot begin to feel like a team until they become familiar with the rules and boundaries of their setting. They don't know whom to trust, who will take initiative, what constitutes normal behavior, or what kinds of interactions are appropriate. They are not yet a real team but only a collection of individuals. Therefore, the task of the team in this stage is less focused on producing an output than on developing the team itself. Helping team members become comfortable with one another takes precedence over task accomplishment. A team faces the following kinds of *task issues* in its first stage of development:

- Orienting members
- Becoming comfortable with team membership
- Establishing trust
- Establishing relationships with the leader
- Establishing clarity of purpose
- Dealing with feelings of dependence

Effective leader behaviors. Teams can remain in the first stage for an extended period, and many do when no clear direction is provided about what the team is to accomplish, what the rules are, or what each member's responsibilities entail. Some teams never move past this stage of development but remain a loose aggregation of individuals without the magnetism or commitment that characterize high-performing teams. The lifespan of such a team is likely to be short. Unless a skillful person takes time to deal with the issues and anxieties of team members, it will become progressively harder for the team to develop beyond this stage. Such teams eventually dissolve. On the other hand, this stage can be relatively brief if a leader of the team takes the following actions:

- Makes introductions
- Answers questions
- Establishes a foundation of trust
- Models expected behaviors
- Clarifies goals, procedures, rules, and expectations

In the initial stage of his own team's development, General Pagonis tackled this challenge head on. He began with the process of recruiting his team members.

> Over the years I have developed a very distinctive leadership style. Gus Pagonis's command style, like everyone else's, is unique. This meant that I had choices to make. Would I rather have the world's best port operation officer, if he was someone who didn't already know my style? Or would I rather have the world's second best port operation officer who knew my style intimately and was comfortable with it? The answer was obvious; we couldn't waste time fighting our own systems. Equally important, we couldn't afford the time that would be wasted as a new person tried to impress me, or get on my good side. We needed an instant body of leaders, strengthened by a united front. We needed to know that we could depend on one another unconditionally. We needed the confidence that the mission, and not personal advancement, would always be paramount in the mind of each participant (p. 78).

In the initial stage of team development, Pagonis needed to bring other team members up to speed on their mission.

> [The team] got down to work with a redoubled sense of urgency. They were soon fully familiar with the plan that had been roughed out by [the highest commanding officers] and me. . . . We quickly got to a joint understanding of what I took to be our role in the theater. . . . Our session . . . was very successful, mainly because from the outset we had a well-defined

structure for invention. We worked toward several clearly expressed goals, and there was an imposed time limit to keep us on track. And finally, our various experiences were complementary. We needed each other and we knew it (pp. 82–83).

Skillful team leaders act more like directors than facilitators in this first stage. This is not a time for team leaders to rely on free and open discussion and consensus decision making to accomplish an outcome. Direction, clarity, and structure are needed instead. The first task is to ensure that all team members know one another and that their questions are answered (even unasked questions which are on the minds of team members). Because relatively little participation may occur during this stage, the temptation is for team leaders to rush ahead or to short-circuit introductions and instructions. Skillful team leaders leave time for questions, however, and they urge team members to reveal their uncertainties. Guidelines, boundaries, and expectations are clarified so that team members understand how they fit in, how much will be required of them, and how much trust they can have in the team.

In the case of the Persian Gulf logistics team, the first critical task undertaken by General Pagonis was to make certain that objectives, rules and regulations, time frames, and resources were clearly laid out. Each member of the team received maximum information in order for each to become comfortable with his or her team membership: "They were soon fully familiar with the plan that had been roughed out, . . . a joint understanding of what I took to be our role in the theater, . . . a well-defined structure for invention, . . . clearly expressed goals, and . . . an imposed time limit to keep us on track."

In the chapter on Empowering and Delegating, we discussed five dimensions upon which trust is built: reliability, fairness, caring, openness, and competence. Team leaders must model these attributes in their own behavior in order to establish this foundation of trust. This means being consistent and dependable in actions and congruent in communication. It means being equitable and fair and showing personal concern for all team members. It means sharing information openly, honestly, and clearly, while exhibiting sensitivity to the needs of all team members. Finally, it means helping team members become aware of the competence and resources available to them.

As stated by General Pagonis (p. 88): "Keeping your [team members] abreast of your actions, as well as the rationale behind those actions, puts everybody on an equal information footing. I believe that information is power, but only if it is shared."

In sum, one of the crucial responsibilities of a team leader is to help clarify for all team members the structure of the team, without which a team will have a difficult time progressing past the forming stage of development. When the team leader successfully provides the necessary clarity and direction, however, the team can progress to the second stage.

The Conforming Stage

Team member questions, interpersonal relationships, and task issues. Once a team has resolved the issues of the forming stage, those issues are replaced by others that lead the team into a new stage of development. When a team begins to function as a unit and team members become comfortable in their setting, team members experience pressure to conform to the emerging norms. For example, recall a time when you became a member of an ongoing team. Chances are that you almost immediately felt pressure to conform. That is because team members become inclined to behave consistently with other team members' expectations. The more team members interact with one another, the more they develop common behaviors and perspectives. This conformity may affect the amount of work done by the team, styles of communicating, approaches to problem solving, and even dress.

Team members also begin to identify a unique role for themselves in this stage. They try to find their own place in the group. In the case of General Pagonis's logistics team, the roles of "firefighter," "fixer," and "cheerleader" began to emerge, even though these roles were not prescribed as part of the formal responsibilities.

The basic problem was that we were trying to set up a logistical structure for reception in the middle of deployment. According to doctrine and common sense, you set up the structure first, and only then do you begin deployment. But the reality of the military situation didn't allow us this luxury. Truth be told, we spent less of our time as logisticians, and more of our time as managers, fixers, firefighters, father confessors, and cheerleaders. There was simply nobody else around to play any of these roles (p. 87).

The major focus of team members, then, shifts from overcoming uncertainty and increasing clarity in the forming stage to becoming unified and identifying roles that can be played by each member in the conforming stage. Typical *questions* in team members' minds during this stage include:

- What are the norms and expectations?
- How much should I conform?
- What role can I perform?
- Will I be supported?
- Where are we headed?
- How much should I invest and commit?

During the conforming stage, team members become contented with team membership and begin to value the team's goals more than their own personal goals. Individual needs begin to be met through the team's accomplishments. The team, rather than the leader or a single person, takes responsibility for solving problems, confronting and correcting mistakes, and ensuring success. Agreement and willingness to go along characterize the climate of the team, since members are willing to put aside personal biases for the good of the group. Individuals experience feelings of loyalty to the team, and the *interpersonal relationships* that most characterize team members include:

- Cooperativeness
- Ignoring disagreements
- Conformity to standards and expectations
- Obedience to leader directions
- Heightened interpersonal attraction
- Commitment to a team vision

In this stage, however, tension arises between forces pushing the team toward cohesion and forces pushing the team toward differentiation. At the same time strong bonds of team unity are being formed, individuals try to differentiate themselves from one another and adopt unique roles in the team. They seek to become complementary to one another rather than duplicative. The presence of differentiated roles in the team may actually foster team cohesion and unity, as illustrated by Pagonis's logistics team, in which members were selected specifically to achieve complementarity. But the potential tension gives rise to the following *task*

issues that must be addressed in this stage of development:

- Maintaining unity and cohesion
- Differentiating and clarifying roles
- Determining levels of personal investment
- Clarifying the future
- Deciding on levels of commitment to the team's future

In identifying which roles to perform in order to contribute the most to the success of the team, members have two main categories of roles from which to choose: **task-facilitating roles** and **relationship-building roles**. It is difficult for team members to emphasize both types of roles equally, and most people tend to contribute in one area more than the other. That is, some team members tend to be more task focused whereas others tend to be more relationship focused. Task-facilitating roles are those that help the team accomplish its outcome objectives—for example, to produce a product or service, solve a problem, or generate a new idea. Among the common task-facilitating roles are:

Direction giving. Identifying ways to proceed or alternatives to pursue and clarifying goals and objectives.

Information seeking. Asking questions, analyzing knowledge gaps, requesting opinions, beliefs, and perspectives.

Information giving. Providing data, offering facts and judgments, and highlighting conclusions.

Elaborating. Building on the ideas expressed by others; providing examples and illustrations.

Coordinating. Pulling ideas together, and helping others examine one another's suggestions and comments; helping members work together.

Monitoring. Developing measures of success and helping to maintain accountability for results.

Process analyzing. Analyzing processes and procedures used by the team in order to improve efficiency and timeliness.

Reality testing. Exploring whether ideas presented are practical or workable.

Enforcing. Keeping the team focused on the task at hand and driving out all side issues.

Summarizing. Combining ideas and summing up points made in the team; helping members understand the conclusions that have been reached.

Relationship-building roles are those that emphasize the interpersonal aspects of the team. They focus on assisting team members to feel good about one another, to enjoy the team's work, and to maintain a tension-free climate. Among the common relationship-building roles are:

Supporting. Praising the ideas of others and pointing out others' contributions.

Harmonizing. Mediating differences between others, and finding a common ground in disputes and conflicting points of view.

Tension relieving. Using jokes and humor to reduce tension and put others at ease.

Confronting. Challenging unproductive or disruptive behaviors; helping to ensure proper behavior in the team.

Energizing. Motivating others toward greater effort and accomplishment; exuding enthusiasm.

Developing. Assisting others to learn, grow, and achieve; orienting and coaching members of the team.

Facilitating. Helping build solidarity among team members and helping interactions to be smooth.

Processing. Reflecting group feelings and helping to smooth out the team's functioning.

Without both types of roles being played, a team does not advance past the second stage of development. Some members must ensure that the team accomplishes its tasks, while others must ensure that members remain bonded together interpersonally. These are usually not the same individuals. Each team member begins to play different roles, with some roles becoming more dominant than others. The key is to have a balance between task-oriented roles and relationship-building roles displayed in the team. The downfall of many teams is that they become unidimensional—for example, they emphasize task accomplishment exclusively—and do not give equal attention to both types of roles.

The next time you are in a team setting, try keeping track of the behaviors displayed by each team member. See if you can identify the "task masters" and the "relationship builders." Which roles do you most naturally play yourself? The advantage of being able to recognize different roles is that team development cannot progress unless many of these roles are present and effectively performed. Knowing which roles are needed and being able to play multiple roles helps perpetuate team effectiveness.

Of course, each role can also have a downside if performed ineffectively or in inappropriate circumstances. For example, elaborating may be disruptive if the team is trying to reach a quick decision; tension relieving may be annoying if the team is trying to be serious; enforcing may create resistance when the team is already experiencing high levels of pressure; facilitating may mask real differences of opinion and tension among team members. However, even more likely is the presence of other unproductive roles that team members play. These roles inhibit the team or its members from achieving what they could have achieved, and they destroy morale and cohesion. They are called **blocking roles.** We point out a few of them here because, as you analyze the teams to which you belong, you may recognize these roles being performed and be able to confront them. Among common blocking roles are:

Overanalyzing. Splitting hairs and examining every detail excessively.

Overgeneralizing. Blowing something out of proportion and drawing unfounded conclusions.

Fault-finding. Unwilling to see the merits of others' ideas or behaviors.

Premature decision making. Making decisions before goals are stated, information is shared, alternatives are discussed, or problems are defined.

Presenting opinions as facts. Failing to examine the legitimacy of proposals and labeling personal opinions as truth.

Rejecting. Rejecting ideas based on the person who stated them rather than on their merits.

Pulling rank. Using status, expertise, or title to get ideas accepted rather than discussing and examining their value.

Dominating. Excessive talking, interrupting, or cutting others off.

Stalling. Not allowing the group to reach a decision or finalize a task by sidetracking the discussion, being unwilling to agree, repeating old arguments, and so on.

Remaining passive. Not being willing to engage in the team's task. Staying on the fringe or refusing to interact with other team members. Expecting others to do the team's work.

Resisting. Blocking all attempts to change, to improve, or to make progress. Being disagreeable and negative about virtually all suggestions from other team members.

Effective leader behaviors. Each of the above-mentioned blocking roles has the potential to inhibit a team from efficiently and successfully accomplishing its task by crushing morale, destroying consensus, creating conflict, and making ill-informed decisions. Effective team leaders work with team members to avoid blocking roles while at the same time ensuring that task-facilitating and relationship-building roles are adequately performed by team members. Maintaining a balance of task and relationship role emphasis and ensuring that roles being performed are not disruptive or destructive is an important responsibility of the team leader. In addition, the following leader behaviors are required in this stage of the team's development:

- Facilitate role differentiation among team members

- Show support to team members

- Provide feedback

- Articulate a vision of the future for the team

- Help generate commitment to the vision

Helping a team develop cohesion relies at least partly on providing feedback to team members. This means giving them information about how they are doing as individuals as well as how the team is doing as a unit. In providing feedback to others, team leaders and team members should use the following guidelines:

Focus feedback on behavior rather than persons. Individuals can control and change their behavior. They cannot change their personalities or physical characteristics.

Focus feedback on observations rather than inferences and on descriptions rather than judgments. Facts and objective evidence is more trustworthy and acceptable than opinions and conjectures.

Focus feedback on behavior related to a specific situation, preferably to the "here-and-now," rather than on abstract or past behavior. It will merely frustrate people if they cannot pinpoint a specific incident or behavior to which you are referring. Similarly, people cannot change something that has already happened and is "water under the bridge."

Focus feedback on sharing ideas and information rather than giving advice. Explore alternatives together. Unless requested, avoid giving directive feedback and demands; instead, help recipients identify changes and improvements themselves.

Focus feedback on the amount of information that the person receiving it can use, rather than on the amount you might like to give. Information overload causes people to stop listening. Not enough information leads to frustration and misunderstanding.

Focus feedback on the value it may have to the receiver, not on the emotional release it provides for you. Feedback should be for the good of the recipient, not merely for you to let off steam.

Focus feedback on time and place so that personal data can be shared at appropriate times. The more specific feedback is, or the more it can be anchored in a specific context, the more helpful it can be.

In addition to providing feedback to help team members become a cohesive unit, the most important thing a team leader can do is to articulate a vision of the future for the team. Peter Senge (1991) asserted that every effective, high-performing team and organization has a clear, inspirational vision. General Pagonis's agreement with this proposition is illustrated by his statement: "Every successful venture grows out of a vision. . . . It's the vision that motivates, embraces, and sets limits, all at once" (p. 171). In one of the best studies published on high-performing teams, Katzenbach and Smith (1993) stated:

> The best teams invest a tremendous amount of time and effort exploring, shaping, and agreeing on a [vision] that belongs to them collectively and individually. . . . With enough time and sincere attention, one or more broad, meaningful aspirations invariably arise that motivate teams to provide a fundamental reason for their extra effort (p. 50).

All teams have specific goals and objectives to achieve, but a vision is something different. It helps illuminate the core values and principles that will guide the team in the future. It gives a sense of direction. It provides a glimpse of possibilities, not just probabilities. It evokes deeper meaning and deeper commitment than task or goal statements. It is intended to help team members think differently about themselves and their future. It serves as a glue to bind the team together. Finally, it does all of this by way of three characteristics:

Left-brained and right-brained. An effective vision statement contains objective targets, goals, and action plans (left-brain components) as well as metaphors, colorful language, and emotion (right-brain components). It captures the head (left-brain) as well as the heart and imagination (right-brain) of team members. The most motivating vision statements—for example, Martin Luther King's "I Have a Dream" speech, Winston Churchill's "Never Give Up" speech, John F. Kennedy's "Ask Not What Your Country Can Do for You" speech, Henry V's "Saint Crispin's Day" speech—contain both left-brained elements (specific objectives) and right-brained elements (emotional imagery). Leaders articulate the vision using stories and metaphors as well as targets and goals.

Interesting. Murray Davis (1971) pointed out that what people judge to be interesting and energizing has little to do with truth or legitimacy. Rather, what's interesting is information that contradicts weakly held assumptions and challenges the status quo. If a vision is consistent with what is already believed or known (e.g., "We will accomplish our work"), people tend to dismiss it as common sense. They don't remember it, and it doesn't motivate them. If a vision is contradictory to strongly held assumptions, or if it blatantly challenges core values of team members (e.g., "Every team member will become rich"), it is labeled ridiculous, silly, or blasphemous. A vision that helps create a new way to view the future, on the other hand, that challenges the current state of things, is viewed as interesting and energizing. For example, "We will land on the moon in 10 years" was just contradictory enough, just outlandish enough, just enough of a stretch to be interesting. It not only made people think, it provided something new to think about. The vision of effective leaders stretches perspectives and contradicts status quo or easily attained targets.

Passion and principles. Effective visions are grounded in core values that team members believe in and about which they feel passionate. Even if a team's

task objective were to vanish, for example, members might still desire to affiliate with the team because of the core principles associated with its vision. Therefore, the principles in the vision must be personal. A vision focused on "increasing productivity" is less magnetic than a vision based on "personal growth." "Achieving profitability" is less magnetic than "building a better world." Furthermore, such principles are best phrased using superlatives. Notice the difference in how you feel about the following comparisons: "exceptional performance" versus "good performance"; "passionately involved" versus "committed"; "explosive growth" versus "substantial growth"; "awesome products" versus "useful products." Visions based on the former phrases engender more enthusiasm and passion than those based on the latter phrases.

Consider as an example of such language the 1987 vision statement of John Scully, former CEO of Apple Computer Company:

> We are all part of a journey to create an extraordinary corporation. The things we intend to do in the years ahead have never been done before. . . . One person, one computer is still our dream. . . . We have a passion for changing the world. We want to make personal computers a way of life in work, education, and the home. Apple people are paradigm shifters. . . . We want to be the catalyst for discovering new ways for people to do things. . . . Apple's way starts with a passion to create awesome products with a lot of distinctive value built in. . . . We have chosen directions for Apple that will lead us to wonderful ideas we haven't as yet dreamed.

Once a vision of the future has been articulated, it is important that leaders ensure that team members commit to it. Although a vision may exist, if team members do not accept the vision as their own, it is worthless and may, in fact, tear apart rather than solidify a team. Team leaders can foster commitment to their vision and, hence, to team cohesion in three principal ways.

Public commitment. When people state their commitments in public, they are motivated to behave consistently with those public declarations (Salancik, 1977). The internal need for congruence enhances the probability that public statements will be followed by consistent actions. For example, during World War II, good cuts of meat were in short supply. Lewin (1951) found a significant difference between the commitment level of shoppers who promised aloud to buy more plentiful but less desirable cuts of meat (e.g., liver, kidneys, brains) compared to those who promised to do so in private. In another study, students in a college class were required to set goals for how much they would read and what kinds of scores they would get on exams. Only half the students were allowed to state these goals publicly to the rest of the class. By mid-semester, the students who stated their goals publicly averaged 86 percent improvement compared to 14 percent improvement for the other students. These findings reinforce the fact that effective team leaders provide opportunities for team members to restate the vision themselves in a public setting. When they do so—that is, when team members are given the opportunity to explain the vision to others—their own commitment increases.

Consensus through participation. Having the opportunity to be involved in formulating plans to accomplish the vision also engenders commitment to it. Effective team leaders therefore foster commitment by involving team members in reaching consensus about various aspects of the vision. For example, in a classic study of how former opponents of a vision came to be supporters, Selznick (1949) studied the resistance of local farmers to the Tennessee Valley Authority's (TVA) plans to build a dam. To elicit farmers' commitment to the project, the TVA made local farmers members of the board that would plan and supervise the construction project. When farmers began to make public statements explaining the TVA project, they became committed to it (Selznick, 1949).

One way to enhance the participation and agreement of all team members is to use a technique such as the Nominal Group Technique (NGT) (Delbecq, Van de Ven, & Gustafson, 1975). This technique ensures that everyone on the team is heard and that consensus is reached. The technique consists of six steps:

1. Team members are presented with a challenge or issue—for example, how to accomplish the vision.

2. Individual team members silently and independently write down their ideas. This is the nominal (noninteracting) phase.

3. Each team member (one at a time, in round-robin fashion) presents an idea to the group. No discussion of ideas occurs. All ideas are recorded for the team to see.

4. After all individuals have presented their ideas, a discussion of the merits of the ideas occurs. Ideas are merged, eliminated, expanded, and modified.

5. Team members privately vote on their preferred ideas. This might be done by having each team member select the top two or three ideas, divide 10 points among alternatives, rank-ordering alternatives, or other decision-making alternatives.

6. A revised list of the best ideas is presented to team members for discussion. If a consensus emerges, the team is finished. If not, the procedure returns to Step 2 and continues through more rounds until the best ideas are identified and agreement is reached.

The point is to help all team members participate and express their own personal opinions while still building team consensus.

Frequent communication. Commitment is enhanced if the vision is communicated frequently. If leaders stop communicating the vision or if they change themes in their interactions with the team, members tend to think that the vision isn't important anymore. Unless leaders continually and consistently articulate, rehearse, and reinforce the vision, it loses its power, and commitment erodes. Leaders must also serve as models of the principles in the vision. No question should exist in the minds of those who interact with team leaders as to what the vision is. One leader who exemplifies this principle is Jan Carlzon, former CEO of Scandinavian Airlines (SAS), a highly touted team leader and executive. Carlzon states:

Good leaders spend more time communicating than anything else. From my first day at SAS I've made communicating, particularly with our employees, a top priority. In fact, during the first year I spent exactly half my working hours out in the field talking to SAS people. The word going around was that any time three employees gathered, Jan Carlzon would probably show up and begin talking with them. . . . When we began reorganizing SAS, our critics scoffed at our efforts as mere promotional gimmicks. They claimed we had become too marketing oriented, but in fact we hadn't increased our marketing budget one cent. Rather, we were spending our money more effectively on messages that were easily understood (Carlzon, 1987, pp. 88, 92).

In summary, skillful managers in the conforming stage of development help build cohesion and unity, help team members engage in productive but differentiated roles, and help create commitment to a motivating vision. When they do so, the team can then move on to the next stage of development.

The Storming Stage

Team member questions, interpersonal relationships, and task issues.   Invariably, the differentiation that begins to occur in the conforming stage leads to conflict and counterdependence in the team. Playing different roles causes team members to develop different perspectives. Virtually every team goes through a stage where team members question the legitimacy of the team's direction, the leader, the roles of other team members, the opinions or decisions being espoused, and the task objectives. This is a natural phase of development in the team because, up to now, the team has largely been characterized by harmony and consensus. Individual differences have been suppressed for the good of the team. However, such a condition will not last forever without team members becoming uncomfortable that they are losing their individual identity, subjugating their feelings, or stifling their differing perspectives. The team, in other words, has never learned how to cope with conflict, differences, and disruptions. It has merely repressed them. Its long-term success, however, will depend on how well it manages this storming stage of development. The team can disintegrate if this stage is not managed well. Typical questions that arise in team members' minds during this stage are:

 ▶ How can we make decisions amidst disagreement?

 ▶ How will we handle dissension?

 ▶ How will we communicate negative information?

 ▶ Can the team be changed?

 ▶ Do we really need this leader?

 ▶ Do I want to maintain my membership in the team?

An old Middle Eastern proverb states: "All sunshine makes a desert." Similarly, team growth implies that some struggles must occur, some discomfort must be experienced, and some obstacles must be overcome for the team to prosper. The team must learn to deal with adversity—especially that produced by its own members. If team members are more interested in keeping peace than in solving problems and accomplishing tasks, the team will never become effective, and its long-term viability will be threatened. No one wants to remain in a team that will not allow for individuality and uniqueness and that wants to maintain harmony more than it wants to accomplish its goals. Consequently, harmony is sometimes sacrificed as the team attacks problems and accomplishes objectives.

Moreover, as team members become more comfortable in their membership and roles as a result of passing through the forming and conforming stages, they begin to participate more openly and more frequently. This increased participation always uncovers differences in perspective. Such expressions of individuality and difference often create conflict. The team therefore experiences a stormy phase of development that, if managed well, can help it be even more effective than if no conflict had been encountered.

Team members in this third stage of development do not cease to care about one another, and they remain committed to the team and its success. But they do begin to take sides on issues, to find that they are more compatible with some team members than with others, and to agree with some points of view rather than with others. This differentiation in roles and perspectives creates interpersonal relationships characterized by:

 ▶ Polarization of team members

 ▶ Coalitions or cliques being formed

 ▶ Competition among team members

 ▶ Disagreement with the leader

 ▶ Challenging others' points of view

 ▶ Violating team norms

The storming stage does not necessarily imply that the team becomes chaotic, self-destructive, or mean-spirited. Rather, the same results occur as when teenagers begin to separate from their parents, when junior managers or interns in companies begin to break away from their mentors, and when pupils begin to challenge their teachers. Separation anxiety, competition, and even resentment may arise, mainly because the old pattern of relationships has changed. The unquestioned authority of the leader is challenged and no longer inviolate. Independence and interdependence replace dependence. Disagreements are common. Therefore, effective conflict management strategies take on added importance as team members are required sometimes to adopt an **initiator role,** sometimes a **responder role,** and sometimes a **mediator role** in addressing inevitable conflicts. Team members must sometimes confront others and express disagreement (initiator), sometimes defend their own point of view against others who disagree with or confront them (responder), and sometimes help referee or mediate a disagreement among other team members (mediator). See the chapter on Managing Conflict for guidelines in performing those three roles.

It is also common in the storming stage for team members to test and challenge the boundaries and norms of the team. This might include small aberrations such as coming late, holding side conversations in team meetings, or interrupting the team's work. It might also encompass more significant challenges, such as trying to oust the team leader, generating new rules to replace the original ones, or building a coalition to alter the team's goals and objectives significantly. During Desert Storm, for example, a relatively rigid military command hierarchy—along with the urgency of the mission to be performed—inhibited large deviations from established norms and rules, but small aberrations occurred constantly. For example, logistics team members painted personal logos on some tanks and trucks, insider code names were given to people and locations as a bit of sarcasm, and challenges to top brass mandates became more common in briefing rooms.

The testing of norms and boundaries is sometimes merely an expression of a need for individuality, while in other instances it is a product of strong feelings that the team can be improved. The main task issues to be addressed by the team in this stage include:

- Managing conflict

- Legitimizing productive expressions of individuality

- Overcoming groupthink

- Examining key work processes of the team

- Turning counterdependence into interdependence

Conflict, coalition formation, and counterdependence create conditions that may lead to the norms and values of the team being questioned. Rather than being stifled, resisted, or shut off, however, effective teams encourage members to turn those challenges into constructive suggestions for improvement. General Pagonis's philosophy about the way to manage differences was to encourage their expression:

> The key is to be open to different experiences and perspectives. If you can't tolerate different kinds of people, you're not likely to learn from different kinds of perspectives. Effective leaders encourage contrary opinions, an important source of vitality. This is especially true in the military where good ideas come in an incredible variety of packages (Pagonis, 1993, p. 24).

The team must be careful during this stage to restate and reinforce the overall vision for the team, and not to confuse it with more specific, short-term goals or processes. Abandoning the core vision will not help the team progress beyond this stage of development; instead, the team will become mired in debates about key values. Coalitions must be reminded of the common vision and principles that bond the overall team, even though different subgroups may take different positions on issues.

General Pagonis ensured that this was the case in his team.

> [Our] strength was flexibility, both as individuals and as a group. Organizations must be flexible enough to adjust and conform when their environments change. But the flexibility can degenerate into chaos in the absence of well-established goals. . . . Once everyone in the organization understands the goals of the organization, then each person sets out several objectives by which to attain those goals within his or her own sphere of activity. . . . When it works, cooperation and collegiality are enhanced, and in-fighting and suboptimization are minimized (p. 83).

It is important for team members to feel that they can legitimately express their personal uniqueness and idiosyncrasies, so long as they are not destructive to the overall team. It is clear from research on teams that they are more effective if membership is heterogeneous than if all team members act, believe, and see things the same way (Murnigham, 1981). Maintaining flexibility in the team implies that tolerance for individuality is acceptable and that changes and improvements are promoted. Note the approach taken by General Pagonis:

> I never tell a subordinate how to carry out a specific goal. Dictating terms to a subordinate undermines innovation, decreases the subordinate's willingness to take responsibility for his or her actions, increases the potential for suboptimization of resources, and increases the chances that the command will be dysfunctional if circumstances change dramatically. Our first month in the theater only underscored my sense that our [team] would have to be incredibly elastic (Pagonis, 1993, p. 119).

Expressing individuality does not mean, of course, that commitment to the overall team's success need be abandoned. In fact, it is important during this stage to reinforce constantly the need for team members to focus on the welfare of the overall group and the achievement of the vision. One of the best ways for this to happen is for the team to make certain that a **win/win philosophy** permeates the team's activities. As discussed in the chapters on Managing Conflict and Communicating Supportively, a win/win philosophy means that team members try to ensure that everyone benefits from their actions. All changes, challenges, or suggestions are pursued for the good of the team, not for self-aggrandizement at the expense of the team. Team members should understand that they are better off only if all team members are better off. Losing and causing others to lose (e.g., not getting rewarded, not accomplishing the objective, not feeling good about oneself) is not acceptable. For example, Pagonis's statement that each of his team members "needed to know that we could depend on one another unconditionally . . . that the mission, and not personal advancement, would always be paramount in the mind of each participant" illustrates the manner in which uniqueness, individuality, and differences are ideally managed.

The advantage of storming: overcoming group-think. One of the potential problems with a win/win philosophy in a team, however, is that it can lead to the emergence of a phenomenon called **groupthink** (Janis, 1972). Groupthink occurs when the cohesiveness and inertia developed in a group or team drives out good decision making or problem solving. The preservation of the team takes precedence over accurate decisions or high-quality task accomplishment. Not enough conflict occurs.

Irv Janis (1972) conducted research in which he chronicled several high-performing teams that in one instance performed in a stellar fashion, but performed disastrously in another instance. His classic example was the cabinet of President John F. Kennedy. This team worked through what is often considered one of the best sets of decisions ever made in handling the Cuban Missile Crisis, in which the former Soviet Union was inhibited from placing warhead missiles in Cuba by means of a high-stakes confrontation by Kennedy and his cabinet. But this was also the same team that made the disastrous decisions related to the Bay of Pigs fiasco, in which a planned overthrow of Fidel Castro's government in Cuba became a logistical nightmare, a confluence of indecision, and an embarrassing defeat for the same formerly high-functioning team.

What was the difference? Why did the same team do so well in one circumstance and so poorly in another? The answer is groupthink. Groupthink typically occurs when the following attributes arise in teams.

Illusion of invulnerability. Members feel assured that the team's past success will continue. ("Because of our track record, we cannot fail.")

Shared stereotypes. Members dismiss disconfirming information by discrediting its source. ("These people just don't understand these things.")

Rationalization. Members rationalize away threats to an emerging consensus. ("The reason they don't agree with us is . . .")

Illusion of morality. Members believe that they, as moral individuals, are not likely to make wrong decisions. ("This team would never knowingly make a bad decision or do anything immoral.")

Self-censorship. Members keep silent about misgivings and try to minimize doubts. ("I must be wrong if others think that way.")

Direct pressure. Sanctions are imposed on members who explore deviant viewpoints. ("If you don't agree, why don't you leave the team?")

Mind-guarding. Members protect the team from being exposed to disturbing ideas. ("Don't listen to them. We need to keep the rabble rousers at bay.")

Illusion of unanimity. Members conclude that the team has reached a consensus because the most vocal members are in agreement. ("If Dave and Melissa agree, there must be a consensus.")

The problem with groupthink is that it leads teams to commit more errors than normal. As an example, consider the following commonly observed scenario. Not wanting to make a serious judgment error, a leader convenes a meeting of his or her team. In the process of discussing an issue, the leader expresses a preference for one option. Other team members, wanting to appear supportive, present arguments justifying the decision. One or two members tentatively suggest alternatives, but they are strongly overruled by the majority. The decision is carried out with even-greater conviction than normal because everyone is in agreement, but the consequences are disastrous. How did this happen? While the leader brought the team together to avoid making a bad decision, the presence of groupthink actually made a bad decision more likely. Without the social support provided by the team, the leader may have been more cautious in implementing a personally preferred but uncertain decision.

To avoid groupthink, each team should make certain that the following characteristics are present:

Critical evaluators. At least one team member should be assigned to perform the role of critic or evaluator of the team's decisions.

Open discussion. The team leader should not express an opinion at the outset of the team meeting but should encourage open discussion of differing perspectives by team members.

Subgroups. Multiple subgroups in the team may be formed to develop independent proposals.

Outside experts. Invite outside experts to listen to the rationale for the team's decision and critique it.

Devil's advocate. Assign at least one team member to play devil's advocate during the discussion if it

seems that too much homogeneity exists in the team's discussion.

Second-chance meetings. Sleep on the team's decision and revisit it afresh the next day. The expression of team members' second thoughts should be encouraged.

Process management. Another highly effective activity to avoid groupthink, enhance the team's task accomplishment, and manage the storming stage of development is for team members to examine carefully the team's processes. **Team processes** are those methods of interacting and doing work that have emerged over the first two stages of development. Such an examination is important because the norms and team processes that the team developed in the forming and conforming stages may become the source of team member dissatisfaction as well as of groupthink. Alternative ways to approach problems and accomplish tasks may be preferred by some members, but no opportunity has existed in previous stages to try them out without creating conflict. Feelings of opposition or counterdependence may therefore begin to arise among team members. This counterdependence can be transformed into interdependence by using **process management** techniques.

Process management was developed as part of the Total Quality Management (TQM) and the reengineering movements. It involves the assessment, analysis, and improvement of sets of activities in which teams engage. A **process** is a sequential set of activities designed to lead to a specific outcome. For example, unloading a ship, transporting ammunition to the front, or feeding troops are among the processes that had to be managed by General Pagonis's team. The importance of process management during the storming stage of development is that it focuses and coordinates team members in a task sequence that minimizes the negative effects of conflict, disruption, and difference. Even though individuals are differentiated, well-managed processes minimize discord by coordinating efforts and capitalizing on team members' unique contributions. Good process management doesn't ignore individuality; it optimizes it. Moreover, it helps position the team to move into the final stage of development. Consider General Pagonis's approach:

I arranged to take a day or two away from headquarters with a group of key people from the command [the team]. We use this brief respite from our everyday activities to take a long look at what our organization is doing. These sessions . . . gave us a chance to work as a group, in a focused way. . . . From Day One, I held large, open classes where we discussed scenarios and potential solutions. I would pose a question to the group: "O.K., you have a ship that docked at Ad Dammam this morning. It's ready to be unloaded, and the onboard crane breaks. What's our response?" Collectively, the group would work toward one of several solutions. . . .These group sessions served several useful purposes at once. Obviously, they brought potential challenges into the open so we could better prepare for them. . . . Equally important, they promoted collaborative discussion across ranks and disciplines (pp. 101, 177).

Process management consists of three main activities: (1) process assessment, (2) process analysis, and (3) process improvement. The objective of the first step, **process assessment,** is to identify the sequence of tasks, activities, and individuals involved in delivering an output. This is done by listing, in sequential order, each identifiable activity performed from the beginning of a process to its completion. Table 4 shows a simplified list of the activities involved in replenishing items used by soldiers at a particular location during Desert Storm. Of course, this single process must be linked closely with other processes such as transporting the supplies to the site (upstream of this process) and distributing the supplies after they have been stored to soldiers in the field (downstream of this process). In other words, a network of processes exists for each team. But all processes cannot be assessed simultaneously. Instead, process assessment articulates specifically what actions and what people are involved in a single, identifiable process.

A "map" of the process is then constructed showing inputs, outputs, and hand-offs between different individuals in the team. A **process map** shows each of the activities in relationship to one another. Different types of symbols indicate decision points, activities, indirect links, and so forth. Reviewing details of map symbols and mapping techniques is beyond the scope of this chapter, however, and interested readers may want to read Morris & Brandon (1993) for a more de-

tailed explanation of process mapping. It doesn't take an expert to generate a useful process map, however, and it can be very helpful in coordinating and improving team members' performance. An effective way to develop a process map is to have each team member identify what he or she does, the person(s) with whom he or she interacts and coordinates, and what information is shared. A simple and effective method for constructing a process map is outlined below, and Figure 2 provides an illustration of a process map for the steps listed in Table 4.

Member jobs. Each team member writes down his or her specific job on a Post-It note. These notes are placed on a wall in the sequence in which they occur in the process. These job descriptions serve as the major categories of activities.

Activities. Each specific activity and hand-off within each job category is written separately on a Post-It

---

The steps involved in replenishing supplies at a military outpost during the Persian Gulf War may include the ones that follow. These same steps are also applicable to most businesses that procure and distribute supplies.

1. Forecast use for each item based on past use.
2. Identify unusual circumstances that will affect future use.
3. Calculate how many of each item to order.
4. Complete a written order form.
5. Determine when to place an order.
6. Submit the order for needed items.
7. Receive ordered items.
8. Confirm received items were ordered.
9. Check off items received from the receipt list.
10. Reconcile order list with receipt list.
11. Contact individuals to transport items received to storage.
12. Move items received to the storage area.
13. Log in items to be stored.
14. Store items in a way that allows for easy access.

Table 4   Process Analysis: A Simplified Process for Replenishing Supplies for Soldiers

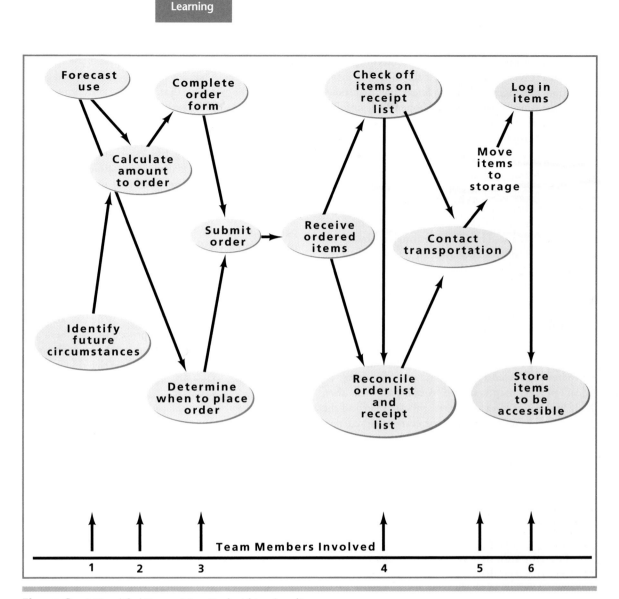

Figure 2   A Simplified Process Map: Replenishing Supplies

note by each team member. These notes are stuck on the wall in the order in which they occur.

Criteria. Measures or indicators of success are attached to each activity. The question is addressed, "How would I know if this activity was highly effective?"

Communication. The information given to and required from someone else is recorded on a Post-It note. These notes are placed next to the activities for which the information is needed.

Differentiation. Different color notes may be used to differentiate information exchanges, activities, and criteria.

Mapping. Construct a map of the task and communication sequence by drawing boxes around each separate activity. Link it with an arrow to other activities from which it receives something or to which it gives something. Do the same for information exchanges. Generate a linear map that shows how the process begins, what happens as it unfolds, and how it concludes. Note who is involved in each separate boxed item.

The second step in process management is **process analysis.** The purpose of this step is to identify a better way to perform a particular process. It involves analyzing the current process and then identifying a target for how much the process can be improved. The question to be asked is, "How much time can be saved, waste reduced, or mistakes avoided by improving the current process?" Ideas for improvements may come from observing others perform the same process (benchmarking), from team members' past experience, from finding small improvements (small wins) that can be made, from customers' recommendations and feedback, or from a radical redesign of the entire sequence of activities (reengineering). Using the ideas for improvement gathered from this variety of sources, an "ideal" process map is drawn. A comparison is then made between the current "as is" process map and the "should be" map. Guidelines for comparing current and ideal process maps include:

▶ Look for *disconnects*—connections that should be present but are not.

▶ Look for *redundancies*—activities that are performed more than once.

▶ Look for *delays* and *waiting time.*

▶ Look for indicators of *poor performance*—errors, mistakes, and defects.

▶ Look for ways to accomplish the process that are *cheaper* or use fewer resources.

▶ Look for ways to *prevent mistakes* before they occur.

The third step in process management is **process improvement,** in which the process itself is changed so as to foster advancement. This means trying out new ways of accomplishing the same outcome, changing the outcome so that it is improved, or providing more value and benefit to those involved. Proposed improvements in the process should generally be tried out in a practice room, a bullpen, or in a pilot test, because it is difficult to revamp an entire

process without evidence that proposed changes will make it better. Changes that promise to speed up or improve the process, that alter the outcome of the process, or that promise to enhance payback for team members usually need to be tried out in advance of wholesale restructuring.

The point of using process management techniques in this stage of team development is to help team members focus their different perspectives and felt need for independence into team-improvement activities. By concentrating on the required interdependence that the team must experience to accomplish its tasks, conflict and disunity are constructively managed. Effective team performance is enhanced, and the team becomes prepared for the next stage of development.

Effective leader behaviors. Whereas all team members must be involved in process management and in reinforcing the vision of the team, the leader has special responsibility to ensure that these two things occur. In addition to those two key factors, other leader behaviors that are most effective in this stage are:

▶ Identify a common enemy to increase feelings of cohesion.

▶ Reinforce the vision.

▶ Generate commitment among team members.

▶ Turn students into teachers.

▶ Provide individual and team recognition.

▶ Foster win/win thinking.

When survival is at stake, internal conflict and individual differences in a team are set aside in favor of the needs of the larger team. For example, Franklin D. Roosevelt was accused of allowing the bombing of Pearl Harbor in 1941 in order to mobilize the American people to stop debating among themselves and enter the war. Saddam Hussein targeted the United States as the "evil empire" in order to remain in power despite widespread hunger, hardship, and repression in Iraq. The loss of U.S. markets to foreign companies in the 1980s mobilized corporate research and development efforts to increase quality and productivity as never before. The National Institute of Education's National Commission on Excellence in Education (1983) chose to report its findings on declining educational excellence as an open letter to the public in order to emphasize the threat to American society and to mobilize public support for change. The report began with the statement:

> If an unfriendly foreign power had attempted to impose on America the mediocre educational performance that exists today, we might well have viewed it as an act of war. As it stands, we have allowed this to happen to ourselves (p. 5).

Effective team leaders can overcome resistance and conflict by identifying factors outside the organization that threaten its welfare. If threats originating inside the organization are pointed out, conflict and rigidity are reinforced. Members tend to blame one another, find scapegoats, and try to reduce their discomfort (see Cameron, Kim, & Whetten, 1987). On the other hand, when threats are external, cooperation increases and individuals mobilize to overcome resistance. Managing the storming stage, therefore, involves raising the consciousness of people inside the organization to the presence of external threats.

Another way to manage storming behavior is to enhance the commitment of team members by *turning students into teachers.* In order to increase the commitment of newly hired engineers, one division within Dow Corning Corporation requires its engineers to spend time recruiting new employees on college campuses. Every other year, engineers are sent to college campuses to attract the best graduating students for positions at Dow Corning. However, recruiting occurs not just in engineering schools but in business schools, law schools, math and chemistry departments, and so on. Those trained to recruit students stay home, and the engineers are assigned to do that task.

Why would Dow Corning do such a thing? Why leave the experts home and send engineers to do a job for which they have not been trained? One reason for this strategy is that it helps increase the commitment of the newly hired engineers. To recruit college students, the engineers must publicly praise Dow Corning, restate the corporate vision, and point out its merits. After making such public pronouncements, individuals become committed to what they have espoused. In other words, new engineers are traditionally treated as students in the company, being recipients of the corporate vision and values. By becoming teachers of others outside the company, however, engineers convert

themselves. Since a core competence of Dow Corning is chemical engineering, the intent is to increase the commitment of this crucial group by turning them into teachers of others.

Figure 3 illustrates a similar system used by Xerox Corporation in order to institutionalize a major change in the company's culture. Resistance to change, conflict, and differences in perspective were all effectively managed by forming teams across the company, labeled "family groups." Each family group engaged in four activities to generate commitment and implement the change:

Learn. Principles were taught and discussed.

Apply. Action plans were formed and an improvement agenda was implemented.

Teach. The principles and successful experiences were taught to others.

Inspect. The performance and action plans of others were measured and monitored.

Teams were exposed to the desired information four times: when they learned it, when they applied it, when they taught it, and when they inspected it. More importantly, team members' commitment to both the information and the team was ensured because of their involvement in each of these four steps.

Throughout this and other stages of team development, the team leader also needs to ensure that rewards and recognition are provided to the team, not just to individuals. A common mistake in teams is for individuals to be singled out for praise or awards instead of the team. "Employee of the month," "top salesperson," and "high scorer" are all awards that can destroy team cohesion and perpetuate team member competition and divisiveness. Team members are motivated to work for individual recognition instead of the good of the team. Consequently, team leaders need to ensure that the team itself is recognized and rewarded for achievement, not just individuals. This might be done, for example, with team-recognition ceremonies, T-shirts or trophies for all team members, or team pictures published in the newspaper. The point is to build commitment and unity in the team in order to counteract the tendency of the team to become fragmented during the storming stage. By so doing, the team is made ready to enter the fourth stage of development: performing.

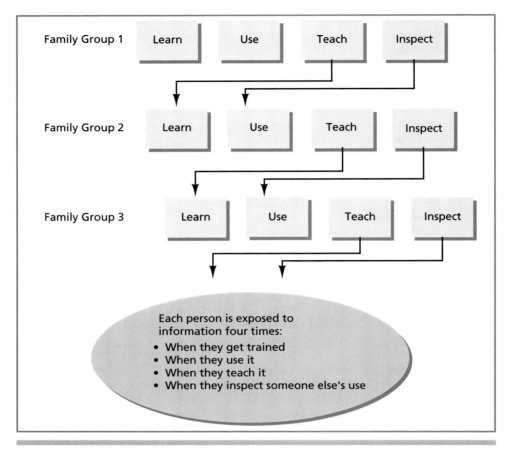

Figure 3 The Xerox Dissemination Process

The Performing Stage

Team member questions, interpersonal relationships, and task issues. When a team reaches the performing stage of development, it is able to function as a highly effective and efficient unit. Because it has worked through the issues embedded in each of the previous stages of development, the team is able to work at a high level of performance. The team has overcome issues of lack of trust, uncertainty, unclear expectations, nonparticipativeness, dependence, and self-centeredness typical of the first, or forming stage of development. It has clarified a vision, team member roles, the degree of personal commitment to the team, and the leader's direction typical of the conforming stage. It has overcome tendencies toward counterdependence, conflict, polarization, and disharmony typical of the storming stage. It now has the potential to develop the attributes of a high-performing team.

As illustrated by General Pagonis's team, the consequence of working through these various stages of development and reaching the stage of high performance was a well-oiled, robust team that pulled off one of the greatest logistical feats in military history.

I meet with skepticism, even disbelief, when I tell people that I didn't issue a single order during the ground war. This is only slightly a stretch of the truth. Yes, people sought and got guidance. But the people in my command knew exactly what they were supposed to do in almost every conceivable circumstance. They had been trained and encouraged to think on their feet. I felt they could even deal with the inconceivable (p. 148).

A listing of attributes of high-performance teams is provided in Table 5, based on the research of Katzenbach and Smith (1993) and Hackman (1990).

- **Performance outcomes**

  High-performing teams *do* things. They *produce* something; they don't just discuss it. Without accomplishment, teams dissolve and become ineffective over time.

- **Specific, shared purpose and vision**

  The more specific the purpose, the more commitment, trust, and coordination can occur. Individuals don't work for themselves; they work for one another in pursuit of the shared purpose. The shared purpose can also be the same as a motivating vision of what the team should achieve.

- **Mutual, internal accountability**

  The sense of internal accountability is far greater than any accountability imposed by a boss or outsider. Self-evaluation and accountability characterize a high-performing team.

- **Blurring of formal distinctions**

  Team members do whatever is needed to contribute to the task, regardless of previous positions or titles. Team membership and team roles are more predominant than outside status.

- **Coordinated, shared work roles**

  Individuals always work in coordination with others on the team. The desired output is a single group product, not a set of individual products.

- **Inefficiency leading to efficiency**

  Because teams allow for lots of participation and sharing, mutual influence about purpose, and blurring of roles, they may initially be inefficient. As the team develops, because they come to know one another so well and can anticipate each other's moves, they become much more efficient than single people working alone.

- **Extraordinarily high quality**

  Teams produce outcomes above and beyond current standards of performance. They surprise and delight their various constituencies with quality levels not expected and never before obtained. An intolerance of mediocrity exists, so standards of performance are very high.

- **Creative continuous improvement**

  Large-scale innovations as well as never-ending small improvements characterize the team's processes and activities. Dissatisfaction with the status quo leads to a constant flow of new ideas, experimentation, and a quest for progress.

- **High credibility and trust**

  Team members trust one another implicitly, defend members who are not present, and form interdependent relationships with one another. Personal integrity and honesty characterize team activities and team member interactions.

- **Clarity of core competence**

  The unique talents and strategic advantages of the team and its members are clear. The ways in which these competencies can be utilized to further the team's objectives are well understood. Extraneous activities and deflections from the team's core mission are given low priority.

Table 5   Some Attributes of High-Performing Teams
Source: Katzenbach and Smith (1993); Petrock (1991); Hackman (1990).

These attributes are those that produce the benefits enumerated earlier in the chapter (e.g., productivity improvements, quality achievements, speed, and cost reductions). By and large, teams produce dramatic successes in organizations only if they reach the performing stage of development.

The team in the performing stage is not, of course, free of issues. Rather, team members still face a set of *questions* that tend to predominate in this stage:

- How can we continuously improve?

- How can we foster innovativeness and creativity?

- How can we build on our core competence?

- What further improvements can be made to our processes?

- How can we maintain a high level of energy and contribution to the team?

Team members' questions in this stage change from being static to being dynamic. They shift in focus from building the team and accomplishing objectives to fostering change and improvement. Continuous improvement replaces accomplishment as a key objective. Up to this point, the team has been trying to manage and resolve issues that lead to three key results in the team: (1) accomplishing tasks or objectives, (2) coordinating and integrating team members' roles, and (3) assuring the personal well-being of all team members. A process was necessary to ensure the collective responsibility and involvement of all team members in the team's tasks and goals. By successfully managing the issues that dominate the first three stages of development, however, the team does not need to continue to focus exclusively on making itself a competent unit. Instead, it can now turn to achieving a level of performance above the ordinary. This leads *interpersonal relationships* to be characterized by:

- High mutual trust

- Unconditional commitment to the team

- Multifaceted relationships among team members

- Mutual training and development

- Entrepreneurship

- Self-sufficiency

Team members in this stage are confident that they have an important role to play in the team and that they are competent enough to perform it and contribute to the team's success. They are self-sufficient. On the other hand, they are also closely connected to other members of the team in terms of their commitment and personal concern for them. This does not mean that all high-performing team members are close personal friends. Rather, they exhibit a sense of mutual responsibility and concern for one another as they carry out their work. Their relationships are not limited merely to accomplishing a task together but also extend to ensuring that each team member is learning, developing, and improving. Coaching and assisting one another is common. In General Pagonis's high-performing team, for

example, team members were continuously briefing one another and helping other team members become more competent. One example is the way Pagonis kept one of his key team members informed even though this team member wasn't invited to some key meetings:

> Very early on I had gotten in the habit of sneaking John Carr into these briefing sessions with CINC [General Schwarzkopf and others] by having Carr flip my slides in and out of the overhead projector. That way, he stayed as smart and as current about the CINC's plans as I did (p. 131).

In addition to multifaceted relationships and unconditional commitment to one another, team members also take responsibility individually for continuously improving the team and its processes. Unlike the storming stage, however, this improvement is not based on counterdependence or needs to display individuality. Rather, it is based on a genuine commitment to seeing the team perform better than it is currently performing. Therefore, experimentation, trial-and-error learning, freewheeling discussions of new possibilities, and personal responsibility by everyone for upgrading performance is typical. The major *task issues* in this stage include:

- Capitalizing on core competence

- Fostering continuous improvement

- Anticipating needs of stakeholders and responding in advance of requests

- Enhancing speed and timeliness

- Encouraging creative problem solving

In this stage of development, the team becomes more aware of its **core competence** (see Prahalad & Hammel, 1990). Over time, teams develop particular areas of expertise or proficiency. Team members' styles, individual skills, patterns of interaction, and the team's vision help produce certain areas of specialty that the team develops as its own. It might be playing defense for a basketball team, solving complicated problems in a NASA team, or producing new ideas in an R&D team. In the case of General Pagonis' logistics team, it was, among other things, the team's ability to communicate clearly even minute details of the operation to all team members, to coordinate a myriad of activities concurrently, and to plan simultaneously for a large number of contingencies. It was these areas of core competence that explain Pagonis' remarkable claim that, once the ground war began, he did not issue a single order. The logistics support simply unfolded like clockwork.

Team core competence refers not only to an aggregation of individual team member skills but also includes knowledge, styles, communication patterns, and ways of behaving that come to characterize a team. They are unique features that are difficult to duplicate and give the team a special strength. By knowing its own core competence, a team can capitalize on these strengths and focus its energies on activities in which it can excel.

In addition to clarifying core competence, the performing stage is also characterized by a focus on the pursuit of both **continuous improvement** and **innovation.** Continuous improvement refers to small, incremental changes team members initiate. Continuous improvement can be represented by a hundred 1 percent changes. Innovation, on the other hand, represents large, visible, discontinuous changes. Innovations are breakthroughs that can be represented by a single 100 percent change. Traditionally, people in Eastern

cultures have been thought to be continuous-improvement oriented; people in Western cultures have been thought to be innovation-oriented (Imai, 1986, p. 32):

We find that the West has been stronger on the innovation side and Japan stronger on the Kaizen [the Japanese word for continuous improvement] side. These differences in emphasis are also reflected in the different social and cultural heritages, such as the Western educational system's stress on individual initiative and creativity as against the Japanese educational system's emphasis on harmony and collectivism.

Table 6 summarizes the differences between a continuous-improvement approach and an innovation approach to team development. Contrary to Imai's claim, high-performing teams in this stage of development emphasize both types of improvement: small and continuous as well as large and dramatic. A discussion of how to

ELEMENT	KAIZEN	INNOVATION
Effect	Long-term, long-lasting, undramatic	Short-term, dramatic
Procedure	Small steps	Large steps
Time frame	Continuous, incremental	Intermittent, nonincremental
Change	Gradual, constant, predictable	Abrupt, unpredictable
Involvement	Everyone	A few champions
Approach	Collectivism, group effort, systems approach	Rugged individualism, individual ideas and effort
Mode	Maintenance and improvement	Scrap and rebuild
Spark	Conventional know-how and state of the art	Technological breakthroughs, new inventions, new theories
Requirements	Little up-front investment, large effort to maintain it	Large up-front investment, little effort to maintain it
Orientation	People	Technology
Evaluation	Process, efforts, systems	Profits, outcomes
Training	Generalist	Specialist
Goal	Adaptability	Creativity
Information	Widely shared, open communication	Not widely shared, proprietary

Table 6　Characteristics of Innovation and Continuous Improvement (Kaizen)
Source: Imai, pp. 24, 32 (1986).

foster creative breakthroughs and innovation is contained in the chapter on Solving Problems Creatively. The implementation of a continuous-improvement approach, on the other hand, mostly depends on team members' orientation or the culture developed in the team. To illustrate this point, we will share a conversation one of the authors had with a Japanese executive who indicated that, as far as he was concerned, the United States had "lost the war." When asked what he meant, the executive clarified his statement by saying it was the economic war that had been lost. The United States was still ahead in economic productivity and size, he said, but Japan was catching up fast. And when Japan overtook the United States, the war would be over. He was challenged to justify this conclusion, and his rationale is noteworthy. He said:

> When you in the West receive a new product or technology, you assume that is the best it will ever be. Durability is at the highest level, no defects are present, and no repairs are needed. On the other hand, when we in the East receive a new product or technology, we assume that is the worst it will ever be, because we haven't had a chance to improve it yet. From now on, it gets better.

This statement illustrates the culture that is needed in high-performing teams, to develop a continuous-improvement approach coupled with an innovation approach to team performance. Addressing this challenge, along with others noted below, are part of the major tasks of the team leader.

Effective leader behaviors. Teams functioning in the performing stage do not require strong, directive leadership in the traditional sense. They become more and more like a self-managing team, able to manage their own processes, training, rewards, and membership. On the other hand, an important role for a leader does exist that relates more to the cultural or cognitive aspects of the team than to its task performance or relationship building. Prescriptions for effective leader behaviors in this stage include:

- Foster innovation and continuous improvement simultaneously.

- Advance the quality culture of the team.

- Provide regular, ongoing feedback on team performance.

- Play sponsor and orchestrator roles for team members.

- Help the team avoid reverting back to earlier stages.

After having moved through the first three stages of development in the Persian Gulf, General Pagonis's logistics team moved into a stage characterized by innovation and continuous improvement. On one occasion, for example, Pagonis directed two team members to generate a solution to the problem of how to provide combat troops the same kinds of meals that support people and civilians were enjoying.

> Imagine that you've been at some remote and desolate desert site for weeks, or even months, consuming dehydrated or vacuum-packed military rations. One day, unannounced, an odd-looking vehicle with the word "Wolfmobile" painted on it comes driving into your camp. The side panels open up, and a smiling crew inside offers to cook you a hamburger to order. "Side of fries? How about a Coke?" Morale shot up everywhere the Wolfmobiles pulled in—a little bit of home in the desert (p. 129).

This incident illustrates the major task of the leader during this high-performance stage of development. It is to help team members expand their focus from merely accomplishing their work and maintaining good interpersonal relationships to seeking to upgrade and elevate the team's performance.

One way to do that is to help the team's approach to quality become more advanced. Table 7 summarizes three different phases of quality culture in which teams and organizations can operate. Few reach the third, most advanced level of quality culture, but if they are to be most successful, teams should do so. High-performing teams strive for this third phase. We briefly explain each of these phases and show how they relate to this stage of team development (see Cameron, 1992; Cameron & Barnett, 1998).

Error detection. Most teams and organizations operate in the first phase of quality culture: error detection. In producing a product or service, they try to avoid mistakes and reduce waste (e.g., minimize rework, repair, scrap). They produce an outcome and then check to make certain that the work was done correctly. In other words, they "inspect-in" quality. In

ERROR DETECTION	ERROR PREVENTION	CREATIVE QUALITY AND CONTINUOUS IMPROVEMENT
Regarding Products	**Regarding Products**	**Regarding Products**
• Inspect and detect errors	• Prevent errors	• Improve and escalate on current standards of performance
• Reduce waste, cost of failure, and rework	• Expect zero defects	• Create new alternatives
• Correct mistakes	• Design and produce it right the first time	• Concentrate on things-gone-right
• Focus on the *output*	• Focus on *processes* and root causes	• Focus on the improving *suppliers* and *customers* as well as *processes*
Regarding Customers	**Regarding Customers**	**Regarding Customers**
• Avoid what may annoy customers	• Satisfy and exceed customer expectations	• Surprise and delight customers
• Respond to complaints quickly and accurately	• Help customers avoid future problems	• Engage in extra-mile restitution
• Reduce dissatisfaction	• Obtain customer preferences in advance, and follow up	• Anticipate customer expectations
• Focus on customer *needs* and requirements	• Focus on customer *preferences*	• *Create customer preferences*

Table 7 Phases of Quality Culture Development
Source: Cameron (1992).

their relationships with customers, they try to avoid annoying or dissatisfying them by responding to complaints in a timely and accurate manner. They focus on what customers need or require, and they ask customers after the product or service has been delivered how satisfied they are with it. By and large, this is a reactive or defensive approach to quality. It assures that the team meets basic requirements, but errors are identified after-the-fact.

Error prevention. In the second phase of quality—error prevention—the team shifts its emphasis toward avoiding mistakes by producing a product or service right the first time. Errors are prevented by focusing on how the task is accomplished (i.e., the process) and by holding all team members, not just inspectors or checkers, accountable for quality. Finding out why mistakes occurred is more important than finding individual errors. In relationships with customers, the emphasis moves from mere customer requirements to preferences and expectations. The team strives to exceed expectations and to help customers reach a high level of satisfaction with the product or service, not just nonannoyance. One way this happens is by training customers before a product or service is delivered to know what to expect and to share their preferences and

expectations before the product or service is produced. That way, customization can occur.

Innovation with continuous improvement. The third phase of quality—innovation coupled with continuous improvement—focuses on improvement rather than preventing errors. The team's standard changes from hitting a target to improving performance. Its objective is to achieve levels of quality in the product or service that are not only unexpected but unrequested. Problems are solved for customers and benefits provided that they don't expect anyone to deliver. New standards are actually created for customers because the team surprises and delights them. It is this third phase of quality culture that characterizes the world's best companies and its highest-performing teams.

The role of the leader in the performing stage of development is to help the team achieve this way of approaching the quality of its work. Team members are encouraged to: (1) strive continuously to improve their own and the team's work processes; (2) deliver extra-mile restitution to customers when mistakes do occur; (3) anticipate requests and respond in advance of receiving them; and (4) help solve problems for customers, and for other team members, that they don't expect anyone to solve for them. Research is clear that the highest levels of commitment and loyalty from customers and from team members, as well as organizational effectiveness, result from such an approach (Cameron, 1992, 1994; Cameron & Barnett, 1998).

Figure 4 illustrates these three phases of quality in the form of a graph. The vertical axis on the graph represents *satisfaction,* and it ranges from high satisfaction ("love it") on the top to low satisfaction ("hate it") on the bottom. The horizontal axis represents *performance* and ranges from low performance ("awful") on the left to high performance ("great") on the right. To understand the figure, consider the experience of purchasing an automobile. If we were to ask you what features are of most interest to you when purchasing a new car, you might list gas mileage, having four doors, roominess, a responsive engine, and good handling. If the auto dealer showed you a car that exactly met your expectations, we would position you at the intersection of the two axes

at point A, that is, in the middle of the satisfaction axis and in the middle of the performance axis. However, if you discovered that the car performed much better than you expected—say, gas mileage was better and the engine was more powerful—satisfaction would also increase to point B in the figure. If, however, the car got terrible gas mileage and rattled and leaked, that is, performed lower than expected, satisfaction would also decrease to point C on the graph. Connecting points A, B, and C results in a **performance curve.** These are the features that the team tries to improve continuously, to drive satisfaction up by finding ways to push performance to the right side of the axis. These features are identifiable and easily recognized.

If, when you got into your new car, however, you discovered that although the features you requested were satisfactory, the car had no carpet and no shock absorbers, you would no doubt be dissatisfied. But, we

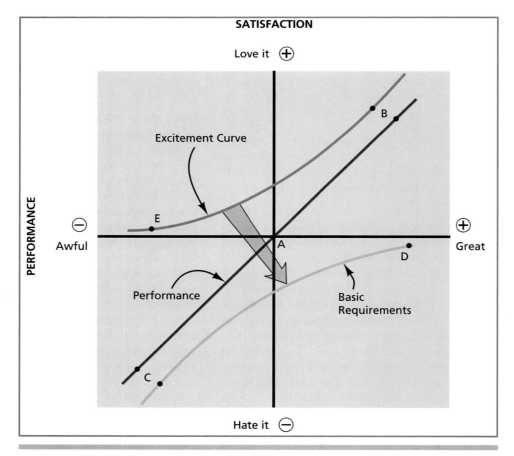

Figure 4   Basic, Performance, and Excitement Factors

suspect, we could ask you for a comprehensive list of features you are looking for in a car and you would probably never list carpet and shock absorbers. That is because you assume that these items are basic features of all new cars. If such basic features are missing, people are dissatisfied. However, no one cares much about whether the shock absorbers are painted red or black, cost $5 or $35, or whether there are one or two on each tire, so long as the ride is smooth. This illustrates the fact that a **basic curve** also exists in the figure. If certain basic features are absent, people are upset (point C). But the presence of additional basic features does not lead to a rise in satisfaction (point D). Having more of a basic feature simply does not add value.

Now assume that when you got into the car, the seat automatically adjusted itself to fit your height and leg length, the mirrors automatically adjusted themselves, and the seat became heated almost immediately on cold winter days. You were given something that you didn't expect—a delightful surprise. Satisfaction would go up to point B. On the other hand, if no such features were present in the car, satisfaction would not decrease, because these features weren't expected in the first place (point E). Connecting points B and E creates an **excitement curve** that shows what happens when innovation and breakthroughs occur. Loyalty and commitment are products of receiving features on the excitement curve.

The point of this figure is simple. Every team must perform its basic work competently and accomplish its basic, required tasks (the basic curve). It should also continuously improve its task accomplishment and strive to generate higher performance and satisfaction with its products or services (the performance curve). However, it can become a high-performance team by producing innovations, delightful surprises, and breakthroughs in task accomplishment and service delivery (the excitement curve). An important task of the team leader in this stage of development is to help the team accomplish all three kinds of activities.

As in previous stages of development, another important task of the team leader is to provide constant feedback to the team on its performance and make certain that adequate information is circulated among team members. Praise and pats on the back cannot be too frequent, but they should not be targeted primarily at individuals. The team as a unit needs to be recognized and kept informed. A common prescription of high-performing team leaders, in fact, is "communicate, communicate, communicate." Most team lead-

ers suggest that this is the key to their success (see Katzenbach & Smith, 1993). Communicating praise and feedback should occur at regularly scheduled intervals (consistency) and should be frequent.

In addition, as discussed in the chapters on Solving Problems Creatively and Empowering and Delegating, good team leaders also play sponsoring and orchestrator roles. This means that they help sponsor the ideas and activities of other team members by obtaining resources, removing obstacles, and providing encouragement to them. They help sponsor others' success. Sponsoring team members means encouraging them, recognizing them, and facilitating their development. Good team leaders also play orchestrator roles by seeing to it that team activities are coordinated, suggestions are fit into the team's plans for the future, and that the innovative suggestions of team members are integrated and harmonized together. Team leaders don't have to be the sources of all good ideas or change efforts. In fact, sponsoring and orchestrating the ideas and actions of their team members makes the entire team, including themselves, more effective.

We have pointed out thus far that teams progress through four different stages of development. The fourth, or final, stage is the one achieved by high-performing teams and the one toward which all teams should aspire. The issues that must be resolved along the way, however, and the changes that team leaders must make to push the team along to the next stage of development are significant. Leaders of effective teams do not become such by accident. They are able to diagnose which stage a team is in and to identify the main issues facing the team. They can therefore answer team members' questions, facilitate effective interpersonal relationships in the team, resolve task issues, and display effective leadership behaviors.

Handling Difficult Team Members

Despite the best efforts of a team leader or the conductor of a meeting, some participants do not always behave in ways that help the team be successful. Some people may be more interested in self-aggrandizement than in team success. They may criticize other team members or try to dominate the meeting agenda. Sometimes, they don't pull their own weight and don't take responsibility. This latter tendency toward "social loafing" is especially common. It has been observed that when three people pull together on a rope, they achieve only two and a half times the power of individuals acting alone. In fact, the larger the group, the less effort put forth by any single individual member (Latane, Williams, & Harkins, 1979). This is because of four factors:

Equity of effort. "No one else is working up to his potential, so why should I?"

Loss of accountability. "I'm an insignificant part of this large group, so no one will notice or care what I do."

Sharing of rewards. "Why should I work harder than others when we will all get the same reward?"

Coordination loss. "The more people involved, the more I have to wait for others, talk to others, and coordinate my work with others, so I'm less efficient."

How do effective team leaders cope with disruptive, difficult, or loafing team members? When students are writing a report together during a semester, how do they assure that all team members will take equal responsibility for the report? How do business task forces ensure that when team members enter a meeting, they will not use it as a forum to impress the boss? If everyone on the team gets the same reward, what is to keep some members from getting a reward that they didn't earn? Table 8 identifies 11 disruptive behaviors that are common in teams, along with suggested responses. The general rule is to avoid embarrassing or intimidating team members, regardless of their disruptive behavior. The way difficult team members are handled not only sets the tone for the kind of discussion that will ensue but also helps determine what kind of feelings will characterize team members. It sets the tone and the culture of the team. In these situations, instead of attacking and being defensive, use supportive communication, collaborative conflict management, and techniques of empowerment (as discussed in the chapters on Communicating Supportively, Managing Conflict, and Empowering and Delegating). Discuss concerns in an open, direct, problem-oriented, and supportive manner.

TYPE	BEHAVIOR	SUGGESTED RESPONSE
Hostile	"It'll never work." "That's a typical engineering viewpoint."	"How do others here feel about this?" "You may be right, but let's review the facts and evidence." "It seems we have a different perspective on the details, but we agree on the principles."
Know-It-All	"I have worked on this project more than anyone else in this room . . ." "I have a Ph.D. in Economics, and . . ."	"Let's review the facts." (Avoid theory or speculation.) "Another noted authority on this subject has said . . ."
Loudmouth	Constantly blurts out ideas or questions. Tries to dominate the meeting.	Interrupt: "Can you summarize your main point/question for us?" "I appreciate your comments, but we should also hear from others." "Interesting point. Help us understand how it relates to our subject."
Interrupter	Starts talking before others are finished.	"Wait a minute, Jim, let's let Jane finish what she was saying."
Interpreter	"What John is really trying to say is . . ." "John would respond to that question by saying . . ."	"Let's let John speak for himself. Go ahead, John, finish what you were saying." "John, how would you respond?" "John, do you think Jim correctly understood what you said?"

Table 8 Suggestions for Handling Difficult Team Members
Source: Adapted from Peoples, 1988, pp. 147–155.

TYPE	BEHAVIOR	SUGGESTED RESPONSE
Gossiper	"Isn't there a regulation that you can't . . ." "I thought I heard the V.P. of Finance say . . ."	"Can anyone here verify this?" (Assuming no response.) "Let's not take the time of the group until we can verify the accuracy of this information."
Whisperer	Irritating side conversation going on between two people.	Hints: 1. Walk up close to the guilty parties and make eye contact. 2. Stop talking and establish dead silence. 3. Politely ask the whisperers to wait until the meeting is over to finish their conversation.
Silent Distractor	Reads newspapers, rolls their eyes, shakes their heads, fidgets.	Hints: Ask them questions to determine their level of interest, support, and expertise. Try to build an alliance by drawing them into the discussion. If that doesn't work, discuss your concerns with them during a break.
Busy-Body	Ducks in and out of the meeting repeatedly, taking messages, dealing with crises.	Hints: Preventive measures include: scheduling the presentation away from the office, checking with common offenders before the meeting to ask if the planned time is OK for minimum interruptions.
Latecomer	Comes late and interrupts the meeting.	Hints: Announce an odd time (8:46) for the meeting to emphasize the necessity for promptness. Make it inconvenient for latecomers to find a seat, and stop talking until they do. Establish a "latecomer's kitty" for refreshments.
Early Leaver	Announces, with regrets, that they must leave for another important activity.	Hints: Before starting, announce the ending time and ask if anyone has a scheduling conflict.

Table 8   *(continued)*

Summary

Because almost everyone is a member of at least one team at work or in nonwork activities, because teams are becoming increasingly prevalent in the workplace, and because teams have been shown to be powerful tools to improve the performance of individuals and organizations, it is important to become proficient in leading and participating in teams. But merely putting people together with an assigned task does not make them into a team. Because teams develop through different stages—each with its own unique challenges and issues—it takes skill to help a team become a high-performing unit. Different behaviors are required in each of the four stages of team development. We have described the different attributes of each of these stages and have provided guidelines for managing the issues that characterize them.

Behavioral Guidelines

1. Determine the stage in which your team is operating by identifying the major questions, interpersonal relationships, and task issues that characterize the team. Use Table 2 for a comprehensive listing. Adopt the appropriate leadership behaviors that correspond to that stage of development.

2. Become familiar with the attributes of high-performing teams and make certain that these attributes characterize your team. In particular, ensure that goals are clear, known by everyone, and achieved in small steps; that standards of excellence, rather than mere acceptability, are applied; that feedback on results is provided; that team members can use all their skills and knowledge, and that they are continuously trained; that adequate equipment and facilities, performance measures, and rules and penalties are available; that performance-based rewards and praise and recognition are prevalent; that team members have autonomy; that plans and tactics to beat a specific competitor are in place; and that team members have a sense of commitment to the team.

3A. When a team is in the forming stage of development:

  ▶ Make certain that all team members are introduced to one another.

  ▶ Answer team members' questions, even those that they don't ask aloud.

  ▶ Work to establish a foundation of trust and openness between yourself and the team members, and among the team members themselves.

  ▶ Model the behaviors that you expect from all team members, such as honesty, openness, friendliness, and so on.

  ▶ Clarify the goals, procedures, and expectations of the team.

3B. When a team is in the conforming stage of development:

  ▶ Facilitate role differentiation among team members by helping them learn to perform various task-facilitating and relationship-building roles.

  ▶ Show support to team members by complimenting and recognizing them.

  ▶ Provide feedback to individuals on the team and to the team as a unit. Feedback may be positive or negative, but make certain that it focuses on behavior rather than people, on observations rather than inferences, on the here-and-now situation rather than the past, on sharing information rather than giving advice, on the amount of information that can be useful to the team members rather than the amount you might like to give, on the value it will have to team members rather than just letting off steam, and on a specific time and place.

  ▶ Articulate a vision of the future for the team that is both left-brain and right-brain oriented, interesting to team members, and that expresses passion regarding core principles.

  ▶ Help generate commitment to the vision by encouraging team members to express public approval of the vision, participate in articulating and implementing it, and communicating it frequently.

3C. When a team is in the storming stage of development:

  ▶ Adopt a mediator role when conflict is encountered.

  ▶ Encourage a win/win philosophy in the team: If a single team member wins, everyone wins.

  ▶ Reemphasize the vision for the team and its core principles in order to maintain a strong team bond.

  ▶ Avoid groupthink by encouraging open discussion, having at least one team member critically evaluate the team's decisions, forming subgroups in the team, formally designating a devil's advocate in the team, having important decisions reviewed by an outside expert, and holding second-chance meetings to review the team's decisions.

  ▶ Encourage the team to assess, analyze, and improve its processes by identifying the sequence of steps used to accomplish each task, mapping those steps, and identifying ways to improve the process by making it faster, more efficient, and of higher quality.

- To enhance team cohesion and commitment, identify a common enemy or external adversary for the team.

- Turn students into teachers by having team members represent team values and goals to outsiders.

- In addition to providing recognition to individuals in the team, make certain that rewards and recognition are given to the team as a unit.

3D. When a team is in the performing stage of development:

- Capitalize on the core competence of the team by articulating clearly what that competence is and building upon those strengths.

- Foster both innovation, or dramatic breakthrough changes, and continuous improvement, or small incremental changes, among all team members.

- Advance the quality culture of the team by moving from an error-detection approach through error-prevention to creative quality. Work toward "excitement" in the team's outputs and services.

- Provide regular, ongoing feedback on team performance.

- Play sponsor and orchestrator roles for team members so that their ideas and changes are integrated with those of others and receive adequate support.

- Help the team avoid reverting back to earlier stages of development by continuing to emphasize the attributes of high-performance teams.

4. Handle difficult team members not by embarrassing or intimidating them, but by helping them to become more productive contributors to the team's effort through supportive communication, conflict management, and empowerment.

Skill Analysis

Cases Involving Building Effective Teams

The *Tallahassee Democrat*'s ELITE Team

Katzenbach and Smith (1993, pp. 67–72), as part of their extensive research on teams, observed the formation of a team at the *Tallahassee Democrat,* the only major newspaper left in Tallahassee, Florida. Here is their description of how the team, which called itself "ELITE Team," performed over time. All incidents and names are factual. As you read the description, look for evidence of team development stages.

Fred Mott, general manager of the *Democrat,* recognized [the declining profitability and distribution of most major metropolitan newspapers] earlier than many of his counterparts. In part, Mott took his lead from Jim Batten, who made "customer obsession" the central theme of his corporate renewal effort shortly after he became Knight-Ridder's CEO. But the local marketplace also shaped Mott's thinking. The Democrat was Tallahassee's only newspaper and made money in spite of its customer service record. Mott believed, however, that further growth could never happen unless the paper learned to serve customers in ways "far superior to anything else in the marketplace." The ELITE

Team story actually began with the formation of another team made up of Mott and his direct reports. The management group knew they could not hope to build a "customer obsession" across the mile-high barriers isolating production from circulation from advertising without first changing themselves. It had become all too common, they admitted, for them to engage in "power struggles and finger pointing."

Using regularly scheduled Monday morning meetings, Mott's group began to "get to know each other's strengths and weaknesses, bare their souls, and build a level of trust." Most important, they did so by focusing on real work they could do together. For example, early on they agreed to create a budget for the paper as a team instead of singly as function heads.

Over time, the change in behavior at the top began to be noticed. One of the women who later joined the ELITE Team, for example, observed that the sight of senior management holding their "Monday morning come-to-Jesus" meetings really made a difference to her and others. "I saw all this going on and I thought, 'What are they so happy about?'"

Eventually, as the team at the top got stronger and more confident, they forged a higher aspiration: to build customer focus and break down the barriers across the broad base of the paper. . . .

A year after setting up the new [team], however, Mott was both frustrated and impatient. Neither the Advertising Customer Service department, a series of customer surveys, additional resources thrown against the problem in the interim, nor any number of top management exhortations had made any difference. Ad errors persisted, and sales reps still complained of insufficient time with customers. In fact, the new unit had turned into another organizational barrier.

Customer surveys showed that too many advertisers still found the *Democrat* unresponsive to their needs and too concerned with internal procedures and deadlines. People at the paper also had evidence beyond surveys. In one instance, for example, a sloppily prepared ad arrived through a fax machine looking like a "rat had run across the page." Yet the ad passed through the hands of seven employees and probably would have found its way into print if it had not been literally unreadable! As someone commented, "It was not anyone's job to make sure it was right. If they felt it was simply their job to type or paste it up, they just passed it along." This particular fax, affectionately know as the "rat tracks fax," came to symbolize the essential challenge at the *Democrat*. . . .

At the time, Mott was reading about Motorola's quality programs and the goal of zero defects. He decided to heed Dunlap's advice by creating a special team of workers charged with eliminating all errors in advertisements. Mott now admits he was skeptical that frontline people could become as cohesive a team as he and his direct reports. So he made Dunlap, his trusted confidante, the leader of the team that took on the name ELITE for "ELIminate The Errors."

A year later, Mott was a born-again believer in teams. Under ELITE's leadership, advertising accuracy, never before tracked at the paper, had risen sharply and stayed above 99 percent. Lost revenues from errors, previously as high as $10,000 a month, had dropped to near zero. Ad sales reps had complete confidence in the Advertising Customer Service department's capacity and desire to treat each ad as though the *Democrat*'s existence were at stake. And surveys showed a huge positive swing in advertiser satisfaction. Mott considered all of this nothing less than a minor miracle.

The impact of ELITE, however, went beyond numbers. It completely redesigned the process by which the *Democrat* sells, creates, produces, and bills for advertisements. More important yet, it stimulated and nurtured the customer obsession and cross-functional cooperation required to make the new process work. In effect, this team of mostly frontline workers transformed an entire organization with respect to customer service.

ELITE had a lot going for it from the beginning. Mott gave the group a clear performance goal (eliminate errors) and a strong mix of skills (12 of the best people from all parts of the paper). He committed himself to follow through by promising, at the first meeting, that "whatever solution you come up with will be implemented." In addition, Jim Batten's customer obsession movement helped energize the task force.

But it took more than a good sendoff and an overarching corporate theme to make ELITE into a high-performance team. In this case, the personal commitments began to grow, unexpectedly, over the early months as the team grappled with its challenge. At first, the group spent more time pointing fingers at one another than coming to grips with advertising errors. Only when one of them produced the famous "rat tracks fax" and told the story behind it did the group start to admit that everyone—not everyone else—was at fault. Then, recalls one member, "We had some pretty hard discussions. And there were tears in those meetings."

The emotional response galvanized the group to the task at hand and to one another. And the closer it got, the more focused it became on the challenge. ELITE decided to look carefully at the entire process by which an ad was sold, created, printed, and billed. When it did, the team discovered patterns in the errors, most of which could be attributed to time pressures, bad communication, and poor attitude. . . .

Commitment to one another drove ELITE to expand its aspirations continually. Having started with the charge to eliminate errors, ELITE moved on to break down functional barriers, then to redesigning the entire advertising process, then to refining new standards and measures for customer service, and, finally, to spreading its own brand of "customer obsession" across the entire *Democrat*. . . . Inspired by ELITE, for example, one production crew started coming to work at 4 a.m., to ease time pressures later in the day. . . .

To this day, the spirit of ELITE lives on at the *Democrat*. "There is no beginning and no end," says Dunlap. "Every day we experience something we learn from." ELITE's spirit made everyone a winner—the customers, the employees, management, and even Knight-Ridder's corporate leaders. CEO Jim Batten was so impressed that he agreed to pay for managers from other Knight-Ridder papers to visit the *Democrat* to learn from ELITE's experience. And, of course, the 12 people who committed themselves to one another and their paper had an impact and an experience none of them will ever forget.

Discussion Questions

1. What were the stages of development of the ELITE Team? Identify specific examples of each of the four stages of development as you progress through the case.

2. How do you explain the team's reaching a high-performance condition? What were the major predictive factors?

3. Why didn't Mott's top management team reach a high level of performance? Why was an ELITE team needed? What was his team lacking?

4. Make recommendations about what Mott should do now to capitalize on the ELITE Team experience. If you were to become a consultant to the *Tallahassee Democrat,* what advice would you give Mott about how he can capitalize on team building?

The Cash Register Incident

A store owner had just turned off the lights in the store when a man appeared and demanded money. The owner opened a cash register. The contents of the cash register were scooped up, and the man sped away. A member of the police force was notified promptly.

This exercise is accomplished in two steps, the first by yourself and the second in a team with four or five other people.

Step 1: Assume that you observed the incident described in the paragraph above. Later, a reporter asks you questions about what you observed in order to write an article for the local newspaper. Answer the questions from the reporter by yourself. Do not talk with anyone else about your answers.

Answer

Y	yes
N	no
DK	don't know

Step 2: The reporter wants to interview your entire team together. As a team, discuss the answers to each question and reach a consensus decision—that is, one with which everyone on the team agrees. Do not vote or engage in horse-trading. The reporter wants to know what you all agree upon.

Statements about the Incident

"Now, as a reporter, I'm interested in what happened here. Can you tell me just what occurred? I'd like to see if you can confirm or deny the following statements that I've picked up by talking to some other people."

Statement

Alone	Team	
Y		1. Did a man appear after the owner turned off his store lights?
Y		2. Was the robber a man?
N		3. Is it true that the man did not demand money?
Y		4. The man who opened the cash register was the owner, right?
Y		5. Did the store owner scoop up the contents of the cash register?
Y		6. OK, so someone opened the cash register, right?
Y		7. Let me get this straight, after the man who demanded the money scooped up the contents of the cash register, he ran away?
Y		8. The contents of the cash register contained money, but you don't know how much?
N		9. Did the robber demand money of the owner?

_____ _____ 10. OK, by way of summary, the incident concerns a series of events in which only three persons are involved: the owner of the store, a man who demanded money, and a member of the police force?

_____ _____ 11. Let me be sure I understand. The following events occurred: Someone demanded money, the cash register was opened, its contents were scooped up, and a man dashed out of the store?

When you have finished your team decision making and mock interview with the reporter, the instructor will provide correct answers. Calculate how many answers you got right as an individual, then calculate how many right answers your team achieved.

Discussion Questions

1. How many individuals did better than the team as a whole? Why?

2. How could your team discussion have been improved?

3. What roles did different members of the team play? Who was most helpful? Who was least helpful?

Team Diagnosis and Leadership Exercise

Consider a team in which you are now a member. If you belong to a team in a college class, select that one. Or you may select a team at your employment, in your church or community, or you may even diagnose your family. Use the following questions to help you determine the stage of development in which your team is operating. Then design a strategy for effectively leading this team to the next higher stage of development or, if in Stage 4, to a high level of performance. Share that strategy with others in class in a small group setting, and add at least one good idea from someone else's strategy to your own design.

Use the following scale in your rating of your team right now.

Rating Scale

1	Not typical at all of my team	3	Somewhat typical of my team
2	Not very typical of my team	4	Very typical of my team

Stage 1

_____ 1. Not everyone is clear about the objectives and goals of the team.

_____ 2. Not everyone is personally acquainted with everyone else in the team.

_____ 3. Only a few team members actively participate.

_____ 4. Interactions among team members are very safe or somewhat superficial.

_____ 5. Trust among all team members has not yet been established.

_____ 6. Many team members seem to need direction from the leader in order to participate.

Stage 2

_____ 7. All team members know and agree with the objectives and goals of the team.

_____ 8. Team members all know one another.

_____ 9. Team members are very cooperative and actively participate in the activities of the team.

_____	10.	Interactions among team members are friendly, personal, and nonsuperficial.
_____	11.	A comfortable level of trust has been established among team members.
_____	12.	Some team members play different roles from others; for example, some push for task accomplishment, others focus on relationships, others help clarify issues, and so on.

Stage 3

_____	13.	Disagreements and differing points of view are openly expressed by team members.
_____	14.	Competition exists among some team members.
_____	15.	Some team members do not follow the rules or the team norms.
_____	16.	Subgroups or coalitions exist within the team.
_____	17.	Discussion issues seem to get polarized—either-or, black-or-white—when examined by the team with some members on one side and others on the other side.
_____	18.	The authority or competence of the team leader is being questioned or challenged.

Stage 4

_____	19.	Team members focus a lot of energy on cooperating actively to improve the team's performance.
_____	20.	Team members feel free to try out new ideas, experiment, share something crazy, or do novel things.
_____	21.	The standards of excellence and expectations for team performance by team members themselves are very high.
_____	22.	Not all team members always agree, but each is given respect and value, and disagreements are resolved productively.
_____	23.	An unconditional commitment exists to the team and its success, so self-aggrandizement is at a minimum.
_____	24.	The team is very fast in making decisions or producing output but maintains very high quality standards.

Scoring

Add up the scores for the items in each stage of team development. Generally, one stage stands out clearly as having the highest scores. If more than one stage receives high scores, it will be necessary for the team leader to manage more than one set of developmental issues. However, because team stages develop sequentially, this is a rare occurrence.

Total of Stage 1 items

Total of Stage 2 items

Total of Stage 3 items

Total of Stage 4 items

Leadership Strategy

1. Identify at least two or three strategies that you can implement to enhance team performance, overcome the obstacles to improvement, and foster higher levels of team effectiveness. Use the guidelines in Table 3 in this chapter for thought-starters, but do not limit

yourself to just those suggested in the table. Stretch yourself to identify an appropriate leadership strategy for improving your team at the stage in which it is performing. Especially focus on what the team should *start doing, stop doing,* and *continue doing*.

Strategies

2. Now identify who will be involved, when you will begin to apply your strategy, and how you will execute the intervention (i.e., the process you will use to implement it).

Who

When

How

3. Share this plan with a small group, receive feedback and suggestions on it, and add at least one new idea from another group member's plan that you had not thought of yourself.

New Idea

Skill Practice

Jimmy Lincoln

Jimmy has a grim background. He is the third child in an inner-city minority family of seven. He has not seen his parents for several years. He recalls that his father used to come home drunk and beat up family members; everyone ran when he came staggering home.

His mother, according to Jimmy, wasn't much better. She was irritable and unhappy, and she always predicted that Jimmy would come to no good end. Yet she worked, when her health allowed, to keep the family in food and clothing. She frequently decried the fact that she was not able to be the kind of mother she would like to be.

Jimmy quit school in the seventh grade. He had great difficulty conforming to the school routine: misbehaving often, playing truant frequently, and getting into fights with schoolmates. On several occasions, he was picked up by the police and, along with members of his group, questioned during investigations into cases of both petty and grand larceny. The police regarded him as a "high-potential troublemaker."

The juvenile officer of the court saw in Jimmy some good qualities that no one else seemed to sense. This man, Mr. O'Brien, took it on himself to act as a father figure to Jimmy. He had several long conversations with Jimmy, during which he managed to penetrate to some degree Jimmy's defensive shell. He represented to Jimmy the first semblance of personal, caring influence in his life. Through Mr. O'Brien's efforts, Jimmy returned to school and obtained a high school diploma. Afterwards, Mr. O'Brien helped him obtain his first job.

Now, at age 22, Jimmy is a stockroom clerk at Costello Pharmaceutical Laboratory. On the whole, his performance has been acceptable, but there have been glaring exceptions. One involved a clear act of insubordination, though the issue was fairly unimportant. On another occasion, Jimmy was accused by a co-worker, on circumstantial grounds, of destroying some expensive equipment. Though the investigation is still open, it appears that the destruction was accidental. He also seems to have lost an extremely important requisition (although he claims never to have seen it). In addition, Jimmy's laid-back attitude and wisecracking ways tend to irritate his co-workers.

It is also important to note that Jimmy is not an attractive young man. He is rather weak and sickly, his appearance is disheveled, and he shows unmistakable signs of long years of social deprivation. Researchers in the lab have commented that his appearance doesn't fit in with the company's image. Others have wondered aloud (half jokingly, half seriously) whether he is counting drugs or taking drugs.

Jimmy's supervisor is fairly new to management and is not sure how to handle this situation. He sees merit in giving Jimmy the benefit of the doubt and helping him out, but he frankly wonders if it is worth the hassle. Seeking advice, the *supervisor* organizes a committee of individuals close to the situation. These include the *crew chief* (who has expressed frustration about the effects of Jimmy's performance and reputation on the morale of the work group), a *seasoned manager* (who has a reputation for being even-handed), a *union representative* (who tends to view most acts of employee discipline as an infringement on employee rights), a *member of the personnel department* (who is concerned about following proper company procedures), and a *member of the company's affirmative action office* (who is concerned that managers at Costello do not fully understand the handicap workers like Jimmy bring with them to the workplace and hence the need to give them special assistance and direction).

Assignment

There are six roles described in this exercise. After reading the case, fill out the "personal preference" part of the worksheet in Appendix I. Do this from the perspective of your assigned role.

When the worksheet has been completed, the supervisor should act as chair of the committee and begin the discussion. The group's assignment is to reach consensus on the rank-ordered options from this list. Group members should stay in character during the discussion. For example, they should not compare their lists and use a statistical process to generate their rank-order. Observers should be assigned to give the group feedback on their performance, using the Meeting Evaluation Worksheet and the Role Evaluation Worksheet.

Worksheet

Identify which of the alternatives you prefer in responding to Jimmy Lincoln. Be prepared to explain and to defend your choices.

Personal Preference	Group Decision	
_____	_____	1. Give Jimmy a warning that at the next sign of trouble a formal reprimand will be placed in his file.
_____	_____	2. Do nothing, as it is unclear that Jimmy has done anything seriously wrong. Back off and give him a chance to prove himself.

_____ _____ 3. Create strict controls (do's and don'ts) for Jimmy with immediate discipline for any misbehavior.

_____ _____ 4. Give Jimmy a great deal of warmth and personal attention (overlooking his annoying mannerisms) so he will feel accepted.

_____ _____ 5. Fire him. It's not worth the time and effort spent for such a low-level position.

_____ _____ 6. Treat Jimmy the same as everyone else, but provide an orderly routine so he can develop proper work habits.

_____ _____ 7. Call Jimmy in and logically discuss the problem with him and ask what you can do to help.

_____ _____ 8. Do nothing now, but watch him so you can reward him the next time he does something good.

Process Assessment

Using the examples in Table 4 and Figure 2 as examples, generate a formal process assessment, analysis, and improvement strategy for one of the following processes. Do this activity in your team, and use the following steps:

1. Identify all the activities involved in the process. Organize them into a sequential flow.

2. Map the activities to show how they are connected to one another, who is involved in the activities, what coordination occurs, and what communication lines are operative.

3. Now generate an ideal process map. That is, generate the same process where time, waste, and errors could be cut in half. Design from scratch a "perfect" process.

4. Based on the ideal map, refine the process map you generated in Step 2 and show the improvements you can make in it.

5. Make a presentation of your process assessment, analysis, and improvement strategy to the larger class. They should critique it in terms of its realism, the accuracy of the assessment and the map, and the amount of improvement you identified.

Potential Processes to Analyze

Select a process in which you are involved that could be improved through process assessment, analysis, and improvement procedures. If none comes readily to mind, you may select one of the following:

1. The process used for course registration in your college.

2. The process used to serve a meal at the college cafeteria.

3. The process used to evaluate students and teachers in your college or training facility.

4. The process used to repair and service your car.

5. The process used to rent an automobile at an airport.

6. The process involved in obtaining a college degree.

7. The process used to restock food on supermarket shelves.

Skill Application

Activities for Building Effective Teams

Suggested Assignments

1. Teach someone else how to determine which stage of development a team is in and what leader behaviors are most effective in each separate stage.

2. Analyze the characteristics of a team in which you are a member. Determine in what ways its functioning could be improved. Based on the attributes of high-performance teams discussed earlier, identify what could be done to improve its performance.

3. Conduct a role analysis of a real team meeting that is trying to make a decision, solve a problem, or examine an issue. Who performed what roles? Which team members were most helpful? Which team members were least helpful? Provide feedback to the team on what roles you saw being played, what roles were missing, and what improvements could have made the team more effective.

4. Write out a formal vision statement for a team you are leading. Make certain that the vision possesses the attributes of effective, energizing vision statements discussed in the chapter. Identify specifically what you can do to get team members to commit to that vision.

5. Use the Nominal Group Technique in a team meeting to reach a consensus decision. Follow precisely the steps outlined in the text.

6. Select a team assigned to perform a task or produce an outcome. Do a formal process assessment and analysis by listing the activities involved in the process and constructing a process map. Then generate ways to improve the process by eliminating redundancies, cutting out time, or finding ways to prevent mistakes.

7. For a team in which you participate, identify the basic services that it must deliver, the performance services that it should deliver, and the excitement services that it could deliver to its customers if it were not only to satisfy, but also surprise and delight them.

Application Plan and Evaluation

The intent of this exercise is to help you apply this cluster of skills in a real-life, out-of-class setting. Now that you have become familiar with the behavioral guidelines that form the basis of effective skill performance, you will improve most by trying out those guidelines in an everyday context. Unlike a classroom activity, in which feedback is immediate and others can assist you with their evaluations, this skill application activity is one you must accomplish and evaluate on your own. There are two parts to this activity. Part 1 helps prepare you to apply the skill. Part 2 helps you evaluate and improve on your experience. Be sure to write down answers to each item. Don't short-circuit the process by skipping steps.

Part 1. Planning

1. Write down the two or three aspects of this skill that are most important to you. These may be areas of weakness, areas you most want to improve, or areas that are most salient to a problem you face right now. Identify the specific aspects of this skill that you want to apply.

2. Now identify the setting or the situation in which you will apply this skill. Establish a plan for performance by actually writing down a description of the situation. Who else will be involved? When will you do it? Where will it be done?

   Circumstances:

   Who else?

   When?

   Where?

3. Identify the specific behaviors you will engage in to apply this skill. Operationalize your skill performance.

4. What are the indicators of successful performance? How will you know you have been effective? What will indicate you have performed competently?

Part 2. Evaluation

5. After you have completed your implementation, record the results. What happened? How successful were you? What was the effect on others?

6. How can you improve? What modifications can you make next time? What will you do differently in a similar situation in the future?

7. Looking back on your whole skill practice and application experience, what have you learned? What has been surprising? In what ways might this experience help you in the long term?

Specific Communi- cation Skills*

*Basic communication principles were discussed in Chapter 4. The purpose of the supplements is to apply those foundation principles to specific communication activities: making oral and written presentations and conducting interviews.

Making Oral and Written Presentations

OBJECTIVES

Increase proficiency in

▶ making effective oral presentations

▶ writing clearly and persuasively

▶ effectively answering questions and challenges

skill development

■ Skill Learning

Making Oral and Written
  Presentations
Essential Elements of Effective
  Presentations
Summary and Behavioral
  Guidelines

⬢ Skill Practice

Speaking as a Leader
Quality Circles at Battle
  Creek Foods

■ Skill Learning

Making Oral and Written Presentations

Taylor Billingsley was hired as a sales representative in the Apex Communications Corporation in 1972. With training and hard work, she advanced through the levels of the corporation, finally landing the position of senior vice-president in charge of personnel. Though she had anticipated that this position would require some adjustments, she was surprised at the kinds of changes she faced during her first few weeks on the job. Taylor had a lot of ideas about how to make the personnel division work more efficiently, but she realized almost immediately that she had to convince others to adopt them. In addition, she had to establish her own credibility—to make her employees and interested outsiders understand and appreciate her personal commitments and management style.

In the first few days on the job, Taylor had several opportunities to communicate her philosophy and expectations during a number of meetings with the departments in her division. Some of these meetings were formal, such as when she first accepted the position; others were more informal, including lunch meetings with the division heads. Immediately following the anouncement of her appointment, she also wrote a memo to her division heads and their employees outlining some of her ideas for moving the department forward. In separate memos she addressed the personnel development and financial benefits departments, introducing a new project and encouraging them to move ahead full speed to develop a new policy on research teams.

Then Taylor began a round of visits with people who worked in her division. She talked individually with several workers and responded to the questions posed by informal groups. She was asked to write up her evaluation of morale among workers in her division and forward it to the corporate chief executive officer. The latest financial reports released by the company's controller's office revealed that quarterly figures were down unexpectedly; it seemed that certain costs had risen dramatically. Taylor was concerned and adjusted a report she had written for a scheduled meeting with the region's top executives to reflect these new developments. Later, she spoke to an assembled employee group in the

cafeteria in an effort to calm their fears about job cuts. At another facility located in a tough urban environment, the task proved more difficult. Workers were outspokenly critical of the company and challenged much of the information she presented. Following these meetings, Taylor was the featured dinner speaker at a regional Chamber of Commerce meeting.

Taylor Billingsley experienced the challenges of management in her new position. During her first two weeks, she addressed dozens of groups on a broad range of subjects; she wrote even more reports and memos. In most of this communication, Taylor was not simply presenting facts. Instead, she was conveying support, pointing a new direction, generating enthusiasm, communicating a sense of caring, building good will, and underscoring the value of teamwork. Some situations called for polite, ceremonial messages; others were confrontational. Some covered familiar material; others stretched her ability to find the right words to convey her ideas. At the end of her first two weeks, Taylor began to appreciate the importance of communication skills.

Managers have to master the basic elements of public communication and be flexible enough to adapt them to varying situations (Barrett, 1977; Mambert, 1976; Peoples, 1988; Sanford & Yeager, 1963; Wilcox, 1967). Like Taylor Billingsley, you may find yourself addressing many different audiences through speeches and in writing. Like Taylor Billingsley, you will probably discover very quickly that your effectiveness as a manager depends in large part upon your ability to communicate with your coworkers and customers. Unfortunately, these skills are often lacking in new managers. According to a recent survey of major business recruiters, the biggest deficiencies in today's college graduates were the lack of good oral communication and writing skills (Endicott Report, 1992). Considering that speaking and writing skills are central to good management and that they are also relatively weak in many new employees, we should turn our attention to how managers can develop these two critical skills. Let's focus first on the core ingredients of good communication and then examine the specific requirements of speaking and writing.

Essential Elements of Effective Presentations

How can one person meet all of the communication demands confronting a good manager? There are five basic steps to making effective presentations—we'll label them the Five Ss. These five Ss are sequential in the sense that each step builds upon the preceding steps. Good communication depends heavily on adequate forethought and preparation. As shown in Figure 1, the first three steps involve preparation, the fourth and fifth focus on the spoken or written presentation itself. Adequate preparation is the cornerstone of effective communication (Collins and Devanna, 1990; Wells, 1989; Gelles-Cole, 1985).

1. Formulate a **strategy** for the specific audience and occasion. This is the phase in which you develop your purposes in relationship to the audience and situation.

2. Develop a clear **structure.** This step translates your broad strategy into specific content.

3. **Support** your ideas with examples, illustrations, and other material adapted to your audience. This will reinforce your ideas.

4. Prepare your material to create a presentation **style** that will enhance your ideas. How you present your ideas is often as important as what you present.

5. **Supplement** your presentation with confident, informed responses to questions and challenges. Your performance in a spontaneous, free-flowing discussion or exchange of memos should be as impressive and informative as your prepared presentation.

We have maintained throughout this book that effective personal performance is a function of skill, knowledge, and practice. This is especially the case with communication. The key to gaining confidence in making oral and written presentations is preparation and practice. If you follow the basic five steps, you should be on your way to delivering effective messages. Specific guidelines for implementing these five steps will be presented in the following sections.

Formulate a Specific Strategy

Identify your purpose. Before collecting information or writing notes, you should clarify your general purpose for speaking or writing. Are you trying to motivate, inform, persuade, demonstrate, or teach? Your general purpose is to inform if you are providing information, demonstrating a technique, or delivering a report. When your purpose is to inform, you are concerned with the transmission and retention of ideas and facts. On the other hand, if you are motivating workers for higher production, convincing others to adopt your ideas, or stimulating pride in the company, your general purpose is to persuade. Persuasion requires the use of motivational language, convincing argument, and audience adaptation. Your general purpose may affect how you structure your message and how you supplement your ideas as well as your style of presentation. That is why it is important to identify your general purpose first.

Your specific purpose should be easier to determine once you have identified your general purpose (see Figure 2). You can discover your specific purpose by asking, "What do I want my listeners to learn?" or "What behaviors or attitudes do I want my listeners to adopt?" You may answer, "I want my listeners or readers to learn the six steps in our new accounting procedure" or "I want them to spend more time with customers." Each of these is a specific purpose. It determines how you will tailor the remainder of your preparation to your audience and the demands of the situation.

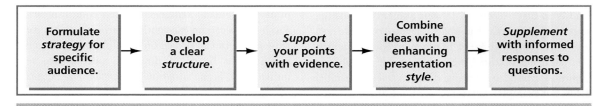

Figure 1 The Five Ss Approach to an Effective Presentation

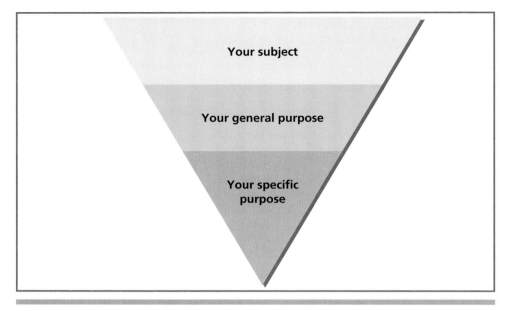

Figure 2 Determining Your Purpose

Tailor your message to your specific audience.
The success of your communication is partially dependent upon your audience's understanding and receptivity. The key to developing an audience-appropriate message is to understand their knowledge of the topic, attitude toward your message, and expectations of your presentation. If they already know what you are trying to teach them, they'll become bored and possibly hostile. Start with what they already know, then expand on it. If you are teaching a new accounting procedure, begin with the one your listeners currently use, then add the new steps. Remember that audiences retain more information if the material is associated with something they already know, rephrased and repeated, reinforced with visual aids, and limited to three to five new ideas. Motivated listeners retain more, so explain how they can use the information early in your message.

Your audience's attitudes toward your message are also critical to consider. Hostile receivers don't learn as readily as eager receivers. If your audience is hostile, start by setting realistic goals. If you try to do too much, you might trigger a boomerang effect in which your audience becomes even more hostile. Emphasize common ground by sharing similar values or parallel goals. For example, you might point out that increased profits are good for everyone in the company or that everyone has a stake in improving plant conditions.

For hostile or uncommitted listeners it is important to develop a two-sided message (see Table 1). Present both sides of the issue. Use strong arguments built on logic and extensive evidence (Sprague & Stuart, 1995). Choose neutral language as you develop your ideas.

For hostile listeners, it is also important to build your credibility. Show yourself to be calm, fair, reasonable, and well informed. Use humor directed at yourself to ease tension (Sprague & Stuart, 1995).

Meet the demands of the situation. Your receivers' expectations of your presentation are also important. The situation frequently determines expectations, such as the level of formality. Some situations clearly demand more formal presentations. If you are expected to address a board meeting, you should prepare carefully. On the other hand, if you are asked for your off-the-cuff comments, a prepared speech is not appropriate or practical. In this case, it is permissible to present more spontaneous remarks. Written communication also involves certain expectations. Invitations to a company picnic can be posted on bulletin boards, but invitations to a board of directors meeting are sent individually. Some situations are tricky. For example, television often appears informal, however you should carefully think out your comments. Banquets and ceremonies may encourage an informal, friendly atmos-

You should use a one-sided message when:

- your audience already favors your position.
- your audience is not well educated in general or on the topic.
- you require a public commitment from your audience.

You should use a two-sided message when:

- your audience initially disagrees with your position.
- your audience is well educated in general or on the topic.
- your audience will experience counter-persuasion on the topic.

Research suggests that the best way to present a two-sided message is to first give the arguments that support your position. Organize those arguments beginning with the weakest and ending with the strongest. Then, present the argument of your opposition. Organize the opposition arguments beginning with the strongest and ending with the weakest. In this way, you take advantage of your listeners' tendency to remember the most recent thing they hear: your strong argument and your opponent's weak argument.

Table 1   One-Sided Versus Two-Sided Messages
Source: Adapted from Michael Sproule, *Speechmaking: An Introduction to Rhetorical Competence* (Dubuque, IA: William C. Brown, 1991).

phere, but don't be fooled. These aren't the same settings as one-on-one or small group events.

The settings of business presentations can create a number of constraints that you must anticipate. (Remember that forethought and preparation are keys to effective communication.) Consider these common occurrences. A meeting schedule runs over so that your 20-minute presentation must be condensed to five minutes. Be prepared with a short version that highlights information that will serve your strategy. After presenting your committee's proposal for changing customer service procedures, which the committee has studied for three months, an influential nonmember distributes an outline of a competing proposal. Be prepared to answer specific criticisms of your proposal while maintaining a tone of cordial professionalism.

Language is also affected by the situation. More formal language choices and more correct sentence structure are demanded by formal situations. Slang, colloquialisms, contractions, and less-rigid grammar can add to the ease of informal settings. Determine your audience's expectations and adapt your language to them. Most experts agree that your language should be one step more intense than your audience's.

Develop a Clear Structure

Begin with a forecast.   In general, an effective introduction does three things. First, it catches the listeners' attention and sets a tone for the message. Second, it provides your listeners with a reason for listening or reading. And, finally, it gives them a road map or quick sketch of the message. At a supervisor's meeting, you might start out your talk on a new plan for production changes this way: "Do you realize that we have not changed our basic production process in four years? In that time, seven new competitors have entered the market, and we've lost 9 percent of market share. But with three changes, we can get more production, which will generate 3 percent more profits and pay raises in the next fiscal year. First, we reorganize Bay 2; second, we install a track between the parts room and the assembly line; and, third, we set up a phone connection between the parts room and the assembly line. Let me spend a few minutes filling out the details of each change and explaining why these changes will save us money." This introduction gets your audience's attention because it portrays the immediacy of the problem and shows why your listeners have an important stake in what you have to say. By setting the larger context of increased competition, you intensify their reason for listening and counter possible resistance to change, which is common in organizations.

Choose an appropriate organizational pattern. Organization is critical because it affects comprehension of the message. Learners retain more when messages are organized. Organization also affects your credibility as a speaker or writer. A person who is organized is viewed more positively than one who is not. And, organization affects attitude change. Your receivers are more likely to be influenced by your viewpoint if it is organized. Finally, an organized message is more likely to be retained, and thus to influence the listener.

There are many patterns of organization to choose from (see Table 2). In general, you should order your thoughts using continua like time, direction, causal process, problem-solving sequence, complexity, space, or familiarity. A related technique is to organize your material as a series of answers to typical questions. Another common technique is called "sandwiching." This involves three steps. First, you emphasize the advantages of the plan. Second, you realistically assess the risks or concerns associated with it. Third, you reinforce the benefits by showing how they outweigh the costs, demonstrate how risks can be minimized with proposed safeguards, or show how resistance to change can be overcome.

As you plan your message consider your listeners' orientation. The main question to ask is "What does my audience already know or think?" Start from that point, then move closer to the desired knowledge or point of view.

Written and spoken communication vary in the amount of detailed information that can be conveyed in a single effort. Because a memo or report can be reread, the receiver doesn't have to remember all the information. However, speeches can't be reheard. It's more important to limit the amount of information presented orally. How many points can you make in a speech? Three main points are preferred by most speakers, but many listeners can remember up to five main points. Seven chunks of information is about the limit of a person's immediate short-term memory at any one time. Since people must remember what you have said if they are to act on it, dividing your speech into no more than five major chunks should make your ideas easier to remember (Miller, 1967). If your presentation is long, consider using visual aids, such as overhead transparencies or handouts, to reinforce the message.

Use transitions or signposts to signal your progress. It is important to give your audience a "road map" at the beginning of your message. Don't stop there but continue to help them follow you

STRATEGY	EXPLANATION
Chronological	Traces the order of events in a time sequence (such as past, present, and future or first step, second step, and third step).
Spatial	Arranges major points in terms of physical distance (such as north, central, and south) or direction from each other (such as internal and external).
Causal	Develops ideas from cause (such as diagnosing a disease from its causes) to effect or results to cause (such as from its symptoms to the disease).
Topical	Enumerates aspects of the topic (such as size, color, shape, or texture).
Monroe's Motivated Sequence	Follows a five-step process: 1. gaining attention 2. showing a need 3. presenting a solution 4. visualizing the results when the solution is implemented 5. calling for action to implement the solution
Familiarity-acceptance order	Begins with what the listener knows or believes and moves on to new ideas.
Inquiry order	Develops the topic in steps the same way you acquire the information or solve a problem.
Question-answer	Raises and answers a series of listeners' questions.
Problem-solution	First establishes that a problem exists then develops a plan to solve the problem.
Elimination order	Surveys all the available solutions and systematically eliminates each possibility until only one remains.

Table 2   Common Patterns of Organization

through it. To do this, signal when you're moving from one idea to another by summarizing the first idea, then forecasting the new idea. This is especially important in oral communication, since listeners will only hear your message once; it is critical that you provide signposts during your speech. You should indicate major transitions between ideas, such as: "We've just seen how the two standard types of data storage operate, now let's look at the advantages and disadvantages of each storage system."

In written form, you can signal transitions by indenting, numbering, or using bullets to highlight information. You can call your reader's attention to key words with italicized or bold print. Take advantage of these devices.

Conclude on a high note. Two important psychological concepts are at work in communication—primacy and recency. Primacy is the first impression received and recency is the last. People tend to remember the first and last things they read or hear in messages. It's easy to understand why the most important parts of any presentation are the first and last impressions it creates. You establish an initial feeling in your introduction that colors the rest of the presentation, and the impression created during the conclusion influences the audiences' overall evaluation of your message. Since these are the most important segments of your presentation, they warrant the most preparation. You should plan your message with the beginning and end in mind, that is, consider your specific purpose statement as you develop your introduction and conclusion. Some people write the conclusion first because this allows them to organize the rest of their material so it naturally flows into the conclusion.

Reach closure at the end of your speech or written message by summarizing your ideas for a final time. Research shows that this kind of reinforcement helps listeners retain information. Normally people remember less than 20 percent of what they hear or read. If you preview the information in your introduction, reinforce it in internal summaries, and then summarize in the conclusion, you will increase the odds that your audience will remember your ideas.

The last statements you make after your summary should create a sense of closure and add to the memorability of your message. These statements can take a variety of forms. You can call for action, reinforce your audiences' commitment to action, or establish feelings of good will (see Table 3 for further sugges-

tions). For example, you might emphasize legitimacy by highlighting several authoritative quotes, emphasize the "I'm here to help" theme, predict conditions in the future, underscore the utility of your proposal by emphasizing its impact on the bottom line, or use an emotional appeal to increase commitment and loyalty.

Support Your Points

Choose a variety of support. There are many reasons to use supporting materials, or evidence, as you develop your message. Most research concludes that supporting material makes a great difference in the impact of ideas. This is true even if you are not well known to your receivers or if they find your credibility moderate to low. What kind of support should you choose? Table 4 illustrates some of the many kinds of supporting materials available. Messages are strongest when they are built upon a variety of supporting materials. For example, reinforce statistics on profit sharing with a specific instance, such as how those numbers will affect a person on the assembly line.

When you select an introduction or conclusion, ask yourself if it orients your audience to your purposes and clearly signals the beginning or ending of your speech.

1. Refer to the subject or occasion.
2. Use a personal reference or greeting.
3. Ask a rhetorical question.
4. Make a startling statement.
5. Use a quotation.
6. Tell a humorous story.
7. Use an illustration.
8. Issue a challenge or appeal.
9. Use suspense.
10. Appeal to the listener's self-interest.
11. Employ a visual aid.
12. Refer to a recent incident.
13. Compliment the audience or a member of the audience.
14. Refer to the preceding speaker.
15. Request a specific action.

Table 3 Types of Introductions and Conclusions

Examples	Specific instances that illustrate the point or clarify the idea: for example, "Our plants in Detroit and Sacramento use Quality Circles."
Statistics	Numbers that express relationships of magnitude, segments, or trends: for example, "Currently, a full 32% of our workforce is involved in Quality Circle decision-making, and that is up 17% over the past two years."
Testimony	The opinions or conclusions of others, particularly experts: for example, "After studying our plants, professor Henry Wilson of the Harvard School of Business observed that American workers are not group motivated. He concluded that 'American workers cannot be expected to respond well to Quality Circles for that reason.'"

Table 4 Types of Supporting Materials

Consider your listeners when choosing your support.   The kind of supporting materials you choose partially depends on your audience. If the evidence is new to them, it will have more impact on them. Live videotapes, recordings, or actual photos also have greater impact. People who are highly dogmatic are more affected by evidence than are persons who are not so dogmatic. Of course, people are likely to believe evidence that agrees with their own position more than evidence that does not. So their initial position determines the extent to which they will find evidence believable. If your receivers find the source or types of evidence to be believable or credible, it will be more effective (see Table 5).

Use visual aids as support.   There are as many reasons to use visual aids as there are types of visual aids (see Table 6). Visual aids help people process and retain data (Seiler, 1971). In addition to enhancing comprehension and memory, visual aids can heighten the persuasive impact of your ideas if they engage receivers actively in the communicative exchange. Your credibility and your persuasiveness are enhanced by good visual aids. With these functions in mind, remember that visual aids should be simple, clear, and professional (see Table 7). The purpose of a visual aid is to augment your presentation, not replace it or distract from it. Unfortunately, this last point is lost by many professionals who treat presentations as slide shows in which

There is a great deal of research on the use of supporting materials or evidence in oral presentations. The following patterns seem to emerge:
1. If you have low to moderate credibility, evidence will probably increase your persuasive effectiveness.
2. There seems to be minimal difference between emotional and logical evidence.
3. Using evidence is usually better than not using it.
4. There seems to be little difference between biased sources and objective sources in their final impact on audiences.
5. Good speech delivery may improve the potency of evidence when sources of the evidence are unknown or have low credibility.
6. Evidence can reinforce the long-term effectiveness of persuasion.
7. Evidence is most effective when listeners are not familiar with it.
8. People are more likely to believe evidence that agrees with their own position.
9. Highly dogmatic people are more affected by evidence than are less-dogmatic people.
10. Evidence produces more attitude change when the course and source qualifications are provided.
11. Speakers with low credibility are seen as more credible when they cite evidence.
12. Using irrelevant evidence or poorly qualified sources may produce an effect opposite to what the speaker intends.

Table 5 Using Supporting Materials

Source: Charles U. Larson, *Persuasion,* 6th ed. (Belmont, CA: Wadsworth, 1992), pp. 202–203. Copyright © 1992 by Wadsworth Publishing Company. Reprinted with the permission of the publishers.

According to research, using effective visual aids in an oral presentation:
- makes your presentation up to 50% more memorable.
- significantly clarifies complex or detailed information.
- portrays you as more professional and better prepared.
- speeds up group decision making.
- shortens meeting time by up to 28%.
- makes your message 43% more persuasive.

Table 6 Functions of Visual Aids

Sources: Michael Osborn and Suzanne Osborn, *Public Speaking* (Boston: Houghton Mifflin, 1991), p. 231; Bruce E. Gronbeck et al., *Principles of Speech Communication,* 11th ed. (New York: HarperCollins, 1992), p. 191.

screen displays and even sound effects—not the presenter—become the center of attention.

Computer-aided graphics make it easier than ever to supplement your main ideas with visual materials. They also make it easier to create cluttered, excessive visual and sound images that distract the audience from your strategic message. Select and design visual aids to reinforce your strategy and ideas, and to make them clearer. Keep in mind that each type of visual aid communicates information in a different way. In general, visual aids such as slides, photographs, and posters can help an audience *feel* the way you do. They enhance the emotional dimension of a presentation. On the other hand, descriptive or written materials help an audience *think* the way you do. Numbers and charts reinforce cognitive processes; photographs reinforce

As you prepare your visual aids, ask yourself the following questions:
- Can I avoid making the visual aid the most important aspect of my speech? Will it be more than just an ornament?
- Can I translate complex numbers into bar or line graphs for easier comprehension?
- Am I comfortable with using the visual aid? Have I practiced with it so using it is natural, and it does not break the flow of ideas in my speech?
- Is it large enough to be seen by everyone without straining?
- Is all the printing short and neat?
- Is the visual aid colorful and involving? Studies show color highlights aid recall of information.
- Are my visual aids professional: neat, attractive, and accurate?
- Have I made the necessary arrangements for special visual aids in advance?
- Can I use the visual aid without blocking my audience's view of it? Will I be able to maintain good eye contact with my listeners while using the visual aid?
- Can I avoid reaching across my body or waving the visual aid in front of my face?
- Can I avoid distracting my listeners by keeping the visual aid covered or out of sight before and after I use it?
- What will I do if the visual aid fails to work? Am I prepared for unexpected contingencies such as a burned-out projector bulb or a room that cannot be darkened?
- Have I planned for assistance or volunteers in advance if they are needed?
- Will a pointer be needed?
- Will all charts be secured so I don't have to hunt for them on the floor in the middle of my speech?
- Am I using a variety of visual aids to increase my listeners' interest?
- If I'm using handouts, can I adjust to the distraction caused by passing them around? Can I compete with listeners who will read the handout rather than listen to me?
- Can I speak over the noise of a projector or other machine?

Table 7 Checklist for Using Visual Aids

affective processes. Use tables and graphs to highlight relationships and patterns, not to convey comprehensive data. If necessary, use supplemental handouts of comprehensive tables and charts.

Use an Enhancing Style

Up to this point, the preparation of oral and written messages is very similar. Whether you intend to deliver a speech or write a memo, you need to develop your strategy by identifying your purposes, structuring your message, and supporting your ideas with evidence. The fourth step requires separate treatment of oral and written messages because they are stylistically very different forms of communication. We'll first focus on oral presentations.

Style in Oral Communication

Prepare your notes. The mark of effective presenters is the appearance of effortlessness. Some speakers have such command of their material it appears they are ad libbing. Most of us prefer such a conversational style (see Table 8), but don't be fooled by appearances. Hours of preparation and practice preceded the actual performance. You've already been introduced to the three steps of preparation, but how do you develop the fourth stage of your preparation for oral communication?

After you have carefully considered your strategy, structure, and support, you should prepare your speaking notes. To do this, simply write your key points in a rough outline following the organizational pattern you have chosen. What you do next depends on your method of presentation. Most often, you will speak in a conversational manner that is not memorized or read; this is referred to as extemporaneous speaking. Extemporaneous presentation is desirable because it is natural and flexible; it applies to most situations. To prepare, copy key words on note cards to stimulate your memory; standard pages are often distracting. Write out quotations, statistics, or anything that requires exact wording. Highlight places where you intend to use visual aids, pause for questions, or present an exhibit. To rehearse, go through the speech, phrasing your ideas in language that seems natural. You may find yourself phrasing ideas with different words each time. That is okay. In fact, it will increase the conversational quality of your speech because your words will be typical of oral style and natural expression. It will help you develop flexibility, allowing you to adjust to different wording and flow of ideas.

If the occasion is formal and demands precise wording or exquisite prose, you should prepare a word-for-word manuscript to memorize or read. Then you should rehearse with the manuscript, trying to achieve as much natural flow in the dialogue as possible. This form of presentation is rare, but it may be required for discussing legal and financial issues, making announcements to the press, or conducting special ceremonies. Otherwise, avoid using written scripts and memorization for presentations because they disrupt the natural flow of conversational style and break eye contact with your listeners. Because manuscripts are

---

Folk wisdom holds that giving a speech is just like talking to another person. While it is true that most people prefer a conversational style of public speaking, there are at least three noteworthy differences between giving speeches and holding conversations:

1. Public speaking is more highly structured. It requires more detailed planning and development. Specific time limits may be imposed, and the speaker does not have the advantage of being able to respond individually to listeners.

2. Public speaking requires more formal language. Slang, jargon, and poor grammar all lower speaker credibility, even in informal speech situations. Listeners usually react negatively to poor language choices. In fact, many studies show that some kinds of language, such as obscene language, dramatically lower a speaker's credibility.

3. Public speaking requires a different method of delivery. The speaker's voice must be adjusted in volume and projection, posture is more correct, and distracting mannerisms and verbal habits are avoided.

Table 8 Differences Between Public Speaking and Conversation
Source: Adapted from Stephen Lucas, *The Art of Public Speaking,* 3rd ed. (New York: Random House, 1989).

prepared in written form first, they usually take on the style of written language. Unless you are a practiced speech writer, your manuscript will sound like written rather than oral speech (see Table 9).

Practice your presentation. It is a good idea to rehearse your presentation under simulated conditions—in a similar room, with listeners who can give you suggestions for improvement. Time your presentation so you know if it is necessary to cut or expand your ideas. Research shows that practicing a speech for short periods of time over the course of several days is more successful in reducing anxiety and improving memory than concentrated practice. So give the speech to yourself during breakfast, at your morning coffee break, as you walk to a mid-afternoon meeting, and before bed. Distributed practice is more efficient and yields better results than massed practice.

Practice using your visual aids. This will help you get used to managing them and give you some idea of how long your speech will take with the visual aids. Prepare for the totally unexpected. What if the roar of an overhead plane drowns out your voice? What if the microphone goes dead, a window blows open, or the room becomes extremely hot? Compensate for minor

disruptions by slowing your rate, raising your volume a little, and continuing. You will encourage listeners to listen to your message rather than be temporarily distracted. For other disruptions, a good rule of thumb is to respond the same way you would if you were in the audience. Take off your jacket if it is too hot, close the window, raise your voice if listeners can't hear you, or pause to allow a complex idea to sink in.

As you practice, think about how you will channel your anxiety. Most speakers report feeling anxious before they speak; it's normal. To manage your anxiety, channel it into positive energy. Prepare well in advance for the speech—develop your ideas, support them, and practice your delivery. Even if you are anxious, you will have something important to say. It may help to visualize the speaking situation. Close your eyes, relax, and think about how it's going to feel and what your audience will look like as they watch you. Expect to feel a little momentary panic as you get up to speak, it will evaporate as you progress into the speech. Remember to think about your ideas rather than how nervous you feel. Focus on your message. Also remember that anxiety about speaking never really goes away. Most experienced speakers still get podium panic. The advantage of experience is that you learn how to cope by converting your

Why do we instantly recognize a memorized speech? Why does a meeting transcript *sound* funny? The answer to both questions is that oral style differs from written style. Memorized speeches from manuscripts reveal their written style, and conversations that are read reveal their oral style. Oral style differs from written style in the following ways:

1. The average sentence length is shorter (about 16 words) in conversations.

2. Vocabulary is more limited in speaking than in writing. "I" and "you" make up almost 8% of the words used in speaking; fewer than 50 words make up almost half of the total vocabulary we use when we speak.

3. Spoken vocabulary consists of more short words.

4. Speakers use more words referring to themselves such as "I," "me," and "we"; listeners rate this as more interesting.

5. More qualifying terms (such as "much," "many," and "a lot") and allness terms (such as "none," "never," and "always") are used in speaking.

6. More phrases and terms indicating hesitation are apparent in speaking, such as "it seems to me," "apparently," "in my opinion," and "maybe."

7. Fewer precise numbers are used in speaking.

8. Speakers use more contractions and colloquial expressions such as "can't," "wouldn't", "wow," and "chill out."

One final note on language: There is some evidence that we use lexical diversity as a cue to a speaker's socioeconomic status, competence, and perceived similarity.

Table 9 Differences Between Oral and Written Styles
Source: Lois Einhorn, "Oral and Written Style: An Examination of Differences," *Southern Speech Communication Journal* (1978): 302–311. Reprinted with the permission of the Southern States Communication Association.

anxiety into energy and enthusiasm. That gives you an extra sparkle as you speak. Above all, don't tell your listeners that you are nervous. This will divert their attention from your ideas to your anxiety. Usually, listeners can't tell that a speaker is nervous—only speakers know, and they should keep that secret.

Convey controlled enthusiasm for your subject. When a survey was given to 1,200 people asking them to identify the characteristics of effective presentations (Peoples, 1988), the results contained adjectives such as flexible, cooperative, audience-oriented, pleasant, and interesting. What was striking about these results is that only the last item on the list of 12 outstanding characteristics was specifically related to the content of the presentations. This suggests that the preceding discussion of effective format, while necessary, is not sufficient to guarantee your success. Put another way, a rambling, poorly organized presentation will surely produce an overall negative evaluation. On the other hand, a well-organized, highly logical, and easy-to-follow presentation that is poorly delivered will also be viewed negatively. This study suggests that style is extremely important in oral communication.

Years of research on student evaluations of classroom teaching performance have consistently shown that enthusiasm is the hallmark of a good teacher. Students will forgive other deficiencies if the teacher obviously loves the subject and is genuinely interested in conveying that appreciation to the students. The same holds true for presenters. Your posture, tone of voice, and facial expressions are all critical indicators of your attitude. Speak standing if you can, move occasionally, and use gestures to convey an attitude of earnestness. Remember, your audience will become infected with your enthusiasm.

Although enthusiasm is important, it must be controlled. Do not confuse enthusiasm with loudness. A good rule is to use vigorous but conversational tones of voice and inflections. Avoid bellowing or preaching at your listeners. Be sure you can be easily heard and that your tone is sufficiently emphatic to convey meaning effectively. In general, your speech should resemble an animated or lively conversation.

Use delivery to enhance your message. Another key to maintaining audience attention is effective delivery. Eye contact is the most important tool for establishing audience involvement. It makes listeners feel as if they are involved in a one-on-one, semiprivate discussion with you. In this culture, we value directness and honesty. One of the expressions of these values is direct eye contact. Effective eye contact means looking directly at members of the audience, one at a time, on a random, rotating basis. Generally, the smaller the group, the longer you can look at each person. Maintaining eye contact is also your primary source of audience feedback as you are presenting. If your audience appears puzzled, you may need to pause and review your key ideas.

It is important to use physical space and body movement to enhance your message. Remember that presentations are like movies, not snapshots. Alternate moving and standing still, speaking and listening, doing and thinking. Intersperse your lecture with chalkboard use, demonstration, audience participation, and audiovisual aids so that no single activity occupies a large portion of the presentation. Add some spice to your presentation by including personal anecdotes, references to members of the group, unusual facts, vital information, and vibrant images. Whenever appropriate, arrange the podium area to accommodate physical movement. Physical movement can be used to punctuate important points, signal transitions, build rapport with a person who asks a question, heighten the interest of particular segments of the audience, and help your listeners stay alert by refocusing their attention.

Other aspects of physical space affect the quality of your presentation. If possible, arrange the podium area and seating in the room to remove distractions. In more intimate settings, group participants so that there is less space between them. Eliminate unnecessary or distracting materials from the podium, such as unused equipment, signs, and displays. Keep your visual aids covered until they are used and keep the chalkboard clean. Focus your listeners' attention on you and your message.

You can use space to convey intimacy or distance. Position yourself roughly in the middle of your audience from left to right and in a spot where you can comfortably maintain eye contact. With this in mind, you can deliberately alter your presentation style to build rapport with members of the audience. Move closer if you intend to build intimacy or tension; move to a comfortable distance when your ideas are neutral.

Gestures can also add to a presentation. They should appear to be spontaneous and natural in order to enhance, rather than distract from, your message. They should be relaxed, not rigid. Use them to accentuate your normal mode of expression. To some extent, when you concentrate on your message, not your movements, the appropriate gestures will come naturally. Remember that your gestures should be smooth, relatively slow, and not too low (below your waist), too high (above your shoulders), or too wide (more than two feet from your body). If you are using a podium, step slightly behind or to the side of the podium so it does not block your listeners' view of your movement. The general rules for gestures change as your audience becomes larger. You must adapt to large groups by making larger, more dramatic gestures.

Avoid any gestures or movement that distracts from your message. Irrelevant movement such as jingling change in a pocket, toying with notes, shifting from foot to foot, twisting hair, or adjusting eyeglasses are annoying. In fact, any movement repeated too often creates a distraction. Practice using a variety of body movements to illustrate or describe, enumerate, add emphasis, or direct attention. For variety, some gestures should involve the entire upper body, not just your dominant hand.

Style in Written Communication

Like oral communication, written communication is a skill; it can be learned. Written communication follows the same three preparation steps as oral communication. The writer determines strategies, structure, and support before actually putting pen to paper. As with effective presentations, good writing draws on careful analysis of the audience and situation. In a business setting, "every document is a response to a problem or opportunity requiring that some consensus be achieved or action taken" (Poor, 1992, p. 38).

There are significant differences between oral and written communication style. Although it lacks the interpersonal dimension of immediacy, written communication offers one tremendous advantage over oral communication—it lasts. Written documents can be retained, studied, duplicated, and filed for the future. This means that they are essentially capable of conveying much more detailed information. While written communication offers these advantages, it also makes different demands on the communicator; written communication demands precision.

Develop mechanical precision in your writing.
Your professional image is judged by the appearance of your written communication. Cross outs, erasures, ty-

pographical errors, or other sloppiness detract from your written message, just as awkward mannerisms can distract from your oral message. Grammatical precision is also required—misspellings, punctuation errors, and poor grammar are marks of uneducated writers. This is certainly not an image you want to convey. You may expect a secretary or clerical worker to catch and correct all these things, and many times that happens. However, when you sign or otherwise endorse the final product, you alone are accountable for any errors it contains. It is essential to develop the habit of proofreading final drafts before you sign them.

Violations of the rules of grammar and punctuation may affect more than just your credibility. They can also disrupt your reader. If the reader is distracted by typos, confusing grammar, or ambiguous pronouns, your ideas may become lost; such errors can cripple the impact of your message. Some recruiters toss out resumes that contain mechanical errors. Their reasoning is that if job applicants can't take the time to proofread a short resume, they may be sloppy on the job, too. Some readers are insulted by poor grammar; others automatically consider themselves superior to the writer. While these may not be logical reactions, they occur, and more important, they block your effectiveness. You may argue that correct grammar and punctuation are not vital. Maybe not, but you take a chance every time you present careless work to another reader. Consider the campaign of Charles Day for a seat on local government. His campaign flyers, delivered house to house, carried the banner, "Vote Charles Day for School Bord." Would you want a man who apparently can't spell making decisions on academic matters for your neighborhood schools? The impression is that if you don't have the time or incentive to check your own writing, you won't pay attention to details in the work of others.

Practice factual precision in your writing.
It's obvious that getting the facts right is important. If you send a memo calling for a meeting but record an incorrect meeting date, you'll suffer the consequences of inconveniencing others. Accuracy is critical but that's just the beginning. It's up to the writer to create sentences so that the meaning is unmistakably clear to the reader. Many times writers know the facts but omit important details in writing. Omission occurs when you have all the facts or circumstances but as you write, you assume the reader knows the facts. Write with your reader in mind. This assumes that you have analyzed

who your readers are and understand what information they need and expect. What basic information is important for readers to know in order to understand your message? Instead of starting with the central part of the message, provide the background first, such as: "In response to your memo of February 2, requesting corrections to our policy on grievances, we have taken three actions. First . . ." If you're not sure what to include, ask someone who doesn't know the details of the situation to read what you have written.

Ambiguity is another barrier to clear writing. Many times we write as we speak, throwing in phrases as we would speak them. Unlike speakers, writers can't use nonverbal cues to convey specific meanings or associations. Since readers may not have the advantage of asking questions or getting immediate feedback, they are left to determine associations for themselves. Consider how ambiguity creates a lack of precise factual meaning in this memo:

> The next meeting of the department is scheduled for next week. Matt Olsen has told Leo Robinson to report on the union elections. His report will follow announcements. We will elect new officers at our upcoming meeting.

This memo doesn't pass the standard test of clear writing. If the memo was sent on Friday and received on Monday, which week contains the meeting? Who is giving the report? The pronoun "his" causes confusion since it could refer to either Matt Olsen or Leo Robinson. Which "upcoming meeting" will result in the election of officers? Will it be the meeting called by the memo or another "upcoming meeting"? Because it can breed confusion, annoyance, and wasted time, such a sloppy memo can have an adverse effect on the relationship between the writer and recipients that can affect their subsequent communication. Seen in this light, the memos a manager routinely writes are an important factor in managing relationships strategically and productively.

Construct written messages with verbal precision.

Achieving verbal precision is different from mechanical or factual precision. Verbal precision is based on the accuracy of the words chosen to express the ideas. In an ideal world, words would provide the exact meaning you intended, but words can't replicate reality. Rather, words are symbols of objects and ideas. Add to this inexact representation the reader's own sub-

tle shadings of meaning, and you can see why it's difficult to achieve verbal precision. Put another way, a word has two levels of meaning: its denotation, or the meaning agreed upon by most people who use the word, and its connotation, or the personal dimension of meaning brought to the word by the receiver.

Communication depends on a blend of both denotative and connotative meanings. Consider the noun "Greenpeace." Its denotative reference is to a specific international environmental organization. The connotative meaning varies widely. For many environmentalists, Greenpeace is leading a worthy crusade. However, for some governments and companies, the organization is, at best, a nuisance. These are the connotative references of a single word. Consider the difficulty in creating the right blend of denotative and connotative meaning in entire documents. You need to be aware of both types of meaning of the words you use. Frequently, you may recognize your own connotative meaning but be unaware of how others may react. While connotation is often a personal matter, you can attempt to judge this meaning by thinking from your receiver's viewpoint. What is their most likely reaction?

The key to verbal precision in writing is clarity. The fundamental questions you must ask yourself are: "Does the word or phrase convey my meaning without confusion?" or "Could anyone reading this memo for the first time understand the ideas directly and simply?" A secondary question is whether the written message conveys unintentional meanings stimulated by connotative meanings of words or phrases. The impact of connotations once more underlines the importance of knowing your audience and of being aware of what is appropriate for one audience or another.

Pay attention to tone.

The tone of your writing is directly related to your diction, or word choices. For example, compare these two statements: "Our company will purchase the product" and "We'll buy it." The second sounds more informal because it uses pronouns and a contraction. In general, longer words and sentences tend to convey a more formal tone.

Using the appropriate level of formality in your writing calls for you to analyze the nature of the writing situation. An invitation to a reception for the company's board of directors calls for formal language. When you are writing to strangers or up the chain of command, it is safer to be formal. When you are communicating across or down the chain, you often may be informal. However, a letter of reprimand to a subordinate should be formal in tone.

Tone in business writing goes beyond its relative formality. It reflects on the nature of the writer as a person and therefore affects how the reader feels about the writer. Its impact can be significant and often unexpected. For example, a terse letter may be interpreted as sarcastic or angry even if the writer did not intend sarcasm or anger. Consider a customer who writes a long letter expressing problems with a product. What would the customer think if this response were mailed back: "Thank you for your letter of January 12. We always enjoy hearing from our customers." Although this response has the trappings of courtesy, it seems insincere and perhaps sarcastic. It hardly seems that the respondent read the customer's letter—there is nothing about its contents—or that the letter was "enjoyed." Although the response shows factual and mechanical precision, the tone is inappropriate and potentially damaging to the relationship with this customer.

In most cases, even disappointing news can be expressed in a positive way. Consider an employer who responds to a job applicant by writing, "In a company as well respected as ours, we rarely have time to consider applications such as yours." Not only is the news bad, the arrogant tone also needlessly humiliates the applicant. A response with a more positive tone might be: "We read your application with interest but currently do not have any openings in your specialties. Best wishes with your continued search." The news is still bad, but the polite tone shows respect for the applicant and promotes a professional image of the company.

Compare the following sentence and its more positive version: "Because of recent heavy demand, we will be unable to ship the items you ordered until July 15," and "Although recent demand has been heavy, we will be able to ship the items you ordered July 15." A slight variation in wording here changes a tone of helplessness to one of helpfulness.

Under most business writing conditions, you should be cordial. You should express tact and friendliness appropriate to your relationship with the reader. This attitude will have a positive effect on your word choices, which in turn will more likely convey an appropriate tone.

One area of modern business writing where failing to pay attention to tone has cost many bad feelings and lost time is electronic mail, or E-mail. By its nature, E-mail encourages rapid-fire exchanges, especially when busy workers face an in box filled with messages, many of which are ill considered and unclear. E-mail is not a phone conversation in which tone of voice and other cues can clarify your meaning and in which you can read the listener's vocal cues. However, many E-mailers seem to forget the difference. They don't state the context of their message; they don't give needed background information; they don't organize their message; they don't make careful word choices that convey a cordial tone. By not taking the time to consider their message in light of the situation and the receiver, E-mailers can convey inappropriately demanding tones or disapproving tones if their requests aren't met promptly. The antagonism created by the poor tone of E-mail messages can delay solving the business problem at hand and affect negatively the work relationships of the E-mailers.

Know the proper format.   Like it or not, first impressions count even in written communication. Sloppiness suggests that the writer doesn't take the message seriously; odd or unconventional formats hint that the writer is ignorant or unprofessional. You should become acquainted with the physical layout of letters, memos, proposals, and other common forms of written business communication. Others expect you to have this basic knowledge; many handbooks and computer software programs are available to guide you in the development of these formats. Some companies have style guides that precisely prescribe the formats for all documents representing the company.

While there are several acceptable formats for written communication such as business letters, the reader should be able to pick up specific information at a glance. In the business letter, this information includes: The intended recipient of the letter, the sender, the sender's address for return correspondence, any enclosures, and recipients of copies of the letter. All of this information is separate from the body of the letter and should be clearly visible.

Because memos are intended to communicate within an organization, their format is different from that of letters. Instead of business letterhead, memo letterhead is used. Basic information can also be obtained at a glance. The top of the memo should include: To, From, Date, and Subject headings. Usually salutations and closings are not considered necessary within an organization.

Proposals are much lengthier and require special attention to supporting information such as tables, graphs, and charts. The best ways to represent such data can be found in readily available resources on business writing.

Whatever the final format, there is one objective in all written business communication: Your message should be simple, direct, and clear. Anything that interrupts your reader's movement through your writing limits its effectiveness. Any imprecision—a mechanical blunder, a factual omission, or a strange word—calls attention to itself and, like an odd gesture in spoken communication, diverts attention away from your ideas. As a writer, you must aim at clear, direct transmission of your message.

Supplement Your Presentation by Responding to Questions and Challenges

Prepare thoroughly to handle questions.
Answering questions and responding to objections is a vital part of the communication process because it allows us to interact directly with our listeners. We can learn about how our listeners are thinking and their responses to our ideas from their questions; it's a two-way street.

The key to formulating effective responses is the same as the key to developing good speeches—careful preparation. Read broadly and talk with experts in your field. Don't read just the material that supports your point of view but also read what the opposition is saying. The best defense can be a good offense, and this is no exception. Ask your colleagues to critique your material, discuss their questions and objections with them, and collect supporting documentation or evidence. You can also practice your responses. Begin by considering what your listeners might ask or find someone opposed to your position who will list questions for you. Then, practice your responses to these questions.

Despite your best efforts, you may get an overwhelmingly hostile response from your listeners. Don't be afraid to take a stand that disagrees with them. People may not agree with you but they will respect your sincerity. If someone throws you a curve, don't apologize or bluff your way through with an inadequate response. Be honest and direct, tell them if you don't have the answer. Invite them to discuss the problem further at a later time and follow up on your invitation. The next time someone asks the same question, you will be prepared.

When challenged, answer in a specific format.
Respond to objections in an orderly manner. In general, answer questions as succinctly as possible. Rambling answers may make it appear as though you are hedging. They also suggest an inability to think concisely. You can answer objections in four steps:

1. **Restate the objection.** This gives you time to think, shows your interest, and makes sure that everyone understands the question. Restatement recognizes the objection and clarifies it for everyone in the audience.

2. **State your position.** Give a concise, direct statement of what you believe to make it clear where you stand.

3. **Offer support for your position.** This is the critical part of the response. Provide evidence that shows your position is the right one.

4. **Indicate the significance of your rebuttal.** Show the impact of adopting your position. Offer reasons for doing so.

Following the four steps we've outlined, a good response to an objection might take this form:

1. "Joe has stated that a management-by-objectives system won't work in our factory because supervisors don't want input from the cutting floor (restatement of the objection).

2. I think that a management-by-objectives system will work and that it will increase worker satisfaction (statement of your position).

3. I'm basing my position on a group of studies done in our Newark plant last year. Output increased 0.5 percent during the first month, and more importantly, workers reported more job satisfaction. They had fewer sick days too (support for the position).

4. If our plant is similar to the Newark plant—and I think it is—then I believe our supervisors will notice the same gains here. Until Joe can provide us with a reason to stick with the current system, I think we ought to give the new one a try—we stand to get more output and better job satisfaction (significance of rebuttal)."

Practice this format until it becomes automatic. It builds up your own case while responding to the objection. Since this format rationally shores up your position, it increases your credibility as well. And, it increases the chances that others will agree with you.

Maintain control of the situation. You need to balance being sensitive to feedback and flexible enough to respond to legitimate concerns with avoiding prolonged, unproductive interchanges. Recognizing everyone's right to ask questions or offer alternative positions is important because it grants audience members respect. On the other hand, you also have every right to decide what is relevant for consideration. You shouldn't allow one or two members of your audience to dictate the pace or direction of your presentation. This places you in a position of weakness that undermines your credibility. If you should alter your position, make certain that the majority of your listeners view it as a responsible shift rather than an effort to placate a minority voice.

Keep exchanges on an intellectual level. Arguments and rebuttals can degenerate into name-calling in which little is settled. Effective communication is more likely to occur when the calm voice of reason dominates than when you squabble with your listeners.

You'll soon learn that people don't always ask questions just because they want information. Some people crave attention; others may sabotage your position if they perceive your ideas as a threat. Planning for these possibilities will give you more options; foresight enables you to respond appropriately. You might answer hostile questions with further questions, drawing out your interrogator and regaining the offensive. Or, you might broaden the discussion. Don't get trapped into an argument with one person. Involve others to determine if this is an isolated concern or a legitimate issue. Finally, you might express your willingness to discuss special or detailed issues but defer extensive discussion until the end of your presentation.

Summary and Behavioral Guidelines

A key aspect of management is communication, and formal presentations are an essential communication tool. Therefore, effective managers must be able to create effective informative and persuasive messages. You can enhance your speaking and writing with thorough prep-

aration and repeated practice. This chapter has outlined a number of guidelines based on the Five Ss model:

1. Formulate a **strategy** for the specific audience and occasion.

2. Develop a clear **structure.**

3. **Support** your points with evidence adapted to your audience.

4. Practice presenting your material in a **style** that will enhance your ideas.

5. **Supplement** your presentation by effectively responding to questions and challenges.

Strategy

1. Identify your general and specific purposes.

2. Tailor your message to your audience.

   ▶ Understand their needs, desires, knowledge level, and attitude toward your topic.

   ▶ Make sure your approach is audience centered.

   ▶ Present both sides of the issue if your audience is hostile or uncommitted.

3. Meet the demands of the situation.

   ▶ More formal situations demand formal language and sentence structure.

   ▶ Informal situations allow slang and less rigid language use.

Structure

4. Begin with a forecast of your main ideas.

   ▶ Catch your audience's attention as you begin.

   ▶ Provide them with a reason for listening or reading.

   ▶ Give them an outline of the message so they can follow along.

5. Choose your organizational pattern carefully.

   ▶ Start with what your listeners already know or think.

   ▶ Use organization to increase your credibility.

   ▶ Move from familiar to unfamiliar, simple to complex, old to new, or use another continua for organizing your thoughts.

▶ Make no more than three to five main points in oral communication.

6. Use transitions to signal your progress.

7. Conclude on a high note.

▶ Take advantage of greater audience attention at the conclusion of your message.

▶ Reach closure by reinforcing through a summary of your ideas.

▶ Use your last statements to call for action, reinforce the commitment to action, or establish a feeling of goodwill.

Support

8. Choose a variety of support.

▶ The most effective support is not well known to your listeners.

▶ Support increases your credibility.

▶ You may use a wide variety of supporting material.

9. Consider your audience when choosing your support.

▶ New evidence and live videotapes have more impact.

▶ The audience's initial position determines the extent to which they find evidence believable.

▶ Using evidence is better than not using evidence.

10. Use visual aids as support.

▶ Visual aids have a dramatic impact on comprehension and retention.

▶ Visual aids also enhance persuasion.

▶ Keep visual aids simple and effective.

Style in Oral Communication

11. Prepare your notes.

▶ Remember, the crucial effect is conversational style.

▶ Extemporaneous presentation requires limited notes combined with frequent delivery practice.

▶ Formal occasions demand precise wording that requires a manuscript or memorized speech.

12. Practice your presentation.

▶ Use distributed practice rather than massed practice.

▶ Practice using your visual aids and plan for the unexpected.

▶ Plan to channel your speaking anxiety.

13. Convey controlled enthusiasm for your subject.

▶ Effective speakers communicate excitement about their topics.

▶ Your posture, tone of voice, and facial expressions all indicate your attitude.

▶ Your speech should resemble an animated conversation.

14. Engage your audience with effective delivery.

▶ Eye contact is the most critical tool.

▶ Use physical space and body movement to enliven your message.

▶ Use space to convey intimacy or distance.

▶ Use gestures to accentuate your normal mode of expression.

▶ Avoid any movement that distracts from your message.

Style In Written Communication

15. Develop mechanical precision in your writing.

▶ Project a professional image.

▶ Errors may distract your readers and disrupt the impact of your message.

16. Practice factual precision in your writing.

▶ Accuracy ensures that your meaning will be communicated clearly.

▶ Ambiguity prevents factual precision.

17. Construct written messages with verbal precision.

▶ Words cannot replicate reality.

▶ Consider denotative and connotative meanings of words as you write them.

▶ The key to verbal precision is clarity.

18. Pay attention to tone.

 ▶ Tone is directly related to word choice.

 ▶ Adjust the tone of your message to the formality of the situation.

 ▶ Tone affects how readers feel about the writer.

 ▶ Writing should express appropriate cordiality.

 ▶ Positive phrasing is preferable to negativity.

19. Know the proper format.

 ▶ You are responsible for creating an impression of professionalism.

 ▶ Business letters, memos, and proposals all have special formats.

Supplement: Questions and Answers

20. Anticipate questions and thoroughly prepare responses.

 ▶ Rehearse answers to difficult questions.

 ▶ Handle hostile listeners with honesty and directness.

21. Respond to objections in an orderly fashion.

 ▶ Restate the objection.

 ▶ State your position.

 ▶ Offer support for your position.

 ▶ Indicate the significance of your rebuttal.

22. Maintain control of the situation.

 ▶ Balance the demands of specific individuals with the interest of the group.

 ▶ Keep exchanges on an intellectual level.

 ▶ Plan for the questioner who has a personal agenda.

Skill Practice

Exercises in Making Effective Oral and Written Presentations

Speaking as a Leader

As illustrated in the opening case about Taylor Billingsley at Apex Communications, one of the major challenges facing leaders is the requirement to deliver a wide range of presentations. Effective communicators must be skilled at both informing and inspiring. They must be able to hold their own with hostile audiences as well as impress content experts and instill confidence in novices. They must be skilled at building consensus, pointing new directions, and explaining complex topics. This exercise, adapted from Richard Linowes, provides an opportunity to practice speaking on a variety of leadership topics.

Assignment

To practice playing this important leadership role, prepare a talk and a memo on one of the following topics. Your speech should last from three to five minutes, unless you are otherwise instructed. Your memo should not exceed two pages. Create a context for your communication by assuming a management role in a familiar organization. Before beginning, explain the details of the context to your audience (either orally or in a written summary). Briefly explain your organizational position, the makeup of the audience, and their expectations of your presentation. (For the memo, attach a one-page background statement.) The specific content of your communication is less important than how well it is prepared and how persuasively it is delivered. Prepare to respond to questions and challenges.

In preparing your presentation, review the behavioral guidelines at the end of the Skill Learning section. The checklist in this exercise may also be useful. You will receive feedback based on the criteria shown in the Observer's Feedback Form in Appendix I.

Topics for Leadership Talks

1. **Taking Charge of an Established Group.** The speaker is a manager newly assigned to a group that has worked together under other managers for some time.

2. **Announcing a New Project.** The speaker is announcing a new undertaking to members of his or her department and is calling on all to rally behind the effort.

3. **Calling for Better Customer Service.** The speaker is motivating all employees to be as attentive and responsive as possible to customers.

4. **Calling for Excellence and High-Quality Work.** The speaker is motivating all employees to perform their jobs with a commitment to meeting the highest-possible standards.

5. **Announcing the Need for Cost Reductions.** The speaker is requesting that everyone look for ways to cut expenditures and immediately begin to slash spending.

6. **Commending for a Job Well Done.** The speaker is extolling a group of people who have worked very hard for an extended period to produce outstanding results.

7. **Calming a Frightened Group of People.** The speaker is endeavoring to restore calm and confidence to those who feel panic in the face of distressing business developments.

8. **Addressing a Challenging Opposition.** The speaker is presenting a heartfelt belief to a critical, even hostile, audience.

9. **Mediating Between Opposing Parties.** The speaker is serving as judge or arbiter between two groups who are bitterly opposed on a key issue.

10. **Taking Responsibility for Error.** The speaker is a spokesperson for an institution whose actions have produced an unfortunate result that affects the audience.

11. **Reprimanding Unacceptable Behavior.** The speaker is taking to task certain individuals who have failed to perform up to required levels.

12. **Petitioning for Special Allowances.** The speaker is presenting the case for an institution seeking certain rights that must be authorized by some external body.

Checklist for Developing Effective Presentations

1. What are my general and specific objectives?

2. What is the context of my communication? (My audience, the situation, etc.)

3. How will I open and close the communication?

4. How will I organize my information?

5. How will I get and keep the attention of my audience?

6. What supporting materials will I use?

7. What visual aids (graphs, charts, objects, etc.) will I use?

8. How will I tailor the presentation to this audience?

9. What format will I use in my presentation?

10. What questions or responses will likely occur?

Quality Circles at Battle Creek Foods

One of the newest innovations in group decision making, quality circles (QCs), has recently received considerable attention among U.S. manufacturers. Their interest in this technique stems from its having been described by the Japanese as critical to their recent manufacturing success. Ironically, Edward Deming, an American, first brought the notion of "statistical quality control," a management tool, to the Japanese in the early post–World War II years. The Japanese combined these ideas with the assumption that the person who performs a job is the one who best knows how to identify and correct its problems. As a result, the Japanese, with Deming's help, developed the "quality circle." A quality circle is a group of people (usually about 10) who meet periodically to discuss and develop solutions to problems related to quality, productivity, or product cost.

The purpose of this exercise is to give you an opportunity to make a presentation on this important topic.

Assignment

You are the Director of Personnel at Battle Creek Foods, a leading manufacturer of breakfast cereal. Productivity has been sagging industry-wide, and your organization is starting to see its effect on profitability. In response, you have been asked by the corporate executive committee to make a 20-minute oral presentation (or prepare a five-page memo) on quality circles. The committee has heard that QCs have been initiated at several plants by your leading competitor, and it would like your recommendation as to whether Battle Creek Foods should follow suit. The committee's only previous exposure to QCs is what each member has read in the popular press. Using the following reference material, prepare a presentation on quality circles. Explain the QC structure and process, and the advantages and disadvantages of QCs. The final section of the presentation should include a recommendation regarding their adoption at your plants. Prepare to respond to questions and challenges.

In preparing your presentation, refer to the behavioral guidelines for effective presentations at the end of the Skill Learning section and the checklist in the preceding exercise. You will receive feedback based on the Observer's Feedback Form in Appendix I.

A Look at Some of the Evidence

Quality circles, on balance, appear to be making a positive contribution to product quality, profits, morale, and even improved employee attendance (Dubrin, 1985, pp. 174–185). The widespread attention QCs have received in recent years has led logically to their evaluation by both businesspeople and researchers. Here we will rely on several types of evaluation methods, sampling first the positive evidence, and then the negative.

Favorable Outcomes with QCs

Honeywell, a high-technology electronics firm, has become a pioneer in the application of QCs in North America. Honeywell currently operates several hundred QCs in the United States. Typically, about a half-dozen assembly workers are brought together every two weeks by a first-level supervisor or team leader. "We feel that this type of participatory management program not only increases productivity," says Joseph Riordan, director of Honeywell Corporate Productivity Services, "but it also upgrades the quality of work life for employees. Line workers feel that they are more a part of the action. As a result, we find that the quality of work improves and absenteeism is reduced. With this kind of involvement, we have, in many cases, been able to increase the capacity of a line without the addition of tooling or extra shifts."

Honeywell used the quality circle method to manage the problem of winning a renewable bid for a government contract. "Here was a situation," Riordan relates, "where we already had cut our rejects down, where all of the learning had effectively gone out of the process." The problem was assigned to the quality circle representing that particular work area. "They came up with a suggestion for further automating the process that enabled us to improve our competitive position by about 20 percent and win the contract."

In an attempt to determine the appropriateness of QCs to North American firms, a team of researchers set up a one-year field experiment at a metal fabricating facility of an electronics firm.

Eleven quality circles, averaging nine production employees each, were established. Performance was measured by a computerized monitoring system created from the company's existing employee performance reporting system. Both quantity and quality measurements were taken. Employee attitudes were also assessed, using the Motivating Potential Score (MPS) of the Hackman-Oldham Job Diagnostic Survey.

The major result of the circle program was its positive impact on reject rate, as shown in the top half of Figure 3. Reject rates per capita for quality-circle participants dropped by one-third to one-half of the former rates by the time the program had run three months. Surprisingly, the reject rates for the control group increased during the same period.

An explanation offered by the researchers for these results is that circle members tackled the issues of internal communication as a top priority item. For example, one of the initial projects implemented by the QCs was improving training manuals and procedures, including translating materials into a worker's native language if the worker desired. Careful attention to better training in fundamentals prevented many errors.

Circle members also made fewer errors. In addition, the defective parts the circle members did make tended to be less expensive to scrap or rework into usable parts. The explanation given for these results is that circle training instructs employees how to prioritize problems on the basis of dollar impact on the company. The cost savings generated by the lower reject rate represented a 300-percent return on the cost of investment in the program.

The impact of QCs on participants' level of work satisfaction was equally impressive. Results shown in Figure 3 indicate that the Motivating Potential Score (MPS) for the circle participants increased, while the control group showed a decrease. No other changes were present in the work environment that would impact the experimental group differently than the control group. The researchers therefore concluded that the improvement in employee job attitudes could be attributed to the circle training program and the problem-solving activity. The job characteristic most influenced by the quality activity was skill variety: the extent to which a job requires a variety of skills.

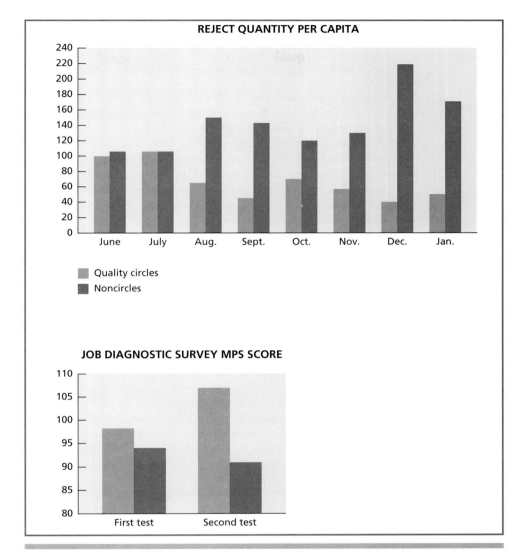

Figure 3 Impact of Quality Circles on Employee Performance and Attitudes

Negative Outcomes with Quality Circles

Despite the favorable outcomes reported, many negative results have also been reported. A review of the results of the first surge of QC activity in the United States revealed that as many as 75 percent of initially successful programs were no longer in operation after a few years. Even Lockheed, one of the American pioneers in this method, had decreased its involvement with quality circles. Robert Cole, a recognized authority on the Japanese workforce, made these pessimistic remarks:

> [The] fact is that the circles do not work very well in many Japanese companies. Even in those plants recognized as having the best operating programs, management knows that perhaps only one-third of the circles are working well, with another third borderline, and

one-third simply making no contribution at all. For all of the rhetoric of voluntarism, in a number of companies the workers clearly perceive circle activity as coercive. Japanese companies face a continuing struggle to revitalize circle activity to ensure that it does not degenerate into ritualistic behavior.

A study of quality circles in 29 companies, conducted by Matthew Goodfellow, found only eight of them to be cost-effective in terms of gains in productivity. Management consultant Woodruff Imberman investigated the 21 unsuccessful QC efforts and found four major causes of failure. First, in many firms, the employees intensely disliked management. Their antagonism carried over into the quality circles, which some employees perceived to be a management ploy to reduce overtime and trim the workforce by increasing productivity. Second, most organizations did a poor job of selling the QCs. Instead of conducting individual discussions with employees, they relied on flip-charts, booklets, and formal management presentations. The workers were left wondering, "What's in it for me?"

Third, the supervisors chosen to lead the circles received some training in human relations and group dynamics, but they felt that little of this information satisfied the specific needs of their own departments. Fourth, most of the 21 firms regarded the QC programs merely as a way of improving the efficiency of production techniques. They did not realize that QCs cannot succeed unless top management is willing to shift its philosophy toward emphasizing good relations among employees and between management and workforce. This last point hints at the importance of establishing the conditions that allow a quality circle program to succeed.

Key Elements of a Successful Program

Quality circle programs show some variation from company to company, whether these companies are engaged in manufacturing or service. They may differ in how frequently they meet, how much authority is granted to the team leader or supervisor, whether they use a group facilitator in addition to a supervisor, and how much coordination there is with the existing quality-control department. Based on the judgments of several observers, the successful programs have certain elements in common.

Quality circles work best in firms where good employee-management relations already exist. QCs are not likely to succeed in organizations suffering from acrimonious union-management conflict or high levels of distrust between employees and management.

Top management is committed to the program. Without commitment from top management, the initiation of a QC program is inadvisable. Instead, the director of a circle project should first prepare reports on other companies where QCs have been successful and present them to top management.

Circle leaders use a participative leadership style. Laurie Fitzgerald, a QC consultant, advocates the "leader as a worker for the members" concept. When the circle leader takes on a highly authoritarian role, the members are usually unresponsive.

The right people and the right area are selected. For quality circles to be effective, the program manager has to be enthusiastic, persistent, and hard-working. The facilitator or team leader must be energetic and cooperative. Also, another important step in getting the program off the ground is to select an area of the company where one can expect cooperation and enthusiasm from participants.

Program goals are stated explicitly. Objectives should be made clear in order to avoid confusion or unreasonable expectations from the circle program. Among the goals of QC programs are improving product quality, increasing productivity, improving communications between workers and supervisors, decreasing product costs, improving the quality of work life, and preparing people for future supervisory assignments.

The program is well publicized throughout the firm.   Once the program is started, information about it should be disseminated widely throughout the company. Better communication results in less resistance and fewer negative rumors about the program. The content of the communication should be open and positive.

The program starts slowly and grows slowly.   A gradual introduction of the program helps expose people to new concepts and helps reduce doubts about its intention and potential merit.

The QC program is customized to meet the needs of the firm.   A subtle source of failure in some QC programs is the use of a canned set of procedures that don't fit local circumstances. A QC participant whose work is data processing may have difficulty with the translation of a case from the aerospace industry. A workable compromise is to use standard training as a framework and build on it with the unique problems of the firm in question.

Quality circles are used as a method of employee development.   A key purpose of these circles is to foster personal development of the participating workers. If managers intend to install a QC as a tool for their own selfish gain, they would do better not to begin.

Management is willing to grant recognition for ideas originating in the circles.   If management attempts to manipulate the circle volunteers or take away from them the credit for improvements, the program most likely will backfire. More will be lost than gained.

Membership is voluntary.   As with job enrichment and all forms of participative management, employee preference is an influential factor. Employees who desire to contribute their ideas will generally perform better than employees who are arbitrarily assigned to a QC.

Achievements of quality circles are recognized as results of group, not individual, effort.   Recognizing them as such decreases showboating and competitiveness and increases cooperation and interdependence within the group or department. Quality circles, not individual employees, receive credit for innovations and suggestions for improvement.

Ample training is provided.   Program volunteers generally need some training in conference techniques or group dynamics. At a minimum, the circle leader will need skills in group-participation methods. Otherwise, he or she will wind up lecturing about topics such as quality improvement and productivity improvement. Leaders and participants will also need training in the use of whatever statistical and problem-solving methods are to be used. Following are eight major problem-solving techniques and their purposes.

1. Brainstorming is used to identify all problems, even those beyond the control of circle members.

2. A check-sheet is used to log problems within the circle's sphere of influence within a certain time frame.

3. A Pareto chart graphically illustrates check-sheet data to identify the most serious problems, that is, the 20 percent of the problems that cause 80 percent of the major mistakes.

4. A cause-and-effect diagram graphically illustrates the cause of a particular problem.

5. Histograms or bar charts are graphed to show the frequency and magnitude of specific problems.

6. Scatter diagrams or "measles charts" identify major defect locations, which show up as dense dot clusters on the pictures of products.

7. Graph-and-control charts monitor a production process and are compared with production samples.

8. Stratification, generally accomplished by inspecting the same products from different production areas, randomizes the sampling process.

Creativity is encouraged.   As illustrated above, brainstorming or variations thereof fit naturally into the quality-circle method and philosophy. Maintaining an attitude of "anything goes" is particularly important, even if rough ideas must be refined later. If half-processed ideas are shot down by the leader or other members, idea generation will extinguish quickly.

Projects are related to members' actual job responsibilities.   Quality circles are not arenas for amateur speculation about other people's work. People make suggestions about improving the quality of work for which they are already responsible. They should, however, be willing to incorporate information from suppliers and customers.

The Arguments For and Against Quality Circles

A major argument for quality circles is that they represent a low-cost, efficient vehicle for unleashing the creative potential of employees. In the process, highly desirable ends are achieved, such as improvements in the quality of both products and work life. Quality circles, in fact, are considered part of the quality of work life movement.

Another favorable feature of these circles is that they are perceived positively by all—management, workers, the union, and stockholders. A firm contemplating implementing such a program thus runs no risk of either internal or external opposition. (It is conceivable, however, that opposition will be forthcoming if management fails to act on quality-circle suggestions.)

Quality circles contribute to organizational effectiveness in another important way. They have emerged as a useful method of developing present and future managers. Recently, a major computing manufacturing firm established a quality circle program. After the program had been operating for two years, the director of training observed that the supervisors who were quality circle leaders were significantly more self-confident, knowledgeable, and poised than other supervisors who were attending the regular training program. The director believed that the supervisors' involvement in the QC training programs and activities had been the major contributor to this difference.

One major criticism of quality circles is that many of them are not cost effective. Furthermore, even more pessimistic is the criticism that the reported successes of QCs may be attributable to factors other than the actual quality circle program. One explanation is that the attention paid to employees by management may be the force behind the gains in productivity and morale (the well-known Hawthorne effect). Another possible explanation of the successes of quality circle programs is that the gains are due to improved group dynamics and problem-solving techniques. Therefore, an entire QC program need not be conducted just to achieve these gains.

A discouraging argument has been advanced that quality circles may not be suited to North American workers. Matsushita Electric, a leading user of the quality circle method in Japan, does not use circles in its U.S. plant (located in Chicago) because it does not consider the American worker suited to circle activities. Perhaps Matsushita management believes that Americans are too self-oriented to be group-oriented.

Quality circles may prove to be breeding grounds for friction and role confusion between the quality-control department and the groups themselves. Unless management carefully defines the relationship of quality circles vis-à-vis the quality-control department, much duplication of effort (and therefore waste of resources) will inevitably result.

Exclusive reliance upon volunteers for the circles may result in the loss of potentially valuable ideas. Many nonassertive people may shy away from participation in the circles despite their having valid ideas for product improvement.

Some employees who volunteer to join quality circles may do so for the wrong reasons. The circle may develop the reputation of being "a good way to get away from the line for a while and enjoy a coffee break and a good bull session." (To counter such an abuse of the quality circle program, QC group members might monitor the quality of input from their own group members.)

Guidelines for Action

An early strategic step in implementing a quality circle is to clarify relationships between the circle and the formal quality-control department. Otherwise, the quality-control department may perceive the circle as a redundancy or threat. One effective arrangement is for the quality circle to complement the quality-control department; the QC department thus does not become subject to the loss of authority.

Membership in the circle should be voluntary and on a rotating basis. In many instances, a team member will soon run out of fresh ideas for quality improvement. Rotating membership will result in a wider sampling of ideas being generated. Experience suggests that group size should be limited to nine.

Quality circles should be implemented on a pilot basis. As the circle produces results and wins the acceptance of managers and employees alike, it can be expanded as the demand for its output increases.

Do not emphasize quick financial returns or productivity increases from the output of the quality circles. The program should be seen as a long-range project that will raise the quality consciousness of the organization. (Nevertheless, as noted in the report from Honeywell, immediate positive results are often forthcoming.)

Management must make good use of many of the suggestions coming from the quality circle yet still define the limits of the power and authority of the circle. On the one hand, if none of the circle's suggestions is adopted, the circle will lose its effectiveness as an agent for change. Circle members will become discouraged because of their lack of clout. On the other hand, if the circle has too much power and authority, it will be seen as a governing body for technical change. Under the latter circumstances, people may use the circle for political purposes. An individual who wants to get a technical modification authorized may try to influence a member of the quality circle to suggest that modification during a circle meeting.

Training in group dynamics and methods of participative management will be particularly helpful. It may also prove helpful at the outset to appoint a group facilitator (an internal or external consultant) who can help the group run more smoothly.

Conducting Interviews

B

OBJECTIVES

Increase proficiency in conducting

▶ general interviews

▶ information gathering interviews

▶ employment selection interviews

▶ performance appraisal interviews

skill development

 Skill Learning

Planning and Conducting
  Interviews
Specific Types of Organizational
  Interviews
Summary and Behavioral
  Guidelines

⬡ Skill Practice

Evaluating the New Employee-
  Orientation Program
Performance Appraisal with
  Chris Jakobsen
Employment Selection Interview
  at Smith Farley Insurance

Skill Learning

Planning and Conducting Interviews

Except for conversations, interviews are perhaps the most frequently occurring form of communication (Sincoff & Goyer, 1984); they certainly occur regularly in organizations. Individuals interview to obtain a position; they interview to gather information to perform their job; and managers interview subordinates to review their performance and provide counseling and coaching (see Chapter 4).

Interviews are so common that they are often taken for granted. People view interviews as simply conversations during which information is gathered. While interviews are similar to conversations, there are important differences. An **interview** is a specialized form of communication conducted for a specific task-related purpose (Lopez, 1975; Downs, Smeyak, & Martin, 1980). Indeed, one reason why some managers perform poorly as interviewers is that they treat this "purposeful communication" too casually, as though it were merely a conversation. As a result of poor planning and lack of attention to managing the interview process, they fail to accomplish their purpose and often alienate the interviewee in the process.

These outcomes are illustrated in the following counseling interview between Joe Van Orden, director of management services, and Kyle Isenbarger, a management consultant on his staff (DuBrin, 1981).

JOE: Kyle, I have scheduled this meeting with you because I want to talk about certain aspects of your work. My comments are not all that favorable.

KYLE: Since you have formal authority over me, I guess I don't have much choice. Go ahead.

JOE: I'm not a judge reading a verdict to you. I want your input.

KYLE: But you called the meeting; go ahead with your complaints. Particularly any with foundation. I remember once when we were having lunch you told me that you didn't like the fact that I wore a brown suit with a blue shirt. I would put that in the category of unfounded.

JOE: I'm glad you brought up appearance. I think you present a substandard impression to clients. A con-

sultant is supposed to look sharp, particularly at the rates we charge clients. You often present the impression that you cannot afford good clothing. Your pants are baggy. Your ties are unstylish and often foodstained.

KYLE: The firm may charge those high rates, but the money I receive does not allow me to purchase fancy clothing. Besides, I have very little interest in trying to dazzle clients with my clothing. I have heard no complaints from them.

JOE: Nevertheless, I think that your appearance should be more businesslike. Now, let's talk about another concern. A routine audit of your expense account shows a practice that I think is improper. You charged one client for a Thursday night dinner for three consecutive weeks, yet your airline ticket receipt shows that you returned home at three in the afternoon each week. That kind of behavior is unprofessional. How do you explain your charges for these phantom dinners?

KYLE: The flight ticket may say 3 P.M., but with our unpredictable weather, the flight could very well be delayed. If I eat at the airport, then my wife won't have to run the risk of preparing a dinner for me that goes to waste. Food is very expensive.

JOE: But how can you eat dinner at 3 P.M. at the airport?

KYLE: I consider any meal after one in the afternoon to be dinner.

JOE: Okay for now. I want to comment on your reports to clients. They are much more careless than they should be. I know that you are capable of more meticulous work. I saw an article you prepared for publication that was first-rate and professional. Yet on one report you misspelled the name of the client company. That's unacceptable.

KYLE: A good secretary should have caught that mistake. Besides, I never claimed that I was able to write perfect reports. There are only so many hours in the working day to spend on writing up reports.

Effective interviews don't just happen. Like other purposeful communication activities, interviews must be properly planned and executed. To help you become an effective interviewer, this supplement includes a series of guidelines, organized according to the schema shown in Figure 1. First, we present broad guidelines for planning and conducting interviews in general. These establish a foundation of general principles, many of which build on more extensive discussions in the chapters on Communicating Supportively, Gaining Power and Influence, and Motivating Employees. These guidelines are divided into two steps: planning the interview and conducting the interview. Following this discussion, we will give more specific guidelines for conducting specialized interviews with limited purposes: gathering information, selecting new employees, and reviewing subordinate performance.

Planning the Interview

Establish the purpose and agenda. As is the case with any kind of planned communication event, you need to define clearly your purpose for holding the interview. In an interview, as in an oral presentation, ask yourself what it is you want to accomplish. Do you want to gather information? Persuade? Counsel? Evaluate? Not only do you need to consider what you want to accomplish in terms of the *content* of the interview, you must also consider the *relationship* you want to develop with the other participant. Consider who your interview partner is and how what you say will affect the already-existing relationship. This resembles the process of adapting your message to your audience in an oral presentation but is somewhat easier since there is only one member in your interview "audience." Also consider the situation in which the interview will occur. Are participants under pressures of deadlines? Can you arrange not to be interrupted?

Once you've determined your purpose, develop an agenda. Consider what kinds of information you need to obtain with respect to your purpose. Based on this, write out a list of topics that need to be covered in the interview. While these topics do not have to be listed in any particular order, you may want to prioritize them.

Create good questions that encourage information sharing. Questions arise out of your purpose and agenda and are the fundamental means by which you obtain information in an interview. Any interviewer can ask questions; only well-prepared interviewers ask effective questions—ones that elicit the information they need. Make sure that the questions are worded clearly and that they ask for the information you want. Adapting to your interviewee is critical. Phrase your questions in language the interviewee can understand and in ways that will enhance your relationship with that person.

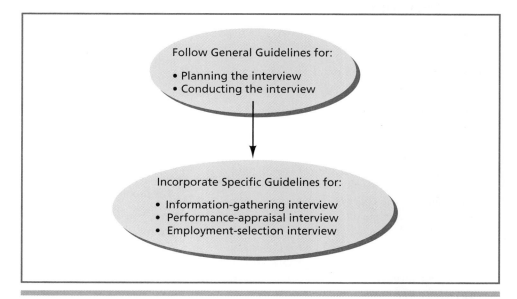

Figure 1 Guidelines for Effective Interviews

Different types of questions can be used for different effects and different types of information-gathering purposes. **Open questions** such as "How is your work going?" or "How has the new regulation affected department morale?" elicit general information. Use open questions when you want to let the interviewee talk without restriction. They allow interviewees freedom to discuss how they feel, what their priorities are, and how much they know about a topic. Thus, open questions are useful for developing rapport. Of course, remembering the answers to open questions is a problem, particularly if the interviewee talks on and on. Open questions are also time-consuming, and using them too often makes it difficult for the interviewer to control the interview. However, if you are looking for broad, general information, ask open questions.

If, on the other hand, you need specific information, ask **closed questions.** Closed questions such as "Where were you last employed?" or "Would you rather work on Project A or Project Z?" restrict the possible answers an interviewee can give. They are appropriate when you have limited time or want to clarify a point made in an answer to an open question. Table 1 suggests when to use open or closed questions.

As you plan your questions, pay close attention to how the questions are worded. Often, an unprepared interviewer will ask questions that are difficult to answer or prevent open, honest answers. One example is the **double-barreled question:**

▶ If there's anything that would make you stay, what would it be?

▶ If you had no choice but to use this system, how would you use it productively?

▶ Why should we adopt this insurance plan when none of our competitors has adopted it?

Each of these questions assumes a condition that the interviewee may not agree with but then calls for the interviewee to support or defend the condition. The first question assumes the interviewee is looking for a reason to stay; the second assumes the system can be used productively; the third suggests something is wrong with the plan. Such questions may lead to hypothetical answers that don't reflect the interviewee's honest position.

Another potentially problematic question is the **false bipolar question.** A bipolar question offers the interviewee two choices: "Did you vote yes or no on the union contract?" This can be a legitimate and appro-

---

Use open questions when you want to:
- discover the interviewee's priorities.
- discover the interviewee's frame of reference.
- let the interviewee talk through his or her opinions without constraints.
- ascertain the depth of the interviewee's knowledge.
- ascertain how articulate the interviewee is.

Use closed questions when you want to:
- save time, energy, and money.
- maintain control over the interview situation.
- obtain very specific information from the interviewee.
- encourage the interviewee to reconstruct a specific event.
- encourage a shy person to talk.
- avoid extensive explanations on the part of the interviewee.
- clarify a point made in answer to an open question.

Table 1   When to Use Open and Closed Questions
Source: Adapted from Downs, Smeyak, & Martin, 1980.

---

priate question. However, suppose you asked this question: "Do you approve or disapprove of overtime work?" Most people do not totally approve or disapprove of overtime work; yet this question forces interviewees to choose from limited, or false, options, neither of which likely represents their true stand on the issue. Thus, if you use bipolar questions, make sure that the options you offer are the only two possible options; otherwise, you will obtain inaccurate information.

A final type of problematic questions is the **leading question,** in which you let the interviewee know the answer you want to hear by how you phrase the question:

▶ Don't you think that using this plan will alleviate the problems we've been having?

▶ Are you in favor of this policy like all your coworkers?

▶ Of course, you want the best for your family, don't you?

It would not take an astute interviewee very long to figure out what you wanted to hear, and so you are likely to get biased responses. Leading questions can be useful when a biased answer is intended and desired. For instance, the last question on the previous page would be useful in a sales interview if the interviewer tries to persuade a potential buyer to buy a set of encyclopedias. However, if you do not realize that you have asked a leading question, you will not know whether you are receiving a biased answer, which can create a serious problem. Table 2 offers ways to reword these three types of badly constructed questions.

Structure the interview using interviewing aids.
After determining the purpose and agenda, and after

DOUBLE-BARRELED QUESTION	PROBLEM	BETTER QUESTION
1. If there's anything that would make you stay, what would it be?	The question ignores the reason behind the interviewee's decision and implies it can be changed.	Why do you want to leave our organization? (Let interviewee respond.) Is there anything I can do to change your mind?
2. If you had no choice but to use this system, how would you use it productively?	The question avoids an open analysis of the system and forces the interviewee to defend it.	What do you feel are the benefits of this system? (Let interviewee respond.) What do you feel are the disadvantages of this system?
3. Why should we adopt this insurance plan when none of our competitors has adopted it?	The question raises a suspicion that something is wrong with the plan and urges the interviewee to put the suspicion to rest rather than to evaluate the plan.	Do you think we should adopt this insurance? (Let interviewee respond.) Do you think that it offers us new benefits? (Let interviewee respond.) Have any of our competitors adopted it?
FALSE BIPOLAR QUESTION	**PROBLEM**	**BETTER QUESTION**
1. Do you prefer working with people or working alone?	The question assumes that there are only two possible choices.	Do you work well with other people? (Can be followed with appropriate probe.)
2. Do you approve or disapprove of the union contract?	The question assumes that there are only two ways to view the issue.	What are your feelings concerning the union contract?
LEADING QUESTION	**PROBLEM**	**BETTER QUESTION**
1. Don't you think that using this plan will alleviate the problems we've been having?	The question identifies the expected answer, making it difficult for the interviewee to disagree.	Do you think this plan will be useful in alleviating the problems we've been having?
2. Are you in favor of this policy like all your coworkers?	The question places interviewee in the position of siding with the "right" side.	What is your attitude toward this policy?
3. Of course, you want the best for your family, don't you?	The question associates response with a desirable goal (getting the best for the family), making it difficult for the interviewee to say no.	This product offers you some real advantages. Could I take some of your time to tell you about them?

Table 2 Rewording Badly Constructed Questions

formulating your questions, the next step in preparing for an interview is to develop a structure. To do this, you need to think about three things: the interview guide, the questioning sequence, and transitions. The interview guide is an outline of the topics and subtopics you want to cover, usually with specific questions listed under each heading. In other words, it is the finalized version of the agenda. Alternative interview guide formats will be discussed later.

While you are constructing the interview guide, you will also need to be concerned with the sequence of questions, that is, how they will interconnect. The two most common types of question sequences are the **funnel sequence** and the **inverted funnel sequence.** The funnel sequence begins with general questions and then moves toward increasingly specific questions. The inverted funnel sequence reverses this order, beginning with specific questions and moving toward more open questions toward the end. Table 3 shows examples of these two sequences. Your choice of which sequence to use depends on what you want to accomplish in the interview. Table 3 also summarizes when you should use each of these sequences, depending on your goals.

After establishing the sequence of your questions, you should consider what kinds of transitions you can use to help the interviewee follow along. The transitions in an interview perform the same function as transitions in an oral presentation: They help listeners maintain focus and keep them aware of where the speaker is in terms of the overall organization. Transitions are difficult to prepare ahead in unstructured interviews, yet a good interviewer will keep in mind that transitions should be used when a topic change occurs. A simple statement such as, "I see what you're saying about that situation. Do you think you could help me with another issue?" allows you to move from one topic into the next. You may also use a brief summary of the interviewee's responses to wrap up one topic before moving to the next one.

Plan the setting to enhance rapport.

The interview location can have a major impact on the interview atmosphere and interview outcome. If you hold the interview in your office or an organizational meeting room, you will create a formal atmosphere. On the other hand, if you conduct the interview in a more neutral area, such as a restaurant, the climate will be more relaxed. The choice of setting depends on your goals for the interview. The most important point to remember about the setting is that, if at all possible,

---

Funnel: From General to Specific

How do you feel about the new regulations concerning smoking in the building?
Are these regulations fair?
How are these regulations curtailing smoking among employees?

Inverted Funnel: From Specific to General

How are these regulations curtailing smoking among employees?
Do you think the new smoking regulations are fair?
In general, how do you feel about these new regulations?

Use the funnel sequence when:

- you want to discover the interviewee's frame of reference.
- you want to avoid leading the interviewee.
- you want to maximize your ability to probe issues.
- the interviewee is willing to talk about the issues.

Use the inverted-funnel sequence when:

- you want to get at specific facts before general reactions.
- you want to motivate a reluctant interviewee.
- you want to jog the interviewee's memory.

Table 3 Funnel and Inverted-Funnel Question Sequences
Source: Adapted from Downs, Smeyak, & Martin, 1980.

---

you should try to hold the interview in a setting that will be conducive to encouraging the kind of communication you seek.

Anticipate problems and prepare responses.

As you prepare for an interview, you should consider what kinds of problems you might encounter. Imagine how the interviewee might respond to what you have to ask, and prepare for his or her objections and questions. Consider the personality of the interviewee and how you might have to adapt to either draw the person out or to control his or her tendency to dominate. Anticipate how much time you will need to ask your questions and how much time your interviewee has to give you. Each interview will offer unique problems. If you can plan for some of these situations, you will be able to handle them better during the actual interview than if you had not considered them at all.

Table 4 provides a checklist for helping prepare for an interview.

Conducting the Interview

Couple thorough preparation with sensitive implementation. Because an interview is an interpersonal communication situation, in this section we will first briefly review the concept of supportive communication (introduced in Chapter 4, Communicating Supportively) as it applies to interviews. Then we will look at the three stages of the interview—the introduction, body, and conclusion—and discuss the functions of each. We will offer suggestions for developing the necessary skills to conduct an interview effectively. Finally, we will discuss ways of recording the interview information.

---

1. Have I determined my general purpose?
2. Have I written out my specific purposes and agenda?
   a. Do I know exactly what I want to accomplish in terms of content?
   b. Do I know exactly what I want to accomplish in terms of the relationship with the interviewee?
3. Do my questions all relate to my purposes and agenda?
4. Are my questions clearly worded in language the interviewee can understand?
5. Are my questions worded in an unbiased manner?
6. Have I chosen an appropriate interview structure for the situation?
7. Have I chosen an appropriate question sequence for the interview situation?
8. Have I developed potential transitions to be used in the interview?
9. Have I chosen a physical setting suited to the topics and the interviewee?
10. Have I planned ways to deal with problems that could develop during the interview?

Table 4   Interview Preparation Checklist

Establish and maintain a supportive communication climate.   The *climate* of the interview refers to the tone of the interview and the general atmosphere in which the interview occurs. An interview, like any other interpersonal communication event, should be a supportive interaction, one in which participants feel free to communicate accurately. As the interviewer, you set the climate of the interview in the introduction when you begin to build rapport with the interviewee. In general, you should seek to build a comfortable, open climate, free of incongruence. Maintaining a supportive and productive climate requires that you constantly analyze and adapt to the interaction as it occurs. When you sense that the climate is no longer supportive, move away from the content level of the interview and address the relational level. Consider this excerpt from an information gathering interview:

INTERVIEWER: Thanks for taking the time to speak with me today.

INTERVIEWEE: Oh, it's no problem at all. What can I do for you?

INTERVIEWER: Well, I was wondering if you could tell me a little about the incident that occurred on the shop floor last week. First, do you have any idea how it started?

INTERVIEWEE: No, not really. I was doing my job and then, all of a sudden, the two of them were at it.

INTERVIEWER: I see. You didn't hear them talking before they began to fight?

INTERVIEWEE: No. Like I said, it seemed to start out of the blue.

INTERVIEWER: Weren't you paying attention?

INTERVIEWEE: How was I to know they were going to fight?!

By now, the questions are obviously beginning to irritate the interviewee. The interviewer has continued to probe an issue that the interviewee seems to think has already been covered sufficiently. The interviewer should move away from this one point and attempt to ease the interviewee's discomfort before continuing.

INTERVIEWER: You're right. You really weren't in a position to anticipate this situation. Perhaps, though, you could describe to me what happened after the fight.

At this point, the interviewee may be hesitant to disclose fully. The interviewer may have to continue to strengthen relational support until the interviewee appears to be comfortable in answering the questions.

Of course, a supportive climate is not maintained solely by verbal behaviors. Listening analytically is also essential to maintaining the climate of an interview. If you do not show that you are listening and responding to what the interviewee is saying, he or she will not want to continue talking with you. In general, you should listen for **comprehension** of the content of the interview, for **empathy** with the interviewee, and for **evaluation** of information and feelings (Stewart & Cash, 1985). Keep in mind the guidelines that discuss listening in Chapter 4, Communicating Supportively. These will help you establish a productive and supportive climate in your interviews.

Introduce the interview. Supportive communication begins immediately in the introduction, where you establish the tone and set the climate of the interview. You should greet the interviewee in such a way as to build positive rapport. The impressions created in the initial minutes of an interview are crucial to its success (Stewart & Cash, 1985). Therefore, you should try to convey as favorable an impression as possible. After the greeting, you need to motivate the interviewee to participate willingly in the interview. Some common ways of doing this are to ask for the interviewee's help or tell the interviewee why he or she was chosen as a source of information. Finally, the introduction should contain an orientation to the total interview. You should tell an interviewee (1) the purpose of the interview, (2) how he or she will help meet that purpose, and (3) how the information obtained during the interview will be used. The introduction should end with a transition into the body of the interview. Using a transition statement, such as "Now then, let me begin by asking . . ." or "Now that you understand what's going to happen during the next few minutes, let's move on to the questions" tells the interviewee that the "real" interview is about to begin.

Conduct the body of the interview. Generally, the body of the interview will follow your interview guide, which is a predetermined sequence of questions. There are three types of guides: structured, semistructured, and unstructured. If the interview guide is structured, you will simply read the questions on the guide and record the interviewee's answers. A semistructured guide lists several recommended questions under each topic. The interviewer then selects the most appropriate questions for a specific candidate. A sample interview guide for a semistructured employment interview is shown in Table 5.

EDUCATION	WORK EXPERIENCE	SELF-EVALUATION
• What was there about your major that appealed to you?	• How did you obtain your current job?	• What do you know about our industry or company?
• What was your most rewarding experience in college?	• What duties occupy most of your time?	• What interests you about our product or service?
• What subjects were the most difficult for you to master? Why?	• What part of your work do you like the most and the least?	• What is your long-term career objective?
• If you were starting college all over again, what courses would you take?	• What has been your greatest frustration and your greatest joy?	• What are your greatest strengths and weaknesses?
• What difficulties did you experience in getting along with other students and faculty?	• What things about your supervisor did you like and dislike?	• What have you done that has demonstrated initiative and willingness to work hard?
• What did you learn from your extracurricular activities?	• What criticisms of your work have you received?	• What do you think determines a person's progress in a good company?
		• What are your plans for self-improvement during this year?
		• What are the three most important things in your life?

Table 5   Sample Interview Questions for an Employment Interview

If the interview guide is unstructured, then you will use the guide only as an agenda. For example, an unstructured interview guide for a termination interview might simply list a few general topics for discussion, for example, "What did he or she like and dislike about the work and the company?" "Why is he or she leaving?" "Any suggestions for improvement?" Particularly in an unstructured interview, an interviewee will need encouragement to answer your questions as fully as possible. In order to encourage complete answers, you will need to follow his or her initial responses with probing questions. Probing well depends directly on your ability to listen well and analyze the content and relational information the interviewee offers you. Probing questions are rarely planned ahead because you cannot predict how the interviewee will respond to your questions. You will want to probe when you feel that, for whatever reason, you are receiving an inadequate response to your question.

The kind of probing you do will depend on the responses given by your interviewee and the kind of information you are looking for. If you feel that the response is superficial or inadequate due to lack of information, you should use an **elaboration probe,** such as:

- "Tell me more about that issue."

- "Why do you suppose it happened that way?"

- "Was there anything else going on at the time?"

If you need to clarify the information given by the interviewee, use a **clarification probe,** such as:

- "What does job satisfaction mean to you?"

- "You said that you are unhappy with this policy. Can you tell me specifically what aspects make you feel this way?"

- "Earlier you mentioned that you enjoyed working with people. Can you provide a specific example?"

A **reflective probe** is also used when you want elaboration or clarification. It is nondirective in nature and generally mirrors or repeats some aspect of the answer the interviewee just gave you:

- "You think, then, that this policy will work?"

- "Are you saying that your supervisor doesn't offer the kind of supervision you need?"

- "Is it correct to assume that you would be willing to relocate?"

If the interviewee does not answer your question, you may need to use a **repetition probe.** Simply paraphrase the question or repeat it verbatim. If you want the interviewee to keep on talking freely, use *silence* to encourage him or her to do so. Silence tends to communicate that you expect more from the interviewee. Be careful not to wait too long, though; give an interviewee enough time to think but not enough time to become uncomfortable. Responses such as "I see," "Hmm mm," and "OK, go on" are nondirective and nonevaluative ways of encouraging the interviewee to speak. Table 6 summarizes these probes and when to use them.

The effective use of probing questions is perhaps the most important skill an interviewer can develop. It is also the most difficult to develop. Too often, an interviewer leaves an interview and thinks about all the things that could have been discussed if only the topic had been followed up with appropriate probes. Or perhaps the interview was ineffective because the interviewer probed into irrelevant topics and thus spent too much time gathering relatively useless information. An effective interviewer needs to learn when to probe and when to stop. If you have planned appropriately, you will be aware of the issues you want to cover and at what depth. Follow your interviewee's cues as well as your agenda in determining when and how much to probe issues.

Conclude the interview. The third stage of the interview is the conclusion. When you conclude an interview, you should accomplish four purposes. First, be sure you indicate explicitly that the interview is about to end. Say something such as, "Well, that's all the questions I have" or "You've been very helpful." This helps the interviewee understand that if he or she has any questions, they should be asked now. Second, try to summarize the information you obtained. This serves as a check on the accuracy of the information you have just obtained: the interviewee can correct your impressions if they seem to be in error. Third, let the interviewee know what's going to happen next: Will you need to meet again? Will you make a report? Finally, make sure you continue to build the relationship by expressing appreciation for his or her time and thoughtful responses.

Record the information. While you may have planned the interview perfectly and asked all the right questions and probes, if you cannot remember accurately the information obtained, the interview cannot

Use an *elaboration* probe when an answer seems superficial or inadequate in some way:	
INTERVIEWER:	How have you been able to adapt to your new job responsibilities?
INTERVIEWEE:	Well, each day I find myself challenged by something new.
INTERVIEWER:	Why don't you tell me more about a specific challenge.
Use a *clarification* probe when you need to clarity information given by the interviewee:	
INTERVIEWER:	How do you feel about working overtime?
INTERVIEWEE:	Well, it's okay some of the time.
INTERVIEWER:	Can you tell me specifically when you would be willing to work overtime?
Use a *reflective* probe when you want elaboration or clarification but want to obtain it in a nondirective manner:	
INTERVIEWER:	So how are you adapting to your new responsibilities?
INTERVIEWEE:	Well, each day I find myself challenged by something new.
INTERVIEWER:	Really? Something new each day?
Use a *repetition* probe when the interviewee doesn't answer your question:	
INTERVIEWER:	What do you believe to be the most difficult aspect of your job?
INTERVIEWEE:	Well, that's not an easy question. My supervisor says I have problems with meeting productivity quotas.
INTERVIEWER:	But what do *you* believe to be the most difficult aspect of your job?
Use *silence* when you want to encourage the interviewee to continue talking:	
INTERVIEWER:	Do you think that we should continue our policy concerning absenteeism?
INTERVIEWEE:	Yes, I do.
INTERVIEWER:	(pauses for 10 seconds)
INTERVIEWEE:	Yes, I think it's good policy because . . .

Table 6   Types of Probes and When to Use Them

be considered a success. After all, you prepared and conducted the interview to get information, not simply because you wanted to have a conversation with someone. The first point that you need to recognize concerning remembering interview information is simple: Memory alone will not work. Relying solely on memory leaves open the possibility of forgetting the information or readjusting it to meet your own needs. Even if you summarize the interview as soon as it is over, you run the risk of reinterpreting the information in ways that the interviewee did not mean. However, if summarizing the interview is your preferred choice, make sure you write your summary immediately after the interview. Additionally, you might want to use your interview guide as a basis for summarizing: Review your questions and write out the interviewee's answers.

A better way to remember information is to take notes during the interview. Make sure you advise the interviewee that you will take notes. Take notes as unobtrusively as possible so as not to make the interviewee uncomfortable. Learn how to write notes while still maintaining eye contact with the interviewee. This is a difficult skill to master, but it can be done; journalists use this skill frequently with great success. Develop your own shorthand so that you are, in fact, taking notes and not recording the interview verbatim. If you need a verbatim account of the interview, then you should use a tape recorder. First ask the interviewee if he or she minds being tape-recorded. Keep the recorder out of sight if possible so that neither you nor the interviewee feels threatened by it. One final way to help you remember the interview information is to have a second interviewer participate in the interview. After the interview, your discussion will function as a check on each other's memory of what occurred.

Specific Types Of Organizational Interviews

The information presented in the preceding sections will help you plan and conduct almost any type of interview. However, there are some special types to plan and consider. In this section, we will briefly describe the most common types of organizational interviews and apply the general principles presented earlier to specific issues and circumstances.

Information Gathering Interviews

The information gathering interview is the one most frequently held in organizations and is also the one that is most like a conversation. You might conduct this type of interview when you need to gather facts about an issue or to help in a problem-solving situation. If you treat these fact-finding missions as interviews, you will be in a better position to gather accurate, useful information because you will take the time to plan ahead. Clearly, you need to follow the planning steps discussed above: Decide on a general purpose and create an agenda; develop questions; develop the structure of the interview; plan the setting; and anticipate problems.

Furthermore, the information gathering interview is the only interview for which you can choose the expert. In other organizational interviews, such as the selection interview or the performance appraisal interview, you have little choice of whom you will see. However, when you want to gather information about some topic or problem, you choose the interviewee. This choice is based on two factors: who *can* give you the information you need and who is *willing* to give you this information (Stano & Reinsch, 1982). Too often, interviewers will talk to interviewees who are willing but who do not have the necessary information. For instance, suppose your organization is considering the implementation of a flex-time work schedule and you have been assigned to write a feasibility report. While you may get some interesting opinions from a colleague on the advantages of such a schedule, it would be better if you could find an expert on flex-time for your interview. On the other hand, if you wanted to find out how well received such a change would be, then you would talk to colleagues rather than an expert.

The nature of an information gathering interview is such that the interviewee may not realize he or she is being interviewed. Thus it may be difficult to keep the interviewee on track and responsive to your questions. More so than in any other interview, you as the interviewer must remain flexible and adaptive to your interviewee. Choose a physical setting that will encourage talk and provide an appropriate climate. In general, the funnel sequence works well in information gathering interviews because of its ability to immediately elicit general information and the interviewee's feelings on the subject. However, the inverted funnel may be a better choice if you will be interviewing a number of people on the same topic and you need to maintain consistency in evaluating their responses.

Employment Selection Interviews

The employment interview is used to help current organizational members choose new members. During the selection interview, the interviewer tries to assess whether job candidates will fit into the organization and if they have the appropriate skills for the job. In addition, the interviewer often tries to sell the organization itself to the interviewee. Questions asked during the selection interview address four general topics: prior work experience, education and training, personality characteristics, and related activities and interests. The nature of the job and the interviewee will dictate which topics will be emphasized.

As Table 7 shows, there are three sources of information you should review when creating questions for a selection interview:

1. Review the *job description* to assess the technical skills and experience needed by the person. Also

- Use the *job description* to formulate questions concerning task-related skills and personality characteristics.
- Use the selection interview *evaluation form* to formulate questions that can help you assess the applicant on the basis of your organization's general criteria for employees.
- Use the applicant's *resume* and *cover letter* to formulate questions concerning the applicant's specific skills and prior work experience.

Table 7 Bases for Selection Interview Questions

review the job environment to determine the desirable personal qualities required. Create your questions based on these reviews; avoid asking merely generic questions.

2. Look at the *evaluation form* your company uses to assess prospective employees. Make sure that some of your questions deal with the topics on this evaluation form. For instance, if one of the topics on this form is communication skills, create questions that specifically address this subject. In this case, you may want to ask the applicant about his or her writing skills and how he or she has used them in the past.

3. One final piece of information you should use for developing questions for a selection interview is the applicant's *resume and cover letter*. Read these documents carefully. If there are gaps in time between jobs, ask the applicant about them. If the information on the resume is too general, develop questions to get at the specifics. Remember that most people create resumes with a very specific goal in mind: to obtain an interview. Therefore, the information tends to be a summary of all the good aspects of that person's career to date. Additionally, all information tends to be written in glowing language. Be prepared to reach beyond this language to obtain clarifying information. For example, suppose you came across this line in a cover letter: "I've had years of experience in leadership positions." Clearly, you would want to ask this applicant for more specific information: "How many years?" "What kinds of positions were these?" "What were your specific leadership responsibilities?"

In constructing interview questions, be sure to include some that focus on specific experiences. For instance, you might want to ask something such as, "Can you tell me about a time when you successfully met a goal you set?" The interviewee may be reluctant to be specific, but you should probe until the interviewee offers you useful, specific, behavioral information.

Why is behavioral information so important? Many experts believe that the best way to assess future job performance is to assess past behavior: past behavior predicts future performance. If you can find out how the interviewees behaved in real situations in the past that are similar to those he or she is likely to face in your organization, you can determine if his or her style will fit into your organization and work well with other members.

Take care that you ask a balanced series of questions: Ask for negative information as well as positive. This will help you obtain a well-rounded picture of the interviewee and also expose hidden bias. For instance, you might want to follow the positive question with something like: "Well, now tell me about a time when you failed to meet a goal you set." Again, make sure the person gives you specific behavioral information.

In conclusion, remember that your primary purpose in a selection interview is to find a person who is qualified for a particular opening in your organization. Table 8 details a six-step process (using the acronym PEOPLE) used by a major firm to help interviewers accomplish this purpose. It follows the general interviewing model outlined in the first half of this supplement.

Performance Appraisal Interviews

The performance appraisal interview is usually part of a larger professional appraisal system. The goal of this system is to evaluate a member of an organization and often to provide feedback to a subordinate concerning ways to improve job performance. While every organization differs in the specifics of carrying out the performance appraisal system, there are some common aspects.

Generally, prior to the performance-appraisal interview, written evaluations are prepared by the subordinate, the superior, or both people. There are any number of types of evaluation forms, including an essay form, where the manager writes a description of the subordinate's work, with no real set format; *forced-choice ratings,* where the manager chooses a statement from many which describes the subordinate in one area; a *graphic rating scale,* where the manager rates the subordinate on various areas on a 1–7 numerical scale. In most cases, though, you will be asked to back up your assessment of the subordinate with specific and concrete information. For instance, if you are using a graphic rating scale and indicate that the employee performed unsatisfactorily, you should write out in objective terms why you have made this assessment. The subordinate has a right to know, and you have the responsibility to back up your decisions with evidence.

It is the responsibility of the interviewer to prepare the structure of the performance appraisal interview. The interviewer should set a definite time and place for the interview, considering the effects these choices will have on the interview and the interviewee. The interviewer must decide on the general purpose of the in-

P = Prepare
1. Review application, resume, transcripts, and other background information.
2. Prepare both general and individual-specific questions.
3. Prepare suitable physical arrangements.

E = Establish Rapport
1. Try to make applicant comfortable.
2. Convey genuine interest.
3. Communicate supportive attitude with voice and manner.

O = Obtain Information
1. Ask questions.
2. Probe.
3. Listen carefully.
4. Observe the person (dress, mannerisms, body language).

P = Provide Information
1. Describe current and future job opportunities.
2. Sell positive features of firm.
3. Respond to applicant's questions.

L = Lead to Close
1. Clarify responses.
2. Provide opportunity for final applicant input.
3. Explain what happens next.

E = Evaluate
1. Assess match between technical qualifications and job requirements.
2. Judge personal qualities (leadership, maturity, team orientation).
3. Make a recommendation.

Table 8 Selection Interview Format (PEOPLE-Oriented Process)

terview and the agenda. Common topics that are often brought up in performance appraisal interviews include job knowledge, job performance, job goals, career goals and opportunities, and interpersonal skills.

The difficult aspect of the performance appraisal interview is that people tend to shy away from evaluating others or being evaluated in face-to-face situations. Both participants in a performance-appraisal interview may be apprehensive. As the interviewer, you need to reassure the interviewee that you are conducting the performance-appraisal interview as a means of assist-

ing in the interviewee's development. Keep in mind that people do not like to be criticized, and balance your criticisms with reassurances and commendations. As noted in Chapter 6, Motivating Employees, when you offer criticisms, work with the interviewee to develop ways to enhance performance in the future.

In conducting a performance-appraisal interview, you must decide beforehand on your objectives. The objectives should then dictate the form of the interview. In general, three types of appraisal interviews seek to meet specific objectives (Maier, 1958), and a fourth type can be used to meet multiple objectives (Beer, 1987). These interview types are summarized in Table 9.

The first type of appraisal interview is called the **tell-and-sell** interview. This approach is evaluative in nature. First, you *tell* the subordinate how you have evaluated him or her, and then you *sell* the subordinate on the ways you have chosen to improve his or her performance. This type of interview should be used when you must be very clear about your expectations. This format is also effective with young employees who find it difficult to evaluate themselves, with very loyal employees or those who strongly identify with the organization or the

Tell-and-Sell Interview
Used for purely evaluative purposes. Manager tells the employee the evaluation and then persuades the employee to follow recommendations for improvement.

Tell-and-Listen Interview
Used for purely evaluative purposes. Manager tells the employee the evaluation and then listens to the employee's reactions to the evaluation in a non-judgmental manner.

Problem-Solving Interview
Used for employee-development purposes. Manager does not offer evaluation but lets employee decide his or her weak areas and works with employee to develop plan for improvement.

Mixed-Model Interview
Used for both evaluative and development purposes. Manager begins interview with problem-solving session and concludes with a more directive tell-and-sell approach.

Table 9 Types of Performance-Appraisal Interviews

appraiser, and with employees who do not want to have a say in how to develop their job and role in the organization (Downs, Smeyak, & Martin, 1980).

If, however, you want to let the subordinate respond to your evaluation, you would use the **tell-and-listen** appraisal format. In this interview, you first *tell* the employee your evaluation; then you *listen* to his or her reactions without displaying any agreement or disagreement. The objective of this interview is also evaluative, but you also want to hear the subordinate's viewpoints and work with the subordinate to help him or her accept your evaluation. Active listening directed at helping the subordinate work through his or her feelings about the evaluation and past performance will help you successfully complete a tell-and-listen appraisal. This type of interview works best with people who have a high need to participate in their jobs, with interviewees who are relatively close in status to the interviewer, and with subordinates who are highly educated (Downs, Smeyak, & Martin, 1980).

The third general type of performance appraisal is the **problem-solving interview.** In this interview, evaluating the person is no longer the goal. Rather, the appraiser's role is to help the employee develop a plan for improving his or her performance. The performance deficiencies are determined by the subordinate, not the supervisor. Your goal as the interviewer is to avoid judgments and evaluations; rather, you offer suggestions for solutions to the problems defined by the interviewee. You form a partnership with the subordinate to solve the problems he or she brings up.

Finally, if your objectives are to both perform an evaluation and offer developmental coaching, you could choose to use a **mixed-model** interview (Beer, 1987). In this type of appraisal interview, you begin with a problem-solving framework and end the interview with a more directive tell-and-sell approach. In this way, you can both help a subordinate meet the development goals as well as offer your own evaluation and plan for development.

No matter which type of interview you choose, a performance-appraisal interview should contain all the elements of a general interview: Build rapport and orient the interviewee to the subject; conduct the body of the interview in a supportive manner; conclude by specifying what is going to happen. Additionally, the performance-appraisal interview generally includes a discussion of a specific plan for improvement or change.

Summary and Behavioral Guidelines

While many people consider interviewing a process that just happens, we have argued that effective interviewing requires planning and thought. The steps shown in Figure 1 provide a framework for enhancing your interviewing skills. The first step, thorough preparation, is essential for a successful interview. Planning involves deciding on your purposes, questions, structure, setting, and responses to anticipated problems. During the actual interview, work toward establishing and maintaining a supportive and productive climate. Keep in mind that every interview should have an introduction, body, and conclusion and that you need to develop ways to record the information you obtain during the interview.

There are a variety of organizational interviews, but the most common are the information-gathering interview, the selection interview, and the performance interview. Each of these interviews has very different objectives and specific means to reach them. Be flexible in how you conduct these interviews. As in any communication activity, you should adapt to the situation, your personality, and the person with whom you are conversing.

Interviewing is a vital management skill. When done well, an interview can provide you with information not otherwise available. This information can then better inform the decisions you make as you act out your role in the organization.

Following are general behavioral guidelines for planning and conducting interviews. Specific guidelines for specialized interviews are incorporated into the Observer's Feedback Forms in the Skill Practice exercises.

Planning the Interview

1. Specify your purposes and plan an agenda.

   ▶ Determine your general purpose: to gather information, persuade, discipline, or evaluate.

   ▶ Compose an agenda, prioritizing all topics.

2. Formulate questions.

   ▶ Determine the type of questions (closed or open) that are consistent with the objectives.

- Write specific questions for each topic on the agenda.

- Use appropriate language in your questions.

- Avoid biased or leading questions.

3. Develop the interview guide.

- Select the appropriate format: structured, semi-structured, or unstructured.

- Use either the funnel or inverted funnel question sequence.

- Formulate transition statements between topics.

4. Select a setting that is consistent with your objectives.

5. Identify potential complications that might occur during the interview and develop contingency plans.

Conducting the Interview

6. Establish and maintain a supportive climate.

- Greet interviewee and initiate a brief social conversation.

- Foster a positive communications climate by constant analysis of, and adaptation to, the interview process.

- Use effective listening skills and nonverbal language (eye contact, posture, and gestures) to foster cooperation.

7. Introduce the interview.

- State the purpose of the interview.

- Clarify interviewee's and interviewer's roles.

- Specify the time frame of the interview.

- Indicate how the information will be used.

- Use a transition to signal the beginning of the interview.

8. Conduct the interview.

- Use the interview guide to manage the flow of the interview.

- Use probing questions when elaboration or clarification are required.

- Be flexible and adapt to the flow of the interview.

9. Conclude the interview.

- Signal that the interview is about to end.

- Summarize the information you have collected.

- Clarify details or technical information.

- Review what will happen as a result of the interview.

- Strengthen the relationship by expressing appreciation.

10. Record the interview content, using the appropriate format.

- Write a summary immediately after the interview.

- Take notes during the interview (sustaining eye contact).

- Use a tape recorder (with the interviewee's permission).

- Use a second interviewer to improve your recall.

Skill Practice

Exercises in Conducting Special-Purpose Interviews

Evaluating the New Employee-Orientation Program

You work for a high-tech electronics firm that was recently purchased by a large, multibusiness conglomerate. Your company produces components for highly sophisticated communications equipment used by the government. This is an exciting, but somewhat confusing, period in the company's history. The new parent company, BETA Products, is known as a Japanese-like firm. It emphasizes high productivity, along with employee commitment and loyalty.

Beta is sending a human resources management team to inspect your organization in two weeks. In advance, they have sent a list of programs they want to review, including your new employee-orientation program. Your boss, the vice-president of Human Resources, has given you the assignment of preparing a 30-minute briefing on this program to the BETA task force. Specifically, she has asked you to interview representatives of various groups in your organization to determine their perceptions of the program's merits and shortcomings.

Currently, when a new employee enters your organization, he or she goes through an extensive orientation session. During this session, the new employee meets with a member of the Human Resources Department to learn about company policies and procedures and receive the Employee's Handbook. This session can last from two to three hours, depending on the participants. At the end of the session, the new employee is assigned a mentor, a member of the new employee's department who has been with the organization for at least one year. The role of the mentor is to help the new employee become familiar with his or her new job and coworkers. The mentor is expected to meet with the new employee on a semiregular basis for at least six months. The relationship can continue if both parties agree. This orientation program has been used for about three years but has never been formally evaluated.

Assignment

To complete this assignment, you have scheduled interviews with several department heads, mentors, and current trainees. Prepare the interview you would conduct with the person from whom you are assigned to gather information about the orientation program. Before beginning this task, review the behavioral guidelines for planning an effective interview at the end of the Skill Learning section. You should also consult Tables 1 through 3, and Table 6. In small groups, compare your questions with others. What did you leave out? What questions need to be reworded? What types of probes may be needed? After this discussion, split up into triads and take turns serving as the interviewer, interviewee, and observer. Do not look at the following role descriptions while planning this exercise. Observers should give feedback using the Observer's Feedback Form in Appendix I.

Role Descriptions for Interviewees

Trainee. You've just found out that you are going to be interviewed on the mentor program with which you've been involved for three months. You've been quite happy with the program and would like to see it continued; in fact, someday, you want to be a mentor to new employees.

Many of your friends have pointed out that you have a tendency to talk too fast, talk a lot, and tend to dominate a conversation. You realize that when you get nervous or involved in an issue, you do talk a lot. You are certainly nervous about this interview because you are very involved in the program and you've heard through the grapevine that the program might be cut. You feel that would be terrible. You really want to let the interviewer know how much you've learned from your mentor and the whole orientation program. What you have to say is important, and you want to make sure the interviewer hears all the good things you have to say about the program.

You are particularly positive about the program because it contrasts with your experience on your former job. In that organization, you were merely given a cursory overview of the company benefits through a videotape presentation. Furthermore, because there was no standardized mentoring program, new employees were left to fend for themselves. They were given no clear picture of what the company expected of them, no encouragement, and no sense of involvement in a group effort. As a result, a great deal of confusion and misunderstanding resulted. Here, in contrast, you have appreciated being able to get answers to your questions from one person. Overall, you feel as though this approach enabled you to become proficient in your job very quickly.

Department head. You've just found out that you are going to be interviewed on the mentor program, and it couldn't have come at a worse time. You've just lost one of your best employees, and you have been scrambling to try to find a replacement. You're really not interested in spending time to think about this interview or participate in it. You'd rather use the time on employment interviews to find a new assistant.

In fact, you tend to be uncomfortable in interviews of any kind. Because you tend to be shy, this kind of one-on-one formal conversation always makes you feel uncomfortable. You don't mind it so much when you are the interviewer—at least then you have some control over the situation. But you don't feel you've ever been a really good interviewee. The direct questions always make you feel as if you are on trial; as a result, you withdraw and appear to be uncooperative, even defensive.

You think that the interviewer should be talking to people more directly involved in the program. You really don't have much to do with it anyway, except for matching up people. The program seems to work okay, but no doubt trainees would learn just as quickly if they sought out their own mentors. You know many of your staff members feel the program is worthwhile, so you'll back it up, albeit reluctantly. However, you would much rather write an evaluation of the program than have to talk about it to a relative stranger.

Mentor. You've just found out that you are going to be interviewed on the mentor program, a program with which you've been involved for six months. When you first became a mentor, you were excited about the possibilities. Now, however, experience has shown that the program is a waste of time. Too often, the trainees use their mentors as a crutch, both at work and in their social lives. The program inspires a dependency that you find counterproductive and time wasting.

You've found yourself in the position of practically taking over trainees' jobs because they got used to relying on your expertise. You've thought that this might simply be a result of your own personality—too willing to help, perhaps—but you've also noticed this behavior in other mentors and trainees.

Furthermore, you haven't noticed any significant difference in productivity between people who have gone through the program and people who haven't. In fact, because of the development of social relationships, your feeling is that productivity has probably declined: There is too much gossip and goofing off and not enough concentration on tasks.

In general, you think the company ought to abandon the program. While a brief orientation might be useful to new hires, you no longer can justify the amount of time you put into the program, given the results. Even this evaluation of the program is taking up your valuable time.

Performance Appraisal Interview with Chris Jakobsen

Background Information for Pat Ginelli

Ginelli, vice-president of the Commercial Loan Division at Firstbank, a medium-sized state-licensed bank. You have been with Firstbank for four years and have conducted a number of performance-appraisal interviews. During your tenure, you have increased your division's profits by 45 percent. Your goal is to increase this level by another 15 percent before the end of next year. In order to do so, you need to have aggressive, dynamic, and dedicated loan officers working for you.

Chris Jakobsen has been with Firstbank for three years. This will be your first review of Chris's performance because he was transferred to your department five months ago to fill a loan officer position vacated by Helen Smith, who had worked in the Personal Loan Division. You agreed to the transfer after reviewing Chris's credentials and past performance appraisal forms. Chris appeared to be qualified for the position, and the performance appraisal reports indicated that Chris's work was rated from above average to outstanding.

Unfortunately, you have been extremely disappointed with Chris's performance in your department. For a long-time bank employee, he seems surprisingly unfamiliar with standard procedures and protocol. Last week, he told a customer there shouldn't be any problem getting approval for her loan application. She wanted to open a boutique in a renovated building downtown. However, the review committee turned it down because the building hadn't met code yet.

There are several other deficiencies in Chris's performance. In contrast to Helen, Chris seems inattentive to detail. He has frequently left out important information on loan applications, causing needless delays in processing. Furthermore, he doesn't seem to be able to keep up with the workload. It takes him twice as long as it should to handle routine paperwork, and he seems totally ill at ease with your department's computerized information system. Due to a favorable investment environment and the recent opening of a local industrial park, your group's workload is up 50 percent from a year ago. You simply can't tolerate having to take extra time to make sure Chris is doing things right the first time.

In Chris's favor, he is extremely punctual and his attendance has been perfect. He also keeps a very neat work area and takes pride in his own appearance. Furthermore, as a native of the community and an active civic leader, he has very good contacts in the business community. It is also clear that everyone likes Chris. He is jovial and easygoing. He has a quick wit that livens up even the most routine and dull staff meeting. He loves treating coworkers during happy hour after work. Unfortunately, he sometimes loses perspective and gets carried away. Indeed, you've wondered at times how this free spirit ended up in a bank job. Certainly his attitude runs counter to your more formal and reserved personality, but it's hard to deny he has charm and class.

In general, Chris seems to have plenty of potential, but at best his current work performance is only average (an "expected" rating on your company's form). He just hasn't applied himself to his new position. You wonder if this is the right work for him or if perhaps he hasn't had adequate training. You spent some time orienting Chris to the group and assigned Jim, a veteran of the department, to act as his mentor. But, in retrospect, the local business boom has made it difficult for you and Jim to help Chris learn the ropes. Your days seem to be filled up with meetings with local investors and city planners. Still, it bugs you that he never asks questions. If he needs help with the technical aspects of the job, why doesn't he ever ask for assistance?

You have scheduled the interview with Chris for later in the day in your office. You know your review will make him very unhappy and probably put him on the defensive. He obviously has high aspirations for advancing in the bank and has received pretty positive feedback in the past. You've got to figure out some way to get him to improve. Your department is short-handed as it is, and everyone must contribute his or her share.

As you contemplate the unpleasant task ahead, you reflect, "Boy, I certainly miss Helen. I never had to have this type of conversation with her."

Assignment for Pat Ginelli

In preparation for this interview, complete a draft of the performance evaluation form in Exhibit 1 in Appendix I. In keeping with standard practice, you have given a blank copy of the form to Chris and asked him to do a self-evaluation. He will bring his completed form to the interview.

After you have completed your draft, identify the type of performance appraisal interview you feel is most appropriate for this situation (see Table 9). Also, review the behavioral guidelines at the end of the Skill Learning section, and the 3 Rs approach to shaping behavior discussed in Chapter 6, Motivating Employees. Then formulate a series of questions consistent with your overall strategy. Finally, anticipate questions and objections Chris might initiate and prepare responses. Compare your plans in small groups and make revisions. Use the Interview Checklist in Table 4 to guide your discussion.

Upon completion of your small-group discussion, prepare to conduct the interview with Chris. Do not look at the background information for Chris's role prior to the interview. An observer will use the Observer's Feedback Form in Appendix I to give you feedback.

Background Information for Chris Jakobsen

You have been with Firstbank, a medium-sized state-licensed bank, for three years. For most of that time, you worked in the Personal Loan Division as a Loan Officer. You liked your job, your clients, and the people with whom you worked. You had hoped that your first move at Firstbank would be a promotion within the Personal Loan Division. However, five months ago, you were transferred to the Commercial Loan Division to replace a loan officer who had worked in that position for 10 years. You did not really want to transfer, but you realized that the move would, in fact, put you in a better position for the next upward move. Your former supervisor indicated that you would not have to stay in this position very long if you kept receiving good ratings on your performance appraisal forms, and you have always received outstanding or above average ratings. He argued that you really needed to gain exposure to other departments in the bank as well as to other managers. Your new boss, Pat Ginelli, is a real rising star in the bank.

You expect your new supervisor, Pat, is going to be pretty tough on you. You feel frustrated and upset because you don't think there has been any change in your effort or commitment. Since you have been in the department, Pat's attitude toward you has seemed very distant and formal. You know that Pat thinks that the person you replaced was an excellent worker who contributed greatly to Pat's goal of achieving a 15 percent increase in profits this year. But certainly she doesn't expect you to immediately pick up where a 10-year veteran left off.

Then there's the problem of training. She promised to give you a thorough orientation when you arrived, but instead you were shunted off to Jim. He seemed sincere and interested in helping out, and he told you to come and ask questions whenever you needed help. However, when you asked about the department's loan-application procedure, he made you feel like an idiot for asking such a basic question, and you've never gone back. Furthermore, Pat always seems to be in meetings. You realize that she is bringing in important business for the bank, so you feel it would be inappropriate to distract her with your basic questions.

This lack of assistance has caused you to make some mistakes. These have primarily been due to the change in procedures between the Personal and Commercial Loan departments. You had much more autonomy and authority over there, probably because the loans were much smaller. In addition, there are many more government regulations to worry about over here. Besides, you really miss the close contact with people that was built into your old job. That's why you took

Supplement B 517

your first job in the bank. You have always been a very people-oriented person and received great satisfaction from helping them. Now, you just seem to be buried in paperwork and committee meetings. Some days, you regret accepting the offer to transfer. You're not sure this stepping-stone to advancement is worth the lost enjoyment you received in your former position.

Assignment for Chris Jakobsen

Your interview with Pat is scheduled for her office. In preparation for the interview, Pat has asked you to complete a copy of the performance-appraisal form as a self-evaluation. Prior to the interview, complete the form in Exhibit 1 in Appendix I. Do not review the background information for Pat's role.

Employment Selection Interview at Smith Farley Insurance

Smith Farley is a rapidly growing insurance firm located in Peoria, Illinois. It offers general lines of insurance, including auto, fire, life, and health. It prides itself on its competitive rates, excellent agent relations, and fast claim service. Employees of the firm appreciate its no-layoff policy, generous pay and benefits, and family-oriented culture. Next to Caterpillar, it is the largest employer in the community, a source of employee pride.

Smith Farley has taken the lead in computerizing the insurance business. Agents and claim handlers conduct much of their business using laptop computers in their offices and in the field. Furthermore, the agents' and claim handlers' offices are all networked with one another as well as with the regional offices. This permits rapid transfer of information, including rate changes, new applications, and claims.

To support this massive computer system, the firm has installed state-of-the-art computer hardware in its 10 regional office centers. In addition, the company has a large software development and maintenance department which has doubled in size in the past five years and now employs 800 programmers. These programmers are generally recruited directly from college. Although they need no previous experience, any relevant experience can help new programmers move quickly into management or senior technical positions.

Programmer/analysts use typical programming languages to develop computer applications for the insurance business (e.g., new claim-handler and customer application forms), for the corporate headquarters staff (e.g., accounting and personnel records), and the computer system itself (internal procedures and controls). Data-processing positions range from extremely technical design of complex computer networks to routine maintenance of existing programs.

All new programmers are put through a 16-week school in which they are oriented to the company and the data processing department, brought up to speed on the relevant programming languages and tools, and socialized into the corporate culture. To meet the heavy demand for computer applications, the data processing department has been authorized to hire two cohorts of 60 programmers a year.

To attract programmers to the firm, Smith Farley offers above-average starting salaries and rapid promotions during the first five years. After that, individuals can continue to pursue the technical career option, which leads to a senior analyst's position that pays about $10,000 above industry average, or they can move into management. The consistently high performance of the firm and its ongoing expansion of data processing afford ample opportunity for promotion into senior positions.

You are J. R. Henderson, a 20-year employee of Smith Farley. For the past 10 years you have been working in the personnel department, primarily interviewing job candidates for the data-processing department. You enjoy your work—the constant contact with young, enthusiastic college graduates is invigorating—but sometimes you find the heavy travel schedule taxing.

For example, during the next week you will be traveling to three cities: first to nearby Bloomington, then to New Orleans and Atlanta. In addition to the regular campus interviews you have scheduled in these areas, you have received several resumes in response to local newspaper ads. In sifting through these inquiries, three resumes caught your interest. You have made arrangements to interview all three applicants during this trip.

Assignment

Review Exhibits 2 through 6 in Appendix I (pp. 578–584) and prepare a list of questions you would ask these three job candidates. Using the Interview Guide planning form in Appendix I, review the general questions you should ask all three. In addition, identify several specific questions you would like to ask the candidate(s) you are assigned, based on their resumes and cover letters.

Review your proposed questions in small groups. What points did you overlook? What questions need to be reworded or discarded?

Using the questions you think are most appropriate, be prepared to conduct selection interviews with these job candidates in class. Prior to each interview, think about the questions each candidate is likely to ask you about the company, the community of Peoria, and the specific jobs available. In addition, identify your "selling points": the specific features of the company, the community, and the jobs that you think each candidate would find most attractive. Also review the general behavioral guidelines and the six-step PEOPLE approach to selection interviews (Table 8). Remember: The interviewing process influences the content of the information exchanged.

Following the interview, take a few minutes and grade the interviewee on each of the seven criteria on the Interview Guide (5 = high, 1 = low). Justify your grades with specific comments. Then make an oral report to the observer assigned to your interview; include a recommendation. (Assume the observer is the director of recruiting for your firm.) After your report, for those criteria related to the interview itself (as compared with the background of the assigned role), discuss your observations with the interviewee. Following this discussion, the observer will give you feedback on your performance as an interviewer using the Observer's Feedback Form in Appendix I (pp. 570–575) as a guide.

Conducting Meetings

OBJECTIVES

▶ Increase proficiency in planning and conducting meetings

▶ Improve the efficiency of meetings you attend

▶ Be a productive contributor to meetings

skill development

 ## Skill Learning

 ## Skill Practice

Skill Learning

Conducting Effective Meetings

Becoming a skillful planner and conductor of meetings is a prerequisite for managerial and organizational effectiveness. This is because so much of a manager's time is spent in meetings. A 3M Company study, for example, found that meetings occupy a large percentage of the typical manager's work week. They found that the number of meetings has doubled over the last decade and their cost has nearly tripled. About 15 percent of the personnel budget of most companies is spent on meetings. In addition, the amount of time spent in meetings is positively associated with the manager's hierarchical level: the more senior the manager, the more meetings he or she attends (3M, 1987).

It is also the case that many people spend a substantial portion of their time in nonwork-oriented meetings. For example, most of the community volunteer work, church activity, participation in arts councils, youth programs, and civic associations are highly dependent on meetings for their success. Because meetings are such a pervasive activity both in and out of work settings, therefore, being a skillful meeting manager has important payoffs beyond just those associated with team building.

The Four P's of Effective Meetings

Effective meeting managers keep in mind four steps in preparing for and conducting meetings: purpose, participants, plan, and process.

Purpose. Purpose refers to the reason for which a meeting is held. When information can be conveyed by a memo or phone call, when people are not prepared, when key people cannot attend, when the cost of a meeting is higher than the potential payoff, and when there is no advantage to holding a meeting even if scheduled, no meeting should be called (3M, 1987). Four main guidelines for determining when to hold meetings are:

Information sharing. When all needed information is not held by any single person, when ideas will be stimulated by getting people together, and when it is not clear what information is needed or available, a meeting should be called.

Commitment building. Because individuals become committed to a course of action when they are involved in its planning and implementation, meetings should be called to foster such participation.

Information disseminating. When many people must receive the same message in the same way, or when updated information must be disseminated quickly, sharing information in a meeting is more efficient than in multiple one-on-one sessions. Furthermore, in a meeting individuals have a chance to provide feedback and to discuss the information being shared.

Problem solving and decision making. Groups outperform the best individuals in accomplishing complex tasks and making high-quality decisions where various pieces of information are needed. Therefore, meetings should be called to solve complex problems and make difficult decisions.

Participants. Participants, the second P, are the individuals invited to attend a meeting. In conducting an effective meeting, it is important to determine the *size* and *composition* of the group to be invited. Meetings can fail because too many or too few participants attend or because the wrong mix of people is present. If a meeting is too large, for example, discussion may be superficial and diffuse, and few people will be able to participate. If a meeting is too small, not enough information will be shared and problems will not be adequately solved. Therefore, certain guidelines should be followed when deciding whom to invite to a meeting. Table 1 identifies types of meetings and the recommended number of participants in each type. The appropriate size depends primarily on the purpose of the meeting.

Meeting composition refers to three main dimensions: homogeneity-heterogeneity, competition-cooperation, and task-process. A homogeneous group is composed of members with similar backgrounds, personalities, knowledge, or values. In general, homoge-

PURPOSE OF THE MEETING	RECOMMENDED NUMBER OF PARTICIPANTS
Decision making and problem solving	5
Problem identification or brainstorming	10
Interactive seminars and training sessions	15
Informational meetings	30
Formal presentations	Unlimited

Table 1   Recommended Meeting Size
Source: 3M (1987).

neous groups produce less conflict and disagreement, but their outcomes may be mundane and unimaginative. Heterogeneous groups, on the other hand, produce more differences among individuals which lead to criticisms and disputes, but, potentially, to more novel, complex solutions to problems as well (Shaw, 1976).

With regard to the competition-cooperation dimension, research on its effect in problem solving meetings is compelling. Studies have consistently shown that groups whose members are working toward a common goal and who adopt a cooperative stance toward one another perform more effectively and produce higher levels of member satisfaction than groups whose members are striving to fulfill individual needs or are pursuing competing goals (Terborg, Castore, & DeNinno, 1976). Cooperative groups demonstrate more effective interpersonal communication, more complete division of labor, higher levels of involvement, and better task performance.

On the task-process dimension, meetings are more effective if they have participants who generate a balance of both. Task-oriented participants are "all business." They have little tolerance for joking or for discussions of feelings and friendships. The task is accomplished efficiently, but satisfaction may be low. Process-oriented participants, on the other hand, emphasize *esprit de corps* and participation. They are sensitive to participants' feelings and satisfaction. Accomplishment may get sacrificed in favor of members' enjoyment.

Planning.   The third P, planning, refers to preparation for the meeting agenda. Often, the justification for a meeting is clear (e.g., we need to determine how to get fuel to troops at the front), and the appropriate individuals are in attendance, but the meeting still seems to flounder, wandering aimlessly, or is unable to

produce a final decision. Such meetings often begin with the leader saying, "We have a problem that I think we all need to sit down and discuss." The leader's erroneous assumption is that because a problem exists and all participants understand it, the meeting will be successful. Unfortunately, participants may come to the meeting unprepared, may be unaware of critical information, may be unclear about their specific roles, may be confused about how the decision will be made, and may be unmotivated to achieve the objective. Conversely, the meeting planner may try to cram too much into a single meeting, schedule too many presentations, handle too many documents, or cover too much business. Tropman (1985) proposed the following rules and guidelines for planning meetings effectively:

The rule of halves. All agenda items for an upcoming meeting must be in the hands of the agenda scheduler no later than one-half of the time interval between the last meeting and the upcoming meeting. Thus, if meetings are held weekly, agenda items for the next meeting should be gathered by the person constructing the agenda by the halfway mark in the week. This allows time to sort and cluster items, handle some items one-on-one outside the meeting, and produce and distribute an agenda in advance of the meeting.

The rule of three-fourths. Packets of information, including minutes from the past meeting and an agenda, should be sent to meeting participants at the three-quarter point between meetings. For example, if a weekly meeting is scheduled, the packet should be sent out approximately two days before the next meeting.

The agenda rule. Agendas for meetings should be written with action verbs or sentence summaries, not with single words. Rather than saying "Minutes," for example, use "Approve Minutes." Rather than "Production Report" use "Determine Production Schedule." This provides clarity and impetus for what the meeting should accomplish.

The rule of sixths. Approximately two-thirds of the meeting should be focused on current agenda items. The remaining third should be subdivided into two sixths. One of those sixths of meeting time should be spent on past agenda items and follow-up. The remaining sixth of the meeting should be spent on future agenda items (i.e., planning or preparation). Continuity is thus maintained and agenda items don't slip through the cracks.

The rule of thirds. All meetings are divided into three parts: (1) a start-up period in which less difficult items are covered, latecomers arrive, and people get on-board; (2) a heavy work period in which the most difficult items are considered; and (3) a decompression period in which the meeting begins to wind down. *Instructional items* should be handled in the first period, *items for decision* should be handled in the second period, and *items for discussion* should be handled in the third period.

The reports rule. Reports circulated to meeting participants should always contain executive summaries or options memos. An executive summary highlights key points and conclusions of the report. An options memo summarizes alternatives to be discussed and decided upon. This eliminates the need to sift through many pages to find relevant information and to spend meeting time shuffling through the report.

The agenda bell rule. This rule is a more specific statement of several previous rules about when certain types of agenda items should be covered. Agenda items should be considered in order of ascending controversiality, then attention should be turned to discussion and decompression items. Figure 1 shows a typical agenda bell for a meeting.

The agenda integrity rule. All items on the agenda should be discussed, and items not on the agenda should not be discussed. This rule helps ensure that meeting participants do not sidetrack the meeting with items that are tangential, for which no one has prepared, or for which insufficient information is available.

The temporal integrity rule. This rule is simple: Start on time and end on time. Follow a time schedule in the meeting itself. This ensures that all agenda items are given adequate time, that latecomers are not rewarded by having the meeting wait for them, and that people can count on finishing at a certain point.

The minutes rule. Minutes of meetings should have three characteristics: agenda relevance (information recorded is related to an agenda item), content relevance (minutes should be written in a form that follows the agenda so that it is easy to find pertinent material with a quick review), and decision focus (minutes should reflect decisions, conclusions, and actions agreed upon, rather than the processes by which the decisions were reached).

These 10 rules of meeting preparation help to ensure that when individuals arrive for a meeting and the meeting begins, a structure and plan will be in place to make the meeting productive and efficient.

Process. The fourth P in meeting preparation is process. Process refers to the actual conducting of meetings and the methods used to ensure that meetings are effective. Huber (1980) outlined seven steps for conducting a meeting.

1. *Review.* At the beginning of the meeting, review the agenda and the tasks to be accomplished as well as progress made to date in previous meetings. This helps meeting participants know precisely what is expected and encourages them to stay focused on the task at hand. It also makes controlling time in the meeting much easier.

2. *Introductions.* Meeting participants should be introduced to each other and helped to feel comfortable together, especially if controversial issues are to be considered. The critical nature of this step is illustrated by an incident in which faculty representatives on the board of a major athletic conference met several times with representatives of a university administration to discuss the eligibility of a star athlete. Both sides were suspicious of the others' motives, and several previous meetings had failed to resolve the dispute. Then, before the next meeting, participants were invited to attend a social gathering featuring an outdoor barbecue.

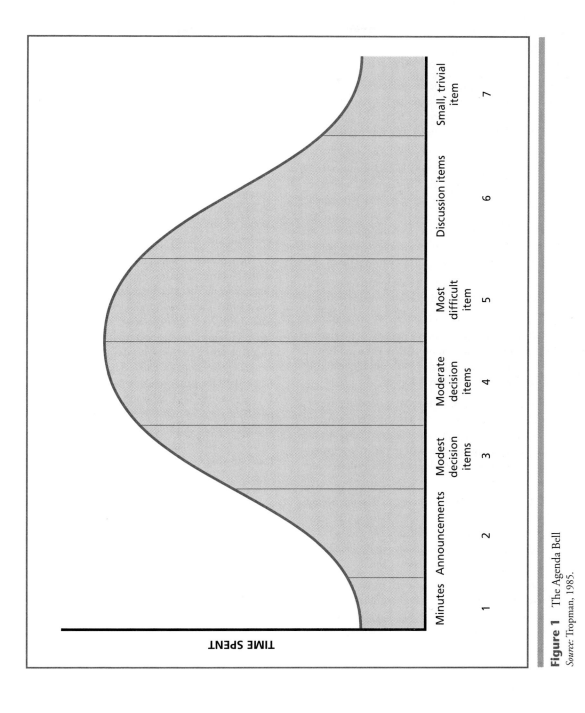

Figure 1 The Agenda Bell
Source: Tropman, 1985.

During this event, participants on both sides got to know one another on a more personal basis, and in the meeting the next day, a breakthrough was achieved to resolve the dispute. Several participants credited the social gathering with playing a major role in breaking down barriers between the two factions.

3. *Ground Rules.* It should be made clear what kind and amount of participation is expected, what variations from the agenda will be tolerated, what the time frame will be, and so on. Establishing a structure for the meeting at the outset helps keep the meeting on track.

In addition, the manner in which decisions are to be made should be determined. For example, will everyone in the meeting have to agree in order to reach a conclusion? Will a majority rule? Will everyone have a vote? Several options exist for making decisions and reaching a conclusion, and it should be determined which will be used in the meeting. Among them are:

Majority rule. Each meeting participant votes on alternatives, and the alternative with a majority of the votes wins.

- *Highest total.* When more than two alternatives are being considered, none may get a majority of the votes. The alternative with the highest number of votes is therefore adopted.

- *Straw vote.* A nonbinding vote is taken to get a sense of the feelings of the participants toward various alternatives. This may happen several times before a decision is reached, in order to eliminate nonsupported alternatives from consideration.

- *Weighted rating.* Meeting participants can divide 100 points among alternatives, so that the strength of their support can be tallied. If four alternatives exist, for example, a participant can give 90 points to one and 5 points to two others. The alternative with the most points wins.

- *Ranking.* Alternatives are rank ordered, and the alternative receiving the highest average ranking is adopted.

- *Consensus.* All participants must agree to adopt one particular alternative.

- *In principle.* Although agreement cannot be obtained on all specific details, certain general principles are identified that can be agreed upon. The principles, rather than the entire proposal, are accepted.

4. *Reports.* Early in the meeting, reports should be heard from those who have been preassigned to make presentations. This helps maintain accountability for assignments, reduces the presenters' apprehension, and assures that presentations will not be tacked onto the end of the meeting. It also allows the presenter to concentrate on other agenda items after the presentation— something that will probably *not* occur before the presenter has made his or her report.

5. *Displays.* To maintain the interest of meeting participants, use various media to present information. Handouts, overhead transparencies, slides, flip charts, videos, blackboard diagrams, and so on are all helpful in maintaining interest and increasing the efficiency with which information is presented. In general, participants should be able to use at least two of their senses during a meeting, for example, seeing and hearing.

6. *Participation.* Participation in a meeting should be equitable among participants, which does not mean that everyone must make exactly the same number of comments. Those with more information will participate more, as will those with vested interests in the topic. However, it is important to control the over-participator or the person who dominates the discussion, as well as to encourage those who may have something to contribute but may not be inclined to share it. Equity should also be maintained among different points of view, so that representatives of one side of an argument don't dominate the discussion. Ways to promote discussion among meeting participants include the following:

- Ask open-ended questions rather than questions that can be answered with a "yes" or "no."

- Ask questions using the language of the participants rather than using jargon or recondite terminology.

- Encourage participants to share personal experiences that relate to the topic being considered.

- Use examples from your own experience to clarify points.

- Make eye contact with those to whom you are talking and summarize their points when they finish their statements.

- Ask group members for their reactions to points made by other meeting participants.

- When appropriate, involve others in answering a question asked of you.

▶ Make certain that, as the leader, you facilitate the discussion rather than dominate it.

7. *Summarize.* Close the meeting by summarizing the decisions reached, tasks assigned, progress accomplished, key points discussed, and what was learned in the meeting. Review action items that will be reported upon at the next meeting. Help meeting participants feel a sense of accomplishment for having spent their time in the meeting. This also may be a good time to anticipate the next meeting by identifying when minutes and the next meeting's agenda will be distributed and what preparation will be required.

Suggestions for Group Members

Throughout this discussion of effective meeting management, we have focused on the role of the leader. This role is key to the success of any group activity. However, meeting participants also bear responsibility for the meeting's effectiveness. It is important for nonleaders attending meetings to appreciate the impact of their contribution, both in shaping the short-term outcomes of meetings and affecting their long-term career opportunities.

Following are several pointers for contributing to the effectiveness of meetings from a nonleader's perspective.

1. Determine if you need to attend the meeting. Don't attend merely because you have been invited. If you have doubts about whether the meeting's agenda applies to you, discuss with the leader why her or she believes your presence is important.

2. Prepare. Acquaint yourself with the agenda, and prepare any reports or information that will facilitate *others'* understanding of the issues. Come prepared with questions that will help *you* understand the issues.

3. Be on time. Stragglers not only waste the time of other participants by delaying the meeting or by requiring summaries of what has happened, but they also hinder effective team building and hurt morale.

4. Ask for clarification on points that are unclear or ambiguous. Most of the time, you will find that others

in the room have the same questions but were too timid to speak out.

5. When giving information, be precise and to the point. Don't bore everyone with anecdotes and details that add little to your point.

6. Listen. Keep eye contact with whoever is speaking, and try to ascertain the underlying ideas behind the comments. Be sensitive to the effect of your nonverbal behavior on speakers, such as slouching, doodling, or reading.

7. Be supportive of other group members. Following the guidelines on supportive communication, acknowledge and build on the comments of others. ("As Jane was saying . . .")

8. Assure equitable participation. Take the lead in involving others so that everyone's talents are used. This is especially important if you know that critical information from particular points of view are not being included in the discussion. This can be rectified by encouraging those who rarely participate. ("Jim, your unit worked on something like this last year. What was your experience like?")

9. Make disagreements principle based. If it is necessary to disagree with, or challenge, the comments of others, follow the guidelines for collaborative conflict management. For example, base your comments on commonly held principles or values. ("That's an interesting idea, Bill, but how does it square with the president's emphasis on cost cutting?")

10. Act and react in a way that will enhance the group performance. In other words, leave your personal agendas at the door and work toward the goals of the group.

Summary and Behavioral Guidelines

Meetings are a pervasive part of organizational life, especially for managers. Few important initiatives are forged without extensive and intensive group efforts. However, meetings are one of the most maligned aspects of organizational membership. To avoid poorly managed meetings, a 4-P's approach was presented.

1. *Purpose.* Use meetings to accomplish the following purposes:

   ▶ A complex problem needs to be resolved using the expertise of several people.

   ▶ Group members' commitment to a decision or to each other needs to be enhanced.

   ▶ Information needs to be shared simultaneously among several people.

2. *Participants.* Make decisions regarding who and how many to invite on the following bases:

   ▶ The size of the group should be compatible with the task. (For interactive groups, five to seven participants tends to work best.)

   ▶ A balance between individuals with strong task orientations and others with strong group process orientations should be sought.

   ▶ Individuals should share some common goals or values.

   ▶ All relevant experience and knowledge need to be represented.

   ▶ The group's composition should reflect the goals of the meeting. (Homogeneity encourages solidarity and commitment; heterogeneity fosters creativity and innovation.)

3. *Plan.* In preparing for the meeting, be sure to do the following:

   ▶ Provide for adequate physical space, audiovisual equipment, and so on.

   ▶ Establish priorities by sequencing agenda items and allotting time limits to each item.

   ▶ Prepare and distribute an agenda before, or at the begging of, the meeting.

   ▶ Choose the most appropriate decision-making format structure for each item (for example, ordinary group discussion, brainstorming, or one of several consensus-building techniques).

4. *Process.* In managing the group dynamics of the meeting, do the following:

   ▶ Present the overall purpose of the meeting, specify the target time length, and highlight specific tasks.

   ▶ Establish process ground rules, such as how decisions will be made.

   ▶ Allow members to become acquainted (if necessary) and make them feel comfortable.

   ▶ Get a report from each member with a preassigned task, preferably early in the meeting.

   ▶ When critical thinking is important, refrain from expressing strong personal opinions. Also, assign the role of critical evaluator to group members.

   ▶ Sustain the flow of the meeting by using informational displays.

   ▶ Encourage the group not to stray from assigned tasks.

   ▶ Manage the discussion to achieve equitable participation.

   ▶ Discourage the premature evaluation of ideas.

   ▶ Prevent "social loafing" by assigning specific responsibilities and stressing the importance of group tasks.

   ▶ Counteract the natural tendency for groups to make risky decisions by polling members prior to the meeting so that discussion-induced trends can be detected.

   ▶ Deal with disruptive members by using supportive communication and collaborative conflict management skills.

   ▶ Conclude the meeting by summarizing what was accomplished, reviewing assignments, and making preparations for subsequent meetings, if necessary.

5. Foster constructive group dynamics as a participant by doing the following:

   ▶ Take time to prepare for the meeting, and gain a clear understanding of the purposes of the meeting.

   ▶ Respect other group members by arriving on time and leaving personal agendas at the door.

   ▶ Listen to other group members, be supportive of them, and clarify and build upon points made by others.

   ▶ Encourage participation by all members.

Skill Practice

Exercises in Conducting Meetings

Preparing and Conducting a Team Meeting at SSS Software

Part 1

Refer back to the SSS Software In-Basket exercise in the Introduction. Assume the role of Chris Perillo. Since you are new to your position, you decide to hold a meeting with some or all of your direct reports tomorrow afternoon (Tuesday). You want to be brought up to date as well as to handle the items of business introduced in your E-mail, phone messages, and memos.

1. Review each of the 16 items in the SSS Software In-Basket exercise. This will remind you again of the tasks to be addressed.

2. Determine three P's: the *purpose* of the meeting, the *participants* (who should attend), and the *plan* (agenda). Also determine how long the meeting should last.

3. Generate an actual meeting agenda showing all items of business that you want to cover, using the 10 rules and guidelines earlier in this chapter.

4. Determine the meeting process you will use, following the seven guidelines discussed in the Skill Learning section, namely, review, introductions, ground rules, reports, displays, participation, and summarize.

5. Have the instructor or another classmate evaluate your agenda and meeting process outline by using the Meeting Evaluation Worksheet in Appendix I. The evaluation should include feedback on what was done especially well, what was incomplete, and what was omitted.

Part 2

6. Now form a team in which each member is assigned to play one of the roles in the Health and Financial Services Group. The team should consist of:

Chris Perillo, Vice President

Bob Miller, Group 1 Manager

Wanda Manners, Group 2 Manager

William Chen, Group 3 Manager

Leo Jones, Group 4 Manager

Mark McIntyre, Group 5 Manager

John Small, Group 6 Manager

Marcus Harper, Group 8 Manager

Armad Marke, Customer Service Manager

Michelle Harrison, Office Administrator

7. Select an agenda for the meeting that was generated by one of the team members in Part 1. Actually work through the agenda with all the staff members. Determine a preset time limit, but do not make the meeting so short that it is superficial. Each team member should realistically play the role assigned to him or her, even if not much specific information exists for the role in the memos. Each team member should play the role as though he or she were beginning a new team meeting with a new leader. What do you recommend that Chris do about each of the items on the meeting agenda?

8. This meeting could be held as a "fish bowl" in the class, or multiple meetings could be conducted at once with several different teams. If the meeting is a fish bowl, observers should (a) analyze the roles being played by different team members and (b) critique the effectiveness of the meeting itself, and identify ways in which the meeting could have been improved. If multiple meetings are held at once, have team members critique the meeting after it concludes.

Role Diagnosis

This exercise is intended to held you identify and practice effective role performance in meetings. You will need to refer back to the chapter on Building Effective Teams to review the roles that team members play in meetings. Some of those roles are helpful, and some are not so helpful.

Listed below are a set of roles organized into three categories. As you are observing a team meeting, put check marks by the roles performed by the team members you are observing each time they make a comment or display behavior that matches one of the roles listed below. If you are analyzing your own team after it has completed its meeting, put names of team members next to the roles they played. (See Chapter 9 for definitions of these roles.)

Task-Facilitating Roles	*Relationship-Building Roles*	*Blocking Roles*
Direction-giving	Supporting	Overanalyzing
Information-seeking	Harmonizing	Overgeneralizing
Information-giving	Tension-relieving	Fault finding
Elaborating	Energizing	Premature decision making
Coordinating	Developing	Presenting opinions as facts
Monitoring	Facilitating	Rejecting
Process-analyzing	Processing	Pulling rank
Reality-testing		Dominating
Enforcing		Stalling
Summarizing		

What suggestions do you have for improvement in the team members' performance? Identify some specific suggestions for more effective role performance in the meeting. Who could have done more of or less of what?

Preparing and Conducting a Team Meeting at SSS Software

Meeting Evaluation Worksheet

1. What is the specific purpose of the meeting?

2. Who was invited to attend? How are they contacted? Was the way in which the meeting announced appropriate (e.g., face to face, E-mail, secretary phone call)?

3. Was the agenda that was constructed consistent with the rules? Specifically, did it follow these rules:

   The Agenda Rule (action words)

   The Rule of Sixths (past and future events)

   The Rule of Thirds (items divided into thirds)

   The Reports Rule (reports from team members early)

   The Agenda Bell Rule (a specific time line)

   The Temporal Integrity Rule (a time line planned)

   The Minutes Rule (someone assigned to keep minutes)

4. What was done especially well in preparing for this meeting?

5. To what extent were the seven rules of effective meeting process followed in the meeting? Rate each step in terms of its effectiveness in the team meeting.

	Effective	Ineffective
1. Review purpose	_____	_____
2. Make introductions	_____	_____
3. Establish ground rules	_____	_____
4. Hear reports	_____	_____
5. Use informational displays	_____	_____
6. Ensure participation	_____	_____
7. Summarize conclusions	_____	_____

6. What could have been improved upon? What was omitted?

Appendixes

Scoring Keys
and Supplemental Materials

Developing Management Skills Web Site

You can take the assessment tests and find useful links at the Whetten and Cameron *Developing Management Skills* web site located at:

http://hepg.awl.com/whetten/dms4/

You will note that Comparison Data scoring keys are provided at the end of each Scoring Key in this section. These data were collected from class tests of the diagnostic surveys by the authors and do not represent a large or representative sample. The web site includes scoring keys that allow users to see their scoring vis-à-vis a more diverse and large sample of their peers. You also will be able to analyze your scores in relation to your peer group, for instance North American undergraduate students or Executive MBA students.

Personal Assessment of Management Skills (page 18)

Scoring Key

Skill Area	Items	Assessment Personal	Associates
Developing Self-Awareness	**1–5**	_____	_____
Self-disclosure and openness	1, 2	_____	_____
Awareness of self	3–5	_____	_____
Managing Stress	**6–11**	_____	_____
Eliminating stressors	6, 7	_____	_____
Developing resiliency	8, 9	_____	_____
Short-term coping	10, 11	_____	_____
Solving Problems Creatively	**12–23**	_____	_____
Rational problem solving	12–14	_____	_____
Creative problem solving	15–19	_____	_____
Fostering innovation and creativity	20–23	_____	_____

Skill Area	Items	Assessment Personal	Associates
Communicating Supportively	**24–32**	_____	_____
Coaching and counseling	24, 25	_____	_____
Effective negative feedback	26–28	_____	_____
Communicating supportively	29–32	_____	_____
Gaining Power and Influence	**33–40**	_____	_____
Gaining power	33–37	_____	_____
Exercising influence	38–40	_____	_____
Motivating Others	**41–49**	_____	_____
Managing Conflict	**50–58**	_____	_____
Initiating	50–52	_____	_____
Responding	53–55	_____	_____
Mediating	56–58	_____	_____
Empowering and Delegating	**59–67**	_____	_____
Empowering	59–62	_____	_____
Delegating	63–67	_____	_____
Building Effective Teams	**68–72**	_____	_____
Team Leadership	67–71	_____	_____
Conducting Team Meetings	72	_____	_____
Total Score		[ ]	[ ]

Comparison Data

Compare your scores with at least four referents: (1) If you asked others to rate you using the Associates' version, compare how you rated yourself with how your associates rated you. (2) Compare the ratings you received to those received by other students in the class. (3) Compare the ratings you received to a norm group of 300 business school students (see the information below). (4) Compare your score against the maximum possible (432).

For the survey as a whole, if you scored

285 or above	you are in the top quartile.
266–284	you are in the second quartile.
251–265	you are in the third quartile.
250 or below	you are in the bottom quartile.

Self-Awareness (page 36)

Scoring Key

Skill Area	Items	Assessment Pre-	Post-
Self-disclosure and openness to feedback from others	1, 2, 3, 9, 11	_22_	_____
Awareness of own values, cognitive style, change orientation, and interpersonal orientation	4, 5, 6, 7, 8, 10	_27_	_____
Total Score		49	

Comparison Data

Compare your scores to three comparison standards: (1) Compare your scores with the maximum possible (66). (2) Compare your scores with the scores of other students in your class. (3) Compare your scores to a norm group consisting of 500 business school students. In comparison to the norm group, if you scored

55 or above	you are in the top quartile.
52–54	you are in the second quartile.
48–51	you are in the third quartile.
47 or below	you are in the bottom quartile.

Interpreting the Defining Issues Test (page 37)

The possibility of misusing and misinterpreting this instrument is high enough that its author, James Rest, maintains control over the scoring procedure associated with its use. Some people may interpret the results of this instrument to be an indication of inherent morality, honesty, or personal worth, none of which the instrument is intended to assess. A scoring manual may be obtained from James Rest, Minnesota Moral Research Center, Burton Hall, University of Minnesota, Minneapolis, MN 55455.

Our purpose is to help you become aware of the stage of moral development you rely on most when facing moral dilemmas. To help determine that, the following lists present the stage of moral development each statement associated with each story reflects. By looking at the four statements you selected as most important in deciding what action to take in each situation, you can determine which stage of development you use most often.

After you have done this, you should discuss which action you would take in each situation and why, and why you selected the statements you did as the most important ones to consider.

The Escaped Prisoner (page 37)

1. Hasn't Mr. Thompson been good enough for such a long time to prove he isn't a bad person? (Stage 3)

2. Every time someone escapes punishment for a crime, doesn't that just encourage more crime? (Stage 4)

3. Wouldn't we be better off without prisons and the oppression of our legal system? (Indicates antiauthoritarian attitudes.)

4. Has Mr. Thompson really paid his debt to society? (Stage 4)

5. Would society be failing what Mr. Thompson should fairly expect? (Stage 6)

6. What benefits would prison be apart from society, especially for a charitable man? (Nonsense alternative, designed to identify people picking high-sounding alternatives.)

7. How could anyone be so cruel and heartless as to send Mr. Thompson to prison? (Stage 3)

8. Would it be fair to all the prisoners who had to serve out their full sentences if Mr. Thompson was let off? (Stage 4)

9. Was Ms. Jones a good friend of Mr. Thompson? (Stage 3)

10. Wouldn't it be a citizen's duty to report an escaped criminal, regardless of circumstances? (Stage 4)

11. How would the will of the people and the public good best be served? (Stage 5)

12. Would going to prison do any good for Mr. Thompson or protect anybody? (Stage 5)

The Doctor's Dilemma (page 38)

1. Whether the woman's family is in favor of giving her an overdose or not. (Stage 3)

2. Is the doctor obligated by the same laws as everybody else if giving her an overdose would be the same as killing her? (Stage 4)

3. Whether people would be much better off without society regimenting their lives and even their deaths. (Indicates antiauthoritarian attitudes.)

4. Whether the doctor could make it appear like an accident. (Stage 2)

5. Does the state have the right to force continued existence on those who don't want to live? (Stage 5)

6. What is the value of death prior to society's perspective on personal values? (Nonsense alternative, designed to identify people picking high-sounding alternatives.)

7. Whether the doctor has sympathy for the woman's suffering or cares more about what society might think. (Stage 3)

8. Is helping to end another's life ever a responsible act of cooperation? (Stage 6)

9. Whether only God should decide when a person's life should end. (Stage 4)

10. What values the doctor has set for himself in his own personal code of behavior. (Stage 5)

| 11. Can society afford to let everybody end their lives when they want to? (Stage 4)

2 12. Can society allow suicides or mercy killing and still protect the lives of individuals who want to live? (Stage 5)

The Newspaper (page 39)

4 1. Is the principal more responsible to students or to the parents? (Stage 4)

2. Did the principal give his word that the newspaper could be published for a long time, or did he promise to approve the newspaper one issue at a time? (Stage 4)

3. Would the students start protesting even more if the principal stopped the newspaper? (Stage 2)

3 4. When the welfare of the school is threatened, does the principal have the right to give orders to students? (Stage 4)

5. Does the principal have the freedom of speech to say "no" in this case? (Nonsense alternative, designed to identify people picking high-sounding alternatives.)

6. If the principal stopped the newspaper, would he be preventing full discussion of important matters? (Stage 5)

7. Whether the principal's order would make Fred lose faith in the principal. (Stage 3)

8. Whether Fred was loyal to his school and patriotic to his country. (Stage 3)

2 9. What effect would stopping the paper have on the students' education in critical thinking and judgments? (Stage 5)

| 10. Whether Fred was in any way violating the rights of others in publishing his own opinions. (Stage 5)

11. Whether the principal should be influenced by some angry parents when it is the principal who knows best what is going on in the school. (Stage 4)

12. Whether Fred was using the newspaper to stir up hatred and discontent. (Stage 3)

The Cognitive Style Instrument (page 41)

Scoring Key

To determine your score on the two dimensions of cognitive style, circle the items on the next page that you checked on this instrument. Then count up the number of circled items and put your scores in the spaces below.

Gathering Information		Evaluating Information	
1a	(1b)	(13a)	13b
(2a)	2b	(14b)	(14a)
3b	(3a)	(15a)	15b
(4b)	4a	(16b)	16a
(5a)	5b	(17b)	17a
(6b)	6a	(18a)	18b
(7b)	7a	(19a)	19b
8a	(8b)	20a	(20b)
(9a)	9b	(21b)	21a
(10b)	10a	(22a)	22b
(11a)	11b	23b	(23a)
(12a)	12b	(24a)	24b

9	3	9	3
Intuitive Score	**Sensing Score**	**Thinking Score**	**Feeling Score**

Comparison Data

	Intuitive	Sensing	Thinking	Feeling
Males	5.98	6.02	6.08	5.20
Females	6.04	5.96	6.94	5.06

Note: The *Instructor's Manual* contains more comparison data from other respondent groups. These will help you compare your own scores with those of others.

The Locus of Control Scale (page 43)

Scoring Key

Count up the number of items you selected of those listed below:

2a	5b	9a	12b	16a	20a	23a	28b
3b	6a	10a	13b	17a	21a	25a	29a
(4b)	7a	(11b) /	15b	18a	22b	26b	

Total Score 2

Comparison Data

Corporate business executives	Ave: 8.29	Sd: 3.57
Elite career military officers	Ave: 8.29	Sd: 3.86

Note: See the *Instructor's Manual* for more comparison data.

Tolerance of Ambiguity Scale (page 45)

Scoring Key

Having intolerance of ambiguity means that an individual tends to perceive situations as threatening rather than promising. Lack of information or uncertainty, for example, would make such a person uncomfortable. Ambiguity arises from three main sources: novelty, complexity, and insolubility. These three subscales exist within the instrument.

High scores indicate a greater *intolerance* for ambiguity. To score the instrument, the *even-numbered* items must be reverse-scored. That is, the 7s become 1s, 6s become 2s, 5s become 3s, and 4s remain the same. After reversing the even-numbered items, sum the scores for all 16 items to get your total score.

The three subscales also can be computed to reveal the major source of intolerance of ambiguity: novelty (N), complexity (C), or insolubility (I). Here are the items associated with each subscale.

Item	Subscale	Item	Subscale	Item	Subscale	Item	Subscale
1 *4*	I	5 *3*	C	9 *6*	N	13 *7*	N
3 2 *5*	N	*6* 6 *2*	C	*4* 10 *4*	C	*5* 14 *3*	C
3 *5*	I	7 *5*	C	11 *5*	N	15 *5*	C
3 4 *5*	C	*6* 8 *2*	C	*6* 12 *2*	I	*4* 16 *4*	C

(N) Novelty score (2, 9, 11, 13)   *23*

(C) Complexity score (4, 5, 6, 7, 8, 10, 14, 15, 16)   *33*

(I) Insolubility score (1, 3, 12)   *11*

Total Score   *67*

Comparison Data

Average range: 44–48

FIRO-B (page 46)

Scoring Key

To derive your interpersonal orientation scores, refer to the table on the next page. Note that there are six columns, each with *items* and *keys*. Each column refers to an interpersonal need listed in the chart at the bottom of the page. *Items* in the column refer to question numbers on the questionnaire; *keys* refer to answers on each of those items. If you answered an item using any of the alternatives in the corresponding key column, circle the item number on this sheet.

When you have checked all of the items for a single column, count up the number of circled items and place that number in the corresponding box in the chart. These numbers will give you your strength of interpersonal need in each of the six areas. The highest possible score is 9. The lowest score is 0. Refer to the explanations in the chapter in order to interpret your scores and for some comparison data.

Expressed Inclusion		*Wanted Inclusion*		*Expressed Control*		*Wanted Control*		*Expressed Affection*		*Wanted Affection*	
Item	Key	Item	Key	Item	Key	Item	Key	Item	Key	Item	Key
1	1-2-3	28	1-2	30	1-2-3	2	1-2-3-4	4	1-2	29	1-2
3	1-2-3-4	31	1-2	33	1-2-(3)	6	1-2-3-4	8	1-2	32	1-2
5	1-2-3-4	34	1-2	36	1-2	10	1-2-3	12	1	35	(5)-6
7	1-2-3	37	1	41	1-2-3-4	14	1-2-3	17	(1)-2	38	1-(2)
9	1-(2)	39	1	44	1-2-3	18	1-(2)-3	19	(4)-5-6	40	(5)-6
11	1-2	42	1-2	47	1-2-(3)	20	1-2-(3)	21	1-2	43	1
13	1-2	45	1-2	50	1-2	22	1-2-3-4	23	1-2	46	(5)-6
15	1	48	1-2	53	1-2	24	1-2-(3)	25	4-5-6	49	1-2
16	1	51	1-2	54	1-2	26	1-2-3	27	1-2	52	(5)-6

Score	Score	Score	Score	Score	Score
1	0	2	3	2	5

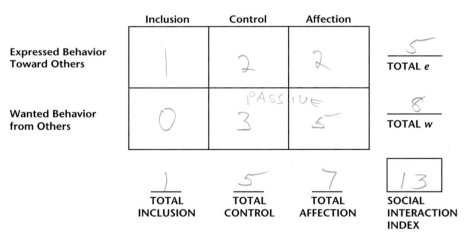

	Inclusion	Control	Affection	
Expressed Behavior Toward Others	1	2	2	5 TOTAL *e*
Wanted Behavior from Others	0	PASSIVE 3	5	8 TOTAL *w*

1	5	7	13
TOTAL INCLUSION	**TOTAL CONTROL**	**TOTAL AFFECTION**	**SOCIAL INTERACTION INDEX**

Comparison Data

Averages: TOTAL *e:*   13.4   5
                 TOTAL *w:*   15,9   8
                 TOTAL INCLUSION: 11.9
                 TOTAL CONTROL: 8.5   5
                 TOTAL AFFECTION: 8.9   7
                 SOCIAL INTERACTION INDEX: 29.3   13

Stress Management (page 82)

Scoring Key

Skill Area	Items	Assessment	
		Pre-	Post-
Eliminating stressors	1, 5, 8, 9	_____	_____
Developing resiliency	2, 3, 6, 7	_____	_____
Short-term coping	4, 10	_____	_____
	Total Score		

Comparison Data

Compare your scores to three comparison standards: (1) Compare your score against the maximum possible (60). (2) Compare your scores with the scores of other students in your class. (3) Compare your scores to a norm group consisting of 500 business school students. In comparison to the norm group, if you scored

50 or above	you are in the top quartile.
45–49	you are in the second quartile.
40–44	you are in the third quartile.
39 or below	you are in the bottom quartile.

Time Management (page 83)

Scoring Key

To determine how effective you are as a manager of your time, give yourself the following number of points for the boxes you checked:

Points	Frequency
0	Never
1	Seldom
2	Sometimes
3	Usually
4	Always

If you completed only Section I of the instrument, double the scores for each category.

Add up your total points for the 40 items. If you scored 120 or above, you are an excellent manager of your time both personally and at work. If you scored between 100 and 120, you are doing a good job of managing your time, and making a few refinements or implementing a few hints will help you achieve excellence. If you scored between 80 and 100, you should consider improving your time management skills. If you scored below 80, training in time management will considerably enhance your efficiency. (See note at top of the next page.)

Note: Sometimes people have markedly different scores in the two sections of this instrument. That is, they are better time managers at the office than in their personal lives, or vice versa. You may want to compute your scores for each section of the instrument and compare them.

Type A Personality Inventory (page 84)

Scoring Key

The Type A personality consists of four behavioral tendencies: extreme competitiveness, significant life imbalance (typically coupled with high work involvement), strong feelings of hostility and anger, and an extreme sense of urgency and impatience.

Scores above 12 in each area suggest this is a pronounced tendency.

Research suggests that the hostility aspect of the Type A personality is the most damaging to personal health.

Competitiveness		Life Imbalance (Work Involvement)		Hostility/Anger		Impatience/Urgency	
Item	Score	Item	Score	Item	Score	Item	Score
1	_____	2	_____	3	_____	4	_____
5	_____	6	_____	7	_____	8	_____
9	_____	10	_____	11	_____	12	_____
13	_____	14	_____	15	_____	16	_____
17	_____	18	_____	19	_____	20	_____
21	_____	22	_____	23	_____	24	_____
Total		Total		Total		Total	

Total Score

Creative Problem Solving (page 138)

Scoring Key

Skill Area	Items	Assessment Pre-	Post-
Rational Problem Solving	1, 2, 3, 4, 5	_____	_____
Creative Problem Solving	6, 7, 8, 9, 10, 11, 12, 13, 14, 15	_____	_____
Fostering Innovation	16, 17, 18, 19, 20, 21, 22	_____	_____

Total Score

Comparison Data

Compare your scores to three comparison standards: (1) Compare your score against the maximum possible (132). (2) Compare your scores with the scores of other students in your class. (3) Compare your scores to a norm group consisting of 500 business school students. In comparison to the norm group, if you scored

105 or above	you are in the top quartile.
94–104	you are in the second quartile.
83–93	you are in the third quartile.
82 or below	you are in the bottom quartile.

How Creative Are You? (page 140)

Scoring Key

Circle and add up the values assigned to each item. The values are as follows:

	A Agree	B Undecided or Don't Know	C Disagree		A Agree	B Undecided or Don't Know	C Disagree
1.	0	1	2	10.	1	0	3
2.	0	1	2	11.	4	1	0
3.	4	1	0	12.	3	0	−1
4.	−2	0	3	13.	2	1	0
5.	2	1	0	14.	4	0	−2
6.	−1	0	3	15.	−1	0	2
7.	3	0	−1	16.	2	1	0
8.	0	1	2	17.	0	1	2
9.	3	0	−1	18.	3	0	−1

	A Agree	B Undecided or Don't Know	C Disagree		A Agree	B Undecided or Don't Know	C Disagree
19.	0	1	2	30.	−2	0	3
20.	0	1	2	31.	0	1	2
21.	0	1	2	32.	0	1	2
22.	3	0	−1	33.	3	0	−1
23.	0	1	2	34.	−1	0	2
24.	−1	0	2	35.	0	1	2
25.	0	1	3	36.	1	2	3
26.	−1	0	2	37.	2	1	0
27.	2	1	0	38.	0	1	2
28.	2	0	−1	39.	−1	0	2
29.	0	1	2				

40. The following have values of 2:

energetic	dynamic	perceptive	dedicated
resourceful	flexible	innovative	courageous
original	observant	self-demanding	curious
enthusiastic	independent	persevering	involved

The following have values of 1:

self-confident	determined	informal	forward-looking
thorough	restless	alert	open-minded

The rest have values of 0.

Total Score [   ]

Comparison Data

95–116	Exceptionally creative
65–94	Very creative
40–64	Above average
20–39	Average
10–19	Below average
Below 10	Noncreative

Innovative Attitude Scale (page 142)

Scoring Key

Add up the numbers associated with your responses to the 20 items. When you have done so, compare that score to the following norm group (consisting of graduate and undergraduate business school students, all of whom were employed full time). Percentile indicates the percent of the people who are expected to score below you.

Score	Percentile
39	5
53	16
62	33
71	50
80	68
89	86
97	95

Applying Conceptual Blockbusting

The Bleak Future of Knowledge (page 179), Keith Dunn and McGuffey's Restaurant (page 180)

Observer's Feedback Form

After the group has completed its problem-solving task, take the time to give the group feedback on its performance. Also provide feedback to each individual group member, either by means of written notes or verbal comments.

Group Observation

1. Was the problem defined explicitly?
    a. To what extent was information sought from all group members?
    b. Did the group avoid defining the problem as a disguised solution?
    c. What techniques were used to expand or alter the definitions of the problem?

2. Were alternatives proposed before any solution was evaluated?
    a. Did all group members help generate alternative solutions without judging them one at a time?
    b. Did people build on the alternatives proposed by others?
    c. What techniques were used to generate more creative alternatives for solving the problem?

3. Was the optimal solution selected?
    a. Were alternatives evaluated systematically?
    b. Was consideration given to the realistic long-term effects of each alternative?

4. Was consideration given to how and when the solution could be implemented?
    a. Were obstacles to implementation discussed?
    b. Was the solution accepted because it solved the problem under consideration, or for some other reason?

5. How creative was the group in defining and solving the problem?

6. What techniques of conceptual blockbusting did the group use?

Individual Observation

1. What violations of the rational problem-solving process did you observe in this person?

2. What conceptual blocks were evident in this person?

3. What conceptual blockbusting efforts did this person make?

4. What was especially effective about the problem-solving attempts of this person?

5. What could this individual do to improve problem-solving skills?

Answers and Solutions to the Creativity Problems

Solution to the Roman numeral problem (page 152).

"S"IX   or   "6"   or   VI

Solution to the matchstick problem in Figure 1 (page 153).

Placing the match at the top turns the figure into a square root sign. The square root of 1 equals 1 ($\sqrt{1} = 1$).

Answer to the Shakespeare problem in Figure 2 (page 154).
5 inches. (Be careful to note where page 1 of Volume 1 is and where the last page of Volume 4 is.)

Common terms applying to both water and finance (page 155):

banks	deposits	capital drain
currency	frozen assets	sinking fund
cash flow	float a loan	liquid assets
washed up	underwater pricing	slush fund

Answer to the Descartes story (page 155).
At the foundation of Descartes' philosophy was the statement, "I think, therefore I am."

Solution to the block of wood problem in Figure 3 (page 155).

Source: McKim, 1972.

By turning the block with the bottom facing us, we see that it becomes a circle and fills the circle hole completely. By turning the block with the dark side toward us, we see that it becomes a square and fills the square hole completely. By turning the block to the side with the light side facing us, we see that it becomes a triangle and fills the triangle hole completely.

Solutions to the nine-dot problem in Figure 4 (page 156).

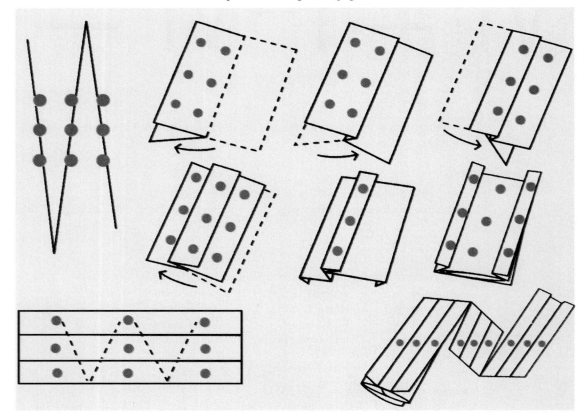

Solutions to embedded-patterns problem in Figure 5 (page 157).

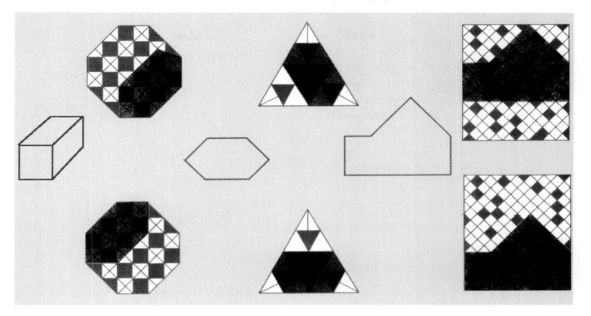

Solution to the fractionation problem in Figure 7 (page 166).

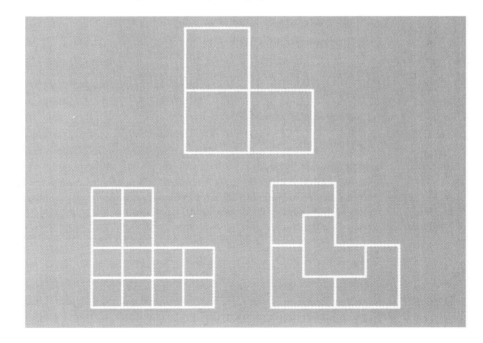

Communicating Supportively (page 190)

Scoring Key

Skill Area	Items	Assessment	
		Pre-	Post-
Knowledge of Coaching and Counseling	1, 2, 20	_____	_____
Providing Effective Negative Feedback	3, 4, 5, 6, 7, 8	_____	_____
Communicating Supportively	9, 10, 11, 12, 13, 14, 15, 16, 17, 18, 19	_____	_____
Total Score		☐	☐

Comparison Data

Compare your scores to three comparison standards: (1) Compare your score against the maximum possible (120). (2) Compare your own scores with the scores of other students in your class. (3) Compare your scores to a norm group consisting of 500 business school students. In comparison to the norm group, if you scored

99 or above	you are in the top quartile.
93–98	you are in the second quartile.
87–92	you are in the third quartile.
86 or below	you are in the bottom quartile.

Communication Styles (page 191)

Scoring Key

Part I: Identify the type of response pattern that you rely on most when required to be a coach or a counselor by adding the numbers you gave to the response alternatives in Part I. The chapter discusses the advantages and disadvantages of each of these response types. The most skilled supportive communicators score 9 or above on Reflecting responses and 6 or more on Probing responses. They score 2 or less on Advising responses and 4 or less on Deflecting responses.

Part II: Circle the alternative that you chose. The most skilled communicators select alternatives 1a, 2b, 3a, 4b, and 5a.

Part I

1. a. Deflecting response _____
   b. Probing response _____
   c. Advising response _____

3. a. Probing response _____
   b. Deflecting response _____
   c. Advising response _____

d. Reflecting response _____	d. Reflecting response _____
e. Deflecting response _____	e. Probing response _____
2. a. Reflecting response _____	4. a. Reflecting response _____
b. Deflecting response _____	b. Probing response _____
c. Advising response _____	c. Deflecting response _____
d. Reflecting response _____	d. Deflecting response _____
e. Probing response _____	e. Advising response _____

Part II

1. a. Problem-oriented statement
   b. Person-oriented statement
2. a. Incongruent/minimizing statement
   b. Congruent statement
3. a. Descriptive statement
   b. Evaluative statement

4. a. Invalidating statement
   b. Validating statement
5. a. Owned statement
   b. Disowned statement

Diagnosing Problems and Fostering Understanding

United Chemical Company (page 219), Byron vs. Thomas (page 221)

Observer's Feedback Form

As the observer, rate the extent to which the role-players performed the following behaviors effectively. Place the initials of each individual beside the number on the scale that best represents performance. Identify specific things that each person can do to improve his or her performance.

Rating
1 = Low
5 = High

Action

Role 1	Role 2	Role 3	
_____	_____	_____	1. Used problem-oriented communication.
_____	_____	_____	2. Communicated congruently.
_____	_____	_____	3. Used descriptive communication.
_____	_____	_____	4. Used validating communication.
_____	_____	_____	5. Used specific and qualified communication.
_____	_____	_____	6. Used conjunctive communication.

_____	_____	_____	7. Owned statements and used personal words.
_____	_____	_____	8. Listened attentively.
_____	_____	_____	9. Used a variety of response alternatives.

Comments:

Gaining Power and Influence (page 226)

Scoring Key

Skill Area	Item	Assessment Pre-	Post-
Gaining power			
(Personal characteristics)			
Expertise	1	_____	_____
	10	_____	_____
Personal attractions	2	_____	_____
	11	_____	_____
Effort	3	_____	_____
	12	_____	_____
Legitimacy	4	_____	_____
	13	_____	_____
(Position characteristics)			
Centrality	5	_____	_____
	14	_____	_____
Criticality	6	_____	_____
	15	_____	_____

Visibility	7	_____	_____
	16	_____	_____
Flexibility	8	_____	_____
	17	_____	_____
Relevance	9	_____	_____
	18	_____	_____
Using influence	19	_____	_____
	20	_____	_____
	21	_____	_____
	22	_____	_____
	23	_____	_____
Resisting influence	24	_____	_____
	25	_____	_____
	26	_____	_____
Increasing authority	27	_____	_____
	28	_____	_____
	29	_____	_____
	30	_____	_____

Total Score ☐ ☐

Comparison Data

Compare your scores to three comparison standards: (1) Compare your score with the maximum possible (180). (2) Compare your own scores with the scores of other students in your class. (3) Compare your scores to a norm group consisting of 500 business school students. In comparison to the norm group, if you scored

147 or above	you are in the top quartile.
138–146	you are in the second quartile.
126–137	you are in the third quartile.
125 or below	you are in the bottom quartile.

Using Influence Strategies (page 228)

Scoring Key

Retribution		Reciprocity		Reason	
Item	**Score**	**Item**	**Score**	**Item**	**Score**
1	_____	2	_____	3	_____
4	_____	5	_____	6	_____
7	_____	8	_____	9	_____
10	_____	11	_____	12	_____
13	_____	14	_____	15	_____
Total	[ ]	**Total**	[ ]	**Total**	[ ]

Primary influence strategy: (highest score) _____

Secondary influence strategy: (second highest score) _____

Neutralizing Unwanted Influence Attempts

Cindy's Fast Foods (page 268), 9:00 to 7:30 (page 269)

Observer's Feedback Form

Rating   *Action*
1 = Low
5 = High

Neutralizing Retribution Strategies

_____ 1. Used countervailing power to shift dependence to interdependence.
(Focused on the value of mutual respect and cooperation. Pointed out the negative consequences to both parties of exploitation. If appropriate, suggested alternatives.)

_____ 2. Confronted exploitative individuals directly.
(Challenged the right to intimidate and threaten. Stated what he/she was willing to do to stop actions.)

_____ 3. If necessary, actively resisted.
(If 1 and 2 failed, did what was necessary to stop retribution attempts. Minimized consequences of resistance on others.)

Neutralizing Reciprocity Strategies

_____ 4. Examined the intent of any gift or favor-giving activity.
(Asked questions to determine the motivation behind favors.)

_____ 5. Confronted unfair bargaining practices, for example, escalating or reciprocally compromising tactics.
(Questioned unfair bargaining tactics. Explored alternative ground rules.)

_____ 6. If necessary, refused to bargain with individuals who used high-pressure tactics.
(If 4 and 5 failed, terminated the negotiation process.)

Neutralizing Reason Strategies

_____ 7. Explained the negative effect of compliance on performance.
(Described effects on personal responsibilities of complying with request. If appropriate, suggested options.)

_____ 8. Defended personal rights.
(Assertively restated position, emphasizing personal rights.)

_____ 9. If necessary, refused to comply with request.
(If 7 and 8 failed, politely but firmly terminated discussion.)

Comments:

Diagnosing Poor Performance and Enhancing Motivation (page 276)

Scoring Key

Skill Area	Item	Assessment Pre-	Post-
Diagnosing performance problems	1	_____	_____
	11	_____	_____
Establishing expectations and setting goals	2	_____	_____
	12	_____	_____
Facilitating performance (Enhancing ability)	3	_____	_____
	13	_____	_____
	20	_____	_____
Liking performance to rewards and discipline	5	_____	_____
	14	_____	_____
	6	_____	_____
	15	_____	_____

Using salient internal and external incentives	7	_____	_____
	16	_____	_____
	8	_____	_____
	17	_____	_____
Distributing rewards equitably	9	_____	_____
	18	_____	_____
Providing timely and straightforward performance feedback	4	_____	_____
	10	_____	_____
	19	_____	_____
Total Score		☐	☐

Comparison Data

Compare your scores to three comparison standards: (1) Compare your score with the maximum possible (120). (2) Compare your scores with the scores of other students in your class. (3) Compare your scores to a norm group consisting of 500 business school students. In comparison to the norm group, if you scored

101 or above	you are in the top quartile.
94–100	you are in the second quartile.
85–93	you are in the third quartile.
84 or below	you are in the bottom quartile.

Work Performance Assessment
(page 277; page 311)

Scoring Key

Step 1: Enter your score from each line below, as follows:
Regular scoring: Enter the number for your response on the survey.
Reverse scoring: Subtract the number of your response from 6 and enter the result.

Items		*Score*	*Items*		*Score*
1.	Reverse	_____	8.	Regular	_____
2.	Reverse	_____	9.	Regular	_____
3.	Reverse	_____	10.	Regular	_____
4.	Reverse	_____	11.	Regular	_____
5.	Reverse	_____	12.	Regular	_____
6.	Reverse	_____	13.	Regular	_____
7.	Reverse	_____	14.	Regular	_____

Step 2: Combine your scores according to the type of performance problem. Problems with scores higher than 7 are obstacles to high performance. Total scores over 50 suggest significant, broad-based motivational deficiencies.

Type of Performance Problem	*Scores on items*		*Total of two items*
Perception	1. _____	8. _____	_____
Training	2. _____	9. _____	_____
Aptitude	3. _____	10. _____	_____
Resources	4. _____	11. _____	_____
Expectations	5. _____	12. _____	_____
Incentives	6. _____	13. _____	_____
Reward salience	7. _____	14. _____	_____

Total Score ☐

Reshaping Unacceptable Behaviors (page 312)

Shaheen Matombo

Observer's Feedback Form

Rating   *Action*
1 = Low
5 = High

Reprimand

_____ 1. Identified the specific inappropriate behavior. Gave examples. Indicated that the action must stop.

_____ 2. Pointed out the impact of the problem on the performance of others, the unit's mission, and so forth.

_____ 3. Asked questions about causes and explored remedies.

Redirection

_____ 4. Described the behaviors or standards expected. Made sure the individual understood and agreed that these are reasonable.

_____ 5. Asked if the individual would comply.

_____ 6. Was appropriately supportive. For example, praised other aspects of the person's work, identified personal and group benefits of compliance, and made sure there were no legitimate obstacles in the way of meeting stated expectations.

Reward

_____ 7. Identified rewards that were salient to the individual.

_____ 8. Linked the attainment of desirable outcomes with incremental, continuous improvement.

_____ 9. Rewarded (including using praise) all improvements in performance in a timely and honest manner.

Comments:

Managing Interpersonal Conflict (page 318)

Scoring Key

Skill Area	Items	Assessment Pre-	Post-
Initiating a complaint	1	_____	_____
	2	_____	_____
	3	_____	_____
	4	_____	_____
	5	_____	_____
	6	_____	_____
	7	_____	_____
	8	_____	_____
Responding to a criticism	9	_____	_____
	10	_____	_____
	11	_____	_____
	12	_____	_____
	13	_____	_____
	14	_____	_____
	15	_____	_____
	16	_____	_____
Mediating a conflict	17	_____	_____
	18	_____	_____
	19	_____	_____
	20	_____	_____
	21	_____	_____
	22	_____	_____
	23	_____	_____
	24	_____	_____
Total Score		☐	☐

Comparison Data

Compare your scores to three comparison standards: (1) Compare your score with the maximum possible (144). (2) Compare your scores with the scores of other students in your class. (3) Compare your scores to a norm group consisting of 500 practicing managers and business school students. In comparison to the norm group, if you scored

120 or above	you are in the top quartile.
116–119	you are in the second quartile.
98–115	you are in the third quartile.
97 and below	you are in the bottom quartile.

Strategies for Handling Conflict (page 319)

Scoring Key

	Forcing		*Accommodating*		*Compromising*
Item	**Score**	**Item**	**Score**	**Item**	**Score**
1	_____	2	_____	3	_____
6	_____	7	_____	8	_____
11	_____	12	_____	13	_____
16	_____	17	_____	18	_____
Total	☐	**Total**	☐	**Total**	☐

	Avoiding		*Integrating*
Item	**Score**	**Item**	**Score**
4	_____	5	_____
9	_____	10	_____
14	_____	15	_____
19	_____	20	_____
Total	☐	**Total**	☐

Primary conflict-management strategy: (highest score) _____

Secondary conflict-management strategy: (next-highest score) _____

Resolving Interpersonal Disputes

Freida Mae Jones (page 356), Can Larry Fit In? (page 359), Hartford Manufacturing Company (page 360)

Observer's Feedback Form

Rating   *Action*
1 = Low
5 = High

Initiator

_____ Maintained personal ownership of the problem, including feelings

_____ Avoided making accusations or attributing motives

_____ Succinctly described the problem (behaviors, outcomes, feelings)

_____ Specified expectations or standards violated

_____ Persisted until understood

_____ Encouraged two-way interaction

_____ Approached multiple issues incrementally (proceeded from simple to complex, easy to hard)

_____ Appealed to what the disputants had in common (goals, principles, constraints)

_____ Made a specific request for change

Respondent

_____ Showed genuine concern and interest

_____ Responded appropriately to the initiator's emotions

_____ Avoided becoming defensive or overreacting

_____ Sought additional information about the problem (shifted general to specific, evaluative to descriptive)

_____ Focused on one issue at a time, gradually broadening the scope of the discussion, searching for integrative solution

_____ Agreed with some aspect of the complaint (facts, perceptions, feelings, or principles)

_____ Asked for suggestions for making changes

_____ Proposed a specific plan of action

Mediator

_____ Treated the conflict and disputants seriously

_____ Broke down complex issues, separated the critical from the peripheral. Began with a relatively easy problem

	Helped disputants avoid entrenched positions by exploring underlying interests
_____	Remained neutral (facilitator, not judge)
_____	Pointed out the effect of the conflict on performance
_____	Kept the interaction issue oriented
_____	Made sure that neither party dominated conversation
_____	Kept conflict in perspective by emphasizing areas of agreement
_____	Helped generate multiple alternatives
_____	Made sure that both parties were satisfied and committed to the proposed resolution

Comments:

Effective Empowerment and Delegation (page 374)

		Assessment	
Skill Area	**Items**	**Pre-**	**Post-**
Personal mastery experiences	1, 2	_____	_____
Modeling	3, 4	_____	_____
Providing support	5, 6	_____	_____
Arousing positive emotions	7, 8	_____	_____
Providing information	9, 10	_____	_____
Providing resources	11, 12	_____	_____
Organizing teams	13, 14	_____	_____
Creating confidence	15, 16	_____	_____
Delegating work	17–26	_____	_____
Total Score		[ ]	[ ]

Comparison Data

Compare your scores to three comparison standards: (1) Compare your score against the maximum possible (156). (2) Compare your scores with the scores of other students in your class.

(3) Compare your scores to a norm group consisting of 500 business school students. In comparison to the norm group, if you scored

above 122	you are in the top quartile.
109 to 122	you are in the second quartile.
95 to 108	you are in the third quartile.
94 or below	you are in the bottom quartile.

Personal Empowerment Assessment (page 376)

Scoring Key

Skill Area	Items	Mean (Total/4)
Self-efficacy (competence)	2, 7, 12, 17	_____
Self-determination (choice)	3, 8, 13, 18	_____
Personal control (impact)	4, 9, 14, 19	_____
Meaningfulness (value)	1, 6, 11, 16	_____
Trust (security)	5, 10, 15, 20	_____

Comparison Data

Scores from approximately 3,000 middle managers in manufacturing and service organizations.

	Mean	Top 1/3	Bottom 1/3
Self-efficacy	5.76	> 6.52	< 5.00
Self-determination	5.50	> 6.28	< 4.72
Personal control	5.49	> 6.34	< 4.64
Meaningfulness	5.88	> 6.65	< 5.12
Trust	5.33	> 6.03	< 4.73

Empowering Chapter, Skill Practice Exercise
Hillside Oaks Advertising Company (page 410)

Customer Scoring Sheet

			Score		
Dimension	Terrific		OK		Ho-Hum
Innovativeness	5	4	3	2	1
Excitement	5	4	3	2	1
Probable effectiveness	5	4	3	2	1
Number of commercials	5	4	3	2	1
Overall quality	5	4	3	2	1
	Great Bargain		OK		Too High
Cost	5	4	3	2	1

Total Scores

Organization 1 _____   Organization 5 _____

Organization 2 _____   Organization 6 _____

Organization 3 _____   Organization 7 _____

Organization 4 _____

Team Development Behaviors (page 418)

Scoring Key

Skill Area	Items	Assessment Pre-	Assessment Post-
Diagnosing team development	1, 16	6	
Managing the forming stage	2–4	16	
Managing the conforming stage	6–9, 13	19	
Managing the storming stage	10–12, 14, 15	25	
Managing the performing stage	5, 17, 18, 19	19	
Total Score		85	

Comparison Data

Compare your scores to three comparison standards: (1) Compare your score against the maximum possible (144). (2) Compare your scores with the scores of other students in your class. (3) Compare your scores to a norm group consisting of 500 business school students. In comparison to the norm group, if you scored

90 or above	you are in the top quartile.
→77 to 89	you are in the second quartile.
63 to 76	you are in the third quartile.
Below 63	you are in the bottom quartile.

Jimmy Lincoln (page 463)

Role-Analysis Worksheet

1. If you are observing a team meeting being conducted, put check marks by the roles performed by the team members you are observing each time they make a comment or display behavior that matches one of the roles listed below. If you are analyzing your own team after it has completed its meeting, put names of team members next to the roles they played. (See pages 433–435 in the text for definitions of these roles.)

Task-Facilitating Roles

Direction-giving   _____

Information-seeking   _____

Information-giving   _____

Elaborating   _____

Coordinating   _____

Monitoring   _____

Process-analyzing   _____

Reality-testing   _____

Enforcing   _____

Summarizing   _____

Relationship-Building Roles

Supporting   _____

Harmonizing   _____

Tension-relieving   _____

Energizing   _____

Developing   _____

Facilitating   _____

Processing   _____

Blocking Roles

Overanalyzing   _____

Overgeneralizing   _____

Fault finding   _____

Premature decision making _____

Presenting opinions as facts _____

Rejecting   _____

Pulling rank   _____

Dominating   _____

Stalling   _____

What suggestions do you have for improvement in the team members' performance?

Making Oral and Written Presentations

Speaking as a Leader (page 489), Battle Creek Foods (page 491)

Observer's Feedback Form

Rating   *Action*
1 = Low
5 = High

Strategy

_____ 1. Identified the general and specific purposes.

_____ 2. Tailored the message to the audience's needs, attitudes, knowledge level, and so forth.

_____ 3. Met the expectations of the audience by using appropriate language and style.

Structure

_____ 4. Began with a forecast of the main ideas and captivated the audience's interest by giving them an important reason to listen.

_____ 5. Chose an appropriate organizational structure, for example, moved from familiar to unfamiliar and simple to complex.

_____ 6. Used transitions, including internal summaries, to signal progress.

_____ 7. Concluded on a high note; reinforced major points; summarized key actions.

Support

_____ 8. Used a variety of supporting information, examples, and so forth, to increase the credibility and understanding of major points.

_____ 9. Used supporting material (both the content and format of evidence and illustrations) appropriate for the audience.

_____ 10. Used effective, simple visual aids to enhance comprehension and retention of the message.

Style in Oral Communications

_____ 11. Used notes to create a conversational style.

_____ 12. Presentation had obviously been well-rehearsed, including the use of visual aids, and so forth.

_____ 13. Conveyed controlled enthusiasm for the subject through the tone of voice, posture, and facial expressions.

_____ 14. Engaged the audience through effective eye contact, physical arrangement of the room, and appropriate gestures.

Style in Written Communication

_____ 15. Document was mechanically precise, that is, it contained no errors that detracted from the message.

_____ 16. Document was factually precise, that is, the content was accurate.

_____ 17. The choice of words communicated the message clearly and unambiguously.

_____ 18. The tone matched the topic and the audience (e.g., formality, emotion, directness).

_____ 19. Used the appropriate format for the type of correspondence.

Supplement: Questions and Answers

_____ 20. Handled questions and challenges thoughtfully, candidly, and assertively.

_____ 21. Responded to objections in an orderly manner, for example, restated the objection, restated your position, offered further support for your position, and explained the significance of your rebuttal.

_____ 22. Maintained control of the meeting by balancing the demands of specific individuals with the interests of the group and keeping the discussion focused on the issues.

Information-Gathering Interview

New Employee-Orientation Program (page 514)

Observer's Feedback Form

Rating   *Action*

1 = Low
5 = High

Introduction

1. Did interviewer

_____   use a friendly greeting?

_____   begin to build rapport?

_____   state purpose?

_____   orient interviewee?

_____   refer to taking notes or recording interview?

Body

2. Did interviewer

_____   use appropriate question sequence?

_____   use a variety of question types?

_____   use internal summaries and transitions?

_____   respond to interviewee with good secondary questions (probes)?

_____   use silence when appropriate?

_____   maintain rapport with interviewee?

_____   handle problematic interviewee well?

Closing

3. Did interviewer

_____   sum up?

_____   maintain/encourage good interpersonal relationship?

_____   indicate what would happen with information?

_____   set up another meeting, if appropriate?

_____   thank interviewee?

Nonverbals

4. Did interviewer

_____ wear appropriate clothing?

_____ maintain eye contact with interviewee?

_____ use purposeful gestures?

_____ use appropriate tone of voice?

_____ maintain good posture?

_____ look enthusiastic and interested in what interviewee had to say?

_____ take notes inconspicuously?

_____ avoid verbal pauses such as uh, uhm, and so forth?

Comments:

Performance-Appraisal Interview

Chris Jakobsen (page 516)

Observer's Feedback Form

Rating   *Action*
1 = Low
5 = High

Introduction

1. Did interviewer

_____ use appropriate greeting?

_____ build rapport?

_____ orient interviewee to the interview?

_____ refer to taking notes?

Body

2. Did interviewer

_____ praise individual's strengths?

	focus on specific concerns?
_____	compare perceptions of the problems?
_____	probe for underlying causes?
_____	reach agreement on performance expectations and goals?
_____	discuss specific plans of action for improving deficiencies?
_____	make specific references to the appraisal form?

Conclusion

3. Did interviewer

_____	provide opportunity for interviewee to make suggestions and ask questions?
_____	summarize interview?
_____	specify when next appraisal interview will be held?

Nonverbals

4. Did interviewer

_____	use nonverbal behaviors to maintain open climate and good rapport?
_____	avoid use of uhs and uhms?
_____	maintain good posture?
_____	maintain eye contact?

Comments:

Employment-Selection Interview

Smith Farley (page 518)

Observer's Feedback Form

Rating   *Action*
1 = Low
5 = High

Opening

1. Did interviewer

_____	use appropriate greeting?

	build rapport?
_____	build rapport?
_____	orient interviewee to the interview?
_____	use appropriate transition to body of interview?

Body

2. Did interviewer

_____	clearly define structure of the interview?
_____	use transitions between topics?
_____	ask questions based on available information and needs?
_____	probe when necessary?
_____	solicit behavioral examples?

Closing

3. Did interviewer

_____	offer organizational or job information?
_____	invite questions?
_____	answer interviewee's questions appropriately and specifically?
_____	state when and how interviewee will be contacted?

Nonverbal

4. Did interviewer

_____	act poised?
_____	dress appropriately?
_____	speak articulately?
_____	act enthusiastically?
_____	use appropriate language style?
_____	maintain eye contact?
_____	use purposeful gestures?

Comments:

Exhibit 1 Interview With Chris Jakobsen (page 516)

Employee Performance Appraisal

DATA COMPLETED _____

NAME   Chris Jakobsen
DATE OF BIRTH   6/22/65
YEARS OF EMPLOYMENT   3
OFFICE LOCATION BRANCH 4   DEPARTMENTAL 9
DEPARTMENT   Commercial

PRESENT JOB TITLE   Loan Officer
CONVERSION CODE   32
YEARS IN PRESENT POSITION   6 months
SOC. SEC. NO.   555–33–9999
EDUCATION   B.A.—Business

Select the statement under each of the following categories that best describes the individual.

Quality of Work   General excellence of output with consideration to accuracy—thoroughness—dependability—without close supervision.

_____   Exceptionally high quality. Consistently accurate, precise, quick to detect errors in own and others' work.

_____   Work sometimes superior and usually accurate. Negligible amount needs to be redone. Work regularly meets standards.

_____   A careful worker. A small amount of work needs to be redone. Corrections made in reasonable time. Usually meets normal standards.

_____   Work frequently below acceptable quality. Inclined to be careless. Moderate amount of work needs to be redone. Excessive time to correct.

_____   Work often almost worthless. Seldom meets normal standards. Excessive amount needs to be redone.

Quantity of Work   Consider the amount of useful work over the period of time since the last appraisal. Compare the output of work to the standard you have set for the job.

_____   Output consistently exceeds standards. Unusually fast worker. Exceptional amount of output.

_____   Maintains a high rate of production. Frequently exceeds standards. More than normal effort.

_____   Output is regular. Meets standards consistently. Works at steady average speed.

_____   Frequently turns out less-than-normal amount of work. A low producer.

_____   A consistently low producer. Excessively slow worker. Unacceptable output.

Cooperation   Consider the employee's attitude toward the work, the employee's coworkers, and supervisors. Does the employee appreciate the need to understand and help solve problems with others?

_____   Always congenial and cooperative. Enthusiastic and cheerfully helpful in emergencies. Well liked by associates.

_____   Cooperates well. Understands and complies with all rules. Usually demonstrates a good attitude. Liked by associates.

_____   Usually courteous and cooperative. Follows orders but at times needs reminding. Gets along well with associates.

_____   Does only what is specifically requested. Sometimes complains about following instructions. Reluctant to help others.

_____   Unfriendly and uncooperative. Refuses to help others.

Knowledge of the Job   The degree to which the employee has learned and understands the various procedures of the job and their objectives.

_____   Exceptional understanding of all phases. Demonstrates unusual desire to acquire information.

_____   Thorough knowledge in most phases. Has interest and potential toward personal growth.

_____   Adequate knowledge for normal performance. Will not voluntarily seek development.

_____   Insufficient knowledge of job. Resists criticism and instruction.

_____   No comprehension of the requirements of job.

Dependability   The reliability of the employee in performing assigned tasks accurately and within the allotted time.

_____   Exceptional. Can be left on own and will establish priorities to meet deadlines.

_____   Very reliable. Minimal supervision required to complete assignments.

_____   Dependable in most assignments. Normal supervision required. A profitable worker.

_____   Needs frequent follow-up. Excessive prodding necessary.

_____   Chronic procrastinator. Control required is out of all proportion.

Attendance and Punctuality   Consider the employee's record, reliability, and ability to conduct the job within the unit's work rules.

_____   Unusual compliance and understanding of work discipline. Routine usually exceeds normal.

_____   Excellent. Complete conformity with rules but cheerfully volunteers time during peak loads.

_____   Normally dependable. Rarely needs reminding of accepted rules.

_____ Needs close supervision in this area. Inclined to backslide without strict discipline.

_____ Unreliable. Resists normal rules. Frequently wants special privileges.

Knowledge of Company Policy and Objectives   Acceptance, understanding, and promotion of company policies and objectives in the area of the employee's job responsibilities.

_____ Thorough appreciation and implementation of all policies. Extraordinary ability to express objectives and encourage others to meet them.

_____ Reflects knowledge of almost all policies related to this position.

_____ Acceptable but fairly superficial understanding of job objectives.

_____ Limited insight into job or company goals. Mentally restricted.

_____ Not enough information or understanding to permit minimum efficiency.

Initiative and Judgment   The ability and interest to suggest and develop new ideas and methods; the degree to which these suggestions and normal decisions and actions are sound.

_____ Ingenious self-starter. Superior ability to think intelligently.

_____ Very resourceful. Clear thinker—usually makes thoughtful decisions.

_____ Fairly progressive, with normal sense. Often needs to be motivated.

_____ Rarely makes suggestions. Decisions need to be checked before implementation.

_____ Needs detailed instructions and close supervision. Tendency to assume and misinterpret.

Supervisory or Technical Potential   Consider the employee's ability to teach and increase skills of others, to motivate and lead, to organize and assign work, and to communicate ideas.

_____ An accomplished leader who can earn respect and inspire others to perform. An articulate and artful communicator, planner, and organizer.

_____ Has the ability to teach and will lead by example rather than technique. Speaks and writes well and can organize and plan with help.

_____ Fairly well informed on job-related subjects but has some difficulty communicating with others. Nothing distinctive about spoken or written word.

_____ Little ability to implement. Seems uninterested in teaching or helping others. Careless speech and writing habits.

_____ Unable to be objective or reason logically. Inarticulate and stilted in expression.

Overall Rating   There are five alternatives in each category. The first alternative is worth 5 points, the last alternative is worth 1 point. Place a number from 1–5 by each of the selected alternatives and total the score for all nine categories. Then select the appropriate overall rating.

_____ Outstanding (45–39)

_____ Above Expected (38–32)

_____ Expected (31–23)

_____ Below Expected (22–16)

_____ Unsatisfactory (15–9)

Exhibit 2 Smith Farley Insurance Companies (page 518)

A. POSITIONS OPEN

1. *Programmer/Analyst*—Auto & Life Company Data Processing Trainee openings leading to Programmer/Analyst positions at the conclusion of *16-week* training program. The DP Trainee is trained in the programming skills necessary to either develop new or to revise data-processing programs that help administer over 10 million auto, life, fire, and health insurance policies.

2. *Analyst*—Computer Operations Support Trainee opening leading to *Analyst* positions at conclusion of a *nine-month* training program. Computer Operations Support is responsible for technical operations support for the Regional Data Processing Offices, including: developing operator procedures, developing and administering training, problem resolution, and coordinating implementation of new systems and major changes for Regional Data Processing Offices.

B. MAJORS CONSIDERED

We are recruiting for three Data Processing Departments (Auto Data Processing, Life Data Processing, and Computer Operations Support), each having different requirements, which are as follows:

1. *Auto Data Processing:* Strongly prefer Applied Computer Science, Computer Technology, and MIS majors, but will consider other majors with 12–15 hours of Computer Science academic background. Strongly prefer *3.0 overall GPA.*
   Logical analysis, problem-solving skills, and communication skills are important for expected job performance. Candidates should possess course work in *COBOL, C, C++,* and/or *Java.*

2. *Life Data Processing:* Most college majors are acceptable (i.e., mathematics, business or related majors, English, music, and science).

   Student must have a sincere interest in and aptitude for data processing. Only students with a *3.5 overall GPA* will be considered.

3. *Computer Operations Support:* Most business majors are acceptable (i.e., Business, Business Administration, Finance, Economics, Accounting, etc., with 6–10 hours of Computer Science academic background). Prefer a *3.0 overall GPA.*

   Student must have a sincere interest in and aptitude for data processing.

C. CITIZENSHIP REQUIREMENTS

Must be citizens or permanent residents.

D. LOCATION

These positions will be located at the corporate headquarters in Peoria, Illinois.

Exhibit 3 Interview Guide for Data Processing (DP) (page 519)

APPLICANT'S NAME _____   SCHOOL _____

INTERVIEW DATE _____   GPA _____

LOCATION _____ TIME _____   MAJOR _____

CRITERION	FOCUS	GENERAL QUESTIONS	APPLICANT-SPECIFIC QUESTIONS
Aptitude/ Knowledge	Determine if exposure to and retention of a high-level computer language and development methods are adequate.	Of the DP courses you have had, which was the most beneficial and why? Explain in detail the most difficult DP assignment you have had. How do you rate yourself as a programmer? Why?	
Interest/ Experience	Determine if interest and record of success in DP studies or work has been sustained (2+ years).	How did you first get interested in DP? What about it do you like the most? The least? Can you give me an example of a DP-related experience you have had that was satisfying? Not satisfying? What is your professional goal?	
Ability to work with others	Determine success of achieving results in team effort.	Do you feel you work more effectively on a one-to-one basis or in a group? Describe a situation in which you worked as a member of a team. What approach did you take to get people together and establish a common approach to the task?	

CRITERION	FOCUS	GENERAL QUESTIONS	APPLICANT-SPECIFIC QUESTIONS
Commitment/ Initiative	Determine level of success in achieving task completion in light of task complexity, adversity, load, level of knowledge, and so forth.	What approaches do you use to get people to accept your ideas or goals? What is a big obstacle you had to overcome to get where you are today? Do you consider yourself a self-starter or are you better at implementing the plans of others?	
Communication	Determine quality of written/spoken word.	Would you rather write a report or give a verbal report? Why? Do you think you are a good listener? What qualities do you need to be a good listener? How do you handle a situation when you are explaining something and the other person doesn't understand?	

Problem solving/ Decision making	Determine if applicant has a record of addressing relatively complex projects.	In your opinion, what are the most difficult problems with which a programmer/analyst must deal? What particular strengths do you have that allow you to deal with these problems? What design methods do you use to create a program? Describe how to use them. Describe the most complex program you have ever written.
Other:	Stability Maturity Leadership Personal appearance	

Exhibit 4 Resume (page 519)

WILLIAM L. HENDERSON II

Campus
700 North Camden #107
Normal, IL 61761
(309) 454–6178

Home
1915 Western Hills
Arlington Heights, IL 60004
(213) 255–5738

OBJECTIVE	*Analyst/Data Processing*
EDUCATION	Illinois Wesleyan University, Bloomington, Illinois—Expected Degree 1997

Major: Computer Science   Major GPA: 3.75
Business Administration   GPA: 3.03

EDUCATIONAL HIGHLIGHTS   Dean's List Spring Semester 1997
ACM Award Spring Semester 1997

STUDENT ACTIVITIES
ILLINOIS WESLEYAN UNIVERSITY
Member of Gamma Ray Social Fraternity (3 years)
    Pledge Class President; In House Activities; Intramurals; Offset Chairman; Social Committee.
Member of Varsity Football Team (2 years)

WORK SUMMARY (Part time during college)
CENTRAL STATES INSURANCE, Bloomington, IL
Auto/Divisional Programming—Corporate
Position: DP—Intern

ILLINOIS WESLEYAN UNIVERSITY, Bloomington, IL
Office of Admissions.
Position: Admissions Counselor Aid
Computer Lab
Position: Lab Assistant

(Summers)	PREMIER CHECK PRINTERS, INC., Des Plaines, IL Printing presses (2 years) *Position:* Press Assistant/Operation
	SOFTWARE, ETC., Arlington Heights, IL Sales, Inventory, Shipping, Ordering, Partial Management *Position:* Salesman
AVAILABILITY	June 1998
REFERENCES	References available upon request

Exhibit 5   Resume (page 519)

Bryan E. Jensen
4364 Peachtree Place
Lilburn, Georgia 30247
Home (404) 381–8909

OBJECTIVE   *Project Leader/Systems Analyst* with supervision potential

BACKGROUND   Anticipated the decline in manufacturing jobs and retrained in computer science. Presently have two associate degrees and four years of in-depth experience. Accepted temporary position at Caterpillar to gain experience. The economic recession in the midwest prompted my relocation to Atlanta. Accepted my present position to broaden my experience. I am now seeking a permanent career position with a midwest employer located in a "smaller" city. I will be an asset to a progressive company. I am well motivated, resourceful, versatile, work well with others, and accept responsibility readily.

HARDWARE   IBM 370—Models 3090E, 3083, 3084, 4341; IBM PC/XT; 486, Power PC

SOFTWARE   Case Tools: Knowledgeware GAMMA

Databases: IMS-DL/I, DBII—SQL, Access, Oracle

Communications: IMS—MFS, TSO—ISPF

Languages: C, C++, Java

Related: BTS, DDLTO, Fileaid-IMS, Datavatage, IMS-Online, SPUFI, QMF, OS/MVS-XA, JES2, Fileaid, Panvalet, Infopac, SDSF, JES-Master, Design/I, All-In-One, Diagram Master, Excel, Word Power Point

EXPERIENCE
03/97–   *Continental Service Corporation,* Macon, Georgia (Corporate)

Senior Systems Analyst/Team Leader

Guided planning, estimating, analysis, and development of major areas of IMB DB/DC Billing System. It has a 2.5 million customer base and is located in 42 states. Used Method/I life cycle/methodology. Utilized Pacdesign (Yourdon) for system design and Pacbase for completion of deliverables and code generation.

01/94–03/97   *Federal Reserve Bank,* Savannah, Georgia (Corporate)

Project Leader (10/96–03/97)

Supervised eight analysts and programmers through the implementation of a billing system for Federal Reserve Districts throughout the United States. Presented written and verbal status reports, employee-performance reviews, and time-planning estimates/schedules to upper management.

(09/95–10/96)
Led development of IMS DB/DC billing system. Analyzed requirements to produce data-flow diagrams and logical data model. Participated in team presentation of system. Created program specifications. Investigated and resolved code-generation problems. Provided support to other team members.

(01/95–08/95)
Received Merit Award for outstanding performance. Designed, programmed, and tested accounting interface to all corporate IBM and branch Unisys applications. Provided training and support during parallel test and acceptance of accounting system. Redirected installation efforts for an accounting deposit module that had fallen behind. Provided production support of newly implemented accounting system.

(04/94–12/94)
Installed accounting software from tape. Modified all JCL to district standards. Installed and modified job-submission system. Documented and instructed the users on the system and the results of each job.

(01/94–03/94)
Designed, wrote, tested, and documented IMB DB/DC programs for system used to report the dollar amount of checks as they clear the Reserve.

03/93–12/93   *Caterpillar Tractor Company,* Chicago, Illinois (Corp.)

Programmer

Programmed, tested, and documented IMS DB/DC programs from specifications for Man and Material Management System. (Due to be laid off 01/94)

04/87–06/91   Skilled Trades Machinist (last position held—layoff)

EDUCATION   Illinois Central College; East Peoria, Illinois—1991, Associate in Applied Science, Data Processing Technology

Bradley University; Peoria, Illinois (1988–1989)

Fifteen hours past Associate toward Manufacturing B.S.

Illinois Central College; East Peoria, Illinois—1985, Associate in Applied Science, Manufacturing Technology.

PERSONAL   Married, one child. Enjoy outdoor activities. Well motivated.

References available upon request.

Exhibit 6 Resume (page 519)

Mary Lynn Smith
3922 North Blair Street
New Orleans, Louisiana 70117
(504) 945–6077

CAREER OBJECTIVES
Entry-level position in Artificial Intelligence research with an industrial firm and eventual managerial capacity in such a firm.

EDUCATION
Dillard University, Division of Natural Sciences, New Orleans, LA.
B.S. degree, Mathematics major with Computer Science minor, May 1989, G.P.A.: 3.58/4.0 (overall), 3.82/4.0 (major)

Courses in Mathematics:

Calculus I, II, III	Complex Variables	
Modern Algebra I & II	Real Algebra	Differential Equations
Advanced Calculus	Linear Algebra	Engineering Statistics

Courses in Computer Science:

Computer Fundamentals	BASIC	Advanced BASIC
Systems Analysis	Pascal	FORTRAN

HONORS AND ACTIVITIES
University academic scholarship, University and National Dean's Lists, Kappa Beta Alpha and Beta Kappa Tau Honor Societies, Kappa Delta Pi Mathematics Society, and Dillard University Concert Choir.

WORK EXPERIENCE

Computer Services, Inc., Systems Operator/Payroll Processor, Summer, 1997.
—Performed system backups, file verification, programming, and payroll processing.
—Verified payroll figures and prepared tax reports.

Black Computer Operators Association, Teacher, 8/96.
—Prepared the South New Orleans Computer Science Team for a national competition. The South New Orleans Team placed first in the national competition.

Washington Elementary School, Summer Mini Camp, Teacher, 7/96–8/96.
—Taught children how to use computers and educational software.

—Responsible for computer lab and equipment.

Dillard University, Math/Computer Science Institute, Student Administrator/Teacher, 6/96–7/96.
—Organized the program and recruited personnel.
—Taught high school students advanced BASIC programming skills.

Preparing and Conducting a Meeting at SSS Software (page 531)

1. To what extent were the seven rules of effective meeting process followed in the meeting? Rate each step in terms of its effectiveness in the team meeting.

Effective			*Ineffective*	
5	4	3	2	1

Effective   **Ineffective**

_____ 1. Review purpose

_____ 2. Make introductions

_____ 3. Establish ground rules

_____ 4. Hear reports

_____ 5. Use informational displays

_____ 6. Ensure participation

_____ 7. Summarize conclusions

2. To what extent were there "difficult team members" in the team? If someone was difficult, was he or she managed effectively using appropriate techniques? Describe what happened.

Meeting Evaluation Worksheet

1. What is the specific purpose of the meeting?
2. Who was invited to attend? How are they contacted? Was the way in which the meeting was announced appropriate (e.g., face-to-face, E-mail, secretary phone call)?
3. Was the agenda that was constructed consistent with the rules? Specifically, did it follow these rules:

_____   The Agenda Rule (action words)

_____   The Rule of Sixths (past and future events)

_____   The Rule of Thirds (items divided into thirds)

_____ The Reports Rule (reports from team members early)

_____ The Agenda Bell Rule (a specific time line)

_____ The Temporal Integrity Rule (a time line planned)

_____ The Minutes Rule (someone assigned to keep minutes)

4. What was done especially well in preparing for this meeting?

5. What could have been improved upon? What was omitted?

Glossary

ability: the product of aptitude multiplied by training and opportunity.

accommodating approach: a response to conflict that tries to preserve a friendly interpersonal relationship by satisfying the other party's concerns while ignoring one's own. It generally ends with both parties losing.

accurate feedback: honest and open appraisal of subordinates' performance that is essential to an effective motivational program.

advising response: a response that provides direction, evaluation, personal opinion, or instructions.

alarm stage: initial response to stress characterized by increases in anxiety, fear, sorrow, or depression.

altruistic-nurturing: a type of personality that seeks gratification through promoting harmony with others and enhancing their welfare without expectation of reward.

ambidextrous thinking: the use of both the left and right sides of the brain, indicative of the most creative problem solvers.

analytic-autonomizing: a type of personality that seeks gratification through the achievement of self sufficiency, self-reliance, and logical orderliness.

anticipatory stressor: the anxious expectation of unfamiliar, uncertain, or disagreeable events.

artificial constraints: arbitrary boundaries placed around a problem that restrict possible alternative approaches and make the problem impossible to solve creatively.

assertive-directing: the type of personality that seeks gratification through self-assertion and directing the activities of others with the expectation of reward.

autonomy: the freedom to choose how and when to do a particular task; one of the characteristics of an intrinsically satisfying job.

avoiding response: an unassertive, uncooperative reaction to conflict that neglects the interests of both parties by side-stepping the issue. The resulting frustration may engender power struggles as others rush to fill the leadership vacuum.

basic curve: representing basic, required work of a team.

benefiting the boss: influencing upward by providing benefits that are not requested or expected.

bias against thinking: the inclination to avoid mental work, one indication of the conceptual block, complacency.

bipolar question: question that gives interviewees only two limited options to choose from in answering. The result may be inaccurate information.

brainstorming: a technique designed to help people solve problems by generating alternative solutions without prematurely evaluating and rejecting them.

centrality: the attribute of a position in which the occupant is a key member of informal networks of task-related and interpersonal relationships. The resulting access to information, resources, and the personal commitment of others is an important source of power.

clarification probe: question(s) designed to clarify information given by the interviewee.

closed questions: interview questions designed to elicit specific information from interviewees by restricting the possible answers the interviewee can give. Useful when time is limited and/or when answers to open questions need clarifying.

585

coaching: interpersonal communication used by managers to pass along advice and information or to set standards for subordinates.

cognitive dissonance reduction: individuals strive to reduce inconsistencies between their own beliefs and behaviors and their expectations of others.

cognitive style: the manner in which an individual gathers and evaluates information he/she receives.

cognitive style strategies: particular problem-solving patterns established in individuals by the way they take in, code, and store information.

collaborating response: the cooperative, assertive, problem-solving mode of responding to conflict. It focuses on finding solutions to the basic problems and issues that are acceptable to both parties rather than on finding fault and assigning blame. Of the conflict-management approaches, this is the only win-win strategy.

commitment: the conceptual block that results when an individual endorses a particular point of view, definition, or solution.

competition-cooperation: studies consistently show that groups whose members are working toward a common goal perform more effectively and produce higher levels of member satisfaction than groups whose members seek to fulfill individual needs or pursue competing goals.

complacency: the conceptual block that occurs not because of poor thinking habits or inappropriate assumptions but because of fear, ignorance, self-satisfaction, or mental laziness.

compression: the conceptual block that results from an individual's looking at a problem too narrowly, screening out too much relevant data, or making assumptions that inhibit solving the problem.

compromising response: a reaction to conflict that attempts to find satisfaction for both parties by "splitting the difference." If overused, it sends the message that settling disputes is more important than solving problems.

conceptual blocks: mental obstacles that restrict the way a problem is defined and limit the number of alternative solutions that might otherwise be considered.

conforming stage: second stage of team development; members experience pressure to conform to the emerging norms.

conformity level: the second level of values maturity, at which moral reasoning is based on agreement with and support of society's conventions and expectations.

congruence: exactly matching the communication, verbally and nonverbally, to what an individual is thinking and feeling.

conjunctive communication: connection of responses to previous messages in such a way that conversation flows smoothly.

constancy: the conceptual block that results from using only one way to look at a problem—to approach, define, describe, or solve it.

continuous improvement: small, incremental changes team members initiate.

core competence: an aggregation of individual team member skills, including knowledge, styles, communication patterns, and ways of behaving.

counseling: interpersonal communication used to help subordinates recognize their own problems rather than offering advice, direction, or a right answer.

creative problem solving: a method of solving problems that involves 4 stages: preparation, incubation, illumination, and verification.

criticality: the attribute of a position that makes it uniquely valuable to an organization. Such a position usually guarantees power to the occupant since it involves specific, highly technical tasks that cannot be shared or delegated.

deep breathing: relaxation technique of taking several successive, slow deep breaths, then exhaling completely.

deep relaxation technique: an approach for use in building psychological resiliency in which both body and mind become completely relaxed.

defensiveness: focusing on self-defense rather than listening; occurs when an individual feels threatened or punished by the communication.

deflecting response: a response that switches the focus from the communicator's subject to one selected by the listener; or simply the change of subject by the listener.

delegation: assignment of responsibility for tasks to subordinates.

descriptive communication: objective description of the event or behavior that needs modification; description of the reaction to the behavior or its consequences; and suggestion of a more acceptable alternative.

dignity (and liberty): the ethical decision principle that a decision is right and proper if it preserves the basic humanity of individuals and provides the opportunity for them to have greater freedom.

direct analogies: a synectic problem-solving technique in which individuals apply facts, technology, and previous experience to solving a problem.

disciplining: a motivational strategy by which a manager reacts negatively to an employee's undesirable behavior in order to discourage further occurrences. Disciplining may be useful up to a point but does not encourage exceptional performance.

disconfirmation: a "put-down"; or the feeling resulting from communication that demeans or belittles the recipient and threatens his or her sense of self-worth.

disjunctive communication: responses that are disconnected from what was stated before. It can result from (1) a lack of equal opportunity to speak; (2) long pauses in a speech or before a response; or (3) when one person decides the topic of conversation.

disowned communication: attribution to an unknown person, group, or some external source; allows the communicator to avoid responsibility for the message and therefore avoid investing in the interaction.

distributive approach: negotiation tactic that requires both parties to sacrifice something to resolve the conflict—to divide up a "fixed pie." (Contrast with the integrative approach.)

distributive justice: the ethical decision principle that a decision is right and proper if it benefits the least advantaged individuals.

dominant personality characteristics: those aspects of an individual's personality, such as altruism, assertiveness, and analyzing, that determine the type of conflict-handling strategy he or she prefers. The most effective managers use a variety of styles, tailoring their response to the situation.

double-barreled question: a problematic question that actually consists of two questions that should be asked separately in order to avoid confusing the interviewee.

effort: an important source of power suggesting personal commitment.

elaboration probe: question(s) designed to pursue a topic further when an interviewee has responded with superficial or inadequate information.

employment-selection interview: an interview designed to help current organizational members choose new members on the basis of experience, work skills, and personal suitability for the job.

empowerment: the use of acquired power to give others power in order to accomplish objectives; it strikes a balance between lack of power and abuse of power.

enactive strategy: a method of managing stress that creates a new environment by eliminating the stressors.

encounter stressor: the type of stressor that results from interpersonal conflict.

enigma of self-awareness: the problem inherent in learning about oneself. Although self knowledge is a prerequisite for growth and improvement, it may also inhibit that growth and improvement because of the individual's fear of and resistance to self-revelation.

environmental stress: conflict-fostering tension induced by such organizational factors as budget-tightening or uncertainty caused by rapid, repeated change.

equity: workers' perceptions of the fairness of rewards based on the comparison of what they are getting out of the work relationship (outcomes) to what they are putting into it (input).

error detection: reactive or defensive approach to quality; errors identified after the fact.

error prevention: second phase of quality, emphasis is on avoiding mistakes by producing a product or service right the first time.

evaluative communication: a statement that makes a judgment about or places a label on other individuals or on their behavior.

excitement curve: representing innovations and breakthroughs in task accomplishment and service delivery.

expertise: cognitive ability resulting from formal training and education or from on-the-job experience;

an important source of power in a technological society.

external locus: the viewpoint of an individual who attributes the outcome of his/her actions to outside forces.

external motivators: rewards for performances that are controlled by someone other than the employee—usually the supervisor—such as appreciation, job security, or good working conditions (Compare with internal motivators.)

extra effort: working extraordinarily hard, especially on behalf of superiors; can gain an individual more power in an organization than his or her position in the hierarchy warrants.

fantasy analogies: a synetic problem-solving technique in which individuals ask, "In my wildest dreams, how would I wish the problem to be resolved?"

feedback: information regularly received by individuals from superiors about their performance on a job. Knowledge of results permits workers to understand how their efforts have contributed to organizational goals.

feeling strategy: a method of interpreting and judging information subjectively or impressionistically rather than objectively; one which defines and redefines a problem on a trial-and-error basis.

flexibility: the freedom to exercise one's judgment—an important prerequisite for gaining power in a position—particularly in tasks that are high in variety and novelty.

flexibility of thought: the diversity of ideas or concepts generated.

flexible communication: the result of the willingness of the coach or counselor to accept the existence of additional data or other alternatives and to acknowledge that other individuals may be able to make significant contributions both to the problem solution and to the relationship.

fluency of thought: the number of ideas or concepts produced in a given length of time.

forcing response: an assertive, uncooperative response to conflict that uses the exercise of authority to satisfy one's own needs at the expense of another's.

forming stage: first stage of team development where team is oriented to each other and establishes clarity of purpose.

funnel sequence: a sequence of interview questions that begins with general questions and moves toward more and more specific questions.

goal characteristics: effective goals are specific, consistent, and appropriately challenging.

goal setting: the foundation of an effective motivational program, which consists of (1) including employees in the goal-setting process; (2) setting specific, consistent, and challenging goals; and (3) providing feedback.

goal-setting process: the critical consideration is that goals must be understood and accepted if they are to be effective.

group shift: the polarization effect that occurs during intensive group discussions as individuals tend to adopt a more extreme version of the position they held at the beginning of the meeting. The tendency is usually toward a risk-taking rather than a conservative stance.

groupthink: one of the pitfalls in group decision making that occurs when the pressure to reach consensus interferes with critical thinking. When the leader or the majority appears to prefer a particular solution, holders of dissenting views are reluctant to speak out.

hardiness: a combination of the three characteristics of a highly stress-resistant personality—control, commitment, and challenge.

high involvement teams: organized to affect an entire organization, function like semi-independent businesses; formed to build empowerment of employees.

homogeneity-heterogeneity: members of a homogeneous group share similar backgrounds, personalities, knowledge, and values. Due to this sameness, these groups tend to produce mundane and unimaginative outcomes. Members of a heterogeneous group are dissimilar and because of their differences are apt to be better at addressing novel, complex tasks.

idea champion: person who comes up with the innovative solutions to problems.

ignoring: a manager's neglect of both the performance and the satisfaction of employees. Such a lack of effective leadership can paralyze a work unit.

ignoring commonalities: a manifestation of the commitment block—the failure to identify similarities among seemingly disparate situations or data.

illumination stage: in creative thought, the third stage, which occurs when an insight is recognized and a creative solution is articulated.

imagery and fantasy: a relaxation technique using visualization to change focus of one's thoughts.

imperviousness in communication: the failure of the communicator to acknowledge the feelings or opinions of the listener.

imposing: a manager's exploitation of employees by assigning tasks with the sole emphasis on performance and without regard to their job satisfaction—usually disastrous in the long term.

incongruence: a mismatch between what one is experiencing and what one is aware of, or a mismatch between what one feels and what one communicates.

incubation stage: an early stage in creative thought in which mostly unconscious mental activity combines unrelated thoughts in pursuit of a solution to a problem.

indifference: a type of communication where the other person's existence or importance is not acknowledged.

indulging: a manager's emphasis on employee satisfaction to the exclusion of employee performance; the resulting country-club atmosphere hinders productivity.

information deficiencies: breakdowns in interorganizational communication. Conflicts based on the resulting misunderstandings tend to be common but easy to resolve.

information-gathering interview: an interview used to gather facts about an issue or to help in a problem-solving situation. Unlike other interviews, the interviewer can choose the interviewee.

initiator role: the part played in a conflict management model by the individual who first registers a complaint with another person who is the "responder." (See Behavioral Guidelines in the chapter on Managing Conflict.)

innovation: large, visible, discontinuous changes; breakthroughs.

innovation with continuous improvement: quality phase focused on improving performance rather than preventing errors.

innovativeness: fostering new ideas among individuals by methods such as placing them in teams and separating them at least temporarily from the normal pressures of organizational life.

instrumental values: those values that prescribe desirable standards of conduct or methods to reach a goal.

integrating: a motivation strategy that emphasizes job performance and job satisfaction equally—a challenging strategy for a manager to implement, but one that can result in both high productivity and high morale of employees.

integrative approach: negotiation tactic in which the focus is on collaborative ways of "expanding the pie" by avoiding fixed, incompatible positions. (Contrast with distributive approach.)

interchange incompatibility: the inability of individuals to communicate effectively owing to their having different interpersonal needs.

internal locus: the viewpoint of an individual who attributes the success or failure of particular behavior to his/her own actions.

internal motivators: job characteristics inherent in the job itself, over which the manager has no control and that determine whether or not a particular employee will find that job interesting and satisfying. (Compare with external motivators.)

interpersonal compatibility: the matching of individuals' needs.

interpersonal competence: the ability to manage conflict, to build and manage high-performance teams, to conduct efficient meetings, to coach and counsel employees, to provide negative feedback in constructive ways, to influence others' opinions, and to motivate and energize employees.

interpersonal orientation: the aspect of self-awareness that relates to behavior and relationships with other people.

interview: a specialized form of communication conducted for a specific task-related purpose.

intuitive strategy: a type of thinking that uses preconceived notions about the sort of information that will be relevant and looks for commonalities among the various elements of data.

invalidating communication: that which denies the other person the possibility of contributing to the communication.

inverted funnel sequence: a sequence of interview questions that begins with specific questions and moves toward more and more general questions.

issue selling: influence strategy characterized by being the champion or representative of an issue.

Janusian thinking: thinking contradictory thoughts at the same time; conceiving two opposing ideas to be true concurrently.

job-involvement teams: self-managing work teams organized to accomplish tasks; team members take responsibility to teach one another their own jobs.

leading question: a tricky interview question that includes the desired answer in the question itself. While useful in a sales interview, it can lead to biased answers in other types of interviews.

left-hemisphere thinking: brain activity concerned with logical, analytic, linear, or sequential tasks.

legitimacy: conformity with an organization's value system and practices, which increases one's acceptance and thus one's influence in that organization.

level of initiative: the extent to which a subordinate is expected to take a task. At least five levels can be identified: (1) wait to be told; (2) ask what to do; (3) recommend, then act; (4) report after acting; and (5) act independently.

life balance: the development of resiliency in all areas of one's life in order to handle stress that cannot be eliminated.

locus of control: the second dimension of orientation toward change; the viewpoint from which an individual judges the extent to which he/she controls his/her own destiny.

mediator role: the conflict-management role played by the third party who intervenes in a dispute between an "initiator" and a "responder."

morphological forced connections: a technique to expand alternative solutions by forcing the integration of seemingly unrelated elements. The four steps are (1) writing down the problem; (2) listing its attributes; (3) listing alternatives to each attribute; and (4) combining different alternatives from the attributes list.

motivation: a combination of desire and commitment demonstrated by effort.

muscle relaxation: technique of relaxation by easing the tension in successive muscle groups.

need for affection: the drive for close personal relationships with others while preserving one's separateness.

need for control: the desire to maintain for oneself a satisfactory balance of power and influence in relationships.

need for inclusion: the basic desire of people to maintain relationships and share activities with others.

negotiation strategies: tactics used in the bargaining phase of negotiation—collaborating, forcing, and accommodating—that are consistent with the related conflict management approaches and have about the same outcomes.

neutralizing influence attempts: techniques of resisting or counteracting the three principal influence strategies: retribution, reciprocity, and reason.

nominal group technique (NGT): a group decision-making technique; a highly structured form of brainstorming. In an NGT session, group members (1) individually write down as many alternative solutions to a problem as they can think of, (2) report their ideas, which are transcribed onto a flip-chart, (3) discuss the ideas briefly for clarification only, and (4) vote for the alternatives they prefer. The process is repeated until a consensus is reached.

noninquisitiveness: the failure to ask questions, obtain information or search for data; an example of the complacency block.

open questions: interview questions designed to elicit general information from interviewees—how they feel, what their priorities are, and how much they know about a topic. Useful for establishing rapport, they can be time consuming.

orchestrator: person who brings together cross-functional groups and necessary political support to facilitate implementation of a creative idea.

orientation toward change: an individual's adaptability to ever-increasing levels of ambiguity and turbulence.

originator incompatibility: the stalemate that occurs when either both people want to initiate in an area or neither does.

owned communication: statements for which a person takes responsibility, acknowledging that he or she is the source of the message; an indication of supportive communication.

participants: individuals invited to attend a meeting.

perceptual stereotyping: defining a problem by using preconceptions based on past experience, thus preventing the problem from being viewed in novel ways.

performance: the product of ability multiplied by motivation.

performance-appraisal interview: an interview designed to evaluate the past performances of a member of the organization and provide that member a means of feedback for the purpose of improving job performance.

performing stage: stage of a team where it is able to function as a highly effective and efficient unit.

personal analogies: recommended as part of synectics, whereby individuals try to identify themselves as the problem, asking the question, "If I were the problem, what would I like? What would satisfy me?"

personal attraction: "likability" stemming from agreeable behavior and attractive physical appearance; a combination of behaviors normally associated with friendship that have been shown to contribute to managerial success.

personal attributes: person's characteristics that determine one's power in an organization.

personal control: empowerment feeling that through one's own actions, a person can influence what happens; a sense of impact.

personal differences: variations among individuals' values and needs that have been shaped by different socialization processes. Interpersonal conflicts stemming from such incompatibilities are the most difficult for a manager to resolve.

personal management interview program: a regularly scheduled, one-on-one meeting between a manager and his or her subordinates.

personal morality: the ethical code that a decision is right and proper if it is consistent with a set of guidelines taught by a religious organization, family, etc.

personal values: an individual's standards that define what is good/bad, worthwhile/worthless, desirable/undesirable, true/false, moral/immoral.

planning: preparation for the meeting agenda.

position characteristics: person's title and rank that determine one's power in an organization.

preparation stage: a stage in creative thought that includes gathering data, defining the problem, generating alternatives, and consciously examining all available information.

principled level: the third and highest level of values maturity in which an individual judges right from wrong by following internalized principles developed from personal experience.

proactive strategy: a method of managing stress that initiates action in order to resist the negative effects of stress.

probing response: a response that asks a question about what the communicator just said or about a topic selected by the listener.

problem-solving teams: small groups of workers who meet for an hour or two each week to discuss ways to improve.

process: a sequential set of activities designed to lead to a specific outcome.

process analysis: step in process management used to identify a better way to perform a particular process.

process assessment: identification of the sequence of tasks, activities, and individuals involved in delivering an output.

process improvement: stage in process management where process itself is changed so as to foster advancement.

process management: the assessment, analysis, and improvement of sets of activities engaged in by teams.

process map: shows each of the activities in relationship to one another.

purpose: the reason a meeting is held, including information sharing, commitment building, information disseminating, and problem solving and decision making.

quality circles: Japanese problem-solving teams who meet to discuss issues and make recommendations to upper management.

rational problem solving: a method of solving problems that involves four steps: (1) defining the problem; (2) generating alternative solutions; (3) evaluating and selecting an alternative; and (4) implementing and following up on the solution.

reactive strategy: a method for managing stress that copes with the stressors immediately, temporarily reducing their effects.

reason: the influence strategy that relies on persuasion and appeal to rational consideration of the inherent merits of the request in order to gain compliance. It is explicit and direct, not manipulative.

reassigning: moving the poor performer to a position more consonant with his or her skill level and aptitude.

reciprocal incompatibility: the stalemate that occurs when there is no match between one person's expressed behavior and another's wanted behavior.

reciprocity: an influence strategy through which a manager uses bargaining as a tool for exacting a subordinate's compliance. This approach operates on the principle of self-interest and respect for the value of the interpersonal relationship.

redirection: a behavior-shaping process that follows a reprimand and gives the offender the opportunity to receive a future reward by modifying his or her behavior.

refitting: adapting the requirements of a job to an employee's abilities in order to improve poor performance.

reflecting response: a response that serves two purposes: (1) to confirm a message that was heard and (2) to communicate understanding and acceptance of the other person.

reflective probe: nondirective question(s) used for either elaboration or clarification of information; it generally mirrors or repeats some aspect of the interviewee's last answer.

reframing: stress reduction technique of redefining a situation as manageable.

rehearsal: relaxation technique of trying out stressful scenarios and alternative reactions.

relational algorithm: a blockbusting technique for combining unrelated attributes in problem solving by connecting words to force a relationship between two elements in a problem.

relationship-building roles: those that emphasize the interpersonal aspects of the team.

releasing: the last management option for solving a problem of poor performance—termination of employment.

relevance: the characteristic of a position whose tasks relate most closely to the dominant competitive goals of an organization and therefore enhance the power of the occupant.

repetition probe: a repeated or paraphrased question used if the interviewee has not directly answered a question the first time.

reprimand: a behavior-shaping approach used to transform unacceptable behaviors into acceptable ones; the discipline should be prompt and it should focus on the specific behavior.

resiliency: one's capacity to cope with stress.

resistance stage: response to stress in which defense mechanisms predominate.

respectful communication: treating subordinates as worthwhile, competent, and insightful by emphasizing joint problem solving rather than projecting a superior position.

responder role: the part played in a conflict-management model by the person who is supposedly the source of the "initiator's" problem.

resupplying: managerial option for overcoming an employee's lack-of-ability problem that focuses on supplying the support needed to do the job.

retraining: a management tool for overcoming the problem of an employee's poor performances, especially needed in rapidly changing technical work environments.

retribution: an influence strategy that involves a threat—the denial of expected rewards or the imposition of punishment. It usually triggers an aversive response in the subordinate and the breakdown of the interpersonal relationship.

reversibility: the ethical decision principle that a decision is right and proper if the individual making the decision would be willing to be treated in the same way.

reverse the definition: a tool for improving and expanding problem definition by reversing the way you think of the problem.

rewarding: the motivational strategy that links desired behaviors with employee-valued outcomes. Such positive reinforcement gives an employee more incentive for exceptional accomplishment than does disciplining.

right-hemisphere thinking: mental activity concerned with intuition, synthesis, playfulness, and qualitative judgment.

rigidity in communication: a type of message that portrays the communication as absolute, unequivocal, or unquestionable.

role incompatibility: the conflict-producing difference between workers whose tasks are interdependent but whose priorities differ because their responsibilities within the organization differ. The mediation of a common superior is usually the best solution.

rule breaker: person who goes beyond organizational boundaries and barriers to ensure the success of an innovation.

self-awareness: a knowledge of one's own personality and individuality.

self-centered level: the first level of values maturity. It contains two stages of values development, moral reasoning and instrumental values, which are based on personal needs or wants and the consequences of an act.

self-determination: feelings of having a choice.

self-disclosure: the revealing to others of ambiguous or inconsistent aspects of oneself, a process necessary for growth.

self-efficacy: empowered feeling of possessing the capability and competence to perform a task successfully.

self-managing teams: most advanced form of teamwork; maintain all responsibilities with the team that are normally spread across multiple levels and functions on an ongoing basis.

sensing strategy: a method of interpreting and judging information that is rational; it uses few preconceptions about what may be relevant and therefore examines the information closely and thoroughly, looking for uniqueness.

sensitive line: an invisible boundary around one's self-image, which if threatened, will evoke a strong defensive reaction.

separating figure from ground: the ability to filter out inaccurate, misleading, or irrelevant information so the problem can be defined accurately and alternative solutions can be generated.

situational stressor: the type of stressor that arises from an individual's environment or circumstances, such as unfavorable working conditions.

skill variety: an attribute of a job that uses an individual's talents and abilities to the maximum and thus makes the job seem worthwhile and important.

small-wins strategy: a strategy for individuals to use for coping with stress; it involves celebrating each small successful step in the attack on a large project.

social loafing: a pitfall in group decision-making performance that occurs when the effort of a large group seems to negate the importance of each member's individual contribution. The result is that each member puts out less than his or her best effort. A group leader can counteract this tendency by emphasizing the importance of individual effort and by expressing positive expectations.

special purpose teams: teams with power to take action and initiate changes in organizations as a result of delegated assignments.

specific goals: goals that are measurable, unambiguous, and behavioral.

sponsor: person who helps provide the resources, environment, and encouragement that the idea champion needs in order to work.

storming stage: team development stage where members question the team's direction, the leader, roles of other members' and task objectives.

stressors: stimuli that cause physiological and psychological reactions in individuals.

subdivision: the breaking apart of a problem into smaller parts.

suggestion teams: teams formed to generate ideas for improvement, used to foster a sense of empowerment.

superiority-oriented communication: a message that gives the impression that the communicator is informed while others are ignorant, adequate while others are inadequate, competent while others are incompetent, or powerful while others are impotent.

supportive communication: communication that helps managers share information accurately and honestly without jeopardizing interpersonal relationships.

symbolic analogies: symbols or images that are imposed on the problem; recommended as part of synectics.

synectics: a technique for improving creative problem solving by putting something you don't know in terms of something you do know.

task-facilitating roles: those that help the team accomplish its outcome objectives.

task identity: an attribute of a job that enables an individual to perform a complete job from beginning to end.

task-process: research indicates that effective groups contain members who are highly task oriented as well as those who are concerned about maintaining the quality of the group's process. Task-oriented members are all business, focusing on outcomes and not worrying about members' feelings and attitudes; process-oriented members encourage everyone to participate and are most concerned with member satisfaction.

task significance: the degree to which the performance of a task affects the work or lives of other people. The greater its significance, the more meaningful the job is to the worker.

terminal values: those values that designate desirable ends or goals for an individual.

thinking languages: the various ways in which a problem can be considered, from verbal to nonverbal or symbolic languages as well as through sensory and visual imagery. Using only one thinking language is one indication of the constancy block.

thinking strategy: a method of interpreting and judging information in which an individual follows a systematic plan with specific sequential steps.

timely rewards: immediate and spontaneous feedback for desired behavior—important for an effective motivational program.

time stressor: the type of stressor generally caused by having too much to do in too little time.

tolerance of ambiguity: an individual's ability to cope with ambiguous, fast-changing, or unpredictable situations in which information is incomplete, unclear, or complex.

two-way communication: the result of respectfulness and flexibility.

Type A personality: a hard-driving, hostile, intense, highly competitive personality.

universalism: the ethical decision principle that a decision is right and proper if everyone would be expected to behave in the same way under the same circumstances.

utilitarianism: the ethical decision principle that a decision is right and proper if it generates the greatest amount of good for the most people while producing little or no harm.

validating communication: a message that helps people feel recognized, understood, accepted, and valued. It is respectful, flexible, two-way, and based on agreement.

verification stage: the final stage in creative thought in which the creative solution is evaluated relative to some standard of acceptability.

vertical thinking: defining a problem in a single way and then pursuing that definition without deviation until a solution is reached.

visibility: the power-enhancing attribute of a position that can usually be measured by the number of influential people one interacts with in the organization.

win-win philosophy: ensuring that everyone benefits from actions.

work design: the process of matching job characteristics and workers' skills and interests.

work processes: methods for interacting and doing work that emerge during team development.

References

Introduction

AACSB. 1985. *Preliminary report on the future of business education and development.* St. Louis, Mo.

Bandura, A. 1977. *A social learning theory.* Englewood Cliffs, N.J.: Prentice-Hall.

Benson, G. 1983. On the campus: How well do business schools prepare graduates for the business world? *Personnel* 60:61–65.

Boyatzis, R. E. 1982. *The competent manager.* New York: Wiley.

Burnaska, R. F. 1976. The effects of behavioral modeling training upon managers' behavior and employees' perceptions. *Personnel Psychology* 29:329–335.

Cameron, K. S., and Tschirhart, M. 1988. Managerial competencies and organizational effectiveness. Working paper, School of Business Administration, University of Michigan.

Cameron, K. S., and Whetten, D. A. 1984. A model for teaching management skills. *Organizational Behavior Teaching Journal* 8:21–27.

Cohen, P. A. 1984. College grades and adult achievement: A research synthesis. *Research in Higher Education* 20:281–291.

Controller of the Currency. 1987. *National bank failure.* U.S. Government Printing Office.

Curtis, D. B.; Winsor, J. L.; and Stephens, D. 1989. National preferences in business and communication education. *Communication Education* 38:6–15.

Davis, T. W., and Luthans, F. 1980. A social learning approach to organizational behavior. *Academy of Management Review* 5:281–290.

Flanders, L. R. 1981. *Report 1 from the federal manager's job and role survey: Analysis of responses by SES and mid-management level executives and management development division.* Washington, D.C., U.S. Office of Personnel Management.

Ghiselli, E. E. 1963. Managerial talent. *American Psychologist* 18:631–642.

Goldstein, A. P., and Sorcher, M. 1974. *Changing supervisor behavior.* New York: Pergammon.

Hanson, G. 1986. Determinants of firm performance: An integration of economic and organizational factors. Ph.D. dissertation, University of Michigan Business School.

Holt, J. 1964. *How children fail.* New York: Pitman.

Katz, R. L. 1974. Skills of an effective administrator. *Harvard Business Review* 51:90–102.

Latham, G. P., and Saari, L. P. 1979. Application of social learning theory to training supervisors through behavioral modeling. *Journal of Applied Psychology* 64: 239–246.

Livingston, S. W. 1971. The myth of the well-educated manager. *Harvard Business Review* 49:79–89.

Luthans, F., Rosenkrantz, S. A.; and Hennessey, H. W. 1985. What do successful managers really do? An observation study of managerial activities. *Journal of Applied Behavioral Science* 21:255–270.

Margerison, C., and Kakabadse, A. 1984. *How American chief executives succeed.* New York: AMA Publications.

Miner, J. B. 1973. The real crunch in managerial manpower. *Harvard Business Review* 51:146–158.

Mintzberg, H. 1975. The manager's job: Folklore and fact. *Harvard Business Review* 53:49–71.

Mintzberg, H. 1987. Training managers, not MBAs. Paper presented at the Macro Organizational Behavior Society meetings, Northwestern University, September.

Moses, J. L., and Ritchie, R. J. 1976. Supervisory relationships training: A behavioral evaluation of a behavioral modeling program. *Personnel Psychology* 29:337–343.

Peterson, D. E. Personal communication. 1990 (October).

Peterson, P. G. 1987. The morning after. *Atlantic Monthly* (October) 43–69.

Pfeffer, J. 1981. *Power in organizations.* Marshfield, Mass.: Pitman.

Pollock, R. H. 1987. Cited in Peters, Thomas. *Thriving on chaos.* New York: Free Press.

Porras, J. I., and Anderson, B. 1981. Improving managerial effectiveness through modeling-based training. *Organizational Dynamics* 9:60–77.

Porter, L. W., and McKibbin, L. E. 1988. *Management education and development: Drift or thrust into the 21st century?* New York: McGraw-Hill.

Prentice, M. G. 1984. An empirical search for a relevant management curriculum. *Collegiate News and Views* (Winter) 25–29.

Rose, S. D.; Crayner, J. J.; and Edleson, J. L. 1977. Measuring interpersonal competence. *Social Work* 22:125–129.

Samuelson, P. J. 1990. What good are B-schools? *Newsweek* (May 14) 49.

Singleton, W. T.; Spurgeon, P.; and Stammers, R. B. 1980. *The analysis of social skill.* New York: Plenum.

Smith, P. E. 1976. Management modeling training to improve morale and customer satisfaction. *Personnel Psychology* 29:351–359.

Staw, B. M.; Sandelands, L.; and Dutton, J. 1981. Threat-rigidity effects in organizational behavior: A multi-level analysis. *Administrative Science Quarterly* 26:501–524.

Thurow, L. C. 1984. Revitalizing American industry: Managing in a competitive world economy. *California Management Review* 27:9–41.

Whetten, D. A., and Cameron, K. S. 1983. Management skill training: A needed addition to the management curriculum. *Organizational Behavior Teaching Journal* 8:10–15.

Wrapp, H. E. Cited in Peters, T. J., and Waterman, R. H. 1982. *In search of excellence.* New York: Harper & Row.

Chapter 1

Allport, G.; Gordon, R.; and Vernon, P. 1931. *The study of values manual.* Boston: Houghton Mifflin Co.

Anderson, C.; Hellriegel, D.; and Slocum, J. 1977. Managerial response to environmentally induced stress. *Academy of Management Journal* 20:260–272.

Anderson, C., and Schneider, C. E. 1978. Locus of control, leader behavior, and leader performance among management students. *Academy of Management Journal* 21:690–698.

Andrews, K. 1989. Ethics in practice. *Harvard Business Review* (September–October) 99–104.

Atwater, L., and Yammarino, F. 1992. Does self–other agreement on leadership perceptions moderate the validity of leadership and performance predictions? *Personnel Psychology* 45:141–164.

Bieri, J.; Atkins, A. L.; Bruar, S.; Leaman, R. L.; Miller, H.; and Tripodi, T. 1966. *Clinical social judgment.* New York: Wiley.

Bonnett, C., and Furnham, A. 1991. Who wants to be an entrepreneur? *Journal of Economic Psychology* 12:465–478.

Blau, G. 1993. Testing the relationship of locus of control to different performance dimensions. *Journal of Occupational and Organizational Psychology* 66:125–138.

Brouwer, P. J. 1964. The power to see ourselves. *Harvard Business Review* 42:156–165.

Budner, S. 1962. Intolerance of ambiguity as a personality variable. *Journal of Personality* 30:29–50.

Cameron, K. S., and Ulrich, D. O. 1986. Transformational leadership in colleges and universities. In *Higher education: Handbook of theory and research,* edited by John Smart. New York: Agathon.

Cavanaugh, G. F. 1980. *American business values in transition.* Englewood Cliffs, N.J.: Prentice-Hall.

Chenhall, R., and Morris, D. 1991. The effect of cognitive style and sponsorship bias on the treatment of opportunity costs in resource allocation decisions. *Accounting, Organizations, and Society* 16:27–46.

Clare, D. A., and Sanford, D. G. 1979. Mapping personal value space: A study of managers in four organizations. *Human Relations* 32:659–666.

Covey, S. R. 1989. *The seven habits of highly effective people.* New York: Simon & Schuster.

Cravens, R. W., and Worchel, P. 1977. The differential effects of rewarding and coercive leaders on group members differing in locus of control. *Journal of Personality* 45:150–168.

Cromie, S., Callaghan, I., and Jansen, M. 1992. The entrepreneurial tendencies of managers. *British Journal of Management* 3:1–5.

DiMarco, N. J. 1974. Supervisor-subordinate life style and interpersonal need compatibilities as determinants of subordinate's attitudes toward the supervisor. *Academy of Management Journal* 17:575–578.

Durand, D., and Shea, D. 1974. Entrepreneurial activity as a function of achievement motivation and reinforcement control. *Journal of Psychology* 88:57–63.

Eckstrom, R. B.; French, J. W.; and Harmon, H. H. 1979. Cognitive factors: Their identification and replication. *Multivariate Behavioral Research Monographs* 72:3–84.

Flower, V.; Hughes, C. I.; Myers, M. S.; and Myer, S. S. 1975. *Managerial values for working.* New York: American Management Association.

Freud, S. 1956. *Collected papers* (Vols. 3 and 4). London: Hogarth.

Fromm, E. 1939. Selfishness and self love. *Psychiatry* 2:507–523.

Gennill, G. R., and Heisler, W. J. 1972. Fatalism as a factor in managerial job satisfaction, job strain, and mobility. *Personnel Psychology* 25:241–250.

Gilligan, C. 1979. Woman's place in man's life cycle. *Harvard Educational Review* 49:431–446.

Gilligan, C. 1980. Moral development in late adolescence: A critique and reconstruction of Kohlberg's theory. *Human Development* 23:77–104.

Gilligan, C. 1982. In a different voice: Women's conceptions of self and morality. *Harvard Educational Review* 47:481–517.

Gilligan, C. 1988. Two moral orientations: Gender differences and similarities. *Merrill-Palmer Quarterly* 34:223–237.

Goodstadt, B. E., and Hjelle, L. A. 1973. Power to the powerless: Locus of control and the use of power. *Journal of Personality and Social Psychology* 72:503–519.

Grayson, J., and O'Dell, C. 1988. *American Business: A Two-Minute Warning.* New York: Free Press.

Graves, C. W. 1970. Levels of existence: An open system theory of values. *Journal of Humanistic Psychology* 10:131–155.

Haan, N.; Smith, M. B.; and Block, J. 1968. Moral reasoning of young adults: Political-social behavior, family background, and personality correlates. *Journal of Personality and Social Psychology* 10:183–201.

Haase, R. F.; Lee, D. Y.; and Banks, D. L. 1979. Cognitive correlates of polychronicity. *Perceptual and Motor Skills* 49:271–282.

Hammer, T. H., and Vardi, Y. 1981. Locus of control and career self-management among nonsupervisory employees in industrial settings. *Journal of Vocational Behavior* 18:13–29.

Haney, W. V. 1979. *Communication and interpersonal relations.* Homewood, Ill.: Irwin.

Harris, S. 1981. *Know yourself? It's a paradox.* Associated Press (October 6).

Harvey, J. M. 1971. Locus of control shift in administrators. *Perceptual and Motor Skills* 33:980–982.

Hayakawa, S. I. 1962. *The use and misuse of language.* New York: Fawcett World Library, Crest, Gold Medal, and Premier Books.

Henderson, J. C., and Nutt, P. C. 1980. The influence of decision style on decision making behavior. *Management Science* 26:371–386.

Hendricks, J. A. 1985. Locus of control: Implications for managers and accountants. *Cost and Management* (May–June) 25–29.

Hewett, T. T.; O'Brien, G. E.; and Hornik, J. 1974. The effects of work organization, leadership style, and member compatibility upon the productivity of small groups working on a manipulative task. *Organizational Behavior and Human Performance* 11:283–301.

Hosmer, L. T. 1987. *The ethics of management.* Homewood, Ill.: Irwin.

Jourard, S. M. 1964. *The transparent self.* Princeton, N.J.: D. Von Nostrand Company.

Jung, K. 1923. *Psychological types.* London: Routledge and Kegan Paul, 1923.

Kohlberg, L. 1969. The cognitive-developmental approach to socialization. In *Handbook of socialization theory and research,* edited by D. A. Goslin.

New York: Houghton Mifflin Company. Copyright © 1969 by Houghton Mifflin Company. Reprinted with the permission of D.A. Goslin.

Kohlberg, L. 1976. Moral stages and moralization, the cognitive-developmental approach. In *Moral development and behavior,* edited by T. Lickona. New York: Holt, Rinehart & Winston.

Kren, L. 1992. The moderating effects of locus of control on performance incentives and participation. *Human Relations* 45:991–1012.

Lawrence, T., and Kleiner, B. 1987. The keys to successful goal achievement. *Journal of Management Development* 6:39–48.

Lickona, T. 1976. Critical issues in the study of moral development and behavior. In *Moral development and behavior: Theory, research, and social issues,* edited by T. Lickona. New York: Holt, Rinehart & Winston.

Liddell, W. W., and Slocum, J. W., Jr. 1976. The effects of individual-role compatibility upon group performance: An extension of Schutz's FIRO theory. *Academy of Management Journal* 19:413–426.

Lobel, S. 1992. A value-laden approach to integrating work and family life. *Human Resource Management Journal* 31:249–265.

Maslow, A. H. 1962. *Toward a psychology of being.* Princeton, N.J.: D. Von Nostrand Company.

McDonald, A. P. 1970. Internal-external locus of control and the practice of birth control. *Psychological Reports* 27:206.

Mendelsohn, G. A., and Rankin, N. O. 1969. Client-counselor compatibility and the outcome of counseling. *Journal of Abnormal Psychology* 74:157–163.

Milgram, S. 1963. Behavioral study of obedience. *Journal of Abnormal and Social Psychology* 67:371–378.

Miller, D.; Kets de Vries, M. F. R.; and Toulouse, J.-M. 1982. Top executive locus of control and its relationship to strategy-making, structure, and environment. *Academy of Management Journal* 25:237–253.

Mitchell, T.; Smyser, C. M.; and Weed, S. 1975. Locus of control: Supervision and work satisfaction. *Academy of Management Journal* 18:623–630.

Moore, T. 1987. Personality tests are back. *Fortune* (March 30) 74–82.

Mulkowsky, G. P., and Freeman, M. J. 1979. The impact of managerial orientation on implementing decisions. *Human Resource Management* 18:6–14.

Newton, T., and Keenan, A. 1990. The moderating effect of the Type A behavior pattern and locus of control upon the relationship between change in job demands and change in psychological strain. *Human Relations* 43:1229–1255.

Organ, D., and Greene, C. N. 1974. Role ambiguity, locus of control, and work satisfaction. *Journal of Applied Psychology* 59:101–102.

Parker, V., and Kram, K. 1993. Women mentoring women. *Business Horizons* 36:42–51.

Peters, T. 1987. *Thriving on chaos.* New York: Knopf.

Posner, B., and Kouzes, J. 1993. Values congruence and differences between the interplay of personal and organizational values. *Journal of Business Ethics* 12:341–347.

Pryer, M. W., and Distefano, M. K. 1971. Perception of leadership behavior, job satisfaction, and interexternal locus of control across three nursing levels. *Nursing Research* 20:534–537.

Reddy, W. B., and Byrnes, A. 1972. Effects of interpersonal group composition on the problem-solving behavior of middle managers. *Journal of Applied Psychology* 56:516–517.

Rest, J. R. 1979. *Revised manual for the Defining Issues Test: An objective test of moral judgment development.* Minneapolis: Minnesota Moral Research Projects.

Rogers, C. R. 1961. *On becoming a person.* Boston: Houghton Mifflin Co.

Rokeach, M. 1973. *The nature of human values.* New York: Free Press. Copyright © 1973 by The Free Press. Reprinted with the permission of The Free Press, an imprint of Simon & Schuster.

Rothenberg, D. L. 1980. Professional achievement and locus of control: A tenuous relationship reconsidered. *Psychological Reports* 46:183–188.

Rotter, J. B. 1966. Generalized expectancies for internal versus external control of reinforcement. *Psychological Monographs* 80:1–28.

Ruble, T., and Cosier, R. 1990. Effects of cognitive styles and decision settings on performance. *Or-*

ganizational Behavior and Human Decision Processes 46:283–295.

Runyon, K. E. 1973. Some interaction between personality variables and management styles. *Journal of Applied Psychology* 57:288–294.

Ryan L. R. 1970. *Clinical interpretation of the FIRO-B.* Palo Alto, Calif.: Consulting Psychologists Press.

Sapolsky, A. 1965. Relationship between patient-doctor compatibility, mutual perception, and outcome of treatment. *Journal of Abnormal Psychology* 70:70–65.

Sayles, L. 1964. *Managerial behavior.* New York: McGraw-Hill.

Schein, E. H. 1960. Interpersonal communication, group solidarity, and social influence. *Sociometry* 23:148–161.

Schere, J. L. 1982. Tolerance of ambiguity as a discriminating variable between entrepreneurs and managers. *Academy of Management Proceedings* 404–409.

Schneier, C. 1979. Measuring cognitive complexity: Developing reliability, validity, and norm tables for a personality instrument. *Educational and Psychological Measurement* 39:599–612.

Schutz, W. 1989. Real teamwork. *Executive Excellence* 6:709.

Schutz, W. C. 1958. FIRO: *A three-dimensional theory of interpersonal behavior.* New York: Holt, Rinehart & Winston.

Seeman, M. 1982. On the personal consequences of alienation in work. *American Sociological Review* 32:273–285.

Shalinsky, W. 1969. Group composition as a factor in assembly effects. *Human Relations* 22:457–464.

Simon, H. A. 1973. Applying information technology to organization design. *Public Administration Review* 34:268–278.

Smith, S., and Haythorn, W. W. 1973. Effects of compatibility, crowding, group size, and leadership seniority on stress, anxiety, hostility, and annoyance in isolated groups. *Journal of Personality and Social Psychology* 22:67–79.

Smith, S., and Leach, C. 1972. A hierarchical measure of cognitive complexity. *British Journal of Psychology* 63:561–568.

Spector, P. E. 1982. Behavior in organizations as a function of employee's locus of control. *Psychological Bulletin* (May) 487–489.

Stabell, C. 1973. The impact of a conversational computer system on human problem solving behavior. Unpublished working paper, Massachusetts Institute of Technology, Sloan School of Management.

Sweeney, P., McFarlin, D., and Cotton, J. 1991. Locus of control as a moderator of the relationship between perceived influence and procedural justice. *Human Relations* 44:333–342.

Toffler, A. 1980. *The third wave.* New York: Morrow.

Vertinsky, I. 1976. Implementation II: A multi-paradigm approach. Working paper presented at International Conference on the Implementation of Management Science in Social Organizations. University of Pittsburgh (February).

Wheeler, R. W., and Davis, J. M. 1979. Decision making as a function of locus of control and cognitive dissonance. *Psychological Reports* 44:499–502.

Wolf, R. N. 1972. Effects of economic threat on autonomy and perceived locus of control. *Journal of Social Psychology* 86:233–240.

Chapter 2

Adler, V. 1989. Little control equals lots of stress. *Psychology Today* 23(4):18–19.

Anderson, C. R. 1977. Locus of control, coping behaviors and performance in a stress setting: A longitudinal study. *Journal of Applied Psychology* 62:446–451.

Antonovsky, A. 1979. *Health, stress, and coping.* San Francisco: Jossey-Bass.

Beary, J. F., and Benson, H. 1977. A simple psychophysiologic technique which elicits the hypometabolic changes in the relaxation response. *Psychosomatic Medicine* 36:115–120.

Beehr, T. A. 1976. Perceived situational moderators of the relationship between subjective role ambiguity and role strain. *Journal of Applied Psychology* 61:35–40.

Benson, H. 1975. *The relaxation response.* New York: William Morrow.

Bramwell, S. T.; Masuda, M.; Wagner, N. N.; and Holmes, T. H. 1975. Psychosocial factors in athletic injuries. *Journal of Human Stress* 1:6.

Brockner, J., and Weisenfeld, B. M. 1993. Living on the edge: The effects of layoffs on those who remain. In *Social psychology in organizations: Advances in theory and research,* edited by J. K. Murnighan. Englewood Cliffs, N.J.: Prentice-Hall.

Cameron, K. S. 1994. Strategies for successful organizational downsizing. *Human Resource Management Journal* 33:189–212.

Cameron, K. S.; Freeman, S.; and Mishra, A. K. 1990. Effective organizational downsizing: Paradoxical processes and best practices. *Academy of Management Meetings, San Francisco.*

Cameron, K. S.; Freeman, S.; and Mishra, A. K. 1991. Best practices in white collar downsizing: Managing contradictions. *Academy of Management Executive* 5:57–73.

Cameron, K. S.; Kim, M. U.; and Whetten, D. A. 1987. Organizational effects of decline and turbulence. *Administrative Science Quarterly* 32:222–240.

Cameron, K. S., and Whetten, D. A. 1987. Organizational dysfunctions of decline. *Academy of Management Journal* 30:126–138.

Carlson, S. 1951. *Executive behavior: A study of the work load and the working methods of managing directors.* Stockholm: Strombergs.

Coddington, R. D., and Troxell, J. R. 1980. The effect of emotional factors on football injury rates—A pilot study. *Journal of Human Stress* 6:3–5.

Cooper, C. L., and Davidson, M. J. 1982. The high cost of stress on women managers. *Organizational Dynamics 11:* 44–53.

Cooper, M. J., and Aygen, M. M. 1979. A relaxation technique in the management of hypocholesterolemia. *Journal of Human Stress* 5:24–27.

Covey, S. R. 1989. *The seven habits of highly effective people.* New York: Simon & Schuster.

Curtis, John D., and Detert, Richard A. 1981. *How to relax: A holistic approach to stress management.* Palo Alto: Mayfield Publishing Co.

Davis, M.; Eshelman, E.; and McKay, M. 1980. *The relaxation and stress reduction workbook.* Richmond, Calif.: New Harbinger Publications.

Dyer, William G. 1981. *Teambuilding.* Reading, Mass.: Addison-Wesley.

Eliot, R. S., and Breo, D. L. 1984. *Is it worth dying for?* New York: Bantam Books.

Farnham, A. 1991. Who beats stress best and how? *Fortune* (October 7) 71–86.

Freedman, J. L., and Fraser, S. C. 1966. Compliance without pressure: The foot-in-the-door technique. *Journal of Personality and Social Psychology* 4:195–202.

French, J. R. R., and Caplan, R. D. 1972. Organizational stress and individual strain. In *The failure of success,* edited by A. J. Marrow. New York: AMACOM.

Friedman, M., and Rosenman, R. H. 1974. *Type A behavior and your heart.* New York: Alfred A. Knopf. Reprinted with the permission of Alfred A. Knopf, Inc.

Friedman, M., and Ulmer, D. 1984. *Treating type A behavior and your heart.* New York: Alfred A. Knopf.

Glaser, W. 1981. *Stations of the mind: New directions for reality therapy.* New York: Harper & Row.

Goldberg, H. 1976. *The hazards of being male.* New York: Nash.

Goldberg, H. 1978. *Executive health.* New York: McGraw-Hill.

Greenberg, J. 1987. *Comprehensive stress management.* 2nd ed. Dubuque, Ia.: Wm. C. Brown Publishers.

Griest, J. H., et al. 1979. Running as treatment for depression. *Comparative Psychiatry* 20:41–56.

Guest, R. H. 1956. Of time and the foreman. *Personnel* 32:478–486.

Hackman, J. R.; Oldham, G. R.; Janson, R.; and Purdy, K. 1975. A new strategy for job enrichment. *California Management Review* 17:57–71.

Hall, D. T. 1976. *Careers in organizations.* Santa Monica, Calif.: Goodyear.

Hamner, W. C., & Organ, D. W. 1978. *Organizational behavior: An applied psychological approach.* Dallas: Business Publications.

Hollander, S. 1965. *The sources of increased efficiency.* Cambridge: MIT Press.

Holmes, T. H., and Masuda, M. 1974. Life change and illness susceptibility. In *Stressful life events: Their nature and effects,* edited by B. S. Dohrenwend and B. P. Dohrenwend. New York: Wiley.

Holmes, T. H., and Rahe, R. H. 1967. The social readjustment rating scale. *Journal of Psychosomatic Research* 11:213–218. Copyright © 1967 by Elsevier

Science, Ltd. Reprinted with the permission of the publishers.

Holmes, T. H., and Rahe, R. H. 1970. The social readjustment rating scale. *Journal of Psychosomatic Research* 14:121–132.

Holmes, T. S., and Holmes T. H. 1970. Short-term intrusions into the lifestyle routine. *Journal of Psychosomatic Research* 14:121–132.

Ivancevich, J. M., and Matteson, Michael T. 1980. *Stress and work: A managerial perspective.* Glenview, Ill.: Scott Foresman.

Jenkins, C. D. 1976. Recent evidence supporting psychological and social risk factors in coronary disease. *New England Journal of Medicine* 294:1033–1034.

Jourard, S. M. 1964. *The transparent self.* Princeton, N.J.: Von Nostrand.

Kahn, R. L. et al. 1964. *Organizational stress: Studies in role conflict and ambiguity.* New York: Wiley.

Kamiya, J. 1978. Conscious control of brain power. *Psychology Today* 1:57–60.

Karasek, R. A.; Theorell, T.; Schwartz, J. E.; Schnall, P. L.; Pieper, C. F.; and Michela, J. L. 1988. Job characteristics in relation to the prevalence of myocardial infarction in the U.S. Health Examination Survey and the Health and Nutrition Examination Survey. *American Journal of Public Health* 78:910–918.

Kobasa, S. C. 1979. Stressful life events, personality, and health: An inquiry into hardiness. *Journal of Personality and Social Psychology* 37:1–12.

Kobasa, S. 1982. Commitment and coping in stress resistance among lawyers. *Journal of Personality and Social Psychology* 42:707–717.

Kopelman, R. 1985. Job redesign and productivity: A review of the evidence. *National Productivity Review* (Summer) 237–255.

Kotter, J. 1987. *The general managers.* New York: Free Press.

Kram, K. 1985. *Mentoring at work.* Glenview, Ill.: Scott, Foresman.

Kuhn, A., and Beam, R. D. 1982. *The logic of organizations.* San Francisco: Jossey-Bass.

Lakein, D. 1989. *How to get control of your time and your life.* New York: McKay.

Levinson, J. D. 1978. *Seasons of a man's life.* New York: Knopf.

Lewin, K. 1951. *Field theory in social science.* New York: Harper & Row.

Likert, R. 1967. *The human organization.* New York: McGraw Hill.

Luthe, W. 1962. Method, research and application of autogenic training. *American Journal of Clinical Hypnosis* 5:17–23.

Maddi, S., and Kobasa, S. C. 1984. *The hardy executive: Health under stress.* Homewood, Ill.: Dow Jones-Irwin.

McNichols, T. J. 1973. *The case of the missing time.* Northwest University Business School.

Mednick, M. T. 1982. Women and the psychology of achievement: Implications for personal and social change. In *Women in the workforce,* edited by H. J. Bernardin. New York: Praeger.

Milgram, S. 1963. Behavioral study of obedience. *Journal of Abnormal and Social Psychology* 63:371–378.

Mintzberg, H. 1973. *The nature of managerial work.* New York: Harper & Row.

Mishra, A. K. 1993. Organizational responses to crisis. Unpublished doctoral dissertation, University of Michigan.

Orme-Johnson, D. W. 1973. Autonomic stability and transcendental meditation. *Psychosomatic Medicine 35:* 341–349.

Perl, L. 1980. *Junk food, fast food, health food.* New York: Clarion Books.

Peters, T. 1988. *Thriving on chaos.* New York: Knopf.

Rahe, R. H. 1974. The pathway between subjects' recent life change and their near future illness reports: Representative results and methodological issues. In *Stressful life events: Their nature and effects,* edited by B. S. Dohrenwend and B. P. Dohrenwend. New York: Wiley.

Rahe, R. H.; Ryman, D. H.; and Ward, H. W. 1980. Simplified scaling for life change events. *Journal of Human Stress* 6:22–27.

Sayles, L. 1964. *Managerial behavior: Administration in complex organizations.* New York: McGraw-Hill.

Schachter, S. 1959. *The psychology of affiliation: Experimental studies of the sources of gregariousness.* Stanford, Calif.: Stanford University Press.

Schein, E. H. 1960. Interpersonal communication, group solidarity, and social influence. *Sociometry* 23:148–161.

Schutz, W. 1958. FIRO: *A three-dimensional theory of interpersonal behavior.* New York: Holt, Rinehart and Winston.

Selye, H. 1976. *The stress of life.* Rev. ed. New York: McGraw-Hill.

Shaw, M. E. 1981. *Group dynamics: The psychology of small group behavior.* 3rd ed. New York: McGraw-Hill.

Staw, B. M.; Sandelands, L.; and Dutton, J. 1981. Threat-rigidity effects in organizational behavior. *Administrative Science Quarterly* 26:501–524.

Stone, R. A., and Deleo, J. 1976. Psychotherapeutic control of hypertension. *New England Journal of Medicine* 294:80–84.

Weick, K. 1979. *The social psychology of organizing.* Reading, Mass.: Addison-Wesley.

Weick, K. 1984. Small wins. *American Psychologist 39:* 40–49.

Weick, K. 1993. The collapse of sensemaking in organizations. *Administrative Science Quarterly* 38:628–652.

Weick, Karl. 1993. The KOR experiment. Working paper, University of Michigan Graduate School of Business.

Wolff, H. G.; Wolf, S. G.; and Hare, C. C. 1950. *Life stress and bodily disease.* Baltimore: Williams & Wilkins.

Wolman, B. B. 1982. *Psychological aspects of obesity: A handbook.* New York: Von Nostrand Reinhold.

Zand, D. E. 1972. Trust and managerial problem solving. *Administrative Science Quarterly* 17:229–239.

Chapter 3

Allen, J. L. 1974. *Conceptual blockbusting.* San Francisco: W. H. Freeman.

Amabile, T. M. 1988. A model of creativity and innovation in organizations. In *Research in organizational behavior,* edited by L. L. Cummings and B. M. Staw, 10:123–167.

Barron, F. X. 1963. *Creativity and psychological health.* New York: Van Nostrand.

Basadur, M. S. 1979. Training in creative problem solving: Effects of deferred judgment and problem finding and solving in an industrial research organization. Ph.D. dissertation, University of Cincinnati.

Beveridge, W. 1960. *The art of scientific investigation.* New York: Random House.

Bower, M. 1965. Nurturing innovation in an organization. In *The creative organization,* edited by G. A. Steiner. Chicago: University of Chicago Press.

Broadwell, M. M. 1972. *The new supervisor.* Reading, Mass.: Addison-Wesley.

Bruner, J. S. 1966. *On knowing: Essays for the left hand.* Cambridge: Harvard University Press.

Campbell, N. 1952. *What is science?* New York: Dover.

Cialdini, R. B. 1988. *Influence: Science and practice.* Glenview, Ill.: Scott, Foresman.

Crovitz, H. F. 1970. *Galton's walk.* New York: Harper & Row.

Dauw, D. C. 1976. *Creativity and innovation in organizations.* Dubuque, Ia.: Kendall Hunt.

deBono, E. 1968. *New think.* New York: Basic Books.

Dellas, M., and Gaier, E. L. 1970. Identification of creativity: The individual. *Psychological Bulletin* 73:55–73.

Drucker, P. F. 1974. *Management.* New York: Harper & Row.

Einstein, A. Fundamental ideas and methods of relativity theory, presented in their development. Unpublished manuscript (c. 1919, G. Holton).

Elbing, A. 1978. *Behavioral decisions in organizations.* Glenview, Ill.: Scott, Foresman.

Ettlie, J.E., and O'Keefe, R.D. 1982. Innovative attitutes, values, and intentions in organizations. *Journal of Management Studies* 19:163–182.

Festinger, L. 1957. *A theory of cognitive dissonance.* Stanford: Stanford University Press.

Filley, A. C.; House, R. J.; and Kerr, S. 1976. *Managerial process and organizational behavior.* Glenview, Ill.: Scott, Foresman.

Freedman, J. L., and Fraser, S. C. 1966. Compliance without pressure: The foot-in-the-door technique. *Journal of Personality and Social Psychology* 4:195–202.

Galbraith, J. R. 1982. Designing the innovating organization. *Organizational Dynamics* (Winter) 5–25.

Gardner, J. W. 1965. *Self-renewal.* New York: Harper & Row.

Gordon, W. J. J. 1961. *Synectics: The development of creative capacity.* New York: Collier.

Greene, R. T. 1993. *Global quality: A synthesis of the world's best management methods.* Homewood, Ill.: Business One Irwin.

Guilford, J. P. 1962. Creativity: Its measurement and development. In *A sourcebook for creative thinking,* edited by S. J. Parnes and H. F. Harding. New York: Scribner.

Heider, Fritz. 1946. Attitudes and cognitive organization. *Journal of Psychology* 21:107–112.

Huber, G. P. 1980. *Managerial decision making.* Glenview, Ill.: Scott, Foresman.

Hyatt, J. 1989. The odyssey of an excellent man. *Inc.* (February) 63–68. Copyright © 1989 by Goldhirsch Group, Inc. Reprinted with permission of the publishers, 38 Commercial Wharf, Boston, MA 02110.

Ichikawa, A. 1986. *Practical strategic TQM for middle management.* Tokyo: Diamond.

Interaction Associates. 1971. *Tools for change.* San Francisco: Interaction Associates.

Janis, Irvin L. 1971. *Groupthink.* New York: Free Press.

Janis, I., and Mann, L. 1977. *Decision making: A psychological analysis of conflict, choice, and commitment.* New York: Free Press. Reprinted with the permission of The Free Press, an imprint of Simon & Schuster. Copyright © 1977 by The Free Press.

Juran, J. 1988. *Juran on planning for quality.* New York: Free Press.

Kanter, R. M. 1983. *The change masters.* New York: Simon & Schuster.

Kobera, D., and Bagnall, J. 1974. *The universal traveler: A soft-system guidebook to creativity, problem solving, and the process of design.* Los Altos, Calif.: William Kaufmann.

Koestler, A. 1967. *The act of creation.* New York: Dell.

Maier, N. R. F. 1967. Assets and liabilities of group problem solving: The need for an integrative function. *Psychological Review* 74:239–249.

Maier, N. R. F. 1970. *Problem solving and creativity in individuals and groups.* Belmont, Calif.: Brooks/Cole.

March, J. G., and Simon, H. A. 1958. *Organizations.* New York: Wiley.

Markoff, John. 1988. For scientists using supercomputers, visual imagery speeds discoveries. New York Times News Service, *Ann Arbor News* (November 2) D3.

McKim, R. H. 1972. *Experiences in visual thinking.* Monterey, Calif.: Brooks/Cole. Reprinted with the permission of Brooks/Cole.

McMillan, Ian. 1985. Progress in research on corporate venturing. Working paper, Center for Entrepreneurial Studies, New York University.

Medawar, P. B. 1967. *The art of the solvable.* London: Methuen.

Nayak, P. Ranganath, and Ketteringham, J. M. 1986. *Breakthroughs!* New York: Rawson Associates.

Nemeth, C. J. 1986. Differential contributions of majority and minority influence. *Psychological Review* 93:23–32.

Newcomb, T. 1954. An approach to the study of communicative acts. *Psychological Review* 60:393–404.

Osborn, A. 1953. *Applied imagination.* New York: Scribner.

Parnes, S. J. 1962. Can creativity be increased? In *A sourcebook for creative thinking,* edited by S. J. Parnes and H. F. Harding. New York: Scribner.

Raudsepp, E. 1981. *How creative are you?* New York: Perigee Books/G.P. Putnam's Sons. Copyright © 1981 by Eugene Raudsepp. Reprinted with the permission of the author, c/o Dominick Abel Literary Agency, Inc.

Raudsepp, E., and Hough, G.P. 1977. Shakespeare riddle. In *Creative growth games.* New York: Putnam.

Rothenberg, A. 1979. Creative contradictions. *Psychology Today* 13:55–62.

Rothenburg, A. 1979. *The emerging goddess.* Chicago: University of Chicago Press.

Schumacher, E. F. 1977. *A guide for the perplexed.* New York: Harper & Row.

Scott, O. J. 1974. *The creative ordeal: The story of Raytheon.* New York: Atheneum.

Steiner, G. 1978. *The creative organization.* Chicago: University of Chicago Press.

Tannenbaum, R., and Schmidt, W. H. 1958. How to choose a leadership pattern. *Harvard Business Review* 3:95–101.

Covey, S. R. 1989. *The seven habits of highly effective people.* New York: Simon & Schuster.

Crocker, J. 1978. Speech communication instruction based on employer's perceptions of the importance of selected communication skills for employees on the job. Paper presented at the Speech Communication Association meeting, Minneapolis, Minn.

Dyer, W. G. 1972. Congruence. In *The sensitive manipulator.* Provo, Utah: Brigham Young University Press.

Egan, E. 1975. *The skilled helper: A model for systematic helping and interpersonal relating.* Belmont, Calif.: Brooks/Cole.

Galbraith, J. K. 1975. Are you Mark Epernay? The literary Galbraith on the art of writing. *Christian Science Monitor* (December 9) 19.

Gibb, J. R. 1961. Defensive communication. *Journal of Communication* 11:141–148.

Glasser, W. 1965. *Reality therapy: A new approach to psychiatry.* New York: Harper & Row.

Golen, S. 1990. A factor analysis of barriers to effective listening. *Journal of Business Communication* 27:25–35.

Gordon, R. D. 1988. The difference between feeling defensive and feeling understood. *Journal of Business Communication* 25:53–64.

Haas, J. W., and Arnold, C. L. 1995. An examination of the role of listening in judgments of communication competence in coworkers. *Journal of Business Communication* 32:123–139.

Haney, W. V. 1979. *Communication and interpersonal relations.* Homewood, Ill.: Irwin.

Hanson, G. 1986. Determinants of firm performance: An integration of economic and organizational factors. Ph.D. dissertation, University of Michigan Business School.

Huseman, R. C.; Lahiff, J. M.; and Hatfield, J. D. 1976. *Interpersonal communication in organizations.* Boston: Holbrook Press.

Jacobs, M. 1973. Levels of confirmation and disconfirmation in interpersonal communication. Ph.D. dissertation, University of Denver.

Loomis, F. 1939. *The consultation room.* New York: Knopf.

Taylor, C. W., and Barron, F. X. 1963. *Scientific creativity: Its recognition and development.* New York: Wiley.

Thompson, J. D., and Tuden, A. 1959. Strategies, structures, and processes or organizational decision. In *Comparative studies in administration,* edited by J. D. Thompson and A. Tuden. Pittsburgh: University of Pittsburgh Press.

Tichy, N. 1983. *Strategic human resource management.* New York: Wiley.

Torrance, E. P. 1965. Scientific views of creativity and factors affecting its growth. *Daedalus* 94:663–682.

von Oech, R. 1986. *A kick in the seat of the pants.* New York: Harper & Row.

Vroom, V. H., and Yetton, P. W. 1973. *Leadership and decision making.* Pittsburgh: University of Pittsburgh Press.

Vygotsky, L. 1962. *Thought and language.* Cambridge: MIT Press.

Weick, K. E. 1979. *The social psychology of organizing.* Reading, Mass.: Addison-Wesley.

Chapter 4

Argyris, C. 1991. Teaching smart people how to learn. *Harvard Business Review* 63:99–109.

Athos, A., and Gabarro, J. 1978. *Interpersonal behavior.* Englewood Cliffs, N.J.: Prentice-Hall.

Barnlund, D. C. 1968. *Interpersonal communication: Survey and studies.* Boston: Houghton Mifflin.

Boss, R. Wayne. 1983. Teambuilding and the problem of regression: The personal management interview as an intervention. *Journal of Applied Behavioral Science* 19:69–83. Copyright © 1983 by NTL Institute of Applied Behavioral Science. Reprinted with the permission of Sage Publications, Inc.

Bowman, G. W. 1964. What helps or harms promotability? *Harvard Business Review* 42:14.

Brownell, J. 1986. *Building active listening skills.* Englewood Cliffs, N.J.: Prentice-Hall.

Brownell, J. 1990. Perceptions of effective listeners: A management study. *Journal of Business Communication* 27:401–415.

Cameron, Kim. 1988. Organizational downsizing and large-scale change. Working paper, University of Michigan.

Maier, N.R.F.; Solem, A. R.; and Maier, A. A. 1973. Counseling, interviewing, and job contacts. In *Psychology of industrial organizations*, edited by N.R.F. Maier. Boston: Houghton Mifflin.

McGregor, D. 1960. *The human side of enterprise.* New York: McGraw-Hill.

Ouchi, W. 1981. *Theory Z.* Reading, Mass.: Addison-Wesley.

Peters, T. 1988. *Thriving on chaos.* New York: Knopf.

Randle, C. W. 1956. How to identify promotable executives. *Harvard Business Review* 34:122.

Rogers, C. W. 1961. *On becoming a person.* Boston: Houghton Mifflin.

Rogers, C., and Farson, R. 1976. *Active listening.* Chicago: Industrial Relations Center.

Ross, D. 1986. Coaching and counseling. Unpublished manuscript, University of Michigan Executive Education Center.

Schnake, M. E.; Dumler, M. P.; Cochran, D. S.; and Barnett, T. R. 1990. Effects of differences in superior and subordinate perceptions of superiors' communication practices. *Journal of Business Communication* 27:37-50.

Sieburg, E. 1969. Dysfunctional communication and interpersonal responsiveness in small groups. Ph.D. dissertation, University of Denver.

Sieburg, E. 1978. Confirming and disconfirming organizational communication. Working paper, University of Denver.

Steil, L. K. 1980. *Your listening profile.* Minneapolis: Sperry Corporation.

Steil, L.; Barker, L.; and Watson, K. 1983. *Effective listening: Key to your success.* New York: Addison-Wesley.

Szilagyi, A. D., and Wallace, M. J. 1983. *Organizational behavior and performance.* 3rd Edition. Glenview: Scott Foresman and Company.

Thorton, B. B. 1966. As you were saying—The number one problem. *Personnel Journal* 45:237-238.

Wiemann, J. M. 1977. Explanation and test of a model of communicative competence. *Human Communication Research* 3:145-213.

Chapter 5

Allen, R. W.; Madison, D. L.; Porter, L. W.; Renwick, P. A.; and Mayer, B. T. 1979. Organizational politics: Tactics and characteristics of actors. *California Management Review* 22:77-83.

Bennis, W., and Nanus, B. 1985. *Leaders.* New York: Harper & Row.

Berry, L.; Parasuraman, A.; and Zeithaml, V. 1994. Ten lessons for improving service quality. *Academy of Management Executive* 8:32-45.

Berscheid, E., and Walster, E. 1974. Physical attractiveness. In *Advances in experimental psychology*, edited by N. N. Berkowitz. New York: Academic Press.

Canfield, F. E., and LaGaipa, J. J. 1970. Friendship expectations at different stages in the development of friendship. Paper read at the annual meeting of the Southeastern Psychological Association, Louisville.

Cialdini, R. B. 1988. *Influence: science and practice.* 2nd ed. Glenview, Ill.: Scott, Foresman.

Cohen, A. R., and Bradford, D. L. 1991. Influence without authority: The use of alliances, reciprocity, and exchange to accomplish work. In *Psychological dimensions of organizational behavior* edited by Barry M. Staw, 378-387. New York: MacMillan.

Cuming, P. 1981. *The power handbook.* Boston: CBI Publishing Co.

Cunningham, M. 1984. *Powerplay.* New York: Simon & Schuster.

Deal, T. E., and Kennedy, A. A. 1982. *Corporate cultures: The rites and rituals of corporate life.* Reading, Mass.: Addison-Wesley.

DeGeorge, Richard T. 1996. *Business Ethics.* New York: Macmillan.

DeLorean, John Z. 1985. *DeLorean.* Grand Rapids, Mich.: Zondervan Publishing House.

Dilenschneider, R. L. 1990. *Power and influence.* New York: Prentice-Hall.

Dion, K. K.; Berscheid, E.; and Walster, E. 1972. What is beautiful is good. *Journal of Personality and Social Psychology* 24:285-290.

Dutton, J. E., and Ashford, S. J. 1993. Selling issues to top management. *Academy of Management Review* 18(3):397-428.

Dutton, J. E., and Duncan, R. B. 1987. The creation of momentum for change through the process of strategic issue diagnosis. *Strategic Management Journal* 83(3):279-295.

Dyer, W. G. 1972. Congruence. In *The sensitive manipulator*. Provo, Utah: Brigham Young University Press.

Fallon, I., and Srodes, J. 1983. *DeLorean: The rise and fall of a dream-maker*. London: Hamish Hamilton.

Gabarro, J. J., and Kotter, J. P. 1980. Managing your boss. *Harvard Business Review* 58:92-100.

Giamatti, A. B. 1981. *The university and the public interest*. New York: Atheneum.

Hickson, D. J.; Hinings, C. R.; Lee, C. A.; Schneck, R. E.; and Pennings, J. M. 1971. Strategic contingencies theory of intraorganizational power. *Administrative Science Quarterly* 16:216-229.

Hinings, C. R.; Hickson, D. J.; Pennings, J. M.; and Schneck, R. E. 1974. Structural conditions of intraorganizational power. *Administrative Science Quarterly* 21:22-44.

Kanter, R. 1979. Power failures in management circuits. *Harvard Business Review* 57:65-75. Copyright © 1979 by The President and Fellows of Harvard College. Reprinted with the permission of Harvard Business Review. All rights reserved.

Kaplan, R. E., and Mazique, M. 1983. *Trade routes: The manager's network of relationships*. Technical Report #22, Center for Creative Leadership, Greensboro, N.C.

Kears, G. R., and Davis, K. E. 1970. The dynamics of sexual behavior of college students. *Journal of Marriage and the Family* 30:390-399.

Kipnis, D. 1976. *The powerholders*. Chicago: University of Chicago Press.

Kipnis, D., and Schmidt, S. M. 1988. Upward-influence styles: Relationship with performance evaluations, salary, and stress. *Administrative Science Quarterly* 33:528-542.

Korda, M. 1975. *Power: How to get it, how to use it*. New York: Ballantine Books.

Kotter, J. P. 1977. Power, dependence, and effective management. *Harvard Business Review* 55:125-136.

Lawrence, P. R., and Lorsch, J. W. 1969. *Organization and environment*. Homewood, Ill.: Richard D. Irwin.

Marwell, G., and Schmitt, D. R. 1967. Dimensions of compliance-gaining behavior: An empirical analysis. *Sociometry* 30:350-364.

May, R. 1972. *Power and innocence*. New York: Norton.

McCall, M. M. Jr., and Lombardo, M. M. 1983. What makes a top executive? *Psychology Today* 26:28-31. Copyright © 1983 by Sussex Publishers Inc. Reprinted with the permission of *Psychology Today*.

Mechanic, D. 1962. Sources of power of lower participants in complex organizations. *Administrative Science Quarterly* 7:349-364.

Mescon, M. H.; Albert, M.; and Khedouri, F. 1977. *Management*. New York: Harper & Row.

Miller, R. 1985. Three who made a difference. *Management Review* 74:16-19.

Mulder, M.; Koppelaar, L.; de Jong, R. V.; and Verhage, J. 1986. Organizational field study. *Journal of Applied Psychology* 71:566-570.

Perrow, C. 1970. Departmental power and perspectives in industrial firms. In *Power in organizations*, edited by M. N. Zold. Nashville: Vanderbilt University Press.

Peters, T. 1978. Symbols, patterns, and settings: An optimistic case for getting things done. *Organizational Dynamics* 7:3-22.

Pfeffer, J. 1977. Power and resource allocation in organizations. In *New direction in organizational behavior*, edited by B. Staw and G. Salancik. Chicago: St. Clair Press.

Pfeffer, J. 1981. *Power in organizations*. Marshfield, Mass.: Pitman.

Pfeffer, J. 1992. *Managing with power*. Boston: Harvard Business School Press.

Pfeffer, J., and Konrad, A. 1991. The effects of individual power on earnings. *Work and Occupations* 18:385-414.

Ross, J., and Ferris, K. R. 1981. Interpersonal attraction and organizational outcomes: A field examination. *Administrative Science Quarterly* 26:617-632.

Schein, E. 1991. The role of the founder in creating organizational culture. In *Psychological dimensions of organizational behavior*, edited by Barry M. Staw, 312-326. New York: MacMillan.

Schlenker, B. R. 1980. *Impression management*. Belmont, Calif.: Wadsworth, Inc.

Schmidt, S., and Kipnis, D. 1987. The perils of persistence. *Psychology Today* 21:32-33.

Scott, W. G., and Hart, D. K. 1979. *Organizational America.* Boston: Houghton Mifflin.

Stewart, T. A. 1992. The search for the organization of tomorrow. *Fortune* (May 18) 92–98.

Tedeschi, J. T. 1974. Attributions, liking and power. In *Foundations of interpersonal attraction*, edited by T. L. Huston. New York: Academic Press.

Tully, S. 1993. The modular corporation. *Fortune* (February 8) 106–114.

Zaleznik, A. 1970. Power and politics in organizational life. *Harvard Business Review* 48:47–48.

Chapter 6

Alderfer, C. P. 1977. A critique of Salancik and Pfeffer's examination need-satisfaction theories. *Administrative Science Quarterly* 22:658–672.

Atkinson, J. W., and Raynor, J. O. 1974. *Motivation and achievement.* Washington, D.C.: V. H. Winston.

Bennis, W. 1984. The four competencies of leadership. *Training and Development Journal* 38:15–19.

Bradford, D. L., and Cohen, A. R. 1984. *Managing for excellence.* New York: John Wiley.

Cropanzano, R., and Folger, R. 1996. Procedural justice and worker motivation. In *Motivation and leadership at work*, edited by R. M. Steers, L. W. Porter, and G. A. Bigley. New York: McGraw-Hill.

Dalton, G.; Lawrence, P.; and Lorsch, J. 1970. *Organizational structure and design.* Homewood, Ill.: Irwin.

Earley, P. C., and Kanfer, R. 1985. The influence of component participation and role models on goal acceptance, goal satisfaction, and performance. *Organizational Behavior and Human Decision Processes* 36:378–390.

Greenberg, J. 1990. Organizational justice: Yesterday, today, and tomorrow. *Journal of Management* 16:606–613.

Hackman, J. R., and Oldham, G. R. 1980. *Work re-design.* Reading, Mass.: Addison-Wesley. Copyright © 1980 by Addison-Wesley Publishing Co., Inc. Reprinted with the permission of Addison Wesley Longman.

House, R. J., and Mitchell, T. R. 1974. Path-goal theory of leadership. *Journal of Contemporary Business* 3:81–97.

Jay, A. 1967. *Management and Machiavelli, an inquiry into the politics of corporate life.* New York: Holt, Rinehart, and Winston.

Kerr, S. 1995. On the folly of rewarding A, while hoping for B. *Academy of Management Executive* 9(1):7–14.

Kerr, S. 1996. Risky business: The new pay game. *Fortune* (July 22) 94–97.

Komaki, J.; Coombs, T.; and Schepman, S. 1996. Motivational implications of reinforcement theory. In *Motivation and leadership at work*, edited by R. M. Steers, L. W. Porter, and G. A. Bigley. New York: McGraw-Hill.

Kopelman, R. E. 1985. Job redesign and productivity: A review of evidence. *National Productivity Review* (Summer) 237–255.

Kotter, J. 1996. Kill complacency. *Fortune* (August 5) 168–170.

Latham, G.; Erez, M.; and Locke, E. 1988. Resolving scientific disputes by the joint design of crucial experiments by the antagonists: Application to the Erez-Latham disputes regarding participation in goal setting. *Journal of Applied Psychology* 73:753–772.

Latham, G. P., and Locke, E. A. 1979. Goal setting—a motivational technique that works. *Organizational Dynamics* 8:68–80.

Lawler, E. E. 1987. The design of effective reward systems. In *Handbook of organizational behavior*, edited by J. Lorsch. Englewood Cliffs, N.J.: Prentice-Hall.

Lawler, E. E. 1988. Gainsharing theory and research: Findings and future directions. In *Research in organizational change and development* (Vol. 2), edited by W. A. Pasmore and E. R. Woodman. Greenwich, Conn.: JAI Press.

Lawler, E. E. 1990. *Strategic pay.* San Francisco: Jossey-Bass.

Lee, C. 1991. Who gets trained in what—1991. *Training* (October) 48–50.

Locke, E. A., and Latham, G. P. 1990. *A theory of goal setting and task performance.* Englewood Cliffs, N.J.: Prentice-Hall.

Lusterman, S. 1985. *Trends in corporate education and training.* The Conference Board, Report No. 870.

McGregor, D. 1960. *The human side of enterprise.* New York: McGraw-Hill.

Michener, H. A.; Fleishman, J. A.; and Vaske, J. J. 1976. A test of the bargaining theory of coalition formulation in four-person groups. *Journal of Personality and Social Psychology* 34:1114–1126.

Murlis, H., and Wright, A. 1985. Rewarding the performance of the eager beaver. *Personnel Management* 17:28–31.

Peters, T., and Waterman, R. H. 1982. *In search of excellence.* New York: Warner Books.

Pfeffer, J. 1995. Producing sustainable competitive advantage through the effective management of people. *Academy of Management Executive* 9:55–71.

Quick, T. L. 1977. *Person to person managing.* New York: St. Martin's Press.

Shamir, B.; House, R. J.; and Arthur, M. B. 1993. The motivational effects of charismatic leadership: A self-concept based theory. *Organization Science* 4(4):577–594.

Staw, B. M. 1986. Organizational psychology and the pursuit of the happy/productive worker. *California Management Review* 28(4):396–407.

Staw, B. M.; McKechnie, P.; and Puffer, S. 1983. The justification of organizational performance. *Administrative Science Quarterly* 28:582–600.

Steers, R. M.; Porter, L. W.; and Bigley, G. A. 1996. *Motivation and leadership at work.* New York: McGraw-Hill.

Thompson, D. W. 1978. *Managing people: Influencing behavior.* St. Louis: C. V. Mosby Co.

Vroom, V. 1964. *Work and motivation.* New York: Wiley.

Wood, R., and Bandura, A. 1989. Social cognitive theory of organizational management. *Academy of Management Review* 14(3):361–383.

Wood, R.; Mento, A. J.; and Locke, E. A. 1987. Task complexity as a moderator of goal effects: A meta-analysis. *Journal of Applied Psychology* 72:416–425.

Chapter 7

Adler, N. J. 1991. *International dimensions of organizational behavior.* 2nd ed. Boston: PWS-KENT Publishing.

Adler, R. B. 1977. Satisfying personal needs: Managing conflicts, making requests, and saying no. In *Con-*

fidence in communication: A guide to assertive and social skills. New York: Holt, Rinehart and Winston.

Bazerman, M. 1986. Why negotiations go wrong. *Psychology Today* (June) 54–58.

Bazerman, M. H., and Neale, M. A. 1992. *Negotiating rationally.* New York: Free Press.

Boulding, E. 1964. Further reflections on conflict management. In *Power and conflict in organizations,* edited by R. L. Kahn and E. Boulding. New York: Basic Books.

Bowers, D. 1983. What would make 11,500 people quit their jobs? *Organizational Dynamics* (Winter) 5–19.

Brown, L. D. 1983. *Managing conflict at organizational interfaces.* Reading, Mass.: Addison-Wesley.

Cameron, K. S.; Kim, M. U.; and Whetten, D. A. 1987. Organizational effects of decline and turbulence. *Administrative Science Quarterly* 32:222–240.

Caudron, S. 1992. Subculture strife hinders productivity. *Personnel Journal* 71(2):60–64.

Cox, T. H. 1994. *Cultural diversity in organizations: Theory, research and practice.* San Francisco: Berrett-Koehler.

Cox, T. H., and Blake, S. 1991. Managing cultural diversity: Implications for organizational competitiveness. *Academy of Management Executive* 5(3):45–56.

Cox, T. H.; Lobel, S.; and McLeod, P. 1991. Effects of ethnic group cultural difference on cooperative versus competitive behavior in a group task. *Academy of Management Journal* 34:827–847.

Filley, A. C. 1975. *Interpersonal conflict resolution.* Glenview, Ill.: Scott, Foresman.

Filley, A. C. 1978. Some normative issues in conflict management. *California Management Review* 71:61–66.

Fisher, R., and Brown, S. 1988. *Getting together: Building a relationship that gets to yes.* Boston: Houghton Mifflin.

Fisher, R., and Ury, W. 1984. *Getting to yes.* Boston: Houghton Mifflin.

Gordon, T. 1970. *Parent effectiveness training.* New York: Wyden.

Hines, J. S. 1980. *Conflict and conflict management.* Athens, Ga.: University of Georgia Press.

Hocker, J. L., and Wilmot, W. W. 1991. *Interpersonal conflict.* Dubuque, Ia.: W. C. Brown.

Hofstede, G. 1980. Motivation, leadership, and organization: Do American theories apply abroad? *Organizational Dynamics* (Summer) 42–63.

Karambayya, R., and Brett, J. M. 1989. Managers handling disputes: Third party roles and perceptions of fairness. *Academy of Management Journal* 32:687–704.

Keashly, L. 1994. Gender and conflict: What does psychological research tell us? In *Conflict and gender,* edited by A. Taylor and J. B. Miller. Cresskill, N.J.: Hampton Press.

Kelly, J. 1970. Make conflict work for you. *Harvard Business Review* (July–August) 48:103–113.

Kilmann, R. H., and Thomas, K. W. 1977. Developing a forced-choice measure of conflict-handling behavior: The MODE instrument. *Educational and Psychological Measurement* 37:309–325.

Kim, S. H., and Smith, R. H. 1993. Revenge and conflict escalation. *Negotiation Journal* 9:37–44.

Kipnis, D., and Schmidt, S. 1983. An influence perspective in bargaining within organizations. In *Bargaining inside organizations,* edited by M. H. Bazerman and R. J. Lewicki. Beverly Hills, Calif.: Sage.

Korabik, D.; Baril, G. L.; and Watson, C. 1993. Managers' conflict management style and leadership effectiveness: The moderating effects of gender. *Sex Roles* 29(5/6):405–420.

Kressel, K., and Pruitt, D. G. 1989. *Mediation research: The process and effectiveness of third party intervention.* San Francisco: Jossey-Bass.

Latham, G., and Wexley, K. 1981. *Increasing production through performance appraisal.* Reading, Mass.: Addison-Wesley.

Mandell, B., and Kohler-Gray, S. 1990. Management development that values diversity. *Personnel* 67:41–47.

Maslow, A. 1965. *Eupsychian management.* Homewood, Ill.: Irwin.

Morrison, A. M. 1996. *The new leaders: Leadership diversity in America.* San Francisco: Jossey-Bass.

Moser, M. R. 1995. Freida Mae Jones: Racism in organizations. In *Understanding diversity: Readings, cases, and exercises,* edited by C. Harvey and M. J. Allard. New York: HarperCollins.

Northcraft, G., and Neale, M. 1994. *Organization behavior: A management challenge.* Chicago: Dryden Press.

Pascale, R. 1990. Creating contention without causing conflict. *Business Month* (February) 69–71.

Phillips, E., and Cheston, R. 1979. Conflict resolution: What works. *California Management Review* 21:76–83.

Porter, E. H. 1973. *Manual of administration and interpretation for strength deployment inventory.* La Jolla, Calif.: Personal Strengths Assessment Service.

Pruitt, D. G. 1983. Integrative agreements: Nature and consequences. In *Negotiating in organizations,* edited by M. H. Bazerman and R. J. Lewicki. Beverly Hills, Calif.: Sage.

Rahim, M. A., and Blum, A. A. 1994. *Global perspectives on organizational conflict.* Westport, Conn.: Praeger.

Robbins, S. P. 1974. *Managing organizational conflict: A nontraditional approach.* Englewood Cliffs, N.J.: Prentice-Hall.

Rubin, J. Z.; Pruitt, D. G.; and Kim, S. H. 1991. *Social conflict: Escalation, stalemate and settlement.* New York: McGraw-Hill.

Ruble, T., and Schneer, J. A. 1994. Gender differences in conflict-handling styles: Less than meets the eye? In *Conflict and gender,* edited by A. Taylor and J. B. Miller. Cresskill, N.J.: Hampton Press.

Ruble, T., and Thomas, K. 1976. Support for a two-dimensional model of conflict behavior. *Organizational Behavior and Human Performance* 16:145.

Savage, G. T.; Blair, J. D.; and Sorenson, R. L. 1989. Consider both relationships and substance when negotiating strategically. *Academy of Management Executive* 3:37–48.

Schmidt, W. H., and Tannenbaum, R. 1965. Management of differences. *Harvard Business Review* (November–December) 38:107–115.

Seybolt, P. M.; Derr, C. B.; and Nielson, T. R. 1996. Linkages between national culture, gender, and conflict management styles. Working paper, University of Utah.

Sillars, A., and Weisberg, J. 1987. Conflict as a social skill. In *Interpersonal processes: New directions in communication research,* edited by M. E. Roloff and G. R. Miller. Beverly Hills: Sage.

Smith, W. P. 1987. Conflict and negotiation: Trends and emerging issues. *Journal of Applied Social Psychology* 17:631–677.

Thomas, K. 1976. Conflict and conflict management. In *Handbook of industrial and organizational psychology*, edited by M. D. Dunnette. London: Routledge and Kegan Paul.

Ting-Toomey, S.; Gao, G.; Trubisky, P.; Yang, Z.; Kim, H. S.; Lin, S. L.; and Nishida, T. 1991. Culture, face maintenance, and styles of handling interpersonal conflict: A study in five cultures. *International Journal of Conflict Management* 2:275–296.

Tjosvold, D. 1991. *The conflict positive organization.* Reading, Mass.: Addison-Wesley.

Trompenaars, F. 1994. *Riding the waves of culture: Understanding diversity in global business.* New York: Irwin.

Walton, R. 1969. *Interpersonal peacekeeping: Confrontations and third party consultation.* Reading, Mass.: Addison-Wesley.

Wanous, J. P., and Youtz, A. 1986. Solution diversity and the quality of group decisions. *Academy of Management Journal* 1:149–159.

Weldon, E., and Jehn, K. A. 1995. Examining cross-cultural differences in conflict management behavior: A strategy for future research. *International Journal of Conflict Management* 6:387–403.

Chapter 8

Adler, A. 1927. *Understanding Human Nature.* Garden City, N.Y.: Garden City Pub. Co.

Alinsky, S. D. 1971. *Rules for radicals: A pragmatic primer for realistic radicals.* New York: Vintage Books.

Alloy, L. B.; Peterson, C.; Abrahamson, L. Y.; and Seligman, M. E. P. 1984. Attributional style and the generality of learned helplessness. *Journal of Personality and Social Psychology* 46:681–687.

Anderson, C.; Hellriegel, D.; and Slocum, J. 1977. Managerial response to environmentally induced stress. *Academy of Management Journal* 20:260–272.

Ashby, R. 1956. *Design for the brain.* London: Science Paperbacks.

Averill, J. R. 1973. Personal control over aversive stimuli and its relationship to stress. *Psychological Bulletin* 80:286–303.

Bandura, A. 1977. Self-efficacy: Toward a unifying theory of behavioral change. *Psychological Review* 84:191–215.

Bandura, A. 1986. *Social foundations of thought and action: A social cognitive theory.* Englewood Cliffs, N.J.: Prentice-Hall.

Bandura, A. 1989. Human agency in social cognition theory. *American Psychologist* 44:1175–1184.

Barber, B. *The logic and limits of trust.* New Brunswick, N.J.: Rutgers University Press.

Bennis, W., and Nanus, B. 1985. *Leaders: The strategies for taking charge.* New York: Harper & Row.

Bernard, C. I. 1938. *The functions of the executive.* Cambridge: Harvard University Press.

Block, P. 1987. *The empowered manager: Positive political skills at work.* San Francisco: Jossey-Bass.

Bookman, A., and Morgan, S. 1988. *Women and the politics of empowerment.* Philadelphia: Temple University Press.

Bramucci, R. 1977. A factorial examination of the self-empowerment construct. Ph.D. dissertation, University of Oregon.

Brehm, J. W. 1966. *Response to loss of freedom: A theory of psychological reactance.* New York: Academic Press.

Byham, W. C. 1988. *Zapp! The lightning of empowerment.* New York: Harmony Books.

Cameron, K. S.; Freeman, S. J.; and Mishra, A. K. 1991. Best practices in white-collar downsizing: Managing contradictions. *Academy of Management Executive* 5:57–73.

Cameron, K. S.; Freeman, S. J.; and Mishra, A. K. 1993. Organization downsizing and redesign. In *Organizational change and design*, edited by G. P. Huber and W. Glick. New York: Oxford University Press.

Cameron, K. S.; Whetten, D. A.; and Kim, M. U. 1987. Organizational dysfunctions of decline. *Academy of Management Journal* 30:126–138.

Chaffee, E. E. 1987. The aftermath of decline. *Review of Higher Education* 10:215–234.

Coch, L., and French, J. R. P. 1948. Overcoming resistance to change. *Human Relations* 11:512–532.

Conger, J. A. 1989. Leadership: The art of empowering others. *Academy of Management Executive* 3:17–24.

Conger, J. A., and Kanungo, R. N. 1988. The empowerment process. *Academy of Management Review* 13:471–482.

Conradt, C. A. 1985. *The game of work.* Salt Lake City: Shadow Mountain Press.

DeCharms, R. 1979. Personal causation and perceived control. In *Choice and perceived control,* edited by L. C. Perlmuter and R. A. Monty. Hillsdale, N.J.: Erlbaum.

Deci, E. L., and Ryan, R. M. 1987. The support of autonomy and control of behavior. *Journal of Personality and Social Psychology* 53:1024–1037.

Deci, E. L.; Connell, J. P.; and Ryan, R. M. 1989. Self-determination in a work organization. *Journal of Applied Psychology* 74:580–590.

Deutsch, M. 1973. *The resolution of conflict: Constructive and destructive processes.* New Haven: Yale University Press.

Drucker, P. 1988. The coming of the new organization. *Harvard Business Review* (January–February).

Durkheim, E. 1964. *Suicide.* New York: Free Press.

Eisenhart, K. M., and Galunic, D. C. 1993. Renewing the strategy-structure-performance paradigm. *Research in Organizational Behavior* 15.

Freire, P., and Faundez, A. 1989. *Learning to question: A pedagogy of liberation.* New York: Continuum Publishing Company.

Geas, V. 1989. The social psychology of self-efficacy. *Annual Review of Sociology* 15:291–316.

Geas, V.; Seff, M. A.; and Ray, M. P. 1988. Injury and depression: The mediating effects of self concept. Paper presented at the Pacific Sociological Association Meetings, Las Vegas.

Gemmill, G. R., and Heisler, W. J. 1972. Fatalism as a factor in managerial job satisfaction. *Personnel Psychology* 25:241–250.

Gibb, J. R., and Gibb, L. M. 1969. Role freedom in a TORI group. In *Encounter theory and practice of encounter groups,* edited by A. Burton. San Francisco: Jossey-Bass.

Golembiewski, R. T., and McConkie, M. 1975. The centrality of trust in group processes. In *Theories of group processes,* edited by C. Cooper. New York: Wiley.

Greenberger, D. B., and Strasser, S. 1991. The role of situational and dispositional factors in the enhancement of personal control in organizations. *Research in Organizational Behavior* 13:111–145.

Greenberger, D. B.; Strasser, S.; Cummings, L. L.; and Dunham, R. B. 1989. The impact of personal control on performance and satisfaction. *Organizational Behavior and Human Decision Processes* 43:29–51.

Hackman, J. R., and Oldham, G. R. 1980. *Work design.* Reading, Mass.: Addison-Wesley.

Hackman, J. R.; Oldham, G. R.; Janson, R.; and Purdy, K. 1975. A new strategy for job enrichment. *California Management Review* 17:57–71.

Hammer, T. H., and Vardi, Y. 1981. Locus of control and career self-management among nonsupervisory employees in industrial settings. *Journal of Vocational Behavior* 18:13–29.

Harter, S. 1978. Effectance motivation reconsidered: Toward a developmental model. *Human Development* 21:34–64.

Kahn, W. A. 1990. Psychological conditions of personal engagement and disengagement at work. *Academy of Management Journal* 33:692–724.

Kanter, R. M. 1968. Commitment and social organization: A study of commitment mechanisms in utopian communities. *American Sociological Review* 33:499–517.

Kanter, R. 1983. *The change masters.* New York: Simon & Schuster.

Langer, E. J. 1983. *The psychology of control.* Beverly Hills: Sage.

Langer, E. J., and Rodin, J. 1976. The effects of choice and enhanced personal responsibility. *Journal of Personality and Social Psychology* 34:191–198.

Lawrence, P., and Lorsch, J. 1967. *Organizations and Environments.* Homewood, Ill.: Irwin.

Lawler, E. E. 1992. *The ultimate advantage: Creating the high involvement organization.* San Francisco: Jossey-Bass.

Locke, E., and Latham, G. 1990. *A theory of goal setting and task performance.* Englewood Cliffs, N.J.: Prentice-Hall.

Locke, E. A., and Schweiger, D. M. 1979. Participation in decision making: One more look. *Research in Organizational Behavior* 1:265–340.

Luhmann, N. 1979. *Trust and power.* New York: Wiley.

Martin, J.; Feldman, M.; Hatch, M. J.; and Sitkin, S. 1983. The uniqueness paradox of organizational stories. *Administrative Science Quarterly* 28:438–452.

Marx, K. 1844. *Early Writings.* Edited and translated by T. B. Bottomore. New York: McGraw-Hill.

McClelland, D. 1975. *Power: The Inner Experience.* New York: Irvington.

Mishra, A. K. 1992. Organizational response to crisis: The role of mutual trust and top management teams. Ph.D. dissertation, University of Michigan.

Neufeld, R.W.J., and Thomas, P. 1977. Effects of perceived efficacy of a prophylactic controlling mechanism on self-control under painful stimulation. *Canadian Journal of Behavioral Science* 9:224–232.

Newman, W. H., and Warren, K. 1977. *The process of management.* Englewood Cliffs, N.J.: Prentice-Hall.

Nielson, E. H. 1986. Empowerment strategies: Balancing authority and responsibility. In *Executive power,* edited by S. Scrivastva et al. San Francisco: Jossey-Bass.

Organ, D., and Greene, C. N. 1974. Role ambiguity, locus of control, and work satisfaction. *Journal of Applied Psychology* 59:101–112.

Ozer, E. M., and Bandura, A. 1990. Mechanisms governing empowerment effects: A self-efficacy analysis. *Journal of Personality and Social Psychology* 58:472–486.

Peters, T. 1992. *Liberation management.* New York: Knopf.

Preston, P., and Zimmerer, T. W. 1978. *Management for supervisors.* Englewood Cliffs, N.J.: Prentice-Hall.

Rappoport, J.; Swift, C.; and Hess, R. 1984. *Studies in empowerment: Steps toward understanding and action.* New York: Haworth Press.

Rose, S. M., and Black, B. L. 1985. *Advocacy and empowerment: Mental health care in the community.* Boston: Routledge and Kegan Paul.

Rothbaum, F.; Weisz, J. R.; and Snyder, S. S. 1982. Changing the world and changing the self: A two-

Runyon, K. E. 1973. Some interaction between personality and management style. *Journal of Applied Psychology* 57:288–294.

Sashkin, M. 1982. *A manager's guide to participative management.* New York: American Management Association.

Sashkin, M. 1984. Participative management is an ethical imperative. *Organizational Dynamics* 12:4–22.

Schwalbe, M. L., and Geas, V. 1988. Social psychological consequences of job-related disabilities. In *Work experience and psychological development through life span,* edited by J. T. Mortimer and K. M. Borman. Boulder, Colo.: Westview.

Seeman, M., and Anderson, C. S. 1983. Alienation and alcohol. *American Sociological Review* 48:60–77.

Seligman, M. E. P. 1975. *Helplessness: On depression, development, and death.* San Francisco: Freeman.

Sewell, Carl. 1990. *Customers for life.* New York: Pocket Books.

Solomon, B. B. 1976. *Black empowerment: Social work in oppressed communities.* New York: Columbia University Press.

Spreitzer, Gretchen M. 1992. When organizations dare: The dynamics of individual empowerment in the workplace. Ph.D. dissertation, University of Michigan.

Staples, L. H. 1990. Powerful ideas about empowerment. *Administration in Social Work* 14:29–42.

Staw, B.; Sandelands, L.; and Dutton, J. 1981. Threat-rigidity effects in organizational behavior: A multilevel analysis. *Administrative Science Quarterly* 26:501–524.

Thomas, K. W., and Velthouse, B. A. 1990. Cognitive elements of empowerment: An interpretive model of intrinsic task motivation. *Academy of Management Review* 15:666–681.

Urwick, L. 1944. *Elements of administration.* New York: Harper and Brothers.

Vogt, J. F., and Murrell, K. L. 1990. *Empowerment in organizations.* San Diego: University Associates.

Vroom, V. H., and Jago, A. G. 1974. Decision making as social process: Normative and descriptive models of leader behavior. *Decision Sciences* 5:743–769.

Vroom, V. H., and Yetton, P. W. 1973. *Leadership and decision making.* Pittsburgh: University of Pittsburgh Press.

White, R. W. 1959. Motivation reconsidered: The concept of competence. *Psychological Review* 66:297–333.

Zand, D. E. 1972. Trust and managerial problem solving. *Administrative Science Quarterly* 17:229–239.

Zimmerman, M. A. 1990. Taking aim on empowerment research: On the distinction between individual and psychological conceptions. *American Journal of Community Psychology* 18:169–177.

Zimmerman, M. A., and Rappaport, J. 1988. Citizen participation, perceived control, and psychological empowerment. *American Journal of Community Psychology* 16:725–750.

Chapter 9

Ancona, D. G., and Caldwell, D. 1992. Bridging the boundary: External activity and performance in organizational teams. *Administrative Science Quarterly* 27:459–489.

Cameron, K.; Whetten, D.; and Kim, M. 1987. Organizational effects of decline and turbulence. *Administrative Science Quarterly* 32:222–240.

Cameron, K. S. 1992. Ways in Which TQM is Implemented. Presentation at the Academy of Management Meetings, Atlanta, Ga.

Cameron, K. S., and Whetten, D. A. 1981. Perceptions of organizational effectiveness in organizational life cycles. *Administrative Science Quarterly* 27:525–544.

Cameron, K. S., and Whetten, D. A. 1984. Organizational life cycle approaches: Overview and applications to higher education. *Review of Higher Education* 6:60–102.

Carlzon, J. 1987. *Moments of truth.* Cambridge, Mass.: Ballinger.

Coch, L., and French, J. R. P. 1948. Overcoming resistance to change. *Human Relations* 1:512–533.

Davis, M. 1971. That's interesting! *Philosophy of the Social Sciences* 1:309–344.

Delbecq, A.; Van de Ven, A.; and Gustafson, D. H. 1975. *Group techniques for program planning.* Glenview, Ill.: Scott Foresman.

Dewey, J. 1933. *How we think.* Boston: Heath.

Dyer, W. G. 1987. *Team building: Issues and alternatives.* Reading, Mass.: Addison-Wesley. Reprinted with the permission of Addison-Wesley, Inc.

Freud, S. 1921. *Group psychology and the analysis of the ego.* Hogarth Press.

Gladstein, D. 1984. Groups in context: A model of task group effectiveness. *Administrative Science Quarterly* 29:497–517.

Greiner, L. 1972. Evolution and revolution as organizations grow. *Harvard Business Review* (July–August) 37–46.

Hackman, J. R. 1990. *Groups that work (and those that don't).* San Francisco: Jossey-Bass.

Hackman, J. R. 1993. Teams and group failure. Presentation at the Interdisciplinary College on Organization Studies, University of Michigan, October.

Hoerr, J. 1989. The payoff from teamwork. *Business Week* (July 10) 56–62.

Huber, G. P. (1980) *Managerial decision making.* Glenview, Ill.: Scott Foresman.

Imai, M. 1986. *Kaizen: The Key to Japan's competitive success.* New York: Random House.

Janis, I. (1972) *Victims of groupthink.* Boston: Houghton Mifflin.

Katzenbach, J. R., and Smith, D. K. 1993. *The wisdom of teams.* Harvard Business School Press.

Latane, B.; Williams, K.; and Harkins, S. 1979. Many hands make light of the work: The causes and consequences of social loafing. *Journal of Personality and Social Psychology* 37:822–832.

Lawler, E. E.; Mohrman, S. A.; and Ledford, G. E. 1992. *Employee involvement and total quality management: Practices and results in Fortune 1000 companies.* San Francisco: Jossey-Bass. Copyright © 1992 by Jossey-Bass, Inc. Reprinted with the permission of the publishers.

Lewin, K. 1951. *Field theory in social science.* New York: Harper.

Macy, B. A.; Norton, J. J.; Bliese, P. O.; and Izumi, H. 1990. The bottom line impact of new design and the design: North America from 1961–1990. Paper presented at the International Conference on Self-Managing Work Teams, Denton, Texas, September.

Maier, N.R.G. 1967. Assets and liabilities of group problem solving: The need for an integrative function. *Psychological Review* 74:239–249.

Morris, D., and Brandon, J. 1993. *Re-engineering your business.* New York: McGraw-Hill.

Moskal, B. S. 1991. Is industry ready for adult relationships? *Industry Week* (January 21) 18–27.

Murnigham, K. 1981. Group decision: What strategies to use? *Management Review* 70:55–61.

National Commission on Excellence in Education. 1983. *A nation at risk.* Washington D.C.: National Institute of Education.

Near, R., and Weckler, D. 1990. Organizational and job characteristics related to self-managing teams. Paper presented at the International Conference on Self-Managing Work Teams, Denton, Texas, September.

Pagonis, W. G. 1993. *Moving mountains.* Cambridge, Mass.: Harvard Business School Press.

Peoples, D.A. 1988. *Presentation Plus.* New York: John Wiley & Sons.

Peters, T. 1987. *Thriving on chaos.* New York: Knopf.

Petrock, F. 1991. Team dynamics: A workshop for effective team building. Presentation at the University of Michigan Management of Managers Program.

Prahalad, C. K., and Hammel, Gary. 1990. The core competence of the corporation. *Harvard Business Review* 90:79–91.

Quinn, R. E., and Cameron, K. S. 1983. Organizational life cycles and shifting criteria of effectiveness: Some preliminary evidence. *Management Science* 29:33–51.

Salancik, G. R. 1977. Commitment and control of organizational behavior and belief. In *New directions in organizational behavior,* edited by B. M. Staw and G. R. Salancik. Chicago: St. Clair Press.

Selznick, P. 1949. *TVA and the grass roots.* Berkeley: University of California Press.

Senge, P. 1991. *The fifth discipline.* New York: Doubleday.

Trist, E. 1969. On sociotechnical systems. In *The planning of change,* edited by W. G. Bennis, K. D. Benne, and R. Chin, 269–282. New York: Holt Rinehart and Winston.

Tropman, J. E. 1985. *Meetings: How to make them work for you.* New York: Van Nostrand Reinhold.

Tuckman, B. W. 1965. Developmental sequence in small groups. *Psychological Bulletin* 63:384–399.

Verespej, M. A. 1990. Yea, teams? Not always. *Industry Week* (June 18) 103–105.

Walton, R. E. 1965. Two strategies for social change and their dilemmas. *Journal of Applied Behavioral Science* 1:167–179.

Wellins, R. S.; Byram, W. C.; and Wilson, J. M. 1991. *Empowered teams.* San Francisco: Jossey-Bass.

Supplement A

Barrett, H. 1977. *Practical uses of speech communication.* 4th ed. New York: Holt, Rinehart, and Winston.

Collins, E., and Devanna, M. 1990. *The portable MBA.* New York: John Wiley.

Endicott Report. 1992. Baton Rouge: Louisiana State University Press.

Gelles-Cole, S. 1985. *The complete guide to executive manners.* New York: Rawson.

Mambert, W. A. 1976. *Effective presentation.* New York: John Wiley and Sons.

Miller, G. A. 1967. *The psychology of communication.* Baltimore: Penguin.

Peoples, D. A. 1988. *Presentations plus.* New York: John Wiley and Sons.

Poor, E. 1992. *The executive writer: A guide to managing words, ideas, and people.* New York: Grove Weidenfeld.

Sanford, W. P., and Yeager, W. H. 1963. *Principles of effective speaking.* 6th ed. New York: Ronald Press.

Seiler, W. J. 1971. The effects of visual materials on attitudes, credibility, and retention. *Speech Monographs* 38:331–334.

Sprague, J., and Stuart, D. 1996. *The speaker's handbook.* 4th ed. Fort Worth: Harcourt Brace College Publishers.

Wells, W. 1989. *Communications in business.* 5th ed. Belmont, Calif.: Wadsworth.

Wilcox, R. P. 1967. *Oral reporting in business and industry.* Englewood Cliffs, N.J.: Prentice-Hall.

Supplement B

Beer, M. 1987. Performance appraisal. In *Handbook of organizational behavior,* edited by J. W. Lorsch, 286–300. Englewood Cliffs, N.J.: Prentice-Hall.

Downs, C. W.; Smeyak, G. P.; and Martin, E. 1980. *Professional interviewing.* New York: Harper & Row.

DuBrin, A. J. 1981. *Human relations: A job-oriented approach.* 2nd ed. Reston, Va.: Reston Publishing Company.

Lopez, F. M. 1975. *Personnel interviewing.* New York: McGraw-Hill.

Sincoff, M. Z., and Goyer, R. S. 1984. *Interviewing.* New York: Macmillan.

Supplement C

Stano, M. E., and Reinsch, N. L., Jr. 1982. *Communication in interviews.* Englewood Cliffs, N.J.: Prentice-Hall.

Stewart, C. J., and Cash, W. B., Jr. 1985. *Interviewing: Principles and practice.* 4th ed. Dubuque, Ia.: W. C. Brown.

Tropman, J. 1985. *Meetings: How to make them work for you.* New York: Van Nostrand Reinhold. Copyright © 1985 by Van Nostrand Reinhold. Reprinted with the permission of the publishers.

Index

Inverted-funnel sequence of questioning, 504, 504t, 513
Involvement
    employee, 381
    management, 286f, 286–287, 287t
Invulnerability, illusion of, 440
IQ, 105, 285
Iron Law of Power, 335
Irvin, Bob, 258
Issue conflicts, 93
Issue selling, 250–252, 251t, 251–252, 256–257
ITT, 237

J

James, William, 205
Janis, Irvin L., 170, 440
Jansky, Karl, 151
Janson, R., 393
Janusian thinking, 163
Japanese management methods, 4–5
    innovation in, 170
    quality circles in, 491, 493–494
    teamwork in, 118
    work units in, 106
Jay, Anthony, 280
Jimmy Lincoln (team building exercise), 463–465
Job description, 509t, 509–510
Job design, 393
    enhancing, 294–296, 295f
    stress management and, 95t, 105–106, 120
Job dimensions, 294–296, 295f
Job factors, order of importance, 293t, 293–294
Job fulfillment, 295
Job strain, 105–106
Jobs, Steven, 230, 329
Jobs, vertical loading of, 296
Joe Chaney (motivation case), 310–311
John DeLorean: Reflections (power and influence case), 264–265
John DeLorean: Why I Quit General Motors (power and influence case), 257–260
John DeLorean: Wild Ride for DeLorean Motors (power and influence case), 261–264
Johnson and Johnson, 111
Johnson Controls, 170
Jones, Jean C., 241
Jones, Tom, 237
Jourard, S.M., 115
Judgment, deferring, 164–165
Jung, Carl, 60–61
Just-in-time inventories, 5

K

Kaizen, 128, 449, 449t
Kakabadse, A., 9t
Kalikow, Peter, 261
Kallmer, Kathleen, 241
Kanter, Rosabeth M., 168
    on empowerment, 387, 389, 391
    on power, 230, 265
Katz, R.L., 8

Katzenbach, J.R., 435, 446, 457
Keashly, 331
Keith Dunn and McGuffey's Restaurant (problem-solving exercise), 180–183
Kekule, Friedrich, 155
Kelleher, Herb, 236
Keller, Helen, 206
Kennedy, John F., 436, 440
Kentucky Fried Chicken, 151
Kerr, William Rolfe, 98t
Kettering, Charles, 144
Kilpatrick, James, 229
King, Martin Luther, 436
Kipnis, D., 336
Knight-Ridder, 457, 459
Kobasa, S.C., 113
Koestler, A., 151
Kohlberg, Lawrence, 55–58
Kotter, John P., 96, 229, 252
Kuhn, A., 116
Kyes, Roger M., 257

L

Language
    in interviews, 501, 513
    in meetings, 526
    in oral presentations, 475, 480–481, 481t
    thinking, 150t, 151–152, 153f
    in written presentations, 475
Lateral thinking, 151
Latham, G.P., 388
Latitude, as source of power, 255
Law and order level of moral development, 55–58
Lawler, E.E., 422
Lawrence, Paul, 242
Leadership
    and management, 13–14
    oral and written presentations and, 489–491
    path-goal theory of, 286f, 286–287, 299–300
    role, exaggerating aspects of, 280
    of teams, 426
        in conforming stage, 428t, 435–438
        in forming stage, 427t, 431–432
        in performing stage, 429t, 450–453
        in storming stage, 428t, 444–445
Leading questions, 502–503, 503t, 513
Leana, C.R., 396
Ledford, G.E., 422
Left-hemisphere thinking, 158–159
Legitimacy, as source of power, 233, 233t, 236–238
Lehman Brothers, 230
Leonard, Stew, 285
Letters, 485, 489, 509t, 510
Levinson, J.D., 95
Lewin, Kurt, 89, 437
Liberation theology, 381
Lickona, T., 58
Life balance, 109–110, 110f
Life-Balance Analysis (stress management exercise), 130

Life-event change, and stress, 94–95
Likability, 234–235, 235t
Listening
    benefiting boss through, 253
    in interviews, 506, 512–513
    in meetings, 527–528
    one-way, 197t
    responses in, 209f, 209–212
    supportive, 197t, 208–212, 209f, 215
Live for Life program, 111
Livingston, S.W., 8
Locke, E.A., 388
Lockheed, 58, 493
Locus of control, 52, 64–66
    external, 64–65
    internal, 64–65, 71, 384
Locus of Control Scale, 43–45, 65
Lorsch, Jay, 242
Louis Harris organization, 377
Loyalty, loss of, 379, 379t
Luthans, F., 9t

M

MacDonald, Kenneth C., 260
Macintosh computer, 168, 324
Macy, B.A., 423
Maddi, S., 113
Magnetron, 149, 151, 153–155, 168
Maier, A.A., 208
Maier, N.R.F., 145, 208, 423
Majority rule, 526
Malcolm Baldrige National Quality Award, 118
Male management role, 115
Management. See also Conflict management; Stress management; Time management
    ability problems in, 280
    effectiveness of, 7–8
    empowerment and, 377–379
    exercise in, 23–32
    ignoring style of, 282f, 282–283
    imposing style of, 282, 282f
    impression, 234–235
    indulging style of, 282, 282f
    innovation and, 168–172, 169t
    integrating style of, 282f, 283
    interaction, 207
    involvement, 286f, 286–287, 287t
    Japanese, 4–5, 106, 118, 170, 491, 493–494
    leadership and, 13–14
    process, 441–444
    responses of, 288–291, 301
    role of, 3–4, 284
    stress and, 88–89
    support and encouragement, 285–287, 389–390, 395t
    Theory X, 204, 281–282
    Theory Y, 204, 282
    time management rules for, 102–103
Management and Machiavelli (Jay), 280
Management by objectives, 107, 284
Management By Walking Around, 236
Management education, 5–7, 12–13
Management skills
    assessment of, 18–32